Western Civilization
A Brief History

Eleventh Edition

Marvin Perry
Baruch College, City University of New York

George W. Bock, *Editorial Associate*

CENGAGE
Learning

Australia • Brazil • Mexico • Singapore • United Kingdom • United States

CENGAGE
Learning®

Western Civilization: A Brief History,
Eleventh Edition
Marvin Perry

Product Manager: Brooke Barbier

Content Developer: Lauren Floyd

Associate Content Developer: Cara Swan

Product Assistant: Andrew Newton

Media Developer: Kate MacLean

Market Development Manager:
  Kyle Zimmerman

Senior Content Project Manager:
  Jane Lee

Senior Art Director: Cate Rickard Barr

Manufacturing Planner: Sandee Milewski

IP Analyst: Alexandra Ricciardi

IP Project Manager: Amber Hosea

Production Service: Lumina Datamatics

Cover Designer: Faith Brosnan

Cover Image: *L'Audition*, detail, Forain,
  Jean Louis (1852–1931). Harper Collins
  Publishers/The Art Archive at Art
  Resource, NY

Compositor: Lumina Datamatics

For product information and technology assistance, contact us at
Cengage Learning Customer & Sales Support, 1-800-354-9706
For permission to use material from this text or product,
submit all requests online at www.**cengage.com/permissions**
Further permissions questions can be emailed to
permissionrequest@cengage.com

Library of Congress Control Number: 2014947313

ISBN: 978-1-305-09146-7

Cengage Learning
20 Channel Center Street
Boston, MA 02210
U.S.A.

Cengage Learning is a leading provider of customized learning solutions with office locations around the globe, including Singapore, the United Kingdom, Australia, Mexico, Brazil and Japan. Locate your local office at **www.cengage.com/global**

Cengage Learning products are represented in Canada by Nelson Education, Ltd.

For your course and learning solutions, visit **www.cengage.com**

Purchase any of our products at your local college store or at our preferred online store **www.cengagebrain.com**

Instructors: Please visit **login.cengage.com** and log in to access instructor-specific resources.

Printed in the United States of America
Print Number: 06   Print Year: 2020

Contents

Part Four

The Modern West: Progress and Breakdown 1789–1914   258

Maps

Chronologies

Preface

Western civilization is a grand but tragic drama. The West has forged the instruments of reason that make possible a rational comprehension of physical nature and human culture, conceived the idea of political liberty, and recognized the intrinsic worth of the individual. But the modern West, though it has unraveled nature's mysteries, has been less successful at finding rational solutions to social ills and conflicts between nations. Science, a great achievement of the Western intellect, while improving conditions of life, has also produced weapons of mass destruction. Though the West has pioneered in the protection of human rights, it has also produced totalitarian regimes that have trampled on individual freedom and human dignity. Although the West has demonstrated a commitment to human equality, it has also practiced brutal racism.

Despite the value that Westerners have given to reason and freedom, they have shown a frightening capacity for irrational behavior and a fascination with violence and irrational ideologies. And they have willingly sacrificed liberty for security or national grandeur. The world wars and the totalitarian movements of the twentieth century have demonstrated that Western Civilization, despite its extraordinary achievements, is fragile and perishable. Yet the West has also shown a capacity to reassert its best values and traditions.

Western Civilization: A Brief History, Eleventh Edition, is an abridged version of *Western Civilization: Ideas, Politics, and Society*, Eleventh Edition. Like the longer text, this volume examines those unique patterns of thought and systems of values that constitute the Western heritage. While focusing on key ideas and broad themes, the text also provides economic, political, and social history for students in Western Civilization courses.

The text is written with the conviction that history is not a meaningless tale. Without knowledge of history, men and women cannot fully know themselves, for all human beings have been shaped by institutions and values inherited from the past. Without an awareness of the historical evolution of reason and freedom, the dominant ideals of Western civilization, commitment to these ideals will diminish. Without knowledge of history, the West cannot fully comprehend or adequately cope with the problems that burden its civilization and the world.

In attempting to make sense out of the past, the author has been careful to avoid superficial generalizations that oversimplify historical events and forces and arrange history into too neat a structure. But the text does strive to interpret and synthesize in order to provide students with a frame of reference with which to comprehend the principal events and eras in Western history.

CHANGES IN THE ELEVENTH EDITION

For the eleventh edition, most chapters have been reworked to some extent. The numerous, carefully selected modifications and additions significantly enhance the text. Some changes deepen the book's conceptual character; others provide useful and illustrative historical details. In several chapters the concluding essays, which strive for meaning and significance, have been enlarged and improved. We have been particularly careful to strengthen the material dealing with intellectual history, a distinguishing feature of the book. The most significant change in recent editions was the insertion in every chapter of a primary source that illuminates the narrative. We retain these primary sources with questions for analysis in the eleventh edition. In several chapters, there is a new primary source.

In Chapter 1, "The Ancient Near East: The First Civilizations," brief inserts strengthen the treatment of prehistory, Sumerian education, Mesopotamian medicine, and the administration of the Persian Empire. Several judicious inserts improve the narrative in Chapter 2, "The Hebrews: A New View of God and the Individual." In Chapter 3, "The Greeks: From Myth to Reason," a discussion of the significance of Greek politics for the Founding Fathers of the United States enriches the section, "The Dilemma of Greek Politics." The coverage of Alexander the Great has also been deepened and, as in past editions, the end piece, "The Greek Achievement: Reason, Freedom, and Humanism," has been strengthened. Significant changes in Chapter 4, "Rome: From City State to World Empire," are the expanded treatment of slavery and the crisis of the Late Roman Empire, and the enhancement of the end piece, "The Roman Legacy." Among the improvements in Chapter 5, "Christianity: A World Religion," are a fuller discussion of the Dead Sea Scrolls and Christianity's appeal in the Roman world, particularly among women.

Most of the changes in Chapter 6, "The Rise of Europe: Fusion of Classical, Christian, and Germanic Traditions," concern the Koran, Islamic interpretations of jihad, and Muslim science. The treatment of economic expansion in medieval Europe now includes a discussion of financial practices that stimulated the growth of capitalism. In Chapter 7, "The Flowering and Dissolution of Medieval Civilization," the discussion of the medieval university has been deepened and a new Primary Source, an excerpt from the writings of Adelard of Bath urging investigating nature, has been inserted; also inserted, in the section on literature, is a brief discussion of Chaucer's *Canterbury Tales*. Consistent with the text's approach, the end piece, "The Middle Ages and the Modern World: Continuity and Discontinuity," has been enriched.

Improvements in Chapter 8, "Transition to the Modern Age: Renaissance and Reformation," are the enrichment of the treatment of Renaissance humanism, the new discussion of Renaissance women, and the expansion of the material dealing with the Peasants' Revolt. In Chapter 9, "Political and Economic Transformation: National States, Overseas Expansion, Commercial Revolution," several inserts elucidate Spain's policy toward Jews and the mistreatment of Native Americans by Spanish colonizers of the New World. Also deepened is the discussion of the acquisition and trading of African slaves. The end piece, "Toward a Global Economy," has been somewhat expanded.

The most significant addition to Chapter 11, "The Era of the French Revolution: Affirmation of Liberty and Equality," is a discussion of the phenomenon of de-Christianization. An illustration of Napoleon's attitude toward women tells us something about the man and his times. And the conceptual character of the end piece, "The Meaning of the French Revolution," has been somewhat improved. A fuller discussion of the ever intriguing question of why the Industrial Revolution began in Britain is the most significant change in Chapter 12, "The Industrial Revolution: The Transformation of Society." In Chapter 13, "Thought and Culture in the Early Nineteenth Century," the treatment of conservatism has been somewhat expanded and a new Primary Source, excerpts from a work of Benjamin Constant illustrating emerging liberalism, has been inserted.

Chapter 14, "Surge of Liberalism and Nationalism: Revolution, Counterrevolution, and Unification," has a new Primary Source—Carl Schurz's description of the revolutionary excitement in Berlin in 1848. Inserted into the narrative is Alexis de Tocqueville's astute analysis of the June Days in Paris and an expanded treatment of the liberal gains of the Revolutions of 1848 in the concluding section assessing the revolutionary failures and gains. A new section, "Religion in a Secular Age," has been added to Chapter 15, "Thought and Culture in the Mid-Nineteenth Century: Realism, Positivism, Darwinism, and Social Criticism." In Chapter 16, "Europe in the Late Nineteenth Century: Modernization, Nationalism, Imperialism," several topics have been expanded: the condition of the working class, the fight for women's suffrage, and the clash of ideologies in France. Now included is an account of the extermination of the Hereros by racist German colonial administrators in German Southwest Africa. In Chapter 17, "Modern Consciousness: New Views of Nature, Human Nature, and the Arts," slight changes have been made in the sections dealing with social thought and the modernist movement.

The principal changes in Chapter 18, "World War I: The West in Despair," are telling examples of the enthusiasm German theologians and intellectuals displayed when war broke out and a strengthening of the treatment of the war itself. The concluding section, "The War and European Consciousness," provides a deeper analysis of the impact of the war on European thought and attitudes. Also added to the section is a discussion of how the war impacted on women. In Chapter 19, "An Era of Totalitarianism," the opening section, "The Nature of Totalitarianism," has been strengthened. Also strengthened is the discussion of Stalin's war on the kulaks and his drive for unchallenged personal power. The treatment of the ordeal faced by German Jews in the new Nazi regime has been expanded. An eyewitness report illustrates the frenzied adoration shown by the German people for their führer. Two significant additions have been made in Chapter 20, "World War II: Western Civilization in the Balance": new material on the war in Russia and a discussion of war criminals in the concluding section, "The Legacy of World War II."

Numerous adjustments have been made in Chapter 21, "Europe After World War II: Recovery and Realignment, 1945–1989." The major changes are improved treatment of the Korean War, the Vietnam War, Stalin's last years, the Soviet Union after Stalin, and the disintegration of the Soviet empire. Much of Chapter 22, "The Troubled Present," has been updated, including the treatment of terrorism, the strife in Afghanistan and Iraq, and the Arab Spring. A new section, "Our Global Age: Promise and Problems," has been added. It treats the themes of globalization, human rights (including the growing persecution of Christians in Muslim lands), the problem of transferring Western democracy to the developing world, the specter of wars, and the march of science and technology. The epilogue, "Reaffirming the Core Ideals of the Western Tradition," is now the chapter's concluding section. Finally, some changes have been made in the art essays.

DISTINCTIVE FEATURES

This brief edition was prepared for Western Civilization courses that run for one term only; for instructors who like to supplement the main text with primary source readers, novels, or monographs; and for humanities courses in which additional works on literature and art will be assigned. In abbreviating the longer text by about a third, the number of chapters has been reduced from thirty-three to twenty-two. The emphasis on the history of ideas and culture has been retained, but the amount of detail has of necessity been reduced.

The text contains several pedagogical features. Chapter introductions and Focus Questions provide comprehensive overviews of key themes and give a sense of direction and coherence to the flow of history. Chronologies at the beginning of most chapters show the sequence of important events discussed in the chapter. Many chapters contain concluding essays that treat the larger meaning of the material. Facts have been carefully selected to illustrate key relationships and concepts and to avoid overwhelming students with unrelated and disconnected data. An annotated bibliography for each chapter can be found online.

This text is published in both single-volume and two-volume editions. Volume I covers the period from the first civilizations in the Near East through the age of Enlightenment in the eighteenth century (Chapters 1–10). Volume II covers the period from the Renaissance and the Reformation to the contemporary age (Chapters 8–22), and incorporates the last three chapters in Volume I: "Transition to the Modern Age: Renaissance and Reformation," "Political and Economic Transformation: National States, Overseas Expansion, Commercial Revolution," and "Intellectual Transformation: The Scientific Revolution and the Age of Enlightenment." Volume II also contains a comprehensive introduction that surveys the ancient world and the Middle Ages; the introduction is designed particularly for students who have not taken the first half of the course.

ANCILLARIES

We are pleased to introduce an expanded ancillary package that will help students in learning and instructors in teaching.

Instructor Resources

CourseMate. Cengage Learning's History CourseMate brings course concepts to life with interactive learning, study tools, and exam preparation tools that support the printed textbook. Use Engagement Tracker to monitor student engagement in the course and watch student comprehension soar as your class works with the printed textbook and the textbook-specific website. An interactive eBook allows students to take notes, highlight, search, and interact with embedded media (such as quizzes, zoomable maps, flashcards, and videos). Learn more at www.cengage.com/coursemate.

Instructor Companion Website. This website is an all-in-one resource for class preparation, presentation, and testing for instructors. Accessible through Cengage.com/login with your faculty account, you will find an Instructor's Manual, PowerPoint presentations (descriptions follow), and test bank files (please see Cognero description).

Instructor's Manual. Prepared by Jan Jenkins of Arkansas Tech University, this manual contains the following for each chapter: summary of the chapter, learning objectives, lecture suggestions, discussion topics, group projects, and film resources.

PowerPoint® Lecture Tools. Prepared by Jan Jenkins of Arkansas Tech University, these presentations are ready-to-use visual outlines of each chapter. They are easily customized for your lectures. There are presentations of only lecture or only images, as well as combined lecture and image presentations. Also available is a per chapter JPEG library of images and maps.

Cengage Learning Testing, powered by Cognero®. Prepared by Stephen Gibson of Allegany College of Maryland and accessible through Cengage.com/login with your faculty account, this test bank contains multiple-choice and essay questions for each chapter. Cognero® is a flexible, online system that allows you to author, edit, and manage test bank content for *Western Civilization: A Brief History*, 11e. Create multiple test versions instantly and deliver through your LMS from your classroom, or wherever you may be, with no special installs or downloads required.

The following format types are available for download from Instructor Companion Site: Blackboard, Angel, Moodle, Canvas, Desire2Learn. You can import these files directly into your LMS to edit, manage questions, and create tests. The test bank is also available in PDF format from the Instructor Companion Website.

MindTap Reader. MindTap Reader is an eBook specifically designed to address the ways students assimilate content and media assets. MindTap Reader combines thoughtful navigation ergonomics, advanced student annotation, note-taking, and search tools, and embedded media assets such as video and MP3 chapter summaries, primary source documents with critical thinking questions, and interactive (zoomable) maps. Students can use the eBook as their primary text or as a multimedia companion to their printed book. The MindTap Reader eBook is available within the CourseMate found at www.cengagebrain.com.

CourseReader: Western Civilization. CourseReader is an online collection of primary and secondary sources that lets you create a customized electronic reader in minutes. With an easy-to-use interface and assessment tool, you can choose exactly what your students will be assigned—simply search or browse Cengage Learning's extensive document database to preview and select your customized collection of readings. In addition to print sources of all types (letters, diary entries, speeches, newspaper accounts, etc.), their collection includes a growing number of images and video and audio clips. Each primary source document includes a descriptive headnote that puts the reading into context and is further supported by both critical thinking and multiple-choice questions designed to reinforce key points. For more information visit www.cengage.com/coursereader.

Reader Program. Cengage Learning publishes a number of readers, some containing exclusively primary sources, others a combination of primary and secondary sources, and some designed to guide students through the process of historical inquiry. Visit Cengage.com/history for a complete list of readers.

Cengagebrain.com. Save your students time and money. Direct them to www.cengagebrain.com for choice in formats and savings and a better chance to succeed in your class. Cengagebrain.com, Cengage Learning's online store, is a single destination for more than 10,000 new textbooks, eTextbooks, eChapters, study tools, and audio supplements. Students have the freedom to purchase a la carte exactly what they need when they need it. Students can save 50 percent on the electronic textbook, and can pay as little as $1.99 for an individual eChapter.

Custom Options. Nobody knows your students like you, so why not give them a text that is tailor-fit to their needs? Cengage Learning offers custom solutions for your course—whether it's making a small modification to *Western Civilization: A Brief History* to match your syllabus or combining multiple sources to create something truly unique. You can pick and choose chapters, include your own material, and add additional map exercises along with the Rand McNally Atlas to create a text that fits the way you teach. Ensure that your students get the most out of their textbook dollar by giving them exactly what they need. Contact your Cengage Learning representative to explore custom solutions for your course.

Student Resources

CourseMate. The more you study, the better the results. Make the most of your study time by accessing everything you need to succeed in one place. Read your textbook, take notes, review flashcards and focus questions, watch videos, and take practice quizzes online with CourseMate.

MindTap Reader. MindTap Reader is an eBook specifically designed to address the ways students assimilate content and media assets. MindTap Reader combines thoughtful navigation ergonomics, advanced student annotation, note-taking, and search tools, and embedded media assets such as video and MP3 chapter summaries, primary source documents with critical thinking questions, and interactive (zoomable) maps. Students can use the eBook as their primary text or as a multimedia companion to their printed book. The MindTap Reader eBook is available within the CourseMate found at www.cengagebrain.com.

Cengagebrain.com. Save time and money! Go to www.cengagebrain.com for choice in formats and savings and a better chance to succeed in your class. Cengagebrain.com, Cengage Learning's online store, is a single destination for more than 10,000 new textbooks, eTextbooks, eChapters, study tools, and audio supplements. Students

have the freedom to purchase a la carte exactly what they need when they need it. Students can save 50 percent on the electronic textbook, and can pay as little as $1.99 for an individual eChapter.

Writing for College History, 1e. Prepared by Robert M. Frakes, Clarion University, this brief handbook guides students through the various types of writing assignments they encounter in a history class. Providing examples of student writing and candid assessments of student work, this text focuses on the rules and conventions of writing for the college history course.

The History Handbook, 1e. Prepared by Carol Berkin of Baruch College, City University of New York, and Betty Anderson of Boston University, this book teaches students both basic and history-specific study skills such as how to read primary sources, research historical topics, and correctly cite sources. Substantially less expensive than comparable skill-building texts, *The History Handbook* also offers tips for Internet research and evaluating online sources.

Doing History: Research and Writing in the Digital Age, 1e. This text was prepared by Michael J. Galgano, J. Chris Arndt, and Raymond M. Hyser of James Madison University. Whether you're starting down the path as a history major or simply looking for a systematic guide to writing a successful paper, you'll find this text to be an indispensable handbook to historical research. This text's approach to researching and writing about history addresses every step of the process, from locating sources and gathering information to writing clearly and citing correctly to avoid plagiarism. You'll also learn how to make the most of every tool available to you—especially the technology that helps you conduct the process efficiently and effectively.

The Modern Researcher, 6e. Prepared by Jacques Barzun and Henry F. Graff of Columbia University, this classic introduction to the techniques of research and the art of expression is not only used widely in history courses but is also appropriate for writing and research methods in other departments. Every aspect of research is covered, from the selection of a topic through the gathering, analysis, writing, revision, and publication of findings, presenting the process not as a set of rules but through actual cases that put the subtleties of research in a useful context.

Acknowledgments

The author would like to thank the following instructors for their critical reading of sections of the manuscript: Andrew Holt, Florida State College at Jacksonville; John Leazer, Carthage College; Kevin O'Connor, Gonzaga University; and Carol Woodfin, Hardin-Simmons University. Several of their suggestions were incorporated into the final version.

In preparing this abridgment, I have made extensive use of the chapters written by my colleagues for *Western Civilization: Ideas, Politics, and Society*. Chapter 8, "Transition to the Modern Age: Renaissance and Reformation," and Chapter 9, "Political and Economic Transformation: National States, Overseas Expansion, Commercial Revolution," are based largely on James R. Jacob's and Margaret C. Jacob's chapters in the longer volume. Parts of Chapter 12, "The Industrial Revolution: The Transformation of Society," and of Chapter 16, "Europe in the Late Nineteenth Century: Modernization, Nationalism, Imperialism," are drawn from Myrna Chase's chapters. Material on tsarist Russia and the Soviet Union and the concluding chapter, "The Troubled Present," are based in part on Theodore H. Von Laue's and Jonathan Daly's contributions to the larger text. To a lesser or greater extent, my colleagues' material has been abridged, restructured, and rewritten to meet the needs of this volume. Therefore, I alone am responsible for all interpretations and any errors. I wish to thank my colleagues for their gracious permission to use their words and thoughts.

I am also grateful to the staff of Cengage Learning who lent their considerable talents to the project. In particular, I wish to thank Lauren Floyd, Content Developer, for her conscientiousness and superb administrative skills and Jane Lee, Senior Content Project Manager, for her careful supervision. Over the years, both Jean Woy, Senior Consulting Editor, who has been affiliated with the book since the first edition, and Nancy Blaine, Senior Sponsoring Editor, with whom I have worked for ten years, continued to recognize and support what I am trying to do—and for this I remain grateful. Although Nancy Blaine is no longer with Cengage Learning, her contribution to the project endures. In addition, I would like to thank Cate Barr, Senior Art Director, and Faith Brosnan, Cover Designer, for their creativity and artistic vision in updating the cover and interior design for this edition. A special thanks to Valarmathy Munuswamy, Senior Project Manager at Lumina Datamatics, who managed the overall production with skill and dedication. Reba Frederics, the photo researcher, deserves praise for her fine eye and enthusiasm for the project. So too do Kristine Janssens, text researcher, who managed the difficult task of obtaining permissions smoothly, and Paula Pyburn, the copy editor, for her careful eye for detail.

I also remain grateful to my good friend George Bock, who passed away in 2012. His creative insights in previous editions continue to contribute to the text's distinguishing character—a concern for crucial concepts and essential relationships. Our often heated but always fruitful discussions demonstrate to me the intrinsic value of the Socratic dialogue. And, as always, I am grateful to my wife, Phyllis Perry, for her encouragement and computer expertise, which has saved me much time and frustration.

M. P.

Geography of Europe

The map on the following pages features the continent of Europe and parts of North Africa and the Middle East. Like most maps, it contains a selected combination of physical and political information. The physical part pertains to the natural world—the shapes of landmasses, mountains, and bodies of water—and serves as a kind of background or screen onto which the political information is projected. Categories of political information commonly featured on historical maps include the location and names of important cities and states, the changing borders of countries and empires, and the routes people traveled as they explored, migrated, traded, and fought with one another.

Europe is one of seven continents; the others are Africa, Asia, North America, South America, Australia, and Antarctica. Europe is bounded in the north by the Arctic Sea, in the west by the Atlantic Ocean, in the south by the Mediterranean Sea, and in the southeast by the Black Sea and the Caspian Sea. Off the mainland but traditionally considered a part of Europe are thousands of islands, from those of the United Kingdom, Ireland, and Iceland in the northwest, to Crete, Sicily, and Sardinia in the southeast.

Europe is quite distinctive in shape. The first thing to notice is that there is no natural border between Europe and Asia. The traditional eastern boundary is the Ural River, but looked at from a purely geographic standpoint, Europe might simply be called western Asia. The second thing to notice is how much of Europe is made up of peninsulas. In fact, Europe itself is one gigantic peninsula, with a coastline equal in distance to one and a half times around the equator (37,877 miles).

North Americans are often surprised to discover the small size of the European continent. The geographic area of France, for example, is less than that of Texas; Britain is similar in size to Alabama. The distance from London to Paris is about the same as from New York to Boston, while the distance from Berlin to Moscow is comparable to that of Chicago to Denver.

MAJOR PENINSULAS AND ISLANDS   There are six major European peninsulas: the Iberian (comprising Portugal and Spain); the Apennine (Italy); the Balkan (Slovenia, Croatia, Bosnia-Herzegovina, Serbia and Montenegro, Albania, Greece, Bulgaria, and Macedonia); the Anatolian (Turkey); the Scandinavian (Norway, Sweden, and Finland); and the Jutland or Danish peninsula. The islands of Iceland, Ireland, and the United Kingdom lie to the Atlantic west, while to the east lie some of the major islands of the Mediterranean, such as Corsica, Sardinia, Sicily, Crete, and Cyprus.

SEAS, LAKES, AND RIVERS   Europe's irregular coastline encloses large areas of water into bays, gulfs, and seas. Moving from west to east in the Mediterranean, we have the Tyrrhenian Sea (between Italy and the islands of Sicily, Sardinia, and Corsica), the Adriatic (between Italy and the nations of the western Balkan peninsula), the Ionian (between Italy and Greece), and the Aegean (between Greece and Turkey). The Baltic Sea is bordered on the east (moving clockwise from the north) by Finland, Russia, Estonia, Latvia, Lithuania, Poland, Germany, and Sweden. It is connected by narrow channels to the North Sea, which lies (moving clockwise from the north) between Norway, Denmark, Germany, the Netherlands, and Belgium in the east and south, to the United Kingdom in the north and west. The English Channel separates England and France; the Bay of Biscay lies between southwestern

France and northern Spain. The Black Sea, on the southern border of Russia and Ukraine, is connected by two straits—the Bosphorous and the Dardanelles—to the Aegean Sea. The Caspian Sea, bordered in the north by Russia and Kazakhstan, is the world's largest saltwater lake and, at 92 feet below sea level, the lowest point in Europe.

Several of Europe's major rivers flow across the Russian plain. At 2,194 miles, the Volga is the longest river in Europe. Linked by canals and other river systems to the Arctic Ocean in the north and the Baltic Sea in the south, the Volga originates west of Moscow and empties into the Caspian Sea after flowing some 2,194 miles. At 1,777 miles, the Danube is Europe's second longest river and the principal waterway in the central part of the continent. It originates in southern Germany and flows through Austria, Slovakia, Hungary, Croatia, Serbia and Montenegro, Bulgaria, Moldova, Ukraine, and Romania, before reaching the Black Sea. The Rhine river comes next, at 766 miles, winding its way from the Swiss Alps to the Netherlands and the North Sea. Other prominent riverways in Europe include the Elbe (678 miles), which originates in the Czech Republic and passes through Germany before it, too, empties into the North Sea, and the Rhône (505 miles), which runs from Switzerland, through France, and into the Mediterranean Sea. The proximity of most areas of the European landmass to the coastline and to major river systems greatly affected the Continent's history.

LAND REGIONS   Despite its relatively small size, the European continent presents a wide range of landforms, from rugged mountains to sweeping plains. These can be separated into four major regions: the Northwest Mountains, the Great European Plain, the Central Uplands, and the Alpine Mountain System. The mountains of the Northwest Region cover most of the region, running through northwestern France, Ireland, northern Great Britain, Norway, Sweden, northern Finland, and the northwest corner of Russia. The Great European Plain covers almost all of the European part of the former Soviet Union, extending from the Arctic Ocean to the Caucasus Mountains. This belt stretches westward across Poland, Germany, Belgium, the western portion of France, and southeastern England. The Central Uplands is a belt of high plateaus, hills, and low mountains. It reaches from the central plateau of Portugal, across Spain, the central highlands of France, to the hills and mountains of southern Germany, the Czech Republic, and Slovakia. The Alpine Mountain System is made up of several mountain ranges, including the Pyrenees between Spain and France, the Alps in southeastern France, northern Italy, Switzerland, and western Austria, and the Apennine range in Italy. Also included are the mountain ranges of the Balkan Peninsula, the Carpathian Mountains in Slovakia and Romania, and the Caucasus Mountains between the Black and Caspian Seas.

When studying the map of Europe, it is important to notice the proximity of Central Asia, the Middle East, and North Africa. Interaction with the peoples and cultures of these regions has had a profound impact on the course of European history.

Western Civilization

A Brief History

Part One

The Ancient World: Foundation of the West

to A.D. 500

The Acropolis of Athens.

Politics and Society	Thought and Culture
3000 B.C.	
Rise of civilization in Sumer (c. 3200)	Cuneiform writing in Sumer; hieroglyphics in Egypt
Union of Upper and Lower Egypt (c. 2900)	
Rise of Minoan civilization (c. 2600)	
2000 B.C.	
Rise of Mycenaean civilization (c. 2000)	*Epic of Gilgamesh* (c. 1900)
Hammurabi of Babylon builds an empire (1792–1750)	Code of Hammurabi (c. 1790)
	Amenhotep IV and a movement toward monotheism in Egypt (1369–1353)
	Moses and the Exodus (1200s)
1000 B.C.	
Creation of a unified Hebrew monarchy under David (1000–961)	Origins of Phoenician alphabet (1000s)
Dark Age in Greece (c. 1100–800)	Homer's *Iliad* and *Odyssey* (700s)
500 B.C.	
Hellenic Age (c. 800–323)	Age of classical prophecy: flowering of Hebrew ethical thought (750–430)
Persian conquest of Near East (550–525)	Law of the Twelve Tables (450)
Formation of Roman Republic (509)	Rise of Greek philosophy: Ionians, Pythagoreans, Parmenides (500s and 400s)
Persian Wars (499–479)	
Peloponnesian War (431–404)	
Conquest of Greek city-states by Philip of Macedonia (338)	Greek dramatists: Aeschylus, Sophocles, Euripides, Aristophanes (400s)
Conquests of Alexander the Great (336–323)	Greek philosophers: Socrates, Plato, Aristotle (400s and 300s)
Hellenistic Age (323–30)	Rise of Hellenistic philosophies: Epicureanism and Stoicism (300s and 200s)
Roman conquest of Carthage and Hellenistic kingdoms (264–146)	
100 B.C.	
Political violence and civil wars in Rome (88–31)	Roman philosophers during the Republic: Lucretius, Cicero (1st cent.)
Assassination of Julius Caesar (44)	Rise and spread of Christianity: Jesus (d. A.D. 29); Paul's missionary activity (c. 34–64)
Octavian takes the title Augustus and becomes first Roman emperor (27)	
Pax Romana: height of Roman Empire (27 B.C.–A.D. 180)	Gospel of Mark (c. 66–70)
	Roman historians, poets, and philosophers during the Pax Romana: Livy, Tacitus, Virgil, Horace, Ovid, Juvenal, Seneca, Marcus Aurelius
A.D. 200	
Military anarchy in Rome (235–285)	Church fathers: Jerome, Ambrose, Augustine (300s and 400s)
Goths defeat Romans at Adrianople (378)	
End of Roman Empire in the West (476)	

Chapter 1

The Ancient Near East: The First Civilizations

- **Prehistory**
- **The Rise to Civilization**
- **Mesopotamian Civilization**
- **Egyptian Civilization**
- **Empire Builders**
- **The Religious Orientation of the Ancient Near East**

Focus Questions

1. What is meant by the term *civilization*? Under what conditions did it emerge?
2. Why was the discovery of agriculture a revolutionary development?
3. What did Mesopotamian and Egyptian civilizations have in common? How did they differ?
4. How did political and cultural universalism characterize the Persian Empire?
5. In what ways did mythopoeic thought characterize Near Eastern civilization? How does this type of thinking differ from that of science?
6. What elements of Near Eastern civilization were passed on to Western civilization?

*C*ivilization was not inevitable; it was an act of human creativity. The first civilizations emerged some five thousand years ago in the river valleys of Mesopotamia and Egypt. There, human beings established cities and states, invented writing, developed organized religion, and constructed large-scale buildings and monuments—all characteristics of civilized life. Humanity's rise to civilization was long and arduous. Some 99 percent of human history took place before the creation of civilization, in the vast ages of prehistory. ❖

PREHISTORY

The period called the Paleolithic Age, or Old Stone Age, began with the earliest primitive, toolmaking human beings who inhabited East Africa some 2.5 million years ago. It ended about ten thousand years ago in parts of the Near East when people discovered how to farm. Our Paleolithic ancestors lived as hunters and food gatherers. Because they had not learned how to farm, they never established permanent villages. When their food supplies ran short, they abandoned their caves or tentlike structures of branches and searched for new dwelling places.

Human social development was shaped by this 2.5 million year experience of hunting and food gathering. Based on fossil evidence found in Ethiopia, it appears that *homo sapiens*, our species, first appeared some 190,000 years ago; it also seems certain that the common ancestor of modern humans originated in Africa and that some 40,000 years ago modern humans began to migrate into Europe and Asia. For survival, groups of families formed bands consisting of around thirty people; members learned how to plan, organize, cooperate, trust, and share. Hunters assisted one another in tracking and killing game, finding cooperative efforts more successful than individual forays. By sharing their kill and bringing some back to their camp for the rest of the group, they reinforced the social bond. So, too, did women, who gathered nuts, seeds, and fruit for the group. Bands that did not cooperate in the hunt, in food gathering, or in food distribution were unlikely to survive.

Although human progress was very slow during the long centuries of the Paleolithic Age, developments occurred that influenced the future enormously. Paleolithic people developed spoken language and learned how to make and use tools of bone, wood, and stone. With these simple tools, they dug up roots; peeled the bark off trees; trapped, killed, and skinned animals; made clothing; and fashioned fishnets. They also discovered how to control fire, which allowed them to cook their meat and provided warmth and protection.

Like toolmaking and the control of fire, language was a great human achievement. Language enabled individuals to acquire and share with one another knowledge, experiences, and feelings. Thus, language was the decisive factor in the development of culture and its transmission from one generation to the next.

Most likely, our Paleolithic ancestors developed mythic-religious beliefs to explain the mysteries of nature, birth, sickness, and death. They felt that living powers operated within and beyond the world they experienced, and they sought to establish friendly relations with these powers. To Paleolithic people, the elements—sun, rain, wind, thunder, and lightning—were alive. The natural elements were spirits; they could feel and act with a purpose. To appease them, Paleolithic people made offerings. Gradually, there emerged shamans, medicine men, and witch doctors, who, through rituals, trances, and chants, seemed able to communicate with these spirits. Paleolithic people also began the practice of burying their dead, sometimes with offerings, which suggests a belief in life after death.

Between thirty thousand and twelve thousand years ago, Paleolithic people sought out the dark and silent interior of caves, which they probably viewed as sanctuaries, and, with only torches for light, they painted remarkably skillful and perceptive pictures of animals on the cave walls. Even prior to civilization, human beings demonstrated artistic talent and an esthetic sense. When these prehistoric artists drew an animal with a spear in its side, they probably believed that this act would make them successful in hunting; when they drew a herd of animals, they probably hoped that this would cause game to be plentiful.

Some ten thousand years ago, the New Stone Age, or Neolithic Age, began in the Near East. During the Neolithic Age, human beings discovered farming, domesticated animals, established villages, polished stone tools, made pottery, and wove cloth. So important were these achievements that they are referred to as the Neolithic Revolution.

Agriculture and the domestication of animals revolutionized life. Whereas Paleolithic hunters and food gatherers had been forced to use

Chronology 1.1 ❖ The Near East

3200 B.C.*	Rise of civilization in Sumer
2900	Union of Upper and Lower Egypt
2686–2181	Old Kingdom: essential forms of Egyptian civilization take shape
2180	Downfall of Akkadian empire
1792–1750	Hammurabi of Babylon brings Akkad and Sumer under his control and fashions a code of laws
1570	Egyptians drive out Hyksos and embark on empire building
1369–1353	Reign of Amenhotep IV: a movement toward monotheism
1200	Fall of Hittite empire
612	Fall of Assyrian empire
604–562	Reign of Nebuchadnezzar: height of Chaldean empire
550–525 B.C.	Persian conquests form a world empire

*Most dates are approximations.

whatever nature made available to them, Neolithic farmers altered their environment to satisfy human needs. Instead of spending their time searching for grains, roots, and berries, women and children grew crops near their homes; instead of tracking animals over great distances, men could slaughter domesticated goats or sheep nearby. Farming made possible a new kind of community. Since farmers had to live near their fields and could store food for the future, farming led to the rise of permanent settlements.

Villages changed the patterns of life. A food surplus freed some people to devote part of their time to sharpening their skills as basket weavers or toolmakers. The demand for raw materials and the creations of skilled artisans fostered trade, sometimes across long distances, and spurred the formation of trading settlements. An awareness of private property emerged. Hunters had accumulated few possessions, since belongings presented a burden when moving from place to place. Villagers, however, acquired property and were determined to protect it from one another and from outsiders, such as nomadic horsemen, who might raid the village. Hunting bands were egalitarian; generally, no one member had more

possessions or more power than another. In farming villages, a ruling elite emerged that possessed wealth and wielded power. Scholars ponder the psychological dimensions of this shift from the hunter's way of life to sedentary farming.

Neolithic people made great strides in technology. By shaping and baking clay, they made pottery containers for cooking and for storing food and water. The invention of the potter's wheel enabled them to form bowls and plates more quickly and precisely. Stone tools were sharpened by grinding them on rock. The discovery of the wheel and the sail improved transportation and promoted trade, and the development of the plow and the ox yoke made tilling the soil easier for farmers.

The Neolithic period also marked the beginning of the use of metals. The first to be used was copper, which was easily fashioned into tools and weapons. Copper implements lasted longer than those of stone and flint, and they could be recast and reshaped if broken. In time, artisans discovered how to make bronze by combining copper and tin in the proper ratio. Bronze was harder than copper, which made a sharper cutting edge possible.

During the Neolithic Age, the food supply became more reliable, village life expanded, and the population increased. Families that acquired wealth gained a higher social status and became village leaders. Religion grew more formal and structured; nature spirits evolved into deities, each with specific powers over nature or human life. Altars were erected in their honor, and ceremonies were conducted by priests, whose power and wealth increased as people gave offerings to the gods. Neolithic society was growing more organized and complex; it was on the threshold of civilization.

THE RISE TO CIVILIZATION

What we call *civilization* arose some five thousand years ago in the Near East (in Mesopotamia and Egypt) and then later in East Asia (in India and China). The first civilizations began in cities that were larger, more populated, and more complex in their political, economic, and social structure than Neolithic villages. Because the cities depended on the inhabitants of adjacent villages for their food, farming techniques must have been sufficiently developed to produce food surpluses. Increased production provided food for urban inhabitants, who engaged in nonagricultural occupations; they became merchants, craftsmen, bureaucrats, and priests.

The invention of writing enabled the first civilizations to preserve, organize, and expand knowledge and to pass it on to future generations. It also allowed government officials and priests to conduct their affairs more efficiently. Moreover, civilized societies possessed organized governments, which issued laws and defined the boundary lines of their states. On a scale much larger than Neolithic communities, the inhabitants erected buildings and monuments, engaged in trade and manufacturing, and used specialized labor for different projects. Religious life grew more organized and complex, and a powerful and wealthy priesthood emerged. These developments—cities, specialization of labor, writing, organized government, monumental architecture, and a complex religious structure—differentiate the first civilizations from prehistoric cultures.

Religion was the central force in these primary civilizations. It provided satisfying explanations for the workings of nature, helped ease the fear of death, and justified traditional rules of morality. Law was considered sacred, a commandment of the gods. Religion united people in the common enterprises needed for survival—for example, the construction and maintenance of irrigation works and the storage of food. In addition, the power of rulers, who were regarded either as gods or as agents of the gods, derived from religion.

The emergence of civilization was a great creative act and not merely the inevitable development of agricultural societies. Many communities had learned how to farm, but only a handful made the leap to civilization. How was it possible for Sumerians and Egyptians, the creators of the earliest civilizations, to make this breakthrough? Most scholars stress the relationship between civilizations and river valleys. Rivers deposited fertile silt on adjoining fields, provided water for crops, and served as avenues for trade. But environmental factors alone do not adequately explain the emergence of civilization. What cannot be omitted is the human contribution: capacity for thought and cooperative activity. Before these rivers could be of any value in producing crops, swamps around them had to be drained; jungles had to be cleared; and dikes, reservoirs, and canals had to be built. To construct and maintain irrigation works required the cooperation of large numbers of people, a necessary condition for civilization.

In the process of constructing and maintaining irrigation networks, people learned to formulate and obey rules and developed administrative, engineering, and mathematical skills. The need to keep records stimulated the invention of writing. These creative responses to the challenges posed by nature spurred the early inhabitants of Sumer and Egypt to make the breakthrough to civilization, thereby altering the course of human destiny.

Civilization also had its dark side. Epidemic disease thrived in urban centers, where people lived close together in unsanitary conditions, drinking contaminated water and surrounded by rotting garbage. Slavery was an essential and accepted feature of early civilization. The authority wielded by rulers and their officials and the habits of discipline acquired by the community's members made possible the construction of irrigation works, but these social structures were also harnessed for destructive conflicts between

Map 1.1 **Mesopotamian and Egyptian Civilizations** The first civilizations emerged in river valleys: Mesopotamia in the valleys of the Tigris and Euphrates rivers, Egypt in the Nile valley.

states. Such warfare, which involved managing large numbers of combatants, was far more lethal than the sporadic and generally disorganized acts of violence that had occurred in Neolithic times. A hostile and aggressive attitude toward members of alien groups has plagued human beings since the rise of civilization. Warfare fascinated the people who created the first civilizations. Scribes recounted battle after battle, warrior-kings boasted of their military conquests, and military heroes were held in the highest esteem.

MESOPOTAMIAN CIVILIZATION

Mesopotamia is the Greek word for "land between the rivers." It was here, in the valleys of the Tigris and Euphrates Rivers, that the first

civilization began. The first people to develop an urban civilization in Mesopotamia (modern-day Iraq) were the Sumerians, who colonized the marshlands of the lower Euphrates, which, along with the Tigris, flows into the Persian Gulf.

Through constant toil and imagination, the Sumerians transformed the swamps into fields of barley and groves of date palms. Around 3000 B.C., their hut settlements gradually evolved into twelve independent city-states, each consisting of a city and its surrounding countryside. Among the impressive achievements of the Sumerians were a system of symbol writing *(Cuneiform)** in which pictures for objects and marks for numbers were

---

**Cuneiform* is the Latin term for "nail-shaped," which the marks inscribed in clay appeared to represent.

engraved on clay tablets with a reed stylus to represent ideas; elaborate brick houses, palaces, and temples; bronze tools and weapons; irrigation works; trade with other peoples; an early form of money; religious and political institutions; schools; religious and secular literature; varied art forms; codes of law; medicinal drugs; and a lunar calendar.

The history of Mesopotamia is marked by a succession of conquests. To the north of Sumer lay a Semitic* city called Akkad. About 2350 B.C., the people of Akkad, led by Sargon the Great, a warrior-king, conquered the Sumerian cities. Sargon built the world's first empire, which extended from the Persian Gulf to the Mediterranean Sea. Establishing a pattern that future despotic rulers would emulate, Sargon stationed garrisons in conquered lands and appointed governors and officials to administer the territories, as well as additional bureaucrats to register and parcel out the precious metals, horses, grain, and other commodities exacted from conquered peoples. He also retained a large standing army to quell revolts and to launch new imperialistic ventures. The Akkadians adopted Sumerian cultural forms, including cuneiform, and spread them beyond the boundaries of Mesopotamia with their conquests. Mesopotamian religion became a blend of Sumerian and Akkadian elements.

Illustrating the confluence of Akkadian and Sumerian culture was Saragon's daughter, Enheduanna, the world's first known poet. Serving as high priestess in the Sumerian city of Ur, Enheduanna wrote numerous poems and hymns to temple deities. In one of her hymns to the Sumerian goddess Ianna, she depicts Ianna as a fierce warrior; in a second, Ianna emerges as an overseer of home and children; and in the third surviving hymn, the poetess appeals to Ianna to help her regain her position as temple priestess after it was taken from her by a male enemy.

In succeeding centuries, the Sumerian cities were incorporated into various kingdoms and empires. The Sumerian language, replaced by a Semitic tongue, became an obscure language

*Semites included Akkadians, Hebrews, Babylonians, Phoenicians, Canaanites, Assyrians, and Aramaeans. Hebrew and Arabic are Semitic languages.

Courtesy of the Oriental Institute, University of Chicago

COUPLE FROM NIPPUR, 2500 B.C. Large eyes and geometrical beard and hair characterize Sumerian figures. Note the intimacy and informality of the pose.

known only to priests, and the Sumerians gradually disappeared as a distinct people. But their cultural achievements endured. Akkadians, Babylonians, Elamites, and others adopted Sumerian religious, legal, literary, and artistic forms. The Sumerian legacy served as the basis for a Mesopotamian civilization, which maintained a distinct style for three thousand years.

Religion: The Basis of Mesopotamian Civilization

Religion lay at the center of Mesopotamian life. Every human activity—political, military, social, legal, literary, or artistic—was generally subordinated to an overriding religious purpose. Religion was the Mesopotamians' frame of reference for understanding nature, society, and themselves; it dominated and inspired all other cultural expressions and human activities. Wars between cities, for instance, were interpreted as conflicts between the gods of those cities, and victory ultimately depended on divine favor, not on human effort. Myths—narratives about the activities of the gods—explained the origins of the human species. According to the earliest Sumerian myths, the first human beings issued forth from the earth like plant life, or were shaped from clay by divine craftsmen and granted a heart by the goddess Nammu, or were formed from the blood of two gods sacrificed for that purpose.

The Mesopotamians believed that people were given life so that they could execute on earth the will of the gods in heaven. No important decisions were made by kings or priests without first consulting the gods. To discover the wishes of the gods, priests sacrificed animals and then examined their entrails, or the priests might find their answers in the stars or in dreams.

The cities of Mesopotamia were sacred communities dedicated to serving divine masters, and people hoped that appeasing the gods would bring security and prosperity to their cities. Each city belonged to a particular god, who was the real owner of the land and the real ruler of the city; often a vast complex of temples was built for the god and the god's family.

Supervised by priests, the temple was the heart of the city's life. The temple probably owned most of the land in its city; temple priests collected rents, operated businesses, and received contributions for festivals. Women priestesses also served the temple. Most inhabitants of the city worked for the temple priests as tenant farmers, agricultural laborers, or servants. Anxious to curry favor with the gods and goddesses who watched over the fields, peasants surrendered part of their crops to the temples. Priests coordinated the city's economic activity, supervising the distribution of land, overseeing the irrigation works, and storing food for emergencies. Temple scribes kept records of expenditures and receipts.

The Mesopotamians believed that the gods controlled the entire universe and everything in it. The moon, the sun, and the storm, the city, the irrigation works, and the fields—each was directed by a god. The Mesopotamians saw gods and demons everywhere in nature. There was a god in the fire and another in the river; evil demons stirred up sandstorms, caused disease, and

endangered women in childbirth. To protect themselves from hostile powers, Mesopotamians wore charms and begged their gods for help. When misfortune befell them, they attributed it to the gods. Even success was not due to their own efforts, but to the intervention of a god who had taken a special interest in them. Compared with the gods, an individual was an insignificant and lowly creature.

Uncertainty and danger filled life in Mesopotamia. Sometimes, the unpredictable waters of the rivers broke through the dikes, flooding fields, ruining crops, and damaging cities. At other times, an insufficient overflow deprived the land of water, causing crops to fail. Mesopotamia had no natural barriers to invasion. Feeling themselves surrounded by incomprehensible and often hostile forces, Mesopotamians lived in an atmosphere of anxiety that permeated their civilization.

Contributing to this sense of insecurity was the belief that the gods behaved capriciously, malevolently, and vindictively. What do the gods demand of me? Is it ever possible to please them? To these questions Mesopotamians had no reassuring answers, for the gods' behavior was a mystery to mere human beings.

A mood of uncertainty and anxiety, an awareness of the cosmos as unfathomable and mysterious, a feeling of dread about the fragility of human existence and the impermanence of human achievement—these attitudes are as old as the first civilization. The *Epic of Gilgamesh,* the finest work of Mesopotamian literature, masterfully depicts this mood of pessimism and despair. The *Gilgamesh* deals with a profound theme: the human protest against death. Confronted with the reality of his own death, Gilgamesh yearns for eternal life. But he learns that when the gods created human beings, they made death part of their lot. "Where is the man who can clamber to heaven? Only the gods live forever . . . but as for us men, our days are numbered, our occupations are a breath of wind."[1] The Mesopotamians had little to look forward to after death. They believed that they would either be confined to a dreary underworld whose rulers would inflict pain on them or be transformed into spirits, flying about and tormenting the living.

Government, Law, and Economy

Kingship, bestowed on a man by the gods, was the central institution in Mesopotamian society. Unlike Egyptian pharaohs, Mesopotamian kings did not see themselves as gods, but rather as great men selected by the gods to represent them on earth. Gods governed through the kings, who reported to the gods about conditions in their land (which was the gods' property) and petitioned the gods for advice. To honor the gods, kings built magnificent temples and adorned sacred statues with lavish dress and fine jewelry.

The king administered the laws, which came from the gods. The principal collection of laws in ancient Mesopotamia was the famous code of Hammurabi (c. 1792–c. 1750 B.C.), the Babylonian ruler. Unearthed by French archaeologists in 1901–1902, the code has provided invaluable insights into Mesopotamian society. In typical Mesopotamian fashion, Hammurabi claimed that his code rested on the authority of the gods; to violate it was to contravene the divine order.

The code reveals social status and mores in that area and time. Women were subservient to men, although efforts were made to protect women and children from abuse. By making death the penalty for adultery, the code probably sought to preserve family life. Punishments were generally severe—"an eye for an eye and a tooth for a tooth." The code prescribed death for housebreaking, kidnapping, aiding the escape of slaves, receiving stolen goods, and bearing false witness, but being forgiven by the wronged party could mitigate the penalty. For example, a wife who committed adultery could be spared execution if she was pardoned by her husband. Class distinctions were expressed in the code. For example, a person received more severe punishment for harming a noble than for harming a commoner. Government officials who engaged in extortion or bribery were harshly punished. The code's many provisions relating to business transactions underscore the importance of trade to Mesopotamian life.

The economy of Mesopotamian cities depended heavily on foreign and domestic trade. To safeguard it, governments instituted regulations to prevent fraud, and business transactions had to be recorded in writing. Enterprising businessmen set up trading outposts in distant lands, making the Mesopotamians pioneers in international trade.

Writing, Mathematics, Astronomy, and Medicine

The Sumerians established schools, which trained the sons of the upper class in the art of cuneiform writing. Hundreds of tablets on which Sumerian students practiced their lessons have been discovered, testifying to the years of disciplines and demanding work required to master the scribal art. Students who completed the course of study successfully were employed as archivists, secretaries, or accountants by the temple palace, the law courts, or merchants.

The Mesopotamians made some impressive advances in mathematics. They devised multiplication and division tables, including even cubes and cube roots. They determined the area of right-angle triangles and rectangles, divided a circle into 360 degrees, and had some understanding of the principles that centuries later would be developed into the Pythagorean theorem and quadratic equations. But the Babylonians, who made the chief contribution in mathematics, barely advanced to the level of devising theories: they did not formulate general principles or furnish proofs for their mathematical operations.

By carefully observing and accurately recording the positions of planets and constellations of stars, Babylonian sky watchers took the first steps in developing the science of astronomy, and they devised a calendar based on the cycles of the moon. As in mathematics, however, they did not form theories to coordinate and illuminate their data. Believing that the position of the stars and planets revealed the will of the gods, astronomers did not examine the heavens to find what we call cause-and-effect connections between the phenomena. Rather, they sought to discover what the gods wanted. With this knowledge, people could organize their political, social, and moral lives in accordance with divine commands, and they could escape the terrible consequences that they believed resulted from ignoring the gods' wishes.

Consistent with their religious worldview, the Mesopotamians believed that gods or demons caused disease. To cure a patient, priest-physicians resorted to magic; through prayers and sacrifices, they attempted to appease the gods and eject the demons from the sick body. Nevertheless, in identifying illnesses and prescribing appropriate remedies, Mesopotamians demonstrated some accurate knowledge of pharmacology and medicine. Physicians most likely utilized splints to set broken bones, lancets to pierce abscesses, and bandages to protect wounds.

EGYPTIAN CIVILIZATION

During the early period of Mesopotamian civilization, the Egyptians developed their civilization in the fertile valley of the Nile. Without this mighty river, which flows more than four thousand miles from central Africa northward to the Mediterranean, virtually all Egypt would be a desert. When the Nile overflowed its banks, as it did reliably and predictably, the floodwaters deposited a layer of fertile black earth, which, when cultivated, provided abundant food to support Egyptian civilization. The Egyptians learned how to control the river—a feat that required cooperative effort and ingenuity, as well as engineering and administrative skills. In addition to water and fertile land, the Nile provided an excellent transportation link between Upper (southern) and Lower (northern) Egypt. Natural barriers—mountains, deserts, cataracts (rapids) in the Nile, and the Mediterranean—protected Egypt from attack, allowing the inhabitants to enjoy long periods of peace and prosperity. Thus, unlike Mesopotamians, Egyptians derived a sense of security from their environment.

From the Old Kingdom to the Middle Kingdom

About 2900 B.C., a ruler of Upper Egypt known as Narmer, or Menes, conquered the Nile Delta and Lower Egypt. By 2686 B.C., centralized rule had been firmly established, and great pyramids, tombs for the pharaohs, were being constructed. The pyramids required rigorous central planning to coordinate the tens of thousands of Egyptian laborers drafted to build these immense monuments. During this Pyramid Age, or Old Kingdom (2686–2181 B.C.), royal power reached its height, and the essential forms of Egyptian civilization crystallized.

The Egyptians believed the pharaoh to be both a man and a god, the earthly embodiment of the deity Horus. He was an absolute ruler who kept the irrigation works in order, maintained justice in the land, and expressed the will of heaven. In time, the nobles who served as district governors gained in status and wealth and gradually came to undermine the divine king's authority. The nobles' growing power and the enormous expenditure of Egypt's human and material resources on building pyramids led to the decline of the Old Kingdom. From 2181 to 2040 B.C., a span of time called the First Intermediate Period, rival families competed for the throne, destroying the unity of the kingdom. The civil wars and collapse of the central authority required to maintain the irrigation system cast a pall over the land.

During what is called the Middle Kingdom (2040–1786 B.C.), strong kings reasserted pharaonic rule and reunited the state. The restoration of political stability reinvigorated cultural life, and economic activity revived. Pharaohs extended Egyptian control south over the land of Nubia (modern Sudan), which became a principal source of gold. A profitable trade was carried on with Palestine, Syria, and Crete.

Around 1800 B.C., central authority again weakened. In the era known as the Second Intermediate Period (1786–1570 B.C.), the nobles regained some of their power, the Nubians broke away from Egyptian control, and the Hyksos (a mixture of Semites and Indo-Europeans) invaded Egypt. The Hyksos dominated Egypt for about a hundred years, until the Egyptians drove them out in 1570 B.C. The period of empire building known as the New Kingdom (1570–1085 B.C.) then began.

The basic features of Egyptian civilization had been forged during the Old and Middle Kingdoms. Egyptians looked to the past, convinced that the ways of their ancestors were best. For almost three thousand years, Egyptian civilization sought to retain a harmony with the order of nature instituted at creation. Believing in a changeless universe, the Egyptians did not value change or development—what we call progress—but venerated the institutions, traditions, and authority that embodied permanence.

Religion: The Basis of Egyptian Civilization

Religion was omnipresent in Egyptian life and accounted for the outstanding achievements of Egyptian civilization. Religious beliefs were the basis of Egyptian art, medicine, astronomy, literature, and government. The great pyramids, which took decades to finish, were tombs for the pharaohs, man-gods. Magical utterances pervaded medical practices, for disease was attributed to the gods. Astronomy evolved to determine the correct time for performing religious rites and sacrifices. The earliest examples of literature dealt wholly with religious themes. A sacrosanct monarch, the pharaoh served as an intermediary between the gods and human beings. The Egyptians developed an ethical code, which they believed the gods had approved.

Egyptian polytheism took many forms, including the worship of animals, for the people believed that gods manifested themselves in both human and animal shapes. The Egyptians also believed the great powers in nature—sky, sun, earth, the Nile—to be gods or the abodes of gods. In the heavens alive with gods, the Egyptians found answers to the great problems of human existence. In their temples, Egyptians prayed and dedicated offerings to their gods. During temple rituals, women chanted and played musical instruments.

A crucial feature of Egyptian religion was the afterlife. Through pyramid-tombs, mummification to preserve the dead, and funerary art, the Egyptians showed their yearning for eternity and their desire to overcome death. Mortuary priests recited incantations to ensure the preservation of the dead body and the continuity of existence. Inscribed on the pyramids' interior walls were "pyramid texts," written in *hieroglyphics*—a form of picture writing in which figures, such as crocodiles, sails, eyes, and so forth, represented

STROLL IN THE GARDEN, EIGHTEENTH DYNASTY, c. 1350 B.C. This relief portrays members of the Egyptian royal family.

words or sounds that would be combined to form words. The texts contained fragments from myths, historical annals, and magical lore and provided spells to assist the king in ascending to heaven.

At first, the Egyptians believed that only the pharaoh and the royal family were immortal. In time, the nobility and then commoners claimed that they too could share in the blessings of the "other world." Prayers hitherto reserved for the pharaoh were, for a fee, recited by priests at the burial of commoners. Believing that their deceased relative would intercede with the gods in their behalf, Egyptians wrote letters to these spirits, petitioning them for help with such problems as infertility, inheritance of property, and family quarrels. To the Egyptians, the other world offered the same pleasures as those enjoyed on earth: friends, servants, fishing, hunting, paddling a canoe, picnicking with family members, entertainment by musicians and dancers, and good food. But since earthly existence was not fundamentally unhappy, Egyptians did not long for death.

Divine Kingship

Divine kingship was the basic institution of Egyptian civilization. The Egyptians saw rule by a god-king as the only acceptable political arrangement: it was in harmony with the order of the universe, and it brought justice and security to the nation.

The pharaoh's power extended to all sectors of society. Peasants were drafted to serve in labor corps as miners or construction workers. Foreign trade was a state monopoly, conducted according to the kingdom's needs. As the supreme overlord, the pharaoh oversaw an army of government officials who collected taxes, supervised construction projects, checked the irrigation works, surveyed the land, kept records, conducted foreign trade, and supervised government warehouses, where grain was stored as insurance against a bad harvest. All Egyptians, including the priesthood and standing army, were subservient to the pharaoh, whose word was regarded as a divine ordinance. Most pharaohs took their responsibilities seriously and tried to govern as benevolent protectors of the people.

The pharaoh was seen as ruling in accordance with *Ma'at*, which means "justice, law, right, and truth." To oppose the pharaoh was to violate the universal and divinely ordained order of Ma'at and to bring disorder to society. Because the Egyptians regarded Ma'at, which was established with the creation of the universe, as the right order of nature, they believed that its preservation must be the object of human activity—the guiding norm of the state and the standard by which individuals conducted their lives. Those who did Ma'at and spoke Ma'at would be justly rewarded. Could anything be more reassuring than this belief that divine truth was represented in the person of the pharaoh, who guaranteed and defended the sacred order of the universe?

Science, Mathematics, and Literature

Like the Mesopotamians, the Egyptians made practical advances in the sciences. They demonstrated superb engineering skills in building pyramids and fashioned an effective system of mathematics, including geometry for measurements, which enabled them to solve relatively simple problems. The Egyptians' solar calendar, which allowed them to predict when the Nile would overflow, was more accurate than the Babylonians' lunar calendar.

In the area of medicine, Egyptian doctors were more capable than their Mesopotamian counterparts. They could identify illnesses and recognized that uncleanliness encouraged contagion. They also had some knowledge of anatomy and performed operations: circumcision and perhaps the draining of abscessed teeth. But their knowledge of medicine, like that of the Mesopotamians, was handicapped by their belief that supernatural forces caused illnesses. Thus sick people were instructed to recite an incantation designed to free the body from the demon's hold and to perform a ritual act such as being burned with hot irons.

Generally only a small percentage of the population—the elite—was literate. Egyptian literature took a wide variety of forms: hymns and other religious texts; love poems; tales of adventure, romance, and fantasy; and collections of maxims prepared by elderly sages for the benefit of young rulers. Containing hymns, litanies, and other religious texts, the *Book of the Dead* was written to guide a deceased person safely between this world and the afterlife. In the "Judgment Hall," before Osiris and other gods who assisted him, deceased individuals proclaimed, among other things, that they had not robbed, murdered, or uttered evil words.

The New Kingdom and the Decline of Egyptian Civilization

The New Kingdom began in 1570 B.C. with the war of liberation against the Hyksos. This war gave rise to an intense militancy, which found expression in empire building. Aggressive pharaohs conquered territory that extended as far east as the Euphrates River. From its subject states, Egypt acquired tribute and slaves. Conquests led to the expansion of the bureaucracy, the development of a professional army, and the increased power of priests, whose temples—which grew larger and more lavish—shared in the spoils. Foreign slaves acquired from imperial conquests provided much of the labor for the construction of new shrines and temples. The formation of the empire ended Egyptian isolation and accelerated commercial and cultural intercourse with other peoples. During this period, Egyptian art, for example, showed the influence of foreign forms.

A growing cosmopolitanism was paralleled by a movement toward monotheism during the reign of Pharaoh Amenhotep IV (c. 1369–1353 B.C.). Amenhotep sought to replace traditional polytheism with the worship of Aton, a single god of all people, who was represented as the sun disk. Amenhotep took the name Akhenaten ("It is well with Aton") and moved the capital from Thebes to a newly constructed holy city called Akhataten (near modern Tell el Amarna). The city had palaces, administrative centers, and a temple complex honoring Aton. Akhenaten and his wife, Nefertiti, who played a prominent role in his court, dedicated themselves to Aton—the creator of the world, the sustainer of life, and the god of love, justice, and peace. Akhenaten also ordered his officials to chisel out the names of Egypt's traditional gods from inscriptions on temples and monuments. With awe, Akhenaten glorified Aton:

> *How manifold are thy works!*
> *They are hidden from man's sight.*
> *O sole god, like whom there is no other.*
> *Thou hast made the earth according to thy*
> *desire.*[2]

Akhenaten's "monotheism" had little impact on the masses of Egyptians, who retained their ancient beliefs, and was resisted by priests, who resented his changes. After Akhenaten's death, a new pharaoh had the monuments to Aton destroyed, along with records and inscriptions bearing Akhenaten's name. The great visionary was now vilified as "the Blasphemer."

The most significant historical questions about Akhenaten are these two: was his religion genuine monotheism, which pushed religious thought in a new direction? And if so, did it influence Moses, who led the Israelites out of Egypt about a century later? These questions have aroused controversy among historians. The principal limitation on the monotheistic character of Atonism is that there were really two gods in Akhenaten's religion: Aton and the pharaoh himself, who was still worshiped as a deity. Nor is there any evidence that Akhenaten influenced the monotheism of Moses. Moreover, the Hebrews never identified their God with the sun or any other object in nature.

Late in the thirteenth century B.C., Libyans, probably seeking to settle in the more fertile land of Egypt, attacked from the west, and the Peoples of the Sea, as unsettled raiders from the Aegean Sea area and Asia Minor were called, launched a series of strikes at Egypt. A weakened Egypt abandoned

Erich Lessing/Art Resource, N.Y.

AKHENATEN. A bas relief found in Tell el-Amarna shows Akhenaten and his family sacrificing to Aton, the sun god.

its empire. In the succeeding centuries, Egypt came under the rule of Libyans, Nubians, Assyrians, Persians, and finally Greeks, to whom Egypt lost its independence in the fourth century B.C.

Egyptian civilization had flourished for nearly two thousand years before it experienced an almost one-thousand-year descent into stagnation, decline, and collapse. During its long history, the Egyptians tried to preserve the ancient forms of their civilization, revealed to them by their ancestors and representing for all time those unchanging values that they believed were the way of happiness.

EMPIRE BUILDERS

The rise of an Egyptian empire during the New Kingdom was part of a wider development in Near Eastern history after 1500 B.C.—the emergence of international empires. Empire building led to the intermingling of peoples and cultural traditions and to the extension of civilization well beyond the river valleys.

One reason for the growth of empires was the migration of peoples known as Indo-Europeans. Originally from a wide area ranging from southeastern Europe to the region beyond the Caspian Sea, Indo-Europeans embarked, around 2000 B.C., on a series of migrations that eventually brought them into Italy, Greece, Asia Minor, Mesopotamia, Persia, and India. From a core Indo-European tongue emerged the Greek, Latin, Germanic, Slavic, Persian, and Sanskrit languages.

Hittites

Several peoples established strong states in the Near East around 1500 B.C.—the Hurrians in northern Mesopotamia, the Kassites in southern Mesopotamia, and the Hittites in Asia Minor. The Hittites wanted to control the trade routes that ran along the Euphrates River into Syria. In the 1300s, the Hittite empire reached its peak. Its leaders ruled Asia Minor and northern Syria, raided Babylon, and challenged Egypt for control of Syria and Palestine.

The Hittites borrowed several features of Mesopotamian civilization, including cuneiform, legal principles, and literary and art forms. Hittite religion blended the beliefs and practices of Indo-Europeans, native inhabitants of Asia Minor, and Mesopotamians. The Hittites were probably the first people to develop a substantial iron industry. Initially, they apparently used iron only for ceremonial and ritual objects and not for tools and weapons. However, because iron ore was more readily available than copper or tin (needed for bronze), after 1200 B.C. iron weapons and tools spread throughout the Near East, although bronze implements were still used. Around 1200 B.C., the Hittite empire fell, most likely to Indo-European invaders from the north.

Small Nations

During the twelfth century B.C., there was a temporary lull in empire building, and this permitted a number of small nations in Syria and Palestine to assert their sovereignty. Three of these peoples—the Phoenicians, the Aramaeans, and the Hebrews*—were originally Semitic desert nomads. The Phoenicians were descendants of the Canaanites, a Semitic people who had settled Palestine around 3000 B.C. The Canaanites who had migrated northwest into what is now Lebanon were called Phoenicians.

Settling in the coastal Mediterranean cities of Tyre, Byblos, Berytus (Beirut), and Sidon, the Phoenicians were naturally drawn to the sea. These daring explorers established towns along the coast of North Africa, on the islands of the western Mediterranean, and in Spain; they became the greatest sea traders of the ancient world. The Phoenicians (or their Canaanite forebears) devised the first alphabet, which was a monumental contribution to writing. Since all words could be represented by combinations of letters, it saved memorizing thousands of diagrams and aided the Phoenicians in transmitting the cultural achievements of the Near East to the western Mediterranean. Adopted by the Greeks, who added vowels, the phonetic alphabet became a crucial component of European languages.

The Aramaeans, who settled in Syria, Palestine, and northern Mesopotamia, performed a role similar to that of the Phoenicians. As great caravan

*The Hebrews are discussed in Chapter 2.

traders, they carried both goods and cultural patterns to various parts of the Near East. The Hebrews and the Persians, for example, acquired the Phoenician alphabet from the Aramaeans.

Assyria

In the ninth century B.C., empire building resumed with the Assyrians, a Semitic people from the region around the upper Tigris River. Although they had made forays of expansion in 1200 and 1100 B.C., the Assyrians began their march to "world" empire three centuries later. In the eighth and seventh centuries, they became a ruthless fighting machine that stormed through Mesopotamia—including Armenia and Babylonia—as well as Syria, Palestine, and Egypt.

The Assyrian king, who was the representative and high priest of the god Ashur, governed absolutely. Nobles appointed by the king kept order in the provinces and collected tribute. The Assyrians improved roads, established messenger services, and engaged in large-scale irrigation projects to facilitate effective administration of their conquered lands and to promote prosperity. They exacted obedience by resorting to terror and by deporting troublemakers from their home territories.

Despite an almost all-consuming concern for war, the Assyrians preserved and spread the culture of the past. They copied and edited the literary works of Babylonia, adopted the old Sumerian gods, and used Mesopotamian art forms. The Assyrian king Ashurbanipal (669–626 B.C.) maintained a great library that housed thousands of clay tablets. After a period of wars and revolts by oppressed subjects weakened Assyria, a coalition of Medes from Iran and Chaldeans, or Neo-Babylonians, sacked the Assyrian capital of Nineveh in 612 B.C., destroying Assyrian power.

Persia: Unifier of the Near East

The destruction of the Assyrian empire made possible the rise of a Chaldean empire that included Babylonia, Assyria, Syria, and Palestine. Under Nebuchadnezzar, who ruled from 604 to 562 B.C., the Chaldean, or Neo-Babylonian, empire reached its height. After Nebuchadnezzar's death, the empire

was torn by civil war and threatened by a new power: the Persians, an Indo-European people who had settled in southern Iran. (Iranians today are descendants of the ancient Persians.) Under Cyrus the Great and his son and successor, Cambyses, the Persians conquered all lands between the Nile in Egypt and the Indus River in India. This conquest took twenty-five years, from 550 to 525 B.C.

The Near Eastern conception of absolute monarchy justified by religion reached its culminating expression in the person of the Persian king, who, with divine approval, ruled a vast empire, "the four quarters of the earth." Persian kings developed an effective system of administration—based in part on an Assyrian model—that gave stability and a degree of unity to their extensive territories. The Persian empire was divided into twenty provinces (*satrapies*), each one administered by a governor (*satrap*) responsible to the emperor. To guard against subversion, the king employed special agents—"the eyes and ears of the emperor"—who supervised the activities of the governors. Persian kings allowed the provincials a large measure of self-rule. They also respected local traditions, particularly in matters of religion, as long as subjects paid their taxes, served in the royal army, and refrained from rebellion.

The empire was bound together by a uniform language, Aramaic (the language of the Aramaeans of Syria), used by government officials and merchants. Aramaic was written in letters based on the Phoenician alphabet. By making Aramaic a universal language, the Persians facilitated written and oral communication within the empire. The empire was further unified by an elaborate network of roads, an efficient postal system, a common system of weights and measures, and an empirewide coinage based on an invention of the Lydians from western Asia Minor. The Persian military was a multinational force recruited and conscripted from numerous lands and the royal bureaucracy was also staffed by a wide range of peoples.

Besides providing impressive political and administrative unity, the Persians fused and perpetuated the various cultural traditions of the Near East. Persian palaces, for example, boasted the terraces of Babylon, the colonnades of Egypt, the winged bulls that decorated Assyrian palace gates, and the craftsmanship of Median goldsmiths.

Map 1.2 **The Assyrian and Persian Empires** In the last part of the sixth century B.C., the Persians established the greatest empire of the ancient Near East, conquering all the lands between the Nile in Egypt and the Indus River in India.

The political and cultural universalism of the Persian empire had its counterpart in the emergence of an ethically oriented religion, Zoroastrianism, which contained both monotheistic and dualistic elements and emphasized the individual's capacity to choose between good and evil. Named for its founder, the Persian prophet Zoroaster, who probably lived in the sixth century B.C. (although some scholars place him much earlier), this religion taught belief in Ahura Mazda—the Wise Lord—the eternal god of light, the creator of the universe, the embodiment of justice, wisdom, and goodness. In addition to Ahura Mazda, however, there existed Ahriman, the spirit of darkness, who was evil and destructive; Ahriman was in conflict with the ultimately triumphant Ahura Mazda. People were free to choose whom they would follow. To serve Ahura Mazda, one had to speak the truth and be good to others; the reward for such behavior was eternal life in paradise, the realm of light and goodness.

Followers of the evil spirit could be cast into a realm of darkness and torment. In contrast to the traditional religions of the Near East, Zoroastrianism rejected magic, polytheism, and blood sacrifices. Instead, it stressed ethics.

Persia unified the nations of the Near East into a world-state, headed by a divinely appointed king. It also synthesized the region's cultural traditions. Soon it would confront the city-states of Greece, whose political system and cultural orientation differed from those of the Near East.

THE RELIGIOUS ORIENTATION OF THE ANCIENT NEAR EAST

Religion dominated, suffused, and inspired all features of Near Eastern society: law, kingship, art, and science. In the first civilizations, the deepest thoughts of human beings were

PERSEPOLIS, IRAN, C. 500 B.C. The Persian ruler Darius (522–486 B.C.) constructed a thirty-acre earthen terrace almost fifty feet above the plain and built there a complex of palaces, reception halls, a treasury, and barracks for his royal guards. Persepolis became the ceremonial center of the vast Persian empire until it was destroyed by Alexander the Great's soldiers.

expressed in the form of religious myths. Priest-kings or god-kings, their power sanctioned by divine forces, furnished the necessary authority to organize large numbers of people in cooperative ventures. Religion also encouraged and justified wars—including enslavements and massacres—which were seen as conflicts between the gods. Religious beliefs and values served as a powerful social force uniting people into a cohesive community.

A Mythmaking Worldview

A religious, or mythopoeic (mythmaking), view of the world gave Near Eastern civilization its distinctive form and allows us to see it as an organic whole. Mesopotamians and Egyptians inherited from their prehistoric ancestors a great variety of communally produced imagery, rituals, and tales accounting for the origin of the world and human life. With unrestrained imagination, they altered the old myths and elaborated new ones to resolve questions that today we try to answer with science. Mythmaking was humanity's first way of thinking; it was the earliest attempt to explain the beginnings of the universe and human history, to make nature's mysteries and life's uncertainties comprehensible.

Originating in sacred rites, ritual dances, feasts, and ceremonies, myths depicted the deeds of gods, who, in some remote past, had brought forth the world and human beings. Holding that human destiny was determined by the gods, Near Eastern people interpreted their experiences through myths. Mesopotamian myths, for example, attributed personal misfortune and the catastrophes that afflicted a city to supernatural forces displeased with people's behavior. These myths gave Near Eastern people a framework with which to pattern their experiences into a meaningful order, justify their rules of conduct, make nature intelligible, and help them to overcome the uncertainty of existence.

The civilizations of the ancient Near East were based on a way of thinking fundamentally different from the modern scientific outlook. The scientific mind views physical nature as an *it*—inanimate, impersonal, and governed by universal law. The mythmaking mind of the Near East saw every object in nature as a *thou*—personified, alive, with an individual will. It saw gods or demons manipulating things. The world was enchanted, imbued with mysterious spirits. The sun and stars, the rivers and mountains, the wind and lightning were either gods or the dwelling places of gods. Live agents were the forces behind natural events. If a river flooded the region, destroying crops, it was because it wanted to; the river or the gods desired to punish the people. The Babylonians attributed drought to the hot breath of the Bull of Heaven. The drought ended when the gigantic bird Imdugud devoured the bull and covered the sky with the storm clouds in its wings.

The Egyptians believed that Nut, the sky goddess, gave birth to the sun, a deity who sailed west across the celestial sea before descending into his mother's womb to be reborn again in the morning. For the Egyptians, the rising and setting of the sun were not natural occurrences—a celestial body obeying an impersonal law—but a religious drama.

The scientific mind holds that natural objects obey universal rules; hence, the location of planets, the speed of objects, and the onset of a hurricane can be predicted. The mythmaking mind of the ancient Near East attributed all occurrences in nature to the actions of gods, whose behavior was often erratic and unpredictable. Shamans employed magic to protect people from evil supernatural forces that surrounded them. Mythical explanations of nature and human experience made life seem less overwhelming and death less frightening.

Of course, Near Eastern people did engage in rational forms of thought and behavior. They certainly employed reason in building irrigation works, in preparing a calendar, in calculating the rise of the Nile, and in performing mathematical operations. Moreover, in their daily life, men and women were often driven by purely pragmatic concerns. Fields had to be planted, goods sold, and household chores attended to. In dealing with these concerns, people did what had to be done in commonsense ways. They planned and prepared; they weighed actions as either beneficial or harmful and behaved accordingly. However, because rational, or logical, thought remained subordinate to a mythic-religious orientation, they did not arrive at a *consistently* and *self-consciously* rational method of inquiring into physical nature and human culture.

Thus, Near Eastern civilization reached the first level in the development of science: observing nature, recording data, and improving technology in mining, metallurgy, and architecture. But it did not advance to the level of self-conscious philosophical and scientific thought—that is, logically deduced abstractions, hypotheses, and generalizations. Mesopotamians and Egyptians did not fashion a body of philosophical and scientific ideas that were logically structured, discussed, and debated. They had no awareness of general laws that govern particular events. These later developments were the singular achievement of Greek philosophy. It gave a "rational interpretation to natural occurrences which had previously been explained by ancient mythologies. . . . With the study of nature set free from the control of mythological fancy, the way was opened for the development of science as an intellectual system."[3]

Mythical Thinking

Mesopotamians and Egyptians believed that their destinies were determined by the gods. Drought, hurricanes, sickness, and foreign invasion were all attributed to divine intervention. In the "Lament for Ur" the assembly of gods decides to punish the Sumerian city-state of Ur. The execution of the assembly's command is left to Enlil.

To the evil storm Enlil gave (his) order;
    The people groan.
To the storm that annihilates the land he called;
    The people groan.
To all the evil winds he called.
    The people groan.
Enlil brings Gibil to his aid;
To the great storm of heaven he called.
    The people groan.
The great storm howls above;
    The people groan.
The land-annihilating storm roars below.
    The people groan.
The evil wind like the rushing torrent cannot
    be restrained;
The boats of the city it attacks (and)
    devours. . . .
In front of the storm *it made fire burn*;
    The people groan. . . .
The destructive storm makes the land tremble
    and quake;
Like the storm of the flood it destroys the cities.

The land-annihilating storm set up (its) decrees
    in the city;
The all-destroying storm came doing evil. . . .
The evil, afflicting storm, the command of
    Enlil, the storm unceasingly undermining
    the land
Covered Ur like a garment, enveloped it like
    linen. . . .
On its walls *they lay prostrate.*
    The people groan.
In its lofty gates where they were won't to
    promenade dead bodies were lying about;
In its boulevards where the feasts were
    celebrated they were *viciously attacked.*
In all its streets where they were wont to
    promenade dead bodies were lying about;
In its places where the festivities of the land
    took place the people were *ruthlessly laid low.*

Questions for Analysis

1. How does mythical thinking differ from scientific thinking?
2. It has been said that humans are myth-making animals and that all human societies sustain themselves by creating myths. Discuss.

Samuel N. Kramer, "Lamentation Over the Destruction of Ur," Assyriological *Studies*, The Oriental Institute of the University of Chicago (University of Chicago Press, 1940), vol 12, pp. 35–41.

Near Eastern Achievements

The Sumerians and the Egyptians demonstrated enormous creativity and intelligence. They built irrigation works and cities, organized governments, charted the course of heavenly bodies, performed mathematical operations, constructed large-scale monuments, engaged in international trade, established bureaucracies and schools, and considerably advanced the level of technology and engineering skills. Without the Sumerian invention of writing—one of the great creative acts in history—what we mean by *civilization* could not have emerged.

Many elements of ancient Near Eastern civilization were passed on to the West. The wheeled vehicle, the plow, and the phonetic alphabet—all important to the development of civilization—derive from the Near East. In the realm of medicine, the Egyptians knew the value of certain drugs, such as castor oil; they also knew how to use splints and bandages. The innovative divisions that gave 360 degrees to a circle and 60 minutes to an hour originated in Mesopotamia. Egyptian geometry and Babylonian astronomy were utilized by the Greeks and became a part of Western knowledge. In Christian art, too, one finds connections to Mesopotamian art forms—for example, the Assyrians depicted winged angel-like beings.

Both the Hebrews and the Greeks borrowed Mesopotamian literary themes. For instance, some biblical stories—the Flood, the quarrel between Cain and Abel, and the Tower of Babel—stem from Mesopotamian antecedents. A similar link exists between the Greek and the earlier Mesopotamian mythologies.

Thus, many achievements of the Egyptians and the Mesopotamians were inherited and assimilated by both the Greeks and the Hebrews, the principal founders of Western civilization. Even more important for an understanding of the essential meaning of Western civilization are the ways in which the Greeks and the Hebrews rejected or transformed elements of the older Near Eastern traditions to create new points of departure for the human mind.

NOTES

1. *Epic of Gilgamesh,* with an introduction by N. K. Sandars (Baltimore: Penguin Books, 1960), 69, 104.

2. Quoted in John A. Wilson, *The Culture of Ancient Egypt* (Chicago: University of Chicago Press, Phoenix Books, 1951), 227.

3. Samuel Sambursky, *The Physical World of the Greeks* (New York: Collier Books, 1962), 18–19.

Chapter 2

The Hebrews: A New View of God and the Individual

- **Early Hebrew History**
- **God: One, Sovereign, Transcendent, Good**
- **The Individual and Moral Autonomy**
- **The Covenant and the Law**
- **The Hebrew Idea of History**
- **The Prophets**
- **The Legacy of the Ancient Jews**

Focus Questions

1. In what ways did the Hebrew view of God mark a revolutionary break with Near Eastern thought?
2. How did Hebrew religious thought promote the ideas of moral autonomy?
3. What were the distinguishing features of Hebrew law?
4. What were the unique achievements of the Hebrew prophets?
5. Why are the Hebrews regarded as a principal source of the Western tradition?

Ancient Mesopotamia and Egypt, the birthplaces of the first civilizations, are not the spiritual ancestors of the West; for the origins of the Western tradition we must turn to the Hebrews (Jews) and the Greeks. Both Greeks and Hebrews, of course, absorbed elements of the civilizations of Mesopotamia and Egypt, but what is more significant is how they transformed this inheritance and shaped worldviews that differed markedly from the outlooks of these first civilizations. As Egyptologist John A. Wilson writes,

> *The Children of Israel built a nation and a religion on the rejection of things Egyptian. Not only did they see God as one, but they ascribed to him consistency of concern for man and consistency of justice to man. . . . Like the Greeks, the Hebrews took forms from their great neighbors; like the Greeks, they used those forms for very different purposes.*[1]

In this chapter, we examine one source of the Western tradition, the Hebrews, whose conception of God broke with the outlook of the Near East and whose ethical teachings helped to fashion the Western idea of the dignity of the individual. ❖

EARLY HEBREW HISTORY

The Hebrews (Israelites or Jews) originated in Mesopotamia and migrated to Canaan, a portion of which was later called Palestine.* The Hebrew patriarchs—Abraham, Isaac, and Jacob, so prominently depicted in the Old Testament—were chieftains of seminomadic clans that roamed Palestine and occasionally journeyed to Mesopotamia and Egypt. The early Hebrews absorbed some features of Mesopotamian civilization. For example, there are parallels between biblical law and the Mesopotamian legal tradition. Several biblical stories, including those of the Garden of Eden and the Flood, derive from Mesopotamian sources. The wise sayings of Egyptian teachers have parallels in Hebrew wisdom literature.

According to Hebrew Scriptures, some Hebrews journeyed from Canaan to Egypt to be herdsmen and farmers, but they eventually

became forced laborers for the Egyptians. Fearful of turning into permanent slaves of the pharaoh, the Hebrews yearned for an opportunity to escape. In the thirteenth century B.C., an extraordinary leader called Moses rose among them and was accepted as a messenger of God. Leading the Hebrews in their flight from Egypt, Moses transformed them during their wanderings in the wilderness of Sinai into a nation, united and uplifted by a belief in Yahweh, the one God. The inspiring biblical narrative of God's liberation of the Hebrews from slavery is the fulcrum of Jewish history.

Some scholars dismiss the Exodus as fiction, arguing that there is no extrabiblical evidence for the Exodus or even for the presence of Hebrews in Egypt; while there are abundant Egyptian hieroglyphics detailing events at the time, none of them refer specifically to Israelites in Egypt. Certainly, say these scholars, the flight of thousands of foreigners would have attracted notice. Moreover, it is highly unlikely that an escape by a large group of slaves could have succeeded when Egypt was at the peak of its power. The biblical account says that Israelites wandered in the Sinai Desert for forty years, but archeologists, who have excavated numerous sites in the Sinai mentioned in the Book of Exodus, have uncovered no traces of Israelite campsites. These scholars, known as biblical minimalists, deny there ever was an Exodus from Egypt. Other scholars reject this position, holding that there is evidence of Asiatic slaves toiling in Egypt, some of whom might have been Hebrews. Moreover, assert these scholars, ancient Hebrew scribes would not have concocted and faithfully preserved such an inglorious history of enslavement unless the biblical account contained a core historical truth along with legend, folklore, and mythic imagery.

The wandering Hebrews returned to Canaan to rejoin other Hebrew tribes that had not migrated to Egypt. The conquest and colonization of Canaan was a gradual process that took many generations. Threatened by the Philistines (originally from the islands of the Aegean Sea and the coast of Asia Minor), the twelve Hebrew tribes united under the leadership of Saul, a charismatic hero, whom they acclaimed as their first king. Under Saul's successor, David, a gifted warrior

---

*Since there is a paucity of references to the early Hebrews in nonbiblical sources, scholars have to rely almost entirely on the Hebrew Bible for reconstructing much of the history of the ancient Israelites. The divergence of scholarly opinion regarding the Bible's accuracy and reliability creates additional uncertainty for the historian.

and poet, the Hebrews (or Israelites) broke the back of Philistine power and subdued neighboring peoples.

David's son Solomon built a royal palace in Jerusalem and beside it a magnificent temple honoring God. Under Solomon, ancient Israel was at the height of its political power and prosperity, but opposition to Solomon's tax policies and his favored treatment of the region of Judah in the south led to the division of the kingdom after his death in 922 B.C. The tribes loyal to Solomon's son belonged to the Kingdom of Judah, whereas the other tribes organized the northern Kingdom of Israel.

In 722 B.C., Israel fell to the Assyrians, who deported many Hebrews to other parts of the Assyrian empire. These transplanted Hebrews merged with neighboring peoples and lost their identity as the people who had made a covenant with God. By 586 B.C., the Chaldeans had conquered Judah, destroyed Solomon's temple, devastated the land, and deported several thousand Hebrews to Babylon. This was the darkest moment in the history of the Hebrews. Their state was gone, and neighboring peoples had overrun their land; their holy temple, built during the reign of King Solomon, was in ruins; thousands had died in battle, had been executed or had fled to Egypt and other lands; and thousands more were in exile in Babylon. This exile is known as the Babylonian Captivity.

Still, the Hebrews, now commonly called Jews, survived as a people—a fact that is a marvel of history. Although many of the exiles in Babylon assimilated Babylonian ways, some remained faithful to their God, Yahweh, and to the Law of Moses, and they longed to return to their homeland. Thus, their faith enabled them to endure conquest and exile. When the Persians conquered Babylon, King Cyrus, in 538 B.C., permitted the exiles to return to Judah, now a Persian province, and to rebuild the temple.

The Jews regained their independence in the second century B.C.; however, in the next century their land fell within the Roman orbit. After failed revolutions in the first and second centuries A.D., they became a dispersed people. But they never relinquished their commitment to God and his Law as recorded in the Hebrew Scriptures. Called *Tanak* by Jews (and the Old Testament by Christians), these Scriptures consist of thirty-nine books by several authors who lived in different centuries. Jews call the first five books—Genesis, Exodus, Leviticus, Numbers, and Deuteronomy—the Torah (which originally meant "teaching" or "instruction"). Often the Torah is referred to as the Pentateuch, a Greek word meaning "five books."

The Hebrew Scriptures represent Jewish written and oral tradition dating from about 1250 to 150 B.C. The record of more than a thousand years of ancient Jewish life, they include Jewish laws,

John C. Trever Family

A DEAD SEA SCROLL, JUDEA, SECOND CENTURY B.C. God's law, as recorded in the Holy Scriptures, still remains a unifying force among Jews. Many ancient Hebrew scrolls were found in caves near the west bank of the Dead Sea beginning in the late 1940s. The scroll depicted here contains the earliest existing copy of a complete Hebrew text of the book of the prophet Isaiah. It barely differs from more modern manuscripts.

wisdom, hopes, legends, and literary expressions. In describing an ancient people's efforts to comprehend the ways of God, the Scriptures emphasize and value the human experience; their heroes are not demigods but human beings. The Scriptures depict human strength as well as weakness. Some passages exhibit cruelty and unseemly revenge against the enemies of Israel and apostates, but others express the highest ethical values.

Compiled by religious devotees, not research historians, the Hebrew Scriptures understandably contain factual errors, imprecisions, and discrepancies. However, they also offer passages of reliable history, and historians find these Scriptures an indispensable source for studying the ancient Near East. Students of literature explore the Old Testament for its poetry, legends, and

themes, all of which are an integral part of the Western literary tradition. But it is as a work of religious inspiration that the Hebrew Bible attains its profoundest importance. As set forth there, the Hebrew idea of God and his relationship to human beings is one of the foundations of the Western tradition.

GOD: ONE, SOVEREIGN, TRANSCENDENT, GOOD

Monotheism, the belief in one God, became the central force in the life of the Hebrews and marked a profound break with Near Eastern religious thought. Near Eastern gods were not truly free; their power was not without limits. Unlike Yahweh, Near Eastern gods were not eternal but were born or created; they issued from some prior realm. They were also subject to biological conditions, requiring food, drink, sleep, and sexual gratification. Sometimes they became ill or grew old or died. When they behaved wickedly, they had to answer to fate, which demanded punishment as retribution; even the gods were subject to fate's power.

The Hebrews regarded God as *fully sovereign.* He ruled all and was subject to nothing. The Hebrews believed that nothing preceded God in time or surpassed him in power. They saw God as eternal and omnipotent, as the source of all in the universe, and as having a supreme will.

Whereas Near Eastern divinities dwelt within nature, the Hebrew God was *transcendent,* above nature and not a part of it. Yahweh was not identified with any natural force and did not dwell in a particular place in heaven or on earth. Since God was the creator and ruler of nature, there was no place for a sun god, a moon god, a god in the river, or a demon in the storm. Nature was God's creation, but was not itself divine. The stars and planets were creations of Yahweh, not divinities or the abodes of divinities. The Hebrews neither regarded them with awe nor worshiped them.

The removal of the gods from nature—the demythicizing of nature—is a necessary prerequisite for scientific thought. But concerned as they were with religion and morality, the Hebrews did not create theoretical science. As testimony to God's greatness, nature inspired them to sing the praises of the Lord; it invoked worship of God, not scientific curiosity. When they gazed at the heavens, they did not seek to discover mathematical relationships but admired God's magnificent handiwork. They did not view nature as a system governed by self-operating physical principles or natural law. Rather, they saw the rising sun, spring rain, summer heat, and winter cold as God intervening in an orderly manner in his creation. The Hebrews, unlike the Greeks, were not philosophical or scientific thinkers. They were concerned with God's will, not the human intellect; with the feelings of the heart, not the power of the mind; with righteous behavior, not abstract thought.

Unlike the Greeks, the Hebrews did not speculate about the origins of all things and the operations of nature; they knew that God had created everything. For the Hebrews, God's existence was based on religious conviction, not on rational inquiry; on revelation, not reason. It was the Greeks, not the Hebrews, who originated self-conscious, systematic, rational thought. But Christianity, born of Judaism, retained the Hebrew view of a transcendent God and the orderliness of his creation concepts that could accommodate Greek science.

The Hebrews also did not speculate about God's nature. They knew only that he was *good* and that he made ethical demands on his people, who were obligated to imitate God's holiness. Unlike Near Eastern gods, Yahweh was not driven by lust or motivated by evil but was "merciful and gracious, long-suffering, and abundant in goodness and truth . . . forgiving inequity and transgression and sin" (Psalm 145:8).[2] In contrast to pagan gods, who were indifferent to human beings, Yahweh was attentive to human needs. By asserting that God was *one, sovereign, transcendent,* and *good,* the Hebrews effected a religious revolution that separated them entirely from the worldview held by the other peoples of the ancient Near East.

THE INDIVIDUAL AND MORAL AUTONOMY

This new conception of God made possible a new awareness of the individual, who was seen as the culmination and centerpiece of God's creation. Created in the image of God, the human being is unique, qualitatively different from the rest of animate nature. Only the human being has the power of volition, the power to make choices. The Hebrews believed that God, who possessed total freedom himself, had bestowed on his people moral freedom—the capacity to take responsibility for one's conduct and to choose between good and evil. Thus, in confronting God, the Hebrews developed an awareness of *self,* or *I:* the individual became conscious of his or her own person, moral autonomy, and personal worth.

Fundamental to Hebrew belief was the insistence that God did not create people to be his slaves. The Hebrews regarded God with awe and humility, with respect and fear, but they did not believe that God wanted people to grovel before him; rather, he wanted them to fulfill their moral potential by freely making the choice to follow or not to follow God's Law. Thus, in creating men and women in his own image, God made them autonomous and sovereign. In God's plan for the universe, human beings were the highest creation, subordinate only to God. Of all his creations, only they had been given the freedom to choose between righteousness and wickedness, between "life and good, and death and evil" (Deuteronomy 30:15).[3] But having the power to choose freely, men and women must bear the responsibility for their choice.

God demanded that the Hebrews have no other gods and that they make no images "nor any manner of likeness, of any thing that is in heaven above, or that is in the earth beneath, . . . thou shalt not bow down unto them nor serve them" (Exodus 20:4–5). The Hebrews believed that the worship of idols deprived people of their freedom and dignity; people cannot be fully human if they surrender themselves to a lifeless idol. Hence, the Hebrews rejected images and all other forms of idolatry. A crucial element of Near Eastern religion was the use of images—art forms that depicted divinities—but the Hebrews believed that God, the Supreme Being, could not be represented by pictures or sculpture fashioned by human hands. The Hebrews rejected entirely the belief that an image possessed divine powers, which could be manipulated for human advantage. Ethical considerations, not myth or magic, were central to Hebrew religious life.

By making God the center of life, Hebrews could become free moral agents; no person, no human institution, and no human tradition could claim their souls. Because God alone was the supreme value in the universe, only he was worthy of worship. Thus, to give ultimate loyalty to a king or a general violated God's stern warning against the worship of false gods. The

first concern of the Hebrews was righteousness, not power, fame, or riches, which were only idols and would impoverish a person spiritually and morally.

There was, however, a condition to freedom. For the Hebrews, people were not free to create their own moral precepts, their own standards of right and wrong. Freedom meant voluntary obedience to commands that originated with God. Evil and suffering were not caused by blind fate, malevolent demons, or arbitrary gods; they resulted from people's disregard of God's commandments. The dilemma is that in possessing freedom of choice, human beings are also free to disobey God, to commit sin, which leads to suffering and death. Thus, in the Genesis story, Adam and Eve were punished for disobeying God in the Garden of Eden.

For the Hebrews, to know God was not to comprehend him intellectually, to define him, or to prove his existence; to know God was to be righteous and loving, merciful and just. When men and women loved God, the Hebrews believed, they were uplifted and improved. Gradually, they learned to overcome the worst elements of human nature and to treat people with respect and compassion. The Jews came to interpret the belief that human beings were created in God's image to mean that each individual has a divine spark in him or her, giving every person a unique dignity that cannot be taken away.

Through their devotion to God, the Hebrews asserted the value and autonomy of human beings. Thus, the Hebrews conceived the idea of moral freedom: that each individual is responsible for his or her own actions. These concepts of human dignity and moral autonomy, which Christianity inherited, are at the core of the Western tradition.

THE COVENANT AND THE LAW

Central to Hebrew religious thought and decisive in Hebrew history was the covenant, God's special agreement with the Hebrew people: if they obeyed his commands, they would "be unto Me a kingdom of priests, and a holy nation" (Exodus 19:6). By this act, the Israelites as a nation accepted God's lordship. Justice was the central theme of Old Testament ethics. The Israelites, liberated from slavery by a righteous and compassionate God, had a moral responsibility to overcome injustice and to care for the poor, the weak, and the oppressed.

The Hebrews came to see themselves as a unique nation, a "chosen people," for God had given them a special honor, a profound opportunity, and (as they could never forget) an awesome responsibility. The Hebrews did not claim that God had selected them because they were better than other peoples or because they had done anything special to deserve God's election. They believed

that God had selected them to receive the Law, including the Ten Commandments, so that their nation would set an example of righteous behavior and ultimately make God and his moral commands known to the other nations. This divinely assigned responsibility to be the moral teachers of humanity weighed heavily on the Hebrews.

Israelite law incorporated many elements from Near Eastern legal codes and oral traditions. But by making people more important than property, by expressing mercy toward the oppressed, and by rejecting the idea that law should treat the poor and the rich differently, Israelite law demonstrated a greater ethical awareness and a more

Art Resource, N.Y.

WALL PAINTING FROM THE SYNAGOGUE OF DURA-EUROPOS, ROMAN SYRIA, EARLY THIRD CENTURY A.D. Although a strict prohibition of the use of images inhibited representational art among the Hebrews, in Hellenistic times scenes from Hebrew history appeared on the walls and floors of Jewish synagogues. Here the prophet Samuel is depicted anointing David as king of Israel.

humane spirit than other legal codes of the Near East as the following passage illustrates:

> *Ye shall not steal; neither shall ye deal falsely, nor lie to one another. . . . Thou shalt not oppress thy neighbour nor rob him. . . . Ye shall do no unrighteousness in judgment; thou shalt not respect [be partial to] the person of the poor, nor favour the person of the mighty; but in righteousness shalt thou judge thy neighbor. . . . And if a stranger sojourn with thee in your land, ye shall not do him wrong. The stranger that sojourneth with you shall be unto you as the home born among you, and thou shalt love him as thyself.* (Leviticus 19:11, 13, 15, 33, 34)

While biblical law valued human life and was concerned with human welfare, it also contained provisions that shock us as cruel, for example, ordering the slaughter of the enemy in war, the stoning to death of one's family members who chose to serve other gods, and the execution of homosexuals. It is not known to what extent these commands were actually carried out. Over the centuries, however, there arose an oral and interpretive tradition that made the written law less rigid and led the Hebrews to adapt to changing cultural traditions.

Like other Near Eastern societies, the Jews placed women in a subordinate position. The husband was considered his wife's master, and she often addressed him as a servant or subject would speak to a superior. A husband could divorce his wife, but she could not divorce him. Only when there was no male heir could a wife inherit property from her husband or a daughter from her father. Outside the home, women were not regarded as competent witnesses in court and played a lesser role than men in organized worship.

On the other hand, the Jews also showed respect for women. Wise women and prophetesses like Judith and Deborah were esteemed by the community and consulted by its leaders. Prophets compared God's love for the Hebrews with a husband's love for his wife. Jewish law regarded the woman as a person, not as property who could be bartered. And women were never barred from worshipping God. Even female captives taken in war were not to be abused or humiliated. The law required a husband to respect and support his wife and never to strike her. One of the Ten Commandments called for honoring both father and mother.

THE HEBREW IDEA OF HISTORY

Their idea of God made the Hebrews aware of the crucial importance of historical time. Holidays commemorating such specific historical events as the Exodus from Egypt, the receiving of the Ten Commandments on Mount Sinai, and the destruction of Solomon's temple kept the past alive and vital. Egyptians and Mesopotamians did not have a similar awareness of the uniqueness of a given event; to them, today's events were repetitions of events experienced by their ancestors. To the Jews, the Exodus and the covenant at Mount Sinai were singular, nonrepetitive occurrences, decisive in shaping their national history. This historical uniqueness and importance of events derived from the idea of a universal God who is profoundly involved in human affairs—a God who cares, teaches, and punishes.

The Jews valued the future as well as the past. Regarding human history as a process leading to a goal, they envisioned a great day when God would establish on earth a glorious age of peace, prosperity, happiness, and human brotherhood. This utopian notion has become deeply embedded in Western thought.

The Hebrews saw history as the work of God; it was a divine drama filled with sacred meaning and moral significance. Historical events revealed the clash of human wills with God's commands. Through history's specific events, God's presence was disclosed and his purpose made known. When the Hebrews suffered conquest and exile, they interpreted these events as divine retribution for violating God's Law and as punishment for their stubbornness, sinfulness, and rebelliousness. For the Hebrews, history also revealed God's compassion and concern. Thus, the Lord liberated Moses and the Israelites at the Red Sea and appointed prophets to plead for the poor and the oppressed. Because historical events revealed God's attitude toward human beings, these events possessed spiritual meaning and therefore were worth recording, evaluating, and remembering.

THE PROPHETS

Jewish history was marked by the emergence of spiritually inspired persons called *prophets,* who felt compelled to act as God's messengers. The prophets believed that God had commanded them to speak and had legitimated their words. The flowering of the prophetic movement—the age of classical, or literary, prophecy—began in the eighth century B.C. Among the prophets were Amos, a shepherd from Judea in the south; his younger contemporary, Hosea, from Israel in the north; Isaiah of Jerusalem; and Jeremiah, who witnessed the siege of Jerusalem by the Chaldeans in the early sixth century B.C. The prophets cared nothing for money or possessions, feared no one, not even the powerful, and preached without invitation. Often emerging in times of social distress and moral confusion, they exhorted the entire nation to make God's moral commands central to its existence and taught that when people forgot God and made themselves the center of all things, they would bring disaster on themselves and their community. The prophets saw national misfortune as an opportunity for penitence and reform.

In attacking oppression, cruelty, greed, and exploitation, the classical prophets added a new dimension to Israel's religious development. These prophets were responding to problems emanating from Israel's changed social structure. A tribal society generally lacks class distinctions, but this situation had been altered by the rise of Hebrew kings, the expansion of commerce, and the growth of cities. By the eighth century, there was a significant disparity between the wealthy and the poor. Small farmers in debt to moneylenders faced the loss of their land or even bondage; the poor were often dispossessed by the greedy wealthy. To the prophets, these social evils were religious sins that would bring ruin to Israel, for God, who intervenes in human affairs, punished the unjust community. In the name of God, they denounced the greed and pomp of the heartless rich and the hypocrisy of pious Jews who worshiped in the prescribed manner but neglected their social obligations to their neighbor. The purpose of worship and ritual was to instill in human beings a passion for justice. God is compassionate, the prophets insisted. He cares for all, especially the poor, the unfortunate, the suffering, and the defenseless.

Prophets also denounced people whose principal concern was the accumulation of possessions and wealth. These objects are only transient, said Isaiah, "but the word of God will stand forever" (Isaiah 40:8).

Prophets stressed the direct spiritual-ethical encounter between the individual and God. The inner person concerned them more than the outer forms of religious activity. Holding that the essence of the covenant was righteousness, the prophets criticized priests whose commitment to rites and rituals was not supported by a deeper spiritual insight or a zeal for morality in daily life. To the prophets, an ethical sin was far worse than a ritual omission. To live unjustly, to mistreat one's neighbors, to act without compassion—these actions violated God's Law and endangered the entire social order.

The prophets thus helped shape a social conscience that has become part of the Western tradition. They held out the hope that life on earth could be improved, that poverty and injustice need not be accepted as part of an unalterable natural order, and that the individual was capable of elevating himself or herself morally and could respect the dignity of others.

Two tendencies were present in Hebrew thought: parochialism and universalism. Parochial-mindedness stressed the special nature, destiny, and needs of the chosen people, a nation set apart from others. This narrow, tribal outlook was offset by universalism: a concern for all humanity, which found expression in those prophets who envisioned the unity of all people under God. All people were equally precious to God.

The prophets were not pacifists, particularly if a war was being waged against the enemies of Yahweh. But some prophets denounced war as obscene and looked forward to its elimination. They maintained that when people glorify force, they dehumanize their opponents, brutalize themselves, and dishonor God. When violence rules, there can be no love of God and no regard for the individual.

Primary Source

Isaiah and Social Justice

The prophets' insistence that rituals were not the essence of the Law and their passion for righteousness are voiced in the Scriptures by Isaiah of Jerusalem, who lived in the mid-eighth century B.C. Scholars agree that Isaiah of Jerusalem did not write all sixty-six chapters that make up the book of Isaiah. Some material appears to have been written by his disciples and interpreters, and Chapters 40 to 55, which were composed two centuries later, are attributed to a person given the name Second Isaiah. The following verses come from Isaiah of Jerusalem.

[11]"What to me is the multitude of your
   sacrifices?
   says the LORD;
I have had enough of burnt offerings of rams
   and the fat of the fed beasts;
I do not delight in the blood of bulls, or of
   lambs, or of he-goats . . .
[13]Bring no more vain offerings;
   incense is an abomination to me.
New moon and sabbath and the calling of
   assemblies—
   I cannot endure iniquity and solemn
   assembly.
[14]Your new moons and your appointed feasts
   my soul hates;
they have become a burden to me;
   I am weary of bearing them.
[15]When you spread forth your hands,
   I will hide my eyes from you;
even though you make many prayers,
   I will not listen;
   your hands are full of blood.

[16]Wash yourselves; make yourselves clean;
   remove the evil of your doings from before
   my eyes;
cease to do evil,
   [17]learn to do good;
seek justice,
defend the fatherless,
   plead for the widow.
(Isaiah 1)

Isaiah denounces the rich and the powerful for exploiting the poor.

[13]The LORD has taken his place to contend, he
   stands to judge his people.
[14]The LORD enters into judgement with the
   elders and princes of his people:
"It is you who have devoured the vineyard, the
   spoil of the poor is in your houses.
[15]What do you mean by crushing my people, by
   grinding the face of the poor?"
   says the LORD GOD of hosts.
(Isaiah 3)

Question for Analysis

1. Discuss the following statement: for Isaiah, ethical conduct was preferable to ritual acts as a way to worship God.

Scripture quotations are from the *Revised Standard Version of the Bible*, copyright © 1946, 1952, and 1971, National Council of the Churches of Christ in the USA.

The prophets' universalism was accompanied by an equally profound awareness of the individual and his or her intrinsic worth. Before the prophets, virtually all religious tradition had been produced communally and anonymously. The prophets, however, spoke as fearless individuals who, by affixing their signatures to their thoughts, fully bore the responsibility for their religious inspiration and conviction.

In coming to regard God's Law as a *command to conscience, an appeal to the inner person,* the prophets heightened the awareness of the human personality. They indicated that the individual could not know God by merely following edicts and performing rituals; the individual must experience God. Precisely this *I–Thou* relationship could make the individual fully conscious of self and could deepen and enrich his or her own personality. During the Exodus, the Hebrews were a tribal people who obeyed the Law largely out of awe and group compulsion. By the prophets' time, the Jews appeared to be autonomous individuals who heeded the Law because of a deliberate, conscious inner commitment.

The ideals proclaimed by the prophets helped sustain the Jews throughout their long and often painful historical odyssey, and they remain a vital force for Jews today. Incorporated into the teachings of Jesus, these ideals, as part of Christianity, are embedded in the Western tradition.

THE LEGACY OF THE ANCIENT JEWS

For the Jews, monotheism had initiated a process of self-discovery and self-realization unmatched by other peoples of the Near East. The great value that Westerners place on the individual and on human dignity derives in part from the ancient Hebrews, who held that men and women were created in God's image and possessed free will and a conscience answerable to God. Inherited by Christianity, the prophets' teachings constitute the core principles of Western morality, and their command to the power structure not to abuse its authority but to pursue justice continues to inspire reformers.

Throughout the centuries the Jewish Bible, with its view of God, human nature, divine punishment, the pursuit of righteousness, and social justice, has played a pivotal and profound role in Jewish life. Moreover, its significance has transcended the Jewish experience; it is also a cornerstone of Western civilization. Christianity, the essential religion of Western civilization, emerged from ancient Judaism, and the links between the two, including monotheism, moral autonomy, prophetic values, and the Hebrew Scriptures as the Word of God, are numerous and strong. The historical Jesus cannot be understood without examining his Jewish background, and his followers appealed to the Hebrew Scriptures in order to demonstrate the validity of their beliefs. For these reasons, we talk of a Judeo-Christian tradition as an essential component of Western civilization.

The Hebrew vision of a future messianic age, a golden age of peace and social justice, is at the root of the Western idea of progress—that people can build a more just society, that there is a reason to be hopeful about the future. This way of perceiving the world has greatly influenced modern reform movements. People longing to escape from oppression—African Americans in particular—have found inspiration in the Hebrews' deliverance from bondage in Egypt, the theme of Exodus.

In seeking to comprehend their relationship to God, the writers of the Hebrew Scriptures produced a treasury of themes, stories, and models of literary style and craftsmanship that have been a source of inspiration for Western religious thinkers, novelists, poets, and artists to the present day. Historians and archaeologists find the Hebrew Scriptures a valuable source in their efforts to reconstruct Near Eastern history.

❖   ❖   ❖

NOTES

1. John A. Wilson, "Egypt—the Kingdom of the 'Two Lands,'" in *At the Dawn of Civilization*, ed. E. A. Speiser (New Brunswick, N.J.: Rutgers University Press, 1964), 267–268. Vol. I in *The World History of the Jewish People.*

2. From *The Holy Scriptures* (Philadelphia: The Jewish Publication Society of America, 1917).

3. From *The Holy Scriptures* (Philadelphia: The Jewish Publication Society of America, 1917).

Chapter 3

The Greeks: From Myth to Reason

- ■ Early Aegean Civilizations
- ■ Evolution of the City-States
- ■ The Decline of the City-States
- ■ Philosophy in the Hellenic Age
- ■ Art
- ■ Poetry and Drama
- ■ History
- ■ The Hellenistic Age: The Second Stage of Greek Civilization
- ■ Hellenistic Thought and Culture
- ■ The Greek Achievement: Reason, Freedom, Humanism

Focus Questions

1. What were the basic features and limitations of Greek democracy?
2. What were the causes and consequences of the Persian Wars?
3. What were the causes and consequences of the Peloponnesian War?
4. How did Greek political life demonstrate both the best and the worst features of freedom as well as both the capabilities and limitations of reason? Why is the Greek political experience crucial to the shaping of the Western tradition?
5. How did the Pre-Socratic thinkers make the transition from myth to reason?
6. How did the Sophists and Socrates advance the tradition of reason and humanism?
7. What do Plato and Aristotle have in common? How do they differ?
8. How did Greek drama, art, and historiography contribute to the tradition of reason and humanism?
9. What are the basic differences between the Hellenic and Hellenistic Ages?

10. What prescription did each of the Hellenistic philosophies offer for achieving happiness?
11. What is the enduring significance of Stoicism for the modern world?

The Hebrew conception of ethical monotheism, with its stress on human dignity, is one principal source of the Western tradition. The second major source is ancient Greece. Both Hebrews and Greeks absorbed the achievements of Near Eastern civilizations, but they also developed their own distinctive viewpoints and styles of thought, which set them apart from the Mesopotamians and Egyptians. The great achievements of the Hebrews lay in the sphere of religious-ethical thought; those of the Greeks lay in the development of philosophical and scientific thought.

The Greeks conceived of nature as following general rules, not acting according to the whims of gods or demons. They saw human beings as having a capacity for rational thought, a need for freedom, and a worth as individuals. Although the Greeks never dispensed with the gods, they increasingly stressed the importance of human reason and human decisions; they came to assert that reason is the avenue to knowledge and that people—not the gods—are responsible for their own behavior. In this shift of attention from the gods to human beings, the Greeks broke with the mythmaking orientation of the Near East and created the rational, humanist outlook that is a distinctive feature of Western civilization. ❖

Chronology 3.1 ❖ The Greeks

1700–1450 B.C.*	Height of Minoan civilization
1400–1230	Height of Mycenaean civilization
1100–800	Dark Age
c. 700	Homer
750–550	Age of Colonization
594	Solon is given power to institute reforms
507	Cleisthenes broadens democratic institutions
480	Xerxes of Persia invades Greece; Greek naval victory at Salamis
479	Spartans defeat Persians at Plataea, ending Persian Wars
431	Start of Peloponnesian War
404	Athens surrenders to Sparta, ending Peloponnesian War
387	Plato founds a school, the Academy
359	Philip II becomes king of Macedonia
338	Battle of Chaeronea: Greek city-states fall under dominion of Macedonia
335	Aristotle founds a school, the Lyceum
323 B.C.	Death of Alexander the Great

*Most dates are approximations.

EARLY AEGEAN CIVILIZATIONS

Until the latter part of the nineteenth century, historians placed the beginning of Greek (or Hellenic) history in the eighth century B.C. Now it is known that two civilizations preceded Hellenic Greece: the Minoan and the Mycenaean. Although the ancient Greek poet Homer spoke of an earlier Greek civilization in his works, historians had believed that Homer's epics dealt solely with myths and legends, not with a historical past. In 1871, however, a successful German businessman, Heinrich Schliemann, began a search for earliest Greece. In excavating several sites mentioned by Homer, Schliemann discovered tombs, pottery, ornaments, and the remains of palaces of what hitherto had been a lost Greek civilization. The ancient civilization was named after Mycenae, the most important city of the time.

In 1900, Arthur Evans, a British archaeologist, excavating on the island of Crete, southeast of the Greek mainland, unearthed a civilization even older than that of the Mycenaean Greeks. The Cretans, or Minoans, were not Greeks and did not speak a Greek language, but their influence on mainland Greece was considerable and enduring. Minoan civilization lasted about 1,350 years (2600–1250 B.C.) and reached its height during the period from 1700 to 1450 B.C.

The centers of Minoan civilization were magnificent palace complexes, whose construction attested to the wealth and power of Minoan kings. The palaces housed royal families, priests, and government officials and contained workshops that produced decorated silver vessels, daggers, and pottery for local use and for export.

Judging by the archaeological evidence, the Minoans were peaceful. Minoan art generally did not depict military scenes, and Minoan palaces, unlike the Mycenaean ones, had no defensive walls or fortifications. Thus, the Minoans were vulnerable to the warlike Mycenaean Greeks, whose invasion contributed to the decline of Minoan civilization.

Who were these Mycenaeans? Around 2000 B.C., Greek-speaking tribes moved southward into the Greek peninsula, where, together with the pre-Greek population, they fashioned the Mycenaean civilization. In the Peloponnesus, in southern Greece, the Mycenaeans built palaces that were based in part on Cretan models. In these palaces, Mycenaean kings conducted affairs of state, and priests and priestesses performed religious ceremonies. Potters, smiths, tailors, and chariot builders practiced their crafts in the numerous workshops, much like their Minoan counterparts. Mycenaean arts and crafts owed a considerable debt to Crete. A script that permitted record keeping probably also came from Crete.

Mycenaean civilization, which consisted of several small states, each with its own ruling dynasty, reached its height in the period from 1400 to 1230 B.C. Following that, constant warfare among the Mycenaean kingdoms (and perhaps foreign invasions) led to the destruction of the palaces and the abrupt disintegration of Mycenaean civilization about 1100 B.C. But to the later Greek civilization, the Mycenaeans left a legacy of religious forms, pottery making, metallurgy, agriculture, language, a warrior culture and code of honor immortalized in the Homeric epics, and myths and legends that offered themes for Greek drama.

EVOLUTION OF THE CITY-STATES

From 1100 to 800 B.C., the Greek world passed through the Dark Age, an era of transition between a dead Mycenaean civilization and a still-unborn Hellenic civilization. The Dark Age saw the migration of Greek tribes from the barren mountainous regions of Greece to more fertile plains and from the mainland to Aegean islands and the coast of Asia Minor. During this period, the Greeks experienced insecurity, warfare, poverty, and isolation.

After 800 B.C., however, town life revived. Writing again became part of the Greek culture, this time with the more efficient Phoenician script. (Other borrowings from the Near East included artistic imagery and motifs, religious practices, craft skills, and mythological tales that were adapted and transformed by Greek poets.) The population increased dramatically, there was a spectacular rise in the use of metals, and overseas trade expanded. Gradually, Greek cities founded settlements on the islands of the Aegean, along the coast of Asia Minor and the Black Sea, and to the west in Sicily and southern Italy. These colonies, established to relieve overpopulation and land hunger, were independent, self-governing city-states, not possessions of the homeland city-states. During these two hundred years of colonization (750–550 B.C.), trade and industry expanded and the pace of urbanization quickened.

Homer: Shaper of the Greek Spirit

The poet Homer lived during the eighth century B.C., just after the Dark Age. His great epics, the *Iliad* and the *Odyssey,* helped shape the Greek spirit and Greek religion. Homer was the earliest molder of the Greek outlook and character. For centuries, Greek youngsters grew up reciting the Homeric epics and admiring the Homeric heroes, who strove for honor and faced suffering and death with courage.

Homer was a poetic genius who could reveal a human being's deepest thoughts, feelings, and conflicts in a few brilliant lines. His characters, complex in their motives and expressing powerful human emotions—wrath, vengeance, guilt, remorse, compassion, and love—would intrigue and inspire Western writers to the present day.

The *Iliad* deals in poetic form with a small segment of the last year of the Trojan War, which had taken place centuries before Homer's time, during the Mycenaean period. Homer's theme is the wrath of Achilles. In depriving "the swift and excellent" Achilles of his rightful war prize (the captive young woman Briseis), King Agamemnon has insulted Achilles' honor and has violated the solemn rule that warrior heroes treat each other with respect. His pride wounded, Achilles refuses to rejoin Agamemnon in battle against Troy. Achilles plans to affirm his honor by demonstrating that the Greeks need his valor and military prowess. Not until many brave men have been slain, including his dearest friend Patroclus, does Achilles set aside his quarrel with Agamemnon and enter the battle.

Homer employs a *particular* event, the quarrel between an arrogant Agamemnon and a revengeful Achilles, to demonstrate a *universal* principle: that "wicked arrogance" and "ruinous wrath" will cause much suffering and death. Homer grasps that there is an internal logic to existence. For Homer, says British classicist H. D. F. Kitto, "actions must have their consequences; ill-judged actions must have uncomfortable results."[1] People, and even the gods, operate within a certain unalterable framework; their deeds are subject to the demands of fate, or necessity. With a poet's insight, Homer sensed what would become a fundamental attitude of the Greek mind: there is a universal order to things. Later Greeks would formulate Homer's poetic insight in scientific and philosophical terms.

Heroism, the pursuit of glory and fame, and war's exhilaration are central to the *Iliad*, but Homer is also sensitive to the suffering caused by war. Battlefields littered with dead and maimed warriors fill soldiers with tears. And the grief of widows, orphans, and parents is unremitting.

Homer grasped war's tragic character: it confers honor and dignity on the victorious, but suffering, grief, enslavement, and death on the defeated. And one day, the hero, who had been lauded for his courage and prowess and had brought glory to his family and city, will also perish by the sword. This is his destiny. Homer's insights into life's tragic nature instructed the great Greek dramatists and future Western writers.

In Homer, we also see the origin of the Greek ideal of *aretē,* excellence. The Homeric warrior expresses a passionate desire to assert himself, to demonstrate his worth, and to gain the glory that poets would immortalize in their songs. In the warrior-aristocrat world of Homer, *excellence* was principally interpreted as bravery and skill in battle. Homer's portrayal also bears the embryo of a larger conception of human excellence, one that combines thought with action. A man of true worth, says the wise Phoenix to the stubborn Achilles, is both "a speaker of words and a doer of deeds." In this passage, we find the earliest statement of the Greek educational ideal: the molding of a man who, says classicist Werner Jaeger, "united nobility of action with nobility of mind," who realized "the whole of human potentialities."[2] Thus, in Homer we find the beginnings of Greek humanism—a concern with man and his achievements.

Essentially, Homer's works are an expression of the poetic imagination and mythical thought. However, his view of the eternal order of the world and his conception of the individual striving for excellence form the foundations of the Greek outlook.

Although Homer did not intend his poetry to have any theological significance, his treatment of the gods had important religious implications for the Greeks. In time, his epics formed the basis of the Olympian religion accepted throughout Greece. The principal gods were said to reside on Mount Olympus, and on its highest peak was the palace of Zeus, the chief deity. Religion pervaded daily life, but in time, traditional religion was challenged and undermined by a growing secular and rational spirit.

The Break with Theocratic Politics

From 750 B.C. to the death of Alexander the Great in 323 B.C., Greek society comprised many independent city-states. The city-state based on tribal allegiances was generally the first political association during the early stages of civilization. Moreover, Greece's many mountains, bays, and islands—natural barriers to political unity—favored this type of political arrangement.

The scale of the city-state, or *polis,* was small; most city-states had fewer than five thousand male citizens. Athens, which was a large city-state, had some thirty-five thousand to forty thousand adult male citizens at its height in the fifth century B.C.; the rest of its population of 350,000 consisted of women, children, resident aliens, and slaves, none of whom could participate in lawmaking. The polis gave individuals a sense of belonging, for its citizens were intimately involved in the political and cultural life of the community.

In the fifth century B.C., at its maturity, the Greeks viewed their polis as the only avenue to the good life—"the only framework within which man could realize his spiritual, moral, and intellectual capacities," in Kitto's words.[3] The mature polis was a self-governing community that expressed the will of free citizens, not the desires of gods, hereditary kings, or priests. In the Near East, religion dominated political activity, and to abide by the mandates of the gods was the ruler's first responsibility. The Greek polis also had begun as a religious institution, in which the citizens sought to maintain an alliance with their deities. Gradually, however, the citizens deemphasized the gods' role in political life and based government not on the magic powers of divine rulers but on human intelligence as expressed through the community. The great innovation that the Greeks introduced into politics and social theory was the principle that law did not derive from gods or divine kings but from the human community. Seers, purported to have supernatural skills, might offer advice but could not override the rulings of the Assembly.

The emergence of rational attitudes did not, of course, spell the end of religion, particularly for the peasants, who retained their devotion to their ancient cults, gods, and shrines. Paying homage to the god of the city remained a required act of patriotism to which Greeks unfailingly adhered. Thus, the religious-mythical tradition never died in Greece but existed side by side with a growing rationalism, becoming weaker as time passed. When Athenian democracy reached its height in the middle of the fifth century B.C., religion was no longer the dominant factor in politics. Athenians had consciously come to rely on human reason, not divine guidance, in their political and intellectual life.

What made Greek political life different from that of earlier Near Eastern civilizations, and also gave it enduring significance, was the Greeks' gradual realization that community problems are caused by human beings and require human solutions. The Greeks also valued free citizenship. An absolute king, a despot who ruled arbitrarily and by decree and who was above the law, was abhorrent to them.

The ideals of political freedom are best exemplified by Athens. But before turning to Athens, let us examine another Greek city, which followed a different political course.

Sparta: A Garrison State

Situated on the Peloponnesian peninsula, Sparta conquered its neighbors, including Messenia, in the eighth century B.C. Instead of selling the Messenians abroad, the traditional Greek way of treating a defeated foe, the Spartans kept them as state serfs, or *helots*. Helots were owned by the state rather than by individual Spartans. Enraged by their enforced servitude, the Messenians, also a Greek people, desperately tried to regain their freedom. After a bloody uprising was suppressed, the fear of a helot revolt became indelibly stamped on Spartan consciousness.

To maintain their dominion over the Messenians, who outnumbered them ten to one, the Spartans—with extraordinary single-mindedness, discipline, and loyalty—transformed their own society into an armed camp. Agricultural labor was performed by helots; trade and crafts were left to the *perioikoi,* conquered Greeks who were free but who had no political rights. The Spartans learned only one craft—soldiering—and were inculcated with only one conception of excellence: fighting bravely for their city, and if needed, dying for it.

The Spartans were trained in the arts of war and indoctrinated to serve the state. Military training for Spartan boys began at age seven; they exercised, drilled, competed, and endured physical hardships. Other Greeks admired the Spartans for their courage, obedience to law, and achievement in molding themselves according to an ideal. Spartan soldiers were better trained and disciplined and were more physically fit than other Greeks. But the Spartans were also criticized for having a limited conception of *aretē*.

Athens: The Rise of Democracy

The contrast between the city-states of Athens and Sparta is striking. Whereas Sparta was a land power and exclusively agricultural, Athens, which was located on the peninsula of Attica near the coast, possessed a great navy and was the commercial leader among the Greeks. The Athenians also were determined to protect their city from enemies, but, unlike the regimented Spartans, they valued political freedom and sought the full development and enrichment of the human personality. Thus, while authoritarian and militaristic Sparta turned culturally sterile, the relatively free and open society of Athens became the cultural leader of Hellenic civilization.

Greek city-states generally moved through four stages: rule by a king (monarchy), rule by landowning aristocrats (oligarchy), rule by one

WRESTLERS: RELIEF FROM A STATUE BASE, ATHENIAN, LATE SIXTH CENTURY B.C.
Physical fitness and athletics were highly prized by the Greeks. Poets sang the
praise of Olympic champions, and sculptors captured the beauty of athletic
physiques for an admiring public.

man who seized power (tyranny), and rule by
the people (democracy). During the first stage,
monarchy, the king, who derived his power
from the gods, commanded the army and judged
civil cases.

Oligarchy, the second stage, was instituted
in Athens during the eighth century B.C. when
aristocrats (*aristocracy* is a Greek word meaning "rule of the best") usurped power from hereditary kings. In the next century, aristocratic
regimes experienced a social crisis. Peasants who
borrowed from the aristocracy, pledging their
lands as security, lost their property and even
became enslaved for nonpayment of their debts.
Merchants and peasants also protested that the
law, which was based on oral tradition and administered exclusively by aristocrats, was unjust.
In Athens, the embittered and restless middle
and lower classes were granted one concession.
In 621 B.C., the aristocrats appointed Draco to
draw up a code of law. Although Draco's code
let the poor know what the law was and reduced
the possibility that aristocratic judges would behave arbitrarily, penalties were extremely severe,
and the code provided no relief for the peasants'
economic woes. As the poor began to organize
and press for the cancellation of their debts and
the redistribution of land, Athens was moving
toward civil war.

Solon, the Reformer. In 594 B.C., Solon
(c. 640–559 B.C.), a traveler and poet with a
reputation for wisdom, was elected chief executive. He maintained that the wealthy landowners,
through their greed, had disrupted community
life and brought Athens to the brink of civil war.
Solon initiated a rational approach to the problems of society by deemphasizing the gods' role
in human affairs and attributing the city's ills to
the specific behavior of individuals; he sought
practical remedies for these ills; and he held that
written law should be in harmony with *Dikē*,
the principle of justice that underlies the human
community. The concept of a just city, a unifying principle of Solon's reforms, became a formative ideal of Greek political thought. At the
same time, he wanted to instill in Athenians of all
classes a sense of working for the common good
of the city.

Solon aimed at restoring a sick Athenian society to health by restraining the nobles and improving the lot of the poor. To achieve this goal,
he canceled debts, freed Athenians enslaved for
debt, and brought back to Athens those who had
been sold abroad; however, he refused to confiscate and redistribute the nobles' land as the extremists demanded. He permitted all classes of
free men, even the poorest, to sit in the Assembly,
which elected magistrates and accepted or

Map 3.1 **The Aegean Basin** This map shows major battle sites. Note also the Hellespont, where Xerxes' forces crossed into Greece, and Ionia, the coast of Asia Minor, where Greek philosophy was born.

rejected legislation proposed by a new Council of Four Hundred. He also opened the highest offices in the state to wealthy commoners, who had previously been excluded from these positions because they lacked noble birth. Thus, Solon undermined the traditional rights of the hereditary aristocracy and initiated the transformation of Athens from an aristocratic oligarchy into a democracy.

Solon also instituted ingenious economic reforms. Recognizing that the poor soil of Attica was not conducive to growing grain, he urged the cultivation of grapes for wine and the growing of olives, whose oil could be exported. To encourage industrial expansion, he ordered that all fathers teach their sons a trade and granted citizenship to foreign craftsmen who were willing to migrate

to Athens. These measures and the fine quality of the native reddish-brown clay allowed Athens to become the leading producer and exporter of pottery. Solon's economic policies transformed Athens into a great commercial center. However, Solon's reforms did not eliminate factional disputes among the aristocratic clans or relieve much of the discontent of the poor.

Pisistratus, the Tyrant. In 546 B.C., Pisistratus (c. 605–527 B.C.), an aristocrat, took advantage of the general instability to become a one-man ruler, driving into exile those who had opposed him. Tyranny thus replaced oligarchy. Tyranny occurred frequently in the Greek city-states. Almost always aristocrats themselves, tyrants generally posed as champions of the poor in their struggle against the aristocracy. Pisistratus sought popular support by having conduits constructed to increase the Athenian water supply; like tyrants in other city-states, he gave to peasants land confiscated from exiled aristocrats and granted state loans to small farmers.

Pisistratus' great achievement was the promotion of cultural life. He initiated grand architectural projects, encouraged sculptors and painters, arranged for public recitals of the Homeric epics, and founded festivals, which included dramatic performances. In all these ways, he made culture, formerly the province of the aristocracy, available to commoners. Pisistratus thus launched a policy that eventually led Athens to emerge as the cultural capital of the Greeks.

Cleisthenes, the Democrat. Shortly after Pisistratus' death, a faction headed by Cleisthenes, an aristocrat sympathetic to democracy, assumed leadership. By an ingenious method of redistricting the city, Cleisthenes ended the aristocratic clans' traditional jockeying for the chief state positions, which had caused much divisiveness and bitterness in Athens. Cleisthenes replaced this practice, rooted in tradition and authority, with a new system, rationally planned to ensure that historic allegiance to tribe or clan would be superseded by loyalty to the city as a whole.

Cleisthenes hoped to make democracy the permanent form of government for Athens. The power to govern Athens, he believed, should rest with the male citizens acting as a body and not with aristocratic factions or a tyrant. To safeguard the city against tyranny, he utilized (or perhaps introduced) the practice of *ostracism*. Once a year, Athenians were given the opportunity to inscribe on a fragment of pottery (*ostracon*) the name of anyone who they felt endangered the state. An individual against whom enough votes were cast was ostracized, that is, forced to leave Athens for ten years.

Cleisthenes firmly secured democratic government in Athens. The Assembly, which Solon had opened to all male citizens, was in the process of becoming the supreme authority in the state. But the period of Athenian greatness lay in the future; the Athenians first had to fight a war of survival against the Persian Empire.

The Persian Wars

In 499 B.C., the Ionian Greeks of Asia Minor rebelled against their Persian overlord. Sympathetic to the Ionian cause, Athens sent twenty ships to aid the revolt. Bent on revenge, Darius I, king of Persia, sent a small detachment to Attica. In 490 B.C., on the plains of Marathon, the citizen army of Athens defeated the Persians—for the Athenians, one of the finest moments in their history. Ten years later, Xerxes, Darius' son, organized a huge invasion force—some 250,000 men and more than 500 ships—with the aim of reducing Greece to a Persian province. Setting aside their separatist instincts, many of the city-states united to defend their independence and their liberty. The historian Herodotus viewed the conflict as an ideological clash between Greek freedom and oriental despotism.

The Persians crossed the waters of the Hellespont (Dardanelles) and made their way into northern Greece. Herodotus describes their encounter at the mountain pass of Thermopylae with three hundred Spartans, who, true to their training and ideal of *aretē*, "resisted to the last with their swords if they had them, and if not, with their hands and teeth, until the Persians, coming on from the front over the ruins of the wall and closing in from behind, finally overwhelmed them."[4] Northern Greece fell to the Persians, who continued south, burning a deserted Athens.

When it appeared that the Greeks' spirit had been broken, the Athenian statesman and general Themistocles (c. 527–460 B.C.), demonstrating in military affairs the same rationality that Cleisthenes had shown in political life, lured the Persian fleet into the narrowest entry to the Bay of Salamis. Unable to deploy its more numerous ships in this cramped space, the Persian armada was destroyed by Greek ships. In 479 B.C., a year after the Athenian naval victory at Salamis, the Spartans defeated the Persians in the land battle of Plataea. The inventive intelligence with which the Greeks had planned their military operations and a fierce desire to preserve their freedom—which, the war made them realize, was their distinguishing attribute—had enabled them to defeat the greatest military power the Mediterranean world had yet seen.

The Persian Wars were decisive in the history of the West. The confidence and pride that came with its astonishing victory propelled Athens into a golden age whose achievements were pivotal in the shaping of European culture. But the conflict also roused the Athenian urge for dominance in Greece. The Persian Wars ushered in an era of Athenian imperialism, which had drastic consequences for the future. Immediately after the wars, more than 150 city-states organized a confederation, the Delian League (named after its treasury on the island of Delos), to protect themselves against a renewed confrontation with Persia. Because of its wealth, its powerful fleet, and the restless energy of its citizens, Athens assumed leadership of the Delian League. Athenians consciously and rapaciously manipulated the league for their own economic advantage, seeing no contradiction between imperialism and democracy. Indeed, they adhered to the principle that strong states had the right to dominate weaker ones in order to acquire wealth, power, honor, and glory. Athens forbade member states to withdraw, stationed garrisons on the territory of confederate states, and used the league's treasury to finance public works in Athens. Although member states did receive protection from both pirates and Persians, were not overtaxed, and enjoyed increased trade, they resented Athenian domination. In converting the Delian League into an instrument of Athenian imperialism, Athens may have lost an opportunity to perform a great creative act—the creation of a broad, voluntary confederation that might have forestalled the intercity warfare that gravely weakened Hellenic civilization.

The Mature Athenian Democracy

Athenian imperialism was one consequence of the Persian Wars; another was the flowering of Athenian democracy and culture. The Athenian state was a direct democracy, in which the citizens themselves, not elected representatives, made the laws. In the Assembly, that was open to all adult male citizens and which met some forty times a year, Athenians debated and voted on key issues of state: They declared war, signed treaties, and spent public funds. The lowliest cobbler, as well as the wealthiest aristocrat, had the opportunity to express his opinion in the Assembly, to vote, to speak before and submit motions to the Assembly, to hold the highest public positions, and to receive equal treatment before the law. By the middle of the fifth century, the will of the people, as expressed in the Assembly, was supreme.

The Council of Five Hundred (which had been established by Cleisthenes to replace Solon's Council of Four Hundred) managed the ports, military installations, and other state properties and prepared the agenda for the Assembly. Because its members were chosen annually by lot and could not serve more than twice in a lifetime, the Council could never supersede the Assembly. Chosen at random, its membership could not become a cabal of the most powerful and ambitious citizens. Some 350 magistrates, also chosen by lot, performed administrative tasks: collecting fines, policing the city, repairing streets, inspecting markets, and so forth. In view of the special competence that their posts required, the ten generals who led the army were not chosen by lot but were elected by the Assembly.

Athens has been aptly described as a government of amateurs: there were no professional civil servants, no professional soldiers and sailors, no state judges, and no elected lawmakers. Ordinary citizens performed the duties of government. Such a system rested on the assumption that the average citizen was capable of participating intelligently in the affairs of state and that he would, in a spirit of civic patriotism, carry out his responsibilities to his city. In Athens of the fifth century B.C., excellence was equated with good citizenship—a concern for the good of the community that outweighs personal aspirations. Indeed, to a surprisingly large number of Athenians, politics was an overriding concern, and they devoted considerable time and thought to civic affairs. Those who allowed private matters to take precedence over the needs of the community were denounced as useless people living purposeless lives.

Athenian democracy achieved its height in the middle of the fifth century B.C. under the leadership of Pericles (c. 495–429 B.C.), a gifted statesman, orator, and military commander. In the opening stage of the monumental clash with Sparta, the Peloponnesian War (431–404 B.C.), Pericles delivered an oration in honor of the Athenian war casualties. The oration, as reported by Thucydides, the great Athenian historian of the fifth century B.C., contains a glowing description of the Athenian democratic ideal:

We are called a democracy, for the administration is in the hands of the many and not of the few. But while the law secures equal justice to all alike in their private disputes, the claim of excellence is also recognized; and when a citizen is any way distinguished, he is [selected for] public service . . . as the reward of merit. Neither is poverty a bar, but a man may benefit his country whatever may be the obscurity of his condition. . . . There is no exclusiveness in our public life, and in our private intercourse we are not suspicious of one another, nor angry with our neighbor if he does what he likes; we do not put on sour looks at him which though harmless are unpleasant. . . . [A] spirit of reverence pervades our public acts; we are prevented from doing wrong by respect for authority and for the laws. . . .[5]

Athenian democracy undoubtedly had its limitations and weaknesses. Modern critics point out that resident aliens were almost totally barred from citizenship and therefore from political participation. Slaves, who constituted about one-fourth of the Athenian population, enjoyed none of the freedoms that Athenians considered so precious. The Greeks regarded slavery as a necessary precondition for civilized life; for some to be free and prosperous, they believed, others had to be enslaved. Slaves were generally prisoners of war or captives of pirates. In Athens, some slaves were Greeks, but most were foreigners. Slaves usually did the same work as Athenian citizens: farming, commerce, manufacturing, and domestic chores. However, those slaves, including preadolescent children, who toiled in the mines suffered a grim fate.

Athenian women were another group denied legal or political rights. Most Greeks, no doubt, agreed with Aristotle, who said: "The male is by nature superior, and the female inferior, and . . . the one rules and the other is ruled."[6] A girl usually was married at fourteen to a man twice her age, and the marriage was arranged by a male relative. The wedding day might be the first time that the young bride saw her future husband.

ATTIC BLACK-FIGURE HYDRIA, C. 510 This hydria, or water jug, shows women drawing water from a fountainhouse. Trips to the fountainhouse provided one of the few opportunities for women to socialize outside the home.

Although either spouse could obtain a divorce, the children remained with the father after the marriage was dissolved. Wives did not dine with their husbands and spent much of their time in the women's quarters.

Athenian women were barred from holding public office and generally could not appear in court without a male representative. They could not act in plays, and when they attended the theater they sat in the rear, away from the men. Greek women received no formal education, although some young women learned to read and write at home. Training in household skills was considered the only education a woman needed. Since it was believed that a woman could not act independently, she was required to have a guardian—normally her father or her husband—who controlled her property and supervised her behavior. Convinced that financial dealings were too difficult for women and that they needed to be protected from strangers, men, not women, did the marketing. When a woman left the house, she was usually accompanied by a male. The Athenian wife was treated as a minor; in effect, she was her husband's ward.

The flaws in Athenian democracy should not cause us to undervalue its extraordinary achievement. The idea that the state represents a community of free, self-governing citizens remains a crucial principle of Western civilization. Athenian democracy embodied the principle of the legal state—a government based not on force but on laws debated, devised, altered, and obeyed by free citizens.

This idea of the legal state could have arisen only in a society that was aware of and respected the rational mind. Just as the Greeks demythicized nature, so too they removed myth from the sphere of politics. Holding that government was something that people create to satisfy human needs, the Athenians regarded their leaders neither as gods nor as priests, but as men who had demonstrated a capacity for statesmanship.

Both democratic politics and systematic political thought originated in Greece. There, people first asked questions about the nature and purpose of the state, rationally analyzed political institutions, speculated about human nature and justice, and discussed the merits of various forms of government. It is to Greece that we ultimately trace the idea of democracy and all that accompanies it: citizenship, constitutions, equality before the law, government by law, reasoned debate, respect for the individual, and confidence in human intelligence.

THE DECLINE OF THE CITY-STATES

Although the Greeks shared a common language and culture, they remained divided politically. A determination to preserve city-state sovereignty prevented the Greeks from forming a larger political grouping that might have prevented the inter-city warfare that ultimately cost the city-state its vitality and independence. But the creation of a Pan-Hellenic union would have required a radical transformation of the Greek character, which for hundreds of years had regarded the independent city-state as the only suitable political system.

The Peloponnesian War

Athenian control of the Delian League frightened the Spartans and their allies in the Peloponnesian League. Sparta and the Peloponnesian states decided on war because they saw a dynamic and imperialistic Athens as a threat to their independence. At stake for Athens was control over the Delian League, which gave Athens political power and contributed to its economic prosperity. Neither Athens nor Sparta anticipated the catastrophic consequences that the war would have for Greek civilization.

The war began in 431 B.C. and ended in 404 B.C. When a besieged Athens, with a decimated navy and a dwindling food supply, surrendered, Sparta dissolved the Delian League, left Athens with only a handful of ships, and forced the city to pull down its long walls—ramparts designed to protect it against siege weapons.

The Peloponnesian War shattered the spiritual foundations of Hellenic society. During its course, men became brutalized; cities were sacked and captives murdered; selfish individualism triumphed over civic duty; moderation gave way to extremism; and in several cities, including Athens, politics degenerated into civil war between oligarchs and democrats. Oligarchs, generally from the wealthier segments of Athenian society, wanted to concentrate power in their own hands by depriving the lower classes of political rights. Democrats, generally from the poorer segment of society, sought to preserve the political rights of all adult male citizens. Strife between oligarchs and democrats was quite common in the Greek city-states even before the Peloponnesian War.

The Fourth Century

The Peloponnesian War was the great crisis of Hellenic history. The golden age of Athenian culture came to an end. The city-states never fully recovered from their self-inflicted spiritual wounds. The civic loyalty and confidence that had marked the fifth century waned, and the fourth century was dominated by a new mentality that the leaders of the Age of Pericles would have abhorred. A concern for private affairs superseded devotion to the general good of the polis. Increasingly, professionals, rather than ordinary citizens, administered the tasks of government, and mercenaries began to replace citizen soldiers.

In the fourth century, the quarrelsome city-states formed new systems of alliances and persisted in their ruinous conflicts. While the Greek cities battered one another in fratricidal warfare, a new power was rising in the north—Macedonia. To the Greeks, the Macedonians, a wild mountain people who spoke a Greek dialect and had acquired a sprinkling of Hellenic culture, differed little from other non-Greeks, whom they called barbarians. In 359 B.C., at the age of twenty-three, Philip II (382–336 B.C.) ascended the Macedonian throne. Converting Macedonia into a first-rate military power, he began a drive to become master of the Greeks.

Incorrectly assessing Philip's strength, the Greeks were slow to organize a coalition against Macedonia. In 338 B.C., Philip's forces decisively defeated the Greeks at Chaeronea, and all of Greece was his. The city-states still existed, but they had lost their independence. The world of the small, independent, and self-sufficient polis was drawing to a close, and Greek civilization was taking a different shape.

The Dilemma of Greek Politics

Philip's conquest of the city-states points to fundamental weaknesses of Greek politics. Despite internal crisis and persistent warfare, the Greeks were unable to fashion any other political framework than the polis. The city-state was fast becoming an anachronism, but the Greeks were unable to see that; in a world moving toward larger states and empires, the small city-state could not compete. An unallied city-state, with its small citizen army, could not withstand the powerful military machine that Philip had created. A challenge confronted the city-states: the need to shape some form of political union, a Pan-Hellenic federation that would end the suicidal internecine warfare,

promote economic well-being, and protect the Greek world from hostile states. Because they could not respond creatively to this challenge, the city-states ultimately lost their independence to foreign conquerors. Learning from the Greek experience, after the American Revolution, astute American statesmen sought to establish a central government strong enough to prevent warfare between states. Moreover, if the thirteen American states remained a weak and disunited assortment of republics, they could lose their independence to a foreign power, duplicating the experience of the Greek city-states with Macedonia.

The waning of civic responsibility among the citizens was another reason for the decline of the city-states. The vitality of the city-state depended on the willingness of its citizens to put aside private concerns for the good of the community. However, although Athens had recovered commercially from the Peloponnesian War, its citizens had suffered a permanent change in character; the abiding devotion to the polis, which had distinguished the Age of Pericles, greatly diminished during the fourth century. The factional strife, the degeneration of politics into personal ambition, the demagoguery, and the fanaticism that Thucydides (see "History" later in the chapter) had described persisted into the fourth century and were aggravated by the economic discontent of the poor. The Periclean ideal of citizenship dissipated as Athenians neglected the community to concentrate on private affairs or sought to derive personal profit from public office. The decline in civic responsibility could be seen in the hiring of mercenaries to replace citizen soldiers and in the indifference and hesitancy with which the Athenians confronted Philip. The Greeks did not respond to the Macedonian threat as they had earlier rallied to fight off the Persian menace because the quality of citizenship had deteriorated.

Greek political life demonstrated the best and worst features of freedom. On the one hand, as Pericles boasted, freedom encouraged active citizenship, reasoned debate, and government by law. On the other, as Thucydides lamented, freedom could degenerate into factionalism, demagoguery, unbridled self-interest, and civil war. Because monarchy deprives people of freedom and self-rule, the Greeks regarded monarchy as a form of government appropriate for uncivilized barbarians. But their political experience showed that free men in a democracy are susceptible to demagogues, will base political decisions on keyed-up emotions rather than on cool reasoning, and are capable of behaving brutally toward political opponents. Moreover, Greek democracy, which valued freedom, was unable to overcome a weakness that afflicts despotic rulers: an incautious attitude toward power that causes the state to overreach itself. Such an attitude demonstrated the self-destructive hubris that Greek moralists warned against. This is how Thucydides interpreted Athens' disastrous Sicilian expedition during the Peloponnesian War. Driven by a mad passion to possess what was beyond their reach, the Athenians brought ruin to their city.

The Athenians, who saw no conflict between imperialism and democracy, considered it natural for stronger states to dominate weaker ones, an attitude that helped to precipitate the destructive Peloponnesian War. A particularly egregious example of this outlook occurred during that war when Athenians decided to invade the island of Melos despite the assurances of the Melians that they represented no threat to Athens. As reported by Thucydides, the Athenian envoys told the Melians that "the strong do what they have the power to do, and the weak accept what they have to accept."[7] When the Melians resisted, the Athenians slaughtered the men, enslaved the women and children, and colonized the territory.

Greek politics also revealed both the capabilities and the limitations of reason. Originally, the polis was conceived as a divine institution, in which the citizen had a religious obligation to obey the law. As the rational and secular outlook became more pervasive, the gods lost their authority. When people no longer regarded law as an expression of sacred traditions ordained by the gods but saw it as a merely human contrivance, respect for the law diminished, weakening the foundations of the society. The results were party conflicts, politicians who scrambled for personal power, and moral uncertainty. Recognizing the danger, conservatives insisted that law must again be conceived as issuing from the gods and the city must again treat its ancient traditions with reverence. Although the Greeks originated the lofty ideal that human beings could regulate their political life according to reason, their history, marred by intercity warfare and internal violence, demonstrates the extreme difficulties involved in creating and maintaining a rational society.

PHILOSOPHY IN THE HELLENIC AGE

The Greeks broke with the mythopoeic outlook of the Near East and conceived a new way of viewing nature and human society that is the basis of the Western scientific and philosophical tradition. By the fifth century B.C., the Greeks had emancipated thought from myth and gradually applied reason to the physical world and to all human activities. This emphasis on reason marks a turning point for human civilization.

The development of rational thought in Greece was a process, a trend, not a finished achievement. The process began when some thinkers rejected mythical explanations for natural phenomena. The nonphilosophical majority of the people never entirely eliminated the language, attitudes, and beliefs of myth from their life and thought. For them, the world remained controlled by divine forces, which were appeased through cultic practices. Even in the mature philosophy of Plato and Aristotle, mythical modes of thought persisted. What is of immense historical importance, however, is not the degree to which the Greeks successfully integrated the norm of reason, but the fact that they originated this norm, defined it, and consciously applied it to intellectual concerns and social and political life.

The first theoretical philosophers in human history emerged in the sixth century B.C. in the Greek cities of Ionia in Asia Minor. Curious about the essential composition of nature and dissatisfied with earlier creation legends, the Ionians sought physical, rather than mythic-religious, explanations for natural occurrences. In the process, they arrived at a new concept of nature and a new method of inquiry. They maintained that nature was not manipulated by arbitrary and willful gods, nor was it governed by blind chance. The Ionians said that there is an intelligible pattern to nature; that nature contains a hidden structure—principles of order or general laws—that govern phenomena; and that these fundamental rules were ascertainable by the human mind. They implied that the origin, composition, and structure of the world can be investigated rationally and systematically. Thus, in seeking to account for rainbows, earthquakes, and eclipses, the Ionians posited entirely naturalistic explanations that relied on observation, showed an awareness of cause and effect, and excluded the gods. This new outlook marks the beginning of scientific thought.

What conditions enabled the Greeks to make this breakthrough? Perhaps their familiarity with Near Eastern achievements in mathematics and science stimulated their ideas. But this influence should not be exaggerated, says Greek scholar John N. Theodorakopoulos, for Egyptians and Mesopotamians "had only mythological systems of belief and a knowledge of practical matters. They did not possess those pure and crystal-clear products of the intellect which we call science and philosophy. Nor did they have any terminology to describe them."[8] Rooted in mythological thinking, the ancient Near East experienced no eruption of theorizing about nature in pristine philosophical and scientific terms as Greece did beginning in the sixth century B.C.

One can only speculate about why the Greeks achieved this breakthrough. Perhaps the poets' conception of human behavior as subject to universal destiny was extended into the philosophers' belief that nature was governed by law. Perhaps the breakthrough was fostered by the Greeks' freedom from a priesthood and rigid religious doctrines that limited thought. Or perhaps Greek speculative thought was an offspring of the city, because if law governed human affairs, providing balance and order, should not the universe also be regulated by principles of order?

The Cosmologists: A Rational Inquiry into Nature

The first Ionian philosophers are called cosmologists because they sought to discover the underlying principles of the universe: how nature came to be the way it was. They held that some single, eternal, and imperishable substance, which

underwent various modifications, gave rise to all phenomena in nature.

Ionian philosophy began with Thales (c. 624–548 B.C.) of Miletus, a city in Ionia. He was a contemporary of Solon of Athens. Concerned with understanding the order of nature, Thales said that water was the basic element, the underlying substratum of nature, and that through some natural process—similar to the formation of ice or steam—water gave rise to everything else in the world.

Thales revolutionized thought because he omitted the gods from his account of the origins of nature and searched for a natural explanation of how all things came to be. Thales also broke with the commonly held belief that earthquakes were caused by Poseidon, god of the sea, and offered instead a naturalistic explanation for these disturbances: that the earth floated on water, and when the water experienced turbulent waves, the earth was rocked by earthquakes.

Anaximander (c. 611–547 B.C.), another sixth-century Ionian, rejected Thales' theory that water was the original substance. He rejected any specific substance and suggested that an indefinite substance, which he called the Boundless, was the source of all things. He believed that from this primary mass, which contained the powers of heat and cold, there gradually emerged a nucleus, the seed of the world. He said that the cold and wet condensed to form the earth and its cloud cover, while the hot and dry formed the rings of fire that we see as the moon, the sun, and the stars. The heat from the fire in the sky dried the earth and shrank the seas. From the warm slime on earth arose life, and from the first sea creatures there evolved land animals, including human beings. Anaximander's account of the origins of the universe and nature understandably contained fantastic elements. Nevertheless, by offering a natural explanation for the origin of nature and life and by holding that nature was lawful, it surpassed the creation myths.

Like his fellow Ionians, Anaximenes, who died about 525 B.C., made the transition from myth to reason. He maintained that a primary substance, air, underlay reality and accounted for the orderliness of nature. Air that was rarefied became fire, whereas wind and clouds were formed from condensed air. If the process of condensation continued, it produced water, earth, and eventually stones. Anaximenes also rejected the old belief that a rainbow was the goddess Iris; instead, he said that the rainbow was caused by the sun's rays falling on dense air.

The Ionians have been called "matter philosophers" because they held that everything issued from a particular material substance. Other thinkers of the sixth century B.C. tried a different approach. Pythagoras (c. 580–507 B.C.) and his followers, who lived in the Greek cities in southern Italy, did not find the nature of things in a particular substance, but rather in mathematical relationships. The Pythagoreans discovered that the intervals in the musical scale can be expressed mathematically. Extending this principle of proportion found in sound to the universe at large, they concluded that the cosmos also contained an inherent mathematical order and harmony. Thus, the Pythagoreans shifted the emphasis from matter to form, from the world of sense perception to the logic of mathematics. The Pythagoreans were also religious mystics who believed in the immortality and transmigration of souls. Consequently, they refused to eat animal flesh, fearing that it contained former human souls.

Parmenides (c. 515–450 B.C.), a native of the Greek city of Elea in southern Italy, argued that the fundamental view of the Ionians that the universe underwent change and development over time was utterly mistaken. In developing his position, Parmenides applied to philosophical argument the logic used by the Pythagoreans in mathematical thinking. In putting forth the proposition that an argument must be consistent and contain no contradictions, Parmenides became the founder of formal logic. Despite appearances, asserted Parmenides, reality—the cosmos and all that is within it—is one, eternal, and unchanging. It is made known not through the senses, which are misleading, but through the mind; not through experience, but through reason. Truth is reached through abstract thought alone. Parmenides' concept of an unchanging reality apprehended by thought alone influenced Plato and is the foundation of metaphysics.

Democritus (c. 460–370 B.C.), from the Greek mainland, renewed the Ionians' concern with the world of matter and reaffirmed their confidence in knowledge derived from sense perception.

But he also retained Parmenides' reverence for reason. His model of the universe consisted of two fundamental realities: empty space and an infinite number of atoms. Eternal, indivisible, and imperceptible, these atoms moved in the void. All things consisted of atoms, and combinations of atoms accounted for all change in nature. In a world of colliding atoms, everything behaved according to mechanical principles.

Concepts essential to scientific thought thus emerged in embryonic form with the early Greek philosophers: natural explanations for physical occurrences (Ionians), the mathematical order of nature (Pythagoras), logical proof (Parmenides), and the mechanical structure of the universe (Democritus). By giving to nature a rational, rather than a mythical, foundation and by holding that theories should be grounded in evidence and that one should be able to defend them logically, the early Greek philosophers pushed thought in a new direction. This new approach made possible theoretical thought and the systematization of knowledge—as distinct from the mere observation and collection of data. It also allowed a critical analysis of theories, whereas myths, accepted unconditionally on faith and authority, did not promote discussion and questioning.

This systematization of knowledge extended into several areas. Greek mathematicians, for example, organized the Egyptians' practical experience with land measurements into the logical and coherent science of geometry. They established mathematics as an ordered system based on fundamental premises and necessary connections, and they developed logical procedures for arriving at mathematical proofs. Both Babylonians and Egyptians had performed fairly complex mathematical operations, but unlike the Greeks, they made no attempt to prove underlying mathematical principles. In another area, Babylonian priests had observed the heavens for religious reasons, believing that the stars revealed the wishes of the gods. The Greeks used the data collected by the Babylonians, but not for a religious purpose; rather, they sought to discover the geometric laws that govern the motions of heavenly bodies.

A parallel development occurred in medicine. No Near Eastern medical text explicitly attacked magical beliefs and practices. In contrast, Greek doctors associated with the medical school of Hippocrates (c. 460–c. 377 B.C.) asserted that diseases have a natural, not a supernatural, cause. The following tract on epilepsy, which was considered a sacred disease, illustrates the development of a scientific approach to medicine:

> I am about to discuss the disease called "sacred." It is not, in my opinion, any more divine or sacred than any other disease, but has a natural cause, and its supposed divine origin is due to men's inexperience, and to their wonder at its peculiar character. Now . . . men continue to believe in its divine origin because they are at a loss to understand it. . . . My own view is that those who first attributed a sacred character to this malady were like the magicians, purifiers, charlatans, and quacks of our own day; men who claim great piety and superior knowledge. Being at a loss, and having no treatment which would help, they concealed and sheltered themselves behind superstition, and called this illness sacred, in order that their utter ignorance might not be manifest.[9]

The Sophists: A Rational Investigation of Human Culture

In their effort to understand the external world, the cosmologists had created the tools of reason. These early Greek thinkers were developing a new and profound awareness of the mind's capacity for theoretical thinking. Equally important, they were establishing the mind's autonomy—its ability to inquire into any subject, relying solely on its own power to think. Greek thinkers then turned away from the world of nature and attempted a rational investigation of people and society, dismissing efforts to explain the social world through inherited beliefs about the gods. The Sophists exemplified this shift in focus. They were professional teachers who wandered from city to city teaching rhetoric, grammar, poetry, gymnastics, mathematics, and music. The Sophists insisted that it was futile to speculate about the first principles of the universe, for such knowledge was beyond the grasp of the human mind. Instead, they urged that individuals improve themselves and their cities by applying

reason to the tasks of citizenship and statesmanship. The Western humanist tradition owes much to the Sophists, who examined political and ethical problems, cultivated the minds of their students, and invented formal secular education.

The Sophists answered a practical need in Athens, which had been transformed into a wealthy and dynamic imperial state after the Persian Wars. Because the Sophists claimed that they could teach *political aretē*—the skill to formulate the right laws and policies for cities and the art of eloquence and persuasion—they were sought as tutors by politically ambitious young men, especially in Athens.

The Sophists were philosophical relativists; that is, they held that no truth is universally valid. Protagoras, a fifth-century Sophist, said that "man is the measure of all things." By this he meant that good and evil, truth and falsehood are matters of individual judgment; there are no universal standards that apply to all people at all times. Human laws and ethical beliefs have evolved according to a particular community's needs; they are simply human contrivances and conventions, not objective truths or standards written into nature. While not based on moral absolutes, hopefully the city's laws derive from the judgment of wise and good men.

In applying reason critically to human affairs, the Sophists challenged the traditional religious and moral values of Athenian society. Some Sophists taught that speculation about the divine was useless; others went further and asserted that religion was just a human invention to ensure obedience to traditions and laws.

The Sophists also applied reason to law, with the same effect: the undermining of traditional authority. The laws of a given city, they asserted, did not derive from the gods; nor were they based on any objective, universal, and timeless standards of justice and good, for such standards did not exist. The more radical Sophists argued that law was merely something made by the most powerful citizens for their own benefit. This view had dangerous implications: since law rested on no higher principle than might, it need not be obeyed.

Some Sophists combined this assault on law with an attack on the ancient Athenian idea of *sophrosyne*—moderation and self-discipline—because it denied human instincts. Instead of moderation, they urged that people should maximize pleasure and trample underfoot those traditions

Hirmer Verlag Fotoarchiv, München.

THE PARTHENON, ATHENS, 447–432 B.C. A masterpiece of the Doric style, the great temple dedicated to Athena Parthenos (the Maiden), the patron goddess of the city, was constructed through the efforts of Pericles. Its cult statue and the sculptural reliefs under its roofline were designed by the outstanding sculptor of the age, Phidias. In post-Hellenistic times, it served as a Christian church and then as a mosque until it was destroyed in 1687. Between 1801 and 1812, the marble reliefs were removed by the Englishman Lord Elgin and now reside in the British Museum in London.

that restricted them from fully expressing their desires.

In subjecting traditions to the critique of reason, the radical Sophists provoked an intellectual and spiritual crisis. Their doctrines encouraged disobedience to law, neglect of civic duty, and selfish individualism. These attitudes became widespread during and after the Peloponnesian War, dangerously weakening community bonds. Conservatives sought to restore the authority of law and a respect for moral values by renewing allegiance to those sacred traditions undermined by the Sophists.

Socrates: Shaping the Rational Individual

Socrates (c. 469–399 B.C.), one of the most extraordinary figures in the history of Western civilization, took a different approach. He attacked the Sophists' relativism, holding that people should regulate their behavior in accordance with universal values. While he recognized that the Sophists taught skills, he felt that they had no insights into questions that really mattered: What is the purpose of life? What are the values by which man should live? How does man perfect his character?

Vanni/Art Resource, N.Y.

PORCH OF THE MAIDENS, ATTIC SCULPTURE FROM THE ACROPOLIS. The architect has incorporated the human form as a functional element in a rationally organized structure. The balance and harmony of the Porch of the Maidens weds humanity with art.

Here the Sophists failed, said Socrates; they taught the ambitious to succeed in politics, but persuasive oratory and clever reasoning do not instruct a man in the art of living. According to Socrates, the Sophists had attacked the old system of beliefs but had not provided the individual with a constructive replacement.

Socrates' central concern was the perfection of individual human character, the achievement of moral excellence. For Socrates, moral values did not derive from a transcendent God, as they did for the Hebrews. Individuals attained them by regulating their lives according to objective standards arrived at through rational reflection, that is, by making reason the formative, guiding, and ruling agency of the soul. For Socrates, true education meant the shaping of character according to values discovered through the active and critical use of reason.

Socrates wanted to subject all human beliefs and behavior to the scrutiny of reason and in this way remove ethics from the realm of authority, tradition, dogma, superstition, and myth. He believed that reason was the only proper guide to the most crucial problem of human existence—the question of good and evil.

Dialectics.   In urging Athenians to think rationally about the problems of human existence, Socrates offered no systematic ethical theory and no list of ethical precepts. What he did supply was a method of inquiry called *dialectics,* or logical discussion. As Socrates used it, a dialectical exchange between individuals or with oneself, a *dialogue,* was the essential source of knowledge. It forced people out of their apathy and smugness and compelled them to examine their thoughts critically; to confront illogical, inconsistent, dogmatic, and imprecise assertions; and to express their ideas in clearly defined terms.

Dialectics demonstrated that the acquisition of knowledge was a creative act. The human mind could not be coerced into knowing; it was not a passive vessel into which a teacher poured knowledge. The dialogue compelled the individual to play an active role in acquiring the ideals and values by which to live. In a dialogue, individuals became thinking participants in a search for knowledge. Through relentless cross-examination, Socrates induced the persons with whom he spoke to explain and justify their opinions rationally, for only thus did knowledge become a part of one's being.

Dialogue implied that reason was meant to be used in relations between human beings and that they could learn from each other, help each other, teach each other, and improve each other. It implied further that the human mind could and should make rational choices. To deal rationally with oneself and others is the distinctive mark of being human.

Condemned to Death. Socrates devoted much of his life to what he believed was his mission, pricking the conscience of uncritical and smug Athenians and persuading them to think critically about how they lived their lives. Through probing questions, he tried to stir people out of their complacency and make them realize how directionless and purposeless their lives were.

For many years, Socrates challenged Athenians without suffering harm, for Athens was generally distinguished by its freedom of speech and thought. However, in the uncertain times during and immediately after the Peloponnesian War, Socrates made enemies. When he was seventy, he was accused of corrupting the youth of the city and of not believing in the city's gods but in other, new divinities. Underlying these accusations was the fear that Socrates was a troublemaker, a subversive who threatened the state by subjecting its ancient and sacred values to the critique of thought.

Socrates denied the charges and conducted himself with great dignity at his trial, refusing to grovel and beg forgiveness. Instead, he defined his creed:

> If you think that a man of any worth at all ought to . . . think of anything but whether he is acting justly or unjustly, and as a good or a bad man would act, you are mistaken. . . . If you were therefore to say to me, "Socrates, we will not listen to [your accuser]. We will let you go, but on the condition that you give up this investigation of yours, and philosophy. If you are found following these pursuits again you shall die." I say, if you offered to let me go on these terms, I should reply: . . . As long as I have breath and strength I will not give up philosophy and exhorting you and declaring the truth to every one of you whom I meet, saying, as I am accustomed, "My good friend, you are a citizen of Athens . . . are you not ashamed of caring so much for making of money and for fame and prestige, when you neither think nor care about wisdom and truth and the improvement of your soul?"[10]

Convicted by an Athenian court, Socrates was ordered to drink poison. Had he attempted to appease the jurors, he probably would have been given a light punishment, but he would not disobey the commands of his conscience and alter his principles even under threat of death.

Socrates did not write down his philosophy and beliefs. We are able to construct a coherent account of his life and ideals largely through the works of his most important disciple, Plato.

Plato: The Rational Society

Plato (c. 429–347 B.C.) used his master's teachings to create a comprehensive system of philosophy that embraced both the world of nature and the social world. Many of the problems discussed by Western philosophers for the past two millennia were first raised by Plato. We focus on two of his principal concerns, the theory of Ideas and the theory of the just state.

Theory of Ideas. Socrates had taught that universal standards of right and justice exist and are arrived at through thought. Building on the insights of his teacher, Plato postulated the existence of a higher world of reality, independent of the world of things that we experience every day. This higher reality, he said, is the realm of Ideas, or Forms—unchanging, eternal, absolute, and universal standards of beauty, goodness, justice, and truth.

Truth resides in this world of Forms and not in the world made known through the senses. For example, a person can never draw a perfect square, but the properties of a perfect square exist in the world of Forms. Similarly, the ordinary person derives an opinion of what beauty is only from observing beautiful things; the philosopher, aspiring to true knowledge, goes beyond what he sees and tries to grasp with his mind the Idea of beauty. The ordinary individual lacks a true conception of justice or goodness; such knowledge is available only to the philosopher, whose mind can leap from worldly particulars to an ideal world beyond space and time.

A champion of reason, Plato aspired to study human life and arrange it according to universally valid standards. In contrast to sophistic relativism, he maintained that objective and eternal standards do exist.

The Just State. In adapting the rational legacy of Greek philosophy to politics, Plato constructed a comprehensive political theory. What the Greeks had achieved in practice—the movement away from mythic and theocratic politics—Plato accomplished on the level of thought: the fashioning of a rational model of the state.

Like Socrates, Plato attempted to resolve the problem caused by the radical Sophists: the undermining of traditional values. Socrates had tried to dispel this spiritual crisis through a moral transformation of the individual based on reason, whereas Plato wanted the entire community to conform to rational principles. Plato said that if human beings are to live an ethical life, they must do so as citizens of a just and rational state. In an unjust state, people cannot achieve Socratic wisdom, for their souls will mirror the state's wickedness.

Plato had experienced the ruinous Peloponnesian War and witnessed Socrates' trial and execution. Disillusioned by the corruption of Athenian morality and democratic politics, he concluded that under the Athenian constitution neither the morality of the individual Athenian nor the good of the state could be enhanced. He became convinced that Athens required moral and political reform founded on Socratic philosophy.

In his great dialogue *The Republic,* Plato devised an ideal state based on standards that would rescue his native Athens from the evils that had befallen it. For Plato, the just state could not be founded on tradition (for inherited attitudes did not derive from rational standards) or on the doctrine of might being right (a principle taught by radical Sophists and practiced by Athenian statesmen). A just state, in his view, had to conform to universally valid principles and aim at the moral improvement of its citizens, not at increasing its power and wealth. Such a state required leaders distinguished by their wisdom and virtue rather than by sophistic cleverness and eloquence.

Fundamental to Plato's political theory as formulated in *The Republic* was his criticism of Athenian democracy. An aristocrat by birth and temperament, Plato believed that it was foolish to expect the common man to think intelligently about foreign policy, economics, or other vital matters of state. Yet the common man was permitted to speak in the Assembly and to vote, and he could also be selected by lot for executive office. A second weakness of democracy for Plato was that leaders were chosen and followed for nonessential reasons, such as persuasive speech, good looks, wealth, and family background.

A third danger of democracy was that it could degenerate into anarchy, said Plato. Intoxicated by liberty, the citizens of a democracy could lose all sense of balance, self-discipline, and respect for law: "The citizens become so sensitive that they resent the slightest application of control as intolerable tyranny, and in their resolve to have no master they end up by disregarding even the law, written or unwritten."[11]

As the democratic city falls into disorder, a fourth weakness of democracy will become evident. A demagogue—often a wealthy, handsome war hero of noble birth with an ability to stir the multitude with words—will be able to gain power by promising to plunder the rich to benefit the poor. Increasingly, the tyrant throws off all constraints and uses his authority to satisfy his desire for power and possessions. To retain his hold over the state, the tyrant "begins by stirring up one war after another, in order that the people may feel their need of a leader."[12] Because of these inherent weaknesses of democracy, Plato insisted that Athens would be governed properly only when the wisest people, the philosophers, attained power.

Plato rejected the fundamental principle of Athenian democracy: that the ordinary citizen is capable of participating sensibly in public affairs. People would not entrust the care of a sick person to just anyone, said Plato, nor would they allow a novice to guide a ship during a storm. Yet in a democracy, amateurs were permitted to run the government and to supervise the education of the young; no wonder Athenian society was disintegrating. Plato believed that these duties should be performed only by the best people in the city, the philosophers, who would approach human problems with reason and wisdom derived from knowledge of the world of unchanging and perfect Ideas. Only those possessors of truth would be competent to rule.

Plato divided people into three groups: those who demonstrated philosophical ability should be rulers; those whose natural bent revealed exceptional courage should be soldiers; and those driven by desire, the great masses, should be producers (tradespeople, artisans, or farmers). In *The Republic,* the philosophers were selected by a rigorous system of education that was open to all children. Those not demonstrating sufficient intelligence or strength of character were to be weeded out to become workers or warriors, depending on their natural aptitudes. After many years of education and practical military and administrative experience, the philosophers were to be entrusted with political power. If they had been properly educated, the philosopher-rulers would not seek personal wealth or personal power; their only concern would be pursuing justice and serving the community. The philosophers were to be absolute rulers. Although the people would have lost their right to participate in political decisions, they would have gained a well-governed state whose leaders, distinguished by their wisdom, integrity, and sense of responsibility, sought only the common good. Only thus, said Plato, could the individual and the community achieve well-being.

Plato wanted to rescue the city-state from disintegration by re-creating the community spirit that had vitalized the polis—and he wanted to re-create it not on the basis of mere tradition but on a higher level, with philosophical knowledge. The social and political institutions of Athens, Plato thought, must be reshaped according to permanent and unalterable ideals of truth and justice, and this could be done only when power and wisdom were joined. He aimed to fashion a just individual and a just state by creating conditions that permitted reason to prevail over the appetites, self-interest, and class and party loyalties.

Aristotle: Synthesis of Greek Thought

Aristotle (384–322 B.C.) stands at the apex of Greek thought because he achieved a creative synthesis of the knowledge and theories of earlier thinkers. The range of Aristotle's interests and intellect is extraordinary. He was the leading expert of his time in every field of knowledge, with the possible exception of mathematics.

Aristotle undertook the monumental task of organizing and systematizing the thought of the Pre-Socratics, Socrates, and Plato. He shared with the natural philosophers a desire to understand the physical universe; he shared with Socrates and Plato the conviction that reason was a person's highest faculty and that the polis was the primary formative institution of Greek life.

Critique of Plato's Theory of Ideas. To the practical and empirically minded Aristotle, the Platonic notion of an independent and separate world of Forms beyond space and time seemed contrary to common sense. To comprehend reality, said Aristotle, one should not escape into another world. For him, Plato's two-world philosophy suffered from too much mystery, mysticism, and poetic fancy; moreover, Plato undervalued the world of facts and objects revealed through sight, hearing, and touch, a world that was important to Aristotle. Like Plato, Aristotle desired to comprehend the essence of things and held that understanding universal principles is the ultimate aim of knowledge. But unlike Plato, he did not turn away from the world of things to obtain such knowledge. Possessing a scientist's curiosity to understand nature, Aristotle respected knowledge obtained through the senses.

For Aristotle, the Forms were not located in a higher world outside and beyond phenomena but existed in things themselves. He said that through human experience with such things as men, horses, and white objects the essence of man, horse, and whiteness can be discovered; through reason, the Form of Man, the Form of Horse, and the Form of Whiteness can be determined. These universals, which apply to all men, all horses, and all white things, were for both Aristotle and Plato the true objects of knowledge. For Plato, these Forms existed independently of particular objects: the Forms for men or horses or whiteness or triangles or temples existed, whether or not representations of these Ideas in the form of material objects were made known to the senses. For Aristotle, however, universal Ideas could not be determined without examination of particular things. Whereas Plato's use of reason tended to stress otherworldliness, Aristotle brought philosophy back to earth.

By holding that certainty in knowledge comes from reason alone and not from the senses, Plato was predisposed toward mathematics and metaphysics—pure thought that transcends the world of change and material objects. By stressing the importance of knowledge acquired through the rational examination of sense experience, Aristotle favored the development of empirical sciences—physics, biology, zoology, botany, and other disciplines based on the observation and investigation of nature and the recording of data.

Ethical Thought. Like Socrates and Plato, Aristotle believed that a knowledge of ethics was possible and that it must be based on reason, for this is what distinguishes human beings from other forms of life. In his *Nicomachean Ethics,* the good life is the examined life; it means making intelligent decisions when confronted with specific problems. People achieve happiness when they exercise the distinctively human trait of reasoning, when they apply their knowledge relevantly to life, and when their behavior is governed by intelligence and not by whim, tradition, or authority.

Aristotle recognized, however, that people are not entirely rational and that the passionate element in the human personality can never be eradicated or ignored. According to Aristotle,

surrendering completely to desire meant descending to the level of beasts, but denying the passions and living as an ascetic was a foolish and unreasonable rejection of human nature. Aristotle maintained that people could attain virtue, when they avoided extremes of behavior and rationally chose the way of moderation, and that children reared and schooled with good habits were more likely to live virtuous lives, that is to choose the path of moderation and to demonstrate self-mastery. "Nothing in excess" was the key to Aristotle's ethics.

Political Thought. Aristotle's *Politics* complements his *Ethics.* To live the good life, he said, a person must do so as a member of a political community. Only the polis would provide people with an opportunity to lead a rational and moral existence, that is, to fulfill their human potential. With this assertion, Aristotle demonstrated a typically Greek attitude. Also in typically Greek fashion, Aristotle held that enhancing the good of the community is nobler and more virtuous than doing good for oneself, however worthy the act.

Like Plato, Aristotle presumed that political life could be rationally understood and intelligently directed. He emphasized the importance of the rule of law. He placed his trust in law rather than in individuals, for individuals are subject to unruly passions. Aristotle recognized that at times laws should be altered, but he recommended great caution; otherwise, people would lose respect for law and legal procedure.

Tyranny and revolution, Aristotle said, can threaten the rule of law and the well-being of the citizen. To prevent revolution, the state must maintain "the spirit of obedience to law. . . . Men should not think it slavery to live according to the rule of the constitution, for it is their salvation."[13]

Aristotle held "that the best political community is formed by citizens of the middle class [that is, those with a moderate amount of property], and that those states are likely to be well-administered in which the middle class is large and stronger if possible than the other classes [the wealthy and the poor]." Both the rich, who excel in "beauty, strength, birth, [and] wealth," and the poor, who are "very weak or very much disgraced," find it "difficult to follow rational

ZEUS, C. 460 B.C. This bronze statue was found off the Greek coast in 1926. Although its face is still stylized, the athletic body pulsates with life, capturing the essence of Zeus as the omnipotent ruler of the gods.

principles. Of these two the one sort grow into violence and great criminals, the other into rogues and petty rascals." The rich are unwilling "to submit to authority . . . for when they are boys, by reason of the luxury in which they are brought up, they never learn even at school, the habit of obedience." Consequently, the wealthy "can only rule despotically." On the other hand, the poor "are too degraded to command and must be ruled like slaves."[14] Middle-class citizens are less afflicted by envy than the poor and are more likely than the rich to view their fellow citizens as equals.

ART

The classical age of Greek art spans the years from the end of the Persian Wars (479 B.C.) to the death of Alexander the Great (323 B.C.). During this period, standards were established that would dominate Western art until the emergence of modern art in the late nineteenth century.

Greek art coincided with Greek achievement in all other areas. Like Greek philosophy and politics, it too applied reason to human experience and made the transition from a mythopoeic-religious worldview to a world perceived as orderly and rational. It gradually transformed the supernatural religious themes with which it was at first preoccupied into secular human themes. Classical art was representational—that is, it strove to imitate reality, to represent the objective world realistically as it appeared to the human eye.

Artists carefully observed nature and human beings and sought to achieve an exact knowledge of human anatomy; they tried to portray accurately the body at rest and in motion. They knew when muscles should be taut or relaxed, one hip lower than the other, the torso and neck slightly twisted—in other words, they succeeded in transforming marble or bronze into a human likeness that seemed alive. Yet although it was realistic and naturalistic, Greek art was also idealistic, aspiring to a finer, more perfect representation of what was seen and depicting the essence and form of a thing more truly than the way it actually appeared. Thus, a Greek statue resembled no specific individual but revealed a flawless human form, without wrinkles, warts, scars, or other imperfections.

In achieving an accurate representation of objects and in holding that there were rules of beauty that the mind could discover, the Greek artist employed an approach consistent with the new scientific outlook. The Greek temple, for example, is an organized unity, obeying nature's laws of equilibrium and harmony; classical sculpture captures the basic laws that govern life in motion.

Greek artists exemplified the humanist spirit that characterized all aspects of Greek culture. They made the human form the focal point of attention and exalted the nobility, dignity, self-assurance, and beauty of the human being.

POETRY AND DRAMA

Like philosophers and artists, Greek poets and dramatists gave expression to the rise of the individual and the emerging humanist values. One of the earliest and best of the Greek poets was Sappho; she lived around 600 B.C., on the island of Lesbos. Sappho established a school to teach music and singing to well-to-do girls and to prepare them for marriage. With great tenderness, Sappho wrote poems of friendship and love.

Pindar (c. 518–438 B.C.) was another Greek lyric poet. In his poem of praise for a victorious athlete, Pindar expressed the aristocratic view of excellence. Although life is essentially tragic—triumphs are short-lived, misfortunes are many, and ultimately death overtakes all—man must still demonstrate his worth by striving for excellence.

The high point of Greek poetry is drama, an art form that originated in Greece. In portraying the sufferings, weaknesses, and triumphs of individuals, Greek dramatists shifted attention from the gods to human beings. Just as a Greek sculptor shaped a clear visual image of the human form, so a Greek dramatist brought the inner life of human beings, their fears and hopes, into sharp focus and tried to find the deeper meaning of human experience. Thus, both art and drama evidenced the growing self-awareness of the individual.

Drama originated in the religious festivals honoring Dionysus, the god of wine and agricultural fertility. A profound innovation in these sacred performances, which included choral songs and dances, occurred in the last part of the sixth century B.C.: Thespis, the first actor known to history, stepped out of the chorus and engaged it in dialogue. By separating himself from the choral group, Thespis demonstrated a new awareness of the individual.

With only one actor and a chorus, however, the possibilities for dramatic action and human conflicts were limited. Then Aeschylus introduced a second actor in his dramas, and Sophocles a third. Dialogue between individuals thus became possible. The Greek actors wore masks, and by changing them, each actor could play several roles in the same performance. This flexibility allowed the dramatists to depict the clash and interplay of human wills and passions on a greater scale. By the middle of the fifth century B.C., tragedies were performed regularly as civic festivals.

A development parallel to Socratic dialectics—dialogue between thinking individuals—occurred in Greek drama. By setting characters in conflict against each other, dramatists showed individuals as active subjects, responsible for their behavior and decisions.

Like the natural philosophers, Greek dramatists saw an inner logic to the universe; they called this logic Fate or Destiny. Both physical and social worlds obeyed laws. When people were stubborn, narrow-minded, arrogant, or immoderate they were punished. The order in the universe required it, said Sophocles:

> *The man who goes his way*
> *Overbearing in the word and deed,*
> *who fears no justice,*
> *Honors no temples of the gods—*
> *May an evil destiny seize him.*
> *And punish his ill-starred pride.*[15]

In being free to make decisions, the dramatists said, individuals have the potential for greatness, but in choosing wrongly and unintelligently they bring disaster to themselves and others.

Also like philosophy, Greek tragedy entailed rational reflection. Tragic heroes were not passive victims of fate. They were thinking human beings who felt a need to comprehend their position, explain the reasons for their actions, analyze their feelings, and respond to their fate with insight.

The essence of Greek tragedy lies in the tragic heroes' struggle against cosmic forces and insurmountable obstacles, which eventually crush them. But what impressed the Greek audience (and impresses us today) was not the vulnerability or weaknesses of human beings, but their courage and determination in the face of these forces.

The three great Athenian tragedians were Aeschylus (525–456 B.C.), Sophocles (c. 496–406 B.C.), and Euripides (c. 485–406 B.C.). Aeschylus believed that the world was governed by divine justice, which could not be violated with impunity; when individuals evinced *hubris* (overweening pride or arrogance), which led them to overstep the bounds of moderation, they had to be punished.

Sophocles maintained that individuals should shape their character in the way a sculptor shapes a form: according to laws of proportion. In his view, when the principles of harmony were violated by immoderate behavior, a person's character would be thrown off balance and misfortune would strike. In *Antigone*, Sophocles raised a question that is timeless: should individual conscience, which is prompted by a higher law, prevail over the laws of the state when the two are in conflict?

The rationalist spirit of Greek philosophy permeated the tragedies of Euripides. Like the Sophists, Euripides subjected the problems of human life to critical analysis and challenged human conventions. His plays carefully scrutinized the role of the gods, women's conflicts, the horrors of war, the power of passion, and the prevalence of human suffering and weakness. Euripides blended a poet's insight with the psychologist's probing to reveal the tangled world of human passions and souls in torment.

Greek dramatists also wrote comedies. Aristophanes (c. 448–c. 380 B.C.), the greatest of the Greek comic playwrights, lampooned Athenian statesmen and intellectuals and censured government policies. Behind Aristophanes' sharp wit lay a deadly seriousness; he sought an end to the ruinous Peloponnesian War and a reaffirmation of traditional values, which the Sophists had undermined.

HISTORY

The Mesopotamians and the Egyptians kept annals that purported to narrate the deeds of gods and their human agents, the priest-kings or god-kings. These chronicles, filled with religious sayings, royal records, and boastful accounts of military campaigns, are devoid of critical analysis and interpretation. The Hebrews valued history, but, believing that God acted in human affairs, they did not remove historical events from the realm of religious-mythical thought. The Greeks initiated a different approach to the study of history. For them, history was not a narrative about the deeds of gods, as it was for the Egyptians and Mesopotamians, or the record of God's wrath or benevolence, as it was for the Hebrews; instead, it dealt with human actions and state policies.

As the gods were eliminated from the nature philosophers' explanations for the origins of things in the natural world, mythical elements were also removed from the writing of history. Greek historians asked themselves questions about the deeds of people, based their answers on available evidence, and wrote in prose, the language of rational thought. They not only narrated events but also examined causes.

Herodotus

Often called the "father of history," Herodotus (c. 484–c. 424 B.C.) wrote a history of the Persian Wars. The central theme of this book, entitled *The Histories*, is the contrast between Near Eastern despotism and Greek freedom and the subsequent clash of these two worldviews in the wars. Though Herodotus found much to praise in the Persian Empire, he was struck by a lack of freedom and by what he considered barbarity. He emphasized that the mentality of the free citizen was foreign to the East, where men were trained to obey the ruler's commands absolutely. Not the rule of law but the whim of despots prevailed in the East.

Another theme evident in Herodotus' work was punishment for hubris. In seeking to become king of both Asia and Europe, Xerxes had acted arrogantly; although he behaved as if he were superhuman, "he too was human, and was sure to be disappointed of his great expectations."[16] Like the Greek tragedians, Herodotus drew universal moral principles from human behavior.

In several ways, Herodotus was a historian rather than a teller of tales. First, he asked questions about the past, instead of merely repeating ancient legends; he tried to discover what had happened and the motivations behind the actions. Second, he demonstrated at times a cautious and critical attitude toward his sources of information. Third, although the gods appeared in his narrative, they played a far less important role than they did in Greek popular mythology. Nevertheless, by retaining a belief in the significance of dreams, omens, and oracles and by allowing divine intervention, Herodotus fell short of being a thoroughgoing rationalist. His writings contain the embryo of rational history. Thucydides brought it to maturity.

Thucydides

Thucydides (c. 460–c. 400 B.C.) also concentrated on a great political crisis confronting the Hellenic world: the Peloponnesian War. Living in Periclean Athens, whose lifeblood was politics, Thucydides regarded the motives of statesmen and the acts of government as the essence of history. He did not just catalogue facts but sought those general concepts and principles that the facts illustrated. His history was the work of an intelligent mind trying to make sense of his times.

Thucydides applied to the sphere of political history a rationalist empiricism. He strove for factual accuracy and drew conclusions based on a critical analysis of events and motives. He searched for the truth underlying historical events and attempted to present it objectively. Thucydides maintained that a proper analysis of the events of the Peloponnesian War would reveal general principles that govern human behavior and relations between states. He intended his history to be a source of enlightenment for future ages, a possession for all time, because the kinds of behavior that caused the conflict between Sparta and Athens would recur regularly through history, for human nature is unchanging and predictable.

In Thucydides' history, there was no place for myths, for legends, for the fabulous—all hindrances to historical truth. He recognized that a work of history was a creation of the rational mind and not an expression of the poetic imagination. The historian seeks to learn and to enlighten, not to entertain.

Rejecting the notion that the gods interfere in history, Thucydides looked for the social forces and human decisions behind events. Where Herodotus occasionally lapsed into supernatural explanations, Thucydides wrote history in which the gods were absent, and he denied their intervention in human affairs. For Thucydides, history was the work of human beings, and the driving force in history was men's will to power and domination.

In addition to being a historian who meticulously examined evidence, Thucydides was also an astute and innovative political thinker with a specific view of government, statesmen, and international relations. He warned against the dangers of extremism unleashed by the strains of war, and he believed that when reason was forsaken, the state's plight would worsen. He had contempt for statesmen who waged war lightly, acting from impulse, reckless daring, and an insatiable appetite for

Primary Source

Euripides: *Medea*

The Greek dramatist Euripides applied a keen critical spirit to the great question of individual life versus the demands of society. His play Medea *focuses on a strong-willed woman whose despair at being cast off by her husband leads her to exact a terrible revenge. But in the following passage, Medea might speak for the deepest feelings of any Greek woman.*

It was everything to me to think well of one
   man,
And he, my own husband, has turned out
   wholly vile.
Of all things which are living and can form a
   judgement
We women are the most unfortunate creatures.
Firstly, with an excess of wealth it is required
For us to buy a husband and take for our bodies
A master; for not to take one is even worse.
And now the question is serious whether we take
A good or bad one; for there is no easy escape.
For a woman, nor can she say no to her
   marriage.
She arrives among new modes of behaviour
   and manners,
And needs prophetic power, unless she has
   learnt at home,

How best to manage him who shares the bed
   with her.
And if we work out all this well and carefully,
And the husband lives with us and lightly bears
   his yoke,
Then life is enviable. If not, I'd rather die.
A man, when he's tired of the company in his
   home,
Goes out of the house and puts an end to his
   boredom
And turns to a friend or companion of his own
   age.
But we are forced to keep our eyes on one alone.
What they say of us is that we have a peaceful
   time
Living at home, while they do the fighting in war:
How wrong they are! I would very much rather
   stand
Three times in the front of battle than bear one
   child.

Question for Analysis

1. According to this passage, what were the difficulties Greek women faced?

Euripedes, *Medea*, trans. Rex Warner (London: The Bodley Head, 1944), 18.

---

territory. Although Thucydides admired Athens for its democratic institutions, rule of law, sense of civic duty, and cultural achievements, he recognized an inherent danger in democracy: the emergence of demagogues who rise to power by stirring up the populace and abuse their power once in office.

Political scientists, historians, and statesmen still turn to Thucydides for insights into the realities of power politics, the dangers of political fanaticism, the nature of imperialism, the methods of demagogues, and the effects of war on democratic politics.

THE HELLENISTIC AGE: THE SECOND STAGE OF GREEK CIVILIZATION

Greek civilization, or Hellenism, passed through three distinct stages: the Hellenic Age, the Hellenistic Age, and the Greco-Roman Age. The Hellenic Age began around 800 B.C. with the early city-states, reached its height in the fifth century B.C., and endured until the death of Alexander the Great in 323 B.C. At that time, the ancient world entered the Hellenistic Age, which ended in 30 B.C. when Egypt, the last major Hellenistic state, fell to Rome. The Greco-Roman Age lasted five hundred years, encompassing the period of the Roman Empire up to the collapse of the Empire's western half in the last part of the fifth century A.D.

Although the Hellenistic Age absorbed the heritage of classical (Hellenic) Greece, its style of civilization changed. During the first phase of Hellenism, the polis was the center of political life. The polis gave Greeks an identity, and only within the polis could a Greek live a good and civilized life. With the coming of the Hellenistic Age, this situation changed. Kingdoms and empires eclipsed the city-state in power and importance. Even though cities retained a large measure of autonomy in domestic affairs, they lost their freedom of action in foreign affairs because they were now dominated by monarchs. Monarchy, the essential form of government in the Hellenistic world, had not been admired by the Greeks of the Hellenic Age. They had agreed with Aristotle that monarchy was suitable only for non-Greeks, who lacked the capacity to govern themselves.

Now, however, as a result of Alexander the Great's conquests of the lands between Greece and India, tens of thousands of Greek soldiers, merchants, and administrators settled in eastern lands. Their encounters with the different peoples and cultures of the Near East widened the Greeks' horizon and weakened their ties to their native cities. Because of these changes, the individual had to define a relationship not to the narrow, parochial society of the polis but to the larger world. The Greeks had to examine their place in a world more complex, foreign, and threatening than the polis. They had to fashion a conception of a community that would be more comprehensive than the city-state.

Hellenistic philosophers struggled with these problems of alienation and community. They sought to give people the inner strength to endure in a world where the polis no longer provided security. In this new situation, philosophers no longer assumed that the good life was tied to the affairs of the city. Freedom from emotional stress—not active citizenship and social responsibility—was the avenue to the good life. This pronounced tendency of people to withdraw into themselves and seek release from anxiety and depression helped shape a cultural environment that contributed to the spread and triumph of Christianity in the Greco-Roman Age.

In the Hellenic Age, Greek philosophers had a limited conception of humanity, dividing the world into Greek and barbarian. In the Hellenistic Age, the intermingling of Greeks and peoples of the Near East—the fusion of different ethnic groups and cultures scattered over great distances—caused a shift in focus from the city to the *oikoumene* (the inhabited world); parochialism gave way to cosmopolitanism and universalism as people began to think of themselves as members of a world community. Philosophers came to regard the civilized world as one city, the city of humanity. This new concept was their response to the decline of the city-state and the quest for an alternative form of community.

Alexander the Great

After the assassination of Philip of Macedon in 336 B.C., his twenty-year-old son, Alexander, succeeded to the throne. Alexander inherited a proud and fiery temperament from his mother. From his tutor Aristotle, Alexander gained an appreciation for Greek culture, particularly the Homeric epics. Undoubtedly, the young Alexander was stirred by these stories of legendary heroes, especially Achilles, and their striving for personal glory. He also acquired military skills and qualities of leadership from his father.

Alexander inherited from Philip an overriding policy of state: the invasion of Persia. Philip had intended to protect his hold on Greece by driving the Persians from Asia Minor. But Alexander, whose ambition knew no bounds, aspired to conquer the entire Persian Empire. Daring, brave, intelligent, and charismatic, Alexander possessed the irrepressible energy of a romantic adventurer. With an army of thirty-five thousand men, Macedonians and Greeks combined, he crossed into Asia Minor in 334 B.C. and eventually advanced all the way to India. In these campaigns, Alexander proved himself to be a superb strategist and leader of men. Winning every battle, his army carved an empire that stretched from Greece to India. Not yet thirty-three years old, Alexander died after a sickness probably exacerbated by excessive drinking.

ALEXANDER THE GREAT ON HORSEBACK. In conquering the lands from Greece to India, Alexander the Great displayed a military genius that would fascinate commanders from Caesar to Napoleon.

The world after Alexander differed sharply from the one that existed before he took up the sword. Alexander's conquests brought West and East closer together, marking a new epoch. Alexander himself helped to implement this transformation, whether intentionally or unwittingly. He took a Persian bride, arranged for eighty of his officers and ten thousand of his soldiers to marry Near Eastern women, and planned to incorporate thirty thousand Persian youths into his army. Alexander founded Greek-style cities in Asia, where Greek settlers mixed with the native population.

As Greeks acquired greater knowledge of the Near East, the parochialism of the polis gave way to a world outlook. As trade and travel between West and East expanded, as Greek merchants and soldiers settled in Asiatic lands, and as Greek culture spread to non-Greeks, the distinctions between barbarian and Greek lessened. Although Alexander never united all the peoples in a world-state, his career pushed the world in a new direction, toward a fusion of disparate peoples and the intermingling of cultural traditions.

The Competing Dynasties

After Alexander's premature death in 323 B.C., his generals engaged in a long and bitter struggle to see who would succeed the conqueror. Since none of the generals or their heirs had enough power to hold together Alexander's vast empire, the wars of succession ended in a stalemate. By 275 B.C., the empire was fractured into three dynasties: the Ptolemies in Egypt, the Seleucids in Asia, and the Antigonids in Macedonia. Macedonia, Alexander's native country, continued to dominate the Greek cities, which periodically tried to break its hold. Later, the kingdom of Pergamum in western Asia Minor emerged as the fourth Hellenistic monarchy.

Rome, a new power, became increasingly drawn into the affairs of the quarrelsome Hellenistic kingdoms. By the middle of the second century B.C., it had built a vast empire and imposed its will over the Hellenistic world. From that time on, the political fortunes of the western and eastern Mediterranean were inextricably linked.

Cosmopolitanism

Hellenistic society was characterized by a growing cosmopolitanism—a mingling of peoples and an interchange of cultures. Greek traditions spread to the Near East, and Mesopotamian, Egyptian, Hebrew, and Persian traditions—particularly religious beliefs—moved westward.

A growing cosmopolitanism replaced the parochialism of the city-state. Although the rulers of the Hellenistic kingdoms were Macedonians and their high officials and generals were Greeks, the style of government was modeled after that of the ancient oriental kingdoms. In the Hellenic Age, the law had expressed the will of the community, but in this new age of monarchy the kings were the law. To promote loyalty, the Macedonian rulers encouraged the oriental cultic practice of worshiping the king as a god or as a representative of the gods. In Egypt, for example, the priests conferred on the Macedonian king the same divine powers and titles traditionally held by Egyptian pharaohs; in accordance with ancient tradition, statues of the divine king were installed in Egyptian temples, suffusing political power with supernatural authority, in marked contrast to the democratic spirit of the Greek Assembly.

Following Alexander's lead, the Seleucids founded cities in the East patterned after the city-states of Greece. The cities, which were often founded to protect trade routes and as fortresses against hostile tribes, adopted the political institutions of Hellenic Greece, including a popular assembly and a council. Hellenistic kings generally did not intervene in the cities' local affairs. Thousands of Greeks settled in these cities, which were Greek in architecture and contained Greek schools, temples, theaters (where performances of classical plays were staged), and gymnasia. Gymnasia were essentially places to exercise, train in sports, and converse, but some had libraries and halls where public lectures and competitions of orators and poets were held. Hellenistic kings brought books, paintings, and statues from Greece to their cities. Hellenistic cities, inhabited by tens of thousands of people from many lands and dominated by a Hellenized upper class, served as centers and agents of Hellenism, which non-Greeks adopted. The cities in Egypt and Syria saw the emergence of a native elite who spoke Greek, wore Greek-style clothing, and adopted Greek customs. *Koine* (or shared language), a form of spoken Greek spread by soldiers, administrators, merchants, teachers, and others, became a common tongue throughout much of the Mediterranean world.

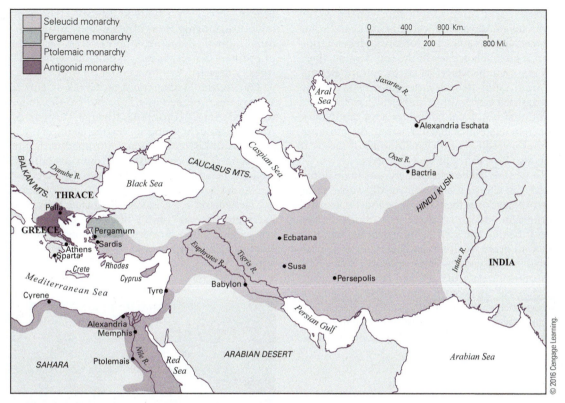

Map 3.2 **The Division of Alexander's Empire and the Spread of Hellenism** None of Alexander's generals could hold together the vast empire, which fractured into competing dynasties.

The greatest city of the time and the one most representative of the Hellenistic Age was Alexandria in Egypt, founded by Alexander the Great. Strategically located at one of the mouths of the Nile, Alexandria became a center of commerce and culture. The most populous city of the Mediterranean world, Alexandria at the beginning of the Christian era contained perhaps a million people: Egyptians, Persians, Macedonians, Greeks, Jews, Syrians, and Arabs. The city was an unrivaled commercial center; goods from the Mediterranean world, East Africa, Arabia, and India circulated in its marketplaces. This cosmopolitan center also attracted poets, philosophers, physicians, astronomers, and mathematicians.

All phases of cultural life were permeated by cultural exchange. Sculpture showed the influence of many lands. Historians wrote world histories, not just local ones. Greek astronomers worked with data collected over the centuries by the Babylonians. The Hebrew Scriptures were translated into Greek for use by Greek-speaking Jews, and some Jewish thinkers, admiring Greek learning, expressed Jewish religious ideas in philosophical terms: God was identified with reason and Moses' Law with the rational order of the universe. Greeks increasingly demonstrated a fascination with oriental religious cults. Philosophers helped to break down the barriers between peoples by asserting that all inhabit a single fatherland.

The spread of Greek civilization from the Aegean to the Indus River gave the Hellenistic world a cultural common denominator, but Hellenization did not transform the East and make it one with the West. Hellenization was limited almost entirely to the cities, and in many urban centers it was often only a thin veneer. Many Egyptians in Alexandria learned Greek, and some assumed Greek names, but for most, Hellenization did not go much deeper. In the countryside, there was not even the veneer of Greek culture. Retaining traditional attitudes, the countryside in the East resisted Greek ways. In the villages, local and traditional law, local languages, and family customs remained unchanged; religion, the most important ingredient of the civilizations of the Near East, also kept its traditional character.

To be sure, Hellenistic society was male dominated, but the status of women did show some improvement over the classical period. Some royal mothers and daughters exercised political power, even if behind the scenes, and royal women had access to great wealth as indicated by their cash contributions to cities. Some nonroyal ladies held important priestly offices, and far more than in the classical era women contributed to high culture as poets, harpists, artists, and architects. Two of the new schools of philosophy, Epicureanism and Cynicism, welcomed female participation.

HELLENISTIC THOUGHT AND CULTURE

Hellenistic culture rested on a Hellenic foundation, but it also revealed new trends: a heightened universalism and a growing individualism.

History, Art, Science

The leading historian of the Hellenistic Age was Polybius (c. 200–118 B.C.), whose history of the rise of Rome is one of the great works of historical literature. Reflecting the universal tendencies of the Hellenistic Age, Polybius endeavored to explain how Rome had progressed from a city-state to a world conqueror. As a disciple of Thucydides, Polybius sought rational explanations for human events. Like Thucydides, he relied on eyewitness accounts (including his own personal experiences), checked sources, and strove for objectivity.

Hellenistic art, like Hellenistic philosophy, expressed a heightened awareness of the individual. Whereas Hellenic sculpture aimed to depict ideal beauty—the perfect body and face—Hellenistic sculpture, moving from idealism to realism, captured individual character and expression, often of ordinary people. Scenes of daily life were realistically depicted.

During the Hellenistic Age, Greek scientific achievement reached its height. When Alexander invaded Asia Minor, the former student of Aristotle brought along surveyors, engineers, scientists, and historians, who continued with him into Asia. The vast amount of data on botany, zoology, geography, and astronomy collected by Alexander's staff stimulated an outburst of activity. Hellenistic science, says historian Benjamin Farrington, stood "on the threshold of the modern world. When modern science began in the sixteenth century, it took up where the Greeks left off."[17]

OLD MARKET WOMAN, C. SECOND CENTURY B.C. Hellenistic genre sculpture depicted people in everyday situations as individuals, rather than as types. This woman's stooped shoulders, weighed down by groceries, also suggest the harsh physical conditions that have worn her down over the years.

Because of its state-supported museum, Alexandria attracted leading scholars and superseded Athens in scientific investigation. The museum contained a library of more than half a million volumes, as well as botanical gardens and an observatory. It was really a research institute, in which some of the best minds of the day studied and worked.

Alexandrian doctors advanced medical skills. They improved surgical instruments and techniques and, by dissecting bodies, added to anatomical knowledge. Through their research, they discovered organs of the body not known until then, made the distinction between arteries and veins, divided nerves into those constituting the motor and the sensory systems, and identified the brain as the source of intelligence. Their investigations brought knowledge of anatomy and physiology to a level that was not significantly improved until the sixteenth century A.D.

Knowledge in the fields of astronomy and mathematics also increased. Eighteen centuries before Copernicus, the Alexandrian astronomer Aristarchus (310–230 B.C.) said that the sun was the center of the universe, that the planets revolved around it, and that the stars were situated at great distances from the earth. But these revolutionary ideas were not accepted, and the belief in an earth-centered universe persisted. In geometry, Euclid, an Alexandrian mathematician who lived around 300 B.C., creatively synthesized earlier developments. Euclid's hundreds of geometric proofs, derived from reasoning alone—his conclusions flowed logically and flawlessly from given assumptions—are a profound witness to the power of the rational mind.

Eratosthenes (c. 275–194 B.C.), an Alexandrian geographer, sought a scientific understanding of the enlarged world. He divided the planet into climatic zones, declared that the oceans are joined, and, with extraordinary ingenuity and accuracy, measured the earth's circumference. Archimedes of Syracuse (287–212 B.C.), who studied at Alexandria, was a mathematician, a physicist, and an ingenious inventor. His mechanical inventions, including war engines, dazzled his contemporaries. However, in typically Greek fashion, Archimedes dismissed his practical inventions, preferring to be remembered as a theoretician.

Philosophy

Hellenistic thinkers preserved the rational tradition of Greek philosophy, but they also transformed it, for they had to adapt their thought to the requirements of a cosmopolitan society. In the Hellenic Age, the starting point of philosophy was the citizen's relationship to the city; in the Hellenistic Age, the point of departure was the solitary individual's relationship to humanity and the individual's destiny in a complex world. Philosophy tried to deal with the feeling of alienation—of not belonging—resulting from the weakening of the individual's attachment to the polis and sought a conception of community that corresponded to the social realities of a world grown larger. It aspired to make people ethically independent so that they could achieve happiness in a hostile and competitive world. As the philosopher Epicurus said: "Empty are the words of that philosopher who offers no therapy for human suffering. For just as there is no use in medical expertise if it does not give therapy for bodily disease, so too there is no use in philosophy if it does not expel the suffering of the soul."[18] To "expel the suffering of the soul"—to conquer fear and anxiety and to achieve happiness—said Hellenistic philosophers, people must not allow themselves to be troubled by cares and concerns that are ultimately trivial. In striving for tranquility of mind and relief from conflict, Hellenistic thinkers reflected the general anxiety that pervaded their society.

Epicureanism. Two principal schools of philosophy arose in the Hellenistic world: Epicureanism and Stoicism. In the tradition of Plato and Aristotle, Epicurus (342–270 B.C.) founded a school in Athens at the end of the fourth century B.C. Epicurus broke with the attitude of the Hellenic Age in significant ways. Unlike classical Greek philosophers, Epicurus, reflecting the Greeks' changing relationship to the city, taught the value of passivity and withdrawal from civic life. To him, citizenship was not a prerequisite for individual happiness. Wise persons, said Epicurus, would refrain from engaging in public affairs, for politics is marred by clashing factions and treachery that could deprive them of their self-sufficiency, their freedom to choose and to act. Nor would wise individuals pursue wealth, power, or fame, as the pursuit would only provoke anxiety. For the same reason, wise persons would not surrender to hate or love, desires that distress the soul. They would also try to live justly, because those who behave unjustly are burdened with troubles. Nor could people find happiness if they worried about dying or pleasing the gods.

To Epicurus, dread that the gods punished people in this life and could inflict suffering after death was the principal cause of anxiety. To remove this source of human anguish, he favored a theory of nature that had no place for supernatural intervention in nature or in people's lives. Therefore, he adopted the physics of Democritus, which taught that all things consist of atoms in motion. In a universe of colliding atoms, there could be no higher intelligence ordering things; there was no room for divine activity. Epicurus taught that the gods probably did exist, but that they did not influence human affairs; consequently, individuals could order their own lives.

People could achieve happiness, said Epicurus, when their bodies were "free from pain" and their minds "released from worry and fear." Although Epicurus wanted to increase pleasure for the individual, he rejected unbridled hedonism. Because he believed that happiness must be pursued rationally, he urged avoidance of the merely sensuous pleasures that have unpleasant aftereffects (such as overeating and excessive drinking). In general, Epicurus espoused the traditional Greek view of moderation and prudence. By opening his philosophy to men and women, slave and free, Greek and barbarian, and by separating ethics from politics, Epicurus fashioned a philosophy adapted to the post-Alexandrian world of kingdoms and universal culture.

A fresco from the Farnesina garden. Museo Nazionale, Rome. Photo Alinari

AN ITINERANT CYNIC. Followers of cynicism, another Hellenistic philosophy, renounced possessions, showed no loyalty to city or kingdom, and dismissed philosophy and religion as nonsense. Cynics embraced asceticism, often wandering from place to place. The above image shows an itinerant Cynic, staff in hand.

Stoicism. Around the time when Epicurus founded his school, Zeno (335–263 B.C.) also opened a school in Athens. Zeno's teachings, called Stoicism (because his school was located in the *stoa*, or colonnade), became the most important philosophy in the Hellenistic world. By teaching that the world constituted a single society, Stoicism gave theoretical expression to the world-mindedness of the age. Through its concept of a world community, the city of humanity, Stoicism offered an answer to the problem of community and alienation posed by the decline of the city-state. By stressing

inner strength in dealing with life's misfortunes, it opened an avenue to individual happiness in a world fraught with uncertainty.

At the core of Stoicism was the belief that built into the universe was a principle of order, variously called Divine Reason (Logos), the Divine Fire, God—more an impersonal force than a living being. This ruling principle underlay reality and permeated all things; it ordered the cosmos according to law. The Stoics reasoned that, being part of the universe, people too shared in the Logos that operated throughout the cosmos.

Inherent in every human soul, and discovered through reason, the Logos enabled people to comprehend the principles of order that governed nature and to act intelligently and virtuously. This natural law provided human beings with an awareness of what is and is not correct behavior, especially when dealing with other human beings. The virtuous person lived in accordance with natural law, which was the avenue to both virtue and happiness. Natural law alone commanded ultimate obedience. Because reason was common to all, human beings were essentially brothers and fundamentally equal. Reason gave individuals dignity and enabled them to recognize and respect the dignity of others. To the Stoics, all people—Greek and barbarian, free and slave, rich and poor—were fellow human beings, and one law, the law of nature, applied to everyone. What people had in common as fellow human beings far outweighed differences based on culture. Thus the Stoics, like the Hebrews, arrived at the idea of the oneness of humanity.

Like Socrates, the Stoics believed that a person's distinctive quality was the ability to reason and that happiness came from the disciplining of emotions by the rational part of the soul. Also like Socrates, the Stoics maintained that individuals should progress morally and perfect their character. In the Stoic view, wise persons ordered their lives according to the natural law, the law of reason, that underlay the cosmos. This harmony with the Logos would give them the inner strength to resist the torments inflicted by others, by fate, and by their own passionate natures. Self-mastery and inner peace, or happiness, would follow. Such individuals would remain undisturbed by life's misfortunes, for their souls would be their own. Even slaves were not denied this inner freedom; although their bodies were subjected to the power of their masters, their minds still remained independent and free.

Stoicism had an enduring influence on the Western mind. To some Roman political and legal thinkers, the Empire fulfilled the Stoic ideal of a world community, in which people of different nationalities held citizenship and were governed by a worldwide law that accorded with the law of reason, or natural law, operating throughout the universe. Stoic beliefs—that by nature we are all members of one family, that each person is

significant, that distinctions of rank and race are of no account, and that human law should not conflict with natural law—were incorporated into Roman jurisprudence, Christian thought, and modern liberalism. There is continuity between the Stoic idea of natural law—a moral order that underlies nature—and the principle of inalienable rights stated in the American Declaration of Independence. In the modern age, the principle of natural law provided theoretical justification for the idea of human rights as the birthright of each individual.

THE GREEK ACHIEVEMENT: REASON, FREEDOM, HUMANISM

Like other ancient peoples, the Greeks warred, massacred, and enslaved; they could be cruel, arrogant, contentious, and superstitious; and they often violated their own ideals. But their achievements were unquestionably of profound historical significance. Western thought essentially begins with the Greeks, who first defined the individual by the capacity to reason. It was the great achievement of the Greek spirit to rise above magic, miracles, mystery, authority, and custom and to discover the procedures and terminology that permit a rational understanding of nature and society. Every aspect of Greek civilization—science, philosophy, art, drama, literature, politics, historical writing—showed a growing reliance on human reason and a diminishing dependence on the gods and mythical thinking. For the Greeks, the pursuit of intellectual concerns was the supreme human activity. They expressed confidence in the mind's capacity to fathom the physical laws that governed nature and to comprehend and cope with the problems afflicting the human community. And they maintained that rational inquiry provides us with the knowledge and inner discipline to live a good life.

In Mesopotamia and Egypt, people had no clear conception of their individual worth and no understanding of political liberty. They were not citizens but subjects marching to the command of a ruler whose power originated with the gods. Such royal power was not imposed on an unwilling population; it was religiously accepted and obeyed.

Unlike in the Near East, monarchs were incidental to Hellenic Greek political history, a development that enabled the Greeks to create both civic politics and political freedom. They saw the state as a community of free citizens who made laws that served the common good and in which disputes between citizens were decided by a jury of one's peers, not by the whims of a ruler or his officials. The citizens had no master other than themselves. The Greeks held that men are capable of governing themselves, and they regarded active participation in public affairs as a duty. For the Greeks, the state was a civilizing agent, permitting people to live the good life. Greek political thinkers arrived at a conception of the rational, or legal, state: a state in which law was an expression of reason, not of whim or divine commands; of justice, not of might; of the general good of the community, not of self-interest.

The Greeks also gave to Western civilization a conception of inner, or ethical, freedom. People were free to choose between shame and honor, cowardice and duty, moderation and excess. The idea of ethical freedom reached its highest point with Socrates, who shifted the focus of thought from cosmology to the human being and the moral life. To shape oneself according to ideals known to the mind—to develop into an autonomous and self-directed person—became for the Greeks the highest form of freedom.

During the Hellenistic Age, the Greeks, like the Hebrews earlier, arrived at the idea of universalism, the oneness of humanity. Stoic philosophers taught that all people, because of their ability to reason, are fundamentally alike and can be governed by the same laws. This idea is at the root of the modern principle of natural or human rights, which are the birthright of each individual.

Underlying everything accomplished by the Greeks was a humanist attitude toward life. The Greeks expressed a belief in the worth, significance, and dignity of the individual. They called for the maximum cultivation of human talent, the full development of human personality, and the deliberate pursuit of excellence. In valuing the human personality, the Greek humanists did not approve of living without restraints. They aimed at creating a higher type of man; such a man would mold himself according to worthy standards and make his life as harmonious and flawless as a work of art. This aspiration required effort, discipline, and intelligence. Despite their lauding of the human being's creative capacities, the Greeks were not naïve about human nature. Rather, intensely aware of the individual's inherent capacity for evil, Greek thinkers repeatedly warned that without the restraining forces of law, civic institutions, moral norms, and character training, society would be torn apart by the savage elements within human nature. But fundamental to the Greek humanist outlook was the belief that human beings could master themselves. Contemporary humanists continue to derive inspiration and guidelines from the literary, artistic, and philosophical creations of the ancient Greeks.

By discovering theoretical reason, by defining political freedom, and by affirming the worth and potential of human personality, the Greeks broke with the past and founded the rational and humanist tradition of the West. "Had Greek civilization never existed," says the poet W. H. Auden, "we would never have become fully conscious, which is to say that we would never have become, for better or worse, fully human."[19]

❖   ❖   ❖

NOTES

1. H. D. F. Kitto, *The Greeks* (Baltimore: Penguin Books, 1957), 60.

2. Werner Jaeger, *Paideia: The Ideals of Greek Culture,* trans. Gilbert Highet (New York: Oxford University Press, 1945), vol. 1, 8.

3. Kitto, *The Greeks,* 78.

4. Herodotus, *The Histories,* trans. Aubrey de Sélincourt (Baltimore: Penguin Books, 1954), 493.

5. Thucydides, *The Peloponnesian War,* trans. B. Jowett (Oxford: Clarendon Press, 1881), bk. 2, chap. 37.

6. Aristotle, *Politics*, in *Basic Works of Aristotle*, ed., Richard McKeon (New York: Random House, 1941), 1132.

7. Thucydides, *History of the Peloponnesian War*, trans. Rex Warner (Baltimore: Penguin Books, 1954), 360.

8. John N. Theodorakopoulos, "The Origins of Science and Philosophy," in *History of the Hellenic World: The Archaic Period* (University Park: Pennsylvania State University Press, 1975), 438.

9. Quoted in George Sarton, *A History of Science* (Cambridge, Mass.: Harvard University Press, 1952), vol. 1, 355–356.

10. Plato, *Apology*, trans. F. J. Church, rev. R. D. Cummings (Indianapolis: Bobbs-Merrill, 1956), secs. 16–17.

11. Plato, *The Republic*, trans. F. M. Cornford (New York: Oxford University Press, 1945), 289.

12. Ibid., 293.

13. Aristotle, *Politics*, 1246, 1251.

14. Ibid., 1220–1221.

15. Sophocles, *Oedipus the King*, trans. Bernard M. W. Knox (New York: Washington Square Press, 1959), 61.

16. Herodotus, *The Histories*, 485.

17. Benjamin Farrington, *Greek Science* (Baltimore: Penguin Books, 1961), 301.

18. Quoted in Anthony Gottlieb, *The Dream of Reason* (New York, W. W. Norton, 2000), 283–284.

19. W. H. Auden, ed., *The Portable Greek Reader* (New York: Viking, 1952), 38.

Chapter 4

Rome: From City-State to World Empire

- **Evolution of the Roman Constitution**
- **Roman Expansion to 146 B.C.**
- **Culture in the Republic**
- **The Collapse of the Republic**
- **Augustus and the Foundations of the Roman Empire**
- **The Pax Romana**
- **Signs of Trouble**
- **The Decline of Rome**
- **The Roman Legacy**

Focus Questions

1. What factors enabled the city-state of Rome to conquer Italy and the Mediterranean world?
2. What was the significance of Roman expansion?
3. What were the reasons for the collapse of the Roman Republic?
4. Why is the Pax Romana regarded as one of the finest periods in world history? What continuity is there between the Pax Romana and the Hellenistic Age?
5. How did Roman law evolve? How did it incorporate Stoic principles?
6. What are the reasons for the decline of the Roman Empire?
7. What is Rome's legacy to Western civilization?
8. Why do you think that over the centuries Rome's demise has intrigued historians and philosophers?

Rome's great achievement was to transcend the narrow political orientation of the city-state and to create a world-state that unified the different nations of the Mediterranean world. Regarding the polis as the only means to the good life, the Greeks had not desired a larger political unit and had almost totally excluded foreigners from citizenship. Although Hellenistic philosophers had conceived the possibility of a world community, Hellenistic politics could not shape one. But Rome overcame the limitations of the city-state mentality and developed an empirewide system of law and citizenship. The Hebrews were distinguished by their prophets and the Greeks by their philosophers. The Romans produced no Amos or Isaiah and no Plato or Aristotle; their genius found expression in law and government and in the transmission of the Greek cultural achievement.

Historians divide Roman history into two broad periods. The period of the Republic began in 509 B.C. with the overthrow of the Etruscan monarchy; the period of the Empire began in 27 B.C., when Octavian (Augustus) became in effect the first Roman emperor, ending almost five hundred years of republican self-government. By conquering the Mediterranean world and extending Roman law and, in some instances, citizenship to different nationalities, the Roman Republic transcended the parochialism typical of the city-state. The Republic initiated the trend toward political and legal universalism, which reached fruition in the second period of Roman history, the Empire. ❖

EVOLUTION OF THE ROMAN CONSTITUTION

By the eighth century B.C., peasant communities existed on some of Rome's seven hills near the Tiber River in central Italy. To the north stood Etruscan cities, and to the south, Greek cities. The more advanced civilizations of both the Etruscans and Greeks were gradually absorbed by the Romans.

The origin of the Etruscans remains a mystery, although some scholars believe that they came from Asia Minor and settled in northern Italy. From them, Romans acquired architectural styles and skills in road construction, sanitation, hydraulic engineering (including underground conduits), metallurgy, ceramics, and portrait sculpture. Etruscan words and names entered the Latin language, and Roman religion absorbed Etruscan gods.

The Etruscans had expanded their territory in Italy during the seventh and sixth centuries B.C., and they controlled the monarchy in Rome. Defeated by Celts, Greeks, and finally Romans, by the third century B.C., the Etruscans ceased to exercise any political power in Italy.

Rome became a republic at the end of the sixth century B.C.—the traditional date is 509 B.C.—when the landowning aristocrats, or patricians, overthrew the Etruscan king. As in the Greek cities, the transition from theocratic monarchy to republic offered possibilities for political and legal growth. In the opening phase of republican history, religion governed the people, dictated the law, and legitimized the rule of the patricians, who regarded themselves as the preservers of sacred traditions. Gradually, the Romans loosened the ties between religion and politics and hammered out a constitutional system that paralleled the Greek achievement of rationalizing and secularizing politics and law. In time, the Romans, like the Greeks, came to view law as an expression of the public will and not as the creation of god-kings, priest-kings, or a priestly caste.

The impetus for the growth of the Roman constitution came from a conflict—known as the Struggle of the Orders—between the patricians and the commoners, or plebeians. At the beginning of the fifth century B.C., the patrician-dominated government consisted of two annually elected executives called consuls, the Centuriate Assembly, and the Senate. Patricians owned most of the land and controlled the army. The two consuls, who came from the nobility, commanded the army, served as judges, and initiated legislation.

The Centuriate Assembly was a popular assembly, but because of voting procedures, it was controlled by the nobility. The Assembly elected consuls and other magistrates and made the laws, which also needed Senate approval. The Senate advised the Assembly but did not itself enact laws; it controlled public finances and foreign policy.

Chronology 4.1 ❖ Rome

509 B.C.	Expulsion of the Etruscan monarch
287	End of the Struggle of the Orders
264–241	First Punic War: Rome acquires provinces
218–201	Second Punic War: Hannibal is defeated
133–122	Land reforms by the Gracchi brothers; they are murdered by the Senate
88–83	Conflict between Sulla and the forces of Marius; Sulla emerges as dictator
49–44	Caesar is dictator of Rome
27 B.C.	Octavian assumes the title *Augustus* and becomes, in effect, the first Roman emperor; start of the Pax Romana
A.D. 180	Marcus Aurelius dies; end of the Pax Romana
212	Roman citizenship is granted to virtually all free inhabitants of Roman provinces
235–285	Military anarchy; Germanic incursions
285–305	Diocletian tries to deal with the crisis by creating a regimented state
378	Battle of Adrianople: Visigoths defeat the Roman legions
406	Borders collapse, Germanic tribes move into the Empire
476	End of the Roman Empire in the West

Senators either were appointed for life terms by the consuls or were former magistrates. The Senate was the principal organ of patrician power.

The tension between patricians and commoners stemmed from plebeian grievances, which included enslavement for debt, discrimination in the courts, prevention of intermarriage with patricians, lack of political representation, and the absence of a written code of laws. Resenting their inferior status and eager for economic relief, the plebeians organized and waged a struggle for political, legal, and social equality.

The plebeians had one decisive weapon: their threat to secede from Rome, that is, not to pay taxes, work, or serve in the army. Realizing that Rome, which was constantly involved in warfare on the Italian peninsula, could not endure without plebeian help, the pragmatic patricians grudgingly made concessions. Thus, the plebeians slowly gained legal equality.

Early in the fifth century, the plebeians won the right to form their own assembly (the Plebeian Assembly, which was later enlarged and called the Tribal Assembly). This assembly could elect tribunes, officials who were empowered to protect plebeian rights. As a result of plebeian pressure, around 450 B.C. the first Roman code of laws was written. Called the Twelve Tables, the code gave plebeians some degree of protection against unfair and oppressive patrician officials, who could interpret customary law in an arbitrary way. Other concessions gained later by the plebeians included the right to intermarry with patricians; access to the highest political, judicial, and religious offices in the state; and the elimination of slavery as payment for debt. In 287 B.C., a date generally recognized as the termination of the plebeian–patrician struggle, laws passed by the Tribal Assembly no longer required the Senate's approval. Now the plebeians had full civil equality and legal protection, and their assembly had full power to enact legislation.

Despite these changes, Rome was still ruled by an upper class. The oligarchy that held power now consisted of patricians and influential plebeians who had joined forces with the old nobility. Marriages between patricians and politically powerful plebeians strengthened this alliance. Generally only wealthy plebeians became tribunes, and they tended to side with the old nobility rather than defend the interests of poor plebeians. By using bribes, the ruling oligarchy maintained control over the Assembly, and the Senate remained a bastion of aristocratic power. Deeming themselves Rome's finest citizens, the ruling oligarchy led Rome during its period of expansion and demonstrated a sense of responsibility and a talent for statesmanship.

During the two-hundred-year Struggle of the Orders, the Romans forged a constitutional system based on civic needs rather than on religious mystery. The essential duty of government ceased to be the regular performance of religious rituals and became the maintenance of order at home and the preservation of Roman might and dignity in international relations. Although the Romans retained the ceremonies and practices of their ancestral religion, public interest, not religious tradition or the prospect of divine punishment, determined the content of law. Public interest was also the standard by which all the important acts of the city were judged. In the opening stage of republican history, law was priestly and sacred, spoken only by priests and known only to men of religious families. Gradually, as law was written, debated, and altered, it became disentangled from religion. Another step in this process of secularization and rationalization occurred when the study and interpretation of law passed from the hands of priests to a class of professional jurists, who analyzed, classified, and systematized it and sought commonsense solutions to legal problems.

The Roman constitution was not a product of abstract thought, nor was it the gift of a great lawmaker, such as the Athenian Solon. Rather, like the unwritten English constitution, the Roman constitution evolved gradually and empirically in response to specific needs. The Romans, unlike the Greeks, were distinguished by practicality and

Scala/Art Resource, N.Y.

STATUE PORTRAIT, FIRST CENTURY A.D. The Romans valued family, city, and tradition. Here a noble proudly exhibits the busts of his ancestors.

common sense, not by a love of abstract thought. In their pragmatic and empirical fashion, they gradually developed the procedures of public politics and the legal state.

ROMAN EXPANSION TO 146 B.C.

At the time of the Struggle of the Orders, Rome was also extending its power over the Italian peninsula. Without the civic harmony and stability gained by patrician concessions, it could not have achieved expansion. By 146 B.C., it had become the dominant power in the Mediterranean world.

Roman expansion occurred in three main stages: the uniting of the Italian peninsula, which gave Rome the manpower that transformed it from a city-state into a great power; the collision with Carthage, from which Rome emerged as ruler of the western Mediterranean; and the subjugation of the Hellenistic states, which brought Romans in close contact with Greek civilization. As Rome expanded territorially, its leaders enlarged their vision. Instead of restricting citizenship to people having ethnic kinship, Rome assimilated other peoples into its political community. As law had grown to cope with the earlier grievances of the plebeians, so too it adjusted to the new situations resulting from the creation of a multinational empire. The city of Rome was evolving into the city of humanity—the cosmopolis envisioned by the Stoics.

The Uniting of Italy

During the first stage of expansion, Rome extended its hegemony over Italy, subduing in the process neighboring Latin kinsmen, semi-civilized Italian tribes, the once-dominant Etruscans, and Greek city-states in southern Italy. Rome's conquest of Italy stemmed in part from superior military organization, training, and iron discipline. Copying the Greeks, the Romans organized their soldiers into battle formations; in contrast, their opponents often fought as disorganized hordes, which were prone to panic and flight. Romans also willingly made sacrifices so that Rome might endure. In conquering Italy, they were united by a moral and religious devotion to their city strong enough to overcome social conflict, factional disputes, and personal ambition. Also fueling

Roman expansion was an aristocratic ethos that placed the highest value on glory. Demonstrating prowess in war, aristocrats believed, was the finest way to win the esteem of fellow Romans, bring honor to their family, and enhance their own political career.

Despite its army's strength, Rome could not have mastered Italy without the cooperation of other Italian peoples. Like other ancient peoples, Rome plundered, enslaved, and brutalized, at times with great ferocity. But it also endeavored, through generous treatment, to gain the loyalty of conquered people. Some defeated communities retained a measure of self-government but turned the conduct of foreign affairs over to Rome and contributed contingents to the army when Rome went to war. Other conquered people received partial or full citizenship. In extending its dominion over Italy, Rome displayed a remarkable talent for converting former enemies into allies and eventually into Roman citizens. No Greek city had ever envisaged integrating nonnatives into its political community.

The Conquest of the Mediterranean World

When Rome finished unifying Italy, there were five great powers in the Mediterranean area: the Seleucid monarchy in the Near East, the Ptolemaic monarchy in Egypt, the kingdom of Macedonia, Carthage in the western Mediterranean, and the Roman-dominated Italian Confederation. One hundred twenty years later—in 146 B.C.—Rome had subjected the other states to its dominion.

Roman expansion beyond Italy did not proceed according to a set plan. Indeed, some Roman leaders considered involvement in foreign adventures a threat to both Rome's security and its traditional way of life. However, as its interests grew, Rome was drawn into conflicts and, without planning it, acquired an overseas empire.

Shortly after asserting supremacy in Italy, Rome engaged Carthage, the other great power in the western Mediterranean, in a prolonged conflict, the First Punic War (264–241 B.C.). Founded about 800 B.C. by Phoenicians, the North African city of Carthage had become a prosperous commercial center. The Carthaginians had acquired an empire comprising North Africa and coastal

A ROMAN WARSHIP WITH LEGIONNAIRES ON A RELIEF FROM THE TEMPLE OF FORTUNA PRIMIGENIA, FIRST CENTURY B.C. Roman soldiers fought on sea as well as on land, conquering nations throughout the Mediterranean area during the eras of the Republic and the Empire.

regions of southern Spain, Sardinia, Corsica, and western Sicily.

War between the two great powers began because Rome feared Carthage's designs on the northern Sicilian city of Messana. Rome was apprehensive about the southern Italian city-states that were its allies, fearing that Carthage would use Messana either to attack them or to interfere with their trade. Rome decided that the security of its allies required intervention in Sicily. Although Rome suffered severe losses—including the annihilation of an army that had invaded North Africa and the destruction of hundreds of ships in battle and storms—the Romans never considered anything but a victor's peace. Drawing manpower from loyal allies throughout Italy, Rome finally prevailed over Carthage, which had to surrender Sicily to Rome. Three years later, Rome seized the islands of Corsica and Sardinia from a weakened Carthage. With the acquisition of these territories

beyond Italy, which were made into provinces, Rome had the beginnings of an empire.

Carthaginian expansion in Spain precipitated the Second Punic War (218–201 B.C.). Coming from Spain, the Carthaginian army was commanded by Hannibal (247–183 B.C.), whose military genius astounded the ancients. Hannibal led a seasoned army, complete with war elephants for charging enemy lines, across mountain passes so steep and icy that men and animals sometimes lost their footing and fell to their deaths. Some twenty-six thousand men survived the crossing into Italy; fifteen thousand more were recruited from Gallic tribesmen of the Po Valley. At the battle of Cannae (216 B.C.), the Carthaginian forces, in a brilliant encircling maneuver, completely destroyed a Roman army of sixty thousand soldiers—the largest single force Rome had ever put into the field. The butchering by hand of the trapped Roman soldiers lasted for hours.

million enslaved aliens were transported to Italy. By the middle of that century, slaves constituted about one-third of Italy's population, compared with about 10 percent before the Second Punic War. The wars of conquest had made the slave trade a vast and lucrative commercial venture. Increasing the market in slaves was the sale of people captured by pirates, and children sold to slave traders by poor parents. Like the Greeks, Romans considered slavery indispensable for the preservation of civilized life. Roman jurists and intellectuals regarded the division of humanity into masters and slaves as a rule of nature and viewed the slave as an animate tool, an object that produced and served; like other forms of property, slaves could be sold or rented out by their masters. The more fortunate or more capable slaves worked as craftsmen and servants; the luckless and more numerous toiled, branded and chained, on the growing number of plantations or died early laboring in mines under inhuman conditions. So brutal was their existence that they begged for death, reported a Roman observer. Roman masters often treated their slaves brutally. Torture was common, and masters sexually exploited both male and female slaves for their own pleasure or compelled them to work as prostitutes. Although slave uprisings were not common, their ferocity terrified the Romans. In 135 B.C., slaves in Sicily revolted and captured some key towns, defeating Roman forces before being subdued. In 73 B.C., gladiators, led by Spartacus, broke out of their barracks and were joined by tens of thousands of runaways. Spartacus aimed to escape into Gaul and Thrace, the homelands of many slaves. His slave army defeated Roman armies and devastated southern Italy before the superior might of Rome prevailed. Some six thousand of the defeated slaves were tortured and crucified on the road from Capua to Rome.

Roman governors, lesser officials, and businessmen found the provinces a source of quick wealth; they were generally unrestrained by the Senate, which was responsible for administering the overseas territories. Exploitation, corruption, looting, and extortion soon ran rampant. "No administration in history has ever devoted itself so whole heartedly to fleecing its subjects for the private benefit of its ruling class as Rome of the last age of the Republic," concludes E. Badian.[1] The Roman nobility proved unfit to manage a world empire.

Despite numerous examples of misrule in the provinces, Roman administration had many positive features. Rome generally allowed its subjects a large measure of self-government and did not interfere with religion and local customs. Usually, the Roman taxes worked out to be no higher, and in some instances were lower, than those under previous regimes. Most important, Rome reduced the endemic warfare that had plagued these regions.

CULTURE IN THE REPUBLIC

One of the chief consequences of expansion was greater contact with Greek culture. During the third century B.C., Greek civilization started to exercise an increasing and fruitful influence on the Roman mind. Greek teachers, both slave and free, came to Rome, many of them as guests of the Roman aristocracy, and instructed Romans in Greek language, philosophy, literature, and art. As they conquered the eastern Mediterranean, Roman generals began to ship libraries and works of art from Greek cities to Rome. Roman sculpture and painting imitated Greek prototypes. In time, Romans acquired from Greece knowledge of scientific thought, philosophy, medicine, and geography. Roman writers and orators used Greek history, poetry, and oratory as models. Adopting the humanist outlook of the Greeks, the Romans came to value human intelligence and eloquent and graceful prose and poetry. Wealthy Romans retained Greek tutors, poets, and philosophers in their households and sent their sons to Athens to study. Thus, Rome creatively assimilated the Greek achievement and transmitted it to others, thereby extending the orbit of Hellenism. To be sure, some conservative Romans were hostile to the Greek influence, which they felt threatened traditional Roman values that had accounted for Rome's greatness. Cato the Elder (234–149 B.C.) and other Roman moralists denounced Socrates for undermining respect for Athenian law and warned that Greek philosophy might lure Roman youth into similar subversive behavior. Moreover, said these moralists, Greek philosophy, with its endless discussions of abstract themes, contrasted with the virtue most cherished by Romans—*gravitas* or seriousness—which enabled Romans to conduct public affairs effectively. Philosophy seemed designed for a life of leisure and inaction, whereas a virtuous Roman was actively involved in practical civic matters.

Plautus (c. 254–184 B.C.), Rome's greatest playwright, adopted features of fourth- and third-century Greek comedy. His plays had Greek characters and took place in Greek settings; the actors wore the Greek style of dress. But the plays also contained familiar elements that appealed to Roman audiences: scenes of gluttony, drunkenness, womanizing, and the pains of love.

Another playwright, Terence (c. 185–159 B.C.), was originally from North Africa and had been brought to Rome as a slave. His owner, a Roman senator, provided the talented youth with an education and freed him. Terence's humor, restrained and refined, lacked the boisterousness of Plautus that Romans liked, but his style was technically superior.

Catullus (c. 84–c. 54 B.C.), a native of northern Italy, is generally regarded as one of the world's great lyric poets. His father provided him with a gentleman's education. Tormented by an ill-fated love, Catullus wrote memorable poems dealing with passion and its anguish.

The leading Roman Epicurean philosopher, Lucretius (c. 96–c. 55 B.C.), was influenced by the conflict fostered by two generals, Marius and Sulla, which is discussed later in this chapter. Distraught by the seemingly endless strife, Lucretius yearned for philosophical tranquility. In his work *On the Nature of Things,* Lucretius expressed his appreciation of Epicurus. Like his mentor, Lucretius denounced superstition and religion for fostering psychological distress and advanced a materialistic conception of nature, one that left no room for the activity of gods—mechanical laws, not the gods, governed all physical happenings. To dispel the fear of punishment after death, Lucretius marshaled arguments to prove that the soul perishes with the body. Like Epicurus, he held that the simple life, devoid of political involvement and excessive passion, was the highest good and the path that would lead from emotional turmoil to peace of mind.

Cicero (106–43 B.C.), a leading Roman statesman, was also a distinguished orator, an unsurpassed Latin stylist, and a student of Greek philosophy. His letters, more than eight hundred of which have survived, provide modern historians with valuable insights into the politics of the late Republic. His Senate speeches have served as models of refined rhetoric for all students of the Latin language. Cicero's discussion of such topics as republicanism, citizenship, friendship, virtue, duty, and justice had an enduring influence on Western moral and political thought. Dedicated to republicanism, Cicero sought to prevent one-man rule. He admired the Stoic goal of the self-sufficient sage who sought to accord his life with standards of virtue inherent in nature. He adopted the Stoic belief that natural law governs the universe and applies to all, that all belong to a common humanity, and that reason is the individual's noblest faculty. Stoicism was the most influential philosophy in Rome. Its stress on virtuous conduct and performance of duty coincided with Roman ideals, and its doctrine of a natural law that applies to all nations harmonized with the requirements of a world empire.

In the eighteenth century, the Founding Fathers of the United States praised Cicero's natural law philosophy, which coincided with their belief in inalienable rights; his condemnation of tyranny; and his advocacy of liberty, republicanism, and constitutional government.

THE COLLAPSE OF THE REPUBLIC

In 146 B.C., Roman might spanned the Mediterranean world. After that year, the principal concerns of the Republic were no longer foreign invasions but adjusting city-state institutions to the demands of empire and overcoming critical social and political problems at home. The Republic proved unequal to either challenge. Instead of developing a professional civil service to administer the conquered lands, Roman leaders attempted to govern an empire with city-state institutions, which had evolved for a different purpose. The established Roman administration proved unable to govern the Mediterranean world. In addition, Rome's ruling elite showed little concern for the welfare of its subjects. Provincial rule worsened as governors, tax collectors, and soldiers shamelessly exploited the provincials.

During Rome's march to empire, all its classes had demonstrated a magnificent civic spirit in fighting foreign wars. With Carthage and Macedonia no longer threatening Rome, this cooperation deteriorated. Internal dissension tore Rome apart as the ferocious drive for domination, formerly directed against foreign enemies, turned inward against fellow Romans. Civil war replaced foreign war.

Neither the Senate nor its opponents could rejuvenate the Republic. Eventually it collapsed, a victim of class tensions, poor leadership, power-hungry demagogues, and civil war. Underlying all these conditions was the breakdown of social harmony and the deterioration of civic patriotism. The Republic had conquered an empire, only to see the spiritual qualities of its citizens decay. In a high moral tone, the historian Sallust (c. 86–34 B.C.) condemned the breakdown of republican values:

> Growing love of money, and the lust for power which followed it, engendered every kind of evil. Avarice destroyed honor, integrity, and every other virtue, and instead taught men to be proud and cruel, to neglect religion, and to hold nothing too sacred to sell. Ambition tempted many to be false. . . . At first these vices grew slowly and sometimes met with punishments; later on, when the disease had spread like a plague, Rome changed: her government, once so just and admirable, became harsh and unendurable.[2]

The Gracchan Revolution

The downhill slide of the Republic began with an agricultural crisis. During the long war with Hannibal in Italy, farms were devastated, and with many Roman soldier-farmers serving in the army for long periods, fields lay neglected. Returning veterans lacked the wealth to restore their land. They were forced to sell their farms to wealthy landowners at low prices.

Another factor that helped to squeeze out the small farm owners was the importation of hundreds of thousands of slaves to work on large plantations, called *latifundia*. This massive use of slave labor was unprecedented in Roman history. Farmers who had formerly increased their meager incomes by working for wages on neighboring large estates were no longer needed. Sinking ever deeper into poverty and debt, they gave up their lands and went to Rome and other cities to seek work. The dispossessed peasantry found little to do in Rome, where there was not enough industry to provide them with employment and where much of the work was done by slaves. The once sturdy and independent Roman farmer, who had done all that his country had asked of him, was becoming part of a vast urban underclass, poor, embittered, and alienated.

In 133 B.C., Tiberius Gracchus (163–133 B.C.), who came from one of Rome's most honored families, was elected tribune. Distressed by the injustice done to the peasantry and recognizing that the Roman army depended on the loyalty of small landowners, Tiberius made himself the spokesman for land reform. He proposed a simple and moderate solution for the problem of the landless peasants: he would revive an old law barring any Roman from using more than 312 acres of the state-owned land obtained in the process of uniting Italy. For many years, the upper class had ignored this law, occupying vast tracts of public land as squatters and treating this land as their own. By enforcing the law, Tiberius hoped to free land for distribution to landless citizens.

Rome's leading families viewed Tiberius as a revolutionary who threatened their property and political authority. They also feared that he was seeking to stir up the poor in order to gain political power for himself. To preserve the status quo, with wealth and power concentrated in the hands of a few hundred families, senatorial extremists killed Tiberius and some three hundred of his followers, dumping their bodies into the Tiber.

The cause of land reform was next taken up by Gaius Gracchus (153–121 B.C.), a younger brother of Tiberius, who was elected tribune in 123 B.C. Gaius aided the poor by reintroducing his brother's plan for land distribution and by enabling them to buy grain from the state at less than half the market price. But like his brother, Gaius aroused the anger of the senatorial class who ordered his murder. A brief civil war raged in Rome, during which Gaius Gracchus (who may have committed suicide) and three thousand of his followers perished.

By killing the Gracchi, the Senate had substituted violence for reason and made murder a means of coping with troublesome opposition. Soon the club and the dagger became common weapons in Roman politics, hurling Rome into an era of political violence that ended with the destruction of the Republic. Although the Senate considered itself the guardian of republican liberty, in reality it was expressing the determination of a few hundred families to retain their control over the state. It is a classic example of a once creative minority clinging tenaciously to power long after it had ceased to govern effectively or to inspire allegiance. In the century after the Gracchi, Roman politics was bedeviled by intrigues, rivalries, personal ambition, and political violence. The Senate behaved like a decadent oligarchy, and the Tribal Assembly, which had become the voice of the urban mob, demonstrated a weakness for demagogues, an openness to bribery, and an abundance of deceit and incompetence. The Roman Republic had passed the peak of its greatness.

Rival Generals

Marius (157–86 B.C.), who became consul in 107 B.C., adopted a military policy that eventually contributed to the wrecking of the Republic. Short of troops for a campaign in Numidia in North Africa, Marius disposed of the traditional property requirement for entrance into the army and filled his legions with volunteers from the urban poor, a dangerous precedent. These new soldiers, disillusioned with Rome, served only because Marius held out the promise of pay, loot, and land grants after discharge. They gave their loyalty not to Rome but to Marius, and they remained loyal to their commander only as long as he fulfilled his promises.

Other ambitious commanders followed the example set by Marius. They saw that a general could use his army to advance his political career—that by retaining the confidence of his soldiers, he could cow the Senate and dictate Roman policy. No longer an instrument of government, the army became a private possession of generals.

Seeing its authority undermined by generals appointed by the Assembly, the Senate was forced to seek army commanders who would champion the cause of senatorial rule. In time, Rome would be engulfed in civil wars, as rival generals used their troops to strengthen their political affiliations and to further their own ambitions.

Meanwhile, the Senate continued to deal ineffectively with Rome's problems. When Rome's Italian allies—who had provided the manpower needed to conquer the empire—pressed for citizenship, the Senate refused to make concessions. The Senate's shortsightedness plunged Italy into a terrible war known as the Social War (91–88 B.C.). As war ravaged the peninsula, the Romans reversed their policy and conferred citizenship on the Italians. The unnecessary and ruinous rebellion petered out.

A conflict over who would command an army in the east broke out between Marius and Sulla (138–78 B.C.), who had distinguished himself in the Social War. In this prolonged civil war, Sulla won the first round, capturing the capital. But then Marius and his troops retook Rome and, in a frenzy, lashed out at Sulla's supporters. The killing lasted for five days and nights. Marius died shortly afterward. Sulla quickly subdued Marius's supporters on his return and instituted a terror that far surpassed Marius's violence.

Sulla believed that only rule by an aristocratic oligarchy could protect Rome from future military adventurers and ensure domestic peace. Consequently, he restored the Senate's right to veto acts of the Assembly, limited the power of the tribunes and the Assembly, and, to prevent any march on Rome, reduced the military authority of provincial governors. To make the Senate less oligarchic, he increased its membership to six hundred. Having put through these reforms, Sulla retired.

Julius Caesar

The Senate, however, failed to wield its restored authority effectively. The Republic was still menaced by military commanders who used their troops for their own political advantage, and underlying problems remained unsolved. In 60 B.C., a triumvirate (a ruling group of three) consisting of Julius Caesar (c. 100–44 B.C.), a politician, Pompey, a general, and Crassus, a wealthy banker, conspired to take over Rome. The ablest of the three was Caesar, who descended from an ancient noble family.

Recognizing the importance of a military command as a prerequisite for political prominence, Caesar gained command of the legions in Gaul in 59 B.C. The following year he began the conquest of the part of Gaul outside of Roman control, bringing the future France into the orbit of Greco-Roman culture. The campaign was brilliantly described in his *Commentaries,* although, to be sure, the work was a deliberate attempt to apprise the Roman public of his military prowess. The successful Gallic campaigns and invasion of Britain revealed Caesar's exceptional talent for generalship: he acted decisively, moved troops rapidly, and had excellent rapport with his men, who admired his battlefield skills and courage and were grateful for the spoils he distributed to them. Lasting eight years, Caesar's conquest of Gaul was marked by brutal massacres and mutilations. Hundreds of thousands of Gauls were killed and hundreds of thousands more were enslaved. By plundering Gaul, he also acquired a fortune that could be used to further his political career, particularly for bribing Roman officials. Indeed, Caesar's victories alarmed the Senate, which feared that the popular general would use his devoted troops and soaring reputation to seize control of the state.

Meanwhile, the triumvirate had fallen apart. In 53 B.C., Crassus had perished with his army in a disastrous campaign against the Parthians in the East. Pompey, who was jealous of Caesar's success and eager to expand his own power, drew closer to the Senate. Supported by Pompey, the Senate ordered Caesar to relinquish his command. Caesar, realizing that without his troops he would be defenseless, decided instead to march on Rome. After he crossed the Rubicon River into Italy in 49 B.C., civil war again ravaged the Republic. Pompey proved no match for so talented a general; the Senate acknowledged Caesar's victory and appointed him to be dictator, a legal office, for ten years.

Caesar realized that republican institutions no longer operated effectively and that only strong and enlightened leadership could permanently end the civil warfare destroying Rome. He fought exploitation in the provinces and generously extended citizenship to more Italians and provincials. To aid the poor in Rome, he began a public works program, which provided employment and beautified the city. He also relocated more than a hundred thousand veterans and members of Rome's lower class to the provinces, where he gave them land.

In February 44 B.C., Rome's ruling class, jealous of Caesar's success and power and afraid of his ambition, became thoroughly alarmed when his temporary dictatorship was converted into a lifelong office. The aristocracy saw this event as the end of senatorial government and their rule, which they equated with liberty, and as the beginning of a hated Hellenistic type of monarchy. On March 15, a group of aristocrats, regarding themselves as defenders of republican traditions and institutions more than four-and-a-half centuries old, assassinated Caesar.

The Republic's Last Years

The assassination of Julius Caesar did not restore republican liberty; rather, it plunged Rome into renewed civil war. Two of Caesar's trusted lieutenants, Mark Antony and Lepidus, joined with Octavian, Caesar's adopted son, and defeated the armies of Brutus and Cassius, conspirators in the plot against Caesar. After Lepidus was forced into political obscurity, Antony and Octavian fought each other, with control of Rome as the prize. In 31 B.C., at the naval battle of Actium in western Greece, Octavian crushed the forces of Antony and his wife, Egypt's Queen Cleopatra. Octavian emerged as master of Rome and four years later became, in effect, the first Roman emperor.

The Roman Republic, which had amassed power to a degree hitherto unknown in the ancient world, was wrecked not by foreign invasion but by internal weaknesses: the degeneration of senatorial leadership and the transformation of political rivalry into violence and terror in which opponents were condemned to death and their property confiscated; the formation of private armies, in which soldiers gave their loyalty to their commander rather than to Rome; the transformation of a self-reliant peasantry into an impoverished and demoralized city rabble; and the deterioration of the ancient virtues that had been the source of the state's vitality. Before 146 B.C., the threat posed by foreign enemies, particularly Carthage, forced Romans to work together for the benefit of the state. This social cohesion broke down when foreign danger had been reduced.

AUGUSTUS AND THE FOUNDATIONS OF THE ROMAN EMPIRE

After Octavian's forces defeated those of Antony and Cleopatra at the battle of Actium, no opponents could stand up to him. The century of civil war, political murder, corruption, and mismanagement had exhausted the Mediterranean world, which longed for order. Like Caesar before him, Octavian recognized that only a strong monarchy could rescue Rome from civil war and anarchy. But, learning from Caesar's assassination, he also knew that republican ideals were far from dead. To exercise autocratic power openly, like a Hellenistic monarch, would have aroused the hostility of the Roman ruling class, whose assistance and good will Octavian desired.

Octavian demonstrated his political genius by reconciling his military monarchy with republican institutions: he held absolute power and direct control over the army without abruptly breaking with a republican past. Magistrates were still elected, and assemblies still met; the Senate administered certain provinces, retained its treasury, and was invited to advise Octavian. With some truth, Octavian could claim that he ruled in partnership with the Senate. By maintaining the facade of the Republic, Octavian camouflaged his absolute power and contained senatorial opposition, which had already been weakened by the deaths of leading nobles in battle or in the purges that Octavian had instituted against his enemies.

In 27 B.C., Octavian shrewdly offered to surrender his power, knowing that the Senate, purged of opposition, would demand that he continue to lead the state. By this act, Octavian could claim to be a legitimate constitutional ruler leading a government of law, not one of lawless despotism, which was hateful to the Roman mentality.

In keeping with his policy of maintaining the appearance of traditional republican government, Octavian refused to be called king or even, like Caesar, dictator. Instead, he cleverly disguised his autocratic rule by taking the inoffensive title *princeps* (first citizen); the rule of Octavian and his successors is referred to as the *principate*. The Senate also honored Octavian by conferring on him the semireligious and revered name of *Augustus*.

The reign of Augustus signified the end of the Roman Republic and the beginning of the Roman Empire—the termination of aristocratic politics and the emergence of one-man rule. Despite his introduction of autocratic rule, however, Augustus was by no means a self-seeking tyrant, but a creative statesman. Heir to the Roman tradition of civic duty, he regarded his power as a public trust delegated to him by the Roman people. He was faithful to the classical ideal that the state should promote the good life by protecting civilization from barbarism and ignorance, and he sought to rescue a dying Roman world by restoring political order and reviving the moral values and civic spirit that had contributed to Rome's greatness.

Augustus instituted reforms and improvements throughout the Empire. He reformed the army to guard against the reemergence of ambitious generals like those whose rivalries and private armies had wrecked the Republic. He maintained the loyalty of his soldiers by ensuring that veterans, on discharge, would receive substantial bonuses and land in Italy or in the provinces. For the city of Rome, Augustus had aqueducts and water mains built, bringing water to most Roman homes. He created a fire brigade, which reduced the danger of great conflagrations in crowded tenement districts, and he organized a police force to contain violence. He improved the distribution of free grain to the impoverished proletariat, and he financed the popular gladiatorial combats out of his own funds.

In Italy, Augustus had roads repaired, fostered public works, and arranged for Italians to play a more important role in the administration of the Empire. He earned the gratitude of the provincials by correcting tax abuses and fighting corruption and extortion, as well as by improving the quality of governors and enabling aggrieved provincials to bring charges against Roman officials. An imperial bureaucracy, which enabled talented and dedicated men to serve the state, gradually evolved.

THE PAX ROMANA

The brilliant statesmanship of Augustus inaugurated Rome's greatest age. For the next two hundred years, the Mediterranean world enjoyed the blessings of the *Pax Romana,* the Roman peace. The ancient world had never experienced such a long period of peace, order, efficient administration, and prosperity. Although both proficient and inept rulers succeeded Augustus, the essential features of the Pax Romana persisted.

The Successors of Augustus

The first four emperors who succeeded Augustus were related either to him or to his third wife, Livia. They constituted the Julio-Claudian dynasty, which ruled from A.D. 14 to 68. Although their reigns were marked by conspiracies, summary executions, and assassinations, the essential achievements of Augustus were preserved.

The Julio-Claudian dynasty came to an end when the emperor Nero committed suicide in A.D. 68. Nero had grown increasingly tyrannical and had lost the confidence of the people, the senatorial class, and the generals, who rose in revolt. In the year following his death, anarchy reigned as military leaders competed for the throne. After a bloody civil war, the execution of two emperors, and the suicide of another, Vespasian gained the principate. His reign (A.D. 69–79) marked the beginning of the Flavian dynasty. By having the great Colosseum of Rome constructed for gladiatorial contests, Vespasian earned the gratitude of the city's inhabitants. He also had nationalist uprisings put down in Gaul and Judea.

In Judea, Roman rule clashed with Jewish religious-national sentiments. Recognizing the tenacity with which Jews clung to their faith, the Roman leaders deliberately refrained from interfering with Hebraic religious beliefs and practices. Numerous privileges, such as exemption

from emperor worship because it conflicted with the requirements of strict monotheism, were extended to Jews not only in Judea but throughout the Empire. Sometimes, however, the Romans engaged in activities that outraged the Jews. For example, the emperor Caligula (A.D. 37–41) ordered that a golden statue of himself be placed in Jerusalem's temple, the central site and focus of Jewish religious life. To the Jews, this display of a pagan idol in their midst was an abomination. The order was rescinded when the Jews demonstrated their readiness to resist.

Relations between the Jews of Judea and the Roman authorities deteriorated progressively in succeeding decades. Militant Jews, who rejected Roman rule as a threat to the purity of Jewish life, urged their people to take up arms. Feeling a religious obligation to reestablish an independent kingdom in their ancient homeland and unable to reconcile themselves to subjection to hated idolaters, the Jews launched a full-scale war of liberation in A.D. 66. In A.D. 70, after a five-month siege had inflicted terrible punishment on the Jews, Roman armies captured Jerusalem, razed the city, destroyed the temple, and massacred survivors.

Vespasian was succeeded by his sons Titus (A.D. 79–81) and Domitian (A.D. 81–96). The reign of Titus was made memorable by the eruption of Mount Vesuvius, which devastated the towns of Pompeii and Herculaneum. After Titus's brief time as emperor, his younger brother Domitian became ruler. Upon crushing a revolt led by the Roman commander in Upper Germany, a frightened Domitian executed many leading Romans. These actions led to his assassination in A.D. 96, ending the Flavian dynasty.

The Senate selected one of its own, Nerva, to succeed the murdered Domitian. Nerva's reign (A.D. 96–98) was brief and uneventful. But he introduced a wise practice that would endure until A.D. 180: he adopted as his son and designated as his heir a man with proven ability, Trajan, the governor of Upper Germany. This adoptive system ensured a succession of competent rulers.

During his rule (A.D. 98–117), Trajan eased the burden of taxation in the provinces, provided for the needs of poor children, and had public works built. With his enlarged army, he conquered Dacia (parts of Romania and Hungary), where he seized vast quantities of gold and silver. He made the territory into a Roman province, adding to the large frontier Rome had to protect. The settlement of the region by many of Trajan's veterans led to its Romanization.

Trajan's successor, Hadrian (A.D. 117–138), strengthened border defenses in Britain and fought the second Hebrew revolt in Judea (A.D. 132–135). After initial successes, including the liberation of Jerusalem, the Jews were again defeated by superior Roman might. The majority of Palestinian Jews were killed, sold as slaves, or forced to seek refuge in other lands. The Romans renamed the province Syria Palestina; they forbade Jews to enter Jerusalem, except once a year; and they encouraged non-Jews to settle the land. Although the Jews continued to maintain a presence in Palestine, they had become a dispossessed and dispersed people.

After Hadrian came another ruler who had a long reign, Antoninus Pius (A.D. 138–161). He introduced humane and just reforms: limits on the right of masters to torture their slaves to obtain evidence and the establishment of the principle that an accused person be considered innocent until proven guilty. During his reign, the Empire remained peaceful and prosperous.

Marcus Aurelius (A.D. 161–180), the next emperor, was also a philosopher; his *Meditations* eloquently expressed Stoic thought. His reign was marked by renewed conflict in the East, with the kingdom of Parthia. The Roman legions were victorious in this campaign but brought back from the East an epidemic that decimated the population of the Empire.

From the accession of Nerva in A.D. 96 to the death of Marcus Aurelius in A.D. 180, the Roman Empire was ruled by the "Five Good Emperors." During this period, the Empire was at the height of its power and prosperity, and nearly all its peoples benefited. The four emperors preceding Marcus Aurelius had no living sons, so they resorted to the adoptive system in selecting successors, which served Rome effectively. But Marcus Aurelius chose his own son, Commodus, to succeed him. With the accession of Commodus, a misfit and a megalomaniac, in A.D. 180, the Pax Romana came to an end.

ARCH OF TITUS, C. A.D. 81, CONCRETE FACED WITH MARBLE , ROME. The arch stands at the crest of the Sacred Way to commemorate Titus' successful capture of Jerusalem in A.D. 70. It was dedicated in A.D. 81 by his brother, the Emperor Domitian.

The "Time of Happiness"

The Romans called the Pax Romana the "Time of Happiness." They saw this period as the fulfillment of Rome's mission: the creation of a world-state that provided peace, security, ordered civilization, and the rule of law. Roman legions defended the Rhine–Danube River frontiers from incursions by German tribesmen, held the Parthians at bay in the East, and subdued the few uprisings that occurred. Nerva's adoptive system of selecting emperors provided Rome with internal stability and a succession of exceptionally able emperors. These Roman emperors did not use military force needlessly but fought for sensible political goals. Generals did not wage war recklessly; instead, they tried to limit casualties, avoid risks, and deter conflicts by a show of force. On balance, the Pax Romana was one of the finest periods in world history.

Constructive Rule. Roman rule was constructive. The Romans built roads—some fifty-three thousand miles of roads from Scotland to the Euphrates—improved harbors, cleared forests, drained swamps, irrigated deserts, and cultivated undeveloped lands. The aqueducts they constructed brought fresh water for drinking and bathing to large numbers of people, and the effective sewage systems enhanced the quality of life. Goods were transported over roads made safe by Roman soldiers and across a Mediterranean Sea swept clear of pirates. A wide variety of goods circulated throughout the Empire. A stable currency, generally not subject to depreciation, contributed to the economic well-being of the Mediterranean world.

Scores of new cities sprang up, and old ones grew larger and wealthier. Although these municipalities had lost their power to wage war and had to bow to the will of the emperors, they retained considerable freedom of action in local matters. Imperial troops guarded against civil wars within the cities and prevented warfare between cities—two traditional weaknesses of city life in the ancient world. The municipalities served as centers of Greco-Roman civilization, which spread to the farthest reaches of the Mediterranean, continuing a process initiated during the Hellenistic Age. Citizenship, generously granted, was finally extended to virtually all free men by an edict of A.D. 212.

Improved Conditions for Slaves and Women. Conditions improved for those at the bottom of society, the slaves. At the time of Augustus, slaves may have accounted for a quarter of the population of Italy. But their numbers declined as Rome engaged in fewer wars of conquest. The freeing of slaves also became more common during the Empire. Freed slaves gained citizenship, with most of the rights and privileges of other citizens; their children suffered no legal disabilities whatsoever. During the Republic, slaves had been terribly abused; they were often mutilated, thrown to wild beasts, crucified, or burned alive. Several emperors issued decrees protecting slaves from cruel masters.

The status of women had gradually improved during the Republic. In the early days of the Republic, a woman lived under the absolute authority first of her father and then of her husband. By the time of the Empire, a woman could own property and, if divorced, keep her dowry. A father could no longer force his daughter to marry against her will. Women could make business arrangements and draw up wills without the consent of their husbands. Unlike their Greek counterparts, Roman women were not secluded in their homes but could come and go as they pleased, and participate in public spectacles and activities. Upper-class women of Rome also had far greater opportunities for education than those of Greece. The history of the Empire—indeed, Roman history in general—is filled with talented and influential women. Cornelia, the mother of Tiberius and Gaius Gracchus, influenced Roman politics through her sons. Livia, the dynamic wife of Augustus, was a successful businesswoman who accumulated estates, mines, granaries, and other properties throughout the Empire and checked to see that they were properly managed. At times, Augustus consulted her on important matters of state. During the third century there were times when women controlled the throne.

Musonius Rufus (c. A.D. 30–100), a Stoic philosopher, evidenced an enlightened view of women, declaring in his lectures that since women have the same reasoning power as men they should have the same upbringing and education.

An Orderly World Community. From Britain to the Arabian Desert, from the Danube River to the sands of the Sahara, some 50 to 70 million people with differing native languages, customs, and histories were united by Roman rule into a world community. Unlike officials of the Republic, when corruption and exploitation in the provinces were notorious, officials of the Empire felt a high sense of responsibility to preserve the Roman peace, institute Roman justice, and spread Roman civilization.

In creating a stable and orderly political community with an expansive conception of citizenship, Rome resolved the problems posed by the limitations of the Greek city-state: civil war, intercity warfare, and a parochial attitude that divided people into Greek and non-Greek. Rome also brought to fruition an ideal of the Greek medicine, and geography. Roman writers used Greek models; sharing in the humanist outlook of the Greeks, they valued human intelligence and achievement and expressed themselves in a graceful and eloquent style. The diffusion of Hellenism throughout the Mediterranean world produced a cultural unity among elites that underlay the Pax Romana.

Literature and History.   Roman cultural life reached its high point during the reign of Augustus, when Rome experienced the golden age of Latin literature. At the request of Augustus, who wanted a literary epic to glorify the Empire and his role in founding it, Virgil (70–19 B.C.) wrote the *Aeneid*, a masterpiece of world literature. The Aeneid is a literary epic of national glory. The profoundest ideas and feelings expressed in the poem are Roman virtues—patriotism, devotion to the family, duty to the state, and a strong sense of religion. Virgil ascribed to Rome a divine mission to bring peace and civilized life to the world, and he praised Augustus as a divinely appointed ruler who had fulfilled Rome's mission. The Greeks might be better sculptors, orators, and thinkers, said Virgil, but only the Romans knew how to govern an empire.

> *For other peoples will, I do not doubt,*
> *still cast their bronze to breathe with softer*
>   *features,*
> *or draw out of the marble living lines, plead*
>   *causes better,*
> *trace the ways of heaven with wands and tell*
>   *the rising*
> *constellations; but yours will be the rulership*
>   *of nations,*
> *remember, Roman, these will be your arts:*
> *to teach the ways of peace to those you*
>   *conquer, to spare*
> *defeated peoples, to tame the proud.*[3]

In his *History of Rome,* Livy (59 B.C.–A.D. 17) also glorified Roman character, customs, and deeds. He praised Augustus for attempting to revive traditional Roman morality, to which Livy felt a strong attachment. Although Livy was a lesser historian than Thucydides or Polybius, his work was still a major achievement, particularly in its depiction of the Roman character, which helped make Rome great.

Alinari/Art Resource, N.Y.

BASALT BUST OF LIVIA Octavian's third wife, Livia (58 B.C.–A.D. 29), was admired for her wisdom and dignity, and the emperor valued her counsel.

city-state: the protection and promotion of civilized life. By constructing a world community that broke down barriers between nations, by preserving and spreading Greco-Roman civilization, and by developing a rational system of law that applied to all humanity, Rome completed the trend toward universalism and cosmopolitanism that had emerged in the Hellenistic Age.

Roman Culture and Law During the Pax Romana

During the late Roman Republic, Rome had acquired Greek scientific thought, philosophy,

Primary Source

Aelius Aristides: The Blessings of the Pax Romana

In the following reading, Aelius Aristides (A.D 117–187), a Greek intellectual, glowingly praises the Pax Romana in an oration that was probably delivered in Rome. In the tradition of Roman orators, Aristides used hyperbole and exaggeration. Nevertheless, the oration does capture the universalism and cosmopolitanism that characterized the Roman Empire.

But the most marvelous and admirable achievement of all, and the one deserving our fullest gratitude, is this. . . . You alone of the imperial powers of history rule over men who are free. You have not assigned this or that region to [an unscrupulous governor] . . . Just as citizens in an individual city might designate magistrates, so you, whose city is the whole world, appoint governors to protect and provide for the governed, as if they were elective, not to lord it over their charges. As a result, so far from disputing the office as if it were their own, governors make way for their successors readily when their term is up, and may not even await their coming. Appeals to a higher jurisdiction are as easy as appeals from parish to county. . . .

But the most notable and praiseworthy feature of all, a thing unparalleled, is your magnanimous conception of citizenship. All of your subjects (and this implies the whole world) you have divided into two parts: the better endowed and more virile, wherever they may be, you have granted citizenship and even kinship; the rest you govern as obedient subjects. Neither the seas nor expanse of land bars citizenship;

Asia and Europe are not differentiated. Careers are open to talent. . . . Rich and poor find contentment and profit in your system; there is no other way of life. Your polity is a single and all-embracing harmony. . . .

. . . [You] established cities in diverse parts. The cities you filled with colonists; you introduced arts and crafts and established an orderly culture. . . . Your military organization makes all others childish. Your soldiers and officers you train to prevail not only over the enemy but over themselves. The soldier lives under discipline daily, and none ever deserts the post assigned him.

You alone are, so to speak, natural rulers. Your predecessors were masters and slaves in turn; as rulers they were counterfeits, and reversed their positions like players in a ball game. . . . You have measured out the world, bridged the rivers, cut roads through mountains, filled the wastes with posting stations, introduced orderly and refined modes of life. . . .

Be all gods and their offspring invoked to grant that this empire and this city flourish forever and never cease until stones float upon the sea and trees forbear to sprout in the springtide. May the great Ruler and his sons be preserved to administer all things well.

Question for Analysis

1. What did Aristides find so admirable in Rome's imperial system?

Moses Hadas, ed., *A History of Rome: From Its Origins to 529 A.D. as Told by the Roman Historians* (Garden City, N.Y.: Doubleday Anchor Books, 1956), 143–145.

Roman writers who excelled in poetry include Horace (65–8 B.C.), the son of a freed slave. He broadened his education by studying literature and philosophy in Athens, and his writings reflect Greek ideals. Horace enjoyed the luxury of country estates, banquets, fine clothes, and courtesans,

along with the simple pleasures of mountain streams and clear skies. His poetry touched on many themes—the joy of good wine, the value of moderation, and the beauty of friendship. Unlike Horace, Virgil, or Livy, Ovid (43 B.C.–A.D. 17) did not experience the civil wars during his adult

Alfredo Dagli Orti/© The Art Archive/Corbis.

MARCUS AURELIUS, ROMAN EMPEROR (A.D.161–180). In this relief, Marcus Aurelius rides through the Roman Forum in ceremonial triumph, after defending the Empire against barbarian incursions.

years. Consequently, he was less inclined to praise the Augustan peace. His poetry showed a preference for romance and humor, and he is best remembered for his advice to lovers.

The writers who lived after the Augustan age were mostly of a lesser quality than their predecessors. The historian Tacitus (A.D. 55–c. 118) was an exception. Sympathetic to republican institutions, Tacitus denounced Roman emperors and the imperial system in his *Histories* and *Annals*. In *Germania,* he turned his sights on the habits of the Germanic peoples, describing the Germans as undisciplined but heroic, with a strong love of freedom. Another outstanding writer was the satirist

Juvenal (A.D. c. 55–138). His works attacked evils of Roman society such as the misconduct of emperors, the haughtiness of the wealthy, the barbaric tastes of commoners, the failures of parents, and the noise, congestion, and poverty of the capital.

Philosophy. Stoicism was the principal philosophy of the Pax Romana, and its leading exponents were Seneca (4 B.C.–A.D. 65), Epictetus (A.D. c. 60–c. 117), and Marcus Aurelius. Perpetuating the rational tradition of Greek philosophy, Rome's early Stoics saw the universe as governed by reason, and they esteemed the human intellect. Like Socrates, they sought the highest good in this world, not in an afterlife, and they envisioned no power above human reason. Moral values were obtained from reason alone. The individual was self-sufficient and depended entirely on rational faculties for knowing and doing good. Stoics valued self-sufficient persons who attained virtue and wisdom by exercising rational control over their lives. The Stoic doctrine that all people, because of their capacity to reason, belong to a common humanity coincided with the requirements of the multinational Roman Empire.

The Stoic conception of God underwent a gradual transformation, reflecting the religious yearnings of the times. For the early Stoics, God was an intellectual necessity, an impersonal principle that gave order to the universe. For later Roman Stoics, God had become a moral necessity, comforting and reassuring people. While maintaining the traditional Stoic belief that the individual can attain virtue through unaided reason, Epictetus and Marcus Aurelius came close to seeking God's help to live properly. And Seneca showed an uncommon compassion for slaves and a revulsion for gladiatorial combat. The gap between Greek philosophy and Christianity was narrowing.

Science. The two most prominent scientists during the Greco-Roman Age were Ptolemy, a mathematician, geographer, and astronomer who worked at Alexandria in the second century A.D., and Galen (A.D. c. 130–c. 201), who investigated medicine and anatomy. Ptolemy's thirteen-volume work, *Mathematical Composition*—more commonly known as the *Almagest*, a Greek-Arabic

AQUEDUCT IN SEGOVIA, SPAIN. This Roman aqueduct in Spain stands as an impressive reminder of the ancient Romans' engineering skills. The discovery and use of concrete allowed the Romans to carry out a vast program of public works—roads, bridges, aqueducts, harbor facilities, and fortifications. Without such aqueducts to bring clean water from distant sources, the Roman style of urban life would have been impossible.

term meaning "the greatest"—summed up antiquity's knowledge of astronomy and became the authoritative text during the Middle Ages. In the Ptolemaic system, a motionless, spherical earth stood in the center of the universe; the moon, sun, and planets moved about the earth in circles or in combinations of circles. The Ptolemaic system was built on a faulty premise, as modern astronomy eventually showed. However, it did work—that is, it provided a model of the universe that adequately accounted for most observed phenomena. The Ptolemaic system was not challenged until the middle of the sixteenth century.

Just as Ptolemy's system dominated astronomy, so the theories of Galen dominated medicine down to modern times. By dissecting both dead and living animals, Galen attempted a rational investigation of the body's working parts. Although his work contains many errors, he made essential contributions to the knowledge of anatomy. Thanks to Arab physicians who preserved his writings during the Middle Ages, Galen's influence continued in the West into early modern times.

Art and Architecture. The Romans borrowed art forms from other peoples, particularly the Greeks, but they borrowed creatively, transforming and enhancing their inheritance. Roman portraiture continued trends initiated during the Hellenistic Age. Imitating Hellenistic models, Roman sculptors realistically carved every detail of a subject's face: unruly hair, prominent nose, lines and wrinkles, a jaw that showed weakness or strength. Sculpture also gave expression to the imperial ideal. Statues of emperors conveyed nobility and authority; reliefs commemorating victories glorified Roman might and grandeur.

The Romans most creatively transformed the Greek inheritance in architecture. The Greek temple was intended to be viewed from the outside; the focus was exclusively on the superbly balanced exterior. By using arches, vaults, and domes, the Romans built structures with large, magnificent interiors. The vast interior, massive walls, and overarching dome of the famous Pantheon, a temple built in the early second century A.D. during the reign of Hadrian, symbolize the power and majesty of the Roman world-state.

Engineering. The Romans excelled at engineering. In addition to amphitheaters and public baths, they built the finest roads in the ancient world. Roman engineers carefully selected routes with an eye for minimizing natural barriers and drainage problems. The great embanked roads constructed during the Empire were designed by military engineers. Stone bridges across rivers, as well as aqueducts that carried water to Roman cities, still survive.

Law. Expressing the Roman yearning for order and justice, law was Rome's great legacy to Western civilization. Roman law passed through two essential stages: the formation of civil law (*jus civile*) and the formation of the law of nations (*jus gentium*). The basic features of the civil law evolved during the two-hundred-year Struggle of the Orders, at the same time as Rome was extending its dominion over Italy. The Twelve Tables, drawn up in the early days of the patrician–plebeian struggle, established written rules of criminal and civil law for the Roman state that applied to all citizens. Over the centuries, the civil law was expanded through statutes enacted by the assemblies and through the legal decisions of jurisdictional magistrates, the rulings of emperors, and the commentaries of professional jurists, who, aided by familiarity with Greek logic, engaged in systematic legal analysis.

During the period of the Republic's expansion outside Italy, contact with the Greeks and other peoples led to the development of the second branch of Roman law, jus gentium, which combined Roman civil law with principles selectively drawn from the legal traditions of Greeks and other peoples. Roman jurists identified the jus gentium with the natural law (*jus naturale*) of the Stoics. The jurists said that a law should accord with rational principles inherent in nature: uniform and universally valid standards that can be discerned by rational people. Serving to bind different peoples together, the law of nations harmonized with the requirements of a world empire and with Stoic ideals. As Cicero pointed out,

> *True law is right reason in agreement with nature; it is of universal application, unchanging and everlasting. And there will not be different laws at Rome and at Athens or different laws now and in the future, but one eternal and unchangeable law will be valid for all nations and all times.*[4]

The law of nations came to be applied throughout the Empire, although it never entirely supplanted local law. In the eyes of the law, a citizen–and by A.D. 212, virtually all free people had been granted citizenship–was not a Syrian or a Briton or a Spaniard, but a Roman.

After the fall of the Western Roman Empire, Roman law fell into disuse in Western Europe. Gradually reintroduced in the twelfth century, it came to form the basis of the common law in all Western lands except Britain and its dependencies. Some provisions of Roman law are readily recognizable in modern legal systems, as the following excerpts illustrate:

> *Justice is a constant, unfailing disposition to give everyone his legal due.*
>
> *No one is compelled to defend a cause against his will.*
>
> *No one suffers a penalty for what he thinks.*
>
> *In the case of major offenses it makes a difference whether something is committed purposefully or accidentally.*
>
> *In inflicting penalties, the age . . . of the guilty party must be taken into account.*[5]

Entertainment.   Despite its many achievements, Roman civilization presents a paradox. On the one hand, Roman culture and law evidence high standards of civilization. On the other, the Romans institutionalized barbaric practices: battles to the death between armed gladiators and the tormenting and slaughtering of wild beasts. The major forms of entertainment in both the Republic and the Empire were chariot races, wild-animal shows, and gladiatorial combat. Chariot races were gala events in which the most skillful riders and the finest and best-trained stallions raced in an atmosphere of rabid excitement. The charioteers, many of them slaves hoping that victory would bring them freedom, became popular heroes.

The Romans craved brutal spectacles. One form of entertainment pitted wild beasts against each other or against men armed with spears. Another consisted of battles, sometimes to the death, between highly trained gladiators. The gladiators, mainly slaves and condemned criminals, learned their craft at schools run by professional trainers. Some gladiators entered the arena armed with a sword; others, with a trident and a net. The spectators were transformed into a frenzied mob that lusted for blood. If they were displeased with a losing gladiator's performance, they would call for his immediate execution. Over the centuries, these spectacles grew more bizarre and brutal. Hundreds of tigers were set against elephants and bulls; wild bulls tore apart men dressed in animal skins; women battled in the arena; dwarfs fought each other. Few Romans questioned these barbarities, which had become a routine part of daily life. Occasionally, however, thoughtful Romans had strong doubts. After watching a public spectacle, the Stoic philosopher Seneca wrote in disgust: "There is nothing more harmful to one's character than attendance at some spectacle, because vices more easily creep into your soul while you are being entertained. When I return from some spectacle, I am greedier, more aggressive and . . . more cruel and inhuman."[6]

SIGNS OF TROUBLE

Most people in the Mediterranean world welcomed Roman rule and could not conceive of a world without the Empire that brought them peace and security. But even during the Time of Happiness, signs of trouble appeared, and they grew to crisis proportions in the third century. Unrest in Egypt, Gaul, and Judea demonstrated that not all people at all times welcomed the grand majesty of the Roman peace, that localist and separatist tendencies persisted in a universal empire. In the centuries that followed, as Rome staggered under the weight of economic, political, and military difficulties, these native loyalties reasserted themselves. Increasingly, the masses and even the Romanized elite of the cities withdrew their support from the Roman world-state.

Social and Economic Weaknesses

A healthy world-state required empirewide trade to serve as an economic base for political unity, expanding agricultural production to feed the cities, and growing internal mass markets to stimulate industrial production. But the economy of the Empire during the Pax Romana had serious defects. The means of communication and transportation were slow, which hindered long-distance commerce. Many nobles, considering it unworthy for a gentleman to engage in business, chose to squander their wealth rather than invest it in commercial or industrial enterprises. Lacking the stimulus of capital investment, the economy could not expand.

Ultimately, only a small portion of the population—the middle and upper classes of the cities, that is, landlords, whose estates were outside the city, merchants, and administrators—reaped the benefits of the Roman peace. They basked in luxury, leisure, and culture. These privileged classes bought off the urban poor with bread and circuses, but occasionally mass discontent expressed itself in mob violence. Outside the cities, the peasantry—still the great bulk of the population—was exploited to provide cheap food for the city dwellers. An enormous cultural gap existed between town and countryside.

Such a parasitical, exploitative, and elitist social system might function in periods of peace and tranquility, but could it survive crises? Would the impoverished people of town and country—the overwhelming majority of the population—remain loyal to a state whose benefits barely extended to them and whose sophisticated culture, which they hardly comprehended, virtually excluded them?

Cultural Stagnation and Transformation

Perhaps the most dangerous sign for the future was the spiritual paralysis that crept over the ordered world of the Pax Romana. A weary and sterile Hellenism underlay the Roman peace. The ancient world was going through a transformation of values that foreshadowed the end of Greco-Roman civilization.

During the second century A.D., Greco-Roman civilization lost its creative energies, and the values of classical humanism were challenged by mythic-religious movements. The application of reason to nature and society was the great achievement of the Greek mind. Yet despite its many triumphs, Greek rationalism never entirely subdued the mythic-religious mentality, which draws its strength from human emotions. The masses of peasants and slaves remained attracted to religious forms. Ritual, mystery, magic, and ecstasy never lost their hold on the ancient world—nor, indeed, have they lost their hold on our own scientific and technological society. During the Hellenistic Age, the tide of rationalism gradually receded, and the nonrational, an ever-present undercurrent, showed renewed vigor. This resurgence of the mythical mentality could be seen in the popularity of the occult, magic, alchemy, and astrology. Burdened by danger and emotional stress, and fearing fate as fixed in the stars, people turned for deliverance to magicians, astrologers, and exorcists.

They also became devotees of the many Near Eastern religious cults that promised personal salvation. The proliferation of Eastern mystery religions was a clear expression of this transformation of classical values. During the Hellenistic era, slaves, merchants, and soldiers brought many religious cults westward from Persia, Babylon, Syria, Egypt, and Asia Minor. The various mystery cults possessed many common features. Converts underwent initiations and were bound by oath to secrecy. The initiates, in a state of rapture, attempted to unite with the deity after first purifying themselves through baptism (sometimes with the blood of a bull), fasting, having their heads shaved, or drinking from a sacred vessel. Communion was achieved by donning the god's robe, eating a sacred meal, or visiting the god's sanctuary. Cultists were certain that their particular savior god would protect them from misfortune and ensure their soul's immortality. More and more people felt that the good life could not be achieved by individuals through their own efforts; they needed outside help.

Like the mystery religions, philosophy reached for something beyond this world in order to edify and comfort the individual. Philosophers eventually sought escape from this world through union with a divine presence greater than human power. In Neo-Platonism, which replaced Stoicism as the dominant school of philosophy in the Late Roman Empire, religious yearnings were transformed into a religious system that transcended reason. Plotinus (A.D. c. 205–c. 270), the most influential spokesman of Neo-Platonism, subordinated philosophy to mysticism and the occult.

Scala/Art Resource, N.Y.

THE COLOSSEUM, ROME, A.D. 70–80. The joint work of the emperor Vespasian and his sons Titus and Domitian, this huge amphitheater was the largest in the ancient world. It was the site of innumerable spectacles, sham sea battles, gladiatorial games, wild beast hunts, and the deaths of Christian martyrs.

Plato's philosophy, we have seen, contained both a major and a minor key. The major key stressed a rational interpretation of the human community and called for reforming the polis on the basis of knowledge, whereas the minor key urged the soul to rise to a higher world of reality. Plotinus was intrigued by Plato's otherworldliness.

What Plotinus desired was union with the One, or the Good, sometimes called God—the source of all existence. Plotinus felt that the intellect could neither describe nor understand the One, which transcended all knowing, and that joining with the One required a mystical leap, a purification of the soul that dispensed with logic, evidence, and proof. This vision, which intends the soul to return to its true home, is for Plotinus

something greater and more compelling than reason. For Plotinus, philosophy became a religious experience, a contemplation of the eternal. Compared with this union with the divine One, of what value was knowledge of the sensible world or a concern for human affairs? For Plotinus, this world was a sea of tears and troubles from which the individual yearned to escape. Reality was not in this world but beyond it, and the principal goal of life was not comprehension of the natural world or the fulfillment of human potential or the betterment of the human community, but knowledge of the One. Thus, his philosophy broke with the essential meaning of classical humanism.

By the time of the Late Roman Empire, mystery religions intoxicated the masses, and mystical philosophy beguiled the educated elite. Classical civilization was being transformed. Philosophy had become subordinate to religious belief; secular values seemed inferior to religious experience. The earthly city had raised its eyes toward heaven. The culture of the Roman world was moving in a direction in which the quest for the divine was to predominate over all human enterprises.

THE DECLINE OF ROME

In the third century A.D., the ordered civilization of the Pax Romana ended. Several elements caused this disruption. The Roman Empire was plunged into military anarchy, raided by Germanic tribes, and burdened by economic dislocations. During these critical times, effective leadership was lacking, for the adoptive system abandoned by Marcus Aurelius was not restored.

Third-Century Crisis

The degeneration of the army was a prime reason for the crisis. During the great peace, the army had remained an excellent fighting force, renowned for its discipline, organization, and loyalty. In the third century, however, there was a marked deterioration in the quality of Roman soldiers. Lacking loyalty to Rome and greedy for spoils, soldiers used their weapons to prey on civilians and to make and unmake emperors. Fearful of being killed by their unruly troops who wanted spoils or of being murdered by a suspicious emperor, generals were driven to seize the throne. Once in power, they had to buy the loyalty of their soldiers and guard against assassination by other generals. From A.D. 235 to 285, military mutiny and civil war raged as legion fought legion. Many emperors were assassinated. The once stalwart army neglected its duty of defending the borders against incursions by Germanic tribes and disrupted the internal life of the Empire.

During the third century, Rome also had to deal with a reborn Persian Empire that forced the Romans to shift large contingents of legions eastward. Taking advantage of the weakened borders and military anarchy, Germanic tribesmen crossed the Rhine—Danube frontier to loot and destroy.

The Persian Empire, led by the Sassanid dynasty, attacked and for a while conquered Roman lands in the East. Some sections of the Empire, notably in Gaul, attempted to break away; these moves reflected an assertion of local patriotism over Roman universalism. The "city of mankind" was crumbling.

These eruptions had severe economic repercussions. Cities were pillaged and destroyed, farmlands ruined, and trade disrupted. To obtain funds and supplies for the military, emperors confiscated goods, exacted forced labor, and debased the coinage, causing inflation. These measures brought ruin to the middle class. Invasions, civil war, rising prices, a debased coinage, declining agricultural production, disrupted transportation, and the excessive demands of the state caused economic havoc and famine in the cities. The urban centers of the ancient world, creators and disseminators of high civilization, were caught in a rhythm of breakdown.

Diocletian and Constantine: The Regimented State

The emperors Diocletian (A.D. 285–305) and Constantine (A.D. 306–337) tried to contain the awesome forces of disintegration. At a time when agricultural production was steadily declining, they had to feed the city poor and an expanded army of more than 500,000 strung out over the Empire. They also had to prevent renewed outbreaks of military anarchy, drive the Germans back across the Rhine–Danube frontier, and secure the eastern region against renewed aggression from Persia. Their solution was to tighten the reins of central government and to squeeze more taxes and requisitions out of the citizens. In the process, they transformed Rome into a bureaucratic, regimented, and militarized state that has been described as "a vast prison."

Cities lost their traditional right of local self-government, consolidating a trend started earlier. To ensure continuous production of food and goods, as well as the collection of taxes, the state forced unskilled workers and artisans to hold their jobs for life and to pass them on to their children. For the same reasons, peasants were turned into virtual serfs, bound to the land that they cultivated. An army of government agents was formed to hunt down peasants who fled the land to escape crushing taxes and poverty.

Also frozen into their positions were city officials *(curiales)*. They often found it necessary to furnish from their own pockets the difference between the state's tax demands and the amount that they could collect from an already overtaxed population. This system of a hereditary class of tax collectors and of crippling taxes to pay for a vastly expanded bureaucracy and military establishment enfeebled urban trade and industry. Such conditions killed the civic spirit of townspeople, who desperately sought escape. By overburdening urban dwellers with taxes and regulations, Diocletian and Constantine helped to shatter the vitality of city life, on which Roman prosperity and civilization depended. During the Pax Romana, municipal authorities enjoyed considerable autonomy; now the state bureaucracy extended its often onerous and rapacious power everywhere.

Rome was now governed by a highly centralized monarchy that regimented the lives of its subjects. Whereas Augustus had upheld the classical ideal that the commonwealth was a means of fostering the good life for the individual, Diocletian adopted the despotic attitude that the individual lives for the state. To guard against military insurrection, he appointed a loyal general as emperor to govern the western provinces of the Empire while he ruled the eastern regions; although both emperors bore the title Augustus, Diocletian remained superior. Constantine furthered this trend of dividing the Empire into eastern and western halves by building an imperial capital, Constantinople, at the Bosporus, a strait where Asia meets Europe. By wining major victories over Germanic tribes and regaining Dacia, which the Romans were forced to abandon in 271 A.D., Constantine did preserve the Empire, although admittedly for a short period.

Tribal Migrations and Invasions

By imposing some order on what had been approaching chaos, Diocletian and Constantine prevented the Empire from collapsing. Rome had been given a reprieve. But in the last part of the fourth century, the problem of guarding the frontier grew more acute.

The Huns, a nomadic people from Central Asia, swept across the plains of Russia and with their formidable cavalry put pressure on the Visigoths, a Germanic tribe that had migrated into southeastern Europe. Terrified of the Huns, the Goths sought refuge within the Roman Empire. Hoping to increase his manpower and unable to stop the panic-stricken Germans, the emperor Valens permitted them to cross the Danube frontier. But enraged by their mistreatment at the hands of Roman officials, the Visigoths took up arms. In A.D. 378, Visigoth cavalry cut to pieces Roman forces in a historic battle at Adrianople. This battle signified that Rome could no longer defend its borders. The Visigoths were on Roman territory to stay, and they now plundered the Balkans at will. The Germanic tribes increased their pressure on the Empire's borders, which finally collapsed at the very end of A.D. 406 as Vandals, Alans, Suebi, and other tribes joined the Goths in devastating and overrunning the Empire's western provinces. In A.D. 410, the Visigoths looted Rome.

Economic conditions continued to deteriorate. Cities in Britain, Gaul, Germany, and Spain lay abandoned. Other metropolises saw their populations dwindle and production stagnate. The great network of Roman roads was not maintained, and trade in the West almost disappeared or passed into the hands of Greeks, Syrians, and Jews from the East. Everywhere famine, the extortion of taxes by government officials, the proliferation of marauding outlaws driven from their homes by the excessive financial demands imposed by the state bureaucracy, and murderous warfare added to the misery of the Roman populace and the decomposition and fragmentation of the Empire.

In A.D. 451, Attila (c. A.D. 406–453), called "the Scourge of God," led his Huns into Gaul, where he was defeated by a coalition of Germans and the remnants of the Roman army. He died two years later, having come within a hairsbreadth of turning Europe into a province of a Mongolian empire. But Rome's misfortunes persisted. In A.D. 455, Rome was again looted, this time by the Vandals. Additional regions fell under the control of Germanic chieftains. And increasingly the old Roman administration was collapsing. Germanic soldiers in the pay of Rome gained control of the government and dictated the choice of emperor. In 476, German officers overthrew the Roman emperor Romulus and placed a fellow German, Odoacer, on the throne. This act is traditionally regarded as the end of the Roman Empire in the West. By the end of the fifth century, the Western Empire had fragmented into separate Germanic kingdoms.

Reasons for Rome's Decline

What were the underlying causes for the decline and fall of the Roman Empire in the West? Surely no other question has intrigued the historical imagination more than this one. Implicit in the answers suggested by historians and philosophers is a concern for their own civilization. Will it suffer the same fate as Rome?

To analyze so monumental a development as the fall of Rome, some preliminary observations are necessary. First, the fall of Rome was a process lasting hundreds of years; it was not a single event that occurred in A.D. 476. Second, only the western half of the Empire fell. The eastern half—wealthier, more populous, less afflicted with civil wars, and less exposed to barbarian invasions—survived as the Byzantine Empire until the middle of the fifteenth century. Third, no single explanation suffices to account for Rome's decline; multiple forces—internal problems and external threats—operated concurrently to bring about the fall.

The Role of the Germanic Tribes. The pressures exerted by the Germans along an immense frontier aggravated Rome's internal problems. The barbarian attacks left border regions depopulated and impoverished, and expenditures for the military drained the western Empire's resources. The Empire imposed high taxes and labor services on its citizens in order to strengthen the armed forces, causing the overburdened middle and lower classes to hate the imperial government that took so much from them.

Spiritual Considerations. The classical mentality, once brimming with confidence about the potentialities of the individual and the power of the intellect, suffered a failure of nerve. The urban upper class, on whom the responsibility for preserving cosmopolitan Greco-Roman culture traditionally rested, became dissolute and apathetic, no longer taking an interest in public life. The aristocrats secluded themselves behind the walls of their fortified country estates; many did not lift a finger to help the Empire. The townspeople demonstrated their disenchantment by avoiding public service and by rarely organizing resistance forces against the barbarian invaders. Hounded by the state and persecuted by the army, many farmers viewed the Germans as liberators. No doubt, a significant number of Christians, focusing on the life to come, showed no interest in supporting the Roman legions charged with defending Rome. The great bulk of the Roman citizenry, apathetic and indifferent, simply gave up, despite the fact that they overwhelmingly outnumbered the barbarian hordes.

Political and Military Considerations. The Roman government itself contributed to this spiritual malaise through its increasingly autocratic tendencies, which culminated in the regimented rule of Diocletian and Constantine. The insatiable demands and regulations of the state in the Late Roman Empire sapped the initiative and civic spirit of its citizens. The ruined middle and lower classes withdrew their loyalty. For many, the state had become the enemy, and its administration was hated and feared more than the Germans.

In the Late Roman Empire, the quality of Roman soldiers deteriorated, and the legions failed to defend the borders even though they outnumbered the German invaders. During the third century, the army consisted predominantly of the provincial peasantry. These nonurban, non-Italian, semi-civilized soldiers, often the dregs of society, were not committed to Greco-Roman civilization. They had little comprehension of Rome's mission, and at times they used their power to attack the cities and towns. The emperors also recruited large numbers of barbarians into the army to fill its depleted ranks—German tribesmen had served as auxiliaries since Julius Caesar. Ultimately, the army consisted mostly of barbarians, as both legionnaires and officers. Although these Germans made brave soldiers, they too had little loyalty to Greco-Roman civilization and to the Roman state. Moreover, barbarian units serving with the Roman army under their own commanders did not easily submit to traditional discipline or training. This deterioration of the Roman army occurred because many young citizens evaded conscription. No longer imbued with patriotism, they considered military service a servitude to be shunned.

Economic Considerations. Among the economic factors contributing to the decline of the Roman Empire in the west were a decrease in population, failure to achieve a breakthrough in technology, the heavy burden of taxation, and economic decentralization, which abetted political decentralization.

Largely because of war and epidemics, the population of the Empire shrank. This decrease adversely affected the Empire in at least three important ways. First, at the same time as the population was declining, the costs of running the Empire were spiraling, which created a terrible burden for taxpayers. Second, fewer workers were available for agriculture, the most important industry of the Empire. Third, population decline reduced the manpower available for the army, forcing emperors to permit the establishment of Germanic colonies within the Empire's borders to serve as feeders for the army. This situation led to the barbarization of the army.

The failure to expand industry and commerce was another economic reason for the Empire's decline. Instead of expanding industry and trade, towns maintained their wealth by exploiting the countryside. The Roman cities were centers of civilized life and opulence, but they lacked industries. They spent, but they did not produce. Provided with food and entertainment—"bread and circuses"—the unproductive city dwellers, driven out of the labor force by economic stagnation and slavery, were a heavy burden for the state. The towns were dominated by landlords whose estates lay beyond the city and whose income derived from grain, oil, and wine. Manufacturing was rudimentary, confined essentially to textiles, pottery, furniture, and glassware. The methods of production—rarely significantly improved—were simple, the market limited, the cost of transportation high, and agricultural productivity low—the labor of perhaps nineteen peasants was required to support one townsman. Such a fundamentally unhealthy economy could not weather the dislocations caused by uninterrupted warfare and the

demands of a mushrooming bureaucracy and the military.

With the barbarians pressing on the borders, the increased military expenditures overstrained the Empire's resources. To pay for the food, uniforms, arms, and armor of the soldiers, taxes were raised, growing too heavy for peasants and townspeople. The state also requisitioned wood and grain and demanded that citizens maintain roads and bridges. The government often resorted to force to collect taxes and exact services. Crushed by these demands, many peasants simply abandoned their farms and sought the protection of large landowners or turned to banditry.

The growth of industries on latifundia, the large, fortified estates owned by wealthy aristocrats, promoted economic decentralization. Producing exclusively for the local market, these estates contributed to the impoverishment of urban centers by reducing the number of customers available to buy goods made in the cities. As life grew more desperate, urban craftsmen and small farmers, made destitute by the state, sought the protection of these large landlords, whose estates grew in size and importance. The growth of latifundia was accompanied by both the decline of cities and the transformation of independent peasants into virtual serfs.

These great estates were also new centers of political power that the imperial government could not curb. A new society was taking shape in the Late Roman Empire. The center of gravity had shifted from the city to the landed estate, from the imperial bureaucrats to the local aristocrats. These developments epitomized the decay of ancient civilization and presaged the Middle Ages.

THE ROMAN LEGACY

Rome left the West a rich heritage that has endured for centuries. In admiration of the Roman Republic's good years, the Founding Fathers of the United States wanted their new country to be a free and self-governing republic in which citizens actively and responsibly participated in civic affairs. The idea of a world empire united by a common law and effective government never died. In the centuries following the collapse of Rome, people continued to be attracted to the idea of a unified and peaceful world-state. To this day, we ask what lessons we can learn from the Pax Romana, which provided a multinational empire with two centuries of relative stability, order, and peace. Indeed, the Roman conception of extended citizenship finds expression in European attempts at integration in the decades after World War II. By preserving and adding to the philosophy, literature, science, and art of ancient Greece, Rome strengthened the foundations of the Western cultural tradition. Latin, the language of Rome, lived on long after Rome perished. The Western church fathers wrote in Latin, and during the Middle Ages, Latin was the language of learning, literature, and law. From Latin came Italian, French, Spanish, Portuguese, and Romanian. Roman law, the quintessential expression of Roman genius, influenced church law and formed the basis of the legal codes of most European states. Finally, Christianity, the core religion of the West, was born within the Roman Empire and was greatly influenced by Roman law (the church's canon law owed much to Roman jurisprudence) and organization (the pope, head of the church and ruling from Rome, was the counterpart of the Roman emperor, and bishoprics were established in regions that coincided with the Empire's administrative structure). The ideal of a single Christian society embracing many different nationalities, so dear to medieval thinkers, was superimposed on the model of the Roman Empire.

NOTES

1. E. Badian, *Roman Imperialism in the Late Republic* (Ithaca, N.Y.: Cornell University Press, 1971), 87.

2. Sallust, *The Conspiracy of Catiline,* trans. S. A. Handford (Baltimore: Penguin Books, 1963), 181–182.

3. From *The Aeneid of Virgil,* trans. Allen Mandelbaum, copyright © 1971 by Allen Mandelbaum. Published by Bantam Books, division of Random House, Inc.

4. Cicero, *De Republica*, trans. Clinton Walker Keyes (Cambridge, Mass.: Harvard University Press, Loeb Classical Library, 1994), 211.

5. Excerpted in Naphtali Lewis and Meyer Reinhold, eds., *Roman Civilization, Sourcebook II: The Empire* (New York: Harper & Row, 1966), 535, 539, 540, 547, 548.

6. Seneca, *The Epistles,* trans. Thomas Morell (London: W. Woodfall, 1786), vol. 1, epistle 7.

Chapter 5

Early Christianity: A World Religion

- **The Origins of Christianity**
- **The Spread and Triumph of Christianity**
- **Development of Christian Organization, Doctrine, and Attitudes**
- **Saint Augustine: The Christian Worldview**
- **Christianity and Classical Humanism: Alternative Worldviews**

Focus Questions

1. Why do you think that over the centuries there have been conflicting interpretations of Jesus' life, thought, and death?
2. How did Saint Paul transform a Jewish sect into a world religion?
3. What factors contributed to the triumph of Christianity in the Roman Empire?
4. What factors contributed to Christian anti-Judaism? What is the historical significance of the negative images of Jews and Judaism taught by early Christians?
5. What are the core features of Saint Augustine's theology.
6. What do the worldviews of Christianity and Greco-Roman humanism have in common? Why are they essentially different?

*A*s confidence in human reason and hope for happiness in this world waned in the last centuries of the Roman Empire, a new outlook began to take hold. Evident in philosophy and in the popularity of Near Eastern religions, this viewpoint stressed escape from an oppressive world and communion with a higher reality. Christianity evolved and expanded within this setting of declining classicism and heightening otherworldliness. As one response to a declining Hellenism, Christianity offered a spiritually disillusioned Greco-Roman world a reason for living: the hope of personal immortality. The triumph of Christianity marked a break with classical antiquity and a new stage in the evolution of the West, for there was a fundamental difference between the classical and the Christian concepts of God, the individual, and the purpose of life. ❖

THE ORIGINS OF CHRISTIANITY

A Palestinian Jew named Jesus was executed by the Roman authorities during the reign of Tiberius (A.D. 14–37), who had succeeded Augustus. At the time, few people paid much attention to what proved to be one of the most pivotal events in world history. In the quest for the historical Jesus, scholars have stressed the importance of both his Jewishness and the religious ferment that prevailed in Palestine in the first century B.C. Jesus' ethical teachings are rooted in the moral outlook of the Old Testament prophets. Jesus, who prayed as a Jew, taught as a Jew to fellow Jews, and valued Jewish Law and prophetic teachings, could only conceive of himself as a Jew. Hans Küng, the prominent Swiss student of religion, elaborates on this point:

> *Jesus was a Jew, a member of a small, poor, politically powerless nation living at the periphery of the Roman Empire. He was active among Jews and for Jews. His mother Mary, his father Joseph, his family, his followers were Jews. His name was Jewish (Hebrew Yeshu'a). . . . His Bible, his worship, his prayers were Jewish. In the situation at that time he could not have thought of any proclamation among the gentiles. His message was for the Jewish people, but for this people in its entirety without any exception. From this basic fact it follows irrevocably that without Judaism there would be no Christianity. The Bible of the early Christians was the "Old Testament." The New Testament Scriptures became part*

> *of the Bible only by being appended to the Old. The gospel of Jesus Christ everywhere quite consciously presupposes the Torah and the Prophets.[1]*

Judaism in the First Century B.C.

In the first century B.C., four principal social-religious parties, or sects, existed among the Palestinian Jews: Sadducees, Pharisees, Essenes, and Zealots. The religiously conservative Sadducees, composed of the upper stratum of Jewish society—influential landed gentry and hereditary priests, who controlled the temple in Jerusalem—insisted on a strict interpretation of Mosaic Law and the perpetuation of temple ceremonies. Claiming to be the descendants of Sadok, the high priest of Solomon, Sadducees believed that they were maintaining the ancient Hebrew teachings concerning the Torah, which they interpreted literally. Rejecting the concepts of the resurrection of the dead and of an afterlife, they held that God meted out rewards and punishments on earth. Challenging the aristocratic Sadducees, the Pharisees adopted a more flexible attitude toward Mosaic Law; they allowed discussion and varying interpretations of the Law and granted authority to oral tradition—an "oral Torah" that was communicated from one generation to another—as well as to written Scripture. The Pharisees had the support of most of the Jewish nation. All later forms of Judaism developed from the Pharisees.

The third religious party, the Essenes, founded by a man they referred to as the "Teacher of Righteousness," established a semimonastic community near the Dead Sea. In 1947, leather scrolls in hermetically sealed cylinders were found near the Essene community of Qumran, about fourteen miles from Jerusalem, close to the Dead Sea. Dated from between c. 200 B.C. and A.D. 66–70, the "Dead Sea Scrolls" contain the oldest extant Hebrew manuscripts and also documents that are unique to the sect of the Essenes. Although the Scrolls make no reference to Jesus or his followers, scholars do find parallels between the Qumran community and the Jesus movement. Like Jesus, for example, the community spoke of the end of days that they believed was imminent. Both the Qumran community and Jesus' early

A.D. 29	Crucifixion of Jesus
c. 34–64	Missionary activity of Saint Paul
c. 66–70	Gospel of Mark is written
250–260	Decade of brutal persecution of Christians by the Romans
313	Constantine grants toleration to Christianity
325	Council of Nicaea rules that God and Christ are of the same substance, coequal and coeternal
391–392	Theodosius I prohibits public acts of pagan worship and the public profession of pagan religions; during his reign, Christianity becomes the state religion
430	Death of Saint Augustine
529	Saint Benedict founds monastery at Monte Cassino

followers considered themselves the true Israel, referred to themselves as the "sons of light," and anticipated the coming of a messianic age.

The fourth sect, the Zealots, demanded that the Jews neither pay taxes to Rome nor acknowledge the authority of the Roman emperor. Devoted patriots, the Zealots engaged in acts of resistance to Rome, which culminated in the great revolt of A.D. 66–70 (see "The Pax Romana" in Chapter 4).

Unlike the Sadducees, the Pharisees believed in life after death. The concept of personal immortality is barely mentioned in the Hebrew Scriptures. A later addition to Hebrew religious thought, probably acquired from Persia, the idea had gained wide acceptance by the time of Jesus. The Essenes, too, believed in the physical resurrection of the body but gave this doctrine a more compelling meaning by tying it to the immediate coming of God's kingdom.

Besides the afterlife, another widely recognized idea in the first century B.C. was the belief in the Messiah, a redeemer chosen by God to liberate Israel from foreign rule. In the days of the Messiah, it was predicted, Israel would be free, the exiles would return, and the Jews would be blessed with peace, unity, and prosperity. The

Messiah, in contrast to wicked Roman rulers, would govern justly and righteously.

Jesus (c. 4 B.C.–A.D. c. 29) performed his ministry within this context of Jewish religious-national expectations and longings. The hopes of Jesus' early followers stemmed from a lower-class dissatisfaction with the aristocratic Sadducees; the Pharisee emphasis on prophetic ideals and the afterlife; the Essene preoccupation with the end-of-days and belief in the nearness of God and the need for repentance; and a conquered people's yearning for the Messiah, who would liberate their land from Roman rule and establish God's reign.

Jesus: Moral Transformation of the Individual

Jesus himself wrote nothing, and nothing was written about him during his lifetime. In the generations following his death, both Roman and Jewish historians paid him scant attention. Consequently, virtually everything we know about Jesus comes from the Bible's New Testament, which was written decades after Jesus' death by devotees seeking to convey a religious truth and to propagate a faith. Modern historians have rigorously and critically analyzed the New Testament; their analyses have provided some insights into Jesus and his beliefs, though much about him remains obscure.

At around the age of thirty, no doubt influenced by John the Baptist, Jesus began to preach the coming of the reign of God and the need for people to repent—to undergo moral transformation so that they could enter God's kingdom. For Jesus, the coming of the kingdom was imminent; the process leading to its establishment on earth had already begun. A new order would soon emerge, in which God would govern his people righteously and mercifully. Hence, the present moment was critical—a time for spiritual preparedness and penitence—because an individual's thoughts, goals, and actions would determine whether he or she would gain entrance into the kingdom. People had to change their lives radically. They had to eliminate base, lustful, hostile, and selfish feelings; stop pursuing wealth and power; purify their hearts; and show their love for God and their fellow human beings. Like the Hebrew prophets, Jesus saw ethics as the core of Mosaic Law: "So whatever you wish that men would do to you, do so to them; for this is the law and the prophets" (Matthew 7:12)[2]. Like the prophets, he denounced injustice and oppression, urged mercy and compassion, and expressed a special concern for the poor and downtrodden.

Although Jesus did not intend to draw away his fellow Jews from their ancestral religion, he was distressed by the Judaism of his day. The rabbis taught the Golden Rule, as well as God's love and mercy for his children, but it seemed to Jesus that these ethical considerations were being undermined by an exaggerated rabbinical concern with ritual, restrictions, and the fine points of the Law. Jesus believed that the center of Judaism had shifted from prophetic values to obeying the rules and prohibitions regulating the smallest details of daily life. (To Jewish leaders, of course, these detailed regulations governing eating, washing, Sabbath observance, family relations, and so forth were God's commands, intended to sanctify all human activities.) To Jesus, such a rigid view of the Law distorted the meaning of prophetic teachings. Rules dealt only with an individual's visible behavior; they did not penetrate to the person's inner being and lead to a moral transformation based on love, compassion, and selflessness.

The inner person concerned Jesus, and it was an inner change that he sought. With the fervor of a prophet, he urged a moral transformation of human character through a direct encounter between the individual and God.

Jewish scribes and priests, guardians of the faith, regarded Jesus as a troublemaker who threatened ancient traditions and undermined respect for the Sabbath. Stated succinctly, Jewish leaders believed that Jesus was setting the authority of his person over Mosaic Law—an unpardonable blasphemy in their eyes. They saw him as a false prophet who was leading the people astray. To the Romans who ruled Palestine, Jesus was a political agitator who could ignite Jewish messianic expectations into a revolt against Rome. After Jewish leaders turned Jesus over to the Roman authorities, the Roman procurator, Pontius Pilate, sentenced him to death by crucifixion, a customary punishment for someone guilty of high treason. Jesus' execution was consistent with Roman policy in Judea, for the Romans routinely arrested and executed Jews suspected of inciting unrest against Roman rule. Inscribed on the cross on which he was crucified were the words "King of the Jews," a seemingly clear indication of why Pilate ordered his death. Although it is questionable if Jesus ever intended to challenge Roman authority, Pilate was taking no chances. He wanted to eliminate the popular leader before he might ignite a popular uprising.

Believing that Jesus was an inspired prophet or even the long-awaited Messiah, some Jews had become his followers; the chief of these were the Twelve Disciples. But at the time of Jesus' death, Christianity was still just a small Hebrew sect, with dim prospects for survival. What established the Christian movement and gave it strength was the belief of Jesus' followers that he was raised from the dead on the third day after his burial. The doctrine of the Resurrection made possible the belief in Jesus as divine, a savior-god who had come to earth to show people the way to heaven. For early Christians, Jesus' death and belief in his resurrection took on an even greater importance than his life. For these Christians, Jesus the savior-god became the center of their emerging church.

There is no evidence that Jesus, who never preached to Gentiles, intended to establish a new church; this was accomplished by his followers. In the years immediately following the Crucifixion, the religion of Jesus was confined almost exclusively to Jews, who could more appropriately be called Jewish-Christians. The word *Christian* derives from a name given Jesus: *Christ* (the Lord's Anointed, the Messiah). Before this new Jewish messianic movement could realize the universal implications of Jesus' teachings and become a world religion, as distinct from a reformist Jewish sect, it had to extricate itself from Jewish ritual, politics, and culture. This achievement was the work of a Hellenized Jew named Saul—known to the world as Saint Paul.

Saint Paul: From a Jewish Sect to a World Religion

Saint Paul (A.D. c. 5–c. 67) came from the Greek city of Tarsus in southeastern Asia Minor. He belonged to the Diaspora, or the "Dispersion"—the millions of Jews living outside Palestine. The non-Jews, or *Gentiles* (from Latin *gens,* or "nation"), who came into contact with Jews of the Diaspora were often favorably impressed by Hebrew monotheism, ethics, and family life. Some Gentiles embraced Hebrew monotheism but refused to adhere to provisions of the Law requiring circumcision and dietary regulations. Among these Gentiles and the non-Palestinian Jews who were greatly influenced by the Greco-Roman milieu, Jesus' Apostles would find receptive listeners.

At first, Saul persecuted the followers of Jesus, but then he underwent a spiritual transformation and became a follower of Jesus. Serving as a zealous missionary of Jewish Christianity in the Diaspora, Saint Paul preached to his fellow Jews in synagogues. Recognizing that the Christian message applied to non-Jews as well, Paul urged spreading it to the Gentiles. In the process of his missionary activity—and he traveled extensively

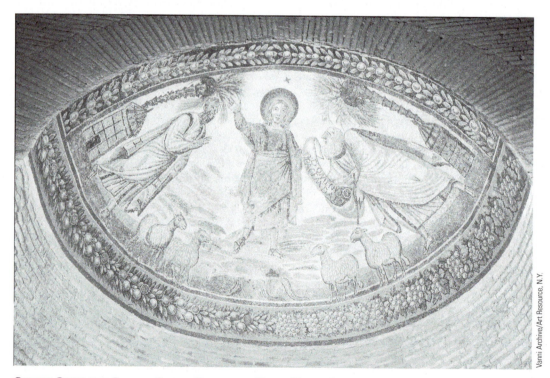

Vanni Archive/Art Resource, N.Y.

Christ Gives the Law to Saints Peter and Paul, Fifth Century, Santa Costanza, Rome. This mosaic portrays a haloed, beardless Christ bestowing the law in the manner of an emperor delivering an edict.

throughout the Roman Empire—Paul formulated ideas that represented a fundamental break with Judaism and became the heart of this new religion. He taught that the crucified Messiah had suffered and died for humanity's sins; that through Jesus God had revealed himself to all people, both Jews and Gentiles; and that this revelation supplanted God's earlier revelation to the Jewish people. Alone, one was helpless, possessed by sin, unable to overcome one's wicked nature. Jesus was the only hope, said Paul.

In attempting to reach the Gentiles, Saint Paul had to disentangle Christianity from a Jewish sociocultural context. Thus, he held that neither Gentile nor Jewish followers of Jesus were bound by the hundreds of rituals and rules that constitute Mosaic Law. As a consequence of Jesus' coming, Paul insisted, Mosaic regulations hindered missionary activity among the Gentiles.* To Paul, the new Christian community was the true fulfillment of Judaism; Jesus' followers were the new Israelites. The Jews regarded their faith as a national religion, bound inseparably with the history of their people. Paul held that Jesus fulfilled not only the messianic aspirations of the Jews, but also the spiritual needs and expectations of all peoples. For Paul, the new Christian community was not a nation, but an *oikoumene,* a world community. To this extent, Christianity shared in the universalism of the Hellenistic Age.

In preaching the doctrine of the risen Savior and insisting that Mosaic Law had been superseded, Paul (whatever his intentions) was breaking with his Jewish roots and transforming a Jewish sect into a new religion. Separating Christianity from Judaism enormously increased its appeal for those non-Jews who were attracted to Hebrew ethical monotheism but repelled by circumcision,

dietary rules, and other strict requirements of Mosaic Law. Paul built on the personalism and universalism implicit in the teachings of Jesus (and the Hebrew prophets) to create a religion intended not for a people with its own particular history, culture, and land but for all humanity.

THE SPREAD AND TRIUMPH OF CHRISTIANITY

By establishing Christianity's independence from Judaism, Saint Paul made the new religion fit for export to the Greco-Roman world. But its growth was slow. Originating in the first century, Christianity took firm root in the second, grew extensively in the third, and became the official religion of the Roman Empire at the end of the fourth century.

The Appeal of Christianity

The triumph of Christianity was linked to a corresponding decline in the vitality of Hellenism and a shift in cultural emphasis—a movement from reason to emotion and revelation. Offering comforting solutions to the existential problems of life and death, religion demonstrated a greater capacity than reason to stir human hearts. Hellenism had invented the tools of rational thought, but the power of mythical thought was never entirely subdued. By the Late Roman Empire, science and philosophy could not compete with mysticism, myth, and the divine. Mystery cults, which promised personal salvation, were spreading and gaining followers. Neo-Platonists yearned for a mystical union with the One. Astrology and magic, which offered supernatural explanations for the operations of nature, were also popular. This recoil from rational and worldly values helped prepare the way for Christianity. In a culturally stagnating and spiritually troubled Greco-Roman world, Christianity gave a new meaning to life and a new hope to disillusioned men and women.

The Christian message of a divine Savior and a concerned Father, as well as of brotherly love, inspired men and women who were dissatisfied with the world of the here-and-now—who felt no

---

*Paul's understanding of Mosaic Law is a matter of controversy. Some scholars argue that he regarded the Law as obsolete and broke with his ancestral faith. Other scholars, arguing that Paul did not forsake the Law, point to a famous passage: "Do we then nullify the law by this faith? Not at all! Rather we uphold the law" (Rom. 3:31). Paul, who continually described himself as a Pharisee, lived an observant life and celebrated Jewish festivals. For these scholars, Paul never stopped revering the Torah, but he taught that Jesus, the Messiah, fulfilled the Torah's higher purpose—the biblical prophecy of the Messiah's coming.

attachment to city or empire, derived no inspiration from philosophy, and suffered from a profound sense of loneliness. Christianity offered the individual what the city and the Roman world-state could not: an intensely personal relationship with God, an intimate connection with a higher world, and membership in a community of the faithful who cared for one another.

Stressing the intellect and self-reliance, Greco-Roman thought did not provide for the emotional needs of the ordinary person. Christianity addressed itself to this defect in the Greco-Roman outlook. The poor, the oppressed, and the slaves were attracted to the personality, life, death, and resurrection of Jesus, his love for all, and his concern for suffering humanity. They found spiritual sustenance in a religion that offered a hand of love and taught that a person need not be well-born, rich, educated, or talented to be worthy, that God draws no distinction between the lowly, poor, and slaves and the mightiest aristocrats. To people burdened with misfortune and terrified by death, Christianity held the promise of eternal life, a kingdom of heaven where they would be comforted by God the Father. Thus, Christianity gave the common person what the aristocratic values of Greco-Roman civilization generally did not: hope, a sense of dignity, and

Map 5.1 **The Spread of Christianity** Aided by dedicated missionaries, Christianity expanded throughout the Mediterranean world and later into Germanic lands.

inner strength. By and large, classical philosophy offered little compassion for the sufferer, but the cardinal principle of Christianity was that Jesus had endured earthly torments because of his love for all human beings and that even the lowliest could be redeemed.

Christianity succeeded not only through the appeal of its message, but also through the power of its institution, the Christian church, which grew into a strong organization uniting the faithful. For city dwellers, lonely, alienated, and disillusioned with public affairs—stranded mortals groping for a sense of community—the church that called its members "brother" and "sister" filled an elemental need of human beings to belong. The church welcomed women converts, who were often the first to join and brought their menfolk after them. Among the reasons that the church drew women was its command to husbands to treat their wives kindly, remain faithful, and provide for the children. Moreover, in the eyes of God, women were spiritually equal with men. The church won new converts and retained the loyalty of its members by furnishing social services for the poor and infirm, welcoming slaves, criminals, sinners, and other outcasts, and offering a hand of brotherhood and comfort during difficult times. While there were some converts from the middle and even upper classes, the earliest Christians were drawn chiefly from the lower classes. Christian churches established in numerous cities insisted that their congregants evidence high moral standards in their daily lives. No doubt people impressed by the behavior of Christians were drawn to the new faith.

The ability of an evolving Christianity to assimilate elements from Greek philosophy and even from the mystery religions also contributed in no small measure to its growth. By utilizing Greek philosophy, Christianity was able to present itself in terms intelligible to those versed in Greek learning and thus attract educated people. Converts to Christianity who were trained in philosophy proved to be able defenders of their newly adopted faith. Because some Christian doctrines (the risen savior-god, the virgin and child, life after death, communion with the divine), practices (purification through baptism), and holy days (December 25 was the birth date of the god Mithras) either paralleled or were adopted from the mystery religions, it became relatively easy to win converts from these rivals.

Christianity and Rome

Generally tolerant of religions, the Roman government at first did not significantly interfere with the Christian movement. Indeed, Christianity benefited in many ways from its association with the Roman Empire. Christian missionaries traveled throughout the Empire, over roads and across seas made safe by Roman arms. The common Greek dialect, Koine, spoken in most parts of the Empire, facilitated the missionaries' task. Had the Mediterranean world been fractured into separate and competing states, the spread of Christianity might well have faced an insurmountable obstacle. The universalism of the Roman Empire, which made citizenship available to peoples of many nationalities, prepared the way for the universalism of Christianity, which welcomed membership from all nations. Early Christians grafted onto Rome's imperial mission a spiritual evangelical cause: "Go ye therefore and teach all nations" (Matthew 28:19).

As the number of Christians increased, Roman officials began to fear the Christians as subversives who preached allegiance to God and not to Rome. To many Romans, Christians were disloyal citizens—a loathsome cabal of enemies of Rome drawn from the dregs of society—and ignorant women who attacked the state gods, would not engage in sacrifices to Roman divinities, scorned gladiatorial combats, stayed away from public baths, glorified nonviolence, refused to honor deceased emperors as gods, and worshiped a crucified criminal as Lord. Romans ultimately found in Christians a universal scapegoat for the ills burdening the Empire, such as famines, plagues, and military reverses. Were not these afflictions divine punishment for Christians' refusal to honor ancestral gods and traditions? In an effort to stamp out Christianity, emperors occasionally resorted to persecution. Christians were imprisoned, beaten, starved, burned alive, beheaded, torn apart by wild beasts in the arena for the amusement of the Roman crowd, and crucified. However, the persecutions did not last long enough to extirpate the new religion. Actually, they strengthened the determination of most of the faithful and won new converts, who were awed by the extraordinary courage of the martyrs willingly dying for their faith. Many Christians embraced the opportunity for martyrdom; they believed that they were reenacting the passion of Jesus, who sacrificed himself for humanity.

Unable to crush Christianity by persecution, Roman emperors decided to gain the support of the growing number of Christians within the Empire. In A.D. 313, Constantine, no doubt drawn to Christianity by its moral force—he was later baptized—issued the Edict of Milan, granting toleration to Christians. By A.D. 392, Theodosius I had made Christianity the state religion of the Empire and declared the worship of pagan gods illegal. With Christians in power, persecution did not end, but its target had shifted from Christians to pagans, Jews, and Christians with unorthodox views. The polytheistic religions of the Roman world did not claim to possess an exhaustive truth—did not assert that a particular god or a particular form of worship should prevail over all others and that wrongful religious expressions should be rooted out. People were relatively free to select their own credo and engage in their own acts of worship. Christianity, in contrast, possessing an exclusive attitude toward truth, felt compelled to cleanse society of false gods and beliefs and often viewed nonbelievers as wicked enemies of God who deserved punishment. Thus mobs, often driven by fanatic clergy, hurled non-Christian writings into bonfires, destroyed pagan altars and sacred images, and squelched pagan rites and festivals. Emperors, often pushed by the clergy, passed decrees calling for fining, imprisoning, torturing, and executing adherents of pagan cults.

Christianity and Greek Philosophy

Christianity synthesized both the Hebrew and the Greco-Roman traditions. Having emerged from Judaism, it assimilated Hebrew monotheism and prophetic morality and retained the Old Testament as the Word of God. As the new religion evolved, it also assimilated elements of Greek philosophy. The ability to combine a historic Judaic monotheism, which had many admirers in the Gentile world, with Greek rational philosophy was a crucial reason for Christianity's triumph in the Roman Empire. But there was a struggle between conservatives, who wanted no dealings with pagan philosophy, and those believers who recognized the value of Greek thought to Christianity.

To conservative church fathers—early Christian writers whose works are accepted as authoritative by the Catholic church—classical philosophy was entirely in error because it did not derive from divine revelation. As the final statement of God's truth, Christianity superseded both pagan philosophy and pagan religions. These conservatives feared that studying classical authors would contaminate Christian morality (did not Plato propose a community of wives, and did not the dramatists treat violent passions?) and promote heresy (was not classical literature replete with references to pagan gods?). For these church fathers, there could be no compromise between Greek philosophy and Christian revelation. They considered their life's mission to be preaching the Gospel of Jesus, which required no reinforcement from pagan ideas. For them, faith was more reliable than all the demonstrations of human reason. "What indeed has Athens to do with Jerusalem?" asked Tertullian (A.D. 150–225). "With our faith, we desire no further belief. For this is our faith that there is nothing which we ought to believe besides."[3]

Some church fathers, including several who had a Greek education, resisted this anti-intellectualism. Defending the value of studying classical literature, they maintained that such literature, properly taught, could aid in the moral development of children because it presented many examples of virtuous deeds. Some church fathers claimed that Greek philosophy contained a dim glimmer of God's truth, a pre-Christian insight into divine wisdom. Christ had corrected and fulfilled an insight reached by the philosophical mind: Christianity had perfected the ethical ideals of the philosopher. Knowledge of Greek philosophy, they also contended, helped Christians explain their beliefs logically and argue intelligently with pagan critics of Christian teachings.

Utilizing the language and categories of Greek philosophy, Christian intellectuals transformed Christianity from a simple ethical creed into a theoretical system, a theology. This effort to express Christian beliefs in terms of Greek rationalism is referred to as the Hellenization of Christianity.

Greek philosophy enabled Christians to explain rationally God's existence and revelation. Christ was depicted as the divine or incarnate Logos (reason) in human form. Educated believers could argue that the fundamental principles that Greek philosophers saw operating in the universe were established by God the Father. The Stoic teaching that all people are fundamentally equal because they share in universal reason could be formulated in Christian terms: that all are united in Christ. Christians could interpret the church to be the true fulfillment of the Stoic idea of a polity embracing the entire world. Stoic ethics, which stressed moderation, self-control, and brotherhood, was compatible with Christianity. Particularly in Platonism, which drew a distinction between a world perceived by the senses and a higher order—a transcendent world that should be the central concern of human existence—Christian thinkers found a congenial vehicle for expressing Christian beliefs. The perfect and universal Forms, or Ideas, which Plato maintained were the true goal of knowledge and the source of ethical standards, were held by Christians to exist in God's mind.

That Greek philosophy exerted an influence on church doctrine is of immense importance: it meant that rational thought, the priceless achievement of the Greek mind, was not lost. However, the Hellenization of Christianity did not mean the triumph of classicism over Christianity, but rather the reverse: Christianity triumphed over Hellenism. Greek philosophy had to sacrifice its essential autonomy—the ability to think freely—to the requirements of Christian revelation; that is, reason had to fit into a Christian framework and serve faith. Although Christianity made use of Greek philosophy, Christian truth ultimately rested on faith, not reason. And in any conflict between reason and faith, faith would prevail.

DEVELOPMENT OF CHRISTIAN ORGANIZATION, DOCTRINE, AND ATTITUDES

Early in its history, the church developed along hierarchical lines. Those members of the Christian community who had the authority to preside over the celebration of the Mass—breaking bread and offering wine as Christ had done at the Last Supper—were called either priests or bishops. Gradually, the designation *bishop* was reserved for the one clergyman in the community with the authority to resolve disputes over doctrines and practices. Regarded as the successors to Jesus' Twelve Disciples, bishops supervised religious activities within their regions. In creating a diocese that was supervised by a bishop and had its center in a leading city, the church adapted Roman administrative techniques.

The Primacy of the Bishop of Rome

The bishop of Rome, later to be called the pope, claimed primacy over the other bishops. In developing the case for their supremacy over the church organization, bishops of Rome increasingly referred to the famous New Testament passage in which Jesus says to his disciple Simon (also called Peter): "'And I tell you, you are Peter, and on this rock I will build my church'" (Matthew 16:18). Because *Peter* in Greek means "rock" *(petra)*, it was argued that Christ had chosen Peter to succeed him as ruler of the universal church. Since it was commonly accepted that Saint Peter had established a church in Rome and was martyred there, it was argued further that the Roman bishop inherited the power that Christ had passed on to Peter.

The Rise of Monasticism

Some devout Christians committed to living a perfect Christian life were distressed by the wickedness of the world about them, including

SAINT PAUL MOSAIC FROM THE BAPTISTRY OF THE ARIANS, RAVENNA, ITALY. Inspired by Jesus' life and death, Paul taught that Jesus was a resurrected redeemer who held the promise of salvation for both Jews and Gentiles.

the moral laxity of those clergy who chased after wealth and pomp. Seeking to escape from the agonies and corruptions of this world, some ardent Christians withdrew to deserts and mountains in search of spiritual renewal. In their zeal for holiness, they sometimes practiced extreme forms of asceticism: self-flogging, wearing spiked corsets, eating only herbs, or living for years on a column high above the ground. They believed that these ascetic practices drew them closer to God. Gradually, colonies of these hermits sprang up, particularly in Egypt; in time, the leaders of these monastic communities drew up written rules that required monks to refrain from bodily abuses and to engage in manual labor.

The monastic ideal spread from East to West. The principal figure in the shaping of monasticism in the West was Saint Benedict (c. 480–c. 543), who founded a monastery at Monte Cassino, Italy, in 529. The Rule of Saint Benedict called for the monks to live in poverty and to study, labor, and obey the abbot, the head of the monastery. Monks were required to pray often, work hard, talk little, and surrender private property. In imposing discipline and regulations, Benedict eliminated the excessive and eccentric individualism of the early monks; he socialized and institutionalized the spiritual impulse that led monks to withdraw from the world. Benedict demonstrated the same genius for administration that the Romans had shown in organizing and governing the Empire. His rule became the standard for monasteries in Western Europe.

The Scriptural Tradition and Doctrinal Disputes

The earliest surviving Christian writings are Paul's Epistles, written some twenty-five to thirty years after the death of Jesus. Jesus' sayings and deeds were preserved by word of mouth. Sometime around A.D. 66–70, about forty years after the Crucifixion, Saint Mark formulated the Christian message from this oral tradition and perhaps from some material that had been put in writing earlier. Later, Saint Matthew and Saint Luke, relying heavily on Mark's account, wrote somewhat longer Gospels. The Gospels of Mark, Matthew, and Luke are called *synoptic* because their approach to Jesus is very similar. The remaining Gospel, written by Saint John around A.D. 110, varies significantly from the synoptic Gospels. The synoptic Gospels, the Gospel of Saint John, the Acts of the Apostles, the twenty-one Epistles (including those written by Saint Paul), and Revelation constitute the twenty-seven books of the Christian New Testament. Christians also accepted the Hebrews' Old Testament as God's Word.

The early Christians had a Bible and a clergy to teach it. But the Holy Writ could be interpreted differently by equally sincere believers, and controversies over doctrine threatened the unity of the early church. The most important controversy concerned how people viewed the relationship between God and Christ. Arius (A.D. 250–336), a Greek priest in Alexandria, led one faction. He denied the complete divinity of Christ, one of the basic tenets of the church. To Arius, Christ was more than man but less than God; there was no permanent union between God and Christ; the Father alone was eternal and truly God.

The Council of Nicaea (A.D. 325), the first assembly of bishops from all parts of the Roman world, was called to settle the controversy. The council condemned Arius and ruled that God and Christ were of the same substance, coequal and coeternal. The position adopted at Nicaea became the basis of the Nicene Creed, which remains the official doctrine of the church. Although Arianism, the name given the heresy of Arius, won converts for a time, it eventually died out, helped along by persecution.

Christianity and Society

Although salvation was their ultimate aim, Christians still had to dwell within the world and deal with its imperfections. In the process, Christian thinkers challenged some of the mores of Greco-Roman society and formulated attitudes that would endure for centuries. Influenced by passages in the New Testament that condemned acts of revenge and the shedding of blood, some early Christians refused military service. Others, however, held that in a sinful world, defense of the state was necessary and served in the army without concealment or apology. After Roman emperors professed Christianity, Christians began to serve the government more often. With the barbarians menacing the borders, these Christian officials could not advocate nonviolence. Christian theorists began to argue that under certain circumstances—to punish injustice or to restore peace—war was just. But even such wars must not entail unnecessary violence.

Women were dedicated followers of Jesus in his ministry. He welcomed their devotion and at times confided in them. As the Christian movement gained momentum it attracted numerous women, and it is likely that more women than men attended church services and participated in church activities; a number of women suffered martyrdom. The early Christian view of women was rooted in the patriarchal tradition of Jewish society. Paul subjected the wife to her husband's authority. "Wives, be subject to your husbands, as to the Lord. For the husband is the head of the wife as Christ is the head of the church" (Ephesians 5:22–23). But Paul also held that all are baptized in Christ: "There is neither Jew nor Greek, there is neither slave nor free, there is neither male nor female; for you are all one in Christ Jesus" (Galatians 3:28). Consequently, both sexes were subject to divine law; both men and women possessed moral autonomy. The early church held to strict standards on sexual matters. It condemned adultery and esteemed virginity pledged for spiritual reasons.

Christians waged no war against slavery, which was widely practiced and universally accepted in the ancient world. Paul commanded slaves to obey their masters, and many Christians, including leaders of local churches, were themselves slave owners. While Christians did not try to alter the legal status of slaves, they did teach that slaves, too, were children of God, sought their conversion, urged owners not to treat them harshly, and considered it a virtue for masters to free their slaves. In the modern world, the Christian teaching that all persons are spiritually equal before God would impel some Christians to fight for the abolition of slavery.

Christian theorists condemned sex outside of marriage, adultery, prostitution, homosexuality, and abortion, and insisted that the sex drive should be confined to reproduction, as Clement of Alexandria wrote: "Yet marriage in itself merits esteem and the highest approval, for the Lord wished men to 'be fruitful and multiply.' He did not tell them, however, to act like libertines, nor did He intend them to surrender themselves to pleasure as though born only to indulge in sexual relations. . . . To indulge in intercourse without intending children is to outrage nature."[4]

Christianity and the Jews

The central theme of the New Testament Gospels is love of both God and fellow human beings. But the Gospels also devote considerable attention to the fallen angel, Satan, and the evil demons that inhabit his kingdom. Increasingly, Christians identified opponents—Jews, pagans, and heretics—with Satan and viewed conflicts in a moral context: a struggle between God's faithful and Satan's servants. Over the centuries, the view that they were participants in a cosmic struggle between good and evil led Christians to demonize adversaries, a practice that exacerbated hatred and justified mistreatment, even massacre. Christian attitudes and behavior toward Jews poignantly illustrate this point.

Numerous links connect early Christianity and Judaism. Jesus himself and his earliest followers, including the Twelve Apostles, were Jews who were faithful to Jewish law. Jesus attended synagogue and frequently quoted the Hebrew scriptures—which to him and his disciples were the authoritative word of God—to support a particular viewpoint. Jesus' message was first spread in synagogues throughout the Roman Empire. Early Christianity's affirmation of the preciousness of the human being created in God's image, its belief that God rules history, its awareness of human sinfulness, its call for repentance, and its appeal to God for forgiveness are rooted in Judaism. The Christian

reference to God as a "merciful Father" derives from Jewish prayer. Also rooted in Judaism are the moral norms proclaimed by Jesus in the Sermon on the Mount and on other occasions. For example, "Thou shalt love thy neighbor as thyself" was the motto of the Jewish sage Hillel, a contemporary of Jesus who founded a school. The great value that the Torah places on charity was inherited by Christianity. Jesus' use of parables to convey his teachings, the concept of the Messiah, respect for the Sabbath, the practice of giving alms to the poor, and congregational worship likewise stem from Judaism. And, of course, Christians viewed the Hebrew Scriptures as God's word. A deeper understanding of the New Testament requires knowledge of the Old Testament, for its thought and language permeated the Christian gospels.

However, over the years, particularly after more and more non-Jews became followers of Christ, Christians forgot, devalued, or denied the Jewish roots of their faith and some thinkers began to show hostility toward Judaism and Jews, which had tragic consequences in later centuries. Several factors fueled this anti-Judaism: resentment against Jews for their refusal to accept Jesus; the polemics of the Jewish establishment against the followers of Jesus; the role in Jesus' death ascribed to Jews by the New Testament; resentment against those Christians who Judaized, that is, continued to observe Jewish festivals and the Jewish Sabbath, to regard the synagogue as holy, and to practice circumcision; and anger that Judaism remained a vital religion, for this undermined the conviction that Christianity was the fulfillment of Judaism and the one true faith.

What made Christian anti-Judaism particularly ominous was the effort of some theologians to demonize the Jewish people. The myth emerged that Jews, murderers of the incarnate God who embodied all that was good, were a cursed nation, children of the Devil, whose suffering was intended by God. Thus Origen (c. 185–c. 251) maintained that "the blood of Jesus [falls] not only upon those who lived then but also upon all generations of the Jewish people following afterwards until the end of the world."[5] In the late fourth century, John Chrysostom

Saint Benedict of Nursia:
The Christian Way of Life

In the following selection from his monastic book of rules, Saint Benedict of Nursia advises his monks on the attitudes and conduct necessary to live a virtuous Christian life.

What Are the Instruments of Good Works?

In the first place, to love the Lord God with the whole heart, whole soul, whole strength, then his neighbor as himself.

Then not to kill, not to commit adultery, not to steal, not to covet, not to bear false witness, to honor all men, and what anyone would not have done to him, let him not do to another. To deny himself, that he may follow Christ, to chasten the body, to renounce luxuries, to love fasting. To relieve the poor, to clothe the naked, to visit the sick, to bury the dead, to help in tribulation, to console the afflicted.

To make himself a stranger to the affairs of the world, to prefer nothing before the love of Christ, not to give way to anger, not to bear any grudge, not to harbour deceit in the heart, not to forsake charity. Not to swear, lest haply he perjure himself, to utter truth from his heart and his mouth. Not to return evil for evil, not to do injuries, but rather to bear them patiently, to love his enemies, not to curse against those that curse him, but rather to bless them, to endure persecution for righteousness' sake. Not to be proud, not given to wine, not gluttonous, not addicted to sleep, not slothful, not given to murmur, not a slanderer. To commit his hope to God; when he sees anything good in himself to attribute it to God, and not to himself, but let him always know that which is evil is his own doing; and impute it to himself. To fear the day of judgment, to dread hell, to desire eternal life with all spiritual longing, to have the expectation of death every day before his eyes. To watch over his actions at all times, to know certainly that in all places the eye of God is upon him; those evil thoughts which come into his heart to dash to pieces on Christ; . . . to pray frequently every day, to confess his past sins to God, in prayer, with tears and groanings; from thence forward to reform as to those sins.

Not to fulfill the desires of the flesh, to hate his own will; . . . every day to fulfill the commands of God in his deeds, to love chastity, to hate no one, not to have jealousy or envy, not to love contention, to avoid self-conceit; to reverence seniors, to love juniors, to pray for enemies in the love of Christ, to be reconciled with his adversary, before the going down of the sun, and never to despair of the mercy of God. . . .

Question for Analysis

1. How might a Christian today react to Saint Benedict's approach to a virtuous life?

Oliver J. Thatcher, ed., *Library of Original Sources* (Milwaukee: University Research Extension, 1907), 4:133–134.

described Jews as "inveterate murderers, destroyers, men possessed by the Devil." "[T]hey murder their offspring and immolate them to the devil." The synagogue, he said, was "the domicile of the devil as is also the soul of the Jews." Their rites are "criminal and impure," their religion is "a disease." For the "odious assassination of Christ," there is "no expiation possible, . . . no pardon." Jews will live "under the yoke of servitude without end."[6] Since the Devil was very real to early and medieval Christians, the Jew became identified with evil. Christians developed a mind-set, concludes the Reverend Robert A. Everett, that was "unable to see anything positive in Judaism. . . . Judaism and the Jewish people came to have no real value for Christians except as a negative contrast to Christianity."[7] Because of this "teaching of contempt" and the "diabolization of the Jew," the Christian ethic of love did not extend to Jews.

> [O]nce it is established that God has cursed the Jews, how can one argue that Christians should love them? If Jews have been fated by God to have . . . a long history of suffering, who are Christians to alter their history by doing anything to relieve Jewish suffering? The theology of victimization thus precludes Christian love as a basis of relating to Jews.[8]

The diabolization of the Jew, which bore no relationship to the actual behavior of Jews or to their highly ethical religion, and the "theology of victimization," which held that the Jews were collectively and eternally cursed for denying Christ, became powerful myths. Over the centuries, these myths poisoned Christians' hearts and minds against Jews, spurring innumerable humiliations, persecutions, and massacres by Christians who believed that their actions were pleasing to God. Alongside this hatred of Jews and antipathy to their suffering, there also evolved the belief that Jews, faithless and perfidious though they were, should be permitted to survive, for their dispersal among the nations was evidence of divine punishment; moreover, one day they would see the light and convert to the true faith.

SAINT AUGUSTINE: THE CHRISTIAN WORLDVIEW

During the early history of Christianity, many learned men, fathers of the church, explained and defended church teachings. Most of the leading early fathers wrote in Greek, but in the middle of the fourth century, three great Latin

THE LADDER OF DIVINE ASCENT, TWELFTH-CENTURY ICON, ST. CATHERINE'S MONASTERY, MOUNT SINAI. Monks climbing a ladder to heaven while demons try to prevent them from leaving earth.

writers—Saint Jerome, Saint Ambrose, and Saint Augustine—profoundly influenced the course of Christianity in the West.

Saint Jerome (A.D. c. 340–420) wrote about the lives of the saints and promoted the spread of monasticism. But his greatest achievement was the translation of the Old and New Testaments from Hebrew and Greek into Latin. Jerome's text, the common, or Vulgate, version of the Bible, became the official edition of the Bible for the Western church.

Saint Ambrose (A.D. 340–397), bishop of Milan, Italy, instructed the clergy to deal humanely with the poor, the old, the sick, and the orphaned. He urged clerics not to pursue wealth but to practice humility and avoid favoring the rich over the poor. Ambrose sought to defend the autonomy of the church against the power of the state. His dictum that "the Emperor is within the church, not above it" became a cardinal principle of the medieval church.

The most important Christian theoretician in the Late Roman Empire was Saint Augustine (A.D. 354–430), bishop of Hippo in North Africa and author of *The City of God.* Augustine became the principal architect of the Christian outlook that succeeded a dying classicism.

In 410, when Augustine was in his fifties, Visigoths sacked Rome—a disaster for which the classical consciousness was unprepared. Throughout the Empire, people panicked. Non-Christians blamed the tragedy on Christianity. Even Christians expressed anxiety. Why were the righteous also suffering? Where was the kingdom of God on earth that had been prophesied? In *The City of God,* Augustine maintained that the worldly city could never be the central concern of Christians. The misfortunes of Rome, therefore, should not distress Christians unduly because the true Christian was a citizen of a heavenly city that could not be pillaged by ungodly barbarians but would endure forever. Compared with God's heavenly city, Rome and its decline were unimportant. What really mattered in history, said Augustine, was not the coming to be or the passing away of cities and empires, but the individual's entrance into heaven or hell.

Augustine did not hold that by his death Christ had opened the door to heaven for all. The majority of humanity remained condemned to eternal punishment, said Augustine; only a handful were blessed with the gift of faith and the promise of heaven. People could not by their own efforts overcome a sinful nature; a moral and spiritual regeneration stemmed not from human will power, but from God's grace. The small number endowed with God's grace constituted the City of God. These people lived on earth as visitors only, for they awaited deliverance to the Kingdom of Christ. Most inhabitants of the earthly city were destined for eternal punishment in hell. A perpetual conflict existed between the two cities and between their inhabitants: one city stood for sin and corruption; the other, for God's truth and perfection.

For Augustine, the highest good was not of this world. Rather, it consisted of eternal life with God. His distinction between this higher world of perfection and a lower world of corruption remained influential throughout the Middle Ages.

Augustine repudiated the distinguishing feature of classical humanism: the autonomy of reason. For him, ultimate wisdom could not be achieved through rational thought alone; reason had to be guided by faith. Without faith, there could be no true knowledge, no understanding. Philosophy had no validity if it did not first accept as absolutely true the existence of God and the authority of his revelation. Thus, Augustine upheld the primacy of faith. But he did not necessarily regard reason as an enemy of faith, and he did not call for an end to rational speculation. What he denied of the classical view was that reason alone could attain wisdom. The wisdom that Augustine sought was Christian wisdom, God's revelation to humanity. The starting point for this wisdom, he said, was belief in God and the Scriptures. To Augustine, secular knowledge for its own sake was of little value; the true significance of knowledge lay in its role as a tool for comprehending God's will. Augustine adapted the classical intellectual tradition to the requirements of Christian revelation.

With Augustine, the human-centered outlook of classical humanism, which for centuries had been undergoing transformation, gave way to a God-centered worldview. The fulfillment of God's will, not the full development of human capacities, became the chief concern of life. *The City of God* encompassed several themes that would concern Christians for centuries: the meaning of history and the place of the individual, the state, and the church in God's plan.

CHRISTIANITY AND CLASSICAL HUMANISM: ALTERNATIVE WORLDVIEWS

Christianity and classical humanism are the two principal components of the Western tradition. The value that modern Western civilization places

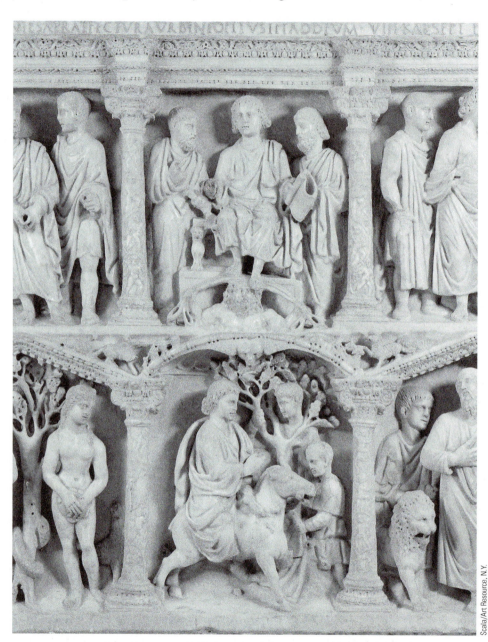

CHRIST ENTHRONED. This detail from the funerary sarcophagus of Junius Bassus, dating from A.D. 359, shows, among other scenes, Christ sitting on a throne (top middle).

on the individual derives ultimately from classical humanism and the Judeo-Christian tradition. Classical humanists believed that human worth came from the capacity of individuals to reason and to shape their character and life according to rational standards. Christianity also places great stress on the individual. In the Christian view, God cares for each person; he wants people to behave righteously and to enter heaven; Christ died for all because he loves humanity. Christianity espouses active love and genuine concern for fellow human beings. Without God, people are as Augustine described them: "foul, crooked, sordid, . . . vicious." With God, the human personality can undergo a moral transformation and become loving, good, and free. The idea of a Christian conscience, prompted by God and transcending all other loyalties, reinforces respect for all human beings regardless of cultural and national differences. Also promoting respect for each person is the presupposition of natural equality stemming from the Christian belief that each individual, regardless of birth, wealth, or talent, is precious to God.

There are striking parallels between Christian and Stoic ethics. Both Stoics and Christians believed that there is an essential "brotherhood of man," that all human beings are related and possess a fundamental dignity. Both urged suppressing wild passions, expressing concern for others, living simply, and heeding the inner voice of conscience that commands human beings to do what is right.

But Christianity and classical humanism also represent two essentially different worldviews. The triumph of the Christian outlook signified a break with the essential meaning of classical humanism; it pointed to the end of the world of antiquity and the beginning of an age of faith, the Middle Ages. With the victory of Christianity, the ultimate goal of life shifted. Life's purpose was no longer to achieve excellence in this world through the full and creative development of human capacities, but to attain salvation in a heavenly city. A person's worldly accomplishments amounted to very little if he or she did not accept God and his revelation. The Christian ideal of the isolated and contemplative monk who rejected the world in order to serve God was alien to the spirit of classical humanism, which valued active citizenship and active participation in worldly activities. Equally foreign to the Greco-Roman mind was another idea introduced by Christianity: the need to escape from a sinful human nature, a consequence of Adam and Eve's defiance of God. This view of a corrupt human nature and an unclean human body, particularly in Augustine's formulation, became deeply embedded in the European mind during the Christian centuries—the Middle Ages.

In the classical view, history had no ultimate end, no ultimate meaning; periods of happiness and misery repeated themselves endlessly. In the Christian view, history is filled with spiritual meaning. It is the profound drama of individuals struggling to overcome their original sin in order to gain eternal happiness in heaven. History began with Adam and Eve's fall and would end when Christ returns to earth, evil is eradicated, and God's will prevails. For the Christian, Christ on the cross was both the central event and a turning point in world history.

Classicism held that there was no authority higher than reason, that individuals had within themselves, through unaided reason, the ability to understand the world and life. Christianity teaches that, without God as the starting point, knowledge is formless, purposeless, and prone to error. Classicism, unlike Judaism or Christianity, possessed no truths or moral precepts revealed by a divine power. Rather, classicism held that ethical standards were expressions of universal reason, laws of nature, which the human mind could discover. Through reason, individuals could discern the norms by which they should regulate their lives. Reason would enable them to govern desires and will; it would show where their behavior was wrong and teach them how to correct it. Because individuals sought what was best for themselves, they would obey the voice of reason. Historically, Christianity maintained that ethical standards emanate from the personal will of God. Without submission to God's commands, people remain wicked forever; the human will, essentially sinful, cannot be transformed by the promptings of reason.

Only when individuals turn to God for forgiveness and guidance can they find the inner strength to overcome their sinful nature. People cannot perfect themselves through scientific knowledge; it is spiritual insight and belief in God that they require and that must serve as the first principle of their lives. For classicism, the ultimate good was sought through independent thought and action; for Christianity, the ultimate good comes through knowing, obeying, and loving God.

Although some Christian thinkers dismissed Greek philosophy as erroneous and useless, others respected the Greek intellectual tradition and rejected attempts to eradicate it. Rather, they sought to fit it into a Christian framework—that is, rational inquiry must be guided by and never conflict with Christian teachings. By holding that the mind is limited in its capacity to think for itself and must be guided by faith and clerical authority, Christianity contributed to the waning of the classical tradition in the Late Roman Empire. Nevertheless, by preserving the Greek philosophical tradition—even if it remained subordinate to the Christian outlook—Christian thinkers performed a task of immense historical significance.

Christianity inherited the Hebrew view of the overriding importance of God for humanity: God, who is both Lawgiver and Judge, makes life intelligible and purposeful. For the Christian, God is a living being, loving and compassionate, in whose company one seeks to spend eternity; one knows God essentially through faith and feeling. Although the Greek philosophers had a conception of God, it was not comparable to the God of Hebrews and Christians. For the Greeks, God was a logical abstraction, a principle of order, the prime mover, the first cause, the mind of the universe, pure thought, the supreme good, the highest truth; God was a concept, impersonal, unfeeling, and uninvolved with human concerns. The Greeks approached God through the intellect, not the heart; they neither loved nor worshiped God. In addition, because religion was at the periphery, not the center, of classical humanism, the idea of God did not carry the same significance as it did for Christianity.

Christianity maintained that there was a prescribed way to worship the one true God, that belief in other gods was an abomination, and that nonbelievers (or infidels) and heretics were wicked sinners hated by God. Over the centuries, this outlook sanctioned fanaticism, persecution, and holy war with accompanying massacres—a terrible legacy that constitutes the dark side of monotheism. Unlike the monotheistic faiths—Judaism, Christianity, and Islam—Greek and Roman polytheism had no concepts of martyrdom for the true faith and holy war against the infidel and consistently tolerated many different religious beliefs and practices as long as they did not threaten the state.

In the classical world, the political community was the avenue to justice, happiness, and self-realization. In Christianity, the good life was identified not with worldly achievement but with life eternal, and the ideal commonwealth could only be one that was founded and ruled by Christ. It was entrance into God's kingdom that each person must make the central aim of life. Christian thinkers viewed the state as an inferior community to their own, the church of Christ, with its ties to a spiritual realm, the highest good. Secular power, they held, should submit to ecclesiastical authority. For the next thousand years, this distinction between heaven and earth, this otherworldly, theocentric outlook, would define the Western mentality.

In the Late Roman Empire, when classical values were in decay, Christianity was a dynamic and creative movement. Possessing both institutional and spiritual strength, Christianity survived the fall of Rome. Because it retained elements of Greco-Roman civilization and taught a high morality, Christianity served as a civilizing agent in the centuries that followed Rome's collapse. Indeed, Christianity was the essential shaper of the European civilization that emerged in the Middle Ages.

❖   ❖   ❖

NOTES

1. Hans Küng, "Christianity and Judaism," in *Jesus' Jewishness,* ed. James H. Charlesworth (New York: Crossroad, 1991), 259.

2. The biblical quotations are from the *Revised Standard Version of the Bible,* copyright © 1946, 1952, and 1971 the National Council of the Churches of Christ in the USA. Used by permission. All rights reserved.

3. Tertullian, "On Prescription against Heretics," in *The Ante-Nicene Fathers,* ed. Alexander Roberts and James Donaldson (New York: Charles Scribner's Sons, 1918), vol. 3, chap. 7, 246.

4. From Clement of Alexandria, *Christ the Educator,* trans. Simon P. Woo, C. P. (New York, Fathers of the Church, 1954), 175.

5. Quoted in Marvin Perry and Frederick M. Schweitzer, *Antisemitism: Myth and Hate from Antiquity to the Present* (New York: Palgrave Macmillan, 2002), 75.

6. Quoted in Edward H. Flannery, *The Anguish of the Jews* (London: Macmillan, 1965), 48.

7. Randolph Braham, ed., *The Origins of the Holocaust: Christian Anti-Semitism* (Boulder, Colo.: Social Science Monographs and Institute for Holocaust Studies of the City University of New York, 1986), 36.

8. Ibid., 37.

Part Two

The Middle Ages: The Christian Centuries

500–1400

Coronation of Charlemagne.

Scala/Art Resource, N.Y.

Politics and Society	Thought and Culture
500 Germanic kingdoms established on former Roman lands (400s and 500s) Saint Benedict founds monastery at Monte Cassino (529) Pope Gregory I sends missionaries to convert the Anglo-Saxons (596)	Boethius, *The Consolation of Philosophy* (523) Law Code of Justinian (529) Cassiodorus establishes a monastic library at Vivarium (540)
600 Spread of Islam (622–732)	The Koran (610)
700 Charles Martel defeats the Muslims at Tours (732)	Bede, *Ecclesiastical History of the English People* (c. 700) Muslim Golden Age (700s and 800s)
800 Charlemagne crowned Emperor of Romans (800) Muslim, Magyar, and Viking invasions of Latin Christendom (9th and early 10th century) Growth of feudalism (800–1100)	Carolingian Renaissance (768–814) Alfred the Great promotes learning in England (871–899)
900 German king Otto I becomes first Holy Roman Emperor (962)	
1000 Split between the Byzantine and Roman churches (1054) Norman conquest of England (1066) Start of First Crusade (1096)	Romanesque style in architecture (1000s and 1100s)
1100 Philip Augustus expands central authority in France (1180–1223) Development of common law and jury system in England (1100s) Pontificate of Innocent III: height of papal power (1198–1216)	Flowering of medieval culture (1100s and 1200s): universities, Gothic architecture, scholastic philosophy, revival of Roman law
1200 Magna Carta (1215) Destruction of Baghdad by Mongols (1258)	Aquinas, *Summa Theologica* (1267–1273)
1300 Hundred Years' War (1337–1453) Black Death (1347–1351) Great Schism of papacy (1378–1417)	Dante, *Divine Comedy* (c. 1307–1321) Chaucer, *Canterbury Tales* (c. 1388–1400)

Chapter 6

The Rise of Europe: Fusion of Classical, Christian, and Germanic Traditions

- **The Medieval East**
- **Latin Christendom in the Early Middle Ages**
- **Feudal Society**
- **Agrarian Society**
- **Economic Expansion During the High Middle Ages**
- **The Rise of States**
- **The Growth of Papal Power**
- **Christians and Jews**

Focus Questions

1. How did Latin Christendom blend Christian, Greco-Roman, and Germanic traditions?
2. What was Byzantium's long-term influence on world history?
3. What does Islam have in common with Christianity? How do they differ?
4. What was the significance of medieval Muslim intellectual life?
5. Why is Charlemagne regarded as an important historical figure?
6. What conditions led to the rise of feudalism and manorialism?
7. What were the signs of vitality and recovery in European economic, political, and religious life during the High Middle Ages?
8. Why was there a conflict between church and state during the Middle Ages?

9. What prompted lords and commoners to heed the papacy's call for a crusade?

10. What conditions led to the rise of states? What were the essential differences characterizing the development of medieval England, France, and Germany?

11. What factors led to the rise of anti-Semitism during the Middle Ages? How does anti-Semitism demonstrate the power of mythical thinking?

*T*he triumph of Christianity and the establishment of Germanic kingdoms on once Roman lands constituted a new phase in Western history: the end of the ancient world and the beginning of the Middle Ages, a period that spanned a thousand years. In the ancient world, the locus of Greco-Roman civilization was the Mediterranean Sea. The heartland of medieval civilization gradually shifted to the north, to regions of Europe that Greco-Roman civilization had barely penetrated. During the Middle Ages, a common European civilization, Latin Christendom, evolved integrating Christian, Greco-Roman, and Germanic traditions: Christianity was at the center of medieval civilization; Rome, the seat of the papacy, was the spiritual capital and Latin, the language of intellectual life; and Germanic customs pervaded social and legal relationships. In the Early Middle Ages (500–1050), the new civilization was struggling to take form; in the High Middle Ages (1050–1300), medieval civilization reached its peak. ❖

THE MEDIEVAL EAST

Three new civilizations based on religion emerged from the ruins of the Roman Empire: Latin Christendom (Western and Central Europe) and two Eastern civilizations, Byzantium and Islam.

Byzantium

Although the Roman Empire in the West fell to the German tribes, the eastern provinces survived. They did so because they were richer, more urbanized, and more populous and because the main Germanic and Hunnish invasions were directed at the western regions. In the eastern parts, Byzantine civilization took shape. Its religion was Christianity; its language and culture Greek; and its machinery of administration Roman. The capital, Constantinople, was a fortress city, perfectly situated to resist attacks from land and sea.

During the Early Middle Ages, Byzantine civilization was economically and culturally far more advanced than that of the Latin West. At a time when few Westerners (Latin Christians) could read or write, Byzantine scholars studied the literature, philosophy, science, and law of ancient Greece and Rome. Whereas trade and urban life had greatly declined in the West, Constantinople was a magnificent Byzantine city of schools, libraries, open squares, and bustling markets.

Over the centuries, many differences developed between the Byzantine church and the Roman church. The pope resisted domination by the Byzantine emperor, and the Byzantines would not accept the pope as head of all Christians. The two churches quarreled over ceremonies, holy days, the display of images, and the rights of the clergy. The final break came in 1054: the Christian church split into the Roman Catholic Church in the West and the Eastern (Greek) Orthodox church in the East, a division that still persists.

Political and cultural differences widened the rift between Latin Christendom and Byzantium. In the Byzantine Empire, Greek was the language of religion and intellectual life; in the West, Latin predominated. Latin Christians refused to recognize that the Byzantine emperors were, as they claimed to be, successors to the Roman emperors. Byzantine emperors were absolute rulers who held that God had chosen them to rule and to institute divine will on earth. As successors to the Roman emperors, they claimed to rule all the lands that had once been part of the Roman Empire.

At its height, under Emperor Justinian, who reigned from 527 to 565, the Byzantine Empire included Greece, Asia Minor, Italy, southern Spain, and parts of the Near East, North Africa, and the Balkans. Over the centuries, the Byzantines faced attacks from the Germanic Lombards and Visigoths, Persians, Muslim Arabs, Seljuk Turks, and Latin Christians. The death blow to the empire was dealt by the Ottoman Turks. Originally from Central Asia, they had accepted Islam and had begun to build an empire. They drove the Byzantines from Asia Minor and conquered much of the Balkans. By the beginning of the fifteenth century, the Byzantine Empire consisted of only two small territories in Greece and the city of Constantinople. In 1453, the Ottoman Turks broke through Constantinople's great walls and plundered the city. After more than ten centuries, the Byzantine Empire had come to an end.

During its thousand years, Byzantium had a significant impact on world history. First, it prevented the Muslim Arabs from advancing into Eastern Europe. Had the Arabs broken through Byzantine defenses, much of Europe might have been converted to the new faith of Islam. Another far-reaching development was the codification of the laws of ancient Rome under Justinian. This monumental achievement, the *Corpus Juris Civilis,* preserved Roman law's principles of reason and justice. Today's legal codes in much of Europe and Latin America trace their roots to the Roman law recorded by Justinian's lawyers. The Byzantines also preserved the philosophy, science, mathematics, and literature of ancient Greece.

Contacts with Byzantine civilization stimulated learning in both the Islamic world to the east and Latin Christendom to the west. Speros Vryonis, a student of Byzantine civilization, states: "The Byzantines carried the torch of civilization unextinguished at a time when the barbarous Germanic and Slav tribes had reduced much of Europe to near chaos: and they maintained this high degree of civilization until Western Europe gradually emerged and began to take

Chronology 6.1 ❖ The Early and High Middle Ages

496	Clovis adopts Roman Christianity
596	Pope Gregory I sends missionaries to convert the Anglo-Saxons
732	Charles Martel defeats the Muslims at Tours
768	Charlemagne becomes king of the Franks
800	Emperor of the Romans
c. 840s	Height of Viking attacks
962	Otto I crowned Emperor of the Romans, beginning the Holy Roman Empire
987	Hugh Capet becomes king of France
1054	Split between the Byzantine and Roman churches
1066	Norman conquest of England
1075	Start of the Investiture Controversy
1096	First Crusade begins
1198–1216	Pontificate of Innocent III: height of the church's power

form."[1] Byzantium exerted an important religious, cultural, and linguistic influence on Latin Romanians, eastern Slavs (Russians and Ukrainians), and southern Slavs (Serbs and Bulgars). From Byzantium, the Slavs acquired legal principles, art forms, and an alphabet (the Cyrillic, based on the Greek) for writing their languages. (On the other hand, the western Slavs—Poles, Czechs, and Slovaks—came under the influence of Latin Christianity and Latin culture.)

Islam

The second civilization to arise after Rome's fall was based on the vital new religion of Islam, which emerged in the seventh century among the Arabs of Arabia. Its founder was Muhammad (c. 570–632), a prosperous merchant in the trading city of Mecca. At times, the introspective Muhammad withdrew from worldly affairs and devoted himself to meditation. He began to experience visions, which he interpreted as messages from God. When Muhammad was about forty, he believed that he was visited in his sleep by the angel Gabriel, who ordered him to "recite in the name of the Lord!" Transformed by this experience, Muhammad came to believe that he had been chosen to serve as a prophet, the carrier of God's revelation. Although most desert Arabs worshiped tribal gods, many Arabs in the towns and trading centers, including Muhammad, were familiar with Judaism and Christianity, and some had accepted the idea of one God. Rejecting the many deities of the tribal religions, Muhammad offered the Arabs a new monotheistic faith, Islam, which means "surrender to Allah (God)."

Islamic standards of morality and rules governing daily life are set by the Koran, which Muslims believe contains the words of Allah as revealed to Muhammad. Muslims see their religion as the completion and perfection of Judaism and Christianity; they believe both of these monotheistic predecessors were superseded by Allah's revelation to Muhammad. Muslims regard the ancient Hebrew prophets as messengers of God and value their message of compassion and the oneness of humanity. They also acknowledge Jesus as a great prophet but do not consider him divine and view the Trinity as a form of polytheism. Muslims view Muhammad as the last and greatest of the prophets and see him as entirely human; they worship only Allah, the creator and ruler of heaven and

127

earth, a single, all-powerful God who is merciful, compassionate, and just. According to the Koran, on the Day of Judgment unbelievers and the wicked will be dragged into a fearful place of "scorching winds and seething water," and "sinners . . . shall eat . . . [bitter] fruit . . . [and] drink boiling water."[2] Faithful Muslims who have lived virtuously are promised paradise, a garden of bodily pleasures and spiritual delights.

An essential feature of Islam is the obligation of the faithful to obey the Five Pillars of the faith: (1) A Muslim must accept and repeat the statement of faith: "There is no God but Allah, and Muhammad is his Prophet." (2) At least five times a day, a believer must face the holy city of Mecca and pray. (3) Muslims have a religious duty to be generous to the poor. (4) During the holy month of Ramadan, believers should not eat or drink

MOSQUE OF CÓRDOBA. The richness of Islamic culture and architecture is evident in Spain, where Muslim rule lingered until the conquest of Granada in 1492. The arch of alternating stone would find its way into Christian churches, most memorably at Vezelay in southern France.

Roger Viollet/Getty Images.

between sunrise and sunset. (5) Muslims are expected to make at least one pilgrimage to the holy city of Mecca. The Koran contains numerous other injunctions designed to promote righteous behavior, including strict modesty for females and the condemnation of polytheism as a vile sin.

In a little more than two decades, Muhammad united the often feuding Arabian tribes into a disciplined, organized and powerful force dedicated to Allah and to spreading the Islamic faith. Muhammad had conveyed to his followers their religious obligation to perform jihad, literally striving in the path of God. *Jihad* is a complex term whose two essential meanings are an internal striving by the individual for moral self-improvement, and a collective military struggle to defend Islam against its enemies and to extend Muslim power over other lands so that all people will be subject to God's laws as revealed to Muhammad. Muhammad glorified jihad and criticized those who did not participate in it. Historically the doctrine of jihad held that the Islamic community (*umma*), the recipient of Allah's revelation, was commanded to make Allah's directives supreme over the whole world. Either by conversion through vigorous missionary activity or conquest, infidels were destined to submit to Islamic jurisdiction. Muslim theologians came to regard jihad as the finest religious act a man can perform.

Muslim warriors believed that they were required to engage in a holy war to spread Islam to nonbelievers and that those who died in the jihad were assured a place in paradise. A desire to escape from the barren Arabian Desert and to exploit the rich Byzantine and Persian lands was another compelling reason for expansion. Conflicts between Persia and Byzantium had greatly weakened both eastern empires, facilitating the Muslim conquest.

After Muhammad's death in 632, his friend and father-in-law, Abu Bakr, became his successor, or caliph. Regarded as the defender of the faith, whose power derived from Allah, the caliph governed in accordance with Muslim law as defined in the Koran. Under the first four caliphs, who ruled from 632 to 661, with breathtaking speed the Arabs, organized and inspired by their faith, overran the Persian Empire, seized some of Byzantine's provinces and invaded Europe. By 750, Islam's territory in the east extended into

India and to the borders of China; in the west, it encompassed North Africa and most of Spain. But the Muslim's northward push lost momentum and was halted in 717 by the Byzantines at Constantinople and in 732 by the Franks at the battle of Tours in central France.

The Islamic state was a theocracy, in which government and religion were inseparable; there could be no distinction between secular and spiritual authority. The separation of church and state, which became firmly rooted in the West in modern times, still remains an alien and hated concept for many Muslims. Muslims viewed God as the source of all law and political authority and the caliph as his earthly deputy. Divine law regulated all aspects of human relations. The ruler who did not enforce Koranic law failed in his duties. Thus, Islam was more than a religion; it was also a system of government, society, law, and thought that bound its adherents into an all-encompassing community. The idea of a single society governed by the Koran and aspiring to extend its power over non-Muslims remained deeply embedded in the Muslim mind over the centuries and for some is still a powerful force today.

Christians and Jews who lived in Islamic lands had to accept a subordinate status—they could not bear arms, were assessed a special tax, could be barred from testifying in court against a Muslim, and were required to wear clothing with distinguishing marks—a sign of humiliation. Over the years, thousands of Christian churches were demolished or converted into mosques. Nevertheless, as "people of the book," Jews and Christians were protected communities, and despite instances of loss of property or life, or both, the two groups generally went about their business and practiced their religions free of persecution. As a rule, Jews were physically safer in Muslim than in Christian lands.

The Arabs who burst into the Byzantine and Persian empires had no tradition of science or philosophy. But they were quick to absorb the learning of others. In the eighth and ninth centuries, under the Abbasid caliphs, Muslim civilization entered its golden age. Islamic civilization creatively integrated Arabic, Byzantine, Persian, and Indian cultural traditions. During the Early Middle Ages, when learning was at a low point in Western Europe, the Muslims forged a high civilization.

Muslim science, philosophy, and mathematics rested largely on the achievements of the ancient Greeks. The Muslims acquired Greek learning from the older Persian and Byzantine civilizations, which had kept alive the Greek inheritance. By translating Greek works into Arabic and commenting on them, Muslim scholars performed the great historical task of preserving and expanding the philosophical and scientific heritage of ancient Greece. This Greek learning, supplemented by original contributions of Muslim scholars and scientists, was eventually passed on to Christian Europe, a transmission of immense historical significance (see next chapter). Muslim achievements in medicine are particularly noteworthy. Building on the Greek inheritance, Muslim physicians became the best trained and most skillful doctors of the time. Surgeons performed amputations, removed cancerous tissue, devised new medicines, and used anesthetics when performing operations. Well ahead of their time were those Muslim doctors who recommended humane treatment for the mentally ill. Persian al-Razi, or Rhazes, who headed the hospital in Baghdad in the ninth century, wrote a medical encyclopedia in which he discussed measles, kidney stones, poisons, skin diseases, and ways of maintaining one's health. The works of Rhazes, translated into Latin, were widely consulted in Latin Christendom.

The Arab empire, stretching from Spain to India, was unified by a common language (Arabic), a common faith, and a common culture. By the eleventh century, however, the Arabs began losing their dominance in the Islamic world. The Seljuk Turks, who had taken Asia Minor from the Byzantines, also conquered the Arabic lands of Syria, Palestine, and much of Persia. Although the Abbasid caliphs remained the religious and cultural leaders of Islam, political power was exercised by Seljuk sultans. In the eleventh and twelfth centuries, the Muslims lost Sicily and most of Spain to Christian knights, and European Crusaders carved out kingdoms in the Near East.

In the thirteenth century, Mongols led by Genghis Khan devastated Muslim lands; in the late fourteenth century, this time led by Tamerlane, they again plundered and massacred their way through Arab territory. After Tamerlane's death in 1404, his empire disintegrated, and its collapse left the way open for the Ottoman Turks.

The Ottoman Empire reached its height in the sixteenth century with the conquest of Egypt, North Africa, Syria, and the Arabian coast. The Ottomans developed an effective system of administration, but they could not restore the cultural brilliance, the thriving trade, or the prosperity that the Muslim world had known under the Abbasid caliphs of Baghdad.

LATIN CHRISTENDOM IN THE EARLY MIDDLE AGES

The centuries of cultural greatness of both the Islamic and the Byzantine civilizations enriched the Western world. However, neither Islam nor Byzantium made the breakthroughs in science, technology, philosophy, the arts, economics, and political thought that gave rise to the modern world. That process was the singular achievement of Europe. During the Early Middle Ages (500–1050), Latin Christendom was culturally far behind the two Eastern civilizations, but by the twelfth century it had caught up. In succeeding centuries, it produced the movements that ushered in the modern age: the Renaissance, the Reformation, the Scientific Revolution, the Age of Enlightenment, the French Revolution, and the Industrial Revolution.

Political, Economic, and Intellectual Transformation

From the sixth to the eighth century, Europeans struggled to overcome the disorder created by the breakup of the Roman Empire and the deterioration of Greco-Roman civilization. In the process, a new civilization, with its own distinctive style, took root. It grew out of the intermingling of Greco-Roman civilization, the Christian outlook, and Germanic traditions. But centuries would pass before it would come to fruition.

In the fifth century, German invaders founded kingdoms in North Africa, Italy, Spain, Gaul, and Britain—lands formerly belonging to Rome. Even before the invasions, the Germans had acquired some knowledge of Roman culture and were attracted to it. Therefore, the new Germanic rulers

sought not to destroy Roman civilization but to share in its advantages. For example, Theodoric the Great (476–526), the Ostrogoth ruler of Italy, retained the Roman Senate, government officials, civil service, and schools, and rich aristocratic Roman families continued to hold high government offices. The Burgundians in Gaul and the Visigoths in Spain maintained Roman law for their conquered subjects. All the Germanic kingdoms tried to keep Roman systems of taxation; furthermore, Latin remained the official language of administration.

But the Germanic kingdoms, often torn by warfare, internal rebellion, and assassination, provided a poor political base on which to revive a decadent and dying classical civilization. Most of the kingdoms survived for only a short time and had no enduring impact. An exception to this trend occurred in Gaul and south-central Germany, where the most successful of the Germanic kingdoms was established by the Franks—the founders of the new Europe.

The Roman world was probably too far gone to be rescued, but even if it had not been, the Germans were culturally unprepared to play the role of restorer. By the end of the seventh century, the old Roman lands in Western Europe showed a marked decline in central government, town life, commerce, and learning. Though vigorous and brave, the German invaders were essentially a rural and warrior people, tribal in organization and outlook. Their native culture, which was without cities or written literature, was primitive compared with the literary, philosophical, scientific, and artistic achievements of the Greco-Roman world. The Germans were not equipped to reform the decaying Roman system of administration and taxation or to cope with the economic problems that had burdened the Empire. Nor could they maintain roads and irrigation systems, preserve skills in the arts of stoneworking and glassmaking, or breathe new life into the dying humanist culture.

The distinguishing feature of classical civilization, its vital urban institutions, had deteriorated in the Late Roman Empire. Under the kingdoms created by Germanic chieftains, the shift from an urban to a rural economy accelerated. Although towns did not vanish altogether, they continued to lose control over the surrounding countryside and to decline in wealth and importance. They were the headquarters of bishops, rather than centers of commerce and intellectual life. Italy remained an exception to this general trend. There, Roman urban institutions persisted, even during the crudest period of the Early Middle Ages. Italian cities kept some metal currency in circulation and traded with one another and with Byzantium.

In retreat since the Late Roman Empire, Greco-Roman humanism continued its decline in the centuries immediately following Rome's demise. The old Roman upper classes abandoned their heritage and absorbed the ways of their Germanic conquerors, the Roman schools closed, and Roman law faded into disuse. Aside from clerics, few people could read and write Latin, and even learned clerics were rare. Knowledge of the Greek language in Western Europe was almost totally lost, and the Latin rhetorical style deteriorated. Many literary works of classical antiquity were either lost or neglected. Raids by Germanic tribes and later by Muslims, Magyars, and Vikings devastated libraries. Works by great authors were lost forever. For example, of the hundred dramas written by Sophocles, only seven survived. Gone were attempts to understand the natural world through reason; magic and the occult prevailed among both pagans and Christians. The literature of the seventh century, concerned principally with the lives of saints, was devoid of the humanist themes that had motivated Greek and Roman poets and dramatists. European culture was much poorer than the high civilizations of Byzantium, Islam, and ancient Rome.

During this period of cultural poverty, the few persons who were learned generally did not engage in original thought but rather salvaged and transmitted remnants of classical civilization. In a rudimentary way, they were struggling to create a Christian culture that combined the intellectual tradition of Greece and Rome with the religious teachings of the Christian church.

An important figure in the intellectual life of this transitional period was Boethius (480– c. 525), a descendant of a noble Italian family. Aspiring to rescue the intellectual heritage of antiquity, Boethius translated into Latin some of Aristotle's treatises on logic and wrote commentaries on Aristotle, Cicero, and Porphyry (a Neo-Platonist philosopher). Until the twelfth century, virtually all that Latin Christendom knew of Aristotle came from Boethius's translations and commentaries. Similarly, his work in mathematics, which contains fragments from Euclid, was the main source for the study of that discipline in the Early Middle Ages. In his theological writings, Boethius tried to demonstrate that reason did not conflict with orthodoxy—an early attempt to attain a rational comprehension of belief, or, as he expressed it, to join faith to reason. Boethius's early effort to examine Christian doctrines rationally, a salient feature of medieval philosophy, was to grow to maturity in the twelfth and thirteenth centuries.

Cassiodorus (c. 490–575), another Italian, collected Greek and Latin manuscripts and helped start the monastic practice of copying classical texts. Without this tradition, many key Christian and pagan works would undoubtedly have perished. In Spain, another preserver of ancient works, Isidore of Seville (c. 576–636), compiled an encyclopedia, *Etymologiae*, covering a diversity of topics from arithmetic and furniture to God. Isidore derived his information from many secular and religious sources. Quite understandably, his work contained many errors, particularly in its references to nature. For centuries, though, the *Etymologiae* served as a standard reference work and was found in every monastic library of note.

The translations and compilations made by Boethius, Cassiodorus, and Isidore, the books collected and copied by monks and nuns, and the schools established in monasteries (particularly those in Ireland, England, and Italy) kept intellectual life from dying out completely in the Early Middle Ages.

The Church: Shaper of Medieval Civilization

Christianity was the integrating principle and the church was the dominant institution of the Middle Ages. During the Late Roman Empire, as the Roman state and its institutions decayed, the church gained in power and importance. Its organization grew stronger, and its membership increased. Unlike the Roman state, the church was a healthy and vital organization. The elite of the Roman Empire had severed their commitment to the values of classical civilization, whereas the church leaders were intensely devoted to their faith.

When the Empire collapsed, the church retained the Roman administrative system and preserved elements of Greco-Roman civilization. A unifying and civilizing agent, the church provided people with an intelligible and purposeful conception of life and death. In a dying world, the church was the only institution capable of reconstructing civilized life. Thus, the Christian outlook, rather than the traditions of the German tribes, formed the foundation of medieval civilization. During the

course of the Middle Ages, people came to see themselves as participants in a great drama of salvation. There was only one truth: God's revelation to humanity. There was only one avenue to heaven, and it passed through the church. Membership in a universal church replaced citizenship in a universal empire. Across Europe, from Italy to Ireland, a new society centered on Christianity was taking shape.

Monks helped build the foundation of medieval civilization. During the seventh century, intellectual life on the European Continent continued its steady decline. In the monasteries of Ireland and England, however, a tradition of learning persisted. Early in the fifth century,

RAVENNA MOSAICS. Theodora, Emperor Justinian's wife, was a strong-willed woman who exercised considerable authority and often advised her husband on matters of state. During his long reign, Justinian succeeded in regaining lands in the western Mediterranean that had been conquered by the Germanic invaders. His lasting achievement was the appointment of a commission of scholars to collect and codify Rome's ancient laws and the commentaries of learned jurists.

INTERFOTO/Personalities/Alamy Limited.

Saint Patrick began the conversion of the Irish to Christianity. In Ireland, Latin became firmly entrenched as the language of both the church and scholars at a time when it was in danger of disappearing in many parts of the Continent. Irish monks preserved and cultivated Latin and even preserved some knowledge of Greek, and during their missionary activities, they revived the use of Latin on the Continent. In England, the Anglo-Saxons, both men and women—who converted to Christianity mainly in the seventh century—also established monasteries that kept learning alive. In the sixth and seventh centuries, Irish and Anglo-Saxon monks became the chief agents for converting people in Northern Europe. Thus, monks and nuns made possible a unitary European civilization based on a Christian foundation. By copying and preserving ancient texts, they also kept alive elements of ancient civilization.

During the Early Middle Ages, when cities were in decay, monasteries, whose libraries contained theological works and ancient Latin classics, were the principal cultural centers; they would remain so until the rebirth of towns in the High Middle Ages. Monasteries also offered succor to the sick and the destitute and served as places of refuge for travelers. To the medieval mind, the monks' and nuns' selfless devotion to God, adoption of apostolic poverty, and dedication to prayer and contemplation represented the highest expression of the Christian way of life; it was the finest and most certain path to salvation. It was not uncommon for both men and women, with old age or even death approaching, to take the vows so they might die as monks or nuns.

The Early Middle Ages were a formative period for the papacy, as well as for society in general. A decisive figure in the strengthening of the papacy was Gregory I, known as the Great (590–604). One of the ablest of medieval popes, Gregory used Roman methods of administration to organize papal property effectively in Italy, Sicily, Sardinia, Gaul, and other regions. He strengthened his authority over bishops and monks, dispatched missionaries to England to win over the Anglo-Saxons, and set his sights on an alliance with the Franks. Finally materializing 150 years later, this alliance helped shape medieval history.

The Kingdom of the Franks

From their homeland in the Rhine River valley, the Frankish tribes had expanded into Roman territory during the fourth and fifth centuries. The ruler Clovis united the various Frankish tribes and conquered most of Gaul. In 496, he converted to Roman Christianity. Clovis's conversion to Catholicism was an event of great significance. A number of other German kings had adopted the Arian form of Christianity, which the church had declared heretical. By embracing Roman Christianity, the Franks became a potential ally of the papacy.

Clovis's successors could not maintain control over their lands, and power passed to the mayor of the palace, the king's chief officer. Serving as mayor of the palace from 717 to 741, Charles Martel subjected all Frankish lands to his rule. In addition, at the battle of Tours in 732, he defeated the Muslims. Although the Muslims continued to occupy the Iberian Peninsula, they would advance no farther north into Europe.

Charles Martel was succeeded by his son Pepin the Short, who in 751 deposed the king. With the approval of the papacy and his nobles, Pepin was crowned king by Boniface, a prominent bishop. Two years later, Pope Stephen II anointed Pepin again as king of the Franks and appealed to him to protect the papacy from the Lombards, the last German tribe to invade formerly Roman territory. Pepin crossed into Italy, defeated the Lombards, and turned over captured lands to the papacy. This famous Donation of Pepin made the pope ruler of the territory between Rome and Ravenna, which became known as the Papal States.

The Era of Charlemagne

The alliance between the Franks and the papacy was continued by Pepin's successor, Charlemagne (Charles the Great), who ruled from 768 to 814. Charlemagne continued the Carolingian (the term refers to Charles Martel and his descendants) policy of expanding the Frankish kingdom. He destroyed the Lombard kingdom and declared himself king of the Lombards. He added Bavaria to his kingdom, and after long, terrible wars, he forced the Saxons to submit to his rule and convert to Christianity—thousands were beheaded when they were slow to choose between baptism or execution. He also conquered a region in northern Spain, the Spanish March, which served as a buffer between the Christian Franks and the Muslims in Spain.

Immense difficulties arose in governing the expanded territories. Size seemed an insuperable obstacle to effective government, particularly since Charlemagne's administrative structure, lacking in trained personnel, was primitive by Islamic, Byzantine, or Roman standards. The empire was divided into about 250 counties, administered by counts—nobles who were personally loyal to the ruler and who implemented the king's decisions.

On Christmas Day in Rome in the year 800, Pope Leo III crowned Charlemagne Emperor of the Romans. The title signified that the tradition of a world empire still survived, despite the demise of the Western Roman Empire three hundred years earlier. But because the pope crowned Charlemagne, the emperor now had a spiritual responsibility to spread and defend the faith. Thus, Roman universalism was fused with Christian universalism.

The Frankish empire, of course, was only a dim shadow of the Roman Empire. The Franks had no Roman law or Roman legions; there were no cities that were centers of economic and cultural activity; and officials were not trained civil servants with a world outlook but uneducated war chieftains with a tribal viewpoint. Yet Charlemagne's empire did embody the concept of a universal Christian empire—an ideal that would endure throughout the Middle Ages.

The crowning of a German ruler as emperor of the Romans by the head of the church represented the merging of German, Christian, and Roman traditions, which is the essential characteristic of medieval civilization. This blending of traditions was also evident on a cultural plane, for Charlemagne, a German warrior-king, showed respect for classical learning and Christianity, both non-Germanic traditions.

Charlemagne believed that it was his religious duty to raise the educational level of the clergy so that they understood and could properly teach the faith. He also fostered education to train administrators who would be capable of overseeing his empire and royal estates; such men had to be literate. He learned Latin and spoke it fluently. To achieve his purpose, Charlemagne gathered some of the finest scholars in Europe. Alcuin of York, England (735–804), was given charge of the palace school attended by Charlemagne and his family, high lords, and youths training to serve the emperor. Throughout Gaul, Alcuin expanded schools and libraries, promoted the copying of ancient manuscripts, and imposed basic literacy standards on the clergy.

The focus of the Carolingian Renaissance—the cultural revival produced by Charlemagne's teachers and scholars—was predominantly Christian: an effort to train clergymen and improve their understanding of the Bible and the writings of the church fathers. This process raised the level of literacy and improved the Latin style. Most important, monastic copyists continued to preserve ancient texts, which otherwise might never have survived. Between the fifth and eighth centuries, as libraries degenerated and books vanished or were burned, most classical literature was lost forever. The oldest surviving manuscripts of many Greek and Roman works are Carolingian copies.

Compared with the Greco-Roman past, with the cultural explosion of the twelfth and thirteenth centuries, or with the great Italian Renaissance of the fifteenth century, the Carolingian Renaissance seems slight indeed. But we must bear in mind the cultural poverty that prevailed before the era of Charlemagne. The Carolingian Renaissance reversed the process of cultural decay that characterized much of the Early Middle Ages. Learning would never again fall to the low level it had reached in the centuries following the decline of Rome.

During the era of Charlemagne, a distinct European civilization emerged. It blended the Roman heritage of a world empire, the intellectual achievement of the Greco-Roman mind, Christian otherworldliness, and the customs of the Germanic peoples. This nascent Western European civilization differed from Byzantine and Islamic civilizations, and Europeans were growing conscious of the difference. But the new medieval civilization was still centuries away from its high point, which would be reached in the twelfth and thirteenth centuries.

Charlemagne's empire also engendered the ideal of a unified Latin Christendom: a single Christian community under one government. Over the centuries, the pursuit of this ideal of a Christian world-state, Christendom, would inspire many people, both clergy and laity.

Map 6.1 **The Carolingian World** Resting more on the personal qualities of
Charlemagne than on any firm economic or political foundation, the Carolingian
empire did not survive the emperor's death in 814.

The Breakup of Charlemagne's Empire

After Charlemagne's death in 814, his son, Louis
the Pious, inherited the throne. Louis aimed to
preserve the empire, but the task was virtually
impossible. The empire's strength rested more
on Charlemagne's personal qualities than on
any firm economic or political foundation. In
particular, it never developed an empire-wide
system of taxation such as had supported the
Roman Empire for centuries. Moreover, the
empire was simply too large and consisted of too
many diverse peoples to be governed effectively.
Besides Frankish nobles, who sought to increase
their own power at the emperor's expense, Louis
had to deal with his own rebellious sons. After
Louis died in 840, the empire was divided among
the three surviving sons.

The Treaty of Verdun in 843 gave Louis the German the eastern part of the empire, which marked the beginning of Germany; to Charles the Bald went the western part, which was the start of France; and Lothair received the Middle Kingdom, which extended from Rome to the North Sea. This Middle Kingdom would be an area of conflict between France and Germany right into the twentieth century. As central authority waned, large landowners increasingly exercised authority in their own regions. Simultaneous invasions from all directions furthered this movement toward localism and decentralization.

In the ninth and tenth centuries, Latin Christendom was attacked on all sides. From bases in North Africa, Spain, and southern Gaul, Muslims ravaged regions of Southern Europe, even as far as the suburbs of Rome. They deported shiploads of Christians to the slave markets of North Africa. The Magyars, originally from western Asia, had established themselves on the plains of the Danube; their horsemen launched lightning raids into northern Italy, western Germany, and parts of France. Defeated in Germany in 933 and again in 955, the Magyars withdrew to what is now Hungary; they ceased their raids and adopted Christianity.

Still another group of invaders, the Northmen, or Vikings, sailed south from Scandinavia in their long, wooden ships to raid the coasts and river valleys of Western Europe. Villages were devastated, ports were destroyed, monasteries were plundered and their libraries set ablaze, and the population was decimated. Trade came to a standstill, coins no longer circulated, and farms turned into wastelands. Already gravely weakened, the European economy collapsed. The political authority of kings disappeared, and cultural life and learning withered.

These terrible attacks heightened political insecurity and accelerated anew the process of decentralization that had begun with the decline of Rome. During these chaotic times, counts came to regard as their own the land that they administered and defended for their king. At a time when monarchs could no longer guarantee the safety of their subjects, the inhabitants of a district looked on the count or local lord, frequently a former Carolingian official, as their ruler, for his men and fortresses protected them. In their regions, nobles exercised public power formerly held by kings. Europe had entered an age of feudalism, in which the essential unit of government was not a kingdom but a local region, and political power was the private possession of local lords.

FEUDAL SOCIETY

Arising during a period of collapsing central authority, invasion, scanty public revenues, and declining commerce and town life, feudalism attempted to provide some order and security. Feudalism was not a planned system derived logically from general principles, but rather an improvised response to the challenge posed by ineffectual central authority. Feudal practices were not uniform; they differed from locality to locality, and in some regions they barely took root. Although it was only a stopgap means of governing, feudalism did bring some order, justice, and law during an era of breakdown, localism, and transition. It remained the predominant political arrangement until kings reasserted their authority in the High and Late Middle Ages.

Vassalage

Feudal relationships enabled lords to increase their military strength. The need for military support was the principal reason for the practice of vassalage, in which a knight, in a solemn ceremony, pledged loyalty to a lord. This feature of feudalism derived from an ancient German ceremony, during which warriors swore personal allegiance to the head of the war-band. Among other things, the vassal gave military service to his lord and received in return a *fief,* which was usually land. This fief was inhabited by peasants, and the crops that they raised provided the vassal with his means of support.

Besides rendering military assistance and supplying knights, the vassal owed several other obligations to his lord in return for the fief and the lord's protection. These duties included sitting in the lord's court and judging cases, such as the breach of feudal agreements between the lord and his other vassals; providing lodgings when

Bishop Adalbero of Laon: The Tripartite Society

Medieval thinkers came to see their society as divided into three different but complementary groups: clergy, lords, and serfs. Each group had its own responsibilities—priests guided the souls of the faithful; lords protected society from its enemies; and the serfs' toil provided sustenance for everyone. Written in about 1020, the following statement by Bishop Adalbero of Laon, France, illustrates the tripartite nature of medieval society.

The community of the faithful is a single body, but the condition of society is threefold in order. For human law distinguishes two classes. Nobles and serfs, indeed, are not governed by the same ordinance. . . . The former are the warriors and the protectors of the churches. They are the defenders of the people, of both great and small, in short, of everyone, and at the same time they ensure their own safety. The other class is that of the serfs. This luckless breed possesses nothing except at the cost of its own labour. Who could, reckoning with an abacus, add up the sum of the cares with which the peasants are occupied, of their journeys on foot, of their hard labours? The serfs provide money, clothes, and food, for the rest; no free man could exist without serfs. Is there a task to be done? Does anyone want to put himself out? We see kings and prelates make themselves the serfs of their serfs; [but in truth] the master, who claims to feed his serf, is fed by him. And the serf never sees an end to his tears and his sighs. God's house, which we think of as one, is thus divided into three; some pray, others fight, and yet others work. The three groups, which coexist, cannot bear to be separated; the services rendered by one are a precondition for the labours of the two others; each in his turn takes it upon himself to relieve the whole. Thus the threefold assembly is none the less united, and it is thus that law has been able to triumph, and that the world has been able to enjoy peace.

Question for Analysis

1. According to Bishop Adalbero, what was the virtue of the tripartite society?

Jacques Le Goff, *Medieval Civilization*, trans. Julia Barrow (Blackwell, 1990), 255.

the lord traveled through the vassal's territory; offering a gift when the lord's son was knighted or when his eldest daughter married; and raising a ransom should the lord be captured by an enemy.

Generally, both lord and vassal felt honorbound to abide by the oath of loyalty. It became an accepted custom for a vassal to renounce his loyalty to his lord if the latter failed to protect the vassal from enemies, mistreated him, or increased his obligations as fixed by the feudal contract. On the other hand, if a vassal did not live up to his obligations, the lord would summon him to his court, where he would be tried for treachery. If found guilty, the vassal could lose his fief and perhaps his life. At times, disputes between vassals and lords erupted into warfare. Because a vassal often held land from more than one lord and sometimes was himself a lord to vassals, situations frequently became awkward, complex, and confusing. On occasion, a vassal had to decide to which lord he owed *liege homage* (prime loyalty).

As feudalism evolved, the king came to be regarded as the chief lord, who had granted fiefs to the great lords, who in turn had divided them into smaller units and regranted them to vassals. Thus, all members of the ruling class, from the lowliest knights to the king, occupied a place in the feudal hierarchy. In theory, the king was the highest political authority and the source of land tenure, but in actual fact he was often less powerful than many other nobles of the realm. Feudalism declined when kings converted their theoretical powers into actual powers. The decline of feudalism was a gradual process; conflict between the crown and the aristocracy persisted, with varying degrees of intensity, for several centuries, but the future belonged to the centralized state being shaped by kings, not to feudal fragmentation.

Feudal Warriors

Feudal lords viewed manual labor and commerce as degrading for men of their rank. They considered only one vocation worthy: that of warrior. Through combat, the lord demonstrated his valor, earned his reputation, measured his individual worth, derived excitement, added to his wealth, and defended his rights. Warfare gave meaning to his life. During the twelfth century, to relieve the boredom of peacetime, nobles staged gala tournaments in which knights, fighting singly (jousting) or in teams, engaged each other in battle to prove their skill and courage and to win honor. The feudal glorification of combat became deeply ingrained in Western society and endured into the twentieth century. Over the centuries, a code of behavior, called *chivalry,* evolved for the feudal nobility. A true knight was expected to fight bravely, demonstrate loyalty to his lord, and treat other knights with respect and courtesy.

In time, the church interjected a religious element into the warrior culture of the feudal knight. It sought to use the fighting spirit of the feudal class for Christian ends: knights could assist the clergy in enforcing God's will. Thus, a Christian component was added to the Germanic tradition of loyalty and courage. As a Christian gentleman, a knight was expected to honor the laws of the church and to wield his sword in the service of God.

Regarding the private warfare of lords as lawless violence that menaced social life, the church, in the eleventh century, imposed strictures called the Peace of God and the Truce of God. These restrictions limited feudal warfare to certain days of the week and certain times of the year. Although only partially effective, these religious restraints did offer Christian society some respite from plundering and incessant warfare.

Noblewomen

Feudal society was very much a man's world. In theory, women were deemed to be physically, morally, and intellectually inferior to men. Although the church taught that both men and women were precious to God and that marriage was a sacred rite, clergymen viewed women as evil temptresses who, like the biblical Eve, lured men into sin. Women were subjected to male authority. Fathers arranged the marriages of their daughters. Girls from aristocratic families were generally married at age sixteen or younger to men often twice their age; frequently, aristocratic girls who did not marry had to enter a convent. The wife of a lord was at the mercy of her

NOBLEWOMEN. At times, medieval ladies joined their husband's hunting party.

husband; if she annoyed him, she might expect a beating. But as the lady of the castle, she performed important duties. She assigned tasks to the servants; made medicines; preserved food; taught young girls how to sew, spin, and weave; and, despite her subordinate position, took charge of the castle when her husband was away.

The nunneries provided an outlet for the talents of unmarried noblewomen. Abbesses demonstrated organizational skills in supervising the convent's affairs. Some nuns acquired an education and, like their male counterparts, copied manuscripts and thus preserved the knowledge of the past. The nun Hroswitha (c. 935–c. 1001) of Gandersheim in Saxony, Germany, produced poetry, history, and plays. Inspired by the Roman poet Terence, she wrote six dramas—the first since Roman times—along with a history of German rulers and one of her own convent.

AGRARIAN SOCIETY

Feudalism was built on an economic foundation known as *manorialism*. Although pockets of free peasantry remained, a village community (manor) consisting of serfs bound to the land became the essential agricultural arrangement for much of the Middle Ages. The manorial village was the means of organizing an agricultural society with limited markets and money. Neither the lords who warred nor the clergy who prayed performed economically productive work. Their ways of life were made possible by the toil of serfs.

The origins of manorialism can be traced in part to the Late Roman Empire, when peasants depended on the owners of large estates for protection and security. This practice developed further during the Early Middle Ages, especially during the invasions of Northmen, Magyars, and Muslims in the ninth and tenth centuries. Peasants continued to sacrifice their freedom in exchange for protection; in some cases, they were too weak to resist the encroachments of local magnates. Like feudalism, manorialism was not an orderly system; it consisted of improvised relationships and practices that varied from region to region.

A lord controlled at least one manorial village; great lords might possess hundreds. A small manor had a dozen families; a large one had as many as fifty or sixty. The manorial village was never completely self-sufficient because salt, millstones, and metalware were generally obtained from outside sources. It did, however, constitute a balanced economic setting. Peasants grew grain and raised cattle, sheep, goats, and hogs; blacksmiths, carpenters, and stonemasons did the building and repairing; the village priest cared for the souls of the inhabitants; and the lord defended the manor and administered the customary law. The serf and his family lived in a dismal, one-room cottage that they shared with chickens and pigs. In the center burned a small fire, the smoke escaping through a hole in the roof. In cold weather when the fire was strong, the room was filled with smoke. When it rained, water came through the thatched roof and turned the earth floor into mud. The odor from animal excrement was ever present. Peasants were often held in contempt by lords, and medieval literature routinely depicted them as repulsive creatures—ugly, dirty, cowardly, and uncouth.

When a manor was attacked by another lord, the peasants found protection inside the walls of their lord's house. By the twelfth century, in many places, this building had become a well-fortified stone castle. Peasants generally lived, worked, and died on the lord's estate and were buried in the village churchyard. Few had any contact with the world beyond the village of their birth.

In return for protection and the right to cultivate fields and to pass these holdings on to their children, the serfs owed obligations to their lord, and their personal freedom was restricted in a variety of ways. Bound to the land, they could not leave the manor without the lord's consent. Before a serf could marry, he had to obtain the lord's permission and pay a fee. The lord could select a wife for his serf and force him to marry her. Sometimes, a serf, objecting to the lord's choice, preferred to pay a fine. These rules also applied to the serf's children, who inherited their parents' obligations. In addition to working their allotted land, the serfs had to tend the fields reserved for the lord. Other services exacted by the lord included digging ditches, gathering firewood, building fences, repairing roads and bridges, and sewing clothes. Probably somewhat more than half of a serf's workweek was devoted to fulfilling these labor obligations. Serfs also paid a variety of dues to the lord, including payments for using the lord's mill, bake-oven, and winepress.

Serfs did derive some benefits from manorial relationships. They received protection from brigands and warring nobles, and they possessed customary rights, which the lord generally respected, to cottages and farmlands. If a lord demanded more services or dues than was customary, or if he interfered with their right to cottages or strips of farmland, the peasants might demonstrate their discontent by refusing to labor for the lord. Until the fourteenth century, however, open rebellion was rare because lords possessed considerable military and legal power. The manorial system promoted attitudes of dependency and servility among the serfs; their hopes for a better life were directed toward heaven.

ECONOMIC EXPANSION DURING THE HIGH MIDDLE AGES

Manorialism and feudalism presupposed a hierarchical, organic, and stable social order: clergy who prayed, lords who fought, and peasants who toiled. People believed that society functioned smoothly when all individuals accepted their status and performed their proper role. Consequently, a person's rights, duties, and relationship to law depended on his or her ranking in the social order. To change position was to upset the organic unity of society. And no one, serfs included, should be deprived of the traditional rights associated with his or her rank. This arrangement was justified by the clergy, who maintained that "God himself has willed that among men, some must be lords and some serfs."[3]

During the High Middle Ages (1050–1300), however, the revival of an urban economy and the reemergence of central authority undermined feudal and manorial relationships. By the end of the eleventh century, Europe showed many signs of recovery. The invasions of Magyars and Vikings had ended, and powerful lords and kings imposed greater order in their territories. A period of economic vitality, the High Middle Ages witnessed an agricultural revolution, a commercial revolution, the rebirth of towns, and the rise of an enterprising and dynamic middle class.

An Agricultural Revolution

Important advances were made in agriculture during the Middle Ages. Many of these innovations occurred in the Early Middle Ages but were only gradually adopted and were not used everywhere. In time, however, they markedly increased production. By the end of the thirteenth century, medieval agriculture had reached a technical level far superior to that of the ancient world.

One innovation was a heavy plow that cut deeply into the soil. This new plow enabled farmers to work more quickly and effectively. As a result, they could cultivate more land, including the heavy, moist soils of northern Europe, which had offered too much resistance to the light plow. Another important advance in agricultural technology was the invention of the collar harness. The old yoke harness worked well with oxen, but it tended to choke horses—and horses, because they move faster and have greater stamina than oxen, are more valuable for agricultural work. The widening use of the water mill by the tenth century and the introduction of windmills in the twelfth century saved labor in grinding grain; these inventions replaced ancient hand-worked mills.

The gradual emergence of the three-field system of managing agricultural land, particularly in Northern Europe, increased production. In the old, widely used two-field system, half the land was planted in autumn with winter wheat, while the other half was left fallow to restore its fertility. In the new three-field system, one-third of the land was planted in autumn with winter wheat, a second third was planted the following spring with oats and vegetables, and the last third remained fallow. The advantages of the three-field system were that two-thirds of the land was farmed and only one-third left unused and that the diversification of crops made more vegetable protein available.

Greater agricultural production reduced the number of deaths from starvation and dietary disease and thus contributed to a population increase. Soon the farmlands of a manorial village could not support its growing population. Consequently, peasants had to look beyond their immediate surroundings and colonize trackless wastelands. Lords vigorously promoted this conversion of uncultivated soil into agricultural land because it increased their incomes. Monastic communities also actively engaged in this enterprise. Almost everywhere, peasants were draining swamps, clearing forests, and establishing new villages. Their endeavors during the eleventh and twelfth centuries brought vast areas of Europe under cultivation for the first time. New agricultural land was also acquired through expansion, the most notable example being the organized settlement of lands to the east by German colonists.

The colonizing and cultivation of virgin lands contributed to the decline of serfdom. Lords owned vast tracts of forests and swamps that would substantially increase their incomes if cleared, drained, and farmed. But serfs were often unwilling to move from their customary homes and fields to do the hard labor needed to cultivate these new lands. To lure serfs away from their villages, lords promised them freedom from most or all personal services. In many cases, the settlers fulfilled their obligations to the lord by paying rent rather than by performing services or providing foodstuffs, thus making the transition from serfs to freemen. In time, they came to regard the land as their own.

The improvement in agricultural technology and the colonization of new lands altered the conditions of life in Europe. Surplus food and the increase in population freed people to work at non-farming occupations, making possible the expansion of trade and the revival of town life.

The Revival of Trade

Expanding agricultural production, the end of Viking attacks, greater political stability, the growth of a considerable money supply, and an increasing population brought about a revival of commerce. During the Early Middle Ages, Italians and Jews kept alive a small amount of long-distance trade between Catholic Europe and the Byzantine and Islamic worlds. In the eleventh century, sea forces of Italian trading cities cleared the Mediterranean of Muslim fleets that preyed on Italian shipping. As in Roman times, goods could circulate once again from one end of the sea to the other. In the twelfth and thirteenth centuries, local, regional, and long-distance trade gained such momentum that some historians describe the period as a commercial revolution that surpassed the commercial activity of the Roman Empire during the Pax Romana. A class of traders emerged, many of them former serfs who started by taking to the road as humble peddlers. Gradually they acquired business contacts in other lands, know-how, and ambition.

Crucial to the growth of trade were international fairs, where merchants and craftspeople set up stalls and booths to display their wares. Because of ever-present robbers, lords provided protection for merchants carrying their wares to and from fairs. Each fair lasted about three to six weeks; then the merchants would move on to another site. The Champagne region in northeastern France was the great center for fairs because the count of Champagne provided protection for merchants both en route and at the fair; judges to guarantee the enforcement of contracts; and the necessary equipment, including covered stalls and accurate scales.

The principal arteries of trade flowed between the eastern Mediterranean and the Italian cities; between Scandinavia and the Atlantic coast; between northern France, Flanders, and England; and from the Baltic Sea in the north to the Black Sea and Constantinople via Russian rivers.

Increased economic activity led to advances in business techniques. Since individual merchants often lacked sufficient capital for large-scale enterprises, groups of merchants formed partnerships. By enabling merchants to pool their capital, reduce their risks, and expand their knowledge of profit-making opportunities, these arrangements furthered commerce. Underwriters insured cargoes; the development of banking and credit instruments made it unnecessary for merchants to carry large amounts of cash. Italian businessmen, taking advantage of the income derived from trade and their numerous business contacts in several lands, pioneered in the growth of banking practices, particularly access to credit that could finance the construction of large trading ships and trading expeditions. The accumulation of capital and the emergence of banking institutions provided a stimulus for the growth of capitalism. The international fairs not only were centers of international trade, but also served as capital markets for international credit transactions. The arrangements made by fair-going merchants to settle their debts were the origin of the bill of exchange, which allowed one currency to be converted into another. The invention of double-entry bookkeeping gave merchants an overview of their financial situation: the value of their goods and their ready cash. Without such knowledge, no large-scale commercial activity could be conducted on a continuous basis. Another improvement in business techniques was the formation of commercial law, which defined the rules of conduct for debts and contracts.

The Rebirth of Towns

In the eleventh century, towns emerged anew throughout Europe, and in the twelfth, they became active centers of commercial and intellectual life. Towns were a new and revolutionary force—socially, economically, and culturally. A new class of merchants and craftspeople came into being. This new class—the middle class—was made up of those who, unlike the lords and serfs, were not affiliated with the land. The townsman was a new man, with a different value system from that of the lord, the serf, and the clergyman.

One reason for town growth was the increased food supply stemming from advances in agricultural technology. Surplus farm production meant that the countryside could support an urban population of artisans and professionals. Another reason for the rise of urban centers was the expansion of trade. Towns emerged in locations that were natural for trade: seacoasts, riverbanks, crossroads, and market sites; they also sprang up outside fortified castles and monasteries and on surviving Roman sites. The colonies of merchants who gathered at these places were joined by peasants skilled in crafts or willing to work as laborers. Most towns had a small population. The largest ones—Florence, Ghent, and Paris—had between fifty thousand and a hundred thousand inhabitants. Covering only small areas, these walled towns were crowded with people.

Merchants and artisans organized guilds to protect their members from outside competition. The merchant guild in a town prevented outsiders from doing much business. A craftsman new to a town had to be admitted to the guild of his trade before he could open a shop. Competition between members of the same guild was discouraged. To prevent one guild member from making significantly more money than another, a guild required its members to work the same number of hours, pay employees the same wages, produce goods of equal quality, and charge customers a just price. These rules were strictly enforced.

Women took an active part in the economic life of towns, working with men, usually their husbands, in the various crafts—as cobblers, tailors, hatters, bakers, goldsmiths, and so forth. Women brewed beer; made and sold charcoal; sold vegetables, fish, and poultry; and ran inns. In many towns, the wives and widows of master craftsmen were admitted to guilds. These guildswomen had many of the privileges of a master, including the right to train apprentices.

Because many towns were situated on land belonging to lords or on the sites of old Roman towns ruled by bishops, these communities at first came under feudal authority. In some instances, lords encouraged the founding of towns, for urban industry and commerce brought wealth to the region. However, tensions soon developed between merchants, who sought freedom from feudal restrictions since they interfered with the pursuit of financial gain, and lords and bishops, who wanted to preserve their authority over the towns. Townspeople, or burghers, refused to be treated as serfs bound to a lord and liable for personal services and customary dues. The burghers wanted to travel, trade, marry, and dispose of their property as they pleased; they wanted to make their own laws and levy their own taxes. Sometimes by fighting, but more often by payments of money, the townspeople obtained charters from the lords giving them the right to set up their own governing councils. These assemblies passed laws, collected taxes, and formed courts that enforced the laws. Towns became more or less self-governing municipalities, the first since Greco-Roman days.

In a number of ways, towns loosened the hold of lords on serfs. Seeking freedom and fortune, serfs fled to the new towns, where, according to custom, lords could no longer reclaim them after a year and a day. Enterprising serfs earned money by selling food to the townspeople. When they acquired a sufficient sum, they bought their freedom from lords, who needed cash to pay for goods bought from merchants. Lords increasingly began to accept fixed cash payments from serfs in place of labor services or foodstuffs. As serfs met their obligations to lords with money, they gradually became rent-paying tenants and, in time, were no longer bound to the lord's land. The manorial system of personal relations and mutual obligations was disintegrating.

The activities of townspeople made them a new breed; they engaged in business and had money and freedom. Their world was the market rather than the church, the castle, or the manor. Townspeople were freeing themselves from the prejudices both of feudal aristocrats, who considered trade and manual work degrading, and of the clergy, who cursed the pursuit of riches as sordid, shameful, and an obstacle to salvation. The townspeople were critical, dynamic, and progressive—a force for change. Medieval towns nurtured the origins of the *bourgeoisie* (literally, "citizens of the burg," the walled town), the urban middle class, which would play a crucial role in modern European history.

THE RISE OF STATES

The revival of trade and the growth of towns were signs of the vitality of Latin Christendom. Another sign of strength was the greater order and security provided by the emergence of states. Aided by educated and trained officials who enforced royal law, tried people in royal courts, and collected royal taxes—all serving to reduce the power of local lords—kings expanded their territory and slowly fashioned strong central governments. These developments laid the foundations of European states. Not all areas followed the same pattern. Whereas England and France achieved a large measure of unity during the Middle Ages, Germany and Italy remained divided into numerous independent territories.

England

In 1066, the Normans—those Northmen who had first raided and then settled in France—conquered Anglo-Saxon England. Normans replaced the Anglo-Saxon aristocracy and ecclesiastical hierarchy. Determined to establish effective control over his new kingdom, William the Conqueror (1027–1087), duke of Normandy, kept a sixth of conquered England for himself. In accordance with feudal practice, he distributed the rest among his Norman nobles, who swore an oath of loyalty to William and provided him with military assistance. But William made certain that no feudal baron had enough land or soldiers to threaten his power. Because he had conquered England in one stroke, his successors did not have to travel the long, painful road to national unity that French monarchs had to take.

To strengthen royal control, William retained some Anglo-Saxon administrative practices. The land remained divided into *shires* (counties) administered by *sheriffs* (royal agents). This structure gave the king control over local government. To determine how much money he could demand, William ordered a vast census to be taken of people and property in every village. These data were compiled in the *Domesday Book,* which listed the number of tenants, cattle, sheep, and pigs and the quantities of farm equipment throughout the realm. Thus, William knew his kingdom's assets better than any other monarch of his day.

A crucial development in shaping national unity was the emergence of common law. During the reigns of Henry I (1100–1135) and Henry II (1154–1189), royal judges traveled to different parts of the kingdom. Throughout England, important cases began to be tried in the king's court rather than in local courts, thereby increasing royal power. The decisions of royal judges were recorded and used as guides for future cases. In this way, a law common to the whole land gradually came to prevail over the customary law of a specific locality. Because common law applied to all England, it served as a force for unity. It also provided a fairer system of justice. Common law remains the foundation of the English legal system and the legal systems of lands settled by English people, including the United States.

Henry II made trial by jury a regular procedure for many cases heard in the king's court, thus laying the foundations of the modern judicial system. Twelve men familiar with the facts of the case appeared before the king's justices and were asked under oath if the plaintiff's statement was true.

The justices based their decisions on the answers. Henry II also ordered representatives of a given locality to report under oath to visiting royal judges any local persons who were suspected of murder or robbery. This indictment jury was the ancestor of the modern grand jury system.

King John (1199–1216) inadvertently precipitated a situation that led to another step in the political development of England. Fighting a costly and losing war with the king of France, John coerced his vassals into giving him more and more revenue; he had also punished some vassals without a proper trial. In 1215, the angry barons rebelled and compelled John to fix his seal to a document called the *Magna Carta,* or Great Charter. The Magna Carta is celebrated as the root of the uniquely English respect for basic rights and liberties. Although essentially a feudal document directed against a king who had violated the rights of feudal barons, the Magna Carta stated certain principles that could be interpreted more broadly.

Over the centuries, these principles were expanded to protect the liberties of the English against governmental oppression. The Magna Carta stated that no unusual feudal dues "shall be imposed in our kingdom except by the common consent of our kingdom." In time, this right came to mean that the king could not levy taxes without the consent of Parliament, the governmental body that represents the English people. The Magna Carta also provided that "no freeman shall be taken or imprisoned . . . save by the lawful judgment of his peers or by the law of the land." The barons who drew up the document had intended it to mean that they must be tried by fellow barons. As time passed, these words were regarded as a guarantee of trial by jury for all men, a prohibition against arbitrary arrest, and a command to dispense justice fully, freely, and equally. Implied in the Magna Carta is the idea that the king cannot rule as he pleases but must govern according to the law—that not even the king can violate the law of the nation. Centuries afterward, when Englishmen sought to limit the king's power, they would interpret the Magna Carta in this way.

Anglo-Saxon England had retained the Germanic tradition that the king should consider the advice of the leading men in the land. Later, William the Conqueror continued this practice by seeking the opinions of leading nobles and bishops. In the thirteenth century, it became accepted custom that the king should not decide major issues without consulting these advisers, who assembled in the Great Council. Lesser nobility and townspeople also began to be summoned to meet with the king. These two groups were eventually called the House of Lords (bishops and nobles) and the House of Commons (knights and burghers). Thus, the English Parliament evolved; by the mid-fourteenth century, it had become a permanent institution of government. Frequently in need of money but unable to levy new taxes without the approval of Parliament, the king had to turn to that body for help. Over the centuries, Parliament would use this control over money matters to increase its power. The tradition grew that the power to govern rested not with the king alone, but with the king and Parliament together.

During the Middle Ages, England became a centralized and unified state. The king, however, did not have unlimited power; he was not above the law. The rights of the people were protected by certain principles implicit in the common law and the Magna Carta and by the emergence of Parliament.

France

In the 150 years after Charlemagne's death, the western part of his empire, which was destined to become France, faced terrible ordeals. Charlemagne's heirs fought one another for the crown; the Vikings raided everywhere their ships would carry them; Muslims from Spain plundered the southern coast; and strong lords usurped power for themselves. With the Carolingian family unable to maintain the throne, the great lords bestowed the title of king on one of their own. In 987, they chose Hugh Capet (987–996), the count of Paris. Because many great lords held territories far larger than those of Hugh, the French king did not seem a threat to noble power. But Hugh strengthened the French monarchy by having the lords also elect his son as his coruler. This practice continued until it became understood that the crown would remain with the Capetian family.

With the accession of Louis VI (1108–1137), a two-hundred-year period of steadily increasing royal power began. Louis started this trend by successfully subduing the barons in his own duchy. A decisive figure in the expansion of royal power was Philip Augustus (1180–1223). Philip struck successfully at King John of England (of Magna Carta fame), who held more territory as feudal lord in France than Philip did. When William, duke of Normandy in western France, conquered England in 1066, he became ruler of England and Normandy; William's great-grandson Henry II acquired much of southern France through his marriage to Eleanor of Aquitaine (c. 1122–1204) in 1152. Thus, as a result of the Norman Conquest and intermarriage, the destinies of France and England were closely intertwined until the end of the Middle Ages. By stripping King John of most of his French territory (Normandy, Anjou, and much of Aquitaine), Philip trebled the size of his kingdom and became stronger than any French lord.

In the thirteenth century, the power of the French monarch continued to grow. Departing from feudal precedent, Louis IX (1226–1270) issued ordinances for the entire realm without seeking the consent of his vassals. Kings added to their lands through warfare and marriage. They also devised new ways of raising money, including taxing the clergy. A particularly effective way of increasing the monarch's power was by extending royal justice; many cases previously tried in lords' courts were transferred to the king's court.

At the beginning of the fourteenth century, Philip IV (the Fair) engaged in a struggle with the papacy. Seeking to demonstrate that he had the support of his subjects, Philip convened a national assembly—the Estates General—representing the clergy, the nobility, and the townspeople. This assembly would be called again to vote funds for the crown. But unlike the English Parliament, the Estates General never became an important body in French political life, and it never succeeded in controlling the monarch. Whereas the basis for limited monarchy had been established in England, no comparable checks on the king's power developed in France. By the end of the Middle Ages, French kings had succeeded in creating a unified state. But regional and local loyalties remained strong and persisted for centuries.

Germany

After the destruction of Charlemagne's empire, its German territories were broken into large duchies. Following an ancient German practice, the ruling dukes elected one of their own as king. The German king, however, had little authority outside his own duchy. Some German kings tried not to antagonize the dukes, but Otto the Great (936–973) was determined to control them. He entered into an alliance with German bishops and archbishops, who could provide him with fighting men and trained administrators—a policy continued by his successors. In 962, emulating the coronation of Charlemagne, the pope crowned Otto "Emperor of the Romans." (Later the title would be changed to Holy Roman Emperor.)

Otto and his successors wanted to dominate Italy and the pope—an ambition that embroiled the Holy Roman Emperor in a life-and-death struggle with the papacy. The papacy allied itself with the German dukes and the Italian cities, enemies of the emperor. The intervention in papal and Italian politics was the principal reason why German territories did not achieve unity in the Middle Ages.

THE GROWTH OF PAPAL POWER

In the High Middle Ages, a growing religious vitality accompanied the economic recovery and increased political stability. It was marked by several developments. Within the church, reform movements attacked clerical abuses, the papacy increased its power, and a holy war against the Muslims drew the Christian community closer together. Furthermore, the church tried with great determination to make society follow divine standards—that is, it tried to shape all institutions and cultural expressions according to a comprehensive Christian outlook.

As the sole interpreters of God's revelation and the sole ministers of his sacraments—sacred rites—the clergy imposed and supervised the moral standards of Christendom. Divine grace was channeled through the sacraments, which could be administered only by the clergy, the indispensable intermediary between the individual and God. On those who resisted its authority, the church could impose the penalty of excommunication—expulsion from the church and denial of the sacraments, without which there could be no salvation.

Gregorian Reform

By the tenth century, the church was Western Europe's leading landholder, owning perhaps a third of the land in Italy and vast properties in other lands. However, the papacy was in no position to exercise commanding leadership over Latin Christendom. The office of pope had fallen under the domination of aristocratic families; they conspired and on occasion murdered in order to place one of their own on the wealthy and powerful throne of Saint Peter. As the papacy became a prize for Rome's leading families, it was not at all unusual for popes themselves to be involved in conspiracies and assassinations. Also weakening the authority of the papacy were local lords, who dominated churches and monasteries by appointing bishops and abbots and by collecting the income from church taxes. These bishops and abbots, appointed by lords for political reasons, lacked the spiritual devotion to maintain high standards of discipline among the priests and monks.

What raised the power of the papacy to unprecedented heights was the emergence of a reform movement, particularly in French and German monasteries. High-minded monks called for a reawakening of spiritual fervor and the elimination of moral laxity among the clergy. They particularly denounced the concern for worldly goods, the taking of mistresses, and the diminishing commitment to the Benedictine rule. Of the many monasteries that took part in this reform movement, the Benedictine monks of Cluny, in Burgundy, France, were the most influential.

In the middle of the eleventh century, popes came under the influence of the monastic reformers. In 1059, a special synod, convened by the reform-minded Pope Nicholas II, moved to end the interference of Roman nobles and German Holy Roman Emperors in choosing the pope. Henceforth, a select group of clergymen in Rome, called *cardinals,* would be responsible for picking a new pontiff.

The reform movement found its most zealous exponent in the person of Hildebrand, who became Pope Gregory VII in 1073. Gregory insisted that human society was part of a divinely ordered universe governed by God's universal law, and as the supreme spiritual leader of Christendom the pope was charged with the mission of establishing a Christian society on earth. As successor to Saint Peter, the pope had the final word on matters of faith and doctrine. All bishops came under his authority; so too did kings, whose powers should be used for Christian ends. Disobeying the pope, God's viceroy on earth, constituted disobedience to God himself. The pope was responsible for instructing rulers in the proper use of their God-given powers, and kings had a solemn duty to obey these instructions. If the king failed in his Christian duty, the pope could deny him his right to rule. Responsible for implementing God's law, the pope could never take a subordinate position to kings.

Like no other pope before him, Gregory VII made a determined effort to assert the preeminence of the papacy over both the church hierarchy and secular rulers. This determination led to a bitter struggle between the papacy and the German monarch and future Holy Roman Emperor Henry IV. The dispute was a dramatic confrontation between two competing versions of the relationship between secular and spiritual authority.

Through his reforms, Gregory VII intended to improve the moral quality of the clergy and to liberate the church from all control by secular authorities. He forbade priests who had wives or concubines to celebrate Mass, deposed clergy who had bought their offices, excommunicated bishops and abbots who had received their estates from a lay lord, and expelled from the church lay lords who invested bishops with their office. The appointment of bishops, Pope Gregory insisted, should be controlled by the church.

This last point touched off the conflict, called the Investiture Controversy, between King Henry and Pope Gregory. Bishops served a dual function. On the one hand, they belonged to the spiritual community of the church; on the other, as members of the nobility and holders of estates, they were also integrated into the feudal order. Traditionally, emperors had both granted bishops their feudal authority and invested them with their spiritual authority. In maintaining that no lay rulers could confer ecclesiastical offices on their appointees, Pope Gregory threatened Henry's authority.

In earlier times, seeking allies in the conflict with feudal nobility, German kings had made vassals of the upper clergy. In return for a fief, bishops had agreed to provide troops for a monarch in his struggle against the lords. But if kings had no control over the appointment of bishops—in accordance with Pope Gregory's view—they would lose the allegiance, military support, and financial assistance of their most important allies. To German monarchs, bishops were officers of the state who served the throne. Moreover, if they agreed to Gregory's demands, German kings would lose their freedom of action and be dominated by the Roman pontiff. Henry IV regarded Gregory VII as a fanatic who trampled on custom, meddled in German state affairs, and challenged legitimate rulers established by God, thereby threatening to subordinate kingship to the papacy.

With the approval of the German bishops, Henry called for Pope Gregory to descend from the throne of Saint Peter. Gregory in turn excommunicated Henry and deposed him as king. German lands were soon embroiled in a civil war, as German lords used the quarrel to strike at Henry's power. Finally, Henry's troops crossed the Alps, successfully attacked Rome, and installed a new pope, who crowned Henry Emperor of the Romans. Gregory died in exile in 1085.

In 1122, the papacy and Emperor Henry V reached a compromise. Bishops were to be elected exclusively by the church and invested with the staff and the ring—symbols of spiritual power—by the archbishop, not the king. This change signified that the bishop owed his role as spiritual leader to the church only. But the king would grant the bishop the scepter, to indicate that the bishop was also the recipient of a fief and the king's vassal, owing feudal obligations to the crown. This compromise, called the Concordat of Worms, recognized the dual function of the bishop as a spiritual leader in the church and a feudal landowner. Similar settlements had been reached with the kings of France and England several years earlier.

The conflict between the papacy and the German rulers continued after the Concordat of Worms—a contest for supremacy between the heir of Saint Peter and the heir of Charlemagne.

German monarchs wanted to control the papacy and the prosperous northern Italian cities. When Frederick I (1152–1190), known as Frederick Barbarossa (Red Beard), tried to assert authority over these cities, they resisted. In 1176, the armies of an alliance of Italian cities, supported by the pope, trounced Frederick's forces at the battle of Legnano. The Italian infantry showed that it could defeat knights on horseback, and Frederick was compelled to recognize the independence of the Italian cities. His numerous expeditions to Italy weakened his authority. German princes strengthened themselves at the expense of the monarchy, thereby continuing to preclude German unity.

The Crusades

Like the movement for spiritual renewal associated with the Cluniac reformers, the Crusades—wars to regain the Holy Land from the Muslims—were an outpouring of Christian zeal and an attempt by the papacy to assert its preeminence. Along with the renewal of commerce and the growth of towns, the Crusades signaled the increased vitality and self-confidence of Western Europe. The victims of earlier Muslim attacks, Latin Christians now took the offensive.

The Crusades were also part of a general movement of expansion that took place in Europe during the High Middle Ages. By the middle of the eleventh century, Genoese and Pisans had driven the Muslims from Sardinia. By 1091, Normans from France had taken Sicily from the Muslims and southern Italy from Byzantium. With the support of the papacy, Christian knights engaged in the long struggle to drive the Muslims from Spain; by 1248, after more than two centuries of conflict, only the small southern kingdom of Granada remained in Muslim hands. Germans conquered and colonized lands south of the Baltic coast inhabited by non-Christian Slavs, Balts, and Prussians. German settlers brought with them Christianity and German language and culture. They cleared vast tracts of virgin land for farming and established towns, bishoprics, and monasteries in a region where urban life had been virtually unknown.

Seeking to regain lands taken from Byzantium by the Seljuk Turks, the Byzantine emperor Alexius appealed to the West for mercenaries.

Pope Urban II, at the Council of Clermont (in France) in 1095, exaggerated the danger confronting Eastern Christianity and called for a holy crusade against the heathen Turks, whom he accused of defiling and destroying Christian churches. A Christian army, mobilized by the papacy to defend the faith and to regain the Holy Land from nonbelievers, accorded with the papal concept of a just war; it would channel the endemic violence of Europe's warrior class in a Christian direction.

What motivated the knights and others who responded to Urban's appeal? No doubt the Crusaders regarded themselves as armed pilgrims dedicated to rescuing holy places from the hated Muslims. Moreover, Urban declared that participation in a crusade was itself an act of penance, an acceptable way of demonstrating sorrow for sin. To the warrior nobility, a crusade was a great adventure promising land, glory, and plunder, but it was also an opportunity to remit sins by engaging in a holy war. The enthusiasm with which knights became Christian warriors revealed the extent to which Christian principles had permeated the warrior mentality of the nobles.

Stirred by popular preachers, the common people also became gripped by the crusading spirit. The most remarkable of the evangelists was Peter the Hermit. Swayed by this old man's eloquence, thousands of poor people abandoned their villages and joined Peter's march to Jerusalem. After reaching Constantinople, Peter's recruits crossed into Turkish territory, where they were massacred.

An army of Christian knights also departed from Constantinople. In June 1099, three years after leaving Europe, this army stood outside the walls of Jerusalem. Using siege weapons, it broke into the city and slaughtered the Muslim and Jewish inhabitants. Besides capturing Jerusalem, the Crusaders carved out four principalities in the Near East.

Never resigned to the establishment of Christian states in their midst, Muslim leaders called for a jihad, or holy war. In 1144, one of the Crusader states, the County of Edessa, fell to the resurgent forces of Islam. Alarmed by the loss of Edessa, Pope Eugenius II called for the Second Crusade, which was a complete failure.

After 1174, Saladin, a brilliant commander, became the most powerful leader in the Muslim Near East. In 1187, he invaded Palestine, annihilating a Christian army near Nazareth and recapturing Jerusalem. This led to the Third Crusade, in which some of Europe's most prominent rulers took part—Richard I, the Lion-Hearted, of England; Philip Augustus of France; and Frederick Barbarossa of Germany. The Crusaders captured Acre and Jaffa, but Jerusalem remained in Muslim hands.

Pope Innocent III, who called the Fourth Crusade (1202–1204), was enraged by the actions of the Crusaders. They had first attacked the Christian port of Zara, controlled by the king of Hungary, and then looted and defiled churches and massacred Byzantines in Constantinople. This shameful behavior, along with the belief that the papacy was exploiting the crusading ideal to extend its own power, weakened both the crusading zeal of Christendom and the moral authority of the papacy. Other Crusades followed, but the position of the Christian states in the Near East continued to deteriorate. In 1291, almost two centuries after Pope Urban's appeal, the last Christian strongholds in the Near East fell.

The Crusades increased the wealth of the Italian cities that furnished transportation for the Crusaders and benefited from the increased trade with the East. They may have contributed to the decline of feudalism and the strengthening of monarchy because many lords were killed in battle or squandered their wealth financing expeditions to the Holy Land. The Crusades sparked an interest in geography and travel; introduced westerners to new foods, clothing, and architecture; and became a theme in literature. Nevertheless, they did not significantly influence European intellectual progress. The Crusaders had no contact with Muslim centers of learning in the Near East; it was through Spain and Sicily that Muslim learning penetrated Latin Christendom and helped stimulate the cultural awakening of the twelfth and thirteenth centuries. Over the centuries, some have praised the Crusades for inspiring idealism and heroism. Others, however, have castigated the movement for corrupting the Christian spirit and unleashing religious intolerance and fanaticism—including the massacre of Jews in the Rhineland and of Muslims and Jews in Jerusalem—that would lead to strife in future centuries. The Crusades remain a crucial component of the ideology of contemporary Islamic extremists.

Dissenters and Reformers

Freedom of religion is a modern concept; it was totally alien to the medieval outlook. Regarding itself as the possessor and guardian of divine truth, the church felt a profound obligation to purge Christendom of heresy—beliefs that challenged Christian orthodoxy. To the church, heretics had committed treason against God and were carriers of a deadly infection. Heresy was the work of Satan; lured by false ideas, people might abandon the true faith and deny themselves salvation. In the eyes of the church, heretics not only obstructed individual salvation but also undermined the foundations of society.

To compel obedience, the church used its power of excommunication. An excommunicated person could not receive the sacraments or attend church services—fearful punishments in an age of faith. In dealing with a recalcitrant ruler, the church could declare an interdict on his territory, which in effect denied the ruler's subjects the sacraments (although exceptions could be made). The church hoped that the pressure exerted by an aroused populace would compel the offending ruler to mend his ways.

The church also conducted heresy trials. Before the thirteenth century, local bishops were responsible for finding heretics and putting them on trial. In 1233, the papacy established the Inquisition, a court specially designed to fight heresy. The accused were presumed guilty until proven innocent; they were not told the names of their accusers, nor could they have legal defense. To wrest a confession from the accused, torture (which had been sanctioned by Roman law) was permitted. Those who persisted in their beliefs might be turned over to the civil authorities to be burned at the stake.

The Waldensians. Religious dissent in the Middle Ages was often reformist in character. Inspired by the Gospels, reformers criticized the church for its wealth and involvement in worldly affairs. They called for a return to the simpler, purer life of Jesus and the Apostles.

In their zeal to emulate the moral purity and material poverty of the first followers of Jesus, these reform-minded dissenters attacked ecclesiastical authority. The Waldensians, followers of Peter Waldo, a rich merchant of Lyons, were a case in point. In the 1170s, Peter distributed his property to the poor and attracted both male and female supporters. Like their leader, the Waldensians committed themselves to poverty and to preaching the Gospel in the vernacular, or native tongue, rather than in the church's Latin, which many Christians did not understand.

The Waldensians considered themselves true Christians, faithful to the spirit of the apostolic church. Repelled by Waldensian attacks against the immorality of the clergy and by the fact that these laypeople were preaching the Gospel without the permission of ecclesiastical authorities, the church condemned the movement as heretical. Despite persecution, however, the Waldensians continued to survive as a group in northern Italy.

The Cathari. Catharism was the most radical heresy to confront the medieval church. This belief represented a curious mixture of Eastern religious movements that had competed with Christianity in the days of the Roman Empire. Cathari tenets differed considerably from those of the church. The Cathari believed in an eternal conflict between the forces of the god of good and those of the god of evil. Because the evil god, whom they identified with the God of the Old Testament, had created the world, this earthly home was evil. The soul, spiritual in nature, was good, but it was trapped in wicked flesh.

The Cathari taught that, since the flesh is evil, Christ would not have taken a human form; hence, he could not have suffered on the cross or have been resurrected. Nor could God have issued forth from the evil flesh of the Virgin. According to Catharism, Jesus was not God but an angel. In order to enslave people, the evil god created the church, which demonstrated its wickedness by pursuing power and wealth. Repudiating the church, the Cathari organized their own ecclesiastical hierarchy.

The center for the Catharist heresy was southern France, where a strong tradition of protest against the moral laxity and materialism of the clergy existed. When the Cathari did not submit to peaceful persuasion, Innocent III called on kings and lords to exterminate Catharism with the sword before the infection spread throughout Europe. Lasting from 1208 to 1229, the war against the Cathari was marked by brutality and fanaticism. Under Innocent's successor, Dominican and Franciscan inquisitors completed the task of exterminating them virtually to the last person, a horrendous slaughter that some refer to as medieval genocide.

The Franciscans and the Dominicans. Driven by a zeal for reform, devout laypeople condemned the clergy for moral abuses. Sometimes their piety and resentment exploded into heresy; at other times, it was channeled into movements that served the church. Such was the case with the two great orders of friars, the Franciscans and the Dominicans.

Like Peter Waldo, Saint Francis of Assisi (c. 1181–1226) came from a wealthy merchant family. After undergoing an intense religious experience, Francis abandoned his possessions and devoted his life to imitating Christ. Dressed as a beggar, he wandered into villages and towns, preaching, healing, and befriending the poor, the helpless, the sick, and even lepers, whom everyone feared to approach. The saintly Francis soon attracted disciples, called Little Brothers, who followed in their leader's footsteps.

As the Franciscans grew in popularity, the papacy exercised greater control over their activities. In time, the order was transformed from a spontaneous movement of inspired laymen into an organized agent of papal policy. The Franciscans served the church as teachers and missionaries in Eastern Europe, North Africa, the Near East, and China. The papacy set aside Francis's prohibition against the Brothers owning churches, houses, and lands corporately. His desire to keep the movement a lay order was abandoned when the papacy granted the Brothers the right to hear confession. Francis's opposition to formal learning as irrelevant to preaching Gospel love was rejected when the movement began to urge university education for its members. Those who protested against these changes as a repudiation of Francis's spirit were persecuted, and a few were even burned at the stake as heretics.

The Dominican order was founded by Saint Dominic (c. 1170–1221), a Spanish nobleman who had preached against the Cathari in southern France. Believing that those who were well versed in Christian teaching could best combat heresy, Dominic, unlike Francis, insisted that his followers engage in study. Eventually, the Dominicans became some of the leading theologians in the universities. Like the Franciscans, they went out into the world to preach the Gospel and to proselytize. Dominican friars became the chief operators of the Inquisition. For their zeal in fighting heresy, they were known as the hounds of the Lord.

Innocent III: The Apex of Papal Power

During the pontificate of Innocent III (1198–1216), papal theocracy reached its zenith. More than any earlier pope, Innocent made the papacy the center of European political life; in the tradition of Gregory VII, he forcefully asserted the theory of papal monarchy. As head of the church, Vicar of Christ, and successor of Saint Peter, Innocent claimed the authority to intervene in the internal affairs of secular rulers when they threatened the good order of Christendom. According to Innocent, the pope, "lower than God but higher than man . . . judges all and is judged by no one."[4]

Innocent applied these principles of papal supremacy in his dealings with the princes of Europe. When King Philip Augustus of France repudiated Ingeborg of Denmark the day after their wedding and later divorced her to marry someone else, Innocent placed an interdict on France to compel Philip to take Ingeborg back. For two decades, Innocent III championed Ingeborg's cause, until she finally became the French queen. When King John of England rejected the papal candidate for archbishop of Canterbury, Stephen Langton, Innocent first laid an interdict on the country. Then he excommunicated John, who expressed his defiance by confiscating church property and by forcing many bishops into exile. However, when Innocent urged Philip Augustus of France to invade England, John backed down.

Innocent called the Fourth Crusade against the Muslims and a crusade against the heretical Cathari. The culminating expression of Innocent's supremacy was the Fourth Lateran Council, convened in 1215. Comprising some twelve hundred clergy and representatives of secular rulers, the council issued several far-reaching decrees. It maintained that the Eastern Orthodox church was subordinate to the Roman Catholic Church. It prohibited the state from taxing the clergy and declared laws detrimental to the church null and void. It also made bishops responsible for ferreting out heretics in their dioceses and ordered secular authorities to punish convicted heretics. Furthermore, the council insisted on high standards of behavior for the clergy and required each Catholic to confess his or her sins to a priest at least once a year and to perform the prescribed penance. Through this directive, the church tightened its control over the conscience of Europe. The council also decreed that in the sacrament of the Eucharist the body and blood of Christ are actually present in the bread and wine used in the sacrament. This meant that the priest at the altar was God's agent in the performance of a wondrous miracle.

CHRISTIANS AND JEWS

In their relations with heretics, pagans, and Muslims, medieval Christians demonstrated a narrow and hostile attitude that ran counter to the Gospel message that all human beings were children of God and that Christ had suffered for all humanity. Muslims were seen, in the words of Pope Urban II, as a "vile breed," "infidels," and "enemies of God."

Medieval Christians also showed hatred for Jews—a visibly alien group in a society dominated by the Christian worldview. The First Crusade was a turning point for medieval Jews. Until then there were few instances of organized violence against Jewish communities. If we are warring against God's enemies, reasoned zealous crusaders, why not annihilate the Lord's enemies living in our midst? In 1096, bands of crusaders, proclaiming that they were seeking vengeance against "Christ-killers," slaughtered Jews in French and German towns. The Crusaders were often aided by townspeople driven by hateful images of Jews and eager to seize Jewish property. The venomous hatred of Jews unleashed by the First Crusade triggered other massacres during the Middle Ages, at times fomented by the clergy. Viewing the Jews as possessions to be exploited, kings and lords taxed and fined them relentlessly and periodically expelled Jews from their territories in order to confiscate

their property. In 1290, Jews were expelled from England, and in 1306, from France. Between 1290 and 1293, expulsions, massacres, and forced conversions led to the virtual disappearance of a centuries-old Jewish community life in southern Italy. In Germany, savage riots periodically led to the torture and murder of Jews. In 1348–1349, when the Black Death (see "The Fourteenth Century: An Age of Adversity" in Chapter 7) raged across Europe, Jews were accused of spreading the plague by poisoning well water; thousands of Jews were burned alive in Basel, Freiburg, Strasbourg, Mainz, and other towns.

Several factors contributed to anti-Jewish feelings during the Middle Ages. To medieval Christians, the refusal of the Jews to embrace Christianity was an act of wickedness, particularly since the church taught that the coming of Christ had been prophesied by the Old Testament. Related to this prejudice was the portrayal of the Crucifixion in the Gospels. In the minds of medieval Christians, the crime of deicide—the killing of God—eternally tainted the Jews as a people; medieval Christians viewed Jews as dangerous sinners rejected by God and deserving of ceaseless punishment. Christian theologians taught they were to remain forever in subjection to Christians. It was just such a view that led town magistrates and princes periodically to confiscate Jewish property, sometimes after burning the helpless Jews alive in a public spectacle. The flames of hatred were fanned by the absurd allegation that Jews, made bloodthirsty by the spilling of Christ's blood, tortured and murdered Christians, particularly children, to obtain blood for ritual purposes. This blood libel was widely believed and incited numerous riots that led to the murder, torture, and expulsion of countless Jews, despite the fact that some popes and emperors condemned the charge as groundless.

The role of Jews as moneylenders also provoked animosity toward them. Increasingly excluded from international trade and most professions, barred from the guilds, and in many areas barred from landholding as well, Jews found that virtually the only means of livelihood open to them was moneylending. This activity, which was in theory forbidden to Christians, aroused the hatred of the individual peasants, clergy, lords, and kings who did the borrowing.

Bibliothèque Royale de Belgique.

ANTI-SEMITISM. Holding the Jews responsible for the Black Death, Christians committed mass murder. In Basel, several hundred Jews were herded into a wooden house and burned to death. Some six thousand Jews were burned alive in Mainz. Flames consumed another two thousand in a huge pyre outside Strasbourg, and their property was distributed to the local townspeople. In this picture depicting the slaughter of the Jews of Strasbourg, the townspeople evidently enjoy the spectacle.

The policy of the church toward the Jews was that they should not be harmed but that they should live in humiliation, a fitting punishment for their presumed act of deicide and continued refusal to embrace Christianity. Thus, the Fourth Lateran Council barred Jews from public office, required them to wear a distinguishing badge on their clothing as a symbol of their degradation, and ordered them to remain off the streets during Christian festivals. Christian art, literature, and religious instruction degraded Jews, depicting them as repulsive and grotesque and identifying them with the Devil, who was very real and very terrifying to medieval Christians. Such people deserved no mercy, reasoned medieval Christians. Indeed, nothing was too bad for them. Because Jews were seen as evil allies of Satan engaged in a diabolical plot against God

and Christendom, Jew-hatred was regarded as an expression of Christian virtue. Deeply etched into the minds and hearts of Christians, the distorted image of the Jew as a contemptible creature persisted in the European mentality into the twentieth century.

Despite their precarious position, medieval Jews maintained their faith, expanded their tradition of biblical and legal scholarship, and developed a flourishing Hebrew literature. The work of Jewish translators, doctors, and philosophers contributed substantially to the flowering of medieval culture in the High Middle Ages.

The foremost Jewish scholar of the Middle Ages was Moses ben Maimon (1135–1204), also called by the Greek name Maimonides. He was born in Cordoba, Spain, then under Muslim rule. After his family emigrated from Spain, Maimonides went to Egypt, where he became physician to the sultan. During his lifetime, Maimonides achieved fame as a philosopher, theologian, mathematician, and physician. He was recognized as the leading Jewish sage of his day, and his writings were respected by Christian and Muslim thinkers as well. Like Christian and Muslim philosophers, Maimonides sought to harmonize faith with reason, to reconcile the Hebrew Scriptures and the Talmud (Jewish biblical commentary) with Greek philosophy. In his writings on ethical themes, Maimonides demonstrated piety, wisdom, and humanity, as when he discussed charity. He held that the highest form of charity was helping someone who has fallen on bad times to become self-supporting by finding him work or providing him with a gift or loan to get started again. Just below that was helping a poor person in such a way that neither the recipient nor the donor knows each other.

NOTES

1. Speros Vryonis, Jr., *Byzantium and Europe* (New York: Harcourt, Brace & World, 1967), 193.

2. The Koran, trans. N. J. Dawood (Baltimore: Penguin Books, 1961), 108–109.

3. Quoted in V. H. H. Green, *Medieval Civilization in Western Europe* (New York: St. Mar-tin's Press, 1971), 35.

4. Excerpted in Brian Tierney, ed., *The Crisis of Church and State, 1050–1300* (Englewood Cliffs, N.J.: Prentice-Hall, 1964), 132.

Chapter 7

The Flowering and Dissolution of Medieval Civilization

- Revival of Learning
- The Medieval Worldview
- Philosophy, Science, and Law
- Literature
- Architecture
- The Fourteenth Century: An Age of Adversity
- The Decline of the Papacy
- Breakup of the Thomistic Synthesis
- The Middle Ages and the Modern World: Continuity and Discontinuity

Focus Questions

1. What conditions contributed to the revival of learning during the High Middle Ages?
2. What were scholastic philosophers trying to accomplish?
3. How does the medieval view of the universe differ from the modern view?
4. How did religion pervade much of the medieval philosophy, science, literature, art, and architecture?
5. Why is the fourteenth century described as an age of adversity?
6. What led to the decline of the medieval papacy? What is the historical significance of this development?

7. What is the legacy of the Middle Ages to the modern world?
8. How does the characteristic outlook of the Middle Ages differ from that of the modern age?

*E*urope in the High Middle Ages showed considerable vitality. The population increased, long-distance trade revived, new towns emerged, states started to take shape, and papal power grew. The culminating expression of this recovery and resurgence was the cultural flowering in philosophy, the visual arts, and literature. Creative intellects achieved on a cultural level what the papacy accomplished on an institutional level: the integration of life around a Christian viewpoint. The High Middle Ages saw the restoration of some of the learning of the ancient world, the rise of universities, the emergence of an original form of architecture (the Gothic), and the erection of an imposing system of thought, called *scholasticism*. Medieval theologian-philosophers fashioned Christian teachings into an all-embracing philosophy that represented the spiritual essence and the distinctive style of medieval civilization. They perfected what Christian thinkers in the Roman Empire had initiated and what the learned men of the Early Middle Ages had been groping for: a synthesis of Greek philosophy and Christian revelation. ❖

Chronology 7.1 ❖ The High and Late Middle Ages

c. 1100	Revival of the study of Roman law at Bologna
1163	Start of the construction of the Cathedral of Notre Dame
1267–1273	Saint Thomas Aquinas writes *Summa Theologica*
1309–1377	Babylonian Captivity: the popes, all French, reside at Avignon and are influenced by the French monarchy
c. 1321	Dante completes *Divine Comedy*
1337–1453	Hundred Years' War between England and France
1347–1351	Black Death reaches Italian ports and ravages Europe
1377	Pope Gregory XI returns the papacy from Avignon to Rome
1378–1417	Great Schism: Christendom has two and then three popes
1415	The battle of Agincourt: Henry V of England defeats the French; Jan Hus, a Bohemian religious reformer, is burned at the stake
1453	The English are driven from France, except Calais; the end of the Hundred Years' War
1460	Pope Pius II condemns the Conciliar Movement as heretical

REVIVAL OF LEARNING

In the late eleventh century, Latin Christendom began to experience a cultural revival; all areas of life showed vitality and creativeness. In the twelfth and thirteenth centuries, a rich civilization with a distinctive style united the educated elite in the lands from Britain to Sicily. Gothic cathedrals, an enduring testament to the creativity of the religious impulse, were erected throughout Europe. Universities sprang up in several cities. Roman authors were again read and their style imitated. The quality of written Latin—the language of the church, learning, and education—improved, and secular and religious poetry, both in Latin and in the vernacular, abounded. Roman law emerged anew in Italy, spread to Northern Europe, and regained its importance (lost since Roman times) as worthy of study and scholarship. Some key works of ancient Greece were translated into Latin and studied in universities. Employing the rational tradition of Greece, men of genius harmonized Christian doctrines and Greek philosophy.

Several conditions contributed to this cultural explosion, known as the Twelfth-Century Awakening. As attacks of Vikings, Muslims, and Magyars ended and kings and great lords imposed more order and stability, people found greater opportunities for travel and communication. The revival of trade and the growth of towns created a need for literacy and provided the wealth required to support learning. Increasing contact with Islamic and Byzantine cultures in Spain, Sicily, and Italy led to the translation into Latin, often by learned Jews, of ancient Greek works preserved by these Eastern civilizations. By preserving Greek philosophy and science—and by producing creative commentaries on these classical works—Islamic civilization acted as a bridge between antiquity and the cultural revival of the High Middle Ages. The Twelfth-Century Awakening was also prompted by the legacy of the Carolingian Renaissance, whose cultural lights had dimmed but never wholly vanished in the period of disorder after the dissolution of Charlemagne's empire.

In the Early Middle Ages, the principal educational centers were the monastic schools. During the twelfth century, cathedral schools in towns gained importance. Their teachers, paid a stipend by a local church, taught grammar, rhetoric, and logic. However, the chief expression of expanding intellectual life was the university, a distinct creation of the Middle Ages. The first universities were not planned but grew spontaneously. They developed as students, eager for knowledge, gathered around prominent teachers. The renewed importance of Roman law for business and politics, for example, drew students to Bologna to study with acknowledged masters.

University students attended lectures, prepared for examinations, and earned degrees. They studied grammar, rhetoric, logic, arithmetic, geometry, astronomy, medicine, music, and, when ready, church law and theology, which was considered the queen of the sciences. The curriculum relied heavily on Latin translations of ancient texts, chiefly the works of Aristotle. Students in mathematics and astronomy read Latin translations of Euclid and Ptolemy, while those in medicine studied the works of two great medical men of the ancient world, Hippocrates and Galen. Latin was the language of instruction.

Universities performed a crucial function in the Middle Ages. Students learned the habit of reasoned argument. Universities trained professional secretaries and lawyers, who administered the affairs of church, state, and the growing cities. These institutions of learning also produced theologians and philosophers, who shaped the climate of public opinion. Since the curriculum and the texts studied were essentially the same in all lands, the learning disseminated by universities tightened the cultural bonds that united Christian Europe. Medieval universities established in the West a tradition of learning that has never died. There is direct continuity between the universities of our own day and medieval centers of learning.

THE MEDIEVAL WORLDVIEW

A distinctive worldview, based essentially on Christianity, evolved during the Middle Ages. This outlook differed from both the Greco-Roman and the modern scientific and secular views of the world. In the Christian view, not the individual but the

Photos 12/Alamy Limited.

GOD AS ARCHITECT OF THE UNIVERSE, FRENCH OLD TESTAMENT MINIATURE PAINTING, THIRTEENTH CENTURY. To the medieval Christian, God was the creator of the world. The universe had a known hierarchical order, a "great chain of being" extending from God downward to the lowest form of being.

Creator determined what constituted the good life. Thus, reason that was not illuminated by revelation was either wrong or inadequate, for God had revealed the proper rules for the regulation of individual and social life. Ultimately, the good life was not of this world but came from a union with God in a higher world. This Christian belief, as formulated by the church, made life and death purposeful and intelligible; it dominated the thought of the Middle Ages.

The Universe: Higher and Lower Worlds

Medieval thinkers sharply differentiated between spirit and matter, between a realm of grace and an earthly realm, between a higher world of perfection and a lower world of imperfection. Moral values derived from the higher world, which was also the final destination for the faithful. Two sets of laws operated in the medieval universe, one for the heavens and one for the earth. The cosmos was a giant ladder, with God at the summit; earth, composed of base matter, stood at the bottom, just above hell, where farthest from God dwelled Satan, his evil spirits, and the souls of the damned.

From Aristotle and Ptolemy, medieval thinkers inherited the theory of an earth-centered universe—the *geocentric theory*—which they imbued with Christian meaning. The geocentric theory held that revolving around the motionless earth at uniform speeds were seven transparent spheres, in which were embedded the seven "planets"—the moon, Mercury, Venus, the sun, Mars, Jupiter, and Saturn. (Because Earth did not move, it was not considered a planet.) A sphere of fixed stars—that is, the stars stayed in a constant relationship to one another—enclosed this planetary system. Above the firmament of the stars were the three heavenly spheres. The outermost, the Empyrean Heaven, was the abode of God and the Elect. Through the sphere below—the Prime Mover—God transmitted motion to the planetary spheres. Beneath this was the lowest sphere, the invisible Crystalline Heaven.

An earth-centered universe accorded with the Christian idea that God had created the universe for men and women and that salvation was the primary aim of life. Because God had created people in his image, they deserved this central position in the universe. Although they might be living at the bottom rung of the cosmic ladder, only they, of all living things, had the capacity to ascend to heaven, the realm of perfection.

Also acceptable to the Christian mentality was the sharp distinction drawn by Aristotle between the world above the moon and the one below it. Aristotle held that terrestrial bodies were made of four elements: earth, water, air, and fire. Celestial bodies, which occupied the region above the moon, were composed of a fifth element, ether—too clear, too pure, and too perfect to be found on earth. The planets and stars

existed in a world apart; they were made of the divine ether and followed celestial laws, which did not apply to earthly objects. Whereas earthly bodies underwent change—ice converting to water, a burning log converting to ashes—heavenly objects were incorruptible, immune to all change. Unlike earthly objects, they were indestructible.

Heavenly bodies also followed different laws of motion from earthly objects. Aristotle said that it was natural for celestial bodies to move eternally in uniform circles, such motion being considered a sign of perfection. According to Aristotle, it was also natural for heavy bodies (stone) to fall downward and for light objects (fire, smoke) to move upward toward the celestial world; the falling stone and the rising smoke were finding their natural place in the universe.

The Individual: Sinful but Redeemable

At the center of medieval belief was the idea of a perfect God and a wretched and sinful human being. God, who had conceived and created the universe, had given Adam and Eve freedom to choose; rebellious and presumptuous, they had used their freedom to disobey God. In doing so, they made evil an intrinsic part of the human personality. But God, who had not stopped loving human beings, showed them the way out of sin. God became man and died so that human beings might be saved. Men and women were weak, egocentric, and sinful. With God's grace, they could overcome their sinful nature and gain salvation; without grace, they were utterly helpless.

The medieval individual's understanding of self stemmed from a comprehension of the universe as a hierarchy instituted by and culminating in God. On earth, the basest objects were lifeless stones, devoid of souls. Higher than stones were plants, endowed with a primitive type of soul that allowed reproduction and growth. Still higher were animals, which had the capacity for motion and sensation. The highest of the animals were human beings; unlike other animals, they could grasp some part of universal truth. Far superior to them were the angels, who apprehended God's truth without difficulty.

SCHOOL OF BOLOGNA MANUSCRIPT ILLUMINATION. The core of the medieval curriculum included the *trivium* and the *quadrivium*. Students mastered grammar, rhetoric, and dialectic—the "three ways" (trivium)—and then proceeded to mathematics, geometry, astronomy, and music (quadrivium). The technique of teaching was the *disputatio*, or oral disputation between master and student.

At the summit of this graduated universe (the Great Chain of Being) was God, who was pure Being, without limitation, and the source of all existence. God's revelation reached down to humanity through the hierarchical order. From God, revelation passed to the angels, who were also arranged hierarchically. From the angels, the truth reached men and women; it was grasped first by prophets and apostles and then by the multitudes. Thus, all things in the universe, from God to angels to men and women to the lowest earthly objects, occupied a place peculiar to their nature and were linked by God in a great, unbroken chain.

Medieval individuals derived a sense of security from this hierarchical universe, in which the human position was clearly defined. True, they were sinners who dwelt on a corruptible earth at the bottom of the cosmic hierarchy. But they could ascend to the higher world of perfection above the moon. As children of God, they enjoyed the unique distinction that each human soul was precious; all Christians commanded respect unless they were heretics. (A heretic forfeited dignity and could be justly executed.)

Medieval thinkers also arranged knowledge in a hierarchical order: knowledge of spiritual things surpassed all worldly knowledge, all human sciences. To know what God wanted of the individual was the summit of self-knowledge and permitted entry into heaven.

PHILOSOPHY, SCIENCE, AND LAW

In the universities, the best minds studied theology, the queen of the sciences, which was closely linked with philosophy. Medieval philosophy, or scholasticism, applied reason to revelation. It explained and clarified Christian teachings by means of concepts and principles of logic derived from Greek philosophy. Scholastics struggled to accommodate Greek philosophy—particularly Aristotle's thought, which was the basis of higher education—to the requirements of Catholic doctrines. They tried to show that the teachings of faith, although not derived from reason, were not contrary to reason; that logic could confirm the truth of church dogma. They tried to prove through reason what they already held to be true through faith. For example, the existence of God and the immortality of the soul, which every Christian accepted as articles of faith, could also, they thought, be demonstrated by reason. In struggling to harmonize faith with reason, medieval thinkers constructed an extraordinary synthesis of Christian revelation and Greek rationalism.

The scholastic masters used reason not to challenge but to serve faith: to elucidate, clarify, and buttress it. They did not break with the central concern of Christianity: earning God's grace and achieving salvation. Although this goal could be realized solely by faith, scholastic thinkers insisted that a science of nature did not obstruct the pursuit of grace and that philosophy could assist the devout in contemplating God. They did not reject those Christian beliefs that were beyond the grasp of human reason and therefore could not be deduced by rational argument. Instead, they held that such truths rested entirely on revelation and were to be accepted on faith.

To medieval thinkers, reason did not have an independent existence but ultimately had to acknowledge a suprarational, superhuman standard of truth; Greek philosophy had to be interpreted to accord with Christian revelation. These thinkers wanted rational thought to be directed by faith for Christian ends and guided by scriptural and ecclesiastical authority. Ultimately, faith had the final word.

Not all Christian thinkers welcomed the use of reason. Regarding Greek philosophy as an enemy of faith (would not reason lead people to question belief in miracles?), a fabricator of heresies (would not reason encourage disbelief in essential church teachings?), and an obstacle to achieving communion of the soul with God (would not a deviation from church teachings, under the influence of pagan philosophy, deprive people of salvation?), conservative theologians opposed the application of reason to Christian revelation. In a sense, the conservatives were right. By giving renewed vitality to Greek thought, medieval philosophy nurtured a powerful force that would eventually shatter the medieval concepts of nature and society and weaken Christianity. Modern Western thought was created by thinkers who refused to subordinate reason to Christian authority. Reason proved a double-edged sword: It both ennobled and undermined the medieval worldview.

Saint Anselm and Abelard

An early scholastic, Saint Anselm (1033–1109) was abbot of the Benedictine monastery of Le Bec in Normandy. He used rational argument to serve the interests of faith. Like Augustine before him and other thinkers who followed him, Anselm said that faith was a precondition for understanding. Without belief there could be no proper knowledge. He developed a philosophical proof for the existence of God. Anselm argued as follows: We can conceive of no being greater than God. But if God were to exist only in thought and not in actuality, his greatness would be limited; he would be less than perfect. Hence, he exists.

Anselm's motive and method reveal something about the essence of medieval philosophy. He

does not begin as a modern might: "If it can be proven that God exists, I will adopt the creed of Christianity; if not, I will either deny God's existence (atheism) or reserve judgment (agnosticism)." Rather, Anselm accepts God's existence as an established fact because he believes what Holy Scripture says and what the church teaches. He then proceeds to employ logical argument to demonstrate that God can be known not only through faith, but also through reason. He would never use reason to subvert what he knows to be true by faith. This attitude would generally characterize later medieval thinkers, who also applied reason to faith.

As a young teacher of theology at the Cathedral School of Notre Dame, Peter Abelard (1079–1142) acquired a reputation for brilliance and combativeness. His tragic affair with Héloise, whom he tutored and seduced, has become one of the great romances in Western literature. Abelard's most determined opponent, Bernard of Clairvaux, accused him of using dialectics—the method of logical argument—to attack faith. To Bernard, a monk and mystic, subjecting revealed truth to critical analysis was fraught with danger. Hearkening to Bernard's powerful voice, the church condemned Abelard and confined him to a monastery for the rest of his days.

Abelard believed that it was important to apply reason to faith and that careful and constant questioning led to wisdom. In *Sic et Non* (Yes and No), he took 150 theological issues and, by presenting passages from the Bible and the church fathers, showed that there were conflicting opinions. He suggested that the divergent opinions of authorities could be reconciled through proper use of dialectics. But like Anselm before him, Abelard did not intend to refute traditional church doctrines. Reason would buttress, not weaken, the authority of faith. He wrote after his condemnation in 1141: "I will never be a philosopher, if this is to speak against St. Paul; I would not be an Aristotle if this were to separate me from Christ. . . . I have set my building on the cornerstone on which Christ has built his Church. . . . I rest upon the rock that cannot be moved."[1] Although he was forced to quit his teaching post, the new scholastic rationalist approach swept across the schools of Europe.

Primary Source

Adelard of Bath:
A Questioning Spirit

In the High and Late Middle Ages, ancient scientific texts, particularly the works of Aristotle, were translated from Greek and Arabic into Latin. Influenced by Aristotle's naturalistic and empirical approach, several medieval scholars devoted greater attention to investigating the natural world. An early exponent of this emerging scientific outlook was Adelard of Bath (c. 1080–c. 1145). Born in England, Adelard studied in France and traveled in Muslim lands, becoming an advocate of Arabic science.

Adelard's Natural Questions *was written before the major Greek works were translated into Latin and made available to western European scholars. But it does show a growing curiosity and a questioning spirit, attitudes that are crucial to scientific thinking.* Natural Questions *is a dialogue between Adelard and his nephew; reproduced below are some of Adelard's responses to his nephew's queries.*

I take nothing away from God, for whatever exists is from Him and because of Him. But the natural order does not exist confusedly and without rational arrangement, and human reason should be listened to concerning those things it treats of. But when it completely fails, then the matter should be referred to God. Therefore, since we have not yet completely lost the use of our minds, let us return to reason. . . .

. . . I have learned one thing, under the guidance of reason, from Arabic teachers; but you, captivated by a show of authority, are led around by a halter. For what should we call authority but a halter? Indeed, just as brute animals are led about by a halter wherever you please, and are not told where or why, but see the rope by which they are held and follow it alone, thus the authority of writers leads many of you, caught and bound by animal-like credulity, into danger.

Whence some men, usurping the name of authority for themselves, have employed great license in writing, to such an extent that they do not hesitate to present the false as true to such animal-like men. For why not fill up sheets of paper, and why not write on the back too, when you usually have such readers today who require no rational explanation and put their trust only in the ancient name of a title? For they do not understand that reason has been given to each person so that he might discern the true from the false, using reason as the chief judge. For if reason were not the universal judge, it would have been given to each of us in vain. It would be sufficient that it were given to one (or a few at most), and the rest would be content with their authority and decisions. . . . I will cut short this discussion of the fact that in my judgment authority should be avoided. But I do assert this, that first we ought to seek the reason for anything, and then if we find an authority it may be added. Authority alone cannot make a philosopher believe anything, nor should it be adduced for this purpose. . . .

I believe that man is dearer to the Creator than all the other animals. Nevertheless it does not happen that he is born with natural weapons or is suited for swift flight. But he has something which is much better and more worthy, reason I mean, by which he so far excels the brutes that by means of it he can tame them, put bits in their mouths, and train them to perform various tasks. You see, therefore, by how much the gift of reason excels bodily defenses.

Question for Analysis

1. In what ways does Adelard of Bath express a scientific attitude in this work?

Richard C. Dales, *The Scientific Achievement of the Middle Ages* (University of Pennsylvania Press, 1973), pp. 40–44.

Saint Thomas Aquinas: The Synthesis of Faith and Reason

The introduction into Latin Christendom of the major works of Aristotle created a dilemma for religious authorities. Aristotle's comprehensive philosophy of nature and man, a product of human reason alone, conflicted in many instances with essential Christian doctrine. Whereas Christianity taught that God created the universe at a specific point in time, Aristotle held that the universe was eternal. Nor did Aristotle believe in the personal immortality of the soul, another cardinal principle of Christianity.

Some church officials feared that the dissemination of Aristotle's ideas and the use of Aristotelian logic would endanger faith. At various times in the first half of the thirteenth century, they forbade teaching the scientific works of Aristotle at the University of Paris. But because the ban did not apply throughout Christendom and was not consistently enforced in Paris, Aristotle's philosophy continued to be studied. Rejecting the position of conservatives, who insisted that philosophy would contaminate faith, Saint Thomas Aquinas (c. 1225–1274) upheld the value of human reason and natural knowledge. Aquinas taught at Paris and in Italy. His greatest work, *Summa Theologica,* is a systematic exposition of Christian thought and the crowning expression of the medieval attempt to integrate Aristotle with Christianity.

Can the teachings of faith conflict with the evidence of reason? For Aquinas, the answer was emphatically no. Since both faith and reason came from God, they were not in competition with each other but, properly understood, supported each other and formed an organic unity. Consequently, reason should not be feared, for it was another avenue to God. Because there was an inherent agreement between true faith and correct reason—they both ultimately stemmed from God—contradictions between them were only a misleading appearance. Although philosophy had not yet been able to resolve the dilemma, for God no such contradictions existed. In heaven, human beings would attain complete knowledge, as well as complete happiness. While on earth, however, they must allow faith to guide reason; they must not permit reason to oppose or undermine faith.

Thus, in exalting God, Aquinas also paid homage to human intelligence, proclaimed the value of rational activity, and asserted the importance of physical reality discovered through human senses. Consequently, he prized the natural philosophy of Aristotle. Correctly used, Aristotelian thought would assist faith. Aquinas's great effort was to synthesize Aristotelianism with the divine revelation of Christianity. That the two could be harmonized he had no doubt. He made use of Aristotelian categories in his five proofs of God's existence. In his first proof, for example, Aquinas argued that a thing cannot move itself. Whatever is moved must be moved by something else, and that by something else again. "Therefore, it is necessary to arrive at a first mover, moved by no other; and this everyone understands to be God."[2]

Aquinas upheld the value of reason. To love the intellect was to honor God and not to diminish the truth of faith. He had confidence in the power of the rational mind to comprehend most of the truths of revelation, and he insisted that in nontheological questions about specific things in nature—those questions not affecting salvation—people should trust only reason and experience. Thus, Aquinas gave new importance to the empirical world and to scientific speculation and human knowledge.

Traditionally, medieval thinkers maintained that knowledge derived from the natural world was insignificant and an obstacle to true knowledge. Aquinas altered this tradition by affirming the importance of knowledge of the social order and the physical world. He gave human reason and worldly knowledge a new dignity. Thus, the City of Man was not merely a sinful place from which people tried to escape in order to enter God's city; it was worthy of investigation and understanding. But Aquinas remained a medieval thinker, for he always maintained that secular knowledge should be supervised and corrected by revealed truth, and he never questioned the truth of the medieval Christian view of the world and the individual.

Science

During the Early Middle Ages, few scientific works from the ancient world were available to Western Europeans. Scientific thought was at its lowest ebb

MILLEFLEURS TAPESTRY: TWO MUSICIANS, SCHOOL OF THE LOIRE, FRANCE, C. 1500. The courtly love tradition, in which women were worshiped and untouchable, inspired poetry. Troubadours sang this poetry, which expressed a changing attitude toward women. By inviting poets to their courts and writing poetry themselves, noblewomen actively influenced the rituals and literature of courtly love.

since its origination more than a thousand years earlier in Greece. In contrast, both the Islamic and Byzantine civilizations preserved and, in some instances, added to the legacy of Greek science. In the High Middle Ages, however, many ancient texts were translated from Greek and Arabic into Latin and entered Latin Christendom for the first time. Spain, where Christian and Muslim civilizations met, was one of the two principal centers of translation. The other was Sicily, which had been controlled by Byzantium up to the last part of the ninth century and then by Islam until Christian Normans completed the conquest of the island by 1091.

In the thirteenth and fourteenth centuries, a genuine scientific movement did occur. Impressed with the naturalistic and empirical approach of Aristotle, some medieval schoolmen spent time examining physical nature. Among them was the Dominican Albert the Great (Albertus Magnus, c. 1206–1280). Born in Germany, he studied at Padua and taught at the University of Paris, where Thomas Aquinas was his student. Albert devoted himself to editing and commenting on the vast body of Aristotle's works.

While retaining the Christian emphasis on God, revelation, the supernatural, and the afterlife, Albert (unlike many earlier Christian thinkers) considered nature a valid field for investigation. In his writings on geology, chemistry, botany, and zoology, Albert, like Aristotle, displayed a respect for the concrete details of nature, utilizing them as empirical evidence. Albert stressed the value of knowledge derived from experience with nature, sought rational explanations for natural occurrences, and held that theological debates should not stop scientific investigations.

Other scholars in the scientific movement included Robert Grosseteste (c. 1175–1253), the chancellor of Oxford University. He insisted that mathematics was necessary in order to understand the physical world, and he carried out experiments on the refraction of light. Another Englishman, the monk and philosopher Roger Bacon (c. 1214–1294), foreshadowed the modern attitude of using science to gain mastery over nature. Bacon maintained that mathematics was crucial for science and read Arabic works on the reflection and refraction of light. Among his achievements were experiments in optics and the observation that light travels much faster than sound. His description of the anatomy of the vertebrate eye and optic nerves was the finest of that era, and he recommended dissecting the eyes of pigs and cows to obtain greater knowledge of the subject.

Medieval scholars did not make the breakthrough to modern science. They retained the belief that the earth was at the center of the universe and that different sets of laws operated on earth and in the heavens. They did not invent analytic geometry or calculus or arrive at the concept of inertia—all crucial for modern science. Moreover, medieval science was never wholly removed from a theological setting.

Medieval scholars and philosophers did, however, advance knowledge about optics, the tides, and mechanics. They saw the importance of mathematics for interpreting nature, and they performed some experiments. By translating and commenting on ancient Greek and Arabic works, medieval scholars provided future ages with ideas to reflect on and to surpass, a necessary precondition for the emergence of modern science. Medieval thinkers also developed an anti-Aristotelian physics, which some historians of science believe influenced Galileo, the creator of modern mechanics, more than two centuries later.

Recovery of Roman Law

During the Early Middle Ages, Western European law essentially consisted of Germanic customs, some of which had been put into writing. Some elements of Roman law endured as custom and practice, but the formal study of Roman law had disappeared. The late eleventh and twelfth centuries saw the revival of Roman law, particularly in Bologna, Italy. Irnerius lectured on the *Corpus Juris Civilis,* codified by Byzantine jurists in the sixth century, and made Bologna the leading center for the study of Roman law. Irnerius and his students employed the methods of organization and logical analysis that scholastic theologians used in studying philosophical texts.

Unlike traditional Germanic law, which was essentially tribal and parochial, Roman law assumed the existence of universal principles that could be grasped by the human intellect and expressed in the law of the state. Roman jurists had systematically and rationally structured the legal experience of the Roman people. The example of Roman law stimulated medieval jurists to organize their own legal tradition. Intellectuals increasingly came to insist on both a rational analysis of evidence and judicial decisions based on rational procedures. Law codes compiled in parts of France and Germany and in the kingdom of Castile were influenced by the recovery of Roman law.

LITERATURE

Medieval literature was written both in Latin and in the vernacular. Much of medieval Latin literature consisted of religious hymns and dramas depicting the life of Christ and saints. In their native tongues, medieval writers created different forms of poetry: *chansons de geste, the roman,* and *troubadour* songs, which emerged during the High Middle Ages.

The French chansons de geste—epic poems of heroic deeds that had first been told orally—were written in the vernacular of northern France. These poems dealt with Charlemagne's battles against the Muslims, with rebellious nobles, and with feudal warfare. The finest of these epic poems, *The Song of Roland,* expressed the feudal ethic—loyalty to one's lord and devotion to Christianity were the highest virtues and treachery an unpardonable crime. Roland, Charlemagne's nephew, who was killed in a battle with the Muslims, is idolized as the brave Christian knight who battles God's enemies. He is a warrior of heroic proportions and great physical prowess, who is loyal to God, the King, and his knightly entourage. The *Nibelungenlied,* the best expression of the heroic epic in Germany, is often called "the *Iliad* of the Germans." Like its French counterpart, it dealt with heroic feats.

The roman—a blending of old legends, chivalric ideals, and Christian concepts—combined love with adventure, war, and the miraculous. Among the romans were the tales of King Arthur and his Round Table. Circulating by word of mouth for centuries, these tales spread from the British Isles to France and Germany. In the twelfth century, they were put into French verse.

Another form of medieval poetry spoken and written in the vernacular dealt with the romantic glorification of women. Known as courtly love, this form of poetry flourished particularly in Provence in southern France. Sung by troubadours, many of them nobles, the courtly love poetry expressed a changing attitude toward women. Although medieval men generally regarded women as inferior and subordinate, courtly love poetry ascribed to noble ladies superior qualities of virtue. To the nobleman, the lady became a goddess worthy of all devotion, loyalty, and worship. He would honor her and serve her as he did his lord; for her love he would undergo any sacrifice.

Noblewomen actively influenced the rituals and literature of courtly love. They often invited poets to their courts and wrote poetry themselves. They demanded that knights treat them with gentleness and consideration and that knights dress neatly, bathe often, play instruments, and compose (or at least recite) poetry. To prove worthy of his lady's love, a knight had to demonstrate patience, charm, bravery, and loyalty. By devoting himself to a lady, it was believed, a knight would ennoble his character.

Courtly love did not involve a husband–wife relationship but rather a noble's admiration of and yearning for another woman of his class. Among nobles, marriages were arranged for political and economic reasons. The rituals of courtly love expanded the skills and refined the tastes of the noble. The rough warrior acquired wit, manners, charm, and skill with words. He was becoming a courtier and a gentleman.

The *Canterbury Tales* by Geoffrey Chaucer (c. 1340–1400), written in Middle English, is a masterpiece of English literature. Chaucer chose as his theme twenty-nine pilgrims en route from London to the religious shrine at Canterbury. In describing the pilgrims, Chaucer displayed humor, charm, an understanding of human nature, and a superb grasp of the attitudes of the English. Few writers have pictured their times better.

The greatest literary figure of the Middle Ages was Dante Alighieri (1265–1321) of Florence. Dante appreciated the Roman classics and wrote not just in Latin, the traditional language of intellectual life, but in Italian, his native tongue. In this respect, he anticipated the Renaissance (see Chapter 8). In the tradition of the troubadours, Dante wrote poems to his beloved Beatrice.

In *The Divine Comedy,* Dante synthesized the various elements of the medieval outlook and summed up, with immense feeling, the medieval understanding of the purpose of life. Written while Dante was in exile, *The Divine Comedy* describes the poet's journey through hell, purgatory, and paradise. Dante arranges hell into nine concentric circles; in each region, sinners are punished in proportion to their earthly sins. The poet experiences all of hell's torments—burning sand, violent storms, darkness, and fearful monsters that whip, claw, bite, and tear sinners apart. The ninth circle, the lowest, is reserved for Lucifer and traitors. Lucifer has three faces, each a different color, and two bat-like wings. In each mouth he gnaws on one of the greatest traitors in history: Judas Iscariot, who betrayed Jesus, and Brutus and Cassius, who assassinated Caesar. Those condemned to hell

Scala/Art Resource, N.Y.

The Visitation, West Portal, Reims Cathedral, c. 1225–1245. The reflection of Roman art exhibited by these statues of the expectant mothers (Mary and Elizabeth) of Jesus and John the Baptist suggests that the sculptor was well versed in the classical tradition. The carving of the draperies and the poses of the figures reveal classical traits, but instead of being idealizations, the figures display human warmth.

are told: "All hope abandon, ye who enter in." In purgatory, Dante meets sinners who, although they undergo punishment, will eventually enter paradise. In paradise, an abode of light, music, and gentleness, the poet, guided by Beatrice, meets the great saints and the Virgin Mary. For an instant, he glimpses the Vision of God. In this mystical experience, the aim of life is realized.

ARCHITECTURE

Two styles of architecture evolved during the Middle Ages: Romanesque and Gothic. The Romanesque style dominated the eleventh century and the greater part of the twelfth. In imitation of ancient Roman structures, Romanesque buildings had massive walls that supported stone barrel-and-groin vaults with rounded arches. The thick walls were needed to hold up the great weight of the roofs. The walls left few spaces for windows, and so little light entered the interior. However, the development of the pointed arch permitted supports that lessened the bearing pressure of the roof on the walls. This new style, called Gothic, allowed buildings to have lofty, vaulted ceilings and huge windows, which permitted sunlight to flood the interiors. The Romanesque building produced an impression of massive solidity; Gothic buildings created an illusion of lightness and soaring energy and an upward reach to the heavens.

The magnificently designed stained-glass windows and complex sculptural decoration of Gothic cathedrals depicted scenes from the Bible and the lives of saints—as well as scenes from daily life—for the worshipers, many of whom were illiterate. The reduction of wall space, which allowed these massive glass illustrations, was made possible by the flying buttresses on the buildings' exteriors. These great arcs of masonry carry the weight and thrust of the stone vaults out to the exterior walls.

The Gothic style was to remain vigorous until the fifteenth century, spreading from France to England, Germany, Spain, and beyond. Revived from time to time thereafter, it has proved to be one of the most enduring styles in Western art and architecture.

THE FOURTEENTH CENTURY: AN AGE OF ADVERSITY

By the fourteenth century, Latin Christendom had experienced more than 250 years of growth. On the economic level, agricultural production had expanded, commerce and town life had revived, and the population had increased. On the political level, kings had become more powerful, bringing

NOTRE-DAME DE CHARTRES, BEGUN C. 1194, CHARTRES, FRANCE. Because the two spires topping the west façade towers were constructed nearly four centuries apart, they provide an interesting contrast between early and late Gothic architecture. The simple north spire was built between 1160 and 1170; the south spire, constructed in the early sixteenth century, is a good example of the flamboyant Gothic style.

Nat Farbman/Time & Life Pictures/Getty Images.

greater order and security to large areas. On the religious level, the papacy had demonstrated its strength as the spiritual leader of Christendom, and the clergy had been reformed. On the cultural level, a unified worldview, blending faith and reason, had been forged.

During the Late Middle Ages (roughly the fourteenth century), however, Latin Christendom was afflicted with severe problems. The earlier increases in agricultural production did not continue. Limited use of fertilizers and limited knowledge of conservation exhausted the topsoil. From 1301 to 1314, there was a general shortage of food, and from 1315 to 1317, famine struck Europe.

People subsisted by scavenging. On roads and in villages, the deceased and those dying of starvation remained unattended. Throughout the century, starvation and malnutrition were widespread.

Adding to the economic crisis was the Black Death, or bubonic plague, a bacillus carried by fleas on black rats. The disease probably first struck Mongolia in 1331–1332, and from there it crossed into Russia. Carried back from Black Sea ports, the plague reached Sicily in 1347 and then spread swiftly throughout much of Europe through human contact. Some historians contend that the Black Death may have consisted of two diseases, the bubonic plague and anthrax, which was transmitted by eating meat from diseased cattle. The first onslaught lasted until 1351, and other serious outbreaks occurred in later decades. The crowded cities and towns, where sewage made rats more fecund, had the highest mortality rate, as much as 60 percent. Perhaps 20 million people—about one-quarter to one-third of the European population—perished in the worst disaster in recorded history caused by natural forces. Contemporaries viewed the plague as divine punishment for humanity's sins.

Overwhelmed by terror, people abandoned their sick children, spouses, and parents. Panic-stricken people drifted into debauchery, law-lessness, and frenzied forms of religious life. Confidence in the church declined as many priests fled, depriving the sick of spiritual comfort and the dying of last rites. Organized bands of flagellants marched from region to region, beating themselves and each other with sticks and whips in a desperate effort to appease God, who they believed had cursed them with the plague. Expressing the pervasive gloom and pessimism of these times, art concentrated on morbid scenes of decaying flesh, open graves laden with worm-eaten corpses—even the Madonna was represented as a corpse being eaten by snakes and frogs—dances of death, and the torments of hell. Sometimes, this hysteria was directed against Jews, who were accused of causing the plague by poisoning wells. Terrible massacres of Jews, often by mass burnings, occurred despite the pleas of the papacy.

The millions of deaths caused production of food and goods to plummet. However, depopulation was a boon for surviving artisans, who found opportunities and higher wages in depopulated towns desperate for skilled workers. A diminishing labor pool also benefited peasants, who were able to attain lighter burdens from strapped lords, and free peasants who toiled as day laborers demanded higher wages. The combination of lower agricultural prices and increasing wages hurt aristocratic landowners. As their agricultural income lessened, nobles tried to make peasants bear the brunt of the crisis. Economic and social tensions, some of them antedating the Black Death, escalated into rebellions. Each rebellion had its own specific causes, but a general pattern characterized the uprisings in the country-side. When kings and lords, breaking with customary social relationships, imposed new and onerous regulations, the peasants rose in defense of their traditional rights.

In 1323, the lords' attempt to reimpose old manorial obligations infuriated the free peasants of Flanders, whose condition had improved in earlier decades. The Peasants' Revolt lasted five bloody years. In 1358, French peasants took up arms in protest against the plundering of the countryside by soldiers. Perhaps twenty thousand peasants died in the uprising known as the *Jacquerie*. In 1381, English peasants revolted, angered over legislation that tied them to the land and imposed new taxes. Like the revolts in Flanders and France, the uprising in England failed. To the landed aristocracy, the peasants were sinners attacking a social system ordained by God. Possessing superior might, the nobility suppressed the peasants, sometimes with savage cruelty.

Social unrest also afflicted towns. The wage earners of Florence (1378), the weavers of Ghent (1382), and the poor of Paris (1382) rose up against the ruling oligarchies. These revolts were generally initiated not by the poorest and most downtrodden but by those who had made some gains and were eager for more. The rebellions of the urban poor were crushed just like the peasant uprisings.

Compounding the adversity was the series of conflicts known as the Hundred Years' War (1337–1453). In earlier centuries, wars in medieval Europe had generally been short and small in scale with limited casualties. This trend changed dramatically with the Hundred Years' War. Because English kings ruled parts of France, conflicts between the two monarchies were common. In the opening phase of the war, the English inflicted terrible defeats on French knights at the battles of Crécy (1346) and Poitiers (1356). Using longbows, which allowed them to shoot arrows rapidly, English archers cut down wave after wave of charging French cavalry. The war continued on and off throughout the fourteenth century. During periods of truce, gangs of unemployed soldiers roamed the French countryside killing and stealing, actions that precipitated the Jacquerie, the peasant uprising.

After the battle of Agincourt (1415), won by the English under Henry V, the English controlled most of northern France. It appeared that England would shortly conquer France and join the two lands under one crown. At this crucial moment in French history, a young, illiterate peasant girl, Joan of Arc (1412–1431), helped rescue France. Believing that God commanded her to drive the English out of France, Joan rallied the demoralized French troops, leading them in battle. In 1429, she liberated the besieged city of Orléans. Later she was captured and imprisoned by the English, and in 1431 she was condemned as a heretic and a witch by a hand-picked church court and was burned at the stake. Inspired by Joan's death, the French drove the English from all French territory except the port of Calais.

During the Hundred Years' War, French kings introduced new taxes, which added substantially to their incomes. These monies furnished them with the means to organize a professional army of well-paid and loyal troops. By evoking a sense of pride and oneness in the French people, the war also contributed to a growing, but still incomplete, national unity. The English, too, emerged from the war with a greater sense of solidarity, and Parliament, because it had to finance the war, gained in stature. However, the war had horrendous consequences for the French peasants. Thousands of farmers were killed, and valuable farmland was destroyed by English armies and marauding bands of mercenaries. In a portentous development, the later stages of the Hundred Years' War saw the use of gunpowder and heavy artillery.

THE DECLINE OF THE PAPACY

The principal sign of the decline of medieval civilization in the Late Middle Ages was the waning authority and prestige of the papacy. In the High Middle Ages, the papacy had been the dominant institution in Christendom, but in the Late Middle Ages, its power weakened. The medieval ideal of a unified Christian commonwealth guided by the papacy was shattered. Papal authority declined in the face of the growing power of kings, who championed the parochial interests of states. As the pope became more embroiled in European politics, papal prestige and the pope's capacity to command diminished. Many pious Christians felt that the pope was behaving more like a secular ruler than like an Apostle of Christ. Political theorists and church reformers further undermined papal authority.

Conflict with France

Philip IV of France (1285–1314) taxed the church in his land to raise revenue for war. In doing so, he disregarded the church prohibition against the taxing of its property without papal permission. In 1296, in the bull *Clericis Laicos*, Pope Boniface VIII (1294–1303) decreed that kings and lords who imposed taxes on the clergy and the clergy who paid them would be excommunicated. Far from bowing to the pope's threat, Philip acted forcefully to assert his authority over the church in his kingdom. Boniface backed down from his position, declaring that the French king could tax the clergy in times of national emergency. Thus, the matter was resolved to the advantage of the state.

A second dispute had more disastrous consequences for Boniface. Philip tried and imprisoned a French bishop despite Boniface's warning that this was an illegal act and a violation of church law and tradition, which held that the church, not the state, must judge the clergy. Philip summoned the first meeting of the Estates General to gain the backing of the nation. Shortly afterward, Boniface threatened to excommunicate Philip. The outraged monarch raided the papal summer palace at Anagni in September 1303 and captured the pope. Although Boniface was released,

© Mary Evans Picture Library/The Image Works.

THE JACQUERIE. Enraged French peasants attack the castle of a lord.

this shocking event proved too much for him, and a month later he died.

Boniface's two successors, Benedict XI (1303–1304) and Clement V (1305–1314), tried to conciliate Philip. In particular, Clement decided to remain at Avignon, a town on the southeastern French frontier, where he had set up a temporary residence.

From 1309 to 1377, a period known as the Babylonian Captivity, the popes were all French and resided in Avignon, not Rome. During this time, the papacy, removed from Rome and deprived of revenues from the Papal States in Italy, was often forced to pursue policies favorable to France. The growing anti-papalism among the laity further damaged the papal image. Laypeople

were repelled by the luxurious style of living at Avignon and by the appointment of high churchmen to lands where they did not know the language and showed little concern for the local population. Criticism of the papacy increased. The conflict between Boniface and Philip provoked a battle of words between proponents of papal supremacy and defenders of royal rights.

The most important critique of clerical intrusion into worldly affairs was *The Defender of the Peace* (1324) by Marsiglio of Padua (c. 1290–c. 1343). Marsiglio held that the state ran according to its own principles, which had nothing to do with religious commands originating in a higher realm. Religion dealt with a supranatural world and with principles of faith that could not be proved by reason, wrote Marsiglio. Politics, on the other hand, dealt with the natural world and the affairs of the human community. Political thinkers should not try to make the earthly realm conform to articles of faith. For Marsiglio, the state was self-sufficient; it needed no instruction from a higher authority. Thus, Marsiglio denied the essential premises of medieval papal political theory: that the pope, as God's vicar, was empowered to guide kings; that the state, as part of a divinely ordered world, must conform to and fulfill supranatural ends; and that the clergy were above the laws of the state. Marsiglio viewed the church as a spiritual institution with no temporal power. Marsiglio's concept of an autonomous state that did not answer to clerical authority anticipated modern political thought.

The Great Schism and the Conciliar Movement

Pope Gregory XI returned the papacy to Rome in 1377, ending the Babylonian Captivity. But the papacy was to endure an even greater humiliation: the Great Schism. Elected pope in 1378, Urban VI abused and imprisoned a number of cardinals. Fleeing from Rome, the cardinals declared that the election of Urban had been invalid and elected Clement VII as the new pope. Refusing to step down, Urban excommunicated Clement, who responded in kind. To the utter confusion and anguish of Christians throughout Europe, there were now two popes: Urban ruling from Rome and Clement from Avignon.

Prominent churchmen urged the convening of a general council—the Council of Pisa—to end the disgraceful schism, which obstructed the papacy from performing its sacred duties. Held in 1409 and attended by hundreds of churchmen, the Council of Pisa deposed both Urban and Clement and elected a new pope. Neither deposed pope recognized the council's decision, so Christendom then had three popes! A new council was called at Constance in 1414. In the struggle that ensued, each of the three popes either abdicated or was deposed in favor of an appointment by the council. In 1417, the Great Schism ended.

During the first half of the fifteenth century, church councils met at Pisa (1409), Constance (1414–1418), and Basel (1431–1449) in order to end schism, combat heresy, and reform the church. The Conciliar Movement attempted to transform the papal monarchy into a constitutional system, in which the pope's power would be regulated by a general council. Supporters of the movement held that the papacy could not reform the church as effectively as a general council representing the clergy. But the Conciliar Movement ended in failure. As the Holy Roman Emperor and then the French monarch withdrew support from the councils, the papacy regained its authority over the higher clergy. In 1460, Pope Pius II condemned the Conciliar Movement as heretical.

Medieval popes claimed both spiritual and temporal powers. They saw this as a sacred duty, fulfilling the wishes of God who was working through them. This outlook deeply embroiled the papacy in European power politics and worldly life at the neglect of its spiritual and moral responsibilities. Many devout Christians longed for a religious renewal, a return to simple piety. The papacy barely heard this cry for reform. Its failure to provide creative leadership for reform made possible the Protestant Reformation of the sixteenth century. By splitting Christendom into Catholic and Protestant, the Reformation destroyed forever the vision of a Christian world commonwealth guided by Christ's vicar, the pope.

Fourteenth-Century Heresies

Another threat to papal power and to the medieval ideal of a universal Christian community guided by the church came from radical reformers who questioned the function and authority of the entire church hierarchy. These heretics in the Late Middle Ages were forerunners of the Protestant Reformation.

The two principal dissenters were the Englishman John Wycliffe (c. 1320–1384) and the Bohemian (Czech) Jan Hus (c. 1369–1415). By stressing a personal relationship between the individual and God and by claiming that the Bible itself, rather than church teachings, was the ultimate Christian authority, Wycliffe challenged the fundamental position of the medieval church: that the avenue to salvation passed through the church alone. He denounced the wealth of the higher clergy and sought a return to the spiritual purity and material poverty of the early church.

To Wycliffe, the wealthy, elaborately organized hierarchy of the church was unnecessary and wrong. The splendidly dressed and propertied bishops had no resemblance to the simple people who first followed Christ. Indeed, these worldly bishops, headed by a princely and tyrannical pope, were really anti-Christians, the "fiends of Hell." Wycliffe wanted the state to confiscate church property and the clergy to embrace poverty. By denying that priests changed the bread and wine of communion into the substance of the body and blood of Christ, Wycliffe rejected the sacramental power of the clergy. The church, in response, deprived the Lollards—an order of poor priests that spread Wycliffe's teachings—of their priestly functions.

Wycliffe's ideas were enthusiastically received by Czech reformers in Bohemia led by Jan Hus. Like Wycliffe, Hus advocated vernacular translations of the Bible, which would be accessible to common people, and upbraided the upper clergy for their luxury and immorality.

Although both movements were declared heretical and some of Wycliffe's followers and Hus were burned at the stake, the church could not crush the dissenters' followers or eradicate their teachings. To some extent, the doctrines of the Reformation would parallel the teachings of Wycliffe and Hus.

BREAKUP OF THE THOMISTIC SYNTHESIS

In the Late Middle Ages, the papacy lost power as kings, political theorists, and religious dissenters challenged papal claims to supreme leadership. The great theological synthesis constructed by the scholastic theologians of the twelfth and thirteenth centuries was also breaking down. The process of fragmentation seen in the history of the church took place in philosophy as well.

Thomas Aquinas' system was the culmination of the scholastic attempt to show the basic agreement of philosophy and religion. In the fourteenth century, a number of thinkers cast doubt on the possibility of synthesizing Aristotelianism and Christianity, that is, reason and faith. Denying that reason could demonstrate the truth of Christian doctrines with certainty, philosophers tried to separate reason from faith. Whereas Aquinas had said that reason proved or clarified much of revelation, fourteenth-century thinkers asserted that the basic propositions of Christianity were not open to rational proof. Whereas Aquinas had held that faith supplemented and perfected reason, some philosophers were now proclaiming that reason often contradicted faith.

To be sure, this new outlook did not urge abandoning faith in favor of reason. Faith had to prevail in any conflict with reason because faith rested on God, the highest authority in the universe. But the relationship between reason and revelation was altered. Articles of faith, it was now held, had nothing to do with reason; they were to be believed, not proved. Reason was not an aid to theology but a separate sphere of activity. This new attitude snapped the link between reason and faith that Aquinas had so skillfully forged. The scholastic synthesis was disintegrating.

The chief proponent of this new outlook was William of Ockham (c. 1285–1349). In contrast to Aquinas, Ockham insisted that natural reason could not prove God's existence, the soul's immortality, or any other essential Christian doctrine. Reason could say only that God probably exists and that he probably endowed human beings with an immortal soul; it could not prove these propositions with certainty. The tenets of faith were beyond the reach of reason, said Ockham; there was no rational foundation to Christianity. For Ockham, reason and faith did not necessarily complement each other as they did for Aquinas; it was neither possible nor helpful to join reason to faith. He did not, however, seek to undermine faith—only to disengage it from reason.

In the process of proclaiming the authority of faith, Ockham also furthered the use of reason to comprehend nature. Ockham's approach, separating natural knowledge from religious dogma, made it easier to explore the natural world empirically, without fitting it into a religious framework. Ockham thus is a forerunner of the modern mentality, which is characterized by the separation of reason from religion and by an interest in the empirical investigation of nature.

THE MIDDLE AGES AND THE MODERN WORLD: CONTINUITY AND DISCONTINUITY

Medieval civilization began to decline in the fourteenth century, but no era of cultural stagnation, economic collapse, and social transformation comparable to the three centuries following Rome's fall descended on Europe; its economic and political institutions and technological skills had grown too strong. Instead, the waning of the Middle Ages opened up possibilities for another stage in Western civilization: the modern age.

The modern world is linked to the Middle Ages in innumerable ways. European cities, the middle class, the state system, English common law, universities—all had their origins in the Middle Ages. During medieval times, important advances were made in business practices, including partnerships, systematic bookkeeping, and the bill of exchange, which paved the way for modern banking. By translating and commenting on the writings of Greek and Arabic thinkers, medieval scholars preserved a priceless intellectual heritage, without which the modern mind could never have evolved. In the universities, scholastic thinkers had established a tradition of critical thinking that in future centuries would nurture intellectual activity in areas other than theology.

Feudal traditions lasted long after the Middle Ages. Up until the French Revolution, for instance, French aristocrats enjoyed special privileges and exercised power over local government. In England, the aristocracy controlled local government until the Industrial Revolution transformed English society in the nineteenth century. Retaining the medieval ideal of the noble warrior, aristocrats continued to dominate the officer corps of European armies through the nineteenth century and even into the twentieth. Aristocratic notions of duty, honor, loyalty, and courtly love have endured into our own day.

During the Middle Ages, Europeans began to take the lead over the Muslims, the Byzantines, the Chinese, and all other peoples in the use of technology. Medieval technology and inventiveness stemmed in part from Christianity, which taught that God had created the world specifically for human beings to subdue and exploit. Consequently, medieval people tried to employ animal power and laborsaving machinery to relieve human drudgery. Moreover, Christianity taught that God was above nature, not within it, so Christians faced no spiritual obstacle to exploiting nature—unlike, for instance, the Hindus. In contrast to classical humanism, the Christian outlook did not consider manual work degrading; even monks combined it with study.

The Christian stress on the sacred worth of the individual (each person had an immortal soul that was God's concern), on human equality (differences in rank and birth were of no account to God on Judgment Day), and on the higher law of God (divine precepts had a greater pull on conscience than did the state's laws) has never ceased to influence Western civilization. Even though in modern times the various Christian churches have not often taken the lead in political and social reform, the ideals identified with the Judeo-Christian tradition have become part of the Western heritage. As such, they have inspired social reformers who may no longer identify with their ancestral religion.

Believing that God's Law was superior to state or national decrees, medieval philosophers provided a theoretical basis for opposing tyrannical kings who violated Christian principles. The idea that both the ruler and the ruled are bound by a higher law would, in a secularized form, become a principal element of modern liberal thought.

Feudalism also contributed to the history of liberty. According to feudal custom, the king, as a member of the feudal community, was duty-bound to honor agreements made with his vassals. Lords possessed personal rights, which the king was obliged to respect. Resentful of a king who ran roughshod over customary feudal rights, lords also negotiated contracts with the crown, such as the famous Magna Carta, to define and guard their customary liberties. To protect themselves from the arbitrary behavior of a king, feudal lords initiated what came to be called *government by consent* and the *rule of law.*

During the Middle Ages, then, there gradually emerged the idea that law was not imposed on inferiors by an absolute monarch but required the collaboration of the king and his subjects; that the king, too, was bound by the law; and that lords had the right to resist a monarch who violated agreements. A related phenomenon was the rise of representative institutions, with which the king was expected to consult on the realm's affairs. The most notable such institution was the British Parliament; although subordinate to the king, it became a permanent part of the state. Later, in the seventeenth century, Parliament would successfully challenge royal authority. Thus, continuity exists between the feudal tradition of a king bound by law and the modern practice of limiting the authority of the head of state.

Although the elements of continuity are clear, the characteristic outlook of the Middle Ages is as different from that of the modern age as it was from the outlook of the ancient world. Religion—which often expressed a disdain for earthly pursuits and a preoccupation with the world to come—was the integrating feature of the Middle Ages, whereas science and secularism—a preoccupation with worldly life—determine the modern outlook. The period from the Italian Renaissance of the fifteenth century through the eighteenth-century Age of Enlightenment constituted a gradual breaking away from the medieval worldview: a rejection of the medieval conception of nature, the individual, and the purpose of life. The transition from medieval to modern was neither sudden nor complete, for there are no sharp demarcation lines separating historical periods. While many distinctively medieval ways endured into the sixteenth, seventeenth, and even eighteenth centuries, these centuries saw as well the rise of new intellectual, political, and economic forms that marked the emergence of modernity.

Medieval thought began with the existence of God and the truth of his revelation as interpreted by the church, which set the standards and defined the purposes for human endeavor. The medieval mind rejected the fundamental principle of Greek philosophy: the autonomy of reason. Without the guidance of revealed truth, reason was seen as feeble. Philosophical inquiry was permissible only if the mind arrived at clerically approved conclusions.

Scholastics engaged in genuine philosophical speculation, but they did not allow philosophy to challenge the basic premises of their faith. For them, the dissemination of views that contradicted church doctrine had to be prohibited lest they corrupt the mind of the faithful, endangering their salvation. Unlike either ancient or modern thinkers, medieval schoolmen ultimately believed that reason alone could not provide a unified view of nature or society. A rational soul had to be guided by a divine light. To understand the natural world properly, it was necessary to know its relationship to the higher world. The discoveries of reason had to accord with Scripture as interpreted by the church. In medieval thought, says the historian-philosopher Ernst Cassirer,

> *neither science nor morality, neither law nor state, can be erected on its own foundations. Supernatural assistance is always needed to bring them to true perfection. . . . Reason is and remains the servant of revelation; within the sphere of natural intellectual and psychological forces, reason leads toward, and prepares the ground for, revelation.*[3]

In the modern view, both nature and the human intellect are self-sufficient. Nature is a mathematical system that operates without miracles or any other form of divine intervention. To comprehend nature and society, the mind needs no divine assistance; it accepts no authority above reason. The modern mentality finds it unacceptable to reject the conclusions of science on the basis of clerical authority and revelation or to ground politics, law, or economics on religious dogma. It refuses to settle public issues by appeals

WISDOM URGES MEDIEVAL SCHOLARS FORWARD. During the Middle Ages, Europeans made considerable advances in technology. The astrolabe, quadrant, sundials, and mechanical clocks shown here exemplify medieval technical skills.

to religious belief, which is now seen as a strictly private concern.

Rejecting the medieval division of the universe into higher and lower realms and superior and inferior substances, the modern view postulates the uniformity of nature and of nature's laws: the cosmos knows no privilege of rank; heavenly bodies follow the same laws of nature as earthly objects. Space is geometric and homogeneous, not hierarchical, heterogeneous, and qualitative. The universe is no longer conceived of as finite and closed but is seen as infinite, and its operations are explained mathematically. The modern thinker studies mathematical law and chemical composition, not grades of perfection. Spiritual meaning is not

sought in an examination of the material world. Roger Bacon, for example, described seven coverings of the eye and then concluded that God had fashioned the eye in this manner in order to express the seven gifts of the Spirit. This way of thinking is alien to the modern outlook. So, too, is the medieval belief that natural disasters, such as plagues and famines, are God's punishments for people's sins.

The outlook of the modern West also broke with the rigid division of medieval society into three orders: clergy, nobles, and commoners. The intellectual justification for this arrangement, as expressed by the English prelate John of Salisbury (c. 1115–1180), has been rejected by modern

Westerners: "For inferiors owe it to their superiors to provide them with service, just as the superiors in their turn owe it to their inferiors to provide them with all things needful for their protection and succor."[4]

Opposing the feudal principle that an individual's obligations and rights are a function of his or her rank in society, the modern view stresses equality of opportunity and equal treatment under the law. It rejects the idea that society should be guided by clergy, who are deemed to possess a special wisdom; by nobles, who are entitled to special privileges; and by monarchs, who are thought to receive their power from God.

The modern West has also rejected the personal and customary character of feudal law. As the modern state developed, law assumed an impersonal and objective character. For example, if a lord demanded more than the customary forty days of military service, a vassal might refuse to comply because he would see the lord's request as an unpardonable violation of custom and agreement, as well as an infringement on his liberties. In the modern state, with a constitution and a representative assembly, if a new law increasing the length of military service is passed, it merely replaces the old law. People do not refuse to obey it because the government has broken faith or violated custom.

In the modern world, the individual's relationship to the universe has been radically transformed. Medieval people lived in a geocentric universe that was finite in space and time. The universe was small, enclosed by a sphere of stars, beyond which were the heavens. The universe, it was believed, was some four thousand years old, and, in the not-too-distant future, Christ would return and human history would end. People in the Middle Ages knew why they were on earth and what was expected of them; they never doubted that heaven would be their reward for living a Christian life. Preparation for heaven was the ultimate aim of life.

This comforting medieval vision is alien to the modern outlook. Today, in a universe more than thirteen billion years old, in which the earth is a tiny speck floating in an endless cosmic ocean, where life evolved over tens of millions of years, many Westerners no longer believe that human beings are special children of God; that heaven is their ultimate goal; that under their feet is hell, where grotesque demons torment sinners; and that God is an active agent in human history. To many intellectuals, the universe seems unresponsive to people's religious supplications, and life's purpose is sought within the limits of earthly existence. Science and secularism have driven Christianity and faith from their central position to the periphery of human concerns.

In the nineteenth and twentieth centuries, Christian thinkers lamented the waning of faith. Distressed by all-consuming secularism, crude materialism, and vicious class and national antagonisms, these thinkers attributed the ills of the modern West to a diminishing commitment to Christianity and called for spiritual renewal. Some of them, looking back nostalgically to the Middle Ages when life had an overriding religious purpose and few doubted the truth of Christian teachings, contended that the modern West would benefit from a reaffirmation of those Christian concerns and values that had energized medieval society.

The modern outlook developed gradually in the period from the Renaissance to the eighteenth-century Age of Enlightenment. Mathematics rendered the universe comprehensible. Economic and political thought broke free of the religious frame of reference. Science became the great hope of the future. The thinkers of the Enlightenment wanted to liberate humanity from superstition, ignorance, and traditions that could not pass the test of reason. They saw themselves as emancipating culture from theological dogma and clerical authority. Rejecting the Christian idea of a person's inherent sinfulness, they held that the individual was basically good and that evil resulted from faulty institutions, poor education, and bad leadership. Thus, the concept of a rational and free society in which individuals could realize their potential slowly emerged.

❖   ❖   ❖

NOTES

1. Quoted in David Knowles, *The Evolution of Medieval Thought* (New York: Vintage Books, 1964), 123.

2. Thomas Aquinas, *Summa Theologica*, Pt. 1, question 2, art. 3. Excerpted in Anton C. Pegis, ed., *Introduction to Saint Thomas Aquinas* (New York: Modern Library, 1948), 25.

3. Ernst Cassirer, *The Philosophy of the Enlightenment* (Boston: Beacon Press, 1955), 40.

4. John of Salisbury, *Policraticus*, trans. John Dickinson (New York: Russell & Russell, 1963), 243–244.

The Art of the Ancient World and the Middle Ages

The art of the classical period (c. fifth century B.C.) was important not only to the ancient Greeks but also to the Romans and to later generations, from the Renaissance to the postmodern period of the late twentieth century. Through the ages, classical art has been kept alive—adopted, adapted, altered, and appreciated—by artists and craftspeople. Why has the classical style remained at the forefront of artistic endeavor?

The classical period has given us the first works of the Western world to represent the human form with accuracy. The body itself was the sculptors' subject. Their aim was to shape their marble so as to make a general and schematic figure lifelike. Classical sculpture has been a powerful learning device for aspiring artisans from Michelangelo to nineteenth-century artists such as Auguste Rodin. Ancient sculptures—and plaster casts made from them—have been used as teaching tools by educators since the Renaissance. Learning to draw from casts of ancient works was the traditional first step in an artist's education; even many abstract artists of the twentieth century had a solid grounding in works of the classical period.

Praxiteles: Hermes with Young Dionysus, c. 350 B.C. Praxiteles (fl. 375–330 B.C.) is renowned for the quality of his marble sculpture, such as the *Hermes with Young Dionysus*, considered one of his finest works. The statue has many of the attributes that distinguish classical sculpture at its best. The stance is relaxed: an S-curve takes the weight off of one leg and shifts it to the opposite hip. This *contrapposto* or counterbalanced pose draws attention to every part of the god's body. The sculpture is so realistic and fluid that viewers might forget they are looking at marble. How does this work express the humanistic outlook of classical Greece? (Archaeological Museum, Olympia, Archaia, Greece/The Bridgeman Art Library International.)

Hellenistic Sculpture: *The Laocoön,* **Second Century** B.C. This Hellenistic sculpture, attributed to three artists, depicts the suffering, anguish, and death of the mythological Laocoön and his sons as divine retribution for his having broken an oath. It presents an interesting contrast to earlier Hellenic art, which was characteristically harmonious and serene. What statement does the shape and arrangement of the figures in the group seem to be making about human destiny? How does it differ from the usual approach of Hellenic art in portraying the human figure? (Scala/Art Resource, N.Y.)

Detail of Pompeian Wall Fresco: Lady Playing the Cithara. Upon the removal of lava and ash from Pompeii, a first-century Roman city appeared, providing historians with data on the daily life of almost twenty centuries ago. What does this fresco scene disclose about the state of Roman culture and the lives of Roman matrons? (© The Art Gallery Collection/Alamy.)

Apse Mosaic: Justinian and Attendants, Church of San Vitale, Ravenna. Emperor Justinian, who ruled Byzantium from 527 to 565, appears in this mosaic as a symbol of Christ rather than as an ordinary ruler on earth. The golden halo and the presence of exactly twelve attendants, reminiscent of the Twelve Apostles, confirm this impression. The way in which an artist depicts the human figure reveals a lot about past cultures. What can we learn about Byzantium by comparing the portrayal of Justinian with that of the Roman matron playing the cithara on the previous page? (Scala/Art Resource, N.Y.)

Byzantine School: *Enthroned Madonna and Child*, **Thirteenth Century.** During the thirteenth century, the Byzantine style, characterized by a blending of the art of Byzantium and the Catholic West, emerged in Italy. An excellent example of this fusion is evident in the *Enthroned Madonna and Child*, probably painted by a Greek artist working in Italy. What is typically Byzantine about this work is the richness of color and the use of gold in the background and in the Madonna's robes. The faces of the figures, the high-backed wooden throne, the halos decorated with floral patterns, and the full-length image of the Virgin on her throne show an Italian influence. Why is Mary seated on a throne? How would a medieval viewer interpret this painting? (National Gallery of Art, Washington, D.C., Gift of Mrs. Otto H. Kahn, 1940.)

April from *Les trés riches heures* of Jean, Duke of Berry. This page from a beautifully illustrated volume of prayers, which was made during 1413 through 1416, is one of the paintings of months appearing in the nobleman's book. What does this scene reveal about the lifestyle of nobles, both men and women? (World History Archive/Newscom)

Domenico Veneziano (c. 1410–1461): *Madonna and Child with Saints,* c. 1445.
This Florentine master painted the altar panel (6' 7-1/2" × 6' 11-7/8") in a new
style, called *sacra conversazione* (sacred conversation). The enthroned Madonna
and child are framed by architectural elements and flanked by the formal, solemn
figures of saints, who seem to converse with her or between themselves, or even
with the onlooker. Saint John, to the left of the child and the Madonna, gazes out
of the painting as he points to them, in effect directing the onlooker's eyes. In his
color scheme, Domenico uses sunlight and spots of bright primary colors, along
with pastels, to present a glowing scene. What elements in the painting indicate
that it is an Early Renaissance work? (DeAgostini/Getty Images)

Hubert or Jan van Eyck: *The Last Judgment*, c. 1420–1425.
The major concern of medieval people was the salvation of
their souls. At the Last Judgment, the good would be drawn
to heaven while the damned would be sealed in hell. In *The
Last Judgment*, the Flemish artist van Eyck depicts this final
division in graphic detail. How does the relationship between
man and the divine portrayed by van Eyck differ from the
classical humanism of ancient Greek art?

Part Three

The Rise of Modernity: From the Renaissance to the Enlightenment

1350–1789

The School of Athens, by Raphael (1483–1520). The ancient Greek philosophers, with Plato and Aristotle at the center, are depicted here, assembled in classical grandeur. Painted to decorate the Vatican, the papal palace in Rome, the picture exudes the Renaissance reverence for classical antiquity and reflects the widely held view that ancient philosophy represented a foreshadowing of Christianity and was essentially in harmony with it.

	Politics and Society	**Thought and Culture**
1300	Hundred Years' War (1337–1453)	Italian Renaissance begins (c. 1350)
1400	War of Roses in England (1455–1485) Rule of Ferdinand and Isabella in Spain (1469–1516) Charles VIII of France (1483–1498) Henry VII, beginning of Tudor dynasty in England (1485–1509) Columbus reaches America (1492)	Early Renaissance artists and architects: Brunelleschi, Masaccio, van Eyck Printing with movable type (c. 1450) Humanists: Valla, Pico della Mirandola Late Renaissance artists: Botticelli, Leonardo da Vinci, Michelangelo, Raphael, Bellini, Giorgione, Titian Renaissance spreads to Northern Europe (late 15th and early 16th cent.)
1500	Henry VIII of England (1509–1547) Francis I of France (1515–1547) Charles V, Holy Roman Emperor (1519–1556) Henry VIII of England breaks with Rome (1529–1536) Council of Trent (1545–1563) Peace of Augsburg in Germany (1555) Philip II of Spain (1556–1598) Elizabeth I of England (1558–1603) Religious wars in France (1562–1598) Revolt of the Netherlands from Spain (1566–1609) Defeat of Spanish Armada (1588)	Humanists: Castiglione, Erasmus, Montaigne, Rabelais, More, Cervantes, Shakespeare Machiavelli, *The Prince* (1513) Luther writes his *Ninety-Five Theses* (1517) Copernicus, *On the Revolution of the Heavenly Spheres* (1543)
1600	Thirty Years' War (1618–1648) English Revolution (1640–1660, 1688–1689) Louis XIV of France (1643–1715) Peter the Great of Russia (1682–1725)	Scientists: Kepler, Galileo, Newton Philosophers: Bacon, Descartes, Hobbes, Locke
1700	War of Spanish Succession (1702–1714) War of Austrian Succession (1740–1748) Frederick the Great of Prussia (1740–1786) Maria Theresa of Austria (1740–1780) Seven Years' War (1756–1763) American Declaration of Independence (1776) American Revolution (1776–1783) Beginning of French Revolution (1789)	Enlightenment thinkers: Voltaire, Montesquieu, Rousseau, Diderot, Hume, Adam Smith, Thomas Jefferson, Kant

Chapter 8

Transition to the Modern Age: Renaissance and Reformation

- ■ **Italy: Birthplace of the Renaissance**
- ■ **The Renaissance Outlook**
- ■ **Renaissance Art**
- ■ **The Spread of the Renaissance**
- ■ **The Renaissance and the Modern Age**
- ■ **Background to the Reformation: The Medieval Church in Crisis**
- ■ **The Lutheran Revolt**
- ■ **The Spread of the Reformation**
- ■ **The Catholic Response**
- ■ **The Reformation and the Modern Age**

Focus Questions

1. What conditions gave rise to the Italian Renaissance?
2. What is the historical significance of Renaissance humanism?
3. How did Machiavelli's political thought mark a break with the medieval outlook?
4. What are the general features of Renaissance art?
5. Why is the Renaissance considered a departure from the Middle Ages and the beginning of modernity?
6. How did Luther's theology mark a break with the church? Why did many Germans become followers of Luther?
7. How did the Reformation contribute to the shaping of the modern world?

*F*rom the Italian Renaissance of the fifteenth century through the Age of Enlightenment of the eighteenth century, the outlook and institutions of the Middle Ages disintegrated and distinctly modern forms emerged. The radical change in European civilization affected every level of society. On the economic level, commerce and industry expanded greatly, and capitalism largely replaced typically medieval forms of economic organization. On the political level, central government grew stronger at the expense of feudalism. On the religious level, the rise of Protestantism fragmented the unity of Christendom. On the social level, middle-class townspeople, increasing in number and wealth, began to play a more important role in economic and cultural life. On the cultural level, the clergy lost its monopoly over learning, and the otherworldly orientation of the Middle Ages gave way to a secular outlook in literature and the arts. Theology, the queen of knowledge in the Middle Ages, surrendered its crown to science, and reason, which had been subordinate to revelation, asserted its independence.

Many of these tendencies manifested themselves dramatically during the Renaissance (1350–1600). The word *renaissance* means "rebirth," and it is used to refer to the attempt by artists and thinkers to recover and apply the ancient learning and standards of Greece and Rome. During the Renaissance, individuals showed an increasing concern for worldly life and self-consciously aspired to shape their own destinies, an attitude that is the key to modernity.

To be sure, the Renaissance was not a complete and abrupt break with the Middle Ages. Many medieval ways and attitudes persisted. Nevertheless, the view that the Renaissance represents the birth of modernity has much to recommend it. Renaissance writers and artists themselves were aware of their age's novelty. They looked back on the medieval centuries as a "Dark Age" that followed the grandeur of ancient Greece and Rome, and they believed that they were experiencing a rebirth of cultural greatness. Renaissance artists and writers were fascinated by the cultural forms of Greece and Rome; they sought to imitate classical style and to capture the secular spirit of antiquity. In the

process, they broke with medieval artistic and literary forms. They valued the full development of human talent and expressed a new excitement about the possibilities of life in this world. This outlook represents a break with the Middle Ages and the emergence of modernity.

The Renaissance, then, was an age of transition. It saw the rejection of certain elements of the medieval outlook, the revival of classical cultural forms, and the emergence of distinctly modern attitudes. This rebirth began in Italy during the fourteenth century and gradually spread north and west to Germany, France, England, and Spain during the late fifteenth and sixteenth centuries.

The Renaissance was one avenue to modernity; another was the Reformation. By dividing Europe into Catholic and Protestant, the Reformation ended medieval religious unity. It also accentuated the importance of the individual person, a distinctive feature of the modern outlook. It stressed individual conscience rather than clerical authority, insisted on a personal relationship between each man or woman and God, and called attention to the individual's inner religious capacities.   ❖

ITALY: BIRTHPLACE OF THE RENAISSANCE

The city-states of northern Italy that spawned the Renaissance were developed urban centers where people had the wealth, freedom, and inclination to cultivate the arts and to enjoy the fruits of worldly life. In Italy, moreover, reminders of ancient Rome's grandeur were visible everywhere: Roman roads, monuments, and manuscripts intensified the Italians' links to their Roman past. Northern Italian city-states had developed into flourishing commercial and banking centers and had monopolized trade in the Mediterranean during the twelfth and thirteenth centuries. The predominance of business and commerce within these city-states meant that the feudal nobility, which held the land beyond the city walls, played a much less important part in government than it did elsewhere in Europe. By the end of the twelfth century, these city-states had adopted a fairly uniform pattern of republican

Chronology 8.1 ❖ The Renaissance and the Reformation

1304–1374	Petrarch, "father of humanism"
c. 1445	Johann Gutenberg invents movable metal type
1513	Machiavelli writes *The Prince*
1517	Martin Luther writes his *Ninety-Five Theses* and the Reformation begins
1520	Pope Leo X excommunicates Luther
1524–1526	German peasants revolt
1529	English Parliament accepts Henry VIII's Reformation
1534	Henry VIII is declared head of the Church of England; King Francis I of France declares Protestants to be heretics; Ignatius Loyola founds the Society of Jesus; Anabaptists, radical reformers, capture Münster in Westphalia
1535	Sir Thomas More, English humanist and author of *Utopia*, is executed for treason
1536–1564	Calvin leads the Reformation in Geneva
1545–1563	Council of Trent
1555	Peace of Augsburg

self-government built around the office of a chief magistrate.

This republicanism proved precarious, however. During the fourteenth and early fifteenth centuries, republican institutions in one city after another toppled, giving way to rule by despots. The city-states had come to rely on mercenary troops, whose leaders, the notorious *condottieri*—unschooled in and owing no loyalty to the republican tradition—simply seized power during emergencies.

Florence, the leading city of the Renaissance, held out against the trend toward despotism for a long time. But by the mid-fifteenth century, even Florentine republicanism was giving way before the intrigues of a rich banking family, the Medici. They had installed themselves in power in the 1430s with the return of Cosimo de' Medici from exile. Cosimo's grandson, Lorenzo the Magnificent, completed the destruction of the republican constitution in 1480 when he managed to set up a government staffed by his supporters.

New ways of life developed within the Italian city-states. Prosperous businesspeople played a leading role in the political and cultural life of the city. With the expansion of commerce and industry, the feudal values of birth, military prowess, and a fixed hierarchy of lords and vassals decayed in favor of ambition and individual achievement, whether at court, in the counting house, or inside the artist's studio.

Art served as a focus of civic pride and patriotism. Members of the urban upper class—patricians—became patrons of the arts, providing funds to support promising artists and writers. Just as they contended on the battlefield, rulers competed for art and artists to bolster their prestige. The popes, too, heaped wealth on artists to enhance their own flagging prestige. They became the most lavish patrons of all, as the works of Michelangelo and Raphael testify.

Some women of wealthy and noble Italian families were educated in classical languages and literature and served as patrons of the arts. Thus, Isabella d'Este, wife of the ruler of a small state in northern Italy, knew Latin and Greek, collected books, and displayed works of artists that she had commissioned.

The result of this new patronage by popes and patricians was an explosion of artistic creativity. The amount, and especially the nature, of this patronage also helped shape both art and the artist. Portraiture became a separate genre for the first time since antiquity and was developed much further than ever before. Patrician rivalry and insecurity of status, fed by the Renaissance ethic of individual achievement and reward, produced a scramble for honor and reputation. This pursuit fostered the desire to be memorialized in a painting if not in a sculpture. Distinguished portrait painters and sculptors were in great demand.

The great artists emerged as famous men by virtue of their exercise of brush and chisel. In the Middle Ages, artists had been regarded as craftsmen who did lowly (manual) labor and who as a result were to be accorded little if any status. Indeed, for the most part they remained anonymous. But the unparalleled Renaissance demand for art brought artists public recognition.

THE RENAISSANCE OUTLOOK

Increasingly, a secular outlook came to dominate Renaissance society. Intrigued by the active life of the city and eager to enjoy the worldly pleasures that their money could obtain, wealthy merchants and bankers moved away from the medieval preoccupation with salvation. Reviving the Greco-Roman view that the complete individual is a political animal who participates actively in civil affairs, many Renaissance figures were critical of monastic withdrawal and asceticism and of the scholastics' purely contemplative life. To be sure, the urban elite were neither nonbelievers nor atheists, but, more and more, religion had to compete with worldly concerns. Consequently, members of the urban upper class paid religion less heed or at least did not allow it to interfere with their quest for the full life. The challenge and pleasure of living well in this world seemed more exciting than the promise of heaven. This outlook found concrete expression in Renaissance art and literature.

Individualism was another hallmark of the Renaissance. In contrast to medieval thinkers, who emphasized the Christian belief in human weakness, sinfulness, and dependency, Renaissance figures revived the classical confidence in human capacities and extolled the infinite possibilities of individual life. The urban elite sought to assert their own personalities, demonstrate their unique talents, and gain recognition for their accomplishments. Traditional feudal values of birth and place in a fixed hierarchy were superseded by the desire for individual achievement. Individual worth was interpreted far more broadly than it had been by feudal lords, who had equated worth with military prowess. Renaissance Italy produced a distinctive human type, the "universal man": a many-sided person who not only showed mastery of the ancient classics, an appreciation of and even talent for the visual arts, and a concern for the day-to-day affairs of his city, but also aspired to mold his life into a work of art. Disdaining Christian humility, Renaissance individuals took pride in their talents and worldly accomplishments—"I can work miracles," said the great Leonardo da Vinci. Renaissance artists portrayed the individual character of human beings, captured the rich diversity of human personality, produced the first portraits since Roman times, and affixed their signatures to their works. Renaissance writers probed their own thoughts and feelings and manifested a self-awareness that characterizes the modern outlook. This new outlook, however, applied almost exclusively to an elite—princes, courtiers, court ladies, wealthy urban families, and exceptionally talented artists and writers.

In later centuries, as the secular outlook gathered strength, it focused even more intently on the individual. It led to the conviction that the individual should be freed from domination by otherworldly concerns, theological dogma, and ecclesiastical authority and should concentrate on the full development of human talents and on improving the quality of earthly existence.

During the Renaissance, the secular spirit and the concern with the individual found expression in the intellectual movement called humanism and in a political theory that separated politics from Christian principles.

Humanism

Humanism, the most characteristic intellectual movement of the Renaissance, was an educational and cultural program based on the study of ancient Greek and Roman literature. The humanist attitude toward antiquity differed from that of medieval scholars, who had taken pains to fit classical learning into a Christian worldview. Renaissance humanists did not subordinate the classics to the requirements of Christian doctrines. Rather, they valued ancient literature for its own sake—for its clear and graceful style and for its insights into human nature. From the ancient classics, humanists expected to learn much that could not be provided by medieval writings: for instance, how to live well in this world and how to perform one's civic duties. For the humanists, the classics were a guide to the good life, the active life. To fulfill one's capabilities to have self-confidence—achieve self-cultivation, to write well, to speak well, and to live well—it was necessary to know the classics. In contrast to scholastic philosophers, who used Greek philosophy to prove the truth of Christian doctrines, Italian humanists used classical learning to nourish their new interest in a worldly life. Whereas medieval scholars were familiar with only some ancient Latin writers, Renaissance humanists restored to circulation every Roman work that could be found. Similarly, knowledge of Greek was very rare in Latin Christendom during the Middle Ages, but Renaissance humanists increasingly cultivated the study of Greek in order to read Homer, Demosthenes, Plato, and other ancients in the original. Fueling their interest in ancient Greece was the entry into Italy of Byzantine scholars fleeing the Turkish threat. Eager Italians sat at the feet of these scholars who taught them Greek language and classical learning. Noble families often employed these learned Greeks to tutor their sons.

Although predominantly a secular movement, Italian humanism was not un-Christian. True, humanists often treated moral problems in a purely secular manner. Yet in dealing with religious and theological issues, they did not challenge Christian belief or question the validity of the Bible. They did, however, attack scholastic philosophy for its hairsplitting arguments and preoccupation with trivial matters. They stressed instead a purer form of Christianity based on the direct study of the Bible and the writings of the church fathers.

One of the early humanists, sometimes called the father of humanism, was Petrarch (1304–1374). Petrarch and his followers carried the recovery of the classics further through their systematic attempt to discover the classical roots of medieval Italian rhetoric. Petrarch's own efforts to learn Greek were largely unsuccessful, but he advanced humanist learning by encouraging his students to master the ancient tongue. Petrarch was particularly drawn to Cicero, the ancient Roman orator. Following Cicero's example, he maintained that education should consist not only of learning and knowing things but also of learning how to communicate one's knowledge and how to use it for the public good. Therefore, the emphasis in education should be on rhetoric and moral philosophy—wisdom combined with eloquence. This was the key to virtue in the ruler, the citizen, and the republic. Petrarch helped to make Ciceronian values dominant among the humanists. His followers set up schools to inculcate the new Ciceronian educational ideal.

Implicit in the humanist educational ideal was a radical transformation of the Christian idea of human beings. According to the medieval (Augustinian) view, men and women, because of their sinful nature, were incapable of attaining excellence through their own efforts. They were completely subject to divine will. In contrast, the humanists, recalling the classical Greek concept of human beings, made the achievement of excellence through individual striving the end not only of education but of life itself. Moreover, because individuals were capable of this goal, it was their duty to pursue it as the end of life. The pursuit was not effortless; indeed, it took extraordinary energy and skill.

People, then, were deemed capable of excellence in every sphere and duty-bound to make the effort. For the humanist, the honor, fame, and even glory bestowed by one's city or patron for meritorious deeds were the ultimate rewards for effort. The humanist pursuit of praise and reputation became something of a Renaissance cult.

This emphasis on human creative powers was one of the most characteristic and influential doctrines of the Renaissance. A classic expression of it is found in the *Oration on the Dignity of Man* (1486) by Giovanni Pico della Mirandola (1463–1494). Man, said Pico, has the freedom to shape his own life. Pico has God say to man: "We have made you a creature" such that "you may, as the free and proud shaper of your own being, fashion yourself in the form you may prefer."[1]

An attack on the medieval scholastics was also implicit in the humanist educational ideal.

Primary Source

Giovanni Pico della Mirandola: *Oration on the Dignity of Man*

Giovanni Pico della Mirandola (1463–1494) was deeply educated in Christian theology, ancient Greek philosophy, and the cabala, a Jewish tradition of biblical interpretation. His most renowned work, Oration on the Dignity of Man *(1486), excerpted below, has been called a humanist manifesto. Its essential theme is that God has bestowed upon human beings a unique distinction and responsibility: the liberty to determine the form and values our lives shall acquire. The notion that people have the power to shape their own lives is a key element in the emergence of the modern outlook.*

At last it seems to me that I have understood why man is the most fortunate living thing worthhy of all admiration and precisely what rank is his lot in the universal chain of being, a rank to be envied. . . . For it is upon this account that man is justly considered and called a great miracle and a truly remarkable being. . . . [God] accepted man as a work of indeterminate nature, and placing him in the center of the world, addressed him thus: . . .

. . . The nature of all other things in the universe is limited and constrained in accordance with the laws prescribed by us. Constrained by no limits, in accordance with your own free will, in whose hands we have placed you, you shall independently determine the bounds of your own nature. We have placed you at the world's center from where you may more easily observe whatever is in the world. We have made you

neither celestial nor terrestrial, neither mortal nor immortal, so that with honor and freedom of choice, as though the maker and molder of yourself, you may fashion yourself in whatever form you prefer. You shall have the power to degenerate into the inferior forms of life which are brutish; you shall have the power, through your soul's judgment, to rise to the superior orders which are divine. . . .

But why do we reiterate all these things? To the end that from the moment we are born into the condition of being able to become whatever we choose, we should be particularly certain that it may never be said of us that, although born to a privileged position, we failed to realize it and became like brutes and mindless beasts of burden. . . . Otherwise, abusing the most indulgent generosity of the Father, we shall make that freedom of choice which He has given to us into something harmful rather than something beneficial.

Let some holy ambition invade our souls, so that, dissatisfied with mediocrity, we shall eagerly desire the highest things and shall toil with all our strength to obtain them, since we may if we wish. . . .

Question for Analysis

1. Why is Pico's *Oration* called a humanist manifesto?

Julia Conaway Bondanella and Mark Musa, eds., *The Italian Renaissance Reader* (New York: Meridian, 1987), pp. 178–183.

Humanists accused scholastics of corrupting the Latin style of ancient Rome and of dealing with useless questions. This humanist emphasis on the uses of knowledge offered a stimulus to science and art.

So hostile were the humanists to things scholastic and medieval that they reversed the prevailing

view of history. According to the Christian view, history was a simple unfolding of God's will and providence. The humanists, however, stressed the importance of human actions and human will in history—the importance of people as active participants in the shaping of events. They characterized the epoch preceding their own as a period of decline from classical heights—a dark age—and saw their own time as a period of rebirth, representing the recovery of classical wisdom and ideals. Thus, the humanists invented the notion of the Middle Ages as the period separating the ancient world from their own. To the humanists, then, we owe the current periodization of history into ancient, medieval, and modern. The humanists' view also contained an element of today's idea of progress: they dared to think that they, "the moderns," might even surpass the ancient glories of Greece and Rome.

The humanist emphasis on historical scholarship yielded a method of critical inquiry that could help to undermine traditional loyalties and institutions. Medieval thinkers generally did not relate a text to its times but accepted it uncritically as an authoritative work of wisdom. In contrast, Renaissance humanists approached ancient civilization with a critical attitude; they studied texts in a historical context and examined them for authenticity and accuracy. The work of Lorenzo Valla (c. 1407–1457) provides the clearest example of this trend. Educated as a classicist, Valla trained the guns of critical scholarship on the papacy in his most famous work, *Declamation Concerning the False Decretals of Constantine*. The papal claim to temporal authority rested on a document that purported to verify the so-called Donation of Constantine, through which the Emperor Constantine, when he moved the capital of the Roman Empire to Constantinople in the fourth century, had given the pope dominion over the entire Western Empire. But Valla proved that the document was based on an eighth-century forgery because the language at certain points was unknown in Constantine's time and did not come into use until much later.

In Renaissance Italy, some upper- and middle-class girls attended elementary school where they learned to read and write and, in some instances, even studied Latin. Believing that learned daughters brought prestige to the family, some fathers hired tutors to instruct their daughters in the classics. Many educated women had been taught by their enlightened humanist fathers who wanted their daughters to share in the richness of classical culture, which they perceived as training in virtue. Often, however, fathers perceived that education for females would simply make them better wives and household managers. Even educated and talented women were barred from entering the professions and teaching in universities. Several educated women wrote works calling for equal education for women and the right to engage in the same scholarly pursuits as men. For example, Moderata Fonte, a wealthy Venetian, wrote the *Worth of Women* whose subtitle—*Wherein Is Clearly Revealed their Nobility and Their Superiority to Men*—shows the author's intent. The work consists of a dialogue among intelligent and articulate noble Venetian ladies who rail against men's behavior, particularly their determination to subjugate women.

A Revolution in Political Thought

By turning away from the religious orientation of the Middle Ages and discussing the human condition in secular terms, Renaissance humanists opened up new possibilities for thinking about political and moral problems. Niccolò Machiavelli (1469–1527), a keen observer of Italian politics, saw the Italian city-states, ruled by men whose authority rested solely on their cunning and effective use of force, as a new phenomenon. He recognized that traditional political theory, concerned with ideal Christian ends, could not adequately explain it. Italian princes made no effort to justify their policies on religious grounds; war was endemic, and powerful cities took over weaker ones; diplomacy was riddled with intrigue, betrayal, and bribery. In such a tooth-and-claw world—where political survival depended on alertness, cleverness, and strength—medieval theorists, who expected the earthly realm to accord with standards revealed by God, seemed utterly irrelevant. Machiavelli simply wanted rulers to understand how to preserve and expand the state's power. In his book *The Prince,* he expounded a new political theory—one that had no place for Christian morality but coincided with the emerging modern secular state. He himself was aware that his study of statecraft in the cold light of reason, free of religious and moral illusions, represented a new departure.

For Machiavelli, survival was the state's overriding aim; it transcended any concern with moral or religious values and the interests of individual subjects. Removing questions of good and evil from the political realm, Machiavelli maintained that the prince may use any means to save the

Scala/Art Resource, N.Y.

NICCOLÒ MACHIAVELLI (1469–1527). Machiavelli looked back to the ancient Roman republic for his ideals and spent his life serving the city-state of Florence, but as the author of *The Prince*, his name became a byword for atheism and deceit. *Machiavellian* is still used to describe an unscrupulous politician.

state when its survival is at stake. Successful princes, he contended, have always been indifferent to moral and religious considerations—a lesson of history that rulers ignore at their peril. Thus, if the situation warrants it, the prince can violate agreements with other rulers, go back on his word with his subjects, and resort to cruelty and terror.

Machiavelli broke with the distinguishing feature of medieval thought: the division of the universe into the higher world of the heavens and a lower earthly realm. To this extent, he did for politics what Galileo accomplished a century later for physics. Medieval thinkers believed that rulers derived their power from God and had a religious obligation to govern in accordance with God's commands. Rejecting completely this otherworldly, theocentric orientation, Machiavelli ascribed no divine origin or purpose to the state.

He saw it as a natural entity; politics had nothing to do with God's intent or with moral precepts originating in a higher world. Machiavelli's significance as a political thinker rests on the fact that he removed political thought from a religious frame of reference and viewed the state and political behavior in the detached and dispassionate manner of a scientist. In secularizing and rationalizing political philosophy, he initiated a trend of thought that we recognize as distinctly modern.

RENAISSANCE ART

The essential meaning of the Renaissance is conveyed through its art, particularly architecture, sculpture, and painting. Renaissance examples of all three art forms reflect a style that stressed proportion, balance, and harmony. These artistic values were achieved through a new, revolutionary conceptualization of space and spatial relations. To a considerable extent, Renaissance art also reflects the values of Renaissance humanism: a return to classical models in architecture, to the rendering of the nude figure, and to a heroic vision of human beings.

Medieval art served a religious function: the world was a veil merely hinting at the other perfect and eternal world. Renaissance artists continued to utilize religious themes, but they shattered the dominance of religion over art by shifting attention from heaven to the natural world and to the human being. Renaissance artists depicted the human qualities of men and women and celebrated the beauty and grace of the human form. The reference was less to the other world and more to this world, and people were treated as creatures who found their spiritual destiny as they fulfilled their human one. By celebrating the dignity, worth, and creative capacity of the individual and the beauty of the human form, Renaissance art gave original expression to classical humanism. Renaissance artists also developed a new conception of visual space, which resulted in a naturalistic, three-dimensional rendering of the real world. It was a quantitative space in which the artist, employing reason and mathematics, portrayed the essential form of the object in perspective, as it would appear to the human eye. Thus, at its most distinctive, Renaissance art represents a conscious revolt against the art of

LEONARDO DA VINCI, *THE PROPORTIONS OF MAN*. Leonardo was fascinated by the human body. In his notebook, his written observations are accompanied by this marvelous drawing of the body, conceived and framed with realism and proportion.

Hulton Archive/Getty Images.

Byzantine painting, he created figures delineated by alterations in light and shade. He also developed several techniques of perspective, representing three-dimensional figures and objects on two-dimensional surfaces so that they appear to stand in space. Giotto's figures look remarkably alive. They are drawn and arranged in space to tell a story, and their expressions and the illusion of movement they convey heighten the dramatic effect. Giotto's best works were *frescoes,* wall paintings painted while the plaster was still wet, or *fresh*. Lionized in his own day, Giotto had no immediate successors, and his ideas were not taken up and developed further for almost a century.

By the early fifteenth century, the revival of classical learning had begun in earnest. In Florence, it had its artistic counterpart among a circle of architects, painters, and sculptors who sought to revive classical art. The leader of this group was an architect, Filippo Brunelleschi (1377–1446). He designed churches reflecting classical models. To him we also owe a scientific discovery of the first importance in the history of art: the rules of perspective. Giotto had revived the ancient technique of foreshortening; Brunelleschi completed the discovery by rendering perspective in mathematical terms.

the Middle Ages. This revolt produced revolutionary discoveries that served as the foundation of Western art up to the twentieth century.

In art, as in literature, the Florentines played a leading role in this esthetic transformation. They, more than anyone else, were responsible for the way artists saw and drew for centuries and for the way most Western people still see or want to see. The first major contributor to Renaissance painting was the Florentine painter Giotto (c. 1276–1337). Borrowing from His devotion to ancient models and his new tool of mathematical perspective set the stage for the further development of Renaissance painting. Brunelleschi's young Florentine friend Masaccio (1401–1428) took up the challenge. Faithful to the new rules of perspective, Masaccio was also concerned with painting statuesque figures and endowing his paintings with a grandeur and simplicity whose inspiration was classical. Perspective came with all the force of religious revelation.

In his work *On Painting*, Leon Battista Alberti (1404–1472), a humanist, scholar, and art theoretician, brought the Renaissance trend toward perspective art to a summation by advancing the first mathematical theory of artistic perspective. By defining visual space and the relationship between the object and the observer in mathematical terms, Renaissance art and artistic theory helped to pave the way for the development of the modern scientific approach to nature, which later found expression in the astronomy of Copernicus and the physics of Galileo.

Renaissance artists were dedicated to representing things as they are, or at least as they are seen to be. Part of the inspiration for this was also classical. The ancient ideal of beauty was the beautiful nude. Renaissance admiration for ancient art meant that for the first time since the fall of Rome artists studied anatomy; they learned to draw the human form by having models pose for them, a practice fundamental to artistic training to this day. Another member of Brunelleschi's circle, the Florentine sculptor Donatello (1386–1466), also showed renewed interest in the human form.

The great Renaissance artists included Leonardo da Vinci (1452–1519), Michelangelo Buonarroti (1475–1564), and Raphael Santi (1483–1520). All of them were closely associated with Florence. Leonardo was a scientist and engineer as well as a great artist. He was an expert at fortifications and gunnery, an inventor, an anatomist, and a naturalist. Bringing careful observation of nature to his paintings, he combined it with powerful psychological insight to produce works of unsurpassed genius, though few in number. Among his most important paintings are *The Last Supper* and *La Gioconda*, or the *Mona Lisa*. The *Mona Lisa* is an example of an artistic invention of Leonardo's—what the Italians call *sfumato*. Leonardo left the outlines of the face a little vague and shadowy; this freed it of any wooden quality that more exact drawing would impart, and thus made it more lifelike and mysterious.

Michelangelo's creation of artistic harmony derived from a mastery of anatomy and drawing. His model in painting came from sculpture: his paintings are sculpted drawings. He was, of course, a sculptor of the highest genius whose approach to his art was poetic and visionary. Instead of trying to impose form on marble, he thought of sculpting as releasing the form from the rock. Among his greatest sculptures are *David, Moses,* and *The Dying Slave*. Michelangelo was also an architect; patronized by the pope, he designed the dome of the new Saint Peter's Basilica in Rome. But perhaps his most stupendous work was the ceiling of the Sistine Chapel in the Vatican, commissioned by Pope Julius II. In four years, working with little assistance, Michelangelo covered the empty space with the most monumental sculpted pictures ever painted, pictures that summarize the Old Testament story. *The Creation of Adam* is the most famous of these superlative frescoes.

Raphael, the last of these three artistic giants, is especially famous for the sweetness of his Madonnas. But he was capable of painting other subjects and conveying other moods, as his portrait of his patron, *Pope Leo X with Two Cardinals*, reveals.

THE SPREAD OF THE RENAISSANCE

Aided by the invention of printing, the Renaissance spread to Germany, France, England, and Spain in the late fifteenth and sixteenth centuries. In its migration northward, Renaissance culture adapted itself to conditions different from those in Italy—particularly the strength of lay piety. For example, the Brethren of the Common Life was a lay movement emphasizing education and practical piety. Intensely Christian and at the same time anticlerical, the people in such lay movements found in Renaissance culture tools for sharpening their wits against the clergy—not to undermine the faith, but rather to restore it to its apostolic purity.

Thus, northern humanists, like those in Italy, were profoundly devoted to ancient learning. But nothing in northern humanism compares with the non-Christian trend of the Italian Renaissance. The northerners were chiefly interested in the question of what constituted original Christianity. They sought a model in the light of which they might reform the corrupted church of their own time.

Humanism outside Italy was less concerned with the revival of classical values than with the reform of Christianity and society through a program of Christian humanism. The Christian humanists cultivated the new arts of rhetoric and history, as well as the classical languages—Latin, Greek, and Hebrew. But the ultimate purpose of these pursuits was more religious than it had been in Italy, where secular interests predominated. Northern humanists used humanist scholarship and language to satirize and vilify medieval scholastic Christianity and to build a purer, more Scriptural Christianity. The discovery of accurate biblical texts, it was hoped, would lead to a great religious awakening. Protestant reformers, including Martin Luther, relied on humanist scholarship.

Erasmian Humanism

To Erasmus (c. 1466–1536) belongs the credit for making Renaissance humanism an international movement. He was educated in the Netherlands by the Brethren of the Common Life, which was one of the most advanced religious movements of the age, combining mystical piety with rigorous humanist pedagogy. Erasmus traveled throughout Europe as a humanist educator and biblical scholar. Like other Christian humanists, he trusted the power of words and used his pen to attack scholastic theology and clerical abuses and promote his philosophy of Christ. His weapon was satire, and his *Praise of Folly* and *Colloquies* won him a reputation for acid wit vented at the expense of conventional religion.

True religion, Erasmus argued, does not depend on dogma, ritual, or clerical power. Rather, it is revealed clearly and simply in the Bible and therefore is directly accessible to all people, from the wise and great to the poor and humble. Erasmian humanism stressed toleration, kindness, and respect for human rationality.

This clear but quiet voice was drowned out by the storms of the Reformation, and the Erasmian emphasis on the individual's natural capacities succumbed to a renewed emphasis on human sinfulness and dogmatic theology. Erasmus was caught in the middle and condemned on all sides; for him, the Reformation was both a personal and a historical tragedy. He had worked for peace and unity, only to experience a spectacle of war and fragmentation. Erasmian humanism, however,

PORTRAIT OF ERASMUS (1523) BY HANS HOLBEIN THE YOUNGER. Erasmus was the leading early sixteenth-century Christian humanist. He insisted that all Christians should strive to think rationally and to live peacefully with one another, despite their differences.

survived these horrors as an ideal, and during the next two centuries, whenever thinkers sought toleration and rational religion, they looked back to Erasmus for inspiration.

French and English Humanism

François Rabelais (c. 1494–c. 1553), a former monk, exemplified the humanist spirit in France. In response to religious dogmatism, he asserted the essential goodness of the individual and the right to enjoy the world rather than being bound by the fear of a punishing God. His folk-epic *Gargantua and Pantagruel* celebrates earthly life and earthly enjoyments, expresses an appreciation for secular learning and a confidence in human nature, and attacks monastic orders and clerical education for stifling the human spirit.

According to Rabelais, once freed from dogmatic theology, with its irrelevant concerns, and narrow-minded clergy, who deprived them of life's joys, people could, by virtue of their native goodness, build a paradise on earth and disregard the one dreamed up by theologians. In *Gargantua and Pantagruel,* Rabelais imagined a monastery where men and women spend their lives "not in laws, statutes, or rules, but according to their own free will and pleasure." They slept and ate when they desired and learned to "read, write, sing, play upon several musical instruments, and speak five or six . . . languages and compose in them all very quaintly." They observed only one rule: "do what thou wilt."[2]

The most influential humanist of the early English Renaissance was Sir Thomas More (1478–1535), who studied at Oxford. His impact came from both his writing and his career. Trained as a lawyer, he was a successful civil servant and member of Parliament. His most famous book is *Utopia,* the first major utopian treatise to be written in the West since Plato's *Republic* and one of the most original works of the entire Renaissance. Many humanists had attacked private wealth as the principal source of pride, greed, and human cruelty. However, only More carried this insight to its ultimate conclusion: in *Utopia,* he called for the elimination of private property. He had too keen a sense of human weakness to think that people could become perfect, but he used *Utopia* to call attention to contemporary abuses and to suggest radical reforms.

More succeeded Cardinal Wolsey as lord chancellor under Henry VIII. But when the king broke with the Roman Catholic church, More resigned, unable to reconcile his conscience with the king's rejection of papal supremacy. Three years later, in July 1535, More was executed for treason because he refused to swear an oath acknowledging the king's ecclesiastical supremacy.

William Shakespeare (1564–1616), widely considered the greatest playwright the world has ever produced, gave expression to conventional Renaissance values: honor, heroism, and the struggle against fate and fortune. But there is nothing conventional about Shakespeare's treatment of characters possessing these virtues. His greatest plays, the tragedies (*King Lear, Julius Caesar,* and others), explore a common theme: men, even heroic men, despite virtue, are able to overcome their human weaknesses only with the greatest difficulty, if at all. What fascinated Shakespeare was the contradiction between the Renaissance image of nobility, which is often the self-image of Shakespeare's heroes, and human beings' capacity for evil and self-destruction. The plays are thus intensely human, but so much so that humanism fades into the background; art transcends doctrine to represent life itself.

THE RENAISSANCE AND THE MODERN AGE

The Renaissance, then, marks the birth of modernity in the conception of the individual. Central to this birth was a bold new view of human nature that departed from the medieval view: individuals in all endeavors are not constrained by a destiny imposed by God from the outside but are free to make their own destiny, guided only by the example of the past, the force of present circumstances, and the drives of their own inner nature. Set free from theology, individuals were seen as the products, and in turn the shapers, of history; their future would be the work of their own free will.

Within the Italian city-states where the Renaissance was born, rich merchants were at least as important as the church hierarchy and the old nobility. Commercial wealth and a new politics produced a new culture that relied heavily on ancient Greece and Rome. This return to antiquity also entailed a rejection of the Middle Ages as dark, barbarous, and rude. The humanists clearly preferred the secular learning of ancient Greece and Rome to the clerical learning of the more recent past. The reason for this was obvious: the ancients had the same worldly concerns as the humanists; the scholastics did not.

The revival of antiquity by the humanists did not mean, however, that they identified completely with it. The revival itself was done too self-consciously for that. In the very act of looking back, the humanists differentiated themselves from the past and recognized that they were different. They were in this sense the first modern historians, because they could study and appreciate the past for its own sake and, to some degree, on its own terms.

In the works of Renaissance artists and thinkers, the world was, to a large extent, depicted and explained without reference to a higher supernatural realm of meaning and ,authority. This is clearly seen in Machiavelli's analysis of politics. Renaissance humanism exuded a deep confidence in the capacities of able people, instructed in the wisdom of the ancients, to understand and change the world.

This new confidence was closely related to another distinctive feature of the Renaissance: the cult of the individual. Both prince and painter were motivated in part by the desire to display their talents and to satisfy their ambitions. This individual striving was rewarded and encouraged by the larger society of rich patrons and calculating princes, which valued ability. Gone was the medieval Christian emphasis on the virtue of self-denial and the sin of pride. Instead, the Renaissance placed the highest value on self-expression and self-fulfillment—on the realization of individual potential, especially of the gifted few. The Renaissance fostered an atmosphere in which talent, even genius, was allowed to flourish.

To be sure, the Renaissance image of the individual and the world, bold and novel, was the exclusive prerogative of a small, well-educated urban elite and did not reach down to include the masses. Nevertheless, the Renaissance set an example of what people might achieve in art and architecture, taste and refinement, education and urban culture. In many fields, the Renaissance set the cultural standards of the modern age.

BACKGROUND TO THE REFORMATION: THE MEDIEVAL CHURCH IN CRISIS

The Renaissance had revitalized European intellectual life and in the process discarded the medieval preoccupation with theology. Similarly, the Reformation marked the beginning of a new religious outlook. The Protestant Reformation, however, did not originate in the elite circles of humanistic scholars. Rather, it was sparked by Martin Luther (1483–1546), an obscure German monk and brilliant theologian. Luther started a rebellion against the church's authority that in less than one decade shattered the religious unity of Christendom. Begun in 1517, the Reformation dominated European history throughout much of the sixteenth century.

The Roman Catholic church, centered in Rome, was the one European institution that transcended geographic, ethnic, linguistic, and national boundaries. For centuries, it had extended its influence into every aspect of European society and culture. As a result, however, its massive wealth and power appeared to take precedence over its commitment to the search for holiness in this world and salvation in the next. Encumbered by wealth, addicted to international power, and protective of their own interests, the clergy, from the pope down, became the focus of a storm of criticism, starting in the Late Middle Ages.

In the fourteenth century, as kings increased their power and as urban centers with their sophisticated laity grew in size and number, people began to question the authority of the international church and its clergy. Political theorists rejected the pope's claim to supremacy over kings. The central idea of medieval Christendom—a Christian commonwealth led by the papacy—increasingly fell into disrepute. Theorists argued that the church was only a spiritual body, and therefore its power did not extend to the political realm. They said that the pope had no authority over kings, that the state needed no guidance from the papacy, and that the clergy were not above secular law. During the late fourteenth century, Latin Christendom witnessed the first systematic attacks ever launched against the church. Church corruption—such as the selling of indulgences (see the upcoming section on "The Break with Catholicism"), nepotism (the practice of appointing one's relatives to offices), the pursuit of personal wealth by bishops, and the sexual indulgence of the clergy—was nothing new. What was new and startling was the willingness of both educated and uneducated Christians to attack these practices publicly.

Thus, the Englishman John Wycliffe and the Bohemian Jan Hus (see "Fourteenth-Century Heresies" in Chapter 7), both learned theologians, denounced the wealth of the clergy as a violation of Christ's precepts and attacked the church's authority at its root by arguing that the church did not control an individual's destiny. They maintained that salvation depends not on participating in the church's rituals or receiving its sacraments but on accepting God's gift of faith.

Wycliffe's and Hus's efforts to initiate reform coincided with a powerful resurgence of religious feeling in the form of mysticism. Late medieval mystics sought an immediate and personal communication with God, and such experiences inspired them to advocate concrete reforms aimed at renewing the church's spirituality. The church hierarchy inevitably regarded mysticism with some suspicion, for if individuals could experience God directly, they would seemingly have little need for the church and its rituals. In the fourteenth century, these mystical movements seldom became heretical. But in the sixteenth and seventeenth centuries, radical reformers often found in Christian mysticism a powerful alternative to institutional control and even to the need for a priesthood.

With the advent of Lutheranism, personal faith, rather than adherence to the practices of the church, became central to the religious life of European Protestants. Renaissance humanists had sought to reinstitute the wisdom of ancient times; Protestant reformers wanted to restore the spirit of early Christianity, in which faith seemed purer, believers more sincere, and clergy uncorrupted by luxury and power. By the 1540s, the Roman Catholic Church had initiated its own internal reformation, but it came too late to stop the movement toward Protestantism in Northern and Western Europe.

THE LUTHERAN REVOLT

The Protestant Reformation of the sixteenth century ushered in a spiritual revolution that had a great impact on the Western world. This reformation was precipitated and largely defined by the Augustinian monk Martin Luther. Luther had no intention of founding a new church or overthrowing the political and ecclesiastical order of his native Germany. Rather, it was a search to resolve his own spiritual crisis that led to the permanent schism within the church. In his youth, Luther at first fulfilled his father's wish and studied law,

but at the age of twenty-one, he suddenly abandoned his legal studies to enter the Augustinian monastery at Erfurt. Luther began his search for spiritual and personal identity, and therefore for salvation, within the strict confinement and discipline of the monastery. He pursued his theological studies there and prepared for ordination.

The Break with Catholicism

As he studied and prayed, Luther grew increasingly terrified by the possibility of his damnation. As a monk, he sought union with God, and he understood the church's teaching that salvation depended on faith, works (meaning acts of charity, prayer, fasting, and so on), and grace—God's influence and favor, which sanctify and regenerate human life. He participated in the sacraments of the church, which, according to its teaching, were intended to give grace. Indeed, after his ordination, Luther administered the sacraments. Yet he still felt the weight of his sins, and nothing the church could offer seemed to relieve that burden. Seeking solace and salvation, Luther increasingly turned to reading the Bible. Two passages seemed to speak directly to him: "For therein is the righteousness of God revealed from faith to faith: as it is written, 'He who through faith is righteous shall live'" (Romans 1:17); and "They are justified [saved] by his grace as a gift, through the redemption which is in Christ Jesus" (Romans 3:24).[3] In these two passages, Luther found, for the first time in his adult life, some hope for his own salvation. Faith, freely given by God through Christ, enables the recipient to receive salvation.

The concept of salvation by faith alone provided an answer to Luther's spiritual quest. Practicing such good works as prayer, fasting, pilgrimages, and participation in the Mass and the other sacraments had never brought Luther peace of mind. He concluded that no amount of good works, however necessary for maintaining the Christian community, would bring salvation. Through reading the Bible and through faith alone the Christian could find the meaning of earthly existence. For Luther, the true Christian was a courageous figure who faced the terrifying quest for salvation armed only with the hope

Kean Collection/Archive Photos/Getty Images.

TETZEL SELLING LETTERS OF INDULGENCE. This engraving shows activities in the pope's audience-viewing room. Peasants and religious men are giving money to the church and receiving blessings after making their payments.

that God had granted him or her the gift of faith. This new Christian served others not to trade good works for salvation but solely to fulfill the demands of Christian love.

The starting point for the Reformation was Luther's attack in 1517 on the church's practice of selling indulgences. The church taught that some individuals go directly to heaven or hell, while others go to heaven only after spending time in purgatory—a period of expiation necessary for those who have sinned excessively in this life but who have had the good fortune to repent before death. To die in a state of mortal sin meant to writhe in hell eternally. Naturally, people worried about how long they might have to suffer in purgatory. Indulgences were intended to remit portions of that time and were granted to individuals by the church for their prayers, attendance at Mass, and almost any acts of charity—including monetary offerings to the church. This last good

work was the most controversial, since it could easily appear that people were buying their way into heaven.

In the autumn of 1517, a Dominican friar named John Tetzel was selling indulgences in the area near Wittenberg. Luther launched his attack on Tetzel and the selling of indulgences by tacking on the door of the Wittenberg castle church his *Ninety-Five Theses*. Luther's theses (propositions) challenged the entire notion of selling indulgences not only as a corrupt practice but also as based on a theologically unsound assumption—namely, that salvation can be earned by good works.

At the heart of Luther's argument in the *Ninety-Five Theses* and in his later writings was the belief that the individual achieves salvation through inner religious feeling, a sense of contrition for sins, and a trust in God's mercy—that church attendance, fasting, pilgrimages, charity, and other good works did not earn salvation. The church, in contrast, held that *both* faith and good works were necessary for salvation. Luther further insisted that every individual could discover the meaning of the Bible unaided by the clergy; the church, however, maintained that only the clergy could read and interpret the Bible properly. Luther argued that in matters of faith there was no difference between the clergy and the laity, for each person could receive faith directly and freely from God. In effect, every baptized Christian was consecrated to the priesthood by Christ. Appointment and ordination by the church were irrelevant. But the church held that the clergy were intermediaries between individuals and God and that, in effect, Christians reached eternal salvation through the clergy. For Luther, no priest, no ceremony, and no sacrament could mediate between the Creator and his creatures. Hope lay only in a personal relationship between the individual and God, as expressed through faith in God's mercy and grace. By declaring that clergy and church rituals do not hold the key to salvation, Luther rejected the church's claim that it alone offered men and women the way to eternal life.

Recognizing that he might be in danger if he continued to preach without a protector, Luther appealed for support to the prince of his district, Frederick, the elector of Saxony. The elector was a powerful man in international politics—one of seven lay and ecclesiastical princes who chose the Holy Roman Emperor. Frederick's support

ICONOCLAST JURY. In the sixteenth century, reformers tore out the statues and stained glass in Protestant churches, arguing that decoration distracts from the Bible and the Word of God. To this day, Protestant churches remain less decorated than Catholic ones.

convinced church officials, including the pope, that this monk would have to be dealt with cautiously. When the pope finally acted against Luther in 1520, it was too late; Luther had been given the needed time to promote his views. He proclaimed that the pope was the Antichrist and that the church was the "most lawless den of robbers, the most shameless of all brothels, the very kingdom of sin, death and Hell."[4] When the papal bull excommunicating him was delivered, Luther burned it.

No longer members of the church, Luther and his followers established congregations for the purpose of Christian worship. Christians outside the church needed protection, and in 1520, Luther published the *Address to the Christian Nobility of the German Nation.* In it he appealed to the emperor and the German princes to reform the church and to cast off their allegiance to the pope, who, he argued, had used taxes and political power to exploit them for centuries. His appeal produced some success; the Reformation flourished on the resentment against foreign papal

intervention that had long festered in Germany. In this and other treatises, Luther made it clear that he wanted to present no threat to legitimate political authority, that is, to the power of the German princes.

In 1521, Charles V, the Holy Roman Emperor, who was a devout Catholic, summoned Luther to Worms, giving him a pass of safe conduct. There, Luther was to answer to the charge of heresy, both an ecclesiastical and a civil offense. When asked to recant, Luther replied: "Unless I am convinced of error by the testimony of Scripture or by clear reason . . . I cannot and will not recant anything, for it is neither safe nor honest to act against one's conscience. God help me. Amen." Shortly after this confrontation with the emperor, Luther went into hiding to escape arrest. During that one-year period, he translated the New Testament into German. His followers, or Lutherans, were eventually called *Protestants*—those who protested against the established church—and the term became generic for all followers of the Reformation.

The Appeal and Spread of Lutheranism

Rapidly disseminated by the new printing press, the tenets of Protestantism offered the hope of revitalization and renewal to Protestantism's adherents. Lutheranism appealed to the devout, who resented the worldliness and lack of piety of many clergy. But the movement found its greatest following among German townspeople, who objected to money flowing from their land to Rome in the form of church taxes and payment for church offices. In addition, the Reformation provided the nobility with an unprecedented opportunity to confiscate church lands, eliminate church taxes, and gain the support of their subjects by serving as leaders of a popular and dynamic religious movement. The Reformation also gave the nobles a way of resisting the Catholic Holy Roman Emperor, Charles V, who wanted to extend his authority over the German princes. Resenting the Italian domination of the church, many other Germans who supported Martin Luther believed that they were freeing German Christians from foreign control.

Lutheranism drew support from the peasants as well, for they saw Luther as their champion against their oppressors—both lay and ecclesiastical lords and the townspeople. Indeed, in his writings and sermons, Luther often attacked the greed of the princes and bemoaned the plight of the poor. Undoubtedly, Luther's successful confrontation with the authorities served to inspire the peasants. Driven to a frenzy by their grievances—taxes, fines, and forced labor services—and religious enthusiasm, in 1524 the German peasants openly rebelled against their lords, seizing their estates. The Peasants' Revolt spread to over one-third of Germany; some 300,000 people took up arms against their masters.

The peasants had hoped that Luther would endorse if not lead their revolt. Luther, however, had no wish to associate his movement with a peasant uprising and risk alienating the nobility who supported him. As a political conservative, he did not want to initiate social revolution and he hesitated to challenge secular authority; to him, the good Christian was an obedient subject. Therefore, he virulently attacked the rebellious peasants, urging the nobility to become "both judge and executioner" and to "knock down, strangle, and stab" the insurgents. By 1525, the peasants

had been put down by the sword. The failure of the Peasants' Revolt meant that the German peasantry remained among the most backward and oppressed until well into the nineteenth century.

Initially, the Holy Roman Emperor, who was at war with France over parts of Italy and whose eastern territories were threatened by the Ottoman Turks, hesitated to intervene militarily in the strife between Lutheran and Catholic princes—a delay that proved crucial. Despite years of warfare, Charles V was unable to subdue the Lutheran princes. The religious conflict was settled by the Peace of Augsburg (1555), which decreed that each territorial prince should determine the religion of his subjects. Broadly speaking, northern Germany became largely Protestant, while Bavaria and other southern territories remained in the Roman Catholic church. The Holy Roman Emperor, who had been successfully challenged by the Lutheran princes, saw his power diminished. The decentralization of the empire and its division into Catholic and Protestant regions would block German unity until the last part of the nineteenth century.

THE SPREAD OF THE REFORMATION

Nothing better illustrates the people's dissatisfaction with the church in the early sixteenth century than the rapid spread of Protestantism. There was a pattern to this phenomenon. Protestantism grew strong in Northern Europe—northern Germany, Scandinavia, the Netherlands, and England. It failed in the Latin countries, although not without a struggle in France. In general, Protestantism was an urban phenomenon, and it prospered where local magistrates supported it and where the distance from Rome was greatest.

Calvinism

The success of the Reformation outside Germany and Scandinavia derived largely from the work of John Calvin (1509–1564), a French scholar and theologian. Sometime in 1533 or 1534, Calvin met French followers of Luther and became convinced of the truth of the new theology. He began to spread its beliefs immediately after his conversion, and within a year he and his friends were in trouble with the civil and ecclesiastical authorities.

Calvin soon abandoned his humanistic and literary studies to become a preacher of the Reformation. Even early in his religious experience, he emphasized the power of God over sinful and corrupt humanity. Calvin's God thundered and demanded obedience, and the terrible distance between God and the individual was mediated only by Christ. Calvin embraced a stern theology, holding that God's laws must be rigorously obeyed, that social and moral righteousness must be earnestly pursued, that political life must be carefully regulated, and that human emotions must be strictly controlled.

Even more than Luther, Calvin explained salvation in terms of uncertain predestination: that God, who grants grace for his own inscrutable reasons, knows in advance who will be saved and who will be condemned to hell. Calvin argued that although people are predestined to salvation or damnation, they can never know their fate with certainty in advance. This terrible decree could and did lead some people to despair. To others—in a paradox difficult for the modern mind to grasp—Calvinism gave a sense of self-assurance and righteousness that made the saint—that is, the truly predestined man or woman—into a new kind of European. Most of Calvin's followers seemed to believe that in having understood the fact of predestination, they had received a bold insight into their unique relationship with God.

Calvinists were individuals who assumed that only unfailing dedication to God's law could be seen as a sign of salvation; thus, Calvinism made for stern men and women, active in their congregations and willing to suppress vice in themselves and others. Calvinism could also produce revolutionaries willing to defy any temporal authorities perceived to be in violation of God's laws. For Calvinists, obedience to Christian law became the dominating principle of life. Forced to flee France, Calvin finally sought safety in Geneva, a small, prosperous Swiss city near the French border. There, he eventually established a Protestant church that closely regulated the citizens' personal and social lives. Elders of the Calvinist church governed the city and imposed strict discipline in dress, sexual mores, church attendance,

and business affairs; they severely punished irreligious and sinful behavior. Prosperous merchants as well as small shopkeepers saw in Calvinism doctrines that justified the self-discipline they already exercised in their own lives and wished to impose on the unruly masses. They particularly approved of Calvin's economic views, for he saw nothing sinful in commercial activities, unlike many Catholic clergy.

Geneva became the center of international Protestantism. Calvin trained a new generation of Protestant reformers of many nationalities, who carried his message back to their homelands. Calvin's *Institutes of the Christian Religion* (1536), in its many editions, became (after the Bible) the leading textbook of the new theology. In the second half of the sixteenth century, Calvin's theology of predestination spread into France, England, the Netherlands, and parts of the Holy Roman Empire.

Calvin always opposed any recourse to violence and supported the authority of magistrates. Yet when monarchy became their persecutor, his followers felt compelled to resist. Calvinist theologians became the first political theoreticians of modern times to publish cogent arguments for opposition to monarchy and eventually for political revolution. In France and later in the Netherlands, Calvinism became a revolutionary ideology, complete with an underground organization composed of dedicated followers who challenged monarchical authority. In the seventeenth century, the English version of Calvinism—Puritanism—performed the same function. Thus, in certain circumstances, Calvinism possessed the moral force to undermine the claims of the monarchical state on the individual.

France

Although Protestantism was illegal in France after 1534, the Protestant minority, the Huguenots, grew, becoming a well-organized underground movement. Huguenot churches, often under the protection of powerful nobles, assumed an increasingly political character in response to monarch-sponsored persecution. French Protestants became sufficiently organized and militant to challenge their persecutors, King Henry II and the Guise, one of the foremost

Catholic families in Europe, and in 1562 civil war erupted between Catholics and Protestants. What followed was one of the most brutal religious wars in the history of Europe. In 1572, on Saint Bartholomew's Day, the gruesome slaughter of thousands of Protestant men, women, and children stained the streets with blood. So intense was the religious hatred at the time that the massacre inspired the pope to have a Mass said in thanksgiving for a Catholic "victory."

After nearly thirty years of brutal fighting throughout France, victory went to the Catholic side—but barely. Henry of Navarre, a Protestant leader, became King Henry IV, though only after he agreed to reconvert to Catholicism. Henry established a tentative peace by granting Protestants limited toleration. In 1598, he issued the Edict of Nantes, the first document in any national state that attempted to institutionalize a degree of religious toleration. In the seventeenth century, the successors of Henry IV (who was assassinated in 1610) gradually weakened and then in 1685 revoked the edict. The theoretical foundations of toleration, as well as its practice, remained tenuous in early modern Europe.

England

The king himself, rather than religious reformers, initiated the Reformation in England. Henry VIII (1509–1547) removed the English church from the jurisdiction of the papacy because the pope refused to grant him an annulment of his marriage to his first wife. The English Reformation thus began as a political act on the part of a self-confident Renaissance monarch. But the Reformation's origins stretched back into the Middle Ages, for England had a long tradition of heresy, as well as anticlericalism, rooted in Wycliffe's actions in the fourteenth century.

When Henry VIII decided that he wanted a divorce from the Spanish princess Catherine of Aragon, in 1527–1528, the pope ignored his request. As the pope stalled, Henry grew more desperate: he needed a male heir and presumed that the failure to produce one lay with his wife. At the same time, he desired the shrewd and tempting Anne Boleyn. Henry VIII arranged to grant himself a divorce by severing England from the

church. In 1534, with Parliament's approval, he had himself declared supreme head of the Church of England. In 1536, he dissolved the monasteries and seized their property, which was distributed or sold to his loyal supporters. In most cases, it went to the lesser nobility and landed gentry—large landowners but not nobles. By involving Parliament and the gentry, Henry VIII turned the Reformation into a national movement. Political considerations, not profound theological differences, were at the root of the English Reformation.

Henry VIII was succeeded by his son, Edward VI (1547–1553), a Protestant, who in turn was succeeded by Mary (1553–1558), the daughter of Henry VIII and Catherine of Aragon. A devout Catholic, Mary severely persecuted Protestants. With the succession of Elizabeth I, Henry's second daughter (by Anne Boleyn), in 1558, England again became a Protestant country. Elizabeth's reign, which lasted until 1603, was characterized by a heightened sense of national identity and the persecution of Catholics, who were deemed a threat to national security. Fear of invasion by Spain, which was bent on returning England to the papacy, contributed to English anti-Catholicism.

In its customs and ceremonies, the English, or Anglican, church as it developed in the sixteenth century differed to only a limited degree from the Roman Catholicism it replaced. The exact nature of England's Protestantism became a subject of growing dispute. Was the Anglican church to be truly Protestant? Were its services and churches to be simple, lacking in "popish" rites and rituals and centered on Scripture and sermon? Obviously, the powerful Anglican bishops would accept no form of Protestantism that might limit their privileges, ceremonial functions, and power. These issues contributed to the English Revolution of the seventeenth century (see Chapter 9).

The Radical Reformation

The leading Protestant reformers generally supported established political authorities, whether they were territorial princes or urban magistrates.

Map 8.1 **The Protestant and Catholic ▶ Reformations** Europe fractured into competing camps, and religious warfare became a way of life.

Safe havens for Protestants

Jesuit establishments

Areas won back from the Reformation

Lutheran

Calvinist (Reformed)

Church of England

Roman Catholic

Huguenot centers

Spread of Calvinism

ATLANTIC OCEAN

400 Mi.

400 Km.

200

200

© 2016 Cengage Learning.

NORWAY 1536

SWEDEN 1527

DENMARK 1536

North Sea

Baltic Sea

LITHUANIA

PRUSSIA

BRANDENBURG

POLAND

Warsaw

Hamburg

Berlin

Wittenberg

Leipzig

Münster

WESTPHALIA

HOLY ROMAN EMPIRE

SAXONY

Prague

BOHEMIA

Nuremberg

MORAVIA

Vienna

AUSTRIA

Buda

Pest

HUNGARY

TRANSYLVANIA

Augsburg

Munich

BAVARIA

Trent

Milan

Venice

Zurich

SWITZERLAND

Geneva

Basel

Strasbourg

Worms

Brussels

NETHERLANDS

Amsterdam

Noyon

Paris

Orléans

FRANCE

Nantes

Bordeaux

Toulouse

Avignon

Loyola

Madrid

SPAIN

PORTUGAL

Lisbon

ITALY

Rome

Naples

Adriatic Sea

Corsica

Sardinia

Mediterranean Sea

Black Sea

OTTOMAN EMPIRE

Bay of Biscay

IRELAND

Dublin

SCOTLAND 1567

Edinburgh

ENGLAND 1534

Oxford

London

199

For the reformers, human freedom was a spiritual, not a political or social, concept. Yet the Reformation did help trigger revolts among the artisan and peasant classes of Central and then Western Europe. By the 1520s, several radical reformers arose, often from the lower classes of European society. They attempted to channel popular religion and folk beliefs into a new version of reformed Christianity that spoke directly to the temporal and spiritual needs of the oppressed.

Radical reformers proclaimed that God's will was known by his saints—those predestined for salvation. They said that the poor would inherit the earth, which at present was ruled by the Antichrist; the saint's task was to purge this earth of evil and thus make it ready for Christ's Second Coming. For the radicals, the Scriptures, which spoke of God's love for the wretched and lowly, became an inspiration for social revolution. Luther, Calvin, and other reformers vigorously condemned the social doctrines preached by the radical reformers.

The largest group in the Radical Reformation before 1550 has the general name of *Anabaptists*. Having received the inner light—the message of salvation—Anabaptists felt born anew and yearned to be re-baptized. Anabaptists were new Christians, new persons led by the light of conscience to seek reform and renewal of all institutions in preparation for Christ's Second Coming.

In 1534, Anabaptists captured the city of Münster in Westphalia, near the western border of Germany. They seized the property of nonbelievers, burned all books except the Bible, and, in a mood of jubilation and sexual excess, openly practiced polygamy. All the while, the Anabaptists proclaimed that the Day of Judgment was close at hand. Provoked by their actions, Lutheran Prince Philip of Hesse and his army crushed the Anabaptists.

In early modern Europe, *Münster* became a byword for dangerous revolution. Determined to prevent these wild enthusiasts from gaining strength in their own territories, princes attacked them with ferocity. In Münster today, the cages still hang from the church steeple where the Anabaptist leaders were tortured and left to die as a warning to all would-be imitators.

By the late sixteenth century, many radical movements had either gone underground or grown quiet. But a century later, during the English Revolution (1640–1660), the beliefs and political goals of the Radical Reformation surfaced again, threatening to push the revolution in a direction that its gentry leaders desperately feared. Although the radicals failed in England as well, they left a tradition of democratic and anti-hierarchical thought. The radical assertion that saints, who have received the inner light, are the equal of anyone, regardless of social status, helped shape modern democratic thought.

THE CATHOLIC RESPONSE

The Protestant threat impelled the Roman Catholic church to institute reforms. At first, the energy for reform came from ordinary clergy, as well as laypeople such as Ignatius Loyola (1491–1556). Trained as a soldier, this pious Spanish reformer sought to create a new religious order, fusing the intellectual excellence of humanism with a reformed Catholicism that would appeal to powerful economic and political groups. Founded in 1534, the Society of Jesus, more commonly known as the Jesuits, became the backbone of the Catholic Reformation in Southern and Western Europe. The Jesuits combined traditional monastic discipline with a dedication to teaching and an emphasis on the power of preaching. They sought to use both to win converts back to the church.

The Jesuits brought hope: a religious revival based on ceremony, tradition, and the power of the priest to offer forgiveness. In addition, they opened some of the finest schools in Europe. Just as the Lutherans in Germany sought to bring literacy to the masses so that they might read the Bible, the Jesuits sought to bring intellectual enhancement to the laity, especially to the rich and powerful. The Jesuits pursued positions as confessors to princes and urged them to intensify their efforts to strengthen the church in their territories.

By the 1540s, the Counter-Reformation was well under way. The leaders of this Catholic movement attacked many of the same abuses that had impelled Luther to speak out, but they avoided a break with the doctrinal and spiritual authority of the clergy. The Counter-Reformation also took aggressive and hostile measures against Protestantism. The church tried to counter the popular appeal of Protestantism by emphasizing spiritual renewal through faith, prayer, and religious ceremony. It also resorted to sterner means. The Inquisition—the church court dealing with heretics—expanded its activities, and wherever Catholic jurisdiction prevailed, unrepentant Protestant heretics were subject to death or imprisonment. Catholics did not hold a monopoly on persecution: wherever Protestantism obtained official status—in England, Scotland, and Geneva, for instance—Catholics or religious radicals at times faced persecution.

One of the Catholic church's main tools was censorship. By the 1520s, the impulse to censor and burn dangerous books intensified dramatically as the church tried to prevent the spread of Protestant ideas. In the rush to eliminate heretical literature, the church condemned the works of reforming Catholic humanists as well as those of Protestants. The Index of Prohibited Books became an institutional part of the church's life. Over the centuries, the works of many leading thinkers were placed on the Index, which was not abolished until 1966.

The Counter-Reformation policies of education, vigorous preaching, church building, persecution, and censorship did succeed in bringing thousands of people, Germans and Bohemians in particular, back into the church. Furthermore, the church implemented some concrete changes in policy and doctrine. In 1545, the Council of Trent met to reform the church and strengthen it for confronting the Protestant challenge. Over the many years that it was convened (until 1563), the council modified and unified church doctrine; abolished many corrupt practices, such as the selling of indulgences; and vested final authority in the papacy, thereby ending the long and bitter struggle within the church over papal authority. The Council of Trent reaffirmed the church's teaching that both faith and good works were necessary for attaining salvation. It passed a decree that the church would be the final arbiter of the Bible. All compromise with Protestantism was rejected (not that Protestants were eager for it). The Reformation had split Western Christendom irrevocably.

THE INQUISITION. This image of the Inquisition came from a French Protestant engraver who had been forced to flee France because of his religion. Clearly he saw the practices of the Inquisition as part of a continuous pattern of religious persecution by authorities with far too much power.

THE REFORMATION
AND THE MODERN AGE

The Renaissance broke with medieval artistic and literary forms and ushered in a vibrant secularism and individualism. Like the Renaissance, the Reformation drew its inspiration from the ancient world. Renaissance humanists and artists sought to imitate and revive classical art and literary forms; Reformation thinkers aspired to restore the spiritual purity of early Christianity, which preceded the growth of a powerful clergy and a dogmatic theology. They used the Gospels in order to undermine the authority of the Church.

At first glance, the Reformation would seem to have renewed the medieval stress on otherworldliness and reversed the direction toward secularism taken by the Renaissance. Attracted to the ancient Stoic doctrine of the autonomous will, Renaissance humanists had broken with Augustine's stern view of original sin, a corrupt human nature, and the individual's inability to achieve salvation through his or her own efforts. Both Luther and Calvin, however, saw human beings as essentially depraved and corrupt and rejected completely the notion that individuals can do something for their own salvation; such an assertion of human will, they held, revealed a dangerous self-confidence in human beings. Whereas the humanists fostered freer discussion and criticism, the Reformation, at times, degenerated into narrow-mindedness and intolerance.

Yet in several important ways, the Reformation contributed to the shaping of modernity. By dividing Christendom into Catholic and Protestant, the Reformation destroyed the religious unity of Europe, the distinguishing feature of the Middle Ages, and weakened the church, the chief institution of medieval society. The Reformation promoted religious pluralism, for in addition to Lutheranism and Calvinism, various other Protestant churches, each with its own distinctive traits, emerged.

During the Middle Ages, popes challenged and at times dominated kings. By strengthening monarchs at the expense of church bodies, the Reformation furthered the growth of the modern secular and centralized state. Protestant rulers repudiated all papal claims to temporal authority and extended their power over the newly established Protestant churches in their lands. In Catholic lands, the weakened church was reluctant to challenge monarchs, whose support it now needed more than ever. This subordination of clerical authority to the throne permitted kings to build strong centralized states, a characteristic of political life of the modern West.

Although absolute monarchy was the immediate beneficiary of the Reformation, indirectly Protestantism contributed to the growth of political liberty—another feature of the modern West. To be sure, neither Luther nor Calvin championed political freedom. For Luther, a good Christian was an obedient subject. Thus, he declared that subjects should obey their rulers' commands: "It is in no wise proper for anyone who would be a Christian to set himself up against his government, whether it act justly or unjustly."[5] And again, "Those who sit in the office of magistrate sit in the place of God, and their judgment is as if God judged from heaven. . . . if the emperor . . . calls me, God calls me."[6] Calvinists created a theocracy in Geneva that closely regulated the citizens' private lives, and Calvin strongly condemned resistance to political authority as wicked. He held that rulers were selected by God and that punishment of bad rulers belonged only to God and not to the ruler's subjects.

Nevertheless, the Reformation also provided a basis for challenging monarchs. Some Protestant theorists, mainly Calvinists, supported resistance to political authorities whose edicts, they believed, contravened God's law as expressed in the Bible. This religious justification for revolution against tyrannical rule helped fuel the resistance of English Calvinists, or Puritans, to the English monarchy in the seventeenth century.

The Reformation advanced the idea of equality. Equality is rooted in the Judeo-Christian belief that all people are the creatures of a single God. In two important ways, however, medieval society contravened the principle of equality. First, feudalism stressed hereditary distinctions between nobles and commoners. Medieval society was hierarchical, arranged in an ascending order of legal ranks, or estates: commoners, nobles, and clergy. Second, the medieval church taught that only the clergy could administer the sacraments, which provided people with the means of attaining salvation; for this reason, they were superior to the laity. Luther, in contrast, held that there was no spiritual distinction between the laity and the clergy. There was a spiritual equality of all believers: all were equally Christian; all were equally priests.

The Reformation also contributed to the creation of an individualistic ethic, which characterizes the modern world. Since Protestants, unlike Catholics, had no official interpreter of Scripture, the individual bore the awesome responsibility of interpreting the Bible according to the dictates of his or her conscience. Protestants confronted the prospect of salvation or damnation entirely on their own. No church provided them with security or certainty, and no priesthood interceded between them and God. Piety was not determined by the church, but by the autonomous individual, whose subjective faith or conscience, illuminated by God, was the source of judgment and authority.

For the Protestant, faith was personal and inward. This new arrangement called for a personal relationship between each individual and God and called attention to the individual's inner religious capacities. Certain that God had chosen them for salvation, many Protestants developed the inner self-assurance and assertiveness that marks the modern individual. Thus, the Protestant emphasis on private judgment in religious matters and on an inner personal conviction accentuated the importance of the individual and helped to mold a new and distinctly modern European.

The Reformation's stress on individual conscience may have contributed to the development of the capitalist spirit, which underlies modern economic life. So argued German sociologist Max Weber in *The Protestant Ethic and the Spirit of Capitalism* (1904). Weber acknowledged that capitalism had existed in Europe before the Reformation; merchant bankers in medieval Italian and German towns, for example, engaged in capitalistic activities. But, he contended, Protestantism (particularly Calvinism) made capitalism more dynamic; it produced a new type of individual who confidently set out to master himself and his environment. Protestant businesspeople believed that they had a religious obligation to prosper, and their faith gave them the self-discipline to do so. Convinced that prosperity was God's blessing and poverty his curse, Calvinists had a spiritual inducement to labor industriously and to avoid laziness.

According to Calvin's doctrine of predestination, God had already determined in advance who would be saved; salvation could not be attained through any worldly actions. Although there was no definite way of discovering who had received God's grace, Calvin's followers came to believe that certain activities were signs that God was working through them, that they had indeed been elected. Thus, Calvinists viewed hard work, diligence, dutifulness, efficiency, frugality, and a disdain for pleasurable pursuits—all virtues that contribute to rational and orderly business procedures and to business success—as signs of election. In effect, Weber argued, Protestantism—unlike Catholicism—gave religious approval to moneymaking and the business people's way of life. Moreover, Calvin's followers seemed to believe that they had attained a special insight into their relationship with God; this conviction fostered a sense of self-assurance and righteousness. Protestantism, therefore, produced a highly individualistic attitude that valued inner strength, self-discipline, and methodical and sober behavior—necessary traits for a middle class seeking business success in a highly competitive world.

❖　　❖　　❖

Notes

1. Giovanni Pico della Mirandola, *Oration on the Dignity of Man,* trans. A. Robert Caponigri (Chicago: Henry Regnery, 1956), 7.

2. François Rabelais, *Gargantua and Pantagruel,* trans. Sir Thomas Urquhart (1883), bk. 1, chap. 57.

3. The biblical quotations are from the *Revised Standard Version of the Bible,* copyright © 1946, 1952, and 1971 the National Council of the Churches of Christ in the USA. Used by permission. All rights reserved.

4. John Dillenberger, ed., *Martin Luther: Selections from His Writings* (Garden City, N.Y.: Doubleday, 1961), 46, taken from *The Freedom of a Christian* (1520).

5. Quoted in George H. Sabine, *A History of Political Thought* (New York: Holt, Rinehart & Winston, 1961), 361.

6. Quoted in Roland Bainton, *Here I Stand* (New York: Abingdon Press, 1950), 23.

Chapter 9

Political and Economic Transformation: National States, Overseas Expansion, Commercial Revolution

- Toward the Modern State
- Hapsburg Spain
- The Growth of French Power
- The Growth of Limited Monarchy and Constitutionalism in England
- The Holy Roman Empire: The Failure to Unify Germany
- European Expansion
- Black Slavery and the Slave Trade
- The Price Revolution
- The Expansion of Agriculture
- The Expansion of Trade and Industry
- The Fostering of Mercantile Capitalism
- Toward a Global Economy

Focus Questions

1. What are key features of the modern state? In what ways did early modern kings help shape the modern state?
2. Why did England move in the direction of parliamentary government while most countries on the Continent embraced absolutism? Describe the main factors.
3. What were the new forces for expansion operating in early modern Europe?
4. How did European expansion give rise to an emerging world economy?
5. What specific torments did Africans suffer in their capture, incarceration in a coastal port, and passage to the New World?

*F*rom the thirteenth to the seventeenth century, a new and unique form of political organization emerged in the West: the dynastic, or national, state. It harnessed the material resources of its territory, directed the energies of the nobility into national service, and increasingly centralized political authority. The national state, a product of dynastic consolidation, is the essential political institution of the modern West.

The disintegration of medieval political forms and the emergence of the modern state coincided with the gradual breakdown of the medieval socioeconomic system, which was based on tradition, hierarchy, and orders or estates. In the medieval system, every group—clergy, lords, serfs, guild members—occupied a particular place and performed a specific function. Society functioned best when each person fulfilled the role allotted to him or her by God and tradition. Early modern times saw the growth of a capitalist market economy whose central focus was the self-sufficient individual, striving, assertive, and motivated by self-interest. This nascent market economy, greatly boosted by the voyages of discovery and the conquest and colonization of other parts of the world, subverted the hierarchically arranged and tradition-bound medieval community. Seeking to enrich their treasuries and extend their power, states promoted commercial growth and overseas expansion. The extension of European hegemony over much of the world was well under way by the eighteenth century. ❖

TOWARD THE MODERN STATE

During the Middle Ages, some kings began to forge national states. However, medieval political forms differed considerably from those that developed later, in the early modern period. In the Middle Ages, kings had to share political power with feudal lords, the clergy, free cities, and representative assemblies. Central authority was tempered by overlapping jurisdictions and numerous and competing allegiances. People saw themselves as members of an estate—clergy, aristocracy, or commoners—rather than as subjects or citizens of a state. Church theorists envisioned Christian Europe as a unitary commonwealth in which spiritual concerns prevailed over secular authority. According to this view, kings, who received their power from God, must never forget their religious obligation to rule in accordance with God's commands as interpreted by the clergy.

In the sixteenth and seventeenth centuries, kings successfully asserted their authority over competing powers, continuing a trend that had begun in the Late Middle Ages. Strong monarchs dominated or crushed the parliaments that had acted as a brake on royal power during the Middle Ages. Increasingly, too, these monarchs subjected lords and ecclesiastical authorities to royal control. They created a bureaucracy to coordinate the activities of the central government. The old medieval political order dissolved. It had been characterized on the one hand by feudal particularism and the strength of local authorities, and on the other by the supranational claims and goals of a universal church. Gradually, the national, territorial state, the hallmark of the modern world, became the essential political unit. Kings were the central figures in the creation of the national state. Strong dynastic states were formed wherever monarchs succeeded in subduing local aristocratic and ecclesiastical power systems. In their struggle to subdue the aristocracy, kings were aided by artillery; the lords' castles quickly became obsolete in the face of royal siege weapons. Where the monarchs failed, as they did in Germany and Italy, no viable states evolved until well into the nineteenth century.

By the early seventeenth century, Europeans had developed the concept of the state: an autonomous political entity to which its subjects owed duties and obligations. The essential prerequisite for the Western concept of the state, as it emerged in the early modern period, was the idea of *sovereignty*. Within its borders, the state was supreme; all other institutions, both secular and religious, had to recognize the state's authority. The art of governing entailed molding the ambitions and strength of the powerful and wealthy so that they could be harnessed to serve the state. Its power growing through war and taxation, the state had become the basic unit of political authority in the West.

Chronology 9.1 ❖ Economic and Political Transformations

1394–1460	Henry the Navigator, prince of Portugal, encourages expansion into Africa for gold and his anti-Muslim crusade
1469	Ferdinand and Isabella begin their rule of Castile and Aragon
1485	Henry VII begins the reign of the Tudor dynasty in England
1488	Bartholomeu Dias reaches the tip of Africa
1492	Christopher Columbus reaches the Caribbean island of Española on his first voyage; the Jews are expelled from Spain; Granada, the last Muslim kingdom in Spain, is conquered, completing the Reconquest
1497	Vasco da Gama sails around the Cape of Good Hope (Africa) to India
1519	Charles V of Spain becomes Hapsburg emperor of the Holy Roman Empire
1519–1521	Hernando Cortés conquers the Aztecs in Mexico
1531–1533	Francisco Pizarro conquers the Incas in Peru
1552	Silver from the New World flows into Europe via Spain, contributing to a price revolution
1556–1598	Philip II of Spain persecutes Jews and Muslims
1562–1598	Religious wars in France
1572	Saint Bartholomew's Day Massacre—Queen Catherine of France orders thousands of Protestants executed
1588	English fleet defeats the Spanish Armada
1598	French Protestants are granted religious toleration by the Edict of Nantes
1624–1642	Cardinal Richelieu, Louis XIII's chief minister, determines royal policies
1640–1660	English Revolution
1648	Treaty of Westphalia ends the Thirty Years' War
1649	Charles I, Stuart king of England, is executed by an act of Parliament
1649–1660	England is co-ruled by Parliament and the army under Oliver Cromwell
1660	Charles II returns from exile and becomes king of England
1685	Louis XIV of France revokes the Edict of Nantes
1688–1689	Revolution in England: end of absolutism
1694	Bank of England is founded
1701	Louis XIV tries to bring Spain under French control

Historically, the modern state has been characterized by a devotion to the nation and by feelings of national pride. A national language is used throughout the land, and the people have a sense of sharing a common culture and history, of being distinct from other peoples. There were some signs of growing national feeling during the sixteenth and seventeenth centuries, but this feature of the modern state did not become a major part of European political life until the nineteenth century. During the early modern period, devotion was largely given to a town, a province, a noble, or to the person of the king rather than to the nation, the people as a whole.

In the sixteenth and seventeenth centuries, the idea of liberty, now so basic to Western political life and thought, was only rarely discussed, and then chiefly by Calvinist opponents of absolutism. Not until the mid-seventeenth century in England was there a body of political thought contending that human liberty was compatible with the new modern state. In general, despite the English (and Dutch) developments, absolutism dominated the political structure of early modern Europe. It was not until the late eighteenth and nineteenth centuries that absolutism was widely challenged by advocates of liberty.

The principle of the balance of power, an integral part of modern international relations, also emerged during early modern times. When one state threatened to dominate Europe, as did Spain under Philip II and France under Louis XIV, other states joined forces and resisted. The fear that one state would upset the balance of power and achieve European domination pervaded international relations in later centuries.

HAPSBURG SPAIN

The Spanish political experience of the sixteenth century was one of the most extraordinary in the history of modern Europe. Spanish kings built a dynastic state that burst through its frontiers and encompassed Portugal, part of Italy, the Netherlands, and enormous areas in the New World. Spain became an intercontinental empire—the first in the West since Roman times.

In the eighth and ninth centuries, the Muslims controlled all of Spain except some tiny Christian kingdoms in the far north. In the ninth century, these Christian states began a five-hundred-year struggle, the Reconquest, to drive the Muslims from the Iberian Peninsula. By the middle of the thirteenth century, Granada in the south was all that remained of Muslim lands in Spain. This long struggle for Christian hegemony in the Iberian Peninsula left the Spanish fiercely religious and strongly suspicious of foreigners. Despite centuries of intermarriage with non-Christians, by the early sixteenth century purity of blood and orthodoxy of faith became necessary for, and synonymous with, Spanish identity.

Ferdinand and Isabella

In 1469, Ferdinand, heir to the throne of Aragon, married Isabella, heir to the throne of Castile. Although Ferdinand and Isabella did not give Spain a single legal and tax system or a common currency, their policies did contribute decisively to Spanish unity and might. They broke the power of aristocrats, who had operated from their fortified castles like kings, waging their private wars at will; they brought the Spanish church into alliance with the state; and in 1492, they drove the Muslims from Granada, the Muslims' last territory in Spain. The crusade against the Muslim infidels accorded with the aims of the militant Spanish church. With a superior army, with the great aristocrats pacified, and with the church and the Inquisition under monarchical control, the Catholic kings expanded their interests and embarked on an imperialist foreign policy that made Spain dominant in the New World.

The Spanish state and church persecuted both Muslims and Jews, who for centuries had contributed substantially to Spanish cultural and economic life. In 1391, thousands of Jews were massacred when anti-Jewish sentiments, fanned by popular preachers, turned to violence in major cities. Under threat of death, many Jews submitted to baptism. In succeeding years, other attacks on Jews led to more conversions. A number of these *conversos,* or New Christians, continued to practice the religion of their fathers in secret, a situation that appalled clerical authorities and the devout Ferdinand and Isabella.

In 1492, in a move to enforce religious uniformity, the crown expelled from Spain Jews who were unwilling to accept baptism. About 150,000 Jews (some estimates are considerably higher) were driven out, including many conversos who opted to stay with their people. The thousands of Jews who underwent conversion and the conversos who remained were watched by the Inquisition— the church tribunal that dealt with insincere converts—for signs of backsliding. Death by fire, sometimes in elaborate public ceremonies, was the ultimate penalty for those of the conversos and their descendants who were suspected of practicing Judaism. Prejudice and discrimination against the conversos had a racial component. Holding that Jews inherited evil character traits that set them apart from other people, Old Christians demanded that purity of blood be a condition for entering the professions, religious orders, universities, and so forth. This racial distinction endured in Spain for centuries. Muslims also bore the pain of forced conversions and investigations, torture, and executions conducted by the Inquisition. Finally, in 1609 through 1614, Spain expelled them.

The Reign of Charles V, King of Spain, and Holy Roman Emperor

Dynastic marriage constituted another crucial part of Ferdinand and Isabella's foreign policy. They strengthened their ties with the Austrian Hapsburg kings by marrying one of their children, Juana (called "the Mad" for her insanity), to Philip the Fair, son of Maximilian of Austria, the head of the ruling Hapsburg family. Philip and Juana's son Charles inherited the kingdom of Ferdinand and Isabella in 1516 and reigned until 1556. Through his other grandparents, he also inherited the Netherlands, Austria, Sardinia, Sicily, the kingdom of Naples, and Franche Comté in eastern France. In 1519, he was elected Holy Roman Emperor Charles V. Charles became the most powerful ruler in Europe. But his reign saw the emergence of political, economic, and social problems that eventually led to Spain's decline.

Charles's inheritance was simply too vast to be governed effectively, but that was only dimly perceived at the time. The Lutheran Reformation proved to be the first successful challenge to Hapsburg power. It was the first phase of a religious and political struggle between Catholic Spain and Protestant Europe, a struggle that would dominate the last half of the sixteenth century.

The achievements of Charles V's reign rested on the twin instruments of army and bureaucracy. The Hapsburg Empire in the New World was vastly extended but, on the whole, effectively administered and policed. Out of this sprawling empire, with its exploited native populations, came the greatest flow of gold and silver ever witnessed by Europeans. Constant warfare in Europe, coupled with the immensity of the Spanish administrative network, required a steady intake of capital. In the long run, however, this easy access to capital seems to have hurt the Spanish economy. There was no incentive for the development of domestic industry, bourgeois entrepreneurship, or international commerce.

Moreover, constant war engendered and perpetuated a social order geared to the aggrandizement of a military class rather than the development of a commercial class. Although war expanded Spain's power in the sixteenth century, it sowed the seeds for the financial crises of the 1590s and beyond and for the eventual decline of Spain as a world power.

Philip II

Philip II inherited the throne from his father, Charles V, who abdicated in 1556. Charles left his son with a vast empire in both the Old World and the New. Although this empire had been administered competently enough, it was facing the specters of bankruptcy and heresy. A zeal for Catholicism ruled Philip's private conduct and infused his foreign policy. In the 1560s, Philip sent the largest land army ever assembled in Europe into the Netherlands with the intention of crushing Protestant-inspired opposition to Spanish authority. The ensuing revolt of the Netherlands lasted until 1609, and the Spanish lost their industrial heartland as a result of it.

The Dutch established a republic governed by the prosperous and progressive bourgeoisie. Rich from the fruits of manufacture and trade in everything from tulip bulbs to ships and slaves, the Dutch merchants ruled their cities and provinces with fierce pride. In the early seventeenth century, this new nation of only 1.5 million people already practiced the most innovative commercial and financial techniques in Europe.

Philip's disastrous attempt to invade England was also born of religious zeal. Philip regarded an assault on England, the main Protestant power, as a holy crusade against the "heretic and bastard" Queen Elizabeth; he particularly resented English assistance to the Protestant Dutch rebels. Sailing from Lisbon in May 1588, the Spanish Armada, carrying twenty-two thousand seamen and soldiers, met with defeat. More than half of the Spanish ships were destroyed or put out of commission. Many ships were wrecked by storms as they tried to return to Spain by rounding the coasts of Scotland and Ireland. The defeat had an enormous psychological effect on the Spanish, who saw it as divine punishment and openly pondered what they had done to incur God's displeasure.

The End of the Spanish Hapsburgs

After the defeat of the Armada, Spain gradually and reluctantly abandoned its imperial ambitions in Northern Europe. The administrative structure built by Charles V and Philip II remained strong throughout the seventeenth century; nevertheless, by the first quarter of the century, enormous weaknesses in Spanish economic and social life had surfaced. In 1596, Philip II was bankrupt, his vast wealth depleted by the cost of foreign wars. Bankruptcy reappeared at various times in the seventeenth century, while the agricultural economy, at the heart of any early modern nation, stagnated. The Spanish in their golden age had never paid enough heed to increasing domestic production.

Despite these setbacks, Spain was still capable of taking a very aggressive posture during the Thirty Years' War (1618–1648). The Austrian branch of the Hapsburg family joined forces with their Spanish cousins, and neither the Swedes and Germans nor the Dutch could stop them. Only French participation in the Thirty Years' War on the Protestant side tipped the balance decisively against the Hapsburgs. Spanish aggression brought no victories, and with the Peace of Westphalia (1648), Spain officially recognized the independence of the Netherlands and severed its diplomatic ties with the Austrian branch of the family.

By 1660, the imperial age of the Spanish Hapsburgs had ended. The rule of the Protestant princes had been secured in the Holy Roman Empire; the largely Protestant Dutch Republic flourished; Portugal and its colony of Brazil were independent of Spain; and dominance over European affairs had passed to France. The quality of material life in Spain deteriorated rapidly, and the ever-present gap between the rich and the poor widened even more drastically. The traditional aristocracy and the church retained their land and power but failed to produce effective leadership.

The Spanish experience illustrates two aspects of the history of the European state. First, the state as empire could survive and prosper only if the domestic economic base remained sound. The Spanish reliance on bullion from its colonies and the failure to cultivate industry and reform the taxation system spelled disaster. Second, states with a vital and aggressive bourgeoisie, such as England and Holland, flourished at the expense of the regions where the aristocracy and the church dominated and controlled society and its mores—as in Spain's situation. The latter social groups tended to despise manual labor, profit taking, and technological progress. Even though they had been created by kings and dynastic families, after 1700, the major dynastic states were increasingly nurtured by the economic activities of merchants and traders—the bourgeoisie. Yet the bureaucracy of the dynastic states continued to be dominated by men drawn from the lesser aristocracy.

THE GROWTH OF FRENCH POWER

Although both England and France effectively consolidated the power of their central governments, each became a model of a different form of statehood. The English model was a constitutional monarchy in which the king's power was limited by Parliament and the rights of the English people were protected by law and tradition. The French model emphasized at every turn the glory of the king and, by implication, the sovereignty of the state and its right to stand above the interests of its subjects. France's monarchy became absolute, and French kings claimed that they had been selected by God to rule, a theory known as the divine right of kings. This theory gave monarchy a sanctity that various French kings exploited to enforce their commands on the population, including rebellious feudal lords.

The evolution of the French state was a very gradual process, completed only in the late seventeenth century. In the Middle Ages, the French monarchs recognized the rights of representative assemblies—the Estates—and consulted with them. These assemblies (whether regional or national) were composed of deputies drawn from the various elites: the clergy, the nobility, and, significantly, the leaders of cities and towns in a given region. Early modern French kings increasingly wrested power from the nobility, reduced the significance of the Estates, and eliminated interference from the church.

Religion and the French State

In every emergent state, tension existed between the monarch and the papacy. At issue was control over the church within that territory—over its personnel, its wealth, and, of course, its pulpits, from which an illiterate majority learned what their leaders wanted them to know not only about religious issues but also about submission to civil authority. The monarch's power to make church appointments could ensure a complacent church—a church willing to preach obedience to royal authority and to comply on matters of taxes.

For the French monarchs, centuries of tough bargaining with the papacy paid off in 1516, when Francis I (1515–1547) concluded the Concordat of Bologna. Under this agreement, Pope Leo X permitted the French king to nominate, and so in effect appoint, men of his choice to all the highest offices in the French church. The Concordat of Bologna laid the foundation for what became known as the *Gallican church*—a term signifying that the Catholic Church in France was sanctioned and overseen by the French kings. Thus, in the early sixteenth century, the central government had been strengthened at the expense of papal authority and of traditional privileges enjoyed by local aristocracy.

The Protestant Reformation, however, challenged royal authority and threatened the very survival of France as a unified state. Fearful that Protestantism would undermine his power, Francis I declared Protestant beliefs and practices illegal and punishable by fines, imprisonment, and even execution. Nevertheless, the Protestant minority (the Huguenots) grew in strength. From 1562 to 1598, France experienced waves of religious wars, which cost the king control over vast areas of the kingdom. The great aristocratic families, the Guise for the Catholics and the Bourbons for the Protestants, drew up armies that scourged the land, killing and maiming their religious opponents and dismantling the authority of the central government.

In 1579, extreme Huguenot theorists published the *Vindiciae contra Tyrannos (A Defense of Liberty Against Tyrants)*. This statement, combined with a call to action, was the first of its kind in early modern times. It justified rebellion against, and even the execution of, an unjust king. European monarchs might claim power and divinely sanctioned authority, but by the late sixteenth century, their subjects had available the moral and theoretical justification for opposing their monarch's will, by force if necessary, and this justification rested on Scripture and religious conviction. Significantly, this same treatise was translated into English in 1648, a year before Parliament publicly executed Charles I, king of England.

The French monarchy foundered in the face of this kind of political and religious opposition. The era of royal supremacy instituted by Francis I came to an abrupt end during the reign of his successor, Henry II (1547–1559). Wed to Catherine de'Medici, a member of the powerful Italian banking family, Henry occupied himself not with the concerns of government but with the pleasures of the hunt. The sons who succeeded Henry—Francis II (1559–1560), Charles IX (1560–1574), and Henry III (1574–1589)—were uniformly weak. Their mother, Catherine, who was the virtual ruler, ordered the execution of thousands of Protestants by royal troops in Paris—the beginning of the infamous Saint Bartholomew's Day Massacre (1572), which, with the bloodbath that followed, became a symbol of the excesses of religious zeal.

The civil wars begun in 1562 were renewed in the massacre's aftermath. They dragged on until the death of the last Valois king in 1589. The Valois failure to produce a male heir to the throne placed

Henry, duke of Bourbon and a Protestant, in line to succeed to the French throne. Realizing that the overwhelmingly Catholic population would not accept a Protestant king, Henry (apparently without much regret) renounced his adopted religion and embraced the church. Henry IV (1589–1610) granted his Protestant subjects and former followers a degree of religious toleration through the Edict of Nantes (1598), but they were never welcomed into the royal bureaucracy in significant numbers. Throughout the seventeenth century, every French king attempted to undermine the Protestants' regional power bases and ultimately to destroy their religious liberties.

The Consolidation of French Monarchical Power

The defeat of Protestantism as a national force set the stage for the final consolidation of the French state in the seventeenth century under the great Bourbon kings, Louis XIII and Louis XIV. Louis XIII (1610–1643) realized that his rule depended on an efficient and trustworthy bureaucracy, a replenishable treasury, and constant vigilance against the localized claims to power by the great aristocracy and Protestant cities and towns. Cardinal Richelieu, who served as Louis XIII's chief minister from 1624 to 1642, became the great architect of French absolutism.

Richelieu's morality rested on one absolute principle, embodied in a phrase he invented: *raison d'état,* reason of state. Richelieu sought to serve the state by bringing under the king's control the disruptive and antimonarchical elements within French society. He increased the power of the central bureaucracy, attacked the power of independent and often Protestant towns and cities, and persecuted the Huguenots. Above all, he humbled the great nobles by limiting their effectiveness as councilors to the king and prohibiting their traditional privileges, such as settling grievances through a duel rather than through court action. Reason of state also guided Richelieu's foreign policy. It required that France turn against Catholic Spain and enter the war that was raging at the time in the Holy Roman Empire on the Protestant—and hence anti-Spanish—side. France's entry into the Thirty Years'

War produced a decisive victory for French power on the Continent.

Richelieu died in 1642, and Louis XIII the following year. Cardinal Mazarin, who took charge during the minority of Louis XIV (who was five years old when Louis XIII died), continued Richelieu's policies. Mazarin's heavy-handed actions produced a rebellious reaction, the *Fronde,* a series of street riots that lasted from 1648 to 1653 and that for a time cost the government control over Paris. Centered in Paris and supported by the great aristocracy, the courts, and the city's poorer classes, the Fronde threatened to develop into a full-scale uprising. It might have done so but for one crucial factor: its leadership was divided. Court judges (lesser nobles who had often just risen from the ranks of the bourgeoisie) deeply distrusted the great aristocrats and refused in the end to make common cause with them, and both groups feared disorders among the urban masses.

When Louis XIV finally assumed responsibility for governing in 1661, he vowed that the events he had witnessed as a child during the Fronde would never be repeated. In the course of his reign, he achieved the greatest degree of monarchical power held during the early modern period. No absolute monarch in Western Europe, before or at that time, had so much personal authority or commanded such a vast and effective military and administrative machine. Louis XIV's reign represents the culmination of the process of increasing monarchical authority that had been under way for centuries. Intelligent, cunning, and possessing a unique understanding of the requirements of his office, Louis XIV worked long hours at being king, and he never undertook a venture without an eye to his personal grandeur. The sumptuous royal palace at Versailles was built for that reason; similarly, etiquette and style were cultivated there on a scale never before seen in any European court.

When Mazarin died, Louis XIV did away with the office of first minister; he would rule France alone. The great nobles, "princes of the blood," enjoyed great social prestige but exercised decreasing political influence. Louis XIV treated the aristocrats to elaborate rituals, processions, displays, and banquets; amid all the clamor, however, their political power dwindled.

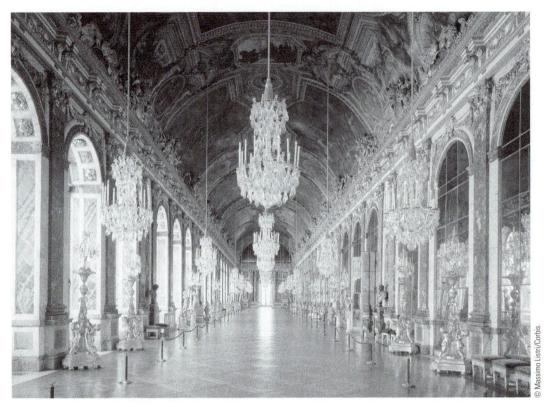

THE HALL OF MIRRORS IN THE ROYAL PALACE AT VERSAILLES. Immense and grand, Versailles was the wonder of the age. Like the person of the king, it said to his subjects: "I am grandeur incarnate." Even by today's standards, it was an impressive building, both inside and out.

Louis XIV's domestic policies centered on his incessant search for new revenues. Not only the building of Versailles but also wars cost money, and Louis XIV waged them to excess. To raise capital, he used the services of Jean Baptiste Colbert, a brilliant administrator who improved the methods of tax collecting, promoted new industries, and encouraged international trade. Operating with a total bureaucracy of about a thousand officials and no longer bothering even to consult the parlements or Estates, Louis XIV ruled absolutely in accordance with the principle of divine right—that the monarch is selected to rule by God.

Yet Louis XIV's system was fatally flawed. Without any effective check on his power and on his dreams of international conquest, no limit was imposed on the state's capacity to make war that inflated the national debt. Louis XIV coveted vast sections of the Holy Roman Empire; he also sought to curb Dutch commercial prosperity and had designs on the Spanish Netherlands (roughly Belgium and Luxembourg). By the 1680s, his domestic and foreign policies turned violently aggressive. In 1685, he revoked the Edict of Nantes, forcing many of the country's remaining Protestants to flee. In 1689, he embarked on a military campaign to secure territory from the Holy Roman Empire. And in 1701, he tried to bring Spain under the control of the Bourbon dynasty. Louis XIV, however, underestimated the power of his northern rivals, England and the Netherlands. Their combined power, in alliance with the Holy Roman Empire and the Austrians, defeated his ambitions.

Louis XIV's participation in these long wars emptied the royal treasury. By the late seventeenth century, taxes had risen intolerably, and they were levied mostly on those least able to pay—the peasants. Absolutism also meant increased surveillance of the population. Royal authorities censored books; spied on suspected heretics, Protestants, and freethinkers; and tortured and executed opponents of state policy.

In the France of Louis XIV, the dynastic state had reached maturity and had begun to display some of its classic characteristics: centralized bureaucracy, royal patronage to enforce allegiance, a system of taxation universally but inequitably applied, and suppression of political opposition either through the use of patronage or if necessary through force. Another important feature was the state's cultivation of the arts and sciences as a means of increasing national power and prestige. Together, these policies enabled the French monarchy to achieve political stability, enforce a uniform system of law, and channel the country's wealth and resources into the service of the state as a whole.

Yet at his death in 1715, Louis XIV left his successors a system of bureaucracy and taxation that was vastly in need of overhaul but was still locked into the traditional social privileges of the church and nobility to an extent that made reform virtually impossible. The pattern of war, excessive taxation of the lower classes, and expenditures that surpassed revenues had severely damaged French finances. Failure to reform the system led to the French Revolution of 1789.

THE GROWTH OF LIMITED MONARCHY AND CONSTITUTIONALISM IN ENGLAND

In 1066, William, duke of Normandy and vassal to the French king, had invaded and conquered England, acquiring at a stroke the entire kingdom. In succeeding centuries, English monarchs continued to strengthen central authority and to tighten the bonds of national unity. At the same time, however, certain institutions and traditions evolved—common law, Magna Carta, and Parliament—that checked royal power and protected the rights of the English people.

Central government in England was threatened after the Hundred Years' War (1337–1453), when English aristocrats brought back from France a taste for warfare. In the ensuing civil war—the War of the Roses (1455–1485)—gangs of noblemen with retainers roamed the English countryside, and lawlessness prevailed for a generation. Only in 1485 did the Tudor family emerge triumphant.

The Tudor Achievement

Victory in the civil war allowed Henry VII (1485–1509) to begin the Tudor dynasty. Henry VII's goal was to check the unruly nobility. To this end, he brought commoners into the government. These commoners, unlike the great magnates, could be channeled into royal service because they craved what the king offered: financial rewards and elevated social status. Although they did not fully displace the aristocracy, commoners were brought into Henry VII's inner circle, into the Privy Council, and into the courts. The strength and efficiency of Tudor government were shown during the Reformation, when Henry VIII (1509–1547) made himself head of the English church.

The Protestant Reformation in England was a revolution in royal, as well as ecclesiastical, government. It attacked and defeated the main obstacle to monarchical authority: the power of the papacy. However, no change in religious practice could be instituted by the monarchy alone. Parliament's participation in the Reformation gave it a greater role and sense of importance than it had ever possessed in the past.

At Henry VIII's death, the Tudor bureaucracy and centralized government were strained to the utmost, yet they survived. The government weathered the reign of Henry's sickly son Edward VI (1547–1553) and the extreme Protestantism of some of his advisers; it also survived the brief and deeply troubled reign of Henry's first daughter, Mary (1553–1558), who attempted to return England to Catholicism. At Mary's death, England had come dangerously close to the religious

HENRY VIII. Although the ruler of a second-rate power, Henry VIII sought to impress upon his subjects that he was a new and powerful monarch. He sought to compete in style, if not in power, with the French and the Spanish kings.

instability and sectarian tension that undermined the French kings during the final decades of the sixteenth century.

Henry's second daughter, Elizabeth I, became queen in 1558 and reigned until her death in 1603. The Elizabethan period was characterized by a heightened sense of national identity. The English Reformation enhanced that sense, as did the increasing fear of foreign invasion by Spain.

That fear was abated only by the defeat of the Spanish Armada in 1588. In the seventeenth century, the English would look back on Elizabeth's reign as a golden age. It was the calm before the storm: a time when a new commercial class was formed that, in the seventeenth century, would demand a greater say in government operations.

Religion played a vital role in this realignment of political interests and forces. Much of the old aristocracy clung to the Anglicanism of the Henrican Reformation and in some cases to Catholicism. The newly risen gentry found in the Protestant Reformation of Switzerland and Germany a form of religious worship more suited to their independent and entrepreneurial spirit. Many of them embraced Puritanism, the English version of Calvinism.

The English Revolution, 1640–1660 and 1688–1689

The forces threatening established authority were dealt with ineffectively by the first two Stuart kings, James I (1603–1625) and Charles I (1625–1649). Like their Continental counterparts, both believed in royal absolutism, and both preached, through the established church, the doctrine of the divine right of kings. James I angered Parliament by conducting foreign policy without consulting it. The conflict between Parliament and Charles I centered on taxes and religion.

Badly needing funds in order to wage war, Charles I exacted "forced loans" from subjects and imprisoned without a specific charge those who would not pay. Fearing that such arbitrary behavior threatened everyone's property and person, Parliament struck back. In 1628, it refused to grant Charles I tax revenues unless he agreed to the Petition of Right, which stated that the king could not collect taxes without Parliament's consent or imprison people without a specific charge. Thus, the monarch had to acknowledge formally the long-established traditions protecting the rights of the English people.

Nevertheless, tensions between the throne and Parliament persisted, and in 1629 Charles I dissolved Parliament, which would not meet again for eleven years. What forced him to reconvene Parliament in 1640 was his need for funds to defend the realm against an invasion from Scotland. The conflict stemmed from Archbishop William Laud's attempt, approved by Charles I, to impose a common prayer book on Scottish Calvinists, or Presbyterians. Infuriated by this effort to impose Anglican liturgy on them, Scottish Presbyterians took up arms. The Long Parliament—so called because it was not disbanded until 1660—abolished the extralegal courts and commissions that had been used by the king to try opponents, provided for regular meetings of Parliament, and strengthened Parliament's control over taxation. When Puritan members pressed to reduce royal authority even more and to strike at the power of the Anglican Church, a deep split occurred in Parliament's ranks: Puritans and all-out supporters of parliamentary supremacy were opposed by Anglicans and supporters of the king. The ensuing civil war was directed by Parliament, financed by taxes and the merchants, and fought by the New Model Army led by Oliver Cromwell (1599–1658), a Puritan squire who gradually realized his potential for leadership.

Parliament's rich supporters financed the New Model Army, gentlemen farmers led it, and religious zealots filled its ranks, along with the usual cross section of poor artisans and day laborers. This army defeated the king, his aristocratic followers, and the Anglican Church's hierarchy. In January 1649, Charles I was publicly executed by order of Parliament. During the interregnum (time between kings), which lasted eleven years, one Parliament after another joined with the army to govern the country as a republic. In the distribution of power between the army and Parliament, Cromwell proved to be a key element. He had the support of the army's officers and some of its rank and file, and he had been a member of Parliament for many years. His control over the army was secured, however, only after its rank and file was purged of radicals, drawn largely from the poor. Some of these radicals wanted to level society, that is, to redistribute property and to give the vote to all male citizens.

Cromwell's death left the country without effective leadership. Parliament, having secured the interests of its constituency (gentry, merchants, and some small landowners), chose to restore court and crown and invited the exiled son of the executed king to return to the kingship. Having

(Equestrian Portrait of Oliver Cromwell (1599–1658) (engraving) (b/w photo), English School, (17th century)/Private Collection/The Bridgeman Art Library.)

OLIVER CROMWELL. Cromwell wore the simple black of the Puritan gentry and sought to portray himself as a pious warrior. Yet in this portrait, he does have a somewhat regal bearing, and his task demanded that he act like a king without ever becoming one.

learned the lesson his father had spurned, Charles II (1660–1685) never restored royal absolutism.

But Charles's brother, James II (1685–1688), was a foolishly fearless Catholic and admirer of French absolutism. He gathered at his court a coterie of Catholic advisers and supporters of royal prerogative and attempted to bend Parliament and local government to the royal will. James II's Catholicism was the crucial element in his failure. The Anglican Church would not back him, and political forces similar to those that in 1640 had rallied against his father, Charles I, descended on him. The ruling elites, however, had learned their lesson back in the 1650s: civil war would produce social discontent among the masses. The upper classes wanted to avoid open warfare and preserve the monarchy, but as a constitutional authority, not an absolute one. Puritanism, with its sectarian fervor and its dangerous association with republicanism, was allowed to play no part in this second and last phase of the English Revolution.

In early 1688, Anglicans, some aristocrats, and opponents of royal prerogative formed a conspiracy against James II. Their purpose was to invite his son-in-law, William of Orange, stadholder (head) of the Netherlands and husband of James's Protestant daughter Mary, to invade England and rescue its government from James's control. Having lost the loyalty of key men in the army, powerful gentlemen in the counties, and the Anglican Church, James II fled the country, and William and Mary were declared king and queen by act of Parliament.

This bloodless revolution—sometimes called the Glorious Revolution—created a new political and constitutional reality. Parliament secured its rights to assemble regularly and to vote on all matters of taxation; the rights of habeas corpus and trial by jury (for men of property and social status) were also secured. These rights were in turn legitimated in a constitutionally binding document, the Bill of Rights (1689). All Protestants, regardless of their sectarian bias, were granted toleration.

The English Revolution, in both its 1640 and its 1688 phases, secured English parliamentary government and the rule of law. Eventually, the monarchical element in that system would yield to the power and authority of parliamentary ministers and state officials. The Revolution of 1688–1689 was England's last revolution. In the nineteenth and twentieth centuries, parliamentary institutions would be gradually and peacefully reformed to express a more democratic social reality. The events of 1688–1689 have rightly been described as "the year one," for they fashioned a system of government that operated effectively in Britain and could also be transplanted elsewhere with modification. The British system became a model for other forms of representative government, adopted in France and in the former British colonies, beginning with the United States.

THE HOLY ROMAN EMPIRE: THE FAILURE TO UNIFY GERMANY

In contrast to the experience of the French, English, Spanish, and Dutch in the early modern period, the Germans failed to achieve national unity. This failure is tied to the history of the Holy Roman Empire. That union of various distinct Central European territories was created in the tenth century when Otto I, in a deliberate attempt to revive Charlemagne's empire, was crowned Emperor of the Romans. Later, the title was changed to Holy Roman Emperor, with the kingdom consisting mainly of German-speaking principalities.

Most medieval Holy Roman Emperors busied themselves not with administering their territories but with attempting to gain control of the rich Italian peninsula and with challenging the rival authority of various popes. In the meantime, the German nobility extended and consolidated their rule over their peasants and over various towns and cities. The feudal aristocracy's power remained a constant obstacle to German unity.

In the medieval and early modern periods, the Holy Roman Emperors were dependent on their most powerful noble lords—including an archbishop or two—because the office of emperor was elective rather than hereditary. German princes, some of whom were electors— for instance, the archbishops of Cologne and Mainz, the Hohenzollern elector of Brandenburg, the landgrave of Hesse, and the duke of Saxony— were fiercely independent. All belonged to the empire, yet all regarded themselves as autonomous powers. These decentralizing tendencies were highly developed by the fifteenth century.

The Hapsburgs had maneuvered themselves into a position from which they could monopolize the imperial elections. The centralizing efforts of the Hapsburg Holy Roman Emperors Maximilian I (1493–1519) and Charles V (1519–1556) were impeded by the Reformation, which bolstered the Germans' already strong propensity for local independence. The German nobility were all too ready to use the Reformation as a vindication of their local power, and indeed,

Map 9.1 Europe, 1648 Europe in 1648, ▶ exhausted by war.

RUSSIA

FINLAND

SWEDEN

NORWAY

Black Sea

POLAND

Vilna

Warsaw

MOLDAVIA

WALLACHIA

TRANSYLVANIA

OTTOMAN EMPIRE

Belgrade

Athens

Lepanto

Crete
(To Rep. of Venice)

ESTONIA

LIVONIA

PRUSSIA

Danzig

POMERANIA

BRANDENBURG

Berlin

SILESIA

MORAVIA

BOHEMIA

Prague

Vienna

AUSTRIA

REPUBLIC OF VENICE

Copenhagen

MECKLEN-BURG

SAXONY

Hamburg

DENMARK

JUTLAND

SCHLESWIG

WEST-PHALIA

HESSE

Mainz

Worms

BAVARIA

Augsburg

SWITZERLAND

MILAN

Genoa

PIEDMONT

GENOA

PAPAL STATES

FLORENCE

Rome

Naples

NAPLES

Palermo

Sicily

Baltic Sea

North Sea

UNITED NETHERLANDS

Amsterdam

Antwerp

Cologne

SPANISH NETHERLANDS

FRANCHE-COMTÉ

Geneva

SAVOY

Corsica
(to Genoa)

Sardinia

Mediterranean Sea

SCOTLAND

Edinburgh

Durham

ENGLAND

London

English Channel

Paris

FRANCE

Nantes

IRELAND

Dublin

ATLANTIC OCEAN

CATALONIA

ARAGON

VALENCIA

CASTILE

SPAIN

Madrid

ANDALUSIA

Granada

PORTUGAL

Lisbon

400 Mi.

400 Km.

200

200

0

0

Austrian Hapsburg lands

Spanish Hapsburg lands

Prussian lands

German states

Swedish lands

Boundary of Holy Roman Empire

© 2016 Cengage Learning.

217

Luther made just such an appeal to their interests. War raged in Germany between the Hapsburgs and the Protestant princes, united for mutual protection in the Schmalkaldic League. The Treaty of Augsburg (1555) conferred on every German prince the right to determine the religion of his subjects. The princes retained their power, and a unified German state was never constructed by the Hapsburgs. Religious disunity and the particularism and provinciality of the German nobility prevented its creation.

When an exhausted Emperor Charles V abdicated in 1556, he gave his kingdom to his son Philip and his brother Ferdinand. Philip inherited Spain and its colonies, as well as the Netherlands, and Ferdinand acquired the Austrian territories; two branches of the Hapsburg family were thus formed. Throughout the sixteenth century, the Austrian Hapsburgs barely managed to control the sprawling and deeply divided German territories. However, they never missed an opportunity to further the cause of Catholicism and to strike at the power of the German nobility.

No Hapsburg was ever more fervid in that regard than the Jesuit-trained Archduke Ferdinand II, who ascended the throne in Vienna in 1619. His policies provoked a war within the empire that engulfed the whole of Europe: the Thirty Years' War. It began when the Bohemians, whose anti-Catholic tendencies could be traced back to Jan Hus, tried to put a Protestant king on their throne. The Austrian and Spanish Hapsburgs reacted by sending an army into the kingdom of Bohemia, and suddenly, the whole empire was forced to take sides along religious lines. Bohemia suffered an almost unimaginable devastation; the ravaging Hapsburg army sacked and burned three-fourths of the kingdom's towns and practically exterminated its aristocracy.

Until the 1630s, it looked as if the Hapsburgs would be able to use the war to enhance their power and promote centralization. But the intervention of Protestant Sweden, led by Gustavus Adolphus and encouraged by France, wrecked Hapsburg ambitions. The ensuing military conflict devastated vast areas of Northern and Central Europe. The civilian population suffered untold hardships. Partly because the French finally intervened directly, the Spanish Hapsburgs emerged from the Thirty Years' War with no benefits. The Treaty of Westphalia gave the Austrian

Hapsburgs firm control of the eastern states of the kingdom, with Vienna as their capital. Austria took shape as a dynastic state, while the German territories in the empire remained fragmented by the independent interests of the feudal nobility.

EUROPEAN EXPANSION

The emergence of the modern state paralleled the gradual disintegration of traditional medieval socioeconomic forms. Medieval society was divided into three principal groups—clergy, lords, and peasants. It was believed that this hierarchically arranged social order worked best when each social group performed a specific function ordained by God: the clergy led according to God's commands; the aristocracy, guided by the church, defended Christian interests; and the peasants toiled to provide sustenance for themselves and their superiors. The focus was on a social group performing its proper role, the one assigned to it by God and tradition. In early modern times, a capitalist market economy arose whose focus was not on the group but on the individual motivated by self-interest. A new European was emerging, striving, assertive, and willing to break with traditional social forms in order to succeed in the market place. The nascent market economy was greatly aided by the expansion of trade and wealth resulting from the voyages of discovery and the conquest and colonization of the New World.

During the period from 1450 to 1750, Western Europe entered an era of overseas exploration and economic expansion that transformed society. European adventurers discovered a new way to reach the rich trading centers of India by sailing around Africa. They also conquered, colonized, and exploited a new world across the Atlantic. These discoveries and conquests brought about an extraordinary increase in business activity and the supply of money, which stimulated the growth of capitalism. People's values changed in ways that were alien and hostile to the medieval outlook. By 1750, the model Christian in northwestern Europe was no longer the selfless saint but the enterprising businessman. The era of secluded manors and walled towns was drawing to a close. A world economy was emerging in which European economic life depended on the market in Eastern spices, African slaves, and American silver. During this age of exploration and commercial expansion, Europe generated a peculiar dynamism unmatched by any other civilization. A process was initiated that by 1900 would give Europe mastery over most of the globe and wide-ranging influence over other civilizations.

Forces Behind the Expansion

A combination of forces propelled Europeans outward and enabled them to dominate Asians, Africans, and American Indians. European monarchs, merchants, and aristocrats fostered expansion for power and profit. As the numbers of the landed classes exceeded the supply of available land, the sons of the aristocracy looked beyond Europe for the lands and fortunes denied them at home. Nor was it unnatural for them to try to gain these things by plunder and conquest; their ancestors had done the same thing for centuries.

Merchants and shippers also had reason to look abroad. Trade between Europe, Africa, and the Orient had gone on for centuries, but always through intermediaries, who increased the costs and decreased the profits on the European end. Gold from the riverbeds of West Africa had been transported across the Sahara by Arab nomads. Spices, which preserved and seasoned food and served a medical function, had been shipped from India and the East Indies by way of Muslim and Venetian merchants. Western European merchants now sought to break those monopolies by going directly to the source: to West Africa for gold, slaves, and pepper, and to India for pepper, spices, and silks.

The centralizing monarchical state was an important factor in the expansion. Monarchs who had successfully established royal hegemony at home, like Ferdinand and Isabella of Spain, sought opportunities to extend their control overseas. From overseas empires came gold, silver, and commerce, which paid for ever more expensive royal government at home and for war against rival dynasties both at home and abroad.

Religion helped in the expansion because the crusading tradition was well established—especially on the Iberian Peninsula, where a five-hundred-year struggle, known as the Reconquest, to drive out the Muslims had taken place. Cortés, the Spanish conqueror of Mexico, for example, saw himself as following in the footsteps of Paladin

Roland, the great medieval military hero who had fought to drive back Muslims and pagans. Prince Henry the Navigator (see the next section) hoped that the Portuguese expansion into Africa would serve two purposes: the discovery of gold and the extension of Christianity at the expense of Islam.

Not only did the West have the will to expand, but it also possessed the technology needed for successful expansion, the armed sailing vessel. This asset distinguished the West from China and the lands of Islam and helps explain why the West, rather than Eastern civilizations, launched an age of conquest resulting in global mastery. Not only were sailing ships more maneuverable and faster in the open seas than galleys (ships propelled by oars), but the addition of guns below deck that could fire on and cripple or sink distant enemy ships gave them another tactical advantage. The galleys of the Arabs in the Indian Ocean and the junks of the Chinese were not armed with such guns. In battle, they relied instead on the ancient tactic of coming up alongside the enemy vessel, shearing off its oars, and boarding to fight on deck.

The gunned ship gave the West naval superiority from the beginning. The Portuguese, for example, made short work of the Muslim fleet sent to drive them out of the Indian Ocean in 1509. That victory at Diu, off the western coast of India, indicated that the West not only had found an all-water route to the Orient, but also was there to stay.

The Portuguese Empire

In the first half of the fifteenth century, a younger son of the king of Portugal, named Prince Henry the Navigator (1394–1460) by English writers, sponsored voyages of exploration and the nautical studies needed to undertake them. The Portuguese first expanded into islands in the Atlantic Ocean. In 1420, they began to settle Madeira and farm there, and in the 1430s, they pushed into the Canaries and the Azores in search of new farmlands and slaves for their colonies. In the middle decades of the century, they moved down the West African coast to the mouth of the Congo River and beyond, establishing trading posts as they went.

By the end of the fifteenth century, the Portuguese had developed a viable imperial economy among the ports of West Africa, their Atlantic islands, and Western Europe—an economy based on sugar,

The Portuguese in India. A charming engraving by a Portuguese traveler in India, this painting mixes what to Western eyes was strange and foreign with the more familiar. The clothes and the elaborate parasols held high by turbaned servants may have seemed exotic, but the horse and the hunting dogs had their counterparts in Western European landed society.

black slaves, and gold. Africans panned gold in the riverbeds of central and western Africa, and the Portuguese purchased it at its source.

The Portuguese did not stop in western Africa. By 1488, Bartholomeu Dias had reached the southern tip of the African continent; a decade later, Vasco da Gama sailed around the Cape of Good Hope and across the Indian Ocean to India. By discovering an all-water route to the Orient, Portugal broke the commercial monopoly on Eastern goods that Genoa and Venice had enjoyed. With this route to India and the islands of the East Indies, the Portuguese found the source of the spices needed to make dried, tough meat palatable. As they had done along the African coast, they established fortified trading posts—most notably at Goa on the western coast of India (Malabar) and at Malacca on the Malay Peninsula.

The Spanish Empire

Spain stumbled onto its overseas empire, and it proved to be the biggest and richest of any until the eighteenth century. Christopher Columbus, who believed that he could reach India by sailing west, won the support of Isabella, queen of Castile. But on his first voyage (1492), he landed on a large Caribbean island, which he named Española (Little Spain). Within decades, two events revealed that Columbus had discovered not a new route to the East, but new continents: Vasco Nuñez de Balboa's discovery of the Pacific Ocean at the Isthmus of Panama in 1513, and the circumnavigation of the globe (1519–1521) by the expedition led by Ferdinand Magellan, which sailed through the strait at the tip of South America that now bears Magellan's name.

Stories of the existence of large quantities of gold and silver to the west lured the Spaniards from their initial settlements in the Caribbean to Mexico. In 1519, Hernando Cortés landed on the Mexican coast with a small army; during two years of campaigning, he managed to defeat the native rulers, the Aztecs, and to conquer Mexico for the Spanish crown. A decade later, Francisco Pizarro achieved a similar victory over the mountain empire of the Incas in Peru.

For good reasons, the Mexican and Peruvian conquests became the centers of the Spanish overseas empire. First, there were the gold hoards accumulated over the centuries by the indigenous rulers for religious and ceremonial purposes. When these supplies were exhausted, the Spanish discovered silver at Potos' in Upper Peru in 1545 and at Zacatecas in Mexico a few years later. From the middle of the century, the annual treasure fleets sailing to Spain became the financial bedrock of Philip II's war against the Muslim Turks and the Protestant Dutch and English.

Not only gold and silver lured Spaniards to the New World. The crusading spirit spurred them on as well. The will to conquer and convert the pagan peoples of the New World stemmed from the crusading tradition developed during the five previous centuries of Spanish history in campaigns against the Muslims. The rewards were what they had always been: the propagation of the true faith, service to the crown, and handsome land grants. The land was especially attractive in the sixteenth century, for the number of *hidalgos* (lesser nobility) was increasing with the general rise in population; as a result, the amount of land available to them at home was shrinking.

In the New World, power and land gradually became concentrated in fewer and fewer hands. In particular, royal officials, their associates, and the church gained substantially in wealth and privilege. As recurrent depressions ruined smaller landowners, they were forced to sell out to their bigger neighbors. Upon their conversion to Christianity, the Indians were persuaded to give more and more land to the church. Thus, Spanish America became permanently divided between the privileged elite and the impoverished masses.

To work the large estates and mines they established in the New Word, the Spanish conquerors reduced the Native Americans to servitude. Outraged by the inhumane treatment of the Amerindians, some Spanish missionaries condemned the settlers in fiery sermons and appealed to the Spanish throne to intercede. Bartolomé de las Casas (1474–1566), a Dominican friar, wrote that on the island of Hispanola (now divided into Haiti and Dominican Republic) the Spanish conquerors "began to carry out massacres and strange cruelties against [the Indians]. They . . . spared neither the children nor the aged, nor pregnant women nor women in childbed, not only stabbing them . . . but cutting them to pieces. . . . They laid bets as to who, with one stroke of the sword, could split a man in two or cut off his head."[1]

Spanish rulers did institute reforms, but the distance separating Spain from its possessions in the New World often prevented effective enforcement of these reforms. Between 1500 and 1600, the number of Native Americans shrank from about 20 million to little more than two million. The major cause of this catastrophe, however, was not forced labor but the diseases introduced from Europe—dysentery, malaria, hookworm, and smallpox—against which the Indians had little or no natural resistance. Beginning in the 1540s, the position of the natives gradually improved as the crown withdrew grants that gave authority over the native population and took increasing responsibility for controlling the Amerindians.

BLACK SLAVERY AND THE SLAVE TRADE

European settlers caused great suffering for another group: the black slaves originally brought over from West Africa. During the long period of their dominance in North Africa and the Middle East (from the seventh to the nineteenth century), the Muslim states relied on slave labor and slave soldiers from black Africa south of the Sahara. Millions of sub-Saharan blacks were captured by Arab slavers and African chiefs and transported by camel caravans across the Sahara or by slave ships from East Africa to the Persian Gulf to be sold in the slave markets. At its height in the eighteenth century, this trans-Saharan trade may have risen to some ten thousand slaves a year. (Muslim pirates also seized Europeans and transported them to slave markets in North Africa.)

But this annual traffic was eventually dwarfed by the slave trade between West Africa and the European colonies in the New World, which began in earnest in the early sixteenth century. As Roland Oliver notes, "By the end of the seventeenth century, stimulated by the growth of plantation agriculture in Brazil and the West Indies, Atlantic shipments had increased to about thirty thousand a year, and by the end of the eighteenth century they were nearly eighty thousand."[2]

The Art Archive/Biblioteca Nacional Madrid/Gianni Dagli Orti.

A NEW WORLD SUGAR REFINERY, BRAZIL. Sugar was the main and most profitable crop of plantation agriculture until the late eighteenth century, when cotton took the lead, at least in some places. On the plantation, the cane was not only grown but also processed into a variety of products—sugar, molasses, and rum— that were exported to Europe to meet a rising demand. Black slaves did the work under efficient but brutal conditions and often at great profit to the plantation owners.

Most slaves were acquired in tribal wars initiated by African chiefs or in raids conducted by African slavers. The victims—with their hands tied behind their backs and necks connected by wooden yokes or chains—marched to the West African coast where they were herded into specially built prisons. These forced marches from the interior, often covering a distance of hundreds of miles, left the trails littered with dead captives. Probably a greater percentage of Africans perished in this journey than in the ocean crossing.

Those accepted for sale were "marked on the breast with a red-hot iron, imprinting the mark of the French, English or Dutch companies so that each nation may distinguish their own property."[3] Across the centuries, some 11 or 12 million blacks in all were exported to the New World. Of these, some 600,000 ended up in the thirteen colonies of British North America, forming the basis of the slave population of the new United States at the end of the American Revolution.

The conditions of the voyage from Africa, the so-called middle passage, were brutal. Crammed into the holds of ships, some 13 to 30 percent of blacks died on board. In all, some 1.4 million Africans died in the passage across the Atlantic. Upon arrival in the New World, slaves were greased with palm oil to improve their appearance and paraded naked into the auction hall for the benefit of prospective buyers, who paid top prices for "the strongest, youthfullest, and most beautiful."[4] Slave traders grew rich; some of them invested their profits in banking, insurance, and plantations. Many of them were devout Christians who did not believe that trafficking in humans sullied their faith. (In the eighteenth century, some Christians, particularly Quakers and Methodists driven by conscience, became outspoken critics of the British and American slave trade.)

The standard workload for slaves everywhere was ten or eleven hours a day, six days a week. But some distinction must be made between slavery in the American South and elsewhere in the New World. In Brazil and the West Indies, slaves were worked to exhaustion and death and then replaced. Slaves formed a large majority there and were concentrated on very large plantations. Revolts were frequent but were always crushed and savagely punished. In the American South, by contrast, slaves were a minority dispersed over relatively small holdings; large plantations were few. As a result, revolts and deadly epidemics were rare. After 1808, when the United States abolished the external slave trade, slaveholders could not ruthlessly exploit their slaves if they were to meet the growing need for workers caused by the increasing industrial demand for raw cotton. (But of course some slave owners and their plantation overseers continued to behave cruelly toward slaves, over whom they had complete authority.) By 1830, the slave population of the southern states rose through natural increase to more than two million, which represented over one-third of all slaves in the New World.

The Atlantic slave trade had grown to such large volume by the eighteenth century because fields and mines had to be worked, but since the native population had been decimated, an enormous labor shortage existed. Black slaves were imported to satisfy the demand. Not only were they plentiful and cheap to maintain, they were also skilled in farming and mining and could withstand tropical heat, insects, and disease, including the infections brought over from Europe to which the Indians had succumbed.

On the African side, how did suppliers continue to meet this growing New World demand? By 1700, guns imported from Europe were now commonly traded for slaves. With the guns, the West African rulers built armies for capturing other peoples to sell to the Europeans while protecting themselves from being enslaved by rival forces. The desire for profit led to the need for more captives to sell for still more firearms to take still more slaves.

THE PRICE REVOLUTION

Linked to overseas expansion was another phenomenon: an unprecedented inflation during the sixteenth century known as the price revolution. For example, cereal prices multiplied by eight times or more in certain regions in the course of that century, and they continued to rise, although more slowly, during the first half of the seventeenth century. Economic historians have generally assumed that the prices of goods other than cereals increased by half as much as grain prices.

The main cause of the price revolution was the population growth during the late fifteenth and sixteenth centuries. The population of Europe almost doubled between 1460 and 1620. Until the middle of the seventeenth century, the

number of mouths to feed outran the capacity of agriculture to supply basic foodstuffs, causing the vast majority of people to live close to subsistence. Until food production could catch up with the increasing population, prices, especially those of the staple food, bread, continued to rise.

The other principal cause of the price revolution was probably the silver that flowed into Europe from the New World via Spain, beginning in 1552. At some point, the influx of silver may have exceeded the necessary expansion of the money supply and may have begun contributing to the inflation. A key factor in the price revolution, then, was too many people with too much money chasing too few goods. The effects of the price revolution were momentous for the European economy.

THE EXPANSION OF AGRICULTURE

The price revolution had its greatest effect on farming. Food prices, which rose roughly twice as much as the prices of other goods, spurred ambitious farmers to take advantage of the situation and to produce for the expanding market. The opportunity for profit drove some farmers to work harder and manage their land better.

All over Europe, landlords held their properties in the form of manors. A particular type of rural society and economy had evolved on these manors in the Late Middle Ages. By the fifteenth century, much manor land was held by peasant tenants according to the terms of a tenure known in England as *copyhold*. The tenants had certain hereditary rights to the land in return for the performance of certain services and the payment of certain fees to the landlord. Principal among these rights was the use of the commons—the pasture, woods, and pond. For the copyholder, access to the commons often made the difference between subsistence and real want because the land tilled on the manor might not produce enough to support a family. Arable land was worked according to ancient custom. The land was divided into strips, and each peasant of the manor was traditionally assigned a certain number of strips. This whole pattern of peasant tillage and rights in the commons was known as the *open-field system*.

Primary Source

Seventeenth-Century Slave Traders: Buying and Transporting Africans

Dealing in slaves was a profitable business that attracted numerous entrepreneurs. The following account was written by a slave trader in the seventeenth century.

As the slaves came down to Fida from the inland country, they are put into a booth, or prison, built for that purpose, near the beach, all of them together; and when the Europeans are to receive them, they are brought out into a large plain, where the surgeons examine every part of every one of them, to the smallest member, men and women being all stark naked. Such as are allowed good and sound, are set on the one side, and the others by themselves; which slaves so rejected are called Mackrons, being above thirty five years of age, or defective in their limbs, eyes or teeth; or grown grey, or that have venereal disease, or any other imperfection. These being so set aside, each of the others, which have passed as good, is marked on the breast, with a red-hot iron, imprinting the mark of the French, English, or Dutch companies, that so each nation may distinguish their own, and to prevent their being chang'd by the natives for worse, as they are apt enough to do. In this particular, care is taken that the women, as tenderest, be not burnt too hard.

The branded slaves, after this, are returned to their former booth, where the factor [agent] is to subsist them at his own charge, which amounts to about two-pence a day for each of them, with bread and water, which is all their allowance. There they continue sometimes ten or fifteen days, till the sea is still enough to send

them aboard; . . . and when it is so, the slaves are carried off by parcels, in bar-canoes, and put aboard the ships in the road. Before they enter the canoes, or come out of the booth, their former Black masters strip them of every rag they have, without distinction of men or women. . . .

The Blacks of Fida are so expeditious at this trade of slaves that they can deliver a thousand every month. . . . If there happens to be no stock of slaves at Fida, the factor must trust the Blacks with his goods, to the value of a hundred and fifty, or two hundred slaves; which goods they carry up into the inland, to buy slaves, at all the markets, for above two hundred leagues up the country, where they are kept like cattle [are kept] in Europe; the slaves sold there being generally prisoners of war, taken from their enemies, like other booty, and perhaps some few sold by their own countrymen, in extreme want, or upon a famine; so also some as a punishment of heinous crimes: tho' many Europeans believe their parent sell their own children, men their wives and relations, which, if it ever happens, is so seldom, that it cannot justly be charged upon a whole nation, as a custom and common practice.

Questions for Analysis

1. How, why, and by whom are the slaves branded?
2. Who are those called "Black masters," and what role do they play in the slave trade?
3. Where do the slaves come from, and how do they initially come to be enslaved?

Elizabeth Donnan, ed., *Documents Illustrative of the Slave Trade*, 293–294. Copyright © 1935 by Carnegie Institution of Washington. Reproduced by permission.

After changing little for centuries, it was met head-on by the incentives generated by the price revolution.

In England, landlords aggressively pursued the possibilities for profit resulting from the inflation

of farm prices. This pursuit required far-reaching changes in ancient manorial agriculture—changes that are called *enclosure*. The open-field system was geared to providing subsistence for the local village and, as such, prevented large-scale farming

THE HARVESTERS, 1565, BY PIETER BRUEGHEL THE ELDER (D. 1569). This painting shows crops being harvested by peasants in the Netherlands. Agriculture was the basis of all economic life in early modern Europe, and the Netherlands was one of the places where advanced farming techniques were applied to maximizing food production to feed a growing population.

for a distant market. In the open-field system, the commons could not be diverted to the production of crops for sale. Moreover, the division of the arable land into strips reserved for each peasant made it difficult to engage in profitable commercial agriculture.

English landlords in the sixteenth century launched a two-pronged attack against the open-field system in an effort to transform their holdings into market-oriented, commercial ventures. First they denied their tenant peasantry the use of the commons, depriving poor tenants of critically needed produce; then they changed the conditions of tenure from copyhold to leasehold. Whereas copyhold was heritable and fixed, leasehold was not. When a lease came up for renewal, the landlord could raise the rent beyond the tenant's capacity to pay. Both acts of the landlord forced peasants off the manor or into the landlord's employ as farm laborers. With tenants gone, fields could be incorporated into larger, more productive units. Landlords could hire labor at bargain prices because of the swelling population and the large supply of peasants forced off the land by enclosure. Subsistence farming gave way to commercial agriculture: the growing of a surplus for the marketplace. But rural poverty increased because of the mass evictions of tenant farmers.

In the fifteenth and sixteenth centuries, the Dutch developed a new kind of farming known as *convertible husbandry* that also expanded production. This farming system employed a series of innovations, including the use of soil-restoring legumes, that replaced the old three-field system of crop rotation, which had left one-third of the land unused at any given time. The new techniques used all the land every year and provided a more diversified agriculture.

THE EXPANSION OF TRADE AND INDUSTRY

The conditions of the price revolution also caused trade and industry to expand. Population growth that exceeded the capacity of local food supplies stimulated commerce in basic foodstuffs—for example, the Baltic trade with Western Europe. Equally important as a stimulus to trade and industry was the growing income of landlords, merchants, and, in some instances, peasants. This income created a rising demand for consumer goods. Another factor in commercial and industrial expansion was the growth of the state. With increasing amounts of tax revenue to spend, the expanding monarchies of the sixteenth and seventeenth centuries bought more and more supplies—ships, weapons, uniforms, paper—and so spurred economic expansion.

Innovations in Business

Markets tended to shift from local to regional or even to international—a condition that gave rise to the merchant capitalist. The merchant capitalists' operations, unlike those of local producers, extended across local and national boundaries. An essential feature of merchant capitalism was the *putting-out system* of production. The manufacture of woolen textiles is a good example of how the system worked. The merchant capitalist would buy the raw wool from English landlords, who had enclosed their manors to take advantage of the rising price of wool. The merchant's agents collected the wool and took it (put it out) to nearby villages for spinning, dyeing, and weaving. The work was done in the cottages of peasants, many

of whom had been evicted from the surrounding manors as a result of enclosure and therefore had to take what work they could get at very low wages. When the wool had been processed into cloth, it was picked up and shipped to market.

A cluster of other innovations in business life accompanied the emergence of the merchant capitalist and the putting-out system. Some of these innovations had roots in the Middle Ages and were important in the evolution of the modern capitalist economy. Banking operations grew more sophisticated, making it possible for depositors to pay their debts by issuing written orders to their banks to make transfers to their creditors' accounts—the origins of the modern check. Accounting methods also improved. The widespread use of double-entry bookkeeping made errors immediately evident and gave a clear picture of the financial position of a commercial enterprise. Very important to overseas expansion was a new form of business enterprise known as the joint-stock company, which allowed small investors to buy shares in a venture. These companies made possible the accumulation of the large amounts of capital needed for large-scale operations, like the building and deployment of merchant fleets, which were quite beyond the resources of one person.

Different Patterns of Commercial Development

England and the Netherlands.   In both England and the United Provinces (the Netherlands), the favorable conditions led to large-scale commercial expansion. In the 1590s, the Dutch devised a new ship, the *fluit* or flyboat, to handle bulky grain shipments at the lowest possible cost. This innovation allowed them to capture the Baltic trade, which became a principal source of their phenomenal commercial expansion between 1560 and 1660.

Equally dramatic was their commercial penetration of the Orient. Profits from the European carrying trade built the ships that allowed the Dutch first to challenge and then to displace the Portuguese in the spice trade with the East Indies during the early seventeenth century. The Dutch chartered the United East India Company in 1602 and established trading posts in the islands, which were the beginnings of a Dutch empire that lasted until World War II.

The English traded throughout Europe in the sixteenth and seventeenth centuries, especially with Spain and the Netherlands. The seventeenth century saw the foundation of a British colonial empire along the Atlantic seaboard in North America, from Maine to the Carolinas, and in the West Indies, where the English managed to dislodge the Spanish in some places.

In both England and the Netherlands, government promoted the interests of business. Political power in the Netherlands passed increasingly into the hands of an urban patriciate of merchants and manufacturers, based in cities like Delft, Haarlem, and especially Amsterdam. There, urban interests pursued public policies that served their pocketbooks. In England, because of the revolutionary transfer of power from the king to Parliament, economic policies also reflected the interests of big business, whether agricultural or commercial. Enclosure, for example, was abetted by parliamentary enactment. The Bank of England, founded in 1694, expanded credit and increased business confidence. The Navigation Acts, which proved troublesome to American colonists, placed restrictions on colonial trade and manufacturing in order to prevent competition with English merchants and manufacturers.

France and Spain. France benefited from commercial and industrial expansion, but not to the same degree as England, mainly because of the aristocratic structure of French society. Family ties and social intercourse between the aristocracy and the merchants, like those that developed in England, were much less common in France. Consequently, the French aristocracy remained contemptuous of commerce. Also inhibiting economic expansion were the guilds—remnants of the Middle Ages that restricted competition and production. In France, there was relatively less room than in England for the merchant capitalist operating outside the guild structures.

Spain presents an even clearer example of the failure to grasp the opportunities afforded by the price revolution. By the third quarter of the sixteenth century, Spain possessed the makings of economic expansion: unrivaled amounts of capital in the form of silver, a large and growing population, rising consumer demand, and a vast overseas empire. These factors did not bear fruit because the Spanish value system regarded business as social heresy. The Spanish held in high esteem gentlemen who possessed land gained through military service and crusading ardor, which enabled them to live on rents and privileges. Commerce and industry remained contemptible pursuits.

Numerous wars in the sixteenth century (with France, the Lutheran princes, the Ottoman Turks, the Dutch, and the English) put an increasing strain on the Spanish treasury, despite the annual shipments of silver from the New World. Spain spent its resources on maintaining and extending its imperial power and Catholicism, rather than on investing in economic expansion. In the end, the wars cost more than Spain could handle. The Dutch for a time and the English and the French for a much longer period displaced Spain as the great power. The English and the Dutch had taken advantage of the opportunities presented by the price revolution; the Spanish had not.

THE FOSTERING OF MERCANTILE CAPITALISM

The changes described—especially in England and the Netherlands—represent a crucial stage in the development of the modern economic system known as *capitalism*. This is a system of *private enterprise*: the main economic decisions (what, how much, where, and at what price to produce, buy, and sell) are made by private individuals in their capacity as owners, workers, or consumers.

From 1450 to 1600, several conditions sustained the incentive to invest and reinvest—a basic factor in the emergence of modern capitalism. One was the price revolution stemming from a supply of basic commodities that could not keep pace with rising demand. Prices continued to climb, creating the most powerful incentive of all to invest rather than to consume. Why spend now, those with surplus wealth must have asked, when investment in commercial farming, mining, shipping, and publishing (to name a few important outlets) is almost certain to yield greater wealth in the future?

Peasant Festival, 1640, by David Teniers the Younger (1610–1690). This scene depicts peasant revelry—the rural village at play. The common folk are eating, drinking, and dancing outside what looks like a country tavern. Hardworking farmworkers no doubt deserved their day off. Notice in the lower left of the picture a small group of gentry who owned the land on which the peasants worked. Such landlords indulged the peasants in their merrymaking, but warily and only up to a point because they feared the possibility of a riot and popular rebellion.

Additional stimuli for investment came from governments. Governments acted as giant consumers, and throughout the early modern period their appetites were expanding. Merchants who supplied governments with everything from guns to frescoes not only prospered but reinvested as well because of the constancy and growth of government demand. Governments also sponsored new forms of investment, whether to supply the debauched taste for new luxuries at the

king's court or to meet the requirements of the military. Moreover, private investors reaped incalculable advantages from overseas empires. Colonies supplied cheap raw materials and cheap (slave) labor and served as markets for exports. They greatly stimulated the construction of both ships and harbor facilities and the sale of insurance.

State policies, known as *mercantilism,* were also aimed at augmenting national wealth and power. According to mercantilist theory, wealth from trade was measured in gold and silver, of which there was believed to be a more or less fixed quantity. The state's goal in international trade became to sell more abroad than it bought, that is, to establish a favorable balance of payments. When the amount received for sales abroad was greater than that spent for purchases, the difference would be an influx of precious metal into the state. By this logic, mercantilists were led to argue for the goal of national sufficiency: a country should try to supply most of its own needs to keep imports to a minimum.

To fuel the national economy, governments subsidized new industries, chartered companies to engage in overseas trade, and broke down local trade barriers, such as guild regulations and internal tariffs. The price revolution, the concentration of wealth in private hands, and government activity combined to provide the foundation for sustained investment and for the emergence of mercantile capitalism. This new force in the world should not be confused with industrial capitalism. The latter evolved with the Industrial Revolution in eighteenth-century England, but mercantile capitalism paved the way for it.

TOWARD A GLOBAL ECONOMY

The transformations considered in this chapter were among the most movements in world history. In an unprecedented development, one small part of the world, Western Europe, had become the lord of the sea-lanes, the master of many lands throughout the globe, and the banker and profit taker in an emerging world economy. Western Europe's global hegemony was to last well into the twentieth century. In conquering and settling new lands, Europeans exported Western culture around the globe, a process that accelerated in the twentieth century.

The effects of overseas expansion were profound. The native populations of the New World were decimated largely because of disease. As a result of the labor shortage, millions of blacks were imported from Africa to work as slaves on plantations and in mines. Black slavery would produce large-scale effects on culture, politics, and society that have lasted to the present day.

The widespread circulation of plant and animal life also had great consequences. Horses and cattle were introduced into the New World. (So amazed were the Aztecs to see men on horseback that at first they thought horse and rider were one demonic creature.) In return, the Old World acquired such novelties as corn, the tomato, and, most important, the potato, which was to become a staple of the Northern European diet. Manioc, from which tapioca is made, was transplanted from the New World to Africa, where it helped sustain the population.

Western Europe was wrenched out of the subsistence economy of the Middle Ages and launched on a course of sustained economic growth. This transformation resulted from the grafting of traditional forms, such as primogeniture—the system of inheritance by the eldest son—and holy war, onto new forces, such as global exploration, price revolution, and convertible husbandry. Out of this change emerged the beginnings of a new economic system, mercantile capitalism. This system, in large measure, paved the way for the Industrial Revolution of the eighteenth and nineteenth centuries and provided the economic thrust for European world predominance. Germs also traversed the Atlantic. Millions of Amerindians perished from diseases imported from Europe and syphilis brought back to Spain by Columbus' men produced a fearsome outbreak of the disease in Europe.

❖   ❖   ❖

NOTES

1. Bartolomé de Las Casas, *The Devastation of the Indies*, trans. Herma Briffault (Baltimore, MD: The Johns Hopkins University Press, 1992), 33.

2. Roland Oliver, *The African Experience* (New York: HarperCollins, 1991), 123.

3. Quoted in Basil Davidson, *Africa in History* (New York: Collier Books, 1991), 215.

4. Quoted in Richard S. Dunn, *Sugar and Slaves* (Chapel Hill: University of North Carolina Press, 1972), 248.

Chapter 10

Intellectual Transformation: The Scientific Revolution and the Age of Enlightenment

- **The Medieval View of the Universe**
- **A New View of Nature**
- **The Newtonian Synthesis**
- **Prophets of Modern Science**
- **The Meaning of the Scientific Revolution**
- **The Age of Enlightenment: Affirmation of Reason and Freedom**
- **Christianity Assailed: The Search for a Natural Religion**
- **Political Thought**
- **Social and Economic Thought**
- **Conflicts and Politics**
- **The Enlightenment and the Modern Mentality**

Focus Questions

1. How did the Scientific Revolution transform the medieval view of the universe?
2. How did the Scientific Revolution contribute to the shaping of the modern mentality?
3. What were the essential concerns of the philosophes of the Enlightenment?
4. How did the Enlightenment contribute to the shaping of the modern mentality?

*T*he movement toward modernity initiated by the Renaissance was greatly advanced by the Scientific Revolution of the seventeenth century. The Scientific Revolution destroyed the medieval view of the universe and established the scientific method—rigorous and systematic observation and experimentation—as the essential means of unlocking nature's secrets. Increasingly, Western thinkers maintained that nature was a mechanical system governed by laws that could be expressed mathematically. The new discoveries electrified the imagination. Science displaced theology as the queen of knowledge, and reason, which had been subordinate to religion in the Middle Ages, asserted its autonomy. The great confidence in reason inspired by the Scientific Revolution helped give rise to the Enlightenment, which explicitly rejected the ideas and institutions of the medieval past and articulated the essential norms of modernity. ❖

THE MEDIEVAL VIEW
OF THE UNIVERSE

Medieval thinkers had constructed a coherent picture of the universe that blended the theories of two ancient Greeks, Aristotle and Ptolemy of Alexandria, with Christian teachings.* To the medieval mind, the cosmos was a giant ladder, a qualitative order, ascending toward heaven. God was at the summit of this hierarchical universe, and the earth, base and vile, was at the bottom, just above hell. It was also the center of the universe. In the medieval view, the earth's central location meant that the universe centered on human beings, that by God's design, human beings—the only creatures on whom God had bestowed reason and the promise of salvation—were lords of the earth. Around the stationary earth revolved seven transparent spheres, each of which carried one of the "planets"—the moon, Mercury, Venus, the sun, Mars, Jupiter, and Saturn. (Since the earth did not move, it was not considered a planet.) The eighth sphere, in which the stars were

* See also Chapter 7

embedded, also revolved about the earth. Beyond the stars was a heavenly sphere, the prime mover, that imparted motion to the planets and the stars, so that in one day the entire celestial system turned around the stationary earth. Enclosing the entire system was another heavenly sphere, the Empyrean, where God sat on his throne, attended by angels.

Medieval thinkers inherited Aristotle's view of a qualitative universe. Earthly objects were composed of earth, water, air, and fire, whereas celestial objects, belonging to a higher world, were composed of ether or quintessence—an element too pure and perfect to be found on earth, which consisted of base matter. In contrast to earthly objects, heavenly bodies were incorruptible; that is, they experienced no change. Since the quintessential heavens differed totally from earth, the paths of planets could not follow the same laws that governed the motion of earthly objects. This two-world orientation blended well with the Christian outlook.

Like Aristotle, Ptolemy held that planets moved around the earth in perfect circular orbits and at uniform speeds. However, in reality, the path of planets is not a circle but an ellipse, and planets do not move at uniform speed but accelerate as they approach the sun. Therefore, problems arose that required Ptolemy to incorporate into his system certain ingenious devices that earlier Greek astronomers had employed. For example, to save the appearance of circular orbits, Ptolemy made use of epicycles, small circles attached to the rims of larger circles. A planet revolved uniformly around the small circle, the epicycle, which in turn revolved about the earth in a larger circle. If one ascribed a sufficient number of epicycles to a planet, the planet could seem to move in a perfectly circular orbit.

The Aristotelian–Ptolemaic model of the cosmos did appear to accord with common sense and raw perception: the earth does indeed seem and feel to be at rest. And the validity of this view seemed to be confirmed by evidence, for the model enabled thinkers to predict with considerable accuracy the movement and location of celestial bodies and the passage of time. This geocentric model and the division of the universe into higher and lower worlds also accorded with passages in Scripture. Scholastic philosophers harmonized Aristotelian and Ptolemaic science with Christian theology, producing an intellectually and emotionally satisfying picture of the universe in which everything was arranged according to a divine plan.

A NEW VIEW OF NATURE

In several ways, the Renaissance contributed to the Scientific Revolution. The revival of interest in antiquity during the Renaissance led to the rediscovery of some ancient scientific texts, including the works of Archimedes (287–212 B.C.), which fostered new ideas in mechanics, and to improved translations of the medical works of Galen, a contemporary of Ptolemy, which stimulated the study of anatomy. Renaissance art, too, was a factor in the rise of modern science, for it linked an exact representation of the human body to mathematical proportions and demanded accurate observation of natural phenomena. By defining visual space and the relationship between the object and the observer in mathematical terms and by delineating the natural world with unprecedented scientific precision, Renaissance art helped to promote a new view of nature, which later found expression in the astronomy of Copernicus and Kepler and the physics of Galileo.

The Renaissance revival of ancient Pythagorean and Platonic ideas, which stressed mathematics as the key to comprehending reality, also contributed to the Scientific Revolution. Extending the mathematical harmony found in music to the universe at large, Pythagoras (c. 580–507 B.C.) and his followers believed that reality consists fundamentally of numerical relations, which the mind can grasp. Plato maintained that beyond the world of everyday objects made known to us through the senses lies a higher reality, the world of Forms, which contains an inherent mathematical order apprehended only by thought. The great thinkers of the Scientific Revolution were influenced by these ancient ideas of nature as a harmonious mathematical system knowable to the mind. The invention of the printing press, which made possible the rapid and wide dissemination of scientific texts, also helped prepare the way for the Scientific Revolution.

COPERNICAN SYSTEM. In his *On the Revolutions of the Heavenly Spheres,* Copernicus proposed a heliocentric model in which the planets orbit around the sun.

Nicolaus Copernicus: The Dethronement of the Earth

Modern astronomy begins with Nicolaus Copernicus (1473–1543), a Polish astronomer, mathematician, and church canon. He proclaimed that earth is a planet that orbits a centrally located sun together with the other planets. This heliocentric theory served as the kernel of a new world picture that eventually supplanted the medieval view of the universe. Copernicus did not base his heliocentric theory on new observations and new data. What led him to remove the earth from the center of the universe was the complexity and cumbersomeness of the Ptolemaic system, which offended his sense of mathematical order. To Copernicus, the numerous epicycles (the number had been increased since Ptolemy, making the model even more cumbersome) violated the Platonic vision of the mathematical symmetry of the universe.

Concerned that his theories would spark a controversy, Copernicus refused to publish his work, but, persuaded by his friends, he finally relented. His masterpiece, *On the Revolutions of the Heavenly Spheres,* appeared in 1543. As Copernicus had feared, his views did stir up controversy, but the new astronomy did not become a passionate issue until the early seventeenth century, more than fifty years after the publication of *On the Revolutions.* The Copernican theory frightened clerical authorities, who controlled the universities as well as the pulpits, for it seemed to conflict with Scripture. For example, Psalm 93 says: "Yea, the world is established, that it cannot be moved." And Psalm 103 says that God "fixed the earth upon its foundation not to be moved forever." In 1616, the church placed *On the Revolutions* and all other works that ascribed motion to the earth on the Index of Prohibited Books.

Galileo: Uniformity of Nature and Experimental Physics

Galileo Galilei (1564–1642) is the principal reason that the seventeenth century has been called "the century of genius." A Pisan by birth, Galileo was a talented musician and artist and a cultivated humanist; he knew and loved the Latin classics and Italian poetry. He was also an astronomer and physicist who helped shatter the medieval conception of the cosmos and shape the modern scientific outlook. Galileo was indebted to the Platonic tradition, which tried to grasp the mathematical harmony of the universe, and to Archimedes, the Hellenistic mathematician-engineer who had sought a geometric understanding of space and motion.

Galileo rejected the medieval division of the universe into higher and lower realms and proclaimed the modern idea of nature's uniformity. Learning that a telescope had been invented in Holland, Galileo built one for himself and used it to investigate the heavens—the first person to do so. From his observations of the moon, Galileo concluded

> *that the surface of the moon is not smooth, uniform, and precisely spherical as a great number of philosophers believe it (and the other heavenly bodies) to be, but is uneven, rough, and full of cavities and prominences, being not unlike the face of the earth, relieved by chains of mountains and deep valleys.*[1]

This discovery of the moon's craters and mountains and of spots on the supposedly unblemished sun led Galileo to break with the Aristotelian notion that celestial bodies were pure, perfect, and unchangeable. For Galileo, there was no difference in quality between celestial and terrestrial bodies. Nature was not a hierarchical order, in which physical entities were ranked according to their inherent quality; rather, it was a homogeneous system, the same throughout.

With his telescope, Galileo discovered the four moons that orbit Jupiter, an observation that overcame a principal objection to the Copernican system. Galileo showed that a celestial body could indeed move around a center other than the earth,

that the earth was not the common center for all celestial bodies, and that a celestial body (the earth's moon or Jupiter's moons) could orbit a planet at the same time that the planet revolved around another body (the sun).

Galileo also pioneered in experimental physics and advanced the modern idea that knowledge of motion should be derived from direct observation and from mathematics. In dealing with problems of motion, he insisted on applying mathematics to the study of moving bodies and did in fact study acceleration by performing experiments, which required careful mathematical measurement. For Aristotelian scholastics, a rock fell because it was striving to reach its proper place in the universe, thereby fulfilling its nature; it was acting in accordance with the purpose God had assigned it. Galileo completely rejected the view that motion is due to a quality inherent in an object. Rather, he said, motion is the relationship of bodies to time and distance. By holding that bodies fall according to uniform and quantifiable laws, Galileo posited an entirely different conceptual system. This system requires that we study angles and distances and search for mathematical ratios but avoid inquiring into an object's quality and purpose—the role God assigned it in a hierarchical universe. Moreover, Galileo's physics implied that celestial objects, which hitherto had belonged to a separate and higher realm, were subject to the same laws that governed terrestrial motion—another sign of nature's uniformity. The traditional belief in a sharp distinction between heavenly and earthly realms was weakened by both Galileo's telescopic observations of the moon and by his mechanistic physics.

For Galileo, the universe was a "grand book which . . . is written in the language of mathematics and its characters are triangles, circles, and other geometric figures without which it is humanly impossible to understand a single word of it."[2] In the tradition of Plato, Galileo sought to grasp the mathematical principles governing reality—reality was physical nature itself, not Plato's higher realm, of which nature was only a poor copy—and ascribed to mathematics absolute authority. Like Copernicus and Kepler (discussed later in this chapter), he believed that mathematics expresses the harmony and beauty of God's creation.

Attack on Authority

Insisting that physical truth is arrived at through observation, experimentation, and reason, Galileo strongly denounced reliance on authority. Scholastic thinkers, who dominated the universities, regarded Aristotle as the supreme authority on questions concerning nature, and university education was based on his works. These doctrinaire Aristotelians angered Galileo, who protested that they sought truth not by opening their eyes to nature and new knowledge but by slavishly relying on ancient texts. In *Dialogue Concerning the Two Chief World Systems—Ptolemaic and Copernican* (1632), Galileo upheld the Copernican view and attacked the unquestioning acceptance of Aristotle's teachings.

Galileo also criticized Roman Catholic authorities for attempting to suppress the Copernican theory. He argued that passages from the Bible had no authority in questions involving nature.

A sincere Christian, Galileo never intended to use the new science to undermine faith. What he desired was to separate science from faith so that reason and experience alone would be the deciding factors on questions involving nature. He could not believe that "God who has endowed us with senses, reason and intellect"[3] did not wish us to use these faculties in order to acquire knowledge. He was certain that science was compatible with Scripture rightly understood, that is, allowing for the metaphorical language of Scripture and its disinterest in conveying scientific knowledge. For Galileo, the aim of Scripture was to teach people the truths necessary for salvation, not to instruct them in the operations of nature, which is the task of science.

Galileo's support of Copernicus aroused the ire of both scholastic philosophers and the clergy, who feared that the brash scientist threatened a world picture that had the support of venerable ancient authorities, Holy Writ, and scholastic tradition. Already traumatized by the Protestant threat, Catholic officials cringed at ideas that might undermine traditional belief and authority.

In 1616, the Congregation of the Index, the church's censorship organ, condemned the teaching of Copernicanism. In 1633, the aging and infirm Galileo was summoned to Rome. Tried and condemned by the Inquisition, he was ordered to abjure the Copernican theory. Not wishing to bring harm to himself and certain that the truth would eventually prevail, Galileo bowed to the Inquisition. He was sentenced to life imprisonment—mostly house arrest at his own villa near Florence—the *Dialogue* was banned, and he was forbidden to write on Copernicanism. Not until 1820 did the church lift the ban on Copernicanism.

Johannes Kepler: Laws of Planetary Motion

Johannes Kepler (1571–1630), a German mathematician and astronomer, combined the Pythagorean–Platonic quest to comprehend the mathematical harmony within nature with a deep commitment to Lutheran Christianity. He contended that God gave human beings the ability to understand the laws of harmony and proportion.

As a true Pythagorean, Kepler yearned to discover the geometric harmony of the planets—what he called the "music of the spheres." Such knowledge, he believed, would provide supreme insight into God's mind. No doubt this mystical quality sparked the creative potential of his imagination, but to be harnessed for science, it had to be disciplined by the rational faculties.

Kepler discovered the three basic laws of planetary motion, which shattered the Ptolemaic cosmology. In doing so, he utilized the data collected by Tycho Brahe, a Danish astronomer, who for twenty years had systematically observed the planets and stars and recorded their positions with far greater accuracy than had ever been done. Kepler sought to fit Tycho's observations into Copernicus's heliocentric model.

Kepler's first law demonstrated that planets move in elliptical orbits—not circular ones, as Aristotle and Ptolemy (and Copernicus) had believed—and that the sun is one focus of the ellipse. This discovery that a planet's path was one simple oval eliminated all the epicycles that had been used to preserve the appearance of circular motion. Kepler's second law showed that planets do not move at uniform speed, as had been believed, but accelerate as they near the sun, and he provided the rule for deciphering a planet's speed at each point in its orbit. His third law

Sir Isaac Newton. The late 18th-century poet and engraver, William Blake imaged Newton as the "first man" who followed the laws of geometry to fashion the world. Here Newton uses the simple compass of the mason to put his design onto the world.

drew a mathematical relationship between the time it takes a planet to complete its orbit of the sun and its average distance from the sun. On the basis of these laws, one could calculate accurately a planet's position and velocity at a particular time—another indication that the planets were linked together in a unified mathematical system.

Derived from carefully observed facts, Kepler's laws of planetary motion buttressed Copernicanism, for they made sense only in a heliocentric universe. But why did the planets move in elliptical orbits? Why did they not fly off into space or crash into the sun? To these questions, Kepler

had no satisfactory answers. It was Isaac Newton (1642–1727), the great British mathematician-scientist, who arrived at a celestial mechanics that linked the astronomy of Copernicus and Kepler with the physics of Galileo and accounted for the behavior of planets.

THE NEWTONIAN SYNTHESIS

The publication in 1687 of Isaac Newton's *Mathematical Principles of Natural Philosophy* marks the climax of the Scientific Revolution. Newton postulated three laws of motion that joined all celestial and terrestrial objects into a vast mechanical system, whose parts worked in perfect harmony and whose connections could be expressed in mathematical terms, and he invented calculus, which facilitated the expression of physical laws in mathematical equations. Since Copernican astronomy was essential to his all-encompassing theory of the universe, Newton provided mathematical proof for the heliocentric system, and opposition to it dissipated.

Newton's first law is the principle of inertia: that a body at rest remains at rest unless acted on by a force and that a body in rectilinear motion continues to move in a straight line at the same velocity unless a force acts on it. A moving body does not require a force to keep it in motion, as ancient and medieval thinkers had believed. Once started, bodies continue to move; motion is as natural a condition as rest. Newton's second law states that a given force produces a measurable change in a body's velocity; a body's change of velocity is proportional to the force acting on it. Newton's third law holds that for every action or force there is an equal and opposite reaction or force. The sun pulls the earth with the same force that the earth exercises on the sun. An apple falling to the ground is being pulled by the earth, but the apple is also pulling the earth toward it. (However, since the mass of the apple is so small in comparison with that of the earth, the force that the apple exercises on the earth causes no visible change in the earth's motion.)

Newton asserted that the same laws of motion and gravitation that operate in the celestial world also govern the movement of earthly bodies. Ordinary mechanical laws explain both why apples fall to the ground and why planets orbit the sun. Both the planet and the apple are subject to the same force, and the very same mathematical formula describes the sun's action on a planet and the earth's pull on an apple. Newtonian physics ended the medieval division of the cosmos into higher and lower worlds, with different laws operating in each realm. The universe is an integrated, harmonious mechanical system held together by the force of gravity. By demonstrating that the universe contains an inherent mathematical order, Newton realized the Pythagorean and Platonic visions. To his contemporaries, it seemed that Newton had unraveled all of nature's mysteries: the universe was fully explicable. It was as if Newton had penetrated God's mind.

Deeply committed to Anglican Christianity, Newton retained a central place for God in his world system. God for him was the grand architect whose wisdom and skill accounted for nature's magnificent clockwork design. Newton also believed that God periodically intervened in his creation to restore energy to the cosmic system and that there was no conflict between divine miracles and a mechanical universe. However, in future generations, thinkers called deists (see the upcoming section "Christianity Assailed: The Search for a Natural Religion") came to regard miracles as incompatible with a universe governed by impersonal mechanical principles.

With his discovery of the composition of light, Newton also laid the foundation of the science of optics. He was a cautious experimentalist who valued experimental procedures, including drawing appropriate conclusions from accumulated data. Both Newton's mechanical universe and his championing of the experimental method were basic premises of the Age of Enlightenment.

PROPHETS OF MODERN SCIENCE

The accomplishments of the Scientific Revolution extended beyond the creation of a new model of the universe. They also included the formulation of a new method of inquiry into nature and the recognition that science could serve humanity. Two thinkers instrumental in articulating the implications of the Scientific Revolution were Francis Bacon and René Descartes. Both repudiated the authority of Aristotle and other ancients in scientific matters and urged the adoption of new methods for seeking and evaluating truth.

Francis Bacon: The Inductive Method

Sir Francis Bacon (1561–1626), an English statesman and philosopher, vigorously supported the advancement of science and the scientific method.

Primary Source

Voltaire: Condemnation of Superstition

The philosophes strongly condemned religious intolerance, fanaticism, persecution, and superstition as the following excerpt from Voltaire's writings indicate.

In 1749 a woman was burned in the Bishopric of Würzburg [a city in central Germany], convicted of being a witch. This is an extraordinary phenomenon in the age in which we live. Is it possible that people who boast of . . . trampling superstition under foot, who indeed supposed that they had reached the perfection of reason, could nevertheless believe in witchcraft . . .?

In 1652 a peasant woman named Michelle Chaudron, living in the little territory of Geneva [a major city in Switzerland], met the devil going out of the city. The devil gave her a kiss, received her homage, and imprinted on her upper lip and right breast the mark that he customarily bestows on all whom he recognizes as his favorites. This seal of the devil is a little mark which makes the skin insensitive, as all the demonographical jurists of those times affirm.

The devil ordered Michelle Chaudron to bewitch two girls. She obeyed her master punctually. The girls' parents accused her of witchcraft before the law. The girls were questioned and confronted with the accused. They declared that they felt a continual pricking in certain parts of their bodies and that they were possessed. Doctors were called, or at least, those who passed for doctors at that time. They examined the girls. They looked for the devil's seal on Michelle's body—what the statement of the case called *satanic marks*. Into them they drove a long needle, already a painful torture. Blood flowed out, and Michelle made it known, by her cries, that satanic marks certainly do not make one insensitive. The judges, seeing no definite proof that Michelle Chaudron was a witch, proceeded to torture her, a method that infallibly produces the necessary proofs: this wretched woman, yielding to the violence of torture, at last confessed every thing they desired.

The doctors again looked for the satanic mark. They found a little black spot on one of her thighs. They drove in the needle. The torment of the torture had been so horrible that the poor creature hardly felt the needle; thus the crime was established. But as customs were becoming somewhat mild at that time, she was burned only after being hanged and strangled.

In those days every tribunal of Christian Europe resounded with similar arrests. The [twigs] were lit everywhere for witches, as for heretics. People reproached the Turks most for having neither witches nor demons among them. This absence of demons was considered an infallible proof of the falseness of a religion.

A zealous friend of public welfare, of humanity, of true religion, has stated in one of his writings on behalf of innocence, that Christian tribunals have condemned to death over a hundred thousand accused witches. If to these judicial murders are added the infinitely superior number of massacred heretics, that part of the world will seem to be nothing but a vast scaffold covered with torturers and victims, surrounded by judges, guards and spectators.

Question for Analysis

1. Voltaire was a great satirist. Which lines do you consider his most effective use of satire? Why?

Voltaire, *Candide and Other Writings*, Haskell M. Block, ed. (New York: Random House, 1956), 374–375.

However, in succeeding centuries, this radical cosmological transformation proved as traumatic for the modern mind as did Adam and Eve's expulsion from the Garden of Eden for the medieval mind. Today, we know that the earth is one of billions and billions of celestial bodies, a tiny speck in an endless cosmic ocean, and that the universe is some 12 billion years old. Could such a universe have been created just for human beings? Could it contain a heaven that assures eternal life for the faithful and a hell with eternal fires and torments for sinners?

Few people at the time were aware of the full implications of the new cosmology. One who did understand was Blaise Pascal (1623–1662), a French scientist and mathematician. A devout Catholic, Pascal was frightened by what he called "the eternal silence of these infinite spaces" and realized that the new science could stir doubt, uncertainty, and anxiety, which threatened belief.

The conception of reason advanced by Galileo and other thinkers of the period differed fundamentally from that of medieval scholastics. Scholastic thinkers viewed reason as a useful aid for contemplating divine truth; as such, reason always had to serve theology. Influenced by the new scientific spirit, thinkers now saw the investigation of nature as reason's principal concern. What is more, they viewed this activity as autonomous and not subject to theological authority.

The Scientific Revolution fostered a rational and critical spirit among the intellectual elite. Descartes's methodical doubt, rejection of authority, and insistence on the clarity, precision, and accuracy of an idea and Francis Bacon's insistence on verification pervaded the outlook of the eighteenth-century Enlightenment thinkers; they denounced magic, spells, demons, witchcraft, alchemy, and astrology as vulgar superstitions. Phenomena attributed to occult forces, they argued, could be explained by reference to natural forces. A wide breach opened up between the intellectual elite and the masses, who remained steeped in popular superstitions and committed to traditional Christian dogma.

The creators of modern science had seen no essential conflict between traditional Christianity and the new view of the physical universe and made no war on the churches. Indeed, they believed that they were unveiling the laws of nature instituted by God at the Creation—that at last the human mind could comprehend God's magnificent handiwork. But the new cosmology and new scientific outlook ultimately weakened traditional Christianity, for it dispensed with miracles and the need for God's presence.

The new critical spirit led the thinkers of the Enlightenment to doubt the literal truth of the Bible and to dismiss miracles as incompatible with what science teaches about the regularity of nature. So brilliantly had God crafted the universe, they said, so exquisite a mechanism was nature, that its operations did not require God's intervention. In the generations after the Scientific Revolution, theology, long considered the highest form of contemplation, was denounced as a barrier to understanding or even dismissed as irrelevant, and the clergy rapidly lost their position as the arbiters of knowledge. To many intellectuals, theology seemed sterile and profitless in comparison with the new science. Whereas science promised the certitude of mathematics, theologians seemed to quibble endlessly over unfathomable and, even worse, inconsequential issues. That much blood had been spilled over these questions discredited theology still more. In scientific academies, in salons, and in coffee houses, educated men and some women met to discuss the new ideas, and journals published the new knowledge for eager readers. European culture was undergoing a great transformation, marked by the triumph of a scientific and secular spirit among the intellectual elite. How different this was from the Islamic world where, after a promising beginning, the study of Greek philosophy and science came to be regarded as a threat to faith and piety. When Western universities were broadening their scholarship to encompass science and secular concerns, Islamic schools focused exclusively on theology.

The Scientific Revolution repudiated reliance on Aristotle, Ptolemy, and other ancient authorities in matters concerning nature and substituted in their place knowledge derived from observation, experimentation, and mathematical thinking. Citing an ancient authority was no longer sufficient to prove a point or win an argument. The new standard of knowledge derived from

THE INQUISITION. In one of the first histories of all the world's religions (published in 1723), the engraver Bernard Picart depicted cold and ruthless interrogators (above) and barbaric torturers (below); at the bottom center is the practice of water-boarding.

Bibliotheque des Arts Decoratifs, Paris, France/Archives Charmet/The Bridgeman Art Library International.

Christian mysteries, prophecies, and miracles—the virgin birth, Jesus walking on water, the Resurrection, and others—as violations of a lawful natural order. They did consider it reasonable that this magnificently structured universe, operating with clockwork precision, was designed and created at a point in time by an all-wise Creator. But in their view, once God had set the universe in motion, he refrained from interfering with its operations. Thus, deists were at odds with Newton, who allowed for divine intervention in the world.

For deists, the essence of religion was morality—a commitment to justice and humanity—and not adherence to rituals, doctrines, or clerical authority. In *The Age of Reason* (1794–1795),

Paine declared: "I believe in the equality of man; and I believe that religious duties consist in doing justice, loving mercy, and endeavoring to make our fellow-creatures happy."[8] Deists deemed it entirely reasonable that after death those who had fulfilled God's moral law would be rewarded, while those who had not would be punished.

POLITICAL THOUGHT

Besides established religion, the philosophes identified another source of the evil that beset humanity: despotism. If human beings were to achieve happiness, they had to extirpate revealed religion and check the power of their rulers. "Every age has its dominant idea," wrote Diderot; "that of our age seems to be Liberty."[9] Eighteenth-century political thought is characterized by a thoroughgoing secularism; an indictment of despotism, the divine right of kings, and the special privileges of the aristocracy and the clergy; a respect for English constitutionalism because it enshrined the rule of law; and an affirmation of John Locke's theory that government had an obligation to protect the natural rights of its citizens. Central to the political outlook of the philosophes was the conviction that political solutions could be found for the ills that afflicted society.

In general, the philosophes favored constitutional government that protected citizens from the abuse of power. With the notable exception of Rousseau, the philosophes' concern for liberty did not lead them to embrace democracy, for they put little trust in the masses. Several philosophes, notably Voltaire, placed their confidence in reforming despots, like Frederick II of Prussia, who were sympathetic to enlightened ideas. However, the philosophes were less concerned with the form of government—monarchy or republic—than with preventing the authorities from abusing their power.

Seventeenth-Century Antecedents: Hobbes and Locke

The political thought of the Enlightenment was greatly affected by the writings of two seventeenth-century English philosophers: Thomas Hobbes (1588–1679) and John Locke (1632–1704). Hobbes witnessed the agonies of the English civil war, including the execution of Charles I in 1649. These developments fortified his conviction that absolutism was the most desirable and logical form of government. Only the unlimited power of a sovereign, Hobbes wrote in his major work, *Leviathan* (1651), could contain the human passions that disrupt the social order and threaten civilized life; only absolute rule could provide an environment secure enough for people to pursue their individual interests.

Influenced by the new scientific thought that saw mathematical knowledge as the avenue to truth, Hobbes aimed at constructing political philosophy on a scientific foundation and rejected the authority of tradition and religion as inconsistent with a science of politics. Thus, although Hobbes supported absolutism, he dismissed the idea advanced by other theorists of absolutism that the monarch's power derived from God. He also rejected the view of medieval theorists that the state, which belonged to a lower temporal order, was subordinate to the commands of a higher spiritual realm and its corollary that the state should not be obeyed when it violates God's law. Like Machiavelli, Hobbes made no attempt to fashion the earthly city in accordance with Christian teachings. As an astute observer of contemporary affairs, Hobbes, of course, recognized religion's importance in European political life. However, his view of human nature and human life rested on no religious presuppositions. Religious thinkers frequently denounced Hobbes as a heretic, if not an atheist. *Leviathan* is a rational and secular political statement; its significance lies in its modern approach, rather than in Hobbes's justification of absolutism.

Hobbes had a pessimistic view of human nature. Believing that people are innately selfish and grasping, he maintained that competition and dissension, rather than cooperation, characterize human relations. When reason teaches that cooperation is more advantageous than competition, said Hobbes, people are still reluctant to alter their ways, because their behavior is governed more by passion than by reason. Without a stringent authority to make and enforce law, life would be miserable, a war of all against all, he said. Therefore, he prescribed a state with unlimited power, since only in this way could people be protected from one another and civilized life preserved. Although the philosophes generally

rejected Hobbes's gloomy view of human nature, they embraced his secular approach to politics, particularly his denunciation of the theory of the divine right of kings. Hobbes's concern with protecting the social order from human antisocial tendencies is still a central consideration of modern political life. His insight that civilization is forever in danger of collapsing into anarchy and savagery is still a poignant message for our times.

In contrast to Hobbes, John Locke maintained that human beings are rational by nature and are moved by a sense of moral obligation; they are capable of transcending a narrow selfishness and of respecting the inherent dignity of others. Viewing people as essentially good and humane, he developed a conception of the state that was fundamentally different from Hobbes's. In the *Two Treatises of Government* (1690), Locke maintained that human beings are born with natural rights to life, liberty, and property, and they establish the state to protect these rights. Consequently, neither executive nor legislature—neither king nor assembly—has the authority to deprive individuals of their natural rights. Whereas Hobbes justified absolute monarchy, Locke explicitly endorsed constitutional government, in which the power to govern derives from the consent of the governed and the state's authority is limited by agreement. Rulers hold their authority under the law; when they act outside the law, they forfeit their right to govern. Thus, if government fails to fulfill the end for which it was established—the preservation of the individual's right to life, liberty, and property—the people have a right to dissolve that government.

Both Hobbes and Locke agreed that the state exists in order to ensure the tranquility, security, and well-being of its citizens. However, they proposed radically different ways of attaining this end. Unlike Hobbes, Locke believed that social well-being encompassed personal freedom. Rejecting Hobbes's view that absolute power can remedy the defects of the state of nature, Locke stated the case for limited government, the rule of law, the protection of fundamental human rights, and the right of resistance to arbitrary power. Underlying Locke's conception of the state is the conviction that people have the capacity for reason and freedom, and that political life can be guided by rational principles: "We are born Free as we are born Rational."[10]

abolition of slavery. During the French Revolution, he attracted the enmity of the dominant Jacobin party and in 1793 was forced to go into hiding. Secluded in Paris, he wrote *Sketch*. Arrested in 1794, Condorcet died during his first night in prison, either from exhaustion or from self-administered poison. In *Sketch,* Condorcet lauded recent advances in knowledge that enabled reason to "lift her chains (and) shake herself free"[27] from superstition and tyranny. Passionately affirming the Enlightenment's confidence in reason and science, Condorcet expounded a theory of continuous and indefinite human improvement. He pointed toward a future golden age, characterized by the triumph of reason and freedom.

> *Our hopes for the future condition of the human race can be subsumed under three important heads: the abolition of inequality between nations, the progress of equality within each nation, and the true perfection of mankind. . . .*
>
> *The time will therefore come when the sun will shine only on free men who know no other master but their reason; when tyrants and slaves, priests and their stupid or hypocritical instruments will exist only in works of history and on the stage; and we shall think of them only to pity their victims and their dupes; to maintain ourselves in a state of vigilance by thinking on their excesses; and to learn how to recognize and so to destroy, by force of reason, the first seeds of tyranny and superstition, should they ever dare to reappear amongst us.*[28]

But the philosophes were not starry-eyed dreamers. They knew that progress was painful, slow, and reversible. Voltaire's *Candide* was a protest against a naïve optimism that ignored the granite might of human meanness, ignorance, and irrationality. "Let us weep and wail over the lot of philosophy," wrote Diderot. "We preach wisdom to the deaf and we are still far indeed from the age of reason."[29]

CONFLICTS AND POLITICS

The major conflicts of the eighteenth century were between Britain and France for control of territory in the New World and between Austria and Prussia for dominance in Central Europe. Then, in the late 1700s, the American and French Revolutions broke out; they helped shape the liberal-democratic tradition.

Warfare and Revolution

In 1740, Prussia, ruled by the aggressive Frederick the Great, launched a successful war against Austria and was rewarded with Silesia, which increased the Prussian population by 50 percent. Maria Theresa, the Austrian queen, never forgave Frederick and in 1756 formed an alliance with France against Prussia. The ensuing Seven Years' War (1756–1763), which involved every major European power, did not significantly change Europe, but it did reveal Prussia's growing might.

At the same time, the French and the English fought over their claims in the New World. England's victory in the conflict (known in American history as the French and Indian War) deprived France of virtually all of its North American possessions and set in motion a train of events that culminated in the American Revolution. The war drained the British treasury, and now Britain had the additional expense of paying for troops to guard the new North American territories that it had gained in the war. As strapped British taxpayers could not shoulder the whole burden, the members of Parliament thought it quite reasonable that the American colonists should help pay the bill; after all, Britain had protected the colonists from the French and was still protecting them in their conflicts with Indians. New colonial taxes and import duties imposed by Parliament produced vigorous protests from the Americans.

The quarrel turned to bloodshed in April and June 1775, and on July 4, 1776, delegates from the various colonies adopted the Declaration of Independence, written mainly by Thomas Jefferson. Applying Locke's theory of natural rights, this document declared that government derives its power from the consent of the governed, that it is the duty of a government to protect the rights of its citizens, and that people have the right to "alter or abolish" a government that deprives them of their "unalienable rights."

Why were the American colonists so ready to throw off British rule? Each of the thirteen colonies had an elected assembly, which acted like a miniature parliament. In these assemblies,

Americans gained political experience and quickly learned to be self-governing.

Familiarity with the thought of the Enlightenment and the republican writers of the English Revolution also contributed to the Americans' awareness of liberty. The ideas of the philosophes traversed the Atlantic and influenced educated Americans, particularly Thomas Jefferson and Benjamin Franklin. Like the philosophes, American thinkers expressed a growing confidence in reason, valued freedom of religion and of thought, and championed the principle of natural rights.

American victory came about in 1783 as a result of several factors. George Washington proved to be a superior leader, able to organize and retain the loyalty of his troops. France, seeking to avenge its defeat in the Seven Years' War, helped the Americans with money and provisions and then, in 1778, entered the conflict. Britain had difficulty shipping supplies across three thousand miles of ocean, was fighting the French in the West Indies and elsewhere at the same time, and ultimately lacked commitment to the struggle.

Reformers in other lands quickly interpreted the American victory as a successful struggle of liberty against tyranny. During the Revolution, the various American states drew up constitutions based on the principle of popular sovereignty and included bills of rights that protected individual liberty. They also managed, somewhat reluctantly, to forge a nation. Rejecting both monarchy and hereditary aristocracy, the Constitution of the United States created a republic in which power derived from the people. A system of separation of powers and checks and balances set safeguards against the abuse of power, and the Bill of Rights provided for protection of individual rights. To be sure, the ideals of liberty and equality were not extended to all people—slaves knew nothing of the freedom that white Americans cherished, and women were denied the vote and equal opportunity. But to reform-minded Europeans, it seemed that Americans were fulfilling the promise of the Enlightenment; they were creating a freer and better society.

Enlightened Despotism

The philosophes used the term *enlightened despotism* to refer to an ideal shared by many of them: rule by a strong monarch who would

Photo by Popperfoto/Getty Images.

CATHERINE THE GREAT. Catherine the Great adorned herself to show her aristocracy that she was its superior.

implement rational reforms and remove obstacles to freedom. Some eighteenth-century monarchs and their ministers—Frederick the Great in Prussia, Catherine the Great in Russia, Charles III in Spain, Maria Theresa and, to a greater extent, her son Joseph II in Austria, and Louis XV in France—did institute educational, commercial, and religious reforms.

Behind the reforms of enlightened despots lay the realization that the struggle for power in Europe called for efficient government administration and ample funds. Enlightened despots appointed capable officials to oversee the administration of their kingdoms, eliminate costly corruption, and collect taxes properly. Rulers strengthened the economy by encouraging the expansion of commerce through reduced taxes on goods and through agricultural reforms. In Central and Eastern Europe, some rulers moved toward abolishing serfdom, or at least improving conditions for serfs. (In Western Europe, serfdom had virtually died out.) Provisions were made to care for widows, orphans, and invalids. Censorship was eased, greater religious freedom was granted to minorities, criminal codes were made less harsh, and there were some attempts at prison reform. By these measures, enlightened despots hoped to inspire greater popular support for the state, an important factor in the European power struggle.

THE ENLIGHTENMENT AND THE MODERN MENTALITY

The philosophes articulated core principles of the modern outlook. Asserting that human beings are capable of thinking independently of authority, they insisted on a thoroughgoing rational and secular interpretation of nature and society. They critically scrutinized authority and tradition and valued science and technology as a means for promoting human betterment. Above all, they sought to emancipate the mind from the bonds of ignorance and superstition and to rescue people from intolerance, cruelty, and oppression. Because of their efforts, torture (which states and Christian churches had endorsed and practiced) was eventually abolished in Western lands, and religious toleration and freedom of speech and of the press became the accepted norms. The arguments that the philosophes marshaled against slavery were utilized by those who fought against the slave trade and called for emancipation. Enlightenment economic thought, particularly Adam Smith's *Wealth of Nations,* gave theoretical support to a market economy based on supply and demand—an outlook that fostered commercial and industrial expansion. The separation of church and state, a basic principle of modern political life, owes much to the philosophes, who frequently cited the dangers of politics inflamed by religious passions. The philosophes' denunciation of despotism and championing of natural rights, equality under the law, and constitutional government are the chief foundations of modern liberal government.

The ideals of the Enlightenment spread from Europe to America and helped shape the political thought of the Founding Fathers. The Declaration of Independence clearly articulated Locke's basic principles: that government derives its authority from the governed; that human beings are born with natural rights, which government has a responsibility to protect; and that citizens have the right to resist a government that deprives them of these rights. The Constitution asserted that the people are sovereign: "We the People of the United States . . . do ordain and establish this Constitution for the United States of America." And it contained several safeguards against despotic power, including Montesquieu's principle of separation of powers, which was also written into several state constitutions. Both the bills of rights drawn up by the various states and the federal Bill of Rights gave recognition to the individual's inherent rights and explicitly barred government from tampering with them—a principal concern of the philosophes.

The *Federalist Papers,* the major American contribution to eighteenth-century political thought, in many ways epitomized Enlightenment thinking. It incorporated specific ideas of Locke, Montesquieu, Hume, and the *Encyclopedia;* analyzed political forms in a rational, secular, and critical spirit; regarded the protection of personal freedom as a principal goal of the state; and expressed a willingness to break with past traditions when they conflicted with good sense. The new American republic, says Peter Gay, was "convincing evidence, to the philosophes . . . that men had some capacity for self-improvement and self-government, that progress might be a reality instead of a fantasy, and that reason and humanity might become governing rather than merely critical principles."[30]

The philosophes broke with the traditional Christian view of human nature and the purpose of life. In that view, men and women were born in sin; suffering and misery were divinely ordained, and relief could come only from God; social inequality was instituted by God; and for many, eternal damnation was a deserved final consequence. In contrast, the philosophes saw injustice and suffering as manmade problems that could be solved through reason; they expressed confidence in people's ability to attain happiness by improving the conditions of their earthly existence and articulated a theory of human progress that did not require divine assistance. Rejecting the idea of a static and immutable order of society instituted by God, the philosophes had confidence that human beings could improve the conditions of their existence, and they pointed to advances in science and technology as evidence of progress.

Thus, the idea of secular progress, another key element of modernity, also grew out of the Enlightenment. After two world wars and countless other conflicts, after Auschwitz and other examples of state-sponsored mass murder, and with the development of weapons of mass destruction, it is difficult to realize that at the beginning of the twentieth century most Westerners were committed to a doctrine of perpetual progress that embodied the hopes of the philosophes.

To be sure, the promise of the Enlightenment has not been achieved. More education for more people and the spread of constitutional government have not eliminated fanaticism and superstition, violence and war, or evil and injustice. In the light of twentieth-century and twenty-first century events, it is difficult to subscribe to Condorcet's belief in linear progress, that history is inexorably carrying humanity toward a golden age.

The worldview of the philosophes has come under attack. Building on the critique of early nineteenth-century romantics, critics have accused the philosophes of overvaluing the intellect at the expense of human feelings. According to this view, the philosophes did not recognize the value of the feelings as a source of creativity and did not call for their creative development. Rather, they viewed the emotions as impediments to clear thinking that had to be overcome.

Another failing of the philosophes, critics argue, is that they did not seek to understand a past age on its own terms but judged it according to preconceived norms, disdaining and rejecting anything that contradicted their idea of truth and their view of the good society. Such an outlook, say the critics, led the philosophes to underestimate the extent to which the past governs the present. Holding with Hume that human nature remains the same in all nations and ages, the philosophes regarded differences between peoples and civilizations as superficial and inconsequential. Since reason was common to humanity, government, law, morality, education, and all other institutions and systems of thought could be based on universal principles and could apply to all peoples throughout the globe regardless of their cultures and history.

In reality, this meant that the outlook of a small party of thinkers would become normative for all peoples and cultures. Such an undervaluing of the complex relationship between past and present, of human diversity, and of the immense appeal of familiar beliefs, traditions, and institutions—even if they seem so blatantly in opposition to reason—promotes the presumptuous and dangerous belief that society and government can be easily and rapidly molded to fit abstract principles and that reformers need pay only scant attention to historically conditioned cultural forms.

The philosophes' belief in universality, in timeless truths that apply to all peoples at all times, also contains an inherent danger. In politics, it could create true believers totally committed to an abstraction, such as the exploited class or the infallible party. To realize their ideal, these devotees will employ terror and mass murder with a clear conscience. Robespierre and the Reign of Terror during the French Revolution might be viewed as an early manifestation of this attempt to make society adhere to a conceptual grid.

Another criticism is that the philosophes' exuberant view of science and reason prevented them from realizing that reason is a double-edged sword: it could demean as well as ennoble human personality. The philosophes believed that removing thought from the realm of myth and religion and eliminating irrational forms of social organization would foster human emancipation. They could not foresee that modern bureaucracy and technology, both creations of the rational mind, could fashion a social order that devalues and depersonalizes the individual. In its determination to make the social world accord with a theoretical model, rationalism strives for uniformity and efficiency; in the process, it threatens to regulate, organize, and manipulate the individual as it would any material object. Future periods would not only reveal the limitations of reason—its inability to cope with powerful irrational drives and instincts that incite acts of inhumanity—but also the dangers of reason—its capacity to subordinate and sacrifice the individual to theoretical systems, particularly political ideologies.

Nevertheless, despite limitations, the philosophes' achievement should not be diminished. Their ideals became an intrinsic part of the liberal-democratic tradition and inspired nineteenth- and twentieth-century reformers. The spirit of the Enlightenment will always remain indispensable to all those who cherish the traditions of reason and freedom. Isaiah Berlin, the distinguished historian of ideas, eloquently summed up the Enlightenment's importance: "the intellectual power, honesty, lucidity, courage, and disinterested love of the truth of the most gifted thinkers of the eighteenth-century remain to this day without parallel. Their age is one of the best and most hopeful episodes in the life of mankind."[31]

NOTES

1. Galileo Galilei, *The Starry Messenger,* in *Discoveries and Opinions of Galileo,* trans. and ed. Stillman Drake (Garden City, N.Y.: Doubleday Anchor Books, 1957), 31.

2. Galileo Galilei, *The Assayer,* in *Discoveries and Opinions,* 237–238.

3. Galileo Galilei, "Letter to the Grand Duchess Christina," in *Discoveries and Opinions,* 183.

4. Quoted in Frank E. Manuel, *Age of Reason* (Ithaca, N.Y.: Cornell University Press, 1951), 28.

5. David Hume, *The Natural History of Religion,* ed. H. E. Root (London: Adam and Charles Black, 1956), 75.

6. Denis Diderot, "Discourse of a Philosopher To a King," in *Diderot, Interpreter of Nature: Selected Writings,* ed., Jonathan Kemp, (New York: International Publishers, 1943), 214.

7. Quoted in Ben Ray Redman, ed., *The Portable Voltaire* (New York: Viking Press, 1949), 26.

8. Thomas Paine, *The Age of Reason* (New York: Eckler, 1892), 5.

9. Quoted in Paul Hazard, *European Thought in the Eighteenth Century* (New Haven, Conn.: Yale University Press, 1954), 174.

10. John Locke, *Two Treatises of Government,* ed. Peter Laslett (New York: New American Library, Mentor Books, 1963), *The Second Treatise,* chap. 6, sec. 61, 350.

11. Jean Jacques Rousseau, *The Social Contract,* in *The Social Contract and Discourses,* ed. and trans. G. D. H. Cole (New York: Dutton, 1950), bk. 1, chap. 1, 3.

12. Quoted in Peter Gay, *The Enlightenment: An Interpretation,* Vol. 2, *The Science of Freedom* (New York: Vintage Books, 1966), 170.

13. Quoted in Steven Seidman, *Liberalism and the Origins of European Social Theory* (Berkeley: University of California Press, 1983), 30.

14. Voltaire, "Letter to M. Bertrand," in *Candide and Other Writings,* ed. Haskell M. Block (New York: Modern Library, 1956), 525.

15. Quoted in Peter Gay, *Voltaire's Politics* (New York: Random House, Vintage Books, 1965), 71.

16. Quoted in Stephen J. Gendzier, ed. and trans., *Denis Diderot's The Encyclopedia Selections* (New York: Harper Torchbooks, 1967), xxv.

17. Ibid., xxvi.

18. Excerpted in Gendzier, *Diderot's Encyclopedia Selections,* 199.

19. Cesare Beccaria, *On Crimes and Punishments,* trans. Henry Paolucci (Indianapolis, Ind.: Library of Liberal Arts, 1963), 32.

20. Voltaire, *Candide,* in *The Portable Voltaire,* ed. Ben Ray Redman (New York: Viking, 1949), 234.

21. Excerpted in Gendzier, *Diderot's Encyclopedia Selections,* 183–184.

22. Excerpted in ibid., 229–230.

23. Quoted in Bonnie S. Anderson and Judith P. Zinsser, *A History of Their Own* (New York: Harper & Row, 1988), Vol. 2, 113.

24. Jean Jacques Rousseau, *Emile,* trans. Barbara Foxley (London: Dent, Everyman's Library, 1974), 370.

25. Mary Wollstonecraft, *Vindication of the Rights of Woman* (London: Dent, 1929), 11–12.

26. Quoted in Charles Taylor, *Sources of the Self* (Cambridge, Mass.: Harvard University Press, 1989), 353.

27. Antoine Nicolas de Condorcet, *Sketch for a Historical Picture of the Progress of the Human Mind,* trans. June Barraclough (London: Weidenfeld & Nicholas, 1955), 124.

28. Ibid., 173, 179.

29. Quoted in Gay, *The Enlightenment,* Vol. 1, *The Rise of Modern Paganism,* 20.

30. Gay, *The Enlightenment, Vol. 2,* 555.

31. Isaiah Berlin, ed., *The Age of Enlightenment* (New York: Mentor Books, 1956), 29.

Part Four

The Modern West: Progress and Breakdown

1789–1914

Storming of the Bastille, July 14, 1789.

Musée Carnavalet/akg-images

Politics and Society	Thought and Culture

1790 French Revolution begins (1789)
Declaration of the Rights of Man
   and of the Citizen (1789)
Reign of Terror (1793–1794)
Napoleon seizes power (1799)
	Kant, *Critique of Pure Reason* (1781)
	Burke, *Reflections on the Revolution in France* (1790)
	Wollstonecraft, *Vindication of the Rights
	   of Woman* (1792)
	Wordsworth, *The Lyrical Ballads* (1798)
	Beethoven, *Fifth Symphony* (1807–1808)
	Goya, *The Third of May* (1808)
	Goethe, *Faust* (1808, 1832)

1810 Napoleon invades Russia (1812)
Napoleon defeated at Waterloo (1815)
Congress of Vienna (1814–1815)
Revolutions in Spain, Italy, Russia,
   and Greece (1820–1829)
	Byron, *Childe Harold's Pilgrimage* (1812)
	Shelley, *Prometheus Unbound* (1820)
	Hegel, *The Philosophy of History*
	   (1822–1831)

1830 First railway built in Britain (1830)
Revolutions in France, Belgium,
   Poland, and Italy (1830–1832)
Reform Act of 1832 in Britain
Irish famine (1845–1849)
Revolutions in France, Germany,
   Austria, and Italy (1848)
	Comte, *Course in Positive Philosophy*
	   (1830–1842)
	De Tocqueville, *Democracy in America*
	   (1835–1840)
	Marx, *Communist Manifesto* (1848)

1850 Second Empire in France
   (1852–1870)
Commodore Perry opens Japan to
   trade (1853)
Unification of Italy (1859–1870)
Civil War in the United States
   (1861–1865)
Unification of Germany (1866–1871)
Opening of Suez Canal (1869)
	Dickens, *Hard Times* (1854)
	Flaubert, *Madame Bovary* (1856)
	Darwin, *Origin of Species* (1859)
	Mill, *On Liberty* (1859)
	Impressionism in art: Manet, Monet,
	   Pissarro, Degas, Renoir (1860–1886)
	Marx, *Capital* (1867)
	Dostoevsky, *The Idiot* (1868)
	Mill, *The Subjection of Women* (1869)

1870 Franco-Prussian War (1870–1871) Third Republic in France (1870–1940) Berlin Conference on Africa (1884) Reform Bill of 1884 in Great Britain	Darwin, *Descent of Man* (1871) Nietzsche, *The Birth of Tragedy* (1872) Ibsen, *A Doll's House* (1879) Zola, *The Experimental Novel* (1880) Nietzsche, *The Anti-Christ* (1888)
1890 Dreyfus affair in France (1894–1899) Sino-Japanese War (1894–1895) Boer War in South Africa (1899–1902)	Chamberlain, *The Foundations of the Nineteenth Century* (1899) Durkheim, *Suicide* (1899)
1900 Russo-Japanese War (1904–1905) Anglo-French Entente Cordiale (1904) Anglo-Russian Entente (1907)	Freud, *The Interpretation of Dreams* (1900) Cubism in art: Picasso, Braque (1909–1914) Planck's quantum theory (1900) Lenin, *What Is to Be Done?* (1902) Einstein's theory of relativity (1905, 1916) Sorel, *Reflections on Violence* (1908)

Chapter 11

The Era of the French Revolution: Affirmation of Liberty and Equality

- **The Old Regime**
- **The Moderate Stage, 1789–1791**
- **The Radical Stage, 1792–1794**
- **Napoleon and France: Return to Autocratic Rule**
- **Napoleon and Europe: Diffusion of Revolutionary Institutions**
- **The Fall of Napoleon**
- **The Meaning of the French Revolution**

Focus Questions

1. What were the causes of the French Revolution?
2. How did the Enlightenment and American Revolution influence the French Revolution?
3. Why are the reforms of the National Assembly described as the death warrant of the Old Regime?
4. Why and how did the French Revolution move from a moderate to a radical stage?
5. How do you evaluate the purpose and significance of the Terror?
6. Why does the career of Napoleon Bonaparte continue to fascinate?
7. How did Napoleon both preserve and undermine the ideals of the French Revolution?
8. How did Napoleon speed up the modernization of Europe?
9. Why is the French Revolution a decisive period in the shaping of the modern West?

*T*he outbreak of the French Revolution in 1789 stirred the imagination of Europeans. Both participants and observers sensed that they were living in a pivotal age. On the ruins of the Old Order, founded on privilege and despotism, a new era that promised to realize the ideals of the Enlightenment was forming. These ideals included the emancipation of the human person from superstition and tradition, the triumph of liberty over tyranny, the refashioning of institutions in accordance with reason and justice, and the tearing down of barriers to equality. It seemed that the natural rights of the individual, hitherto a distant ideal, would now reign on earth, ending centuries of oppression and misery. Never before had people shown such confidence in the power of human intelligence to shape the conditions of existence. Never before had the future seemed so full of hope. ❖

THE OLD REGIME

Eighteenth-century French society was divided into three orders, or Estates, which were legally defined groupings. The clergy constituted the First Estate, the nobility the Second Estate, and everyone else the Third Estate. The clergy and nobility, totaling about five hundred thousand out of a population of 26 million, enjoyed special privileges, receiving pensions and profitable positions from the king. The social structure of the Old Regime, based on privileges and inequalities sanctioned by law, produced tensions that contributed to the Revolution.

The First Estate

The powers and privileges of the French Catholic church made it a state within a state. As it had done for centuries, the church registered births, marriages, and deaths; collected tithes (a tax on products from the soil); censored books considered dangerous to religion and morals; operated schools; and distributed relief to the poor. Although its land brought in an immense revenue, the church paid no taxes. Instead, it made a "free

gift" to the state—the church determined the amount—which was always smaller than direct taxes would have been.

The clergy reflected the social divisions in France. The upper clergy shared the attitudes and way of life of the nobility from which they sprang. The parish priests, commoners by birth, resented the haughtiness and luxurious living of the upper clergy. In 1789, when the Revolution began, many priests sympathized with the reform-minded people of the Third Estate.

The Second Estate

Like the clergy, the nobility was a privileged order. Nobles held the highest positions in the church, the army, and the government. They were exempt from most taxes (or used their influence to evade paying taxes), collected manorial dues from peasants, and owned between one-quarter and one-third of the land. In addition to the income that they drew from their estates, nobles were becoming increasingly involved in such nonaristocratic enterprises as banking and finance. Nobles were the leading patrons of the arts. Many key philosophes—Montesquieu, Condorcet, d'Holbach—were nobles. Most nobles, however, were suspicious and intolerant of the liberal ideas advanced by the philosophes.

All nobles were not equal; there were gradations of dignity among the 350,000 members of the nobility. Enjoying the most prestige were *nobles of the sword:* families that could trace their aristocratic status back several centuries. The highest of the ancient nobles were engaged in the social whirl at Versailles and Paris, receiving pensions and sinecures from the king but performing few useful services for the state. Most nobles of the sword, unable to afford the gilded life at court, remained on their provincial estates, the poorest of them barely distinguishable from prosperous peasants.

Alongside this ancient nobility, a new nobility created by the monarchy had arisen. To obtain money, reward favorites, and weaken the old nobility, French kings had sold titles of nobility to members of the bourgeoisie and had conferred noble status on certain government offices bought by wealthy bourgeois. Particularly significant

Chronology 11.1 ❖ The French Revolution

July 1788	Calling of the Estates General
June 17, 1789	Third Estate declares itself the National Assembly
July 14, 1789	Storming of the Bastille
Late July 1789	The Great Fear
August 4, 1789	Nobles surrender their special privileges
April 20, 1792	Legislative Assembly declares war on Austria
Sept. 21–22, 1792	Abolition of the monarchy
June 1793	Jacobins replace Girondins as the dominant group in the National Convention
July 28, 1794	Robespierre is guillotined

were the *nobles of the robe,* whose ranks included many former bourgeois who had purchased judicial offices in the *parlements*, or high law courts.

Opinion among the aristocrats was divided. Some nobles, influenced by the liberal ideals of the philosophes, sought to reform France; they wanted to end royal despotism and establish a constitutional government. To this extent, the liberal nobility had a great deal in common with the bourgeoisie. These liberal nobles saw the king's difficulties in 1788 as an opportunity to regenerate the nation under enlightened leadership. When they resisted the king's policies, they claimed that they were opposing royal despotism. But, at the same time, many nobles remained hostile to liberal ideals and opposed reforms that threatened their privileges and honorific status.

The Third Estate

The Third Estate comprised the bourgeoisie, the peasants, and the urban workers. Although the bourgeoisie provided the leadership for the Revolution, its success depended on the support given by the rest of the Third Estate.

The Bourgeoisie. The bourgeoisie consisted of merchant manufacturers, wholesale merchants, bankers, master craftsmen, doctors, lawyers, intellectuals, and government officials below the top

ranks. Although the bourgeoisie had wealth, they lacked social prestige. A merchant, despite his worldly success, felt that his occupation denied him the esteem enjoyed by the nobility.

Influenced by the aristocratic values of the day and envious of the nobility's lifestyle, the bourgeoisie sought to erase the stigma of common birth and to rise socially by becoming landowners. By 1789, the bourgeoisie owned about 20 percent of the land. Traditionally, some of its members had risen socially either by purchasing a judicial or political office that carried with it a title of nobility or by gaining admission to the upper clergy or the officer ranks of the army. Access to the nobility remained open throughout the eighteenth century. Nevertheless, since the highest and most desired positions in the land were reserved for the nobility, able bourgeois were often excluded for a variety of reasons: the high cost of purchasing an office, the limited number of new offices created, the resistance of nobles to their advancement, or the hostility of the older nobility toward those recently ennobled. No doubt these men felt frustrated and came to resent a social system that valued birth more than talent. For most of the century, however, the bourgeoisie did not challenge the existing social structure, including the special privileges of the nobility.

By 1789, the bourgeois had many grievances. They wanted all positions in the church, army, and state to be open to men of talent regardless of birth. They sought a parliament that would make laws for the nation; a constitution that would limit the king's power and guarantee freedom of thought, fair trials, and religious toleration; and administrative reforms that would eliminate waste, inefficiency, and interference with business.

The Peasantry. The condition of the more than 21 million French peasants was a paradox. On the one hand, they were better off than peasants in Austria, Prussia, Poland, and Russia, where serfdom still predominated. In France, serfdom had largely disappeared; many peasants owned their land, and some were even prosperous. On the other hand, most French peasants lived in poverty, which worsened in the closing years of the Old Regime.

The typical peasant holding was barely large enough to eke out a living. The rising birthrate (between 1715 and 1789, the population may have increased from 18 million to 26 million) led to the continual subdivision of farms among heirs. Moreover, many peasants did not own land but rented it from a nobleman or a prosperous neighbor. Others worked as sharecroppers, turning over a considerable portion of the harvest to their creditors.

An unjust and corrupt system of taxation weighed heavily on the peasantry. Louis XIV had maintained his grandeur and financed his wars by milking ever more taxes from the peasants, a practice that continued throughout the eighteenth century. An army of tax collectors victimized the peasantry. In addition to royal taxes, peasants paid the tithe to the church and manorial dues to lords.

Although serfdom had ended in most parts of France, lords continued to demand obligations from peasants as they had done in the Middle Ages. Besides performing labor services on the lord's estate, peasants still had to grind their grain in the lord's mill, bake their bread in his oven, press their grapes in his winepress, and give him part of their produce in payment. (These fees were called *banalities.*) In addition, the lord exercised exclusive hunting rights on lands tilled by peasants. Those rights were particularly onerous, for the lord's hunting parties damaged crops. Lords

"LET'S HOPE THAT THE GAME FINISHES WELL." This political cartoon shows a laborer carrying smug representatives of the privileged orders on his back.

were determined to hold on to these privileges not only because of the income they brought but also because they were symbols of authority and social esteem.

Urban Laborers. The urban laboring class in this preindustrial age consisted of journeymen working for master craftsmen, factory workers in small-scale industries, and wage earners such as day laborers, gardeners, handymen, and deliverymen, who were paid by those whom they served. Conditions for the urban poor, like those for the peasant wage earners, worsened in the late eighteenth century. From 1785 to 1789, the cost of living increased by 62 percent, while wages rose only by 22 percent. For virtually the entire decade of the Revolution, urban workers struggled to keep body and soul together in the face of food shortages and rising prices, particularly the price of their staple food, bread. Material want drove the urban poor to acts of violence that affected the course of the Revolution.

Inefficient Administration and Financial Disorder

The administration of France was complex, confusing, and ineffective. The practice of buying state offices from the king, introduced as a means of raising money, resulted in many incompetent officeholders. Tariffs on goods shipped from one province to another and differing systems of weights and measures hampered trade. No single law code applied to all the provinces; instead, there were overlapping and conflicting law systems based on old Roman law or customary feudal law, which made the administration of justice slow, arbitrary, and unfair. To admirers of the philosophes, the administrative system was an insult to reason. The Revolution would sweep the system away.

Financial disorders also contributed to the weakness of the Old Regime. In the regime's last years, the government could not raise sufficient funds to cover expenses. By 1787, it still had not paid off the enormous debt incurred during the wars of Louis XIV, let alone the costs of succeeding wars during the eighteenth century, particularly France's aid to the colonists in the American Revolution. The king's gifts and pensions to court nobles and the extravagant court life further drained the treasury.

Finances were in a shambles not because France was impoverished but because of an inefficient and unjust tax system. Although serious, the financial crisis could have been solved if the clergy, nobility, and bourgeoisie had paid their fair share of taxes. With France on the brink of bankruptcy, some of the king's ministers proposed that the nobility and church surrender some of their tax exemptions, but the privileged orders resisted. Some nobles resisted because they were steadfast defenders of noble prerogatives; the more liberal nobles resisted because they saw an opportunity to check absolutism and introduce fundamental reforms that would regenerate the nation.

The resistance of the nobility forced the government, in July 1788, to call for a meeting of the Estates General—a medieval representative assembly that had last met in 1614—to deal with the financial crisis. The body was to convene in May 1789. Certain that they would dominate the Estates General, the nobles intended to weaken the power of the throne. Once in control of the government, they would introduce financial reforms. But the revolt of the nobility against the crown had unexpected consequences. It opened the way for a revolution by the Third Estate that destroyed the Old Regime and with it the aristocracy and its privileges.

The Roles of the Enlightenment and the American Revolution

Revolutions are born in the realm of the spirit. Revolutionary movements, says George Rudé, a historian of the French Revolution, require "some unifying body of ideas, a common vocabulary of hope and protest, something, in short, like a common 'revolutionary psychology.' "[1] For this reason, many historians see a relationship between the Enlightenment and the French Revolution. The philosophes were not revolutionaries themselves, but their attacks on the pillars of the established order and their appeals for a freer, more tolerant society helped to create a revolutionary psychology. As Henri Peyre observes,

> Eighteenth-century philosophy taught the Frenchman to find his condition wretched, or in any case, unjust and illogical and made him disinclined to the patient resignation to his troubles that had long characterized his ancestors. . . . The propaganda of the "Philosophes" perhaps more than any other factor accounted for the fulfillment of the preliminary condition of the French Revolution, namely discontent with the existing state of things.[2]

As the Revolution progressed, its leaders utilized the philosophes' ideas and language to attack the foundations of the old order and to justify their own reform program.

The American Revolution, which gave practical expression to the liberal philosophy of the philosophes, also helped to pave the way for the French Revolution. The Declaration of Independence (1776), which proclaimed the natural rights of man and sanctioned resistance against a government that deprived men of these rights, influenced the framers of the Declaration of the Rights of Man and of the Citizen (1789) (see the upcoming section "Reforms of the National Assembly"). The United States showed that a nation could be established on the principle that sovereign power derived from the people. The Americans set an example of social equality unparalleled in Europe. In the United States, there was no hereditary aristocracy, no serfdom, and no state church. Liberal French aristocrats, such as the Marquis de Lafayette, who had fought in the American Revolution, returned to France more optimistic about the possibilities of reforming French society.

A Bourgeois Revolution?

Because the bourgeois were the principal leaders and chief beneficiaries of the French Revolution, many historians have viewed it, along with the English revolutions of the seventeenth century and the growth of capitalism, as "an episode in the general rise of the bourgeoisie."[3] Those who regard the Revolution as a "bourgeois revolution" argue that in the last part of the eighteenth century it became increasingly difficult for the bourgeoisie to gain the most honored offices in the land. According to this view, in the eighteenth century, a decadent and reactionary aristocracy sought to regain the powers that it had lost under Louis XIV. Through parlements, aristocrats blocked reforms proposed by the king that threatened their privileges, and they united to prevent commoners from entering their ranks.

The nobility's determination to safeguard its power and social exclusiveness collided head-on with the aspirations of a wealthy, talented, and progressive bourgeoisie. Finding the path to upward mobility and social dignity barred, the bourgeoisie, imbued with the rational outlook of the Enlightenment, came to perceive nobles as an obstacle to its advancement and the nation's progress. "The essential cause of the Revolution," concludes French historian Albert Soboul, "was the power of a bourgeoisie arrived at its maturity and confronted by a decadent aristocracy holding tenaciously to its privileges."[4] Thus, when the bourgeois found the opportunity during the Revolution, they ended the legal division of France into separate orders.

In recent decades, some historians have challenged this interpretation. These revisionists argue that before 1789 France did not have a self-conscious bourgeois class aspiring to take control of the state in order to promote a capitalist economy—that the nobles and the bourgeoisie did not represent antagonistic classes divided by sharp differences. On the contrary, they were not clearly distinguishable from each other. The bourgeois aspired to noble status, and many nobles were involved in business enterprises—mining, metallurgy, textiles, and overseas trading companies—traditionally considered the province of the bourgeoisie. Abandoning a traditional aristocratic disdain for business, many nobles had acquired the capitalist mentality associated with the middle class. Some nobles also shared with the bourgeois the liberal values of the philosophes and a desire to do away with monarchical despotism and reform France according to rational standards. Thus, French nobles, particularly those who lived in urban centers or had traveled to Britain and the American colonies, were receptive both to new means of livelihood and to progressive ideas.

Moreover, the French nobility was constantly infused with new blood from below. During the eighteenth century, thousands of bourgeois, through marriage, the purchase of an office, or service as local officials—mayors, for example—had some entitlement of nobility. As British historian William Doyle puts it, "the nobility was an open elite, not a hereditary class apart. Nor is it now possible to maintain that this elite grew less open as the eighteenth century went on thanks to some exclusive 'aristocratic reaction.'"[5]

Just prior to 1789, revisionists contend, nobles and prosperous bourgeois were no longer clearly differentiated; the traditional distinctions that had set them apart were now obsolete. France's social elite actually consisted not of a hereditary nobility, but of *notables*—both nobles and bourgeois—distinguished more by wealth than by birth. Bourgeois notables were essentially moderate; they did not seek the destruction of the aristocracy that was accomplished in the opening stage of the Revolution. The elimination of aristocratic privileges was not part of a preconceived bourgeois program, revisionists maintain, but an improvised response to the violent upheavals in the countryside in July and August 1789. Moreover, not until early 1789, when a struggle erupted over the composition of the Estates General (see the next section), did the bourgeoisie start to become conscious of itself as a class with interests that clashed with those of the aristocracy. Until then, both the bourgeoisie and many aristocrats were united around a common and moderate reform program.

Finally, revisionists argue that the feudal nobility was not as decadent or reactionary as traditional accounts would have it. The nobles resisted the king's reforming ministers because they doubted the ability of a despotic and incompetent state to solve the financial crisis. To be sure, there were aristocrats who selfishly wanted to cling to their privileges, but many also aspired to serve the public good by instituting structural changes that would liberate the nation from despotic and inefficient rule and reform its financial and administrative system. It was this desire to institute crucial changes in French political life, say revisionists, that led nobles to press for the convening of the Estates General.

THE MODERATE STAGE, 1789–1791

Since a significant number of nobles were sympathetic to reform, there was no insuperable gulf between the Second and Third Estates as the Estates General prepared to meet. However, it soon became clear that the hopes of reformers clashed with the intentions of many aristocrats.

What had started as a struggle between the crown and the aristocracy was turning into something far more significant: a conflict between the two privileged orders on one side and the Third Estate on the other. One pamphleteer, Abbé Sieyés (1748–1836), expressed the hatred that members of the bourgeoisie felt for the aristocracy. "The privileged order has said to the Third Estate: 'Whatever be your services, whatever be your talents, you shall go thus far and no farther. It is not fitting that you be honored.'" The higher positions in the land, said Sieyés, should be the "reward for talents," not the prerogative of birth. Without the Third Estate, "nothing can progress"; without the nobility, "everything would proceed infinitely better."[6]

Formation of the National Assembly

The Estates General convened at Versailles on May 5, 1789, but was stalemated by the question of procedure. Seeking to control the assembly, the nobility insisted that the three Estates follow the traditional practice of meeting separately and voting as individual bodies. Since the two privileged orders were likely to stand together, the Third Estate would always be outvoted two to one. But the delegates from the Third Estate, unwilling to allow the nobility and the higher clergy to dominate the Estates General, proposed instead that the three Estates meet as one body and vote by head. There were some six hundred and ten delegates from the Third Estate; the nobility and clergy together had an equivalent number. Since the Third Estate could rely on the support of sympathetic parish priests and liberal nobles, it would be assured a majority if all the orders met together. As aristocrats and bourgeois became more polarized, anti-noble rhetoric gained a growing audience among all segments of the Third Estate. Many commoners now saw the aristocracy as the chief obstacle to reform.

On June 17, the Third Estate made a revolutionary move. It declared itself the National Assembly. On June 20, locked out of their customary meeting hall (apparently by accident), the Third Estate delegates moved to a nearby tennis court and took a solemn oath not to disband until a constitution had been drawn up for France. Louis XVI commanded the National Assembly to separate into orders, but the Third Estate held firm. The steadfastness of the delegates and the menacing actions of Parisians who supported the National Assembly forced Louis XVI to yield. On June 27, he ordered the nobility (some had already done so) and the clergy (a majority had already done so) to join with the Third Estate in the National Assembly.

But the victory of the bourgeoisie was not yet secure, for most nobles had not resigned themselves to a bourgeois-dominated National Assembly. It appeared that Louis XVI, influenced by court aristocrats, had resolved to use force against the National Assembly and stop the incipient revolution. At this point, uprisings by the common people of Paris and peasants in the countryside saved the National Assembly, exacerbated hostilities between the Third Estate and the nobility, and ensured the victory of the forces of reform.

Storming of the Bastille

In July 1789, the level of tension in Paris was high for three reasons. First, the calling of the Estates General had aroused hopes for reform. Second, the price of bread was soaring: in August 1788, a Parisian laborer had spent 50 percent of his income on bread; by July 1789, he was spending 80 percent. A third element in the tension was the fear of an aristocratic plot to crush the National Assembly. Afraid that royal troops would bombard and pillage the city, Parisians searched for weapons.

On July 14, eight hundred to nine hundred Parisians gathered in front of the Bastille, a fortress used as a prison and a reviled symbol of royal despotism. They gathered primarily to obtain gunpowder and to remove the cannon

that threatened a heavily populated working-class district. As the tension mounted, the Parisians stormed and captured the Bastille. The fall of the Bastille had far-reaching consequences: a symbol of the Old Regime's darkness and despotism had fallen; some court nobles hostile to the Revolution decided to flee the country; the frightened king told the National Assembly that he would withdraw the troops ringing Paris. The revolutionary act of the Parisians had indirectly saved the National Assembly and its bourgeois leadership.

The Great Fear

Revolution in the countryside also served the interests of the reformers. Inflamed by economic misery and stirred by the uprisings of the Parisians, peasants began to burn manor houses and destroy the registers on which their obligations to the lords were inscribed. The flames of the peasants' insurrection were fanned by rumors that aristocrats were organizing bands of brigands

WOMEN'S MARCH TO VERSAILLES. A bread shortage and high prices sparked the protest march of thousands of women to Versailles in October 1789. The king was compelled to return to Paris, a sign of his diminishing power, and many aristocrats hostile to the Revolution fled the country.

to attack the peasants. The mythical army of brigands never materialized, but the Great Fear, as this episode is called, led more peasants to take up arms. Suspicious of an aristocratic plot to thwart efforts at reform and releasing years of stored-up hatred for the nobles, the peasants attacked the lords' chateaux with great fury.

Like the insurrection in Paris, the peasant upheavals in late July and early August worked to the advantage of the reformers. The attacks provided the National Assembly with an opportunity to strike at noble privileges by putting into law what the peasants had accomplished with the torch—the destruction of feudal remnants. On the night of August 4, 1789, aristocrats seeking to restore calm in the countryside surrendered their special privileges: exclusive hunting rights, tax exemptions, monopoly of highest offices, manorial courts, and the right to demand labor services from peasants.

In the decrees of August 5 and 11, the National Assembly implemented the resolutions of August 4. The Assembly also declared that the planned constitution should be prefaced by a declaration of rights. On August 26, it adopted the Declaration of the Rights of Man and of the Citizen.

October Days

Louis XVI, cool to these reforms, postponed his approval of the August Decrees and the Declaration of Rights. It would require a second uprising by the Parisians to force the king to agree to the reforms and to nail down the victory of the reformers.

On October 5, 1789, Parisian housewives and men marched twelve miles to Versailles to protest the lack of bread to the National Assembly and the king. A few hours later, twenty thousand Paris Guards, a citizen militia sympathetic to the Revolution, also set out for Versailles in support of the protesters. The king had no choice but to promise bread and to return with the demonstrators to Paris. Aware that he had no control over the Parisians and fearful of further violence, Louis XVI approved the August Decrees and the Declaration of Rights. Nobles who had urged the king to use force against the Assembly and had tried to block reforms fled the country in large numbers.

Reforms of the National Assembly

With resistance weakened, the National Assembly continued the work of reform begun in the summer of 1789. Its reforms, which are summarized below, destroyed the Old Regime.

1. *Abolition of special privileges.* By ending the special privileges of the nobility and the clergy in the August Decrees, the National Assembly legalized the equality that the bourgeoisie had demanded. The aristocratic structure of the Old Regime, a remnant of the Middle Ages that had hindered the progressive bourgeoisie, was eliminated.

2. *Statement of human rights.* The Declaration of the Rights of Man and of the Citizen expressed the liberal and universal goals of the philosophes. In proclaiming the inalienable right to liberty of person, freedom of religion and thought, and equal treatment under the law, the declaration affirmed the dignity of the individual. It asserted that government belonged not to any ruler but to the people as a whole, and that its aim was the preservation of the natural rights of the individual. Because the declaration contrasted sharply with the principles espoused by an intolerant clergy, a privileged aristocracy, and a despotic monarch, it has been called the death warrant of the Old Regime. A significant example of the new leadership's commitment to equality and religious toleration was the law passed in 1791 granting civil rights to Jews. Jews were now free to leave the ghettos, to which they had been forcibly confined for centuries to keep them apart from Gentiles, and, in theory, to participate in French society as equal citizens.

3. *Subordination of church to state.* The National Assembly also struck at the privileges of the Roman Catholic Church. The August Decrees declared the end of tithes. To obtain badly needed funds, the Assembly in November 1789 confiscated church lands and put them up for sale. In 1790, the Assembly passed the Civil Constitution of the Clergy, which reduced the number of bishops and priests and transformed the clergy into government officials elected by the people and paid by the state.

Almost all bishops and many priests opposed the Civil Constitution. It divided the French and gave opponents of the Revolution an emotional issue around which to rally supporters. Many devout Catholic peasants, resentful of the Revolution's treatment of the church, would join with aristocrats and clergy in the counterrevolution that would soon emerge.

4. *A constitution for France.* In September 1791, the National Assembly issued a constitution limiting the power of the king and guaranteeing all French citizens equal treatment under the law. Citizens paying less than a specified amount in taxes could not vote. Probably about 30 percent of the males over the age of twenty-five were excluded by this stipulation, and only the more well-to-do citizens were qualified to sit in the Legislative Assembly, a unicameral parliament created to succeed the National Assembly. The drafters of the constitution did not trust illiterate and propertyless men to vote and enact legislation. Nevertheless, the suffrage requirements under the constitution of 1791 were far more generous than those in Britain.

5. *Administrative and judicial reforms.* The National Assembly replaced the patchwork of provincial units with eighty-three new administrative units, or departments, approximately equal in size. Judicial reforms complemented the administrative changes. A standardized system of courts replaced the innumerable jurisdictions of the Old Regime, and the sale of judicial offices was ended. The penal code completed by the National Assembly abolished torture and barbarous punishments.

6. *Aid for business.* The National Assembly abolished all tolls and duties on goods transported within the country, established a uniform system of weights and measures, eliminated the guilds (medieval survivals that blocked business expansion), and forbade workers to form unions or to strike.

By ending absolutism, striking at the privileges of the nobility, and preventing the mass of people from gaining control over the government, the National Assembly consolidated the rule of the bourgeoisie. With one arm, it broke the power of aristocracy and throne; with the other, it held back the common people. Although the reforms benefitted the bourgeoisie, it would be a mistake to view them merely as a selfish expression of bourgeois interests. The Declaration of the Rights of Man and of the Citizen was addressed to all; it proclaimed liberty and equality as the right of all and called on citizens to treat one another with respect.

THE RADICAL STAGE, 1792–1794

Pleased with their accomplishments—equality before the law, careers open to talent, a written constitution, parliamentary government—the men of 1789 wished the Revolution to go no further. But revolutionary times are unpredictable. Soon the Revolution moved in a direction neither anticipated nor desired by the reformers. A counterrevolution, led by irreconcilable nobles and alienated churchmen, gained the support of the strongly Catholic peasants. It threatened the Revolution, forcing the revolutionary leadership to resort to extreme measures.

The Sans-Culottes

The discontent of the *sans-culottes**—small shopkeepers, artisans, and wage earners—also propelled the Revolution toward radicalism. Although they had played a significant role in the Revolution, particularly in the storming of the Bastille and in the October Days, they had gained little. The sans-culottes, says French historian Albert Soboul, "began to realize that a privilege of wealth was taking the place of a privilege of birth. They foresaw that the bourgeoisie would succeed the fallen aristocracy as the ruling

*Literally, *sans-culottes* means "without culottes" and refers to the people who wore the simple trousers of a laborer and not the knee breeches that aristocrats wore before the Revolution.

enthusiasm for political democracy. It contained a new Declaration of Rights, which affirmed and amplified the principles of 1789. By giving all adult males the right to vote, it overcame sans-culotte objections to the constitution of 1791. However, the threat of invasion and the revolts caused the implementation of the new constitution to be postponed, and it was never put into effect. By abolishing both slavery in the French colonies and imprisonment for debt and by making plans for free public education, the Jacobins revealed their humanitarianism and their debt to the philosophes. To halt inflation and gain the support of the poor—both necessary for the war effort—the Jacobins decreed the *law of the maximum,* which fixed prices on bread and other essential goods and raised wages.

The Nation in Arms

To fight the war against foreign invaders, the Jacobins, in an act that anticipated modern conscription, drafted unmarried men between eighteen and twenty-five years of age. They mobilized the country's resources, infused the army with a love for *la patrie* (the nation), and, in a remarkable demonstration of administrative skill, equipped an army of more than 800,000 men. In creating the nation in arms, the Jacobins heralded the emergence of modern warfare. Inspired by the ideals of liberty, equality, and fraternity and commanded by officers who had proved their skill on the battlefield, the citizen soldiers of the Republic won decisive victories. In May and June 1794, the French routed the allied forces on the vital northern frontier, and by the end of July, France had become the triumphant master of Belgium.

By demanding complete devotion to the nation, the Jacobin phase of the Revolution also heralded the rise of modern nationalism. In the schools, in newspapers, speeches, and poems, on the stage, and at rallies and meetings of patriotic societies, the French people were told of the glory won by republican soldiers on the battlefield and were reminded of their duties to *la patrie.* "The citizen is born, lives, and dies for the fatherland"—these words were written in public places for all citizens to read and ponder. The soldiers of the Revolution fought not for money or for a king but for the nation. Could this heightened sense of nationality, which concentrated on the special interests of the French people, be reconciled with the Declaration of the Rights of Man, whose principles were addressed to all humanity? The revolutionaries themselves did not understand the implications of the new force that they had unleashed.

The Republic of Virtue and the Reign of Terror

While forging a revolutionary army to deal with external enemies, the Jacobins were also waging war against internal opposition. The pivotal personality in this struggle was Maximilien Robespierre (1758–1794), who had a fervent faith in the rightness of his beliefs and a total commitment to republican democracy. In the early stage of Revolution, Robespierre had strongly supported liberal reforms. He attacked—at times with great fervor—slavery, capital punishment, and censorship; he favored civil rights for Jews; and, in what was considered a radical measure, he supported giving all men the vote regardless of how much property they owned. Robespierre wanted to create a better society founded on reason, good citizenship, and patriotism. In his Republic of Virtue, there would be no kings or nobles; men would be free, equal, and educated; and reason would be glorified and superstition ridiculed. There would be no extremes of wealth or poverty; people's natural goodness would prevail over vice and greed; and laws would preserve, not violate, inalienable rights. In this utopian vision, an individual's duties would be "to detest bad faith and despotism, to punish tyrants and traitors, to assist the unfortunate, to respect the weak, to defend the oppressed, to do all the good one can to one's neighbor, and to behave with justice towards all men."[8] Robespierre pursued his ideal society with religious zeal. Knowing that the Republic of Virtue could not be established while France was threatened by foreign and civil war, and certain that counterrevolutionaries were everywhere, Robespierre urged harsh treatment for enemies of the Republic, who "must be prosecuted by all not as ordinary enemies, but as rebels, brigands, and assassins."[9]

With Robespierre playing a key role, the Jacobin leadership executed those they considered enemies of the Republic: Girondins who challenged Jacobin authority; federalists who opposed a strong central government emanating from Paris; counterrevolutionary priests and nobles and their peasant supporters; and profiteers who hoarded food. The Jacobins even sought to discipline the ardor of the sans-culottes, who had given them power. Fearful that, uncontrolled, the sans-culottes would undermine central authority and promote anarchy, Robespierrists brought about the dissolution of sans-culotte societies. They also executed sans-culotte leaders known as the *enragés* (literally, madmen), who threatened insurrection against Jacobin rule and pushed for more social reforms than the Jacobins would allow. The enragés wanted to set limits on income and on the size of farms and businesses—policies considered far too extreme by the supporters of Robespierre.

Robespierre and his fellow Jacobins did not make terror a deliberate government policy because they were bloodthirsty or power mad. Instead, they sought to establish a temporary dictatorship in a desperate attempt to save the Republic and the Revolution. Deeply devoted to republican democracy, the Jacobins viewed themselves as bearers of a higher faith. Like all other true believers, Robespierre was convinced that he knew the right way and that the new society he envisaged would benefit all humanity. He saw those who impeded its implementation not just as opponents, but as sinners who had to be liquidated for the general good.

Special courts were established in Paris and other cities to try suspects. The proceedings were carried on in haste, and most judgments called for either acquittal or execution. In the Vendée, where civil war raged, many of the arrested were executed by firing squads without trial. Ironically, most of the executions took place after the frontiers had been secured and the civil war crushed. Of the five hundred thousand people imprisoned for crimes against the Republic, some sixteen thousand were sentenced to death by guillotine and another twenty thousand perished in prison before they could be tried. More than two hundred thousand died in the civil war in the provinces, and forty thousand were summarily executed by firing squad, guillotine, and mass

M.M.J. ROBERSPIERRE

*Député de l'Artois,
à l'Assemblée Nationale en 1789.*

A Paris, chez l'AUTEUR, quay des Augustins Nº 71. au 5º

ROBESPIERRE, AN ENGRAVING BY FIÉSINGER AFTER A DRAWING BY PIERRE-NARCISSE GUÉRIN. To create a Republic of Virtue where men would be free and equal, Maximilien Robespierre considered terror necessary. Robespierre lost favor with his own party and was himself guillotined.

drownings ordered by military courts authorized by the Convention.

The Terror was particularly brutal in the Vendée, where the counterrevolution was fought by deeply religious Catholic peasants led by aristocrats who wanted an end to conscription and the mistreatment of their priests. Although untrained and poorly armed, the Vendéans succeeded in capturing a major town in the Loire Valley; in the process, they killed some one hundred and fifty republican soldiers and took eight thousand prisoners. The Republic was imperiled, but in June 1793, seasoned republican forces defeated the Vendéans in the port city of Nantes. This was followed up in October by a crushing defeat in the town of Chalet. Then the mass murders began.

Primary Source

Robespierre: The Necessity for Terror

In notes written in the style of a Catholic catechism, Robespierre advocated terror against the enemies of the Revolution

What is our goal? The enforcement of the constitution for the benefit of the people. Who will our enemies be? The vicious and the rich.

What means will they employ? Slander and hypocrisy.

What things may be favorable for the employment of these? The ignorance of the *sans-culottes*.

The people must therefore be enlightened. But what are the obstacles to the enlightenment of the people? Mercenary writers who daily mislead them with impudent falsehoods.

What conclusions may be drawn from this? 1. These writers must be proscribed as the most dangerous enemies of the people. 2. Right-minded literature must be scattered about in profusion.

What are the other obstacles to the establishment of liberty? Foreign war and civil war.

How can foreign war be ended? By putting republican generals in command of our armies and punishing those who have betrayed us.

How can civil war be ended? By punishing traitors and conspirators, particularly if they are deputies or administrators; by sending loyal troops under patriotic leaders to subdue the aristocrats of Lyon, Marseille, Toulon, the Vendée, the Jura, and all other regions in which the standards of rebellion and royalism have been raised; and by making frightful examples of all scoundrels who have outraged liberty and spilled the blood of patriots.

1. Proscription of perfidious and counterrevolutionary writers and propagation of proper literature.

2. Punishment of traitors and conspirators, particularly deputies and administrators.

3. Appointment of patriotic generals; dismissal and punishment of others.

4. Sustenance and laws for the people.

Question for Analysis

1. On what grounds did Robespierre justify terror?

E. L. Higgins , ed., *The French Revolution as Told by Contemporaries* (Boston: Houghton Mifflin, 1938), p. 301.

Regarding the Vendéans as superstitious fanatics who fought against the Revolution's ideals and as traitors in league with France's enemies, frenzied republican soldiers, under orders from their superiors, burned villages, slaughtered livestock, and indiscriminately killed tens of thousands of peasants. Some five thousand Vendéans were loaded onto barges that were then sunk in the middle of the Loire River. Perhaps one-quarter of the region's population, women and children included, perished in 1793 and 1794. (To this day, the Vendéans mourn these losses and express contempt for the Revolution.)

Anticlericalism reinforced by the exigencies of war fostered a phenomenon known as de-Christianization. In many regions, priests were dismissed and churches were closed, policies supported by the belief that the clergy helped instigate the counterrevolution. Removed from churches were items including metal crosses, which could be channeled into the war effort. One district decreed that "the throne of error and falsehood be overthrown at the same time as that of the tyrant, to be replaced by the eternal reign of reason and philosophy."[10]

To purge the Republic of Christianity, which many deputies regarded as superstition and fanaticism that undermined liberty, the Convention drew up a Republican calendar in which the year one started, not with Christ's birth, but with the founding of the French Republic on September 22, 1792. On November 10, 1793, a celebration honoring the goddess Reason took place in the cathedral of Notre Dame. Maintaining that belief in God strengthened civic order and that attacking the church drove people to support the counter-revolution, Robespierre was a staunch opponent of de-Christianization.

The Jacobins expelled foreign armies, crushed the federalist uprisings, contained the counter-revolutionaries in the Vendée, and prevented anarchy. Without the discipline, order, and unity imposed on France by the Jacobins, it is likely that the Republic would have collapsed under the twin blows of foreign invasion and domestic anarchy.

Nonetheless, the Reign of Terror poses fundamental questions about the meaning of the French Revolution and the validity of the Enlightenment conception of the individual. To what extent did the feverish passions and lust for violence demonstrated in the mass executions in the provinces and in the public spectacles in Paris—vast crowds watching and applauding the beheadings—indicate a darker side of human nature beyond the control of reason? Did Robespierre's religion of humanity revive the fanaticism and cruelty of the wars of religion, which had so disgusted the philosophes? Did the Robespierrists, who considered themselves the staunchest defenders of the Revolution's ideals, soil and subvert these ideals by their zeal? The Jacobins mobilized the might of the nation, created the mystique of *la patrie,* imposed dictatorial rule in defense of liberty and equality, and legalized and justified terror committed in the people's name. In so doing, were they unwittingly unleashing new forces—total commitment to a political ideology that promised to regenerate the nation and mass executions carried out in good conscience—that would be harnessed by totalitarian ideologies that were consciously resolved to stamp out the liberal heritage of the Revolution?

The Fall of Robespierre

Feeling the chill of the guillotine blade on their own necks, Robespierre's opponents in the Convention ordered his arrest and the arrest of some of his supporters. On July 28, 1794, the tenth of Thermidor according to the new republican calendar, Robespierre was guillotined. After the fall of Robespierre, the machinery of the Jacobin republic was dismantled.

Leadership passed to the property-owning bourgeois who had endorsed the constitutional ideas of 1789 to 1791, the moderate stage of the Revolution. The new leadership, known as Thermidoreans until the end of 1795, wanted no more of the Jacobins or of Robespierre's society. They had viewed Robespierre as a threat to their political power because he would have allowed the common people a considerable voice in the government. They had also deemed him a threat to their property because he would have introduced some state regulation of the economy to aid the poor.

The Thermidorean reaction was a counterrevolution. The new government purged the army of officers who were suspected of Jacobin leanings, abolished the law of the maximum, and declared void the constitution of 1793. A new constitution, approved in 1795, reestablished property requirements for voting. The counterrevolution also produced a counterterror, as royalists and Catholics massacred Jacobins in the provinces.

At the end of 1795, the new republican government, the Directory, was burdened by war, a sagging economy, and internal unrest. The Directory crushed insurrections by Parisian sans-culottes, maddened by hunger and hatred of the rich (1795, 1796), and by royalists seeking to restore the monarchy (1797). As military and domestic pressures increased, power began to pass into the hands of generals. One of them, Napoleon Bonaparte, seized control of the government in November 1799, pushing the Revolution into yet another stage.

NAPOLEON AND FRANCE: RETURN TO AUTOCRATIC RULE

Napoleon was born on August 15, 1769, on the island of Corsica, the son of a petty noble. After finishing military school in France, he became an artillery officer. The wars of the French Revolution afforded him an opportunity to advance his career; in 1796, he was given command of the French Army of Italy. In Italy, against the Austrians, Napoleon demonstrated a dazzling talent for military planning and leadership, which

Chronology 11.2 ❖ Napoleon's Career

1796	Napoleon gets command of the French Army of Italy
November 10, 1799	He helps to overthrow the Directory's rule, establishing a strong executive in France
December 2, 1804	He crowns himself emperor of the French
October 21, 1805	Battle of Trafalgar—French and Spanish fleets are defeated by the British
October 1806	Napoleon defeats the Prussians at Jena, and French forces occupy Berlin
1808–1813	Peninsular War—Spaniards, aided by the British, fight against French occupation
October–December 1812	Grand Army retreats from Russia
October 1813	Allied forces defeat Napoleon at Leipzig
1814	Paris is captured and Napoleon is exiled to Elba
March 20, 1815	Escaping, he enters Paris and begins "hundred days" rule
June 1815	Defeated at Waterloo, Napoleon is exiled to St. Helena

earned him an instant reputation. Having tasted glory, he could never do without it. Since he had experienced only success, nothing seemed impossible; he sensed that he was headed for greatness.

In 1799, Napoleon was leading a French army in Egypt when he decided to return to France and make his bid for power. He joined a conspiracy that overthrew the Directory and created an executive office of three consuls. As first consul, Napoleon monopolized power. In 1802, he was made first consul for life, with the right to name his successor. And on December 2, 1804, in a magnificent ceremony at the Cathedral of Notre Dame in Paris, Napoleon crowned himself "Emperor of the French." General, first consul, and then emperor—it was a breathless climb to the heights of power. Napoleon, who once said that he loved "power as a musician loves his violin," was determined never to lose it.

An Enlightened Despot

Napoleon did not identify with the republicanism and democracy of the Jacobins; rather, he belonged to the tradition of eighteenth-century enlightened despotism. Like the reforming despots, he admired administrative uniformity and efficiency; disliked feudalism, religious persecution, and civil inequality; and favored government regulation of trade and industry. He saw in enlightened despotism a means of ensuring political stability and strengthening the state. Napoleon did preserve several gains of the Revolution: equality under the law, careers open to men of talent, promotion of secular education, and the weakening of clerical power. But he suppressed political liberty.

Napoleon succeeded in giving France a strong central government and administrative uniformity. An army of officials subject to the emperor's will reached into every village, linking together the entire nation. This centralized state suited Napoleon's desire for orderly government and rational administration, enabled him to concentrate power in his own hands, and provided him with the taxes and soldiers needed to fight his wars. To suppress irreconcilable opponents, primarily diehard royalists and republicans, Napoleon used the instruments of the police state—secret agents, arbitrary arrest, summary trials, and executions.

Erich Lessing/Art Resource, N.Y.

CORONATION OF NAPOLEON AND JOSEPHINE, BY DAVID. Napoleon crowned himself emperor in a magnificent ceremony. To French émigrés and nobles throughout Europe, he was the "crowned Jacobin" who threatened aristocratic privileges and European stability.

In still another way he was a precursor of twentieth-century dictators. To prevent hostile criticism of his rule and to promote popular support for his policies and person, Napoleon also shaped public opinion. Liberty of the press came to an end. Printers swore an oath of obedience to the emperor, and newspapers were converted into government mouthpieces.

Napoleon tried to close the breach between the state and the Catholic Church that had opened during the Revolution. Such a reconciliation would gain the approval of the mass of the French people, who still remained devoted to their faith and would also reassure the peasants and bourgeois who had bought confiscated church lands. For these reasons, Napoleon negotiated an agreement with the pope. The Concordat of 1801 recognized Catholicism as the religion of the great majority of the French, rather than as the official state religion (the proposal that the pope desired). Napoleon had achieved his aim. The Concordat made his regime acceptable to Catholics and to owners of former church lands.

Legal, Educational, and Financial Policies

Under the Old Regime, France was plagued by numerous and conflicting law codes. Reflecting local interests and feudal traditions, these codes obstructed national unity and administrative efficiency. Efforts by the revolutionaries to draw up a unified code of laws bogged down. Recognizing the value of such a code in promoting effective administration throughout France, Napoleon pressed for the completion of the project. The Code Napoléon incorporated many principles of the Revolution: equality before the law, the right to choose one's profession, religious freedom, protection of property rights, the abolition of serfdom, and the secular character of the state.

The code also had its less liberal side, denying equal treatment to workers in their dealings with employers, to women in their relations with their husbands, and to children in their relations with their fathers. In making wives inferior to their husbands in matters of property, adultery, and divorce, the code reflected both Napoleon's personal attitude and the general view of the times toward women and family stability. The restoration of slavery in the French colonies—which the Jacobins had abolished—was another violation of equality.

Napoleon's educational policy was in many ways an elaboration of the school reforms initiated during the Revolution. Like the revolutionaries, Napoleon favored a system of public education with a secular curriculum and a minimum of church involvement. For Napoleon, education served a dual purpose: it would provide him with capable officials to administer his laws and trained officers to lead his armies, and it would indoctrinate the young in obedience and loyalty. He established the University of France, a giant board of education that placed education under state control. To this day, the French school system, unlike that in the United States, is strictly centralized, with curriculum and standards set for the entire country.

The emperor did not consider education for girls important, holding that "marriage is their whole destination."[11] In his view, whatever education girls did receive should stress religion. "What we ask of education is not that girls should think but that they should believe. The weakness of women's brains, the instability of their ideas, the place they fill in society, their need for perpetual resignation . . . all this can be met by religion."[12]

Napoleon's financial and economic policies were designed to strengthen France and enhance his popularity. To stimulate the economy and to retain the favor of the bourgeois who supported his seizure of power, Napoleon aided industry through tariffs and loans, and he fostered commerce (while also speeding up troop movements) by building or repairing roads, bridges, and canals. To protect the currency from inflation, he established the Bank of France, which was controlled by the nation's leading financiers. By keeping careers open to talent, he endorsed one of the key demands of the bourgeoisie during the Revolution. Fearing a revolution based on lack of bread, he provided food at low prices and stimulated employment for the laboring poor. He endeared himself to the peasants by not restoring feudal privileges and by allowing them to keep the land they had obtained during the Revolution.

NAPOLEON AND EUROPE: DIFFUSION OF REVOLUTIONARY INSTITUTIONS

Napoleon, the Corsican adventurer, realized Louis XIV's dream of French mastery of Europe. Between 1805 and 1807, he decisively defeated Austria, Prussia, and Russia, becoming the virtual ruler of Europe. In these campaigns, as in his earlier successes in Italy, Napoleon demonstrated his greatness as a military commander.

By 1810, Napoleon dominated the Continent, except for the Balkan Peninsula. The Grand Empire comprised lands annexed to France, vassal states, and cowed allies.

With varying degrees of determination and success, Napoleon extended the reforms of the Revolution to other lands. His officials instituted the Code Napoléon, organized an effective civil service, opened careers to talent, and equalized the tax burden. Besides abolishing serfdom, manorial payments, and the courts of the nobility, they did away with clerical courts, promoted freedom of religion, permitted civil marriage, pressed for civil rights for Jews, and fought clerical interference with secular authority. They also abolished the medieval guilds, introduced a uniform system of weights and measures, eliminated internal tolls, and built roads, bridges, and canals. They promoted secular education and improved public health. Napoleon had launched a Europe-wide social revolution that attacked the privileges of the aristocracy and the clergy—who regarded him as "that crowned Jacobin"—and worked to the advantage of the bourgeoisie. This diffusion of revolutionary institutions weakened the old regime irreparably in much of Europe and speeded up the modernization of nineteenth-century Europe.

Pleased by the overhaul of feudal practices and the reduction of clerical power, many Europeans, particularly the progressive bourgeoisie, welcomed Napoleon as a liberator. But there was another side to Napoleon's rule. Napoleon, the tyrant of Europe, turned conquered lands into satellite kingdoms and exploited them for the benefit of France—a policy that gained him the enmity of many Europeans.

THE FALL OF NAPOLEON

In addition to the hostility of subject nationals, Napoleon had to cope with the determined opposition of Great Britain, whose subsidies and encouragements kept resistance to the emperor alive. But perhaps Napoleon's greatest obstacle was his own boundless ambition, which warped his judgment. From its peak, the emperor's career soon slid downhill to defeat, dethronement, and deportation.

Failure to Subdue England

Britain was Napoleon's most resolute opponent. It could not be otherwise, for any power that dominated the Continent could organize sufficient naval might to threaten British commerce, challenge its sea power, and invade the island kingdom. Britain would not make peace with any state that sought European hegemony, and Napoleon's ambition would settle for nothing less.

Unable to invade Britain while British warships commanded the English Channel, Napoleon decided to bring what he called "the nation of shopkeepers" to its knees by damaging the British economy. His plan, called the Continental System, was to bar all countries under France's control from buying British goods. However, by smuggling goods onto the Continent and increasing trade with the New World, Britain, although hurt, escaped economic ruin. Besides, the Continental System also punished European lands that were dependent on British imports; the bourgeoisie, generally supportive of Napoleon's social and administrative reforms, turned against him because of the economic distress it caused. Furthermore, Napoleon's efforts to enforce the system enmeshed him in two catastrophic blunders: the occupation of Spain and the invasion of Russia.

The Spanish Ulcer

An ally of France since 1796, Spain proved a disappointment to Napoleon. It failed to prevent the Portuguese from trading with Britain, and it contributed little military or financial aid to France's war effort. Napoleon decided to incorporate Spain into his empire; in 1808, he deposed the Spanish ruler and designated his own brother Joseph as king of Spain.

Napoleon believed that the Spanish would rally round the gentle Joseph and welcome his liberal reforms. This confidence was a fatal illusion. Spanish nobles and clergy feared French liberalism; the overwhelmingly peasant population—illiterate and credulous, intensely proud, fanatically religious, and easily aroused by the clergy—viewed Napoleon as the Devil's agent. Loyal to the Spanish monarchy and faithful to the church, the Spanish fought a "War to the Knife" against the invaders.

Seeking to keep the struggle against Napoleon alive, Britain came to the aid of the Spanish insurgents. The intervention of British troops, commanded by Sir Arthur Wellesley, the future duke of Wellington, led to the ultimate defeat of Joseph in 1813. The "Spanish ulcer" drained Napoleon's treasury, tied down hundreds of thousands of French troops, enabled Britain to gain a foothold on the Continent from which to invade southern France, and inspired patriots in other lands to resist the French emperor.

Disaster in Russia

Deteriorating relations between Russia and France led Napoleon to his fatal decision to attack the Eastern giant. His creation of the Grand Duchy of Warsaw irritated the tsar, who feared a revival of Polish power and resented French influence on Russia's border. Another source of friction between the tsar and Napoleon was Russia's illicit trade with Britain, in violation of the Continental System. No doubt, Napoleon's inexhaustible craving for glory and power also compelled him to strike at Russia.

In June 1812, the Grand Army, 614,000 men strong, crossed the Neman River into Russia. Fighting mainly rearguard battles and retreating according to plan, the tsar's forces lured the invaders into the vastness of Russia, far from their lines of supply. On September 14, the Grand Army, its numbers greatly reduced by disease, hunger, exhaustion, desertion, and battle, entered Moscow, which the Russians had virtually evacuated. To show their contempt for the French conquerors

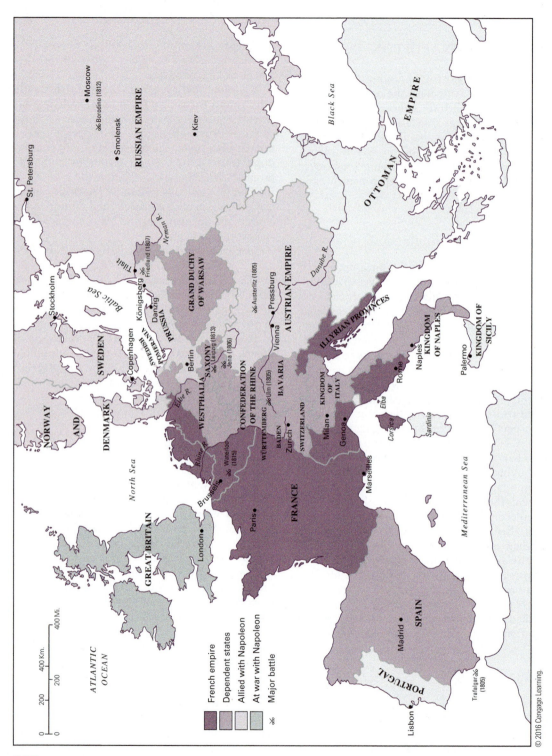

St. Petersburg

Moscow
Borodino (1812)
Smolensk

RUSSIAN EMPIRE

Kiev

Black Sea

OTTOMAN EMPIRE

Stockholm

Baltic Sea

Tilsit
Königsberg   Friedland (1807)
Danzig
POMERANIA

Neman R.

GRAND DUCHY OF WARSAW

PRUSSIA

Austerlitz (1805)
Pressburg

AUSTRIAN EMPIRE

Vienna

Danube R.

SWEDEN

NORWAY

AND

DENMARK

Copenhagen

Berlin
Elbe R.
Jena (1806)
Leipzig (1813)

WESTPHALIA

SAXONY

CONFEDERATION OF THE RHINE

Ulm (1805)

BAVARIA

ILLYRIAN PROVINCES

KINGDOM OF NAPLES

Naples
Rome

KINGDOM OF SICILY

Palermo

North Sea

WÜRTTEMBERG
BADEN
Zürich

SWITZERLAND

KINGDOM OF ITALY

Milan

Genoa

Elba

Corsica

Sardinia

Mediterranean Sea

Rhine R.
Waterloo (1815)

Brussels

FRANCE

Paris

Marseilles

GREAT BRITAIN

London

ATLANTIC OCEAN

SPAIN

Madrid

PORTUGAL

Lisbon

Trafalgar (1805)

400 Mi.
400 Km.
200
200
0
0

French empire
Dependent states
Allied with Napoleon
At war with Napoleon
Major battle

280

© 2016 Cengage Learning.

and to deny the French shelter, the Russians set fire to the city, which burned for five days. Taking up headquarters in Moscow, Napoleon waited for Alexander I to admit defeat and come to terms. But the tsar remained intransigent.

Napoleon was in a dilemma: to penetrate deeper into Russia was certain death; to stay in Moscow with winter approaching meant possible starvation. Faced with these alternatives, Napoleon decided to retreat westward. On October 19, 1812, ninety-five thousand troops and thousands of wagons loaded with loot left Moscow for the long trek back. In early November came the first snow and frost. Army stragglers were slaughtered by Russian Cossacks and peasant partisans. In the middle of December, with the Russians in pursuit, the remnants of the Grand Army staggered across the Neman River into East Prussia.

The German War of Liberation

Napoleon's disastrous Russian campaign helped to trigger uprisings in the German states where anti-French feeling was high. Hatred of the French invaders evoked a feeling of national outrage among some Germans, who up to this time had thought only in terms of their own particular state and prince. Some German intellectuals, using the emotional language of nationalism, called for a war of liberation against Napoleon and, in some instances, for the creation of a unified Germany.

Besides kindling a desire for national independence and unity, the disastrous defeat of the Prussians at Jena (1806) and French domination of Germany stimulated a movement for reform among members of the Prussian high bureaucracy and officer corps. To survive in a world altered by the French Revolution, Prussia would have to learn the principal lessons of the Revolution: that aroused citizens fighting for a cause make better soldiers than mercenaries and oppressed serfs, and that officers selected for daring and intelligence command better than nobles possessing only a gilded birthright. The reformers believed that the

◀ *Map 11.1* **Napoleon's Europe, 1810** By 1810, Napoleon dominated much of the Continent. His Grand Empire comprised lands annexed to France, vassal states, and cowed allies.

elimination of social abuses would overcome defeatism and apathy and encourage Prussians to serve the state willingly and to fight bravely for national honor. A revitalized Prussia could then deal with the French.

Among the important reforms introduced in Prussia between 1807 and 1813 were the abolition of serfdom, the granting to towns of a large measure of self-administration, the awarding of army commissions on the basis of merit instead of birth, the elimination of cruel punishment in the ranks, and the establishment of national conscription. In 1813, the reform party forced King Frederick William III to declare war on France. The military reforms did improve the quality of the Prussian army. In the War of Liberation (1813), Prussian soldiers demonstrated far more enthusiasm and patriotism than they had at Jena in 1806, and the French were driven from Germany. The German War of Liberation came on the heels of Napoleon's disastrous Russian campaign.

Final Defeat

After the destruction of the Grand Army, the empire crumbled. Although Napoleon raised a new army, he could not replace the equipment, cavalry horses, and experienced soldiers squandered in Russia. Now he had to rely on schoolboys and overage veterans. Most of Europe joined in a final coalition against France. In October 1813, allied forces from Austria, Prussia, Russia, and Sweden defeated Napoleon at Leipzig; in November, Anglo-Spanish forces crossed the Pyrenees into France. Finally, in the spring of 1814, the allies captured Paris. Napoleon abdicated and was exiled to the tiny island of Elba, off the coast of Italy. The Bourbon dynasty was restored to the throne of France in the person of Louis XVIII, younger brother of the executed Louis XVI and the acknowledged leader of the émigrés.

Only forty-four years of age, Napoleon did not believe that it was his destiny to die on Elba. On March 1, 1815, he landed on the French coast with a thousand soldiers, and three weeks later he entered Paris to a hero's welcome. Raising a new army, Napoleon moved against the allied forces in Belgium. There, the Prussians, led by Field Marshal Gebhard von Blücher, and the

British, led by the Duke of Wellington, defeated Napoleon at Waterloo in June 1815. Napoleon's desperate gamble to regain power—the famous "hundred days"—had failed. This time the allies sent Napoleon to Saint Helena, a lonely island in the South Atlantic a thousand miles off the coast of southern Africa. On this gloomy and rugged rock, Napoleon Bonaparte, emperor of France and would-be conqueror of Europe, spent the last six years of his life. Napoleon's drive, military genius, and charisma had propelled him to the peak of power; his inability to moderate his ambition bled Europe, distorted his judgment, and led to his downfall.

THE MEANING OF
THE FRENCH REVOLUTION

The French Revolution was a decisive period in the shaping of the modern West. It implemented the thought of the philosophes, destroyed the hierarchical and corporate society of the Old Regime, which was a legacy of the Middle Ages, promoted the interests of the bourgeoisie, and quickened the growth of the modern state.

The French Revolution weakened the aristocracy. With their feudal rights and privileges eliminated, the nobles became simply ordinary citizens. Throughout the nineteenth century, France would be governed by both aristocrats and bourgeoisie; property, not noble birth, determined the composition of the new ruling elite.

The principle of careers being open to talent gave the bourgeois access to the highest positions in the state. Having wealth, talent, ambition, and now opportunity, the bourgeois would play an ever more important role in French political life. Throughout Continental Europe, the reforms of the French Revolution served as a model for progressive bourgeois, who sooner or later would challenge the old regimes in their own lands.

The French Revolution transformed the dynastic state, on which the Old Regime was based, into the modern state: national, liberal, secular, and rational. When the Declaration of the Rights of Man and of the Citizen stated that "the source of all sovereignty resides essentially in the nation," the concept of the state took on a new meaning. The state was no longer merely a territory or a federation of provinces, nor was it the private possession of a king who claimed to be God's lieutenant on earth. In the new conception, the state belonged to the people as a whole. For a government to be legitimate it had to derive its power from the people. And the individual, formerly a subject, was now a citizen with both rights and duties and was governed by laws that permitted no legal distinction between commoners and nobles.

The liberal thought of the Enlightenment found practical expression in the reforms of the Revolution. Absolutism and divine right of monarchy, repudiated in theory by the philosophes, were invalidated by constitutions affirming that sovereignty resides with the people, not with a monarch, and setting limits to the powers of government and by elected parliaments that represented the governed. By providing for equality before the law and the protection of human rights—habeas corpus, trial by jury, civil rights for Protestants and Jews, and freedom of speech and the press—the Revolution struck at the abuses of the Old Regime. Because of violations and interruptions, these gains seemed at times more theoretical than actual. Nevertheless, these liberal ideals reverberated throughout the Continent. In the early nineteenth century, revolutionaries in France and other lands, aspiring for political and social change, took the French Revolution as their inspiration, and the pace of reform quickened.

Prior to the Revolution, religion was still closely linked to the state. As a general rule each state had an official religion, a state church that legitimated the ruling power. By disavowing any divine justification for the monarch's power, by depriving the church of its special position, and by no longer limiting citizenship to members of a state church, the Revolution accelerated the secularization of European political life.

Sweeping aside the administrative chaos of the Old Regime, the Revolution attempted to impose rational norms on the state. The sale of public offices, which had produced ineffective and corrupt administrators, was eliminated, and the highest positions in the land were opened to men of talent, regardless of birth. The Revolution abolished the peasantry's manorial obligations, which had hampered agriculture, and swept away barriers to

AND THERE IS NO REMEDY, ETCHING BY FRANCISCO GOYA (1746–1828). Spaniards resisted the installation of Joseph, Napoleon's brother, as king of Spain. Both sides engaged in terrible atrocities in the ensuing Peninsular War. The Spanish painter Francisco Goya captured the war's brutality.

economic expansion. It based taxes on income and streamlined their collection. The destruction of feudal remnants, internal tolls, and the guilds speeded up the expansion of a competitive market economy. In the nineteenth century, reformers in the rest of Europe would follow the lead set by France.

By spreading revolutionary ideals and institutions, Napoleon made it impossible for the traditional rulers to restore the Old Regime intact after the emperor's downfall. He had solidified in France what the Revolution had initiated— the destruction of a society based on orders and legal privileges and the opening of careers to talent regardless of birth. In conquered lands, his administrators undermined the authority of aristocrats and clergy. Napoleon's reforms furthered the rationalization and secularization of society and contributed to the transformation of the dynastic state into the modern national state and to the prominence of the bourgeoisie.

By showing that a decadent old order could be toppled and supplanted by a new one, the French Revolution inspired generations of revolutionaries aspiring to end longstanding abuses and to remodel society. In the process, it unleashed three potentially destructive forces identified with the modern state: total war, nationalism, and a fanatic utopian mentality. All these forces contradicted the rational and universal aims of the reformers as stated in the Declaration of the Rights of Man and of the Citizen. Whereas the restrained wars of the eighteenth century were fought by a limited number of professional soldiers for limited aims, the French Revolution brought conscription and the mobilization of all the state's resources for armed conflict, practices continued by Napoleon. The French emperor raised armies of unprecedented size and sought the complete destruction of the enemy force. The battle of Leipzig, for example, involved 500,000 combatants on both sides, of whom 150,000 were killed or wounded. Almost a million Frenchmen perished in Napoleon's wars. The world wars of the twentieth century were the terrible fulfillment of this new development in warfare.

The French Revolution also gave birth to modern nationalism. During the Revolution, loyalty was directed to the entire nation, not to a village or province or to the person of the king. The whole of France became the fatherland. Under the Jacobins, the French became converts to a secular faith preaching total reverence for the nation. "In 1794 we believed in no supernatural religion; our serious interior sentiments were all summed up in the one idea, how to be useful to the fatherland. Everything else . . . was, in our eyes, only trivial. . . . It was our only religion."[13] Few suspected that the new religion of nationalism was fraught with danger. Louis-Antoine de Saint-Just, a young, ardent Robespierrist, was gazing into the future when he declared: "There is something terrible in the sacred love of the fatherland. This love is so exclusive that it sacrifices everything to the public interest, without pity, without fear, with no respect for the human individual."[14] The philosophes would have deemed nationalism, which demanded total dedication of body and soul to the nation and stifled clear thinking, to be a repudiation of their universalism and hopes for rational solutions to political conflicts. It was a new dogma capable of evoking wild and dangerous passions and a setback for the progress of reason.

The French Revolution gave rise to still another potentially destructive force: a revolutionary mentality that sought to demolish an unjust traditional society and create a new social order that would restore individuals to their natural goodness. The negative side of this lofty vision was its power to whip up an extremism that demonized opponents as irredeemably evil and that justified mass murder in the name of a supposedly higher good. Such was the case with Robespierre and other Jacobins. In the twentieth century, Nazis in Germany and radical socialists in Russia, China, and Cambodia, seeing themselves as idealists striving for a social regeneration of humanity, oppressed, terrorized, and murdered with intense dedication—and a clear conscience.

The Revolution attempted to reconstruct society on the basis of Enlightenment thought. The Declaration of the Rights of Man and of the Citizen—whose spirit permeated the reforms of the Revolution—upheld the dignity of the individual, demanded respect for the individual, attributed to each person natural rights, and barred the state from denying these rights. It insisted that society and the state have no higher duty than to promote the freedom and autonomy of the individual. "It is not enough to have overturned the throne," said Robespierre; "our concern is to erect upon its remains holy Equality and the sacred Rights of Man."[15] The tragedy of the Western experience is that this humanist vision, brilliantly expressed by the Enlightenment and given recognition in the reforms of the French Revolution, would be undermined in later generations. And, ironically, by its fanatical commitment to a seductive ideology that promised worldly salvation—the creation of the Republic of virtue and truth—the French Revolution itself contributed to the shattering of this vision. It had spawned total war, including mass conscription, aggressive nationalism, terror as government policy, and a revolutionary mentality that sought to change the world through coercion and terror, including mass murder. In the twentieth century, these dangerous forces almost succeeded in crushing the liberty and equality so valued by the French reformers.

❖   ❖   ❖

Notes

1. George Rudé, *Revolutionary Europe, 1783–1815* (New York: Harper Torchbooks, 1966), 74.

2. Henri Peyre, "The Influence of Eighteenth-Century Ideas on the French Revolution," *Journal of the History of Ideas,* 10 (1949), 73.

3. George Lefebvre, *The French Revolution from 1793 to 1799,* trans. John Hall Stewart and James Friguglietti (New York: Columbia University Press, 1964), Vol. 2, 360.

4. Quoted in T. C. W. Blanning, *The French Revolution: Aristocrats Versus Bourgeois?* (Atlantic Highlands, N.J.: Humanities Press, 1987), 9. Reprinted with permission from the author.

5. William Doyle, *Origins of the French Revolution* (London: Oxford University Press, 1980), 21.

6. Excerpted in John Hall Stewart, ed., *A Documentary Survey of the French Revolution* (New York: Macmillan, 1951), 43–44.

7. Albert Soboul, *The Parisian Sans-Culottes and the French Revolution, 1793–94,* trans. Gwynne Lewis (London: Oxford University Press, 1964), 28–29.

8. Excerpted in George Rudé, ed., *Robespierre* (Englewood Cliffs, N.J.: Prentice-Hall, 1976), 72.

9. Ibid., 57.

10. Excerpted in Philip G. Dwyer and Peter McPhee, *The French Revolution and Napoleon: A Sourcebook* (London: Routledge, 2002), 88.

11. Quoted in Robert B. Holtman, *Napoleonic Revolution* (Philadelphia: J. B. Lippincott, 1967), 143.

12. Excerpted in Maurice Hutt, ed., *Napoleon* (Englewood Cliffs, N.J.: Prentice Hall, 1972), 49–50.

13. Quoted in Carlton J. H. Hayes, *The Historical Evolution of Modern Nationalism* (New York: Richard R. Smith, 1931), 55.

14. Quoted in Hans Kohn, *Making of the Modern French Mind* (New York: D. Van Nostrand, 1955), 17.

15. Quoted in Christopher Dawson, *The Gods of Revolution* (New York: New York University Press, 1972), 83.

Chapter 12

The Industrial Revolution: The Transformation of Society

- **Britain First**
- **Society Transformed**
- **The Rise of Reform in Britain**
- **Responses to Industrialization**
- **Industrialism in Perspective**

Focus Questions

1. What were the causes of the Industrial Revolution? Why did it begin in Britain?
2. How did the Industrial Revolution transform social structure?
3. How did the Industrial Revolution affect the middle class? Laborers?
4. Why are Saint-Simon, Fourier, and Owen regarded as early socialists? Do any of their ideas appeal to you?
5. The Industrial Revolution was a principal force in the shaping of the modern world. Discuss this statement.

*I*n the last part of the eighteenth century, as a revolution for liberty and equality swept across France and sent shock waves through Europe, a different kind of revolution—a revolution in industry—was transforming life in Great Britain. In the nineteenth century, the Industrial Revolution spread to the United States

ARPL/Topham/The Image Works.

WOMAN AT HARGREAVES'S SPINNING JENNY. The cotton textile trade was one of the first to be mechanized. In cottage industries, the whole family contributed to the making of thread and cloth. James Hargreaves's spinning jenny, one of the early inventions made by the workers themselves, was an adaptation of his wife's thread-spinning tool.

and to the European continent. Today, it encompasses virtually the entire world; everywhere the drive to substitute machines for human labor continues at a rapid pace.

After 1760, dramatic changes occurred in Britain in the way goods were produced and labor organized. New forms of power, particularly steam, replaced animal strength and human muscle. Better ways of obtaining and using raw materials were discovered, and a new way of organizing production and workers—the factory—came into use. In the nineteenth century, technology moved from triumph to triumph. The resulting explosion in economic production and productivity transformed society.

Industrial development did not proceed at the same pace everywhere. The changes began in England in the mid-1700s but moved slowly in France until the 1840s. Committed to traditional forms of production, French artisans resisted working in factories. In the German states, the lack of political unity slowed the growth of industrialization until the 1840s. The sharp economic divisions between north and south, the comparative lack of natural resources, and Italy's slow political unification hampered industrialization. ❖

BRITAIN FIRST

Britain possessed several advantages that enabled it to take the lead in industrialization. Large, easily developed supplies of coal and iron had given the British a long tradition of metallurgy and mining. In the early stages of industrialization, Britain's river transportation system was supplemented by canals and toll roads (turnpikes), which private entrepreneurs financed and built for profit. In addition, the enclosure movement provided factories with a labor pool. During the eighteenth century, great landlords enclosed, or fenced off and claimed as their own, land formerly used in common by villagers for grazing farm animals. Once the peasants were gone, lords could bring this land under cultivation for their own private gain. No longer able to earn a living from the land, these

M'CORMICK'S AMERICAN REAPING MACHINE.

© Mary Evans Picture Library/The Image Works.

THE AGRICULTURAL REVOLUTION: THE MCCORMICK REAPER. Harvesting grain with a horse-drawn machine released great numbers of laborers from farms to work in factories or cities. The great demand for labor may explain, in part, the constant search for and investment in mechanical devices for farm and factory in the United States, a major food exporter even today.

dispossessed farmers sought work in emerging factories.

Britain also had capital available for investment in new industries. These funds came from wealthy landowners and merchants who had grown rich through commerce, including the slave trade. Interest rates on loans fell in the eighteenth century, stimulating investment, which was aided by an effective banking system. Britain's expanding middle class provided a home market for emerging industries. So, too, did its overseas colonies, which also supplied raw materials—particularly cotton, needed for the developing textile industry. Exports to the American colonies (and later the young United States) and the West Indies rose dramatically in the last part of the eighteenth century. A vigorous spirit of enterprise and the opportunity for men of ability to rise from common origins to riches and fame also help explain the growth of industrialization.

Finally, two European cultural traditions in which Britain shared played crucial roles in the rise of industrialism. One was individualism, which had its roots in both the Renaissance and the Reformation; during the era of the commercial revolution, it manifested itself in hard-driving, ambitious merchants and bankers. This spirit of individualism, combined with the wide latitude states gave to private economic activity, fostered the development of dynamic capitalist entrepreneurs. The second cultural tradition promoting industrialization was the high value Westerners placed on the rational understanding and control of nature. Both individualism and the tradition of reason, concludes historian David S. Landes, "gave Europe a tremendous advantage in the invention and adoption of new technology. The will to mastery, the rational approach to problems that we call scientific method, the competition for wealth and power—together these broke down the resistance of inherited ways and made change a positive good."[1]

Changes in Technology

The Cotton Industry. The unprecedented technological breakthroughs in eighteenth-century Britain were the immediate cause of the Industrial Revolution. Expanding markets, both at home and abroad, provided the impetus for finding better and faster methods of manufacturing. Both inventors and investors recognized that machines that increased productivity and reduced costs held the promise of considerable financial gain. Long the home of an important wool trade, Britain in the eighteenth century jumped ahead in the production of cotton, the industry that first showed the possibility of unprecedented growth rates. British cotton production expanded tenfold between 1760 and 1785, and another tenfold between 1785 and 1825. A series of inventions revolutionized the industry and drastically altered the social conditions of the work.

In 1733, long before the expansion started, a simple invention—John Kay's flying shuttle—made it possible for weavers to double their output. The flying shuttle enabled weavers to produce faster than spinners could spin—until James Hargreaves's spinning jenny, perfected by 1768, allowed an operator to work several spindles at once, powered only by human energy. Within five years, Richard Arkwright's water frame spinning machine could be powered by water or animals, and Samuel Crompton's spinning mule (1779) powered many spindles, first by human and later by animal and water energy. These changes improved spinning productivity so much that it caused bottlenecks in weaving until Edmund Cartwright developed a power loom in 1785.* To the end of the century, there was a race to speed up the spinning part of the process and then the

weaving part by applying water power to looms or new, larger devices to the spinning jenny.

Arkwright's water frame made it more efficient to bring many workers together, rather than sending work out to individuals in their own homes. This development was the beginning of the factory system, which within a generation would revolutionize the conditions of labor. Because water power drove these early machines, mills were located near rivers and streams. Towns thus grew up where machinery could be powered by water; the factory system concentrated laborers and their families near the factories.

The Steam Engine. James Watt, a Scottish engineer, developed the steam engine in the 1760s. A loom powered by steam could produce seven times as much cloth as a hand loom. Because steam engines ran on coal or wood, not water power, they allowed greater flexibility in locating textile mills. Factories were no longer restricted to the power supplied by a river or a stream or to the space available beside flowing water; they could be built anywhere. With steam, the whole pattern of work changed because weaker, younger, and less skilled workers could be taught the few simple tasks necessary to tend the machine. The employment of female and child labor was a major social change.

The Iron Industry. Although steam power allowed employers to hire weaker people to operate machinery, it required machines made of stronger metal to withstand the forces generated by the stronger power source. By the 1780s, trial and error had perfected the production of wrought iron, which became the most widely

---

*Technological developments in America helped to meet the growing demand for raw cotton. Eli Whitney's cotton gin (1793) removed the seeds from raw cotton quickly and cheaply, leading farmers and plantation owners to devote more land to cotton. Within a generation, more laborers were required for the fields and fewer to process the cotton. The increased demand for slave labor had far-reaching repercussions.

used metal until steel began to be cheaply produced in the 1860s.

The iron industry made great demands on the coal mines to fuel its furnaces. Because steam engines enabled miners to pump water from the mines more efficiently and at a much deeper level, rich veins in existing mines became accessible for the first time. The greater productivity in coal allowed the continued improvement of iron smelting. Then, in 1856, Henry Bessemer developed a process for converting pig iron into steel by speedily removing the impurities in the iron. In the 1860s, William Siemens and the brothers Pierre and Émile Martin developed the open-hearth process, which could handle much greater amounts of metal than Bessemer's converter. Steel became so cheap to produce that it quickly replaced iron in industry because of its greater tensile strength and durability.

Transportation. The steam engine and iron and steel brought a new era in transport. As machines speeded up factory production, methods of transportation also improved. In 1830, the first railway line was built in England, connecting Manchester and Liverpool; this sparked an age of railway building throughout much of the world. Shipping changed radically with the use of vessels without sails, which had greater tonnage capacity.

SOCIETY TRANSFORMED

The innovations in agricultural production, business organization, and technology had revolutionary consequences for society, economics, and politics. People were drawn from the countryside into cities, and traditional ways of life changed. Much of the old life persisted, however, particularly during the first half of the nineteenth century. Landed property was still the principal form of wealth, and large landowners continued to exercise political power. From England to Russia, families of landed wealth (often the old noble

RAILROAD LINE FROM NUREMBERG TO FURTH. The spectacle of the arrival and departure of the train attracts townspeople of all classes. Central Europe followed England and France in railroad mania.

Primary Source

James Phillips Kay: Moral and Physical Dissipation

In 1832 James Phillips Kay, a physician, published a pamphlet describing the moral and physical condition of the working class in Manchester. His study, excerpted below, provided additional evidence of the painful effects industrialization had on factory workers and their families.

The township of Manchester chiefly consists of dense masses of houses, inhabited by the population engaged in the great manufactories of the cotton trade. . . . Prolonged and exhausting labour, continued from day to day, and from year to year, is not calculated to develop the intellectual or moral faculties of man. [The factory worker is subject to the] dull routine of a ceaseless drudgery, in which the same mechanical process is incessantly repeated. . . .

To condemn man to such severity of toil is, in some measure, to cultivate in him the habits of an animal. . . . He neglects the comforts and delicacies of life. He lives in squalid wretchedness, on meagre food, and expends his superfluous gains in debauchery. . . .

[T]he population. . . . is crowded into one dense mass, in cottages separated by narrow, unpaved, and almost pestilential streets; in an atmosphere loaded with the smoke and exhalations of a large manufacturing city. The operatives are congregated in rooms and workshops during twelve hours in the day, in an enervating, heated atmosphere, which is frequently loaded with dust or filaments of cotton. . . . [Their work] absorbs their attention, and unremittingly employs their physical energies. They are drudges who watch the movements, and assist the operations, of a [machine] . . . ever unconscious of fatigue. The persevering labour of the operative must rival the mathematical precision . . . of the machine.

Hence, besides the total abstraction of every moral and intellectual stimulus—the absence of variety—[and] banishment from the grateful air and the cheering influences of light, the physical energies are exhausted by incessant toil, and imperfect nutrition. Having been subjected to the prolonged labour of an animal—his physical energy wasted—his mind in supine inaction—the artisan has neither moral dignity nor intellectual nor organic strength to resist the seductions of [the pursuit of bodily pleasures] . . . Domestic economy is neglected, domestic comforts are unknown. A meal of the coarsest food is prepared with heedless haste, and devoured with equal precipitation. Home has no other relation to him than that of shelter. . . . Himself impotent of all the distinguishing aims of his species, he sinks into sensual sloth, or revels in more degrading licentiousness. His house is ill furnished, uncleanly, often ill ventilated, perhaps damp; his food, from want of forethought and domestic economy, is meagre and innutritious; he is debilitated. . . .

The absence of religious feeling, the neglect of all religious ordinances, we conceive to afford substantive evidence of so great a moral degradation of the community, as generally to ensure a concomitant civic debasement. . . .

Question for Analysis

1. What is Doctor Kay's description of the mental and physical health of a worker in a Manchester cotton mill?

James Phillips Kay, M.D., *Moral and Physical Condition of the Working Classes Employed in the Cotton Manufacture in Manchester* (London: James Ridgway, 1832), pp. 6–8, 10–11, 39.

families) still constituted the social elite. European society remained overwhelmingly rural; as late as the midcentury, only England was half urban. Nevertheless, contemporaries were so overwhelmed by industrialization that they saw it as a sudden and complete break with the past: the shattering of traditional moral and social patterns.

Cities grew in number, size, and population as a result of industrialization. For example, between 1801 and 1851, the population of Birmingham rose from 73,000 to 250,000 and that of Liverpool from 77,000 to 400,000. Industrial cities expanded rapidly, without planning or much regulation by local or national government. So much growth with so little planning or control led to cities with little sanitation, no lighting, wretched housing, poor transportation, and little security.

The poor lived in houses located as close to the factories as possible. The houses were several stories high and built in rows close to each other. Sometimes a whole family huddled together in one room or even shared a room with another family. Open sewers, polluted rivers, factory smoke, and filthy streets allowed disease to spread. In Britain, about twenty-six out of every one hundred children died before the age of five. Almost universally, those who wrote about industrial cities—England's Manchester, Leeds, and Liverpool and France's Lyons—described the stench, the filth, the inhumane crowding, the poverty, the crime, and the immorality.

Changes in Social Structure

The Industrial Revolution destroyed forever the old division of society into clergy, nobility, and commoners. The development of industry and commerce caused a corresponding development of the bourgeoisie, a middle class comprising people of common birth who engaged in trade and other capitalist ventures. The wealthiest bourgeois were bankers, factory and mine owners, and merchants, but the middle class also included shopkeepers, managers, lawyers, and doctors. The virtues of work, thrift, ambition, and prudent behavior characterized the middle class as a whole, as did the perversion of these virtues into materialism, selfishness, callousness, and smugness.

From the eighteenth century on, as industry and commerce developed, the middle class grew in size, first in England and then throughout Western Europe. During the eighteenth and nineteenth centuries, the middle class struggled against the entrenched aristocracy to end political, economic, and social discrimination. By the end of the nineteenth century, bourgeois politicians held the highest offices in much of Western Europe and shared authority with aristocrats, whose birth no longer guaranteed them the only political and social power in the nation. As industrial wealth grew more important, the middle class became more influential. Its wealthy members also tended to imitate the aristocracy: it was common throughout Europe for rich bourgeois to spend fortunes buying great estates and emulating aristocratic manners and pleasures.

Industrialization may have reduced some barriers between the landed elites and the middle class, but it sharpened the distinctions between the middle class and the laboring class. Like the middle class, the lower class encompassed different economic levels: rural laborers, miners, and city workers. Many gradations existed among city workers, from artisans to factory workers and servants. Factory workers were the newest and most rapidly growing social group; at midcentury, however, they did not constitute most of the laboring people in any major city. For example, as late as 1890, they made up only one-sixth of London's population.

The artisans were the largest group of workers in the cities for the first half of the nineteenth century, and in some places for much longer than that. They worked in construction, printing, small tailoring or dressmaking establishments, food preparation and processing, and crafts producing such luxury items as furniture, jewelry, lace, and velvet. Artisans were distinct from factory workers; their technical skills were difficult to learn, and traditionally their crafts were acquired in guilds, which still functioned as both social and economic organizations. Artisans were usually educated (they could read and write), lived in one city or village for generations, and maintained stable families, often securing places for their children in their craft. As the Industrial Revolution progressed, however, they found it hard to compete with cheap, factory-produced goods, and their livelihoods were threatened.

© Hulton-Deutsch Collection/CORBIS.

LONDON ROW HOUSES. This painting by the French artist Gustave Doré depicts the overcrowded and unsanitary conditions in industrial London. Workers and their families lived in row houses, each just one room wide with a tiny yard in back.

Servants were especially numerous in capital cities. In the first half of the nineteenth century in cities like Paris and London, where the number of factories was not great, there were more servants than factory workers. Servants usually had some education. If they married and had a family, they taught their children to read and write and sometimes to observe the manners and values of the household in which the parent had worked.

Working-Class Life

Usually, factory workers were recent arrivals from agricultural areas, where they had been driven off the land. They frequently moved to the city without their families, leaving them behind until they could afford to support them in town. These people entered rapidly growing industries, where

long hours—sometimes fifteen a day—were not unusual. Farming had meant long hours, too, as had the various forms of labor for piecework rates in the home, but the pace of the machine, the dull routine, and dangerous conditions in factories and mines made work even more oppressive. Miners, for example, labored under the hazards of cave-ins, explosions, and deadly gas fumes. Deep beneath the earth's surface, life was dark, cold, wet, and tenuous. Their bodies stunted and twisted, their lungs wrecked, miners toiled their lives away in "the pits."

Sometimes, compared with their lives in the country, the factory workers' standard of living rose, particularly if the whole family found work; the pay for a family might be better than they could have earned for agricultural labor. But working conditions were terrible, as were living conditions. The factories were dirty, oppressively

ENGRAVING FROM THE *ILLUSTRATED TIMES,* 1859. As unemployed workers flooded into the great cities of Europe, homelessness became a pressing social problem. To keep dry and warm, homeless men sometimes slept in coffins made for the living and lined up in a factory or prisonlike building. These facilities were charitable institutions—not the poor-law workhouses—but they too reflected the common belief of the day that poverty was the fault of the poor, who should learn to help themselves.

hot, unventilated, and frequently dangerous. Workers toiled long hours, were fined for mistakes and even for accidents, were fired at the will of the employer or foreman, and were laid off during slowdowns. They often lived in overcrowded and dirty housing. If they were unmarried or had left their family in the country, they often lived in barracks with other members of their sex. If they lost their jobs, they also lost their shelter.

In the villages they had left, they had been poor, but they were socially connected to family, church, and even local landlords. But in the cities, factory workers labored in plants with twenty to a hundred workers and had little contact with their employers. Instead, they were pushed by foremen to work hard and efficiently to keep up with the machines. Workers had little time on the job to socialize with others; they were fined for talking to one another, for lateness, and for many petty infringements. Lacking organization, a sense

of comradeship, education, and experience of city life, factory workers found little comfort when times were hard.

Workers often developed a life around the pub, the café, or some similar gathering place, where there were drinks and games and the gossip and news of the day. On Sundays, their one day off, workers drank and danced; absenteeism was so great on Monday that the day was called "holy Monday." Both workers and reformers denounced gin-drinking and urged temperance. Social organizations grew up around the workers' sporting games. In these and other ways, workers developed a culture of their own—a culture that was misunderstood and often deplored by middle-class reformers.

Many contemporaries felt that the poor—those who were so unfortunate that they needed the assistance of others—were growing in numbers, that their condition was woeful, and that it had actually deteriorated in the midst of increased wealth. If machines could produce so much wealth and so many products, then why, social observers wondered, were there so many poor people? Parliamentary reports and investigations of civic-minded citizens documented the suffering for all to read.

Many reformers believed that the only hope for the workers lay in unified action through trade unions. In England and Western Europe, trade unions grew even when they were illegal. Unions made some headway in protecting their members from unemployment and dangerous working conditions, but strikes were rarely successful. The general public, which was imbued with individualist and laissez-faire principles, saw strikes as an attack on the businessman's right to carry on trade. Not until the 1870s and 1880s was widespread discontent expressed by militant trade unions. In the early stages of industrialization, most workers experienced periods of acute distress, but historians generally conclude that the standard of living slowly improved and take an optimistic view of the long-term effects of industrialization.

THE RISE OF REFORM IN BRITAIN

Although it was the freest state in Europe in the early decades of the nineteenth century, Britain was far from democratic. A constitutional monarchy, with many limits on the powers of king and state, Britain was nonetheless dominated by landed aristocrats who controlled both the House of Lords and the House of Commons—the House of Lords because they constituted its membership and the House of Commons because they patronized or sponsored men favorable to their interests. The vast majority of people, from the middle class as well as from the working class, could not vote. Many towns continued to be governed by corrupt groups. New industrial towns were not allowed to elect representatives to Parliament; often they lacked a town organization and could not even govern themselves effectively.

The social separation of noble and commoner was not as rigid in Britain as on the Continent. Younger sons of aristocrats did not inherit titles and were therefore obliged to make careers in law, business, the military, and the church. The upper and middle classes mingled much more freely than on the Continent, and the wealthiest merchants tended to buy lands, titles, and husbands for their daughters. However, Parliament, the courts, local government, the established Anglican Church, and the monarchy were all part of a social and political system dominated by aristocratic interests and values. This domination persisted despite the vast changes in social and economic structure that had taken place in the process of industrialization during the second half of the eighteenth century.

Some members of Parliament urged timely reforms. In 1828, Parliament repealed a seventeenth-century act that in effect barred Nonconformists (non-Anglican Protestants) from government positions and from universities; the following year, Catholics gained the right to sit in Parliament. In 1833, slavery was abolished within the British Empire. (The British slave trade had been abolished earlier.) The Municipal Corporations Act (1835) granted towns and cities greater authority over their affairs. This measure created town and city governments that could, if they wished, begin to solve some of the problems of urbanization and industrialization. These municipal corporations could institute reforms such as sanitation, which Parliament encouraged by passing the first Public Health Act in 1848.

Increasingly, reform centered on extending suffrage and enfranchising the new industrial towns. Middle-class men, and even workers, hoped to gain the right to vote. Because of population shifts, some sparsely populated regions—called rotten boroughs—sent representatives to the House of Commons, while many densely populated factory towns had little or no representation. Often a single important landowner controlled many seats in the Commons. Voting was public, which allowed intimidation, and candidates frequently tried to influence voters with drinks, food, and even money.

Intense and bitter feelings built up during the campaign for the Reform Bill of 1832. The House of Commons passed the bill to extend the suffrage by some two hundred thousand, almost double the number who were then entitled to vote. The House of Lords, however, refused to pass the bill. There were riots and strikes in many cities, and mass meetings, both of workers and of middle-class people, took place all over the country. King William IV (1830–1837) became convinced, along with many politicians, that the situation was potentially revolutionary. To defuse it, he threatened to increase the number of the bill's supporters in the House of Lords by creating new peers. This threat brought reluctant peers into line, and the bill was passed. The Reform Act of 1832 extended the suffrage to the middle class and made the House of Commons more representative. The rotten boroughs lost their seats, which were granted to towns. However, because there were high property qualifications, workers did not gain the right to vote.

Workers did obtain some relief when humanitarians pressured Parliament to pass the Factory Act (1833), which legislated that no child under thirteen could work more than nine hours a day and that no one aged thirteen to eighteen could work more than sixty-nine hours a week. The act also provided some inspectors to investigate infractions and punish offenders. That same year, Parliament also banned children under ten from the mines. The Factory Act of 1847 stipulated that boys under eighteen and women could work no more than ten hours a day in factories. At first, workers resented the prohibition of child labor, since their family income would be greatly reduced if their children could not work, but they gradually came to approve of this law. The ten-hour day for adult male workers was not enacted until 1874.

The Chartist reform movement, whose adherents came from the ranks of both intellectual radicals and workers, pressed for political, not economic, reforms. During the 1830s and 1840s, the Chartists agitated for democratic measures such as universal manhood suffrage, the secret ballot, salaries and the abolition of property qualifications for members of Parliament, and annual meetings of Parliament.

The last political effort by the Chartists was led by Feargus O'Connor, a charismatic Irishman who organized a mass demonstration to present a huge petition of demands to Parliament in 1848. The cabinet ignored the great "People's Charter," which had signatures of at least two million names, and the movement died out. But the Chartist platform remained the democratic reform program for the rest of the century, long after the death of Chartism itself at midcentury. All of the Chartists' demands, except for annual elections for members of Parliament, were eventually realized.

At the beginning of the nineteenth century, elementary education in Britain was managed by private individuals and church organizations. Schools were financed by contributions, grants, and fees paid by students. The government neither financed nor promoted education. As a result, very few poor children attended school. Indeed, many government officials feared that educating the poor would incite unrest. If the lower classes read publications attacking Christianity and challenging authority, they would become insolent to their superiors; education would lead them to reject their rank in society. However, many Britons, inheriting the Enlightenment's confidence in education, favored schooling for the poor. In 1833, Parliament began to allocate small sums for elementary education. These funds were inadequate; in 1869, only about half of all children of school age attended school. The Education Act of 1870 gave local governments the power to establish elementary schools. By 1891, these schools were free and attendance was required.

Many workers and democratic leaning liberals believed that the only hope for their class lay in unified action through trade unions. At first, Parliament fought the unions, passing the Combination Acts (1799–1800), which made unions illegal. In 1825, Parliament allowed workers to unionize but forbade them to strike. Unions made some headway in protecting their members from unemployment and dangerous working conditions, but strikes (which remained officially illegal until 1875) were rarely successful and were often suppressed by force.

Unlike the Continental states, England avoided revolution. British politicians thought that it was because they had made timely reforms in the 1830s and 1840s. The political experience of the first half of the nineteenth century laid the foundation for British parliamentary practices, which came to be the model of liberal, progressive, and stable politics. Britain was the symbol for all those who argued for reform rather than revolution.

RESPONSES TO INDUSTRIALIZATION

The problems created by rapid industrialization profoundly influenced political and social thought. Liberalism, which began as an attempt to safeguard individual rights from oppressive state authority, now had to confront an unanticipated problem: the distress caused by rapid industrialization and urbanization. Also responding to this ordeal was a new group of thinkers, called socialists.

Liberalism

Adopting the laissez-faire theory of Adam Smith, liberals* maintained that a free economy, in which private enterprise would be unimpeded by government regulations, was as important as political freedom to the well-being of the individual and the community. When people acted from self-interest, liberals said, they worked harder and achieved more; self-interest and natural competitive impulses spurred economic activity and ensured the production of more and better goods at the lowest possible price, benefitting the entire nation. For this reason, the government must neither block free competition nor deprive individuals of their property, which was their incentive to work hard and efficiently.

Convinced that individuals were responsible for their own misfortunes, liberals were often unmoved by the misery of the poor. Indeed, they used the principle of laissez-faire—that government should not interfere with the natural laws of supply and demand—to justify their opposition to humanitarian legislation intended to alleviate the suffering of the factory workers. These liberals regarded such social reforms as unwarranted and dangerous meddling with the natural law of supply and demand.

They drew comfort from the theory advanced by Thomas Malthus (1766–1834) in his *Essay on the Principle of Population* (1798), which supported laissez-faire economics. Malthus asserted that population always grows at a faster rate than the food supply; consequently, government programs to aid the poor and provide higher wages would only encourage larger families and thus perpetuate poverty. Malthus seemed to supply "scientific" justification for opposing state action to help the poor. Poverty, argued Malthusians, was not the fault of factory owners. It was an iron law of nature—the result of population pressure on resources—and could not be eliminated by state policies. According to Malthus, the state could not ameliorate the poor's misery; "the means of redress," he said, "are in their own hands, and in the hands of no other persons whatever."[4] This "means of redress" would be a lowering of the birthrate through late marriages and chastity, but Malthus believed that the poor lacked the self-discipline to refrain from

sexual activity. When they received higher wages, they had more children, thereby upsetting the population–resource balance and bringing misery to themselves and others.

A fellow economist, David Ricardo (1772–1823), gave support to Malthus's gloomy outlook. Wages, he said, tended to remain at the minimum needed to maintain workers. Higher wages encouraged workers to have more children, causing an increase in the labor supply, and greater competition for jobs would then force down wages. Ricardo's disciples made his law inflexible. This "iron law of wages" meant bleak prospects for the working poor. Many workers felt that the new science of economics offered them little hope. They argued that the liberals were concerned only with their class and national interests and that they were callous and apathetic toward the sufferings of the poor.

Liberals of the early nineteenth century saw poverty and suffering as part of the natural order and beyond the scope of government. They feared that state intervention in the economy to redress social ills would disrupt the free market, threatening personal liberty and hindering social well-being. In time, however, the liberals modified their position, allowing for government action to protect the poor and the powerless against the economy's ravages.

Early Socialism

Reformers called utopian socialists argued that the liberals' concern for individual freedom and equality had little impact on the poverty, oppression, and gross inequality of wealth that plagued modern society. Liberal ideals, socialists claimed, protected the person and property of the wealthy, while the majority was mired in poverty and helplessness. Asserting that the liberals' doctrine of individualism degenerated into selfish egoism, which harmed community life, socialists demanded the creation of a new society based on cooperation rather than competition. Reflecting the spirit of the Enlightenment and the French Revolution, socialists, like liberals, denounced the status quo for perpetuating injustice and held that people could create a better world. Like liberals, too, they placed the highest value on a rational analysis of society and on transforming society in line with scientifically valid premises whose truth

*See also the following chapter.

rational people could grasp. Socialists believed that they had discerned a pattern in human society that, if properly understood and acted upon, would lead men and women to an earthly salvation. Thus, utopian socialists were also romantics, for they dreamed of a new social order, a future utopia, where each individual could find happiness and fulfillment. Although they sought to replace the existing social order with a more just arrangement, these early socialists, unlike Karl Marx, did not advocate class warfare. Rather, they aspired to create a new harmonious social order that would reconcile different classes.

Saint-Simon. Henri Comte de Saint-Simon (1760–1825) renounced his title during the French Revolution and enthusiastically preached the opportunity to create a new society. His mission, he believed, was to set society right by instilling an understanding of the new age that science and industry were shaping. He argued that just as Christianity had provided social unity and stability during the Middle Ages, so scientific knowledge would bind the society of his time. The scientists, industrialists, bankers, artists, and writers would replace the clergy and the aristocracy as the social elite and would harness technology for the betterment of humanity. Saint-Simon's disciples championed efforts to build great railway and canal systems, including the Suez and Panama Canals. His vision of a scientifically organized society led by trained experts was a powerful force among intellectuals in the nineteenth century.

Fourier. Another early French socialist, Charles Fourier (1772–1837), believed that society conflicted with the natural needs of human beings and that this tension was responsible for human misery. Only the reorganization of society so that it would satisfy people's desire for pleasure and contentment would end that misery. Fourier sought to create small communities that would let men and women enjoy life's simple pleasures.

These communities of about sixteen hundred people, called *phalansteries,* would be organized according to the unchanging needs of human nature. All the people would work at tasks that interested them and would produce things that brought them and others pleasure. Fourier understood that specialization, with its deadening routine, bred boredom and alienation from work and life. In the phalansteries, money and goods would not be equally distributed; those with special skills and responsibilities would be rewarded accordingly, a system that conformed to nature because people have a natural desire to be rewarded.

Fourier thought that marriage distorted the natures of both men and women, since monogamy restricted their sexual needs and narrowed the scope of their lives to just the family, depriving them of greater community involvement. Because married women had to devote all their strength and time to household and children, they had no time or energy left to enjoy life's pleasures. Fourier did not call for the abolition of the family, but he did hope that it would disappear of its own accord as society adjusted to his theories. Men and women would find new ways of fulfilling themselves sexually, and the community would be organized so that it could care for the children. Fourier's ideas found some acceptance in the United States, where in the 1840s at least twenty-nine communities were founded on Fourierist principles. None, however, lasted more than five or six years.

Owen. In 1799, Robert Owen (1771–1858) became part owner and manager of the New Lanark cotton mills in Scotland. Distressed by the widespread mistreatment of workers, Owen resolved to improve the lives of his employees and show that it was possible to do so without destroying profits. He raised wages, upgraded working conditions, refused to hire children under ten, and provided workers with neat homes, food, and clothing, all at reasonable prices. He set up schools for children and for adults. In every way, he demonstrated his belief that healthier, happier workers produced more than the less fortunate ones. Visitors came from all over Europe to see Owen's factories.

Just like many philosophes, Owen was convinced that the environment was the principal shaper of character—that the ignorance, alcoholism, and crime of the poor derived from bad living conditions. Public education and factory reform, said Owen, would make better citizens of the poor. Owen came to believe that the entire social and economic order must be replaced by a new system based on harmonious group living rather than on competition. He established a model community at New Harmony, Indiana, but it was short-lived.

INDUSTRIALISM IN PERSPECTIVE

Like the French Revolution, the Industrial Revolution helped to modernize Europe. Eventually, it transformed every facet of society. In preindustrial society—Europe in the mid-eighteenth century—agriculture was the dominant economic activity and peasants were the most numerous class. Peasant life centered on the family and the village, which country folk rarely left. The new rational and critical spirit associated with the Enlightenment hardly penetrated rural Europe; there, religious faith, clerical authority, and ancient superstition remained firmly entrenched.

Traditional society was predominantly rural. By the start of the nineteenth century, 20 percent of the population of Britain, France, and Holland lived in cities; in Russia, the figure was only 5 percent. Artisan manufacturing in small shops and trade for local markets were the foundations of the urban economy, although some cities did produce luxury goods for wider markets. Textile manufacturing was conducted through the putting-out system, in which wool was turned into cloth in private dwellings, usually the homes of peasants.

The richest and most powerful class was the aristocracy, whose wealth stemmed from land. Nobles dominated the countryside and enjoyed privileges protected by custom and law. Eighteenth-century aristocrats, like their medieval forebears, viewed society as a hierarchy, in which a person's position in life was determined by his or her inherited status. By championing the ideals of liberty and equality, the French Revolution undermined the traditional power structure of king, aristocracy, and clergy. French reformers further dismantled the religious and political pillars of traditional society by advocating the rational and secular outlook of the Enlightenment.

The Industrial Revolution transformed all areas of society. Eventually, agricultural villages and handicraft manufacturing were eclipsed in importance by cities and factories. In the society fashioned by industrialization and urbanization, aristocratic power and values declined; at the same time, the bourgeoisie increased in number, wealth, importance, and power. More and more, a person was judged by talent rather than by birth, and opportunities for upward social mobility expanded. The Industrial Revolution became a great force for democratization: during the nineteenth century, first the middle class and then the working class gained the vote. The Industrial Revolution also hastened the secularization of European life. In the cities, former villagers, separated from traditional communal ties, drifted away from their ancestral religion. In a world being reshaped by technology, industry, and science, Christian mysteries lost their force, and for many salvation became a remote concern. Modernization did not proceed everywhere at the same pace and with the same thoroughness. Generally, pre-modern social and institutional forms remained deeply entrenched in Eastern and Southern Europe, persisting well into the twentieth century.

Although the Industrial Revolution created many problems, some of which still endure, it was a great triumph. Ultimately, it made possible the highest standard of living in human history and created new opportunities for social advancement, political participation, and educational and cultural development. It also widened the gap between the West and the rest of the world in terms of science and technology. By 1900, Western states, aided by superior technology, extended their power over virtually the entire globe, completing the trend that had begun with the Age of Exploration.

NOTES

1. David S. Landes, *The Unbound Prometheus: Technological Change and Industrial Development in Western Europe from 1750 to the Present* (Cambridge, Mass.: Harvard University Press, 1969), 33.

2. Thomas Robert Malthus, *First Essay on Population,* reprinted for the Royal Economic Society (London: Macmillan, 1926), 17.

Chapter 13

Thought and Culture in the Early Nineteenth Century

- **Romanticism: A New Cultural Orientation**
- **German Idealism**
- **Conservatism: The Value of Tradition**
- **Liberalism: The Value of the Individual**
- **Nationalism: The Sacredness of the Nation**

Focus Questions

1. How was the Romantic Movement a reaction against the dominant ideas of the Enlightenment?
2. What was the impact of romanticism on European life?
3. What were the attitudes of conservatives and liberals toward the Enlightenment and the French Revolution?
4. What is the relationship between nationalism and liberalism? How do you explain nationalism's great appeal?

After the defeat of Napoleon, the traditional rulers of Europe, some of them just restored to power, were determined to protect themselves and society from future revolutions. As defenders of the status quo, they attacked the reformist spirit of the philosophes, which, they thought, had produced the French Revolution. In *conservatism*, which championed tradition over reason, hierarchy over equality, and the community over the individual, they found a philosophy to justify their assault on the Enlightenment and the Revolution.

But the forces unleashed by the Revolution had penetrated European consciousness too deeply to be eradicated. One of them was *liberalism,* which aimed to secure the liberty and equality proclaimed by the Revolution. Another was *nationalism,* which sought to free subject peoples and unify fragmented nations. Captivated by the dream to redeem humanity, idealistic youth and intellectuals joined in the revolutionary struggle for liberty and nationhood.

The postrevolutionary period also witnessed the flowering of a new cultural orientation. *Romanticism,* with its plea for the liberation of human emotions and the free expression of personality, challenged the Enlightenment stress on rationalism. Although primarily a literary and artistic movement, romanticism also permeated philosophy and political thought, particularly conservatism and nationalism. ❖

ROMANTICISM: A NEW CULTURAL ORIENTATION

The Romantic Movement, which began in the closing decades of the eighteenth century, dominated European cultural life in the first half of the nineteenth century. Most of Europe's leading cultural figures came under its influence. Among the exponents of romanticism were the poets Shelley, Wordsworth, Keats, and Byron in England; the novelist Victor Hugo and the Catholic novelist and essayist Chateaubriand in France; and the writers A. W. and Friedrich Schlegel, the dramatist and poet Schiller, and the philosopher Schelling in Germany. Caspar David Friedrich in Germany and John Constable in England expressed the romantic mood in art, and Beethoven, Schubert, Chopin, and Wagner expressed it in music.

Exalting Imagination and Feelings

Perhaps the central message of the romantics was that the imagination and emotions of the individual should determine the form and content of an artistic creation. This outlook ran counter to the

TRAVELER LOOKING OVER A SEA OF FOG, BY CASPAR DAVID FRIEDRICH. A prominent German romantic landscape painter, Friedrich frequently portrayed individuals lost in thought as they confronted fogs, clouds, stars, and other powerful and mysterious natural wonders.

rationalism of the Enlightenment, which itself had been a reaction against the otherworldly Christian orientation of the Middle Ages. The philosophes had attacked religion because it thwarted and distorted reason; romantic poets, philosophers, and artists now denounced the rationalism of the philosophes because it crushed the emotions and impeded creativity.

The philosophes, said the romantics, had turned flesh-and-blood human beings into soulless thinking machines. For human beings to be restored to their true nature, to become whole again, they must be emancipated from the tyranny of excessive intellectualizing; the feelings must be nurtured and expressed. Taking up one of Rousseau's ideas, romantics yearned to rediscover in the human soul the pristine freedom and insight that had been squashed by habits, values, rules, and standards imposed by civilization.

***Dante's Inferno: The Whirlwind of Lovers*, by William Blake (1757–1827).** A radical romantic painter and poet, Blake totally rejected the artistic conventions of the past. His religious and political beliefs were as unique as his art; he spent his life trying to convey tormented inward visions. A prolific illustrator, his imaginative genius was stimulated by great literature such as Dante's *Divine Comedy*.

Abstract reason and scientific knowledge, said the romantics, are insufficient guides to knowledge. They provide only general principles about nature and people; they cannot penetrate to what really matters—the uniqueness of each person, of each robin, of each tree, cloud, and lake. The philosophes had concentrated on people in general, focusing on the elements of human nature shared by all people. Romantics, on the other hand, emphasized human diversity and uniqueness—those traits that set one human being apart from others. Discover and express your true self, the romantics urged: play your own music; write your own poetry; paint your own vision of nature; live, love, and suffer in your own way.

Whereas the philosophes had asserted the mind's autonomy—its capacity to think for itself and not depend on authority—romantics gave primary importance to the autonomy of the personality—the individual's need and right to find and fulfill an inner self. To the philosophes, feelings were an obstacle to clear thinking, but to the romantics they were the essence of being human. People could not live by reason alone, said the romantics. They agreed with Rousseau, who wrote: "For us, to exist is to feel and our sensibility is incontestably prior to our reason."[1] For the romantics, reason was cold and dreary, and its understanding of people and life meager and inadequate. Reason could not grasp or express the complexities of human nature or the richness of human experience. By always dissecting and analyzing, by imposing deadening structure and form, and by demanding adherence to strict rules, reason crushed inspiration and creativity and barred true understanding. "The Reasoning Power in Man," wrote William Blake (1757–1827), the British poet, artist, and mystic, is "an Incrustation [scab] over my Immortal Spirit."[2]

The romantics saw spontaneous, unbounded feelings, rather than the constricted intellect, as the avenue to truth. By cultivating emotions, intuition, and the imagination, individuals could experience reality and discover their authentic selves. The romantics wanted people to feel and to experience— "To bathe in the Waters of Life," said Blake.[3] Consequently, they insisted that imaginative poets had a greater insight into life than analytical philosophers. "I am certain of nothing but of the holiness of the Heart's affections and the truth of Imagination," wrote John Keats (1795–1821). "O for a Life of Sensations rather than of Thoughts." [4]

The Enlightenment mind had been clear, critical, and controlled. It had adhered to standards of esthetics, thought to be universal, that had dominated European cultural life since the Renaissance. Romantic poets, artists, and musicians broke with these traditional styles and uniform rules—essentially those inherited from the classical tradition—and created new cultural forms and techniques. "We do not want either Greek or Roman Models," Blake declared, "but [should be] just & true to our own Imaginations."[5] Victor Hugo (1802–1885), the dominant figure among French romantics, urged in the Preface to his play *Cromwell*, "Freedom in art! . . . Let us take the hammer to the theories, the poetics [the analysis of poetry] and the systems."[6] The romantics felt deeply that one did not learn how to write poetry or paint pictures by following textbook rules, nor could one grasp the poet's or artist's intent by judging works according to fixed standards.

Only by trusting their own feelings could individuals attain their creative potential and achieve self-realization. Hence, the most beautiful works of art were not photographic imitations of nature but authentic and spontaneous expressions of the artist's feelings, fantasies, and dreams. It was the artist's inner voice that gave a work of art its supreme value. The romantics also explored the inner life of the mind, which Freud would later call the unconscious. It was this layer of the mind— the wellspring of creativity, mysterious, primitive, more elemental and more powerful than reason— that the romantics yearned to revitalize and release. Like Freud, some romantics had an intuitive awareness of the dark side of the unconscious. Buried there, they sensed, were our worst fears and most hideous desires.

Nature, God, History

The philosophes had viewed nature as a lifeless machine: a giant clock, all of whose parts worked together with precision and in perfect harmony. Nature's laws, operating with mathematical certainty, were uncovered by the methodology of science. To the romantics, nature was alive and suffused with God's presence. Nature stimulated the creative energies of the imagination; it taught human beings a higher form of knowledge. As William Wordsworth (1770–1850) wrote in his poem "The Tables Turned,"

> One impulse from a vernal wood
> [spring greenery]
> May teach you more of man,
> Of moral evil and of good,
> Than all the sages can.[7]

Regarding God as a great watchmaker—a detached observer of a self-operating mechanical universe—the philosophes tried to reduce religion to a series of scientific propositions. Many romantics, on the contrary, viewed God as an inspiring spiritual force and condemned the philosophes for weakening Christianity by submitting its dogmas to the test of reason. For the romantics, religion was not science and syllogism but a passionate and authentic expression of human nature. They called for acknowledgment of the individual as a spiritual being and for cultivation of the religious side of human nature. This appeal accorded with their goal of restoring the whole personality, which, they were convinced, had been fragmented and distorted by the philosophes' excessive emphasis on the intellect.

The philosophes and the romantics viewed the Middle Ages very differently as well. To the former, that period was a time of darkness, superstition, and fanaticism; surviving medieval institutions and traditions only barred progress. The romantics, on the other hand, revered the Middle Ages. To the romantic imagination, the Middle Ages abounded with spiritual sensitivity, Christian mysteries, heroic deeds, and social harmony.

The romantics also disagreed with the philosophes on their conception of history. For the philosophes, history served a didactic purpose by providing examples of human folly. Such knowledge helped people to prepare for a better future, and for that reason alone history was worth studying. To the romantics, a historical period, like an individual, was a unique entity with its own soul. They wanted the historian to portray and analyze the variety of nations, traditions, and institutions that constituted the historical experience, always recognizing what is particular and unique to a given time and place. The romantics' insistence on comprehending the specific details of history and culture within the context of the times is the foundation of modern historical scholarship.

Searching for universal principles, the philosophes had dismissed folk traditions as peasant superstitions and impediments to progress. The romantics, on the other hand, rebelling against the standardization of culture, saw native languages, songs, and legends as the unique creations of a people and the deepest expression of national feeling. The romantics regarded the legends, myths, and folk traditions of a people as the fount of poetry and art and the spiritual source of a people's cultural vitality, creativity, and identity. Consequently, they examined these earliest cultural expressions with awe and reverence. In this way, romanticism played a part in shaping modern nationalism.

The Impact of the Romantic Movement

The romantic revolt against the Enlightenment had an important and enduring impact on European history. By focusing on the creative capacities inherent in the emotions—intuition, instinct, passion, will, empathy—the romantics shed light on a side of human nature that the philosophes had often overlooked or undervalued. By encouraging personal freedom and diversity in art, music, and literature, they greatly enriched European cultural life. Future artists, writers, and musicians would proceed along the path opened by the romantics. Modern art, for example, owes much to the Romantic Movement's emphasis on the legitimacy of human feeling and

Lord Byron (1788–1824). One of the leading romantic poets, Byron created the "Byronic hero," a lonely and mysterious figure. His own short life exalted the emotions and the senses. He went to Greece in 1824 to aid the revolutionaries and died there from poor health.

its exploration of the hidden world of dreams and fantasies. Romantics were among the first to attack the emerging industrial capitalism for subordinating individuals to the requirements of the industrial process and treating them as mere things. By recognizing the distinctive qualities of historical periods, peoples, and cultures, they helped create the modern historical outlook. Because it valued a nation's past, romanticism also contributed to modern nationalism and conservatism.

However, the Romantic Movement had a potentially dangerous side: it served as background to the extreme nationalism of the twentieth century. As Ernst Cassirer has pointed out, the romantics "never meant to politicize but to 'poeticize' the world," and their deep respect for human individuality and national diversity was not compatible with Hitler's racial nationalism. Yet by waging their attack on reason with excessive zeal, the romantics undermined respect for the

the progress of the consciousness of Freedom . . . [It is] the absolute goal of history."[9]

According to Hegel, Spirit manifests itself in history through a dialectical confrontation between opposing ideas or forces; the struggle between one idea (thesis) and its adversary (antithesis) is evident in all spheres of human activity. This clash of opposites gains in intensity, eventually ending in a resolution (synthesis) that unifies and surpasses both opposing views. Thought and history thus enter a new and higher stage, that of synthesis, which, by absorbing the truths within both the thesis and the antithesis, achieves a higher level of truth and a higher stage of history. Soon this synthesis itself becomes a thesis that enters into another conflict with another opposing force; this conflict, too, is resolved by a still higher synthesis. Thus, the dynamic struggle between thesis and antithesis—sometimes expressed in revolutions and war, sometimes in art, religion, and philosophy—and its resolution into a synthesis accounts for movement in history. Or, in Hegelian language, Spirit is closer to realization: its rational essence is progressing from potentiality to actuality. The dialectic is the march of Spirit through human affairs. Historical change is often instituted by world-historical individuals who, unknown to themselves, are agents of Spirit in its progress through history. Since Hegel held that freedom is the essence of Spirit, it is through history that human beings progress toward consciousness of their own freedom. They become self-consciously aware of their own self-determination—their ability to regulate their lives rationally according to their own consciousness.

But for individual freedom to be realized, said Hegel, social and political institutions must be rationally determined and organized: that is, the will of the individual must be harmonized with the needs of the community. For Hegel, freedom is not a matter of securing abstract natural rights for the individual, the goal of the French Revolution. Rather, true freedom is attained only within the social group. Thus, in Hegel's view, human beings discover their essential character—their moral and spiritual potential—only as citizens of a cohesive political community. This view goes back to the city-states of ancient Greece, which Hegel admired. In the state's laws and institutions, which are manifestations of reason and the objectivization of Spirit, individuals find a basis for rationally determining their own lives. In this way, the private interests of citizens become one with the interests of the community.

For Hegel, Absolute Spirit, which is also Ultimate Reason, realizes itself in the state, the highest form of human association. The state joins fragmented individuals together into a community and substitutes a rule of justice for the rule of instincts. It permits individuals to live the ethical life and to develop their human potential. An individual cannot achieve these goals in isolation. Hegel's thought reveals a powerful undercurrent of statism: the exaltation of the state and the subordination of the individual to it. For Hegel, the national state was the embodiment of Universal Reason and the supreme achievement of Absolute Spirit.

German conservatives used Hegel's idea that existing institutions have a rational legitimacy to support their opposition to rapid change. Existing reality, even if it appears cruel and hateful, is the actualization of Absolute Spirit. Therefore, it is inherently necessary and rational and should not be altered.

Some of Hegel's followers, known as Young Hegelians, interpreted Hegel in a radical sense. They rejected his view that the Prussian state, or any German state, was the goal of world history, the realization of freedom. The Germany of their day, held the Young Hegelians, had not attained a harmony between the individual and society; it was not rationally organized and did not foster freedom. These Young Hegelians saw Hegel's philosophy as a means of radically altering the world to make existing society truly rational. The most important of the radical Young Hegelians was Karl Marx. Marx retained Hegel's overarching principle that history contains an inner logic, that it is an intelligible process, and that a dialectical struggle propels history from a lower to a higher stage (see Chapter 15).

CONSERVATISM: THE VALUE OF TRADITION

To the traditional rulers of Europe—kings, aristocrats, and clergy—the French Revolution was a great evil that had inflicted a near-fatal wound on civilization. Disgusted and frightened by the revolutionary violence, terror, and warfare,

Primary Source

Benjamin Constant: On the Limits of Popular Sovereignty

Benjamin Constant (1767–1830), a leading French liberal theorist, feared the danger posed to liberty by democratic revolutionaries like Robespierre and his fellow Jacobins, who would exercise unlimited authority to establish liberty. Constant embraced the principle of popular sovereignty (that government derives its legitimacy and authority from the people), but warned against the danger of unlimited popular sovereignty. Neither the people as a whole nor their delegated representatives, said Constant, can possess total authority over the lives of individuals. The following passage is taken from his book On the Sovereignty of the People, *published in 1815.*

When you establish that the sovereignty of the people is unlimited, you create and toss at random into human society a degree of power which is too large in itself, and which is bound to constitute an evil, in whatever hands it is placed. Entrust it to one man, to several, to all, you will still find that it is equally an evil. . . .

In a society founded upon the sovereignty of the people, it is certain that no individual, no class, are entitled to subject the rest to their particular will. But it is not true that society as a whole has unlimited authority over its members. . . .

There is, on the contrary, a part of human existence which by necessity remains individual and independent, and which is, by right, outside any [governmental authority]. Sovereignty has only a limited and relative existence. At the point where independence and individual existence begin, the jurisdiction of sovereignty ends. If society oversteps this line, it is as guilty as the despot who has, as his only title, his exterminating sword. . . .

When sovereignty is unlimited, there is no means of sheltering individuals from governments. . . .

This is what we must declare; this is the important truth, the eternal principle which we must establish.

No authority upon earth is unlimited, neither that of the people, nor that of the men who declare themselves their representatives. . . .

The citizens possess individual rights independently of all social and political authority, and any authority which violates these rights becomes illegitimate. The rights of the citizens are individual freedom, religious freedom, freedom of opinion, which includes the freedom to express oneself openly, the enjoyment of property, a guarantee against all arbitrary power. No authority can call these rights into question without destroying its own credentials. . . .

Let us now sum up the consequences of our principles. The sovereignty of the people is not unlimited: it is, on the contrary, circumscribed within the limits traced by justice and by the rights of individuals.

Questions for Analysis

1. What did Benjamin Constant mean by unlimited sovereignty? Why did he fear it?
2. Provide examples in American history when people protested that the government was interfering with their liberties.

Benjamin Constant Political Writings, translated and edited by Biancamaria Fontana (Cambridge: Cambridge University Press, 1988), pp. 176–177, 179–180, 182.

the traditional rulers sought to refute the philosophes' worldview, which had spawned the Revolution. To them, natural rights, equality, the goodness of man, and perpetual progress were perverse doctrines that had produced the Jacobin "assassins." In conservatism, they found a political philosophy to counter the Enlightenment ideology.

Edmund Burke's *Reflections on the Revolution in France* (1790) was instrumental in shaping conservative thought. Burke (1729–1797), an Anglo-Irish statesman and political theorist, wanted to warn his countrymen of the dangers inherent in the ideology of the revolutionaries. Written during the early and still moderate stage of the Revolution, Burke astutely predicted that it would end with civil war, terror, and the seizure of power by a military leader. To Burke, fanatics armed with pernicious principles—abstract ideas divorced from historical experience—had dragged France through the mire of revolution. Burke developed a coherent political philosophy that served as a counterweight to the ideology of the Enlightenment and the Revolution.

Hostility to the French Revolution

Entranced by the great discoveries in science, the philosophes and French reformers had believed that the human mind could also transform social institutions and ancient traditions according to rational models. Progress through reason became their faith. Dedicated to creating a new future, the revolutionaries abruptly dispensed with old habits, traditional authority, and familiar ways of thought. For them, these traditional ways were a form of bondage that stifled progress.

To the conservatives, who like the romantics venerated the past, this was supreme arrogance and wickedness. They regarded the revolutionaries as presumptuous men who recklessly severed society's links with ancient institutions and traditions and condemned venerable religious and moral beliefs as ignorance. By attacking time-honored ways, the revolutionaries had deprived French society of moral leadership and had opened the door to anarchy and terror. "You began ill," wrote Burke of the revolutionaries, "because you began by despising everything that belonged to you. . . . When ancient opinions and rules of life are taken away, the loss cannot possibly be estimated. From that moment we have no compass to govern us; nor can we know distinctly to what port we steer."[10]

The philosophes and French reformers had expressed unlimited confidence in the power of human reason to understand and to improve society. While appreciating human rational capacities, conservatives also recognized the limitations of reason. They saw the Revolution as a natural outgrowth of an arrogant Enlightenment philosophy that overvalued reason and sought to reshape society according to abstract principles. An overly critical spirit promotes discontent, fosters atheism, and undermines established authority.

Conservatives did not view human beings as good by nature. Human wickedness was not caused by a faulty environment, as the philosophes had proclaimed, but lay at the core of human nature, as Christianity taught. Evil was held in check not by reason, but by tried and tested institutions—monarchy, church, and aristocracy—traditions, and beliefs. Without these habits inherited from ancestors, said conservatives, sinful human nature threatened the social order.

Because monarchy, aristocracy, and the church had endured for centuries, argued the conservatives, they had worth. By despising and uprooting these ancient institutions, revolutionaries had hardened the people's hearts, perverted their morals, and caused them to commit terrible outrages upon one another and upon society. As conservatives saw it, revolutionaries had divorced people and society from their historical settings and reduced them to abstractions. They were fanatics who had destroyed time-honored patterns that seemed to conflict with their metaphysical theories. They had drawn up constitutions based on the unacceptable principle that government derives its power from the consent of the governed.

For conservatives, God and history were the only legitimate sources of political authority. States were not made; rather, they were an expression of the nation's moral, religious, and historical experience. No legitimate or sound constitution could be drawn up by a group assembled for that purpose. Scraps of paper with legal terminology and philosophical visions could not produce an effective government. Instead, a sound political system evolved gradually and inexplicably in response to circumstances.

The Quest for Social Stability

The liberal philosophy of the Enlightenment and the French Revolution started with the individual. The philosophes and the revolutionaries envisioned a society in which the individual was free and autonomous. Conservatives, on the other hand, began with the community, which they considered more important than the individual. They believed that society was not a mechanical arrangement of disconnected individuals but a living organism held together by centuries-old bonds. Individualism would imperil social stability, destroy obedience to law, and fragment society into self-seeking, isolated atoms. Whereas the philosophes had attacked Christianity for promoting superstition and fanaticism, conservatives saw religion as the basis of civil society. Without Christianity, they said, people become brutalized and civilization degenerates into anarchy. For this reason, they maintained that the guidance of education must be returned to religious authorities. Catholic conservatives, in particular, held that God had constituted the church and monarchy to check sinful human nature.

Conservatives viewed equality as another pernicious abstraction that contradicted all historical experience. For conservatives, society was naturally hierarchical, and they believed that some men, by virtue of their intelligence, education, wealth, and birth, were best qualified to rule and instruct the less able. They said that by denying the existence of a natural elite and uprooting the long-established and divinely ordained ruling elite, which had learned its art through experience, the revolutionaries had deprived society of effective leaders, brought internal disorder, and prepared the way for Napoleon's military despotism.

Conservatism pointed to a limitation of the Enlightenment. It showed that human beings and social relationships are far more complex than the philosophes had imagined. People do not always accept the rigorous logic of the philosopher and are not eager to break with ancient ways, however illogical those ways appear. They often find familiar customs and ancestral religions more satisfying guides to life than the blueprints of philosophers. The granite might of tradition remains an obstacle to all the visions of reformers. Conservative theorists warned that revolutionary violence in the pursuit of utopian dreams transforms politics into an ideological crusade that ends in terror and despotism. These warnings bore bitter fruit in the twentieth century.

LIBERALISM: THE VALUE OF THE INDIVIDUAL

The decades after 1815 saw a spectacular rise of the bourgeoisie. Talented and ambitious bankers, merchants, manufacturers, professionals, and officeholders wanted to break the stranglehold of the landed nobility—the traditional elite—on political power and social prestige. They also wanted to eliminate restrictions on the free pursuit of profits. The political philosophy of the bourgeoisie was most commonly liberalism. While conservatives sought to strengthen the foundations of traditional society, which had been severely shaken in the period of the French Revolution and Napoleon, liberals strove to alter the status quo and to realize the promise of the Enlightenment and the French Revolution.

The Sources of Liberalism

In the long view of Western civilization, liberalism is an extension and development of the democratic practices and rational outlook that originated in ancient Greece. Also flowing into the liberal tradition is Judeo-Christian respect for the worth and dignity of the individual endowed by God with freedom to make moral choices. But nineteenth-century liberalism had its immediate historical roots in seventeenth-century England. At that time, the struggle for religious toleration by English Protestant dissenters established the principle of freedom of conscience, which is easily translated into freedom of opinion and expression in all matters. The Glorious Revolution of 1688 set limits on the power of the English monarchy. At the same time, John Locke's natural rights philosophy declared that the individual was by nature entitled to freedom, and it justified revolutions against rulers who deprived citizens of their lives, liberty, or property.

The French philosophes helped to shape liberalism. From Montesquieu, liberals derived the theory of the separation of powers and of checks and balances—principles intended to guard against despotic government. The philosophes supported religious toleration and freedom of thought, expressed confidence in the capacity of the human mind to reform society, maintained that human beings are essentially good, and believed in the future progress of humanity—all fundamental principles of liberalism.

The American and French Revolutions were crucial phases in the history of liberalism. The Declaration of Independence gave expression to Locke's theory of natural rights, the Constitution of the United States incorporated Montesquieu's principles and demonstrated that people could create an effective government, and the Bill of Rights protected the person and rights of the individual. In destroying the special privileges of the aristocracy and opening careers to talent, the French National Assembly of 1789 had implemented the liberal ideal of equality under the law. It also drew up the Declaration of the Rights of Man and of the Citizen, which affirmed the dignity and rights of the individual, and a constitution that limited the king's power. Both revolutions explicitly called for the protection of property rights, another basic premise of liberalism.

Individual Liberty

The liberals' primary concern was the enhancement of individual liberty. They agreed with Kant that every person exists as an end in himself and not as an object to be used arbitrarily by others. If uncoerced by government and churches and properly educated, a person can develop into a good, productive, and self-directed human being.

Liberals rejected a legacy of the Middle Ages, the classification of an individual as a commoner or aristocrat on the basis of birth. They held that individuals were not born into a certain station in life but made their way through their own efforts. Taking their cue from the French Revolution, liberals called for an end to all privileges of the aristocracy.

In the tradition of the philosophes, liberals stressed the preeminence of reason as the basis of political life. Unfettered by ignorance and tyranny, the mind could eradicate evils that had burdened people for centuries and begin an age of free institutions and responsible citizens. For this reason, liberals supported the advancement of education.

Liberals attacked the state and other authorities that prevented the individual from exercising the right of free choice, interfered with the right of free expression, and blocked the individual's self-determination and self-development. They agreed with John Stuart Mill (1806–1873), the British philosopher, who declared that "over his own body and mind, the individual is sovereign. . . . that the only purpose for which power can be rightfully exercised over any member of a civilized community, against his will, is to prevent harm to others."[11]

To guard against the absolute and arbitrary authority of kings, liberals demanded written constitutions that granted freedom of speech, the press, and religion; freedom from arbitrary arrest; and the protection of property rights. To prevent the abuse of political authority, they called for a freely elected parliament and the distribution of power among the various branches of government. Liberals held that a government that derived its authority from the consent of the governed, as given in free elections, was least likely to violate individual freedom. A corollary of this principle was that the best government is one that governs least—that is, one that interferes as little as possible with the economic activities of its citizens and does not involve itself in their private lives or their beliefs.

Liberalism and Democracy

Many bourgeois liberals viewed with horror the democratic creed that all people should share in political power. To them, the participation of commoners in politics meant a vulgar form of despotism and the end of individual liberty. They saw the masses—uneducated, unpropertied, inexperienced, and impatient—as lacking both the ability and the temperament to maintain liberty and protect property.

Because bourgeois liberals feared that democracy could crush personal freedom as ruthlessly as any absolute monarch, they called for property requirements for voting and officeholding. They wanted political power to be concentrated in the hands of a safe and reliable—that is, a propertied and educated—middle class. Such a government would prevent revolution from below, a prospect that caused anxiety among bourgeois liberals.

To be sure, early nineteenth-century liberals engaged in revolutions, but their aims were always limited. Once they had destroyed absolute monarchy and gained a constitution and a parliament or a change of government, they quickly tried to end the revolution. When the fever of revolution spread to the masses, liberals either withdrew or turned counterrevolutionary, for they feared the stirrings of the multitude.

Although liberalism was the political philosophy of a middle class that was generally hostile to democracy, the essential ideals of democracy flowed logically from liberalism. Eventually, democracy became a later stage in the evolution of liberalism because the masses, their political power enhanced by the Industrial Revolution, pressed for greater social, political, and economic equality. Thus, by the early twentieth century, many European states had introduced universal suffrage, abandoned property requirements for office-holding, and improved conditions for workers.

The confidence of liberal-democrats was shaken in the twentieth century. Growing impatient, in turbulent times, with parliamentary procedures, people in some European countries gave their support to demagogues who promised swift and decisive action. They were willing to trade freedom for economic security, state authority, and national power. Liberalism is based on the assumption that human beings can and do respond to rational argument and that reason will prevail over base human feelings. Recent history shows that this may be an overly optimistic assessment of human nature.

NATIONALISM: THE SACREDNESS OF THE NATION

Nationalism is a conscious bond shared by a group of people who feel strongly attached to a particular land and who possess a common language, culture, and history, marked by shared glories and sufferings. Nationalists contend that one's highest loyalty and devotion should be given to the nation. They exhibit great pride in their people's history and traditions and often feel that their nation has been specially chosen by God or history. They assert that the nation—its culture and history—gives meaning to an individual's life and actions. Like a religion, nationalism provides the individual with a sense of community and with a cause worthy of self-sacrifice. Identifying with the nation's collective achievements and its past greatness enhances feelings of self-worth.

In an age when Christianity was in retreat, nationalism became the dominant spiritual force in nineteenth-century European life. Nationalism provided new beliefs, martyrs, and "holy" days that stimulated reverence; it offered membership in a community that satisfied the overwhelming psychological need of human beings for fellowship and identity. And nationalism gave a mission—the advancement of the nation—to which people could dedicate themselves.

The Emergence of Modern Nationalism

The essential components of modern nationalism emerged at the time of the French Revolution. The Revolution asserted the principle that sovereignty derived from the nation, from the people as a whole: the state was not the private possession of the ruler but the embodiment of the people's will. The nation-state was above king, church, estate, guild, or province; it superseded all other loyalties. The French people must view themselves not as subjects of the king, not as Bretons or Normans, not as nobles or bourgeois, but as citizens of a united fatherland, *la patrie*. These two ideas—that the people possess unlimited sovereignty and that they are united in a nation—were crucial in fashioning a nationalist outlook.

As the Revolution moved from the moderate to the radical stage, French nationalism intensified. In 1793 and 1794, when foreign invasion threatened the Republic, the Jacobins created a national army, demanded ever greater allegiance to and sacrifice for the nation, and called for the expansion of France's borders to the Alps and the Rhine. With unprecedented success, the Jacobins used every means—press, schoolroom, and rostrum—to instill a love of country, to forge a sense of national unity that would supersede attachment to local regions.

The Romantic Movement also awakened nationalist feelings. By examining the language, literature, and folkways of their people, romantic thinkers instilled a sense of national pride in their compatriots. Johann Gottfried Herder (1744–1803), a prominent German writer, conceived the idea of the *Volksgeist*, the soul of the people. For Herder, each people was unique and creative; each expressed his or her peculiar genius in language, literature, monuments, and folk traditions. Herder did not make the theoretical jump from a spiritual or cultural nationalism to political nationalism; he did not call for the formation of states based on nationality. But his emphasis on the unique culture of a people stimulated a national consciousness among Germans and the various Slavic peoples who lived under foreign rule. Fascination with the Volksgeist prompted intellectuals to investigate the past of their own people, to rediscover their ancient traditions, and to extol their historic language and culture. From this cultural nationalism, it was only a short step to a political nationalism that called for national liberation, unification, and statehood.

The romantics were the earliest apostles of German nationalism. Resisting the French philosophes, who sought to impose universal norms on all peoples, German romantics stressed the uniqueness of the German nation and its history. They restored to consciousness memories of the German past, and they emphasized the peculiar qualities of the German folk and the special destiny of the German nation. The romantics glorified medieval Germany and valued hereditary monarchy and aristocracy as vital links to the nation's past. They saw the existence of each individual as inextricably bound up with folk and fatherland, and they found the self-realization for which they yearned in the uniting of their own egos with the national soul. To these romantics, the national community was the source of artistic and spiritual creativity and the vital force, giving the individual both an identity and a purpose in life. The nation stood above the individual; the national spirit linked isolated souls into a community of brethren.

To the philosophes, the state was a human institution, a rational arrangement between individuals that safeguarded their rights and permitted them to realize their individual goals. To German romantics, such a state was an artificial and lifeless construction. The true German state was something holy, the expression of the divine spirit of the German people; it could not be manufactured to order by the intellect. The state's purpose was neither the protection of natural rights nor the promotion of economic well-being; rather, the state was a living organism that linked each person to a sacred past and reconciled and united heterogeneous wills, imbuing them with a profound sense of community, with which one entered into mystical communion. "This 'Romantic' image of a state founded not on any rational idea of the functions and purposes of a state but on love and perfect communion, is of course a formula for totalitarianism," observes R. J. Hollingdale, "and it was towards a state modeled on this formula that German nationalism continually moved."[12] Building on the romantics' views, radical German nationalists came to propound the dangerous racist idea that national identity was an inherited characteristic—that being and feeling German depended on birth, on blood—rather than acculturation. Holding this belief, some German nationalists maintained that Jews, no matter how many generations they had resided in Germany, could never be truly German.

Nationalism and Liberalism

In the early 1800s, liberals were the principal leaders and supporters of nationalist movements. They viewed the struggle for national rights—the freedom of a people from foreign rule—as an extension of the struggle for the rights of the individual. There could be no liberty, said liberal nationalists, if people were not free to rule themselves in their own land.

Liberals called for the unification of Germany and Italy, the rebirth of Poland, the liberation of Greece from Turkish rule, and the granting of autonomy to the Hungarians of the Austrian Empire. Liberal nationalists envisioned a Europe of independent states based on nationality and popular sovereignty. Free of foreign domination and tyrant princes, these newly risen states would protect the rights of the individual and strive to create a brotherhood of nationalities in Europe.

In the first half of the nineteenth century, few intellectuals recognized the dangers inherent in nationalism or understood the fundamental contradiction between liberalism and nationalism. For the liberal, the idea of universal natural rights transcended all national boundaries. Inheriting the cosmopolitanism of the Enlightenment, liberalism emphasized what all people had in common, demanded that all individuals be treated equally under the law, and preached toleration. As they grew more extreme, nationalists manifested a narrow, tribal outlook and came to regard the nation as the essential fact of existence. Consequently, they often willingly subverted individual liberty for the sake of national grandeur. Whereas the liberal sought to protect the rights of all within the state, the nationalist often ignored or trampled on the rights of individuals and national minorities.

Liberalism grew out of the rational tradition of the West, but nationalism derived from an emotional attachment to ancient customs and bonds. Because it fulfilled an elemental yearning for community and kinship, nationalism exerted a powerful hold over human hearts, often driving people to political extremism. Liberalism demanded objectivity in analyzing tradition, society, and history; nationalism, however, evoked a mythic and romantic past, frequently a heroic golden age, that often distorted history.

"Nationalism requires . . . much belief in what is patently not so," wryly observes British historian E. J. Hobsbawm.[13] Thus nationalists inflated their people's past achievements and attributed to the nation a peculiar inner spirit that set it apart from others and accounted for its superiority. While constantly declaiming the wrongs that others had inflicted on them, they turned a blind eye to their own mistreatment of other nationalities. Nationalists interpreted history to serve political ends: the unity of their people and the creation of a powerful nation-state.

In the last part of the nineteenth century, the irrational and mythic quality of nationalism intensified. By stressing the unique qualities and history of a particular people, nationalism promoted hatred between nationalities. By kindling deep love for the past, including a longing for ancient borders, glories, and power, nationalism led to wars of expansion. When it roused the emotions to fever pitch, nationalism shattered rational thinking, dragged the mind into a world of fantasy and myth, and introduced extremism into politics. Love of nation became an overriding passion, threatening to extinguish the liberal ideals of reason, freedom, and equality.

❖   ❖   ❖

Notes

1. Quoted in H. G. Schenk, *The Mind of the European Romantics* (Garden City, N.Y.: Doubleday, 1969), 4.

2. William Blake, "Milton," in *The Poetry and Prose of William Blake*, ed. David V. Erdman (Garden City, N.Y.: Doubleday, 1965), plate 40, lines 34–36, 141.

3. Ibid., plate 41, line 1.

4. Letter of John Keats, November 22, 1817, in *The Letters of John Keats*, ed. Hyder E. Rollins (Cambridge, Mass.: Harvard University Press, 1958), vol. 1, 184–185.

5. Blake, "Milton," Preface, bk. 1, plate 1, 95.

6. Quoted in Robert T. Denommé, *Nineteenth-Century French Romantic Poets*, 28. Copyright © 1969 by Southern Illinois University Press. All rights reserved. Reprinted with permission.

7. From "The Tables Turned," in *The Complete Poetical Works of Wordsworth*, ed. Andrew J. George (Boston: Houghton Mifflin, 1904, rev. ed., 1982), 83.

8. Horst von Maltitz, *The Evolution of Hitler's Germany* (New York: McGraw-Hill, 1973), 217.

9. G. W. F. Hegel, *The Philosophy of History*, trans. J. Sibree (New York: Dover, 1956), 19, 23.

10. Edmund Burke, *Reflections on the Revolution in France* (New York: Liberal Arts Press, 1955), 40, 89.

11. John Stuart Mill, *On Liberty*, ed. Currin V. Shields (Indianapolis, Ind.: Bobbs-Merrill, 1956), chap. 1.

12. R. J. Hollingdale, *Nietzsche* (London: Routledge & Kegan Paul, 1973), 25.

13. E. J. Hobsbawm, *Nations and Nationalism Since 1780* (Cambridge, Eng.: Cambridge University Press, 1992), 12.

Chapter 14

Surge of Liberalism and Nationalism: Revolution, Counterrevolution, and Unification

- ■ **The Congress of Vienna**
- ■ **Revolutions, 1820–1829**
- ■ **Revolutions, 1830–1832**
- ■ **The Revolutions of 1848: France**
- ■ **The Revolutions of 1848: Germany, Austria, and Italy**
- ■ **The Revolutions of 1848: An Assessment**
- ■ **The Unification of Italy**
- ■ **The Unification of Germany**
- ■ **Nationality Problems in the Hapsburg Empire**

Focus Questions

1. Why did Metternich fear liberalism and nationalism?
2. What were the accomplishments and failures of the Congress of Vienna?
3. What were the principal reasons for the revolutions that broke out in Europe in the decades after the Congress of Vienna?
4. Why did the revolutions of 1848 essentially fail?
5. What were the liberal gains in 1848? Why were liberals and nationalists disappointed?
6. What was the historical significance of the unification of Germany?
7. How did nationalism promote unity in some lands and division in others?

*D*uring the years 1815 through 1848, the forces unleashed by the French Revolution clashed with the traditional outlook of the old regime. The period opened with the Congress of Vienna, which drew up a peace settlement after the defeat of Napoleon, and closed with the revolutions that swept across much of Europe in 1848. Outside France, much of the old regime had survived the stormy decades of the French Revolution and Napoleon. Monarchs still held the reins of political power. Aristocrats, particularly in Central and Eastern Europe, retained their traditional hold on the army and administration, controlled the peasantry and local government, and enjoyed tax exemptions. Determined to enforce respect for traditional authority and to smother liberal ideals, the conservative ruling elites resorted to censorship, secret police, and armed force. But the liberals and nationalists, inspired by the revolutionary principles of liberty, equality, and fraternity, continued to engage in revolutionary action. ❖

THE CONGRESS OF VIENNA

After the defeat of Napoleon, a congress of European powers met at Vienna (1814–1815) to draw up a peace settlement. The delegates wanted to restore stability to a continent torn by revolution and war and to reestablish the balance of power shattered by Napoleonic France.

Statesmen and Issues

The pivotal figure at the Congress of Vienna was Prince Klemens von Metternich (1773–1859) of Austria. A man of the old order, Metternich believed that both domestic and international stability depended on rule by monarchs and respect for the aristocracy. The misguided liberal belief that society could be reshaped according to the ideals of liberty and equality, said Metternich, had led to twenty-five years of revolution, terror, and war. To restore stability and peace, the old Europe must suppress liberal ideas and quash the first signs of revolution.

Metternich also feared the new spirit of nationalism. As a multinational empire, Austria was particularly vulnerable to nationalist unrest. If its ethnic groups—Poles, Czechs, Magyars, Italians, South Slavs, and Romanians—became infected with the nationalist virus, they would destroy the Hapsburg Empire. Moreover, by arousing the masses and setting people against people, nationalism could undermine the foundations of the European civilization that he cherished.

Determined to end the chaos of the Napoleonic period and restore stability to Europe, Metternich wanted to return to power the ruling families deposed by more than two decades of revolutionary warfare. He also sought to reestablish the balance of power in Europe so that no one country could be in a position to dominate the Continent as Napoleon had done. There must be no more Napoleons who obliterate states, topple kings, and dream of European hegemony.

Other nations at the Congress of Vienna included Britain, Russia, France, and Prussia. Representing Britain was Robert Stewart, Viscount Castlereagh (1769–1822), the British foreign secretary, who was realistic and empirically minded. Although an implacable enemy of Napoleon, Castlereagh demonstrated mature statesmanship by not seeking to punish France severely. Tsar Alexander I (1777–1825) attended the congress himself. Steeped in Christian mysticism, the tsar wanted to create a European community based on Christian teachings. Alexander regarded himself as the savior of Europe, an attitude that caused other diplomats to view him with distrust. Representing France was Prince Charles Maurice de Talleyrand-Périgord (1754–1838). A devoted patriot, Talleyrand sought to remove from France the stigma of the Revolution and Napoleon. Prince Karl von Hardenberg (1750–1822) represented Prussia. Like Metternich, Castlereagh, and Talleyrand, the Prussian statesman believed that the various European states, besides pursuing their own national interests, should concern themselves with the well-being of the European community as a whole.

Two interrelated issues threatened to disrupt the conference and enmesh the Great Powers in another war. One was Prussia's intention to annex the German kingdom of Saxony; the other was Russia's demand for Polish territories. The tsar wanted to combine the Polish holdings of Russia, Austria, and Prussia into a new Polish kingdom under Russian control. Both Britain and Austria regarded such an extension of Russian domination into Central Europe as a threat to the balance of power.

Talleyrand suggested that Britain, Austria, and France join in an alliance to oppose Prussia and Russia. This clever move restored France to the family of nations. Now France was no longer the hated enemy but a necessary counterweight to Russia and Prussia. Threatened with war, Russia and Prussia moderated their demands and the crisis ended.

The Settlement

After months of discussion, quarrels, and threats, the delegates to the Congress of Vienna finished their work. Resisting Prussia's demands for a punitive peace, the allies did not punish France severely. They feared that a humiliated France would only prepare for a war of revenge. Besides, Metternich continued to need France to balance the power of both Prussia and Russia. France had to pay a large indemnity over a five-year period and submit to allied occupation until the obligation was met.

Although it lost most of its conquests, France emerged with somewhat more land than it had possessed before the Revolution. To guard against a resurgent France, both Prussia and Holland received territories on the French border. Holland obtained the southern Netherlands (Belgium); Prussia gained the Rhineland and part of Saxony, but not as much as the Prussians had desired. Nevertheless, Prussia emerged from the settlement significantly larger and stronger. Russia obtained Finland and a considerable part of the Polish territories, but not as much as the tsar had anticipated; the congress prevented further Russian expansion into Central Europe. The northern Italian province of Lombardy was restored to Austria, which also received adjacent Venetia. England obtained strategic naval bases: Helgoland in the North Sea, Malta and the Ionian Islands in the Mediterranean, the Cape Colony in South Africa, and Ceylon in the Indian Ocean. Germany was organized into a confederation of thirty-eight (later thirty-nine) states. Norway was given to Sweden. The legitimate rulers, who had been displaced by the Revolution and the wars

of Napoleon, were restored to their thrones in France, Spain, Portugal, the Kingdom of the Two Sicilies, the Papal States, and many German states.

The conservative delegates at the Congress of Vienna have often been criticized for ignoring the liberal and nationalist aspirations of the different peoples and turning the clock back to the old regime. Critics have castigated the congress for dealing only with the rights of thrones and not the rights of peoples. But after the experience of two world wars in the twentieth century, some historians today are impressed by the peacemakers' success in restoring a balance of power that effectively stabilized international relations. No one country was strong enough to dominate the Continent, and no Great Power was so unhappy that it resorted to war to undo the settlement. Not until the unification of Germany in 1870–1871 was the balance of power upset; not until World War I in 1914 did Europe have another general war of the magnitude of the Napoleonic wars.

REVOLUTIONS, 1820–1829

Russia, Austria, Prussia, and Great Britain agreed to act together to preserve the territorial settlement of the Congress of Vienna and the balance of power. After paying its indemnity, France was admitted into this Quadruple Alliance, also known as the Concert of Europe. Metternich intended to use the Concert of Europe to maintain harmony between nations and internal stability within nations. Toward this end, conservatives in their respective countries censored books and newspapers and imprisoned liberal and nationalist activists.

But repression could not contain the liberal and nationalist ideals unleashed by the French Revolution. The first revolution after the restorations of legitimate rulers occurred in Spain in 1820. Fearing that the Spanish uprising, with its quasi-liberal overtones, would inspire revolutions in other lands, the Concert of Europe empowered France to intervene. In 1823, a hundred thousand French troops crushed the revolution.

Revolutionary activity in Italy also frightened the Concert of Europe. In 1815, Italy consisted of several separate states. In the south, a Bourbon king ruled the Kingdom of the Two Sicilies; the

Chronology 14.1 ❖ The Surge of Nationalism

1821	Austria crushes revolts in Italy
1823	French troops crush revolt in Spain
1825	Uprising in Russia crushed by Nicholas I
1829	Greece gains its independence from Ottoman Empire
1830	The July Ordinances in France are followed by a revolution, which forces Charles X to abdicate
1831	The Polish revolution fails
1831–1832	Austrian forces crush a revolution in Italy
1848	The Year of Revolution
1862	Bismarck becomes chancellor of Prussia
1864	Austria and Prussia defeat Denmark in a war over Schleswig-Holstein
1866	Seven Weeks' War between Austria and Prussia: Prussia emerges as the dominant power in Germany
1870–1871	Franco-Prussian War: German unification completed
January 18, 1871	William I becomes German kaiser

pope governed the Papal States in central Italy; and Hapsburg Austria ruled Lombardy and Venetia in the north. Hapsburg princes subservient to Austria ruled the duchies of Tuscany, Parma, and Modena. Piedmont in the northwest and the island of Sardinia were governed by an Italian dynasty, the House of Savoy.

Besides all these political divisions, Italy was split economically and culturally. Throughout the peninsula, attachment to the local region was stronger than devotion to national unity. Economic ties between north and south were weak; inhabitants of the northern Italian cities felt little closeness to Sicilian peasants. Except for the middle class, most Italians clung to the values of the old regime.

Through novels, poetry, and works of history, an expanding intellectual elite awakened interest in Italy's glorious past. They insisted that a people who had built the Roman Empire and produced the Renaissance must not remain weak and divided, their land occupied by Austrians. These sentiments appealed particularly to university students and the middle class. But the rural masses, illiterate and preoccupied with the hardships of daily life, showed little interest in this struggle for national revival.

Secret societies kept alive the hopes for liberty and independence from foreign rule in the period after 1815. The most important of these societies was the Carbonari, which had clubs in every state in Italy and a membership drawn largely from the middle class and the army. In 1820, the Carbonari enjoyed a few months of triumph in the Kingdom of the Two Sicilies. Supported by the army and militia, they forced King Ferdinand I to grant a constitution and a parliamentary government. But Metternich feared that the germ of revolution would spread to other countries. Supported by Prussia and Russia, Austria suppressed the constitutional government in Naples and another revolution that broke out in Piedmont. In both cases, Austria firmly fixed an absolute ruler on the throne.

A revolution also failed in Russia. During the Napoleonic wars and the occupation of France, Russian officers were introduced to French ideas. Contrasting French liberal attitudes with Russian autocracy, some officers resolved to change conditions in Russia. Like their Western counterparts, they organized secret societies and disseminated liberal ideas within Russia. When Alexander

Congress of Vienna, 1815, by Jean Baptiste Isabey (1767–1855). The delegates to the Congress of Vienna sought to reestablish many features of Europe that had existed before the French Revolution and Napoleon. They can be accused of shortsightedness; nevertheless, the balance of power that they formulated preserved international peace. Metternich is standing before a chair at the left.

I died, these liberal officers struck. Their uprising in December 1825 was easily smashed by the new tsar, Nicholas I, and the leaders were severely punished.

The revolutions in Spain, Italy, and Russia were suppressed, but the Metternich system also suffered setbacks. Stimulated by the ideals of the French Revolution, the Greeks revolted against their Turkish rulers in 1821. Although the Turkish sultan was the legitimate ruler, Russia, France, and Britain aided the Greek revolutionaries, for they were Christians, whereas the Turks were Muslims; moreover, pro-Greek sentiments were very strong among educated Western Europeans, who had studied the literature and history of ancient Greece. To them, the Greeks were struggling to regain the freedom of their ancient forebears. Not only the pressure of public opinion but also fear of Russian motives led Britain to join in intervention. If Russia carried out its intention of aiding the Greeks on its own, no doubt it would never surrender control. Britain could not permit this extension of Russian power in the eastern Mediterranean. Despite Metternich's objections, Britain, France, and Russia took joint action against the Turks, and in 1829 Greece gained its independence.

REVOLUTIONS, 1830–1832

After Napoleon's defeat, a Bourbon king, Louis XVIII (1814–1824), younger brother of the executed Louis XVI, ascended the throne of France. Recognizing that the French people would not accept a return to the old order, Louis pursued a moderate course. Although his pseudo-constitution, the Charter, declared that the king's power

LIBERTY LEADING THE PEOPLE, 1830, BY EUGÈNE DELACROIX (1799–1863). Early-nineteenth-century reformers found their rallying cry in "liberty," a legacy of the French Revolution. In this painting, Delacroix, the leader of the French romantic artists, glorifies liberty.

RMN–Grand Palais/Art Resource, N.Y.

rested on divine right, it acknowledged that citizens possessed fundamental rights: freedom of thought and religion and equal treatment under the law. It also set up a two-house parliament. But peasants, urban workers, and most bourgeois could not meet the property requirements for voting. Louis XVIII was resisted by diehard aristocrats, called *ultras*, who wanted to erase the past twenty-five years of French history and restore the power and privileges of church and aristocracy. It was said of them that "they had forgotten nothing and learnt nothing." Their leader was the king's younger brother, the Comte d'Artois, who after Louis's death in 1824 ascended the throne as Charles X (1824–1830).

The new government aroused the hostility of the bourgeoisie by indemnifying the émigrés for the property they had lost during the Revolution, censoring the press, and giving the church greater control over education. In the election of 1830, the liberal opposition to Charles X won a decisive victory. Charles responded with the July Ordinances, which dissolved the newly elected chamber; the Ordinances also deprived the upper bourgeois of the vote and severely curbed the press.

The bourgeois, students, and workers rebelled. Viewing themselves as heirs of the Jacobins, they hoped to establish a republic, but the wealthy bourgeois who took control of the revolution feared republican radicalism. They offered the throne to the Duc d'Orléans; Charles X abdicated and went into exile in Britain. The new king, Louis Philippe (1830–1848), never forgot that he owed his throne to the rich bourgeois. And the Parisian workers who had fought for a republic and economic reforms to alleviate poverty felt betrayed by the outcome, as did the still disenfranchised petty bourgeois.

The Revolution of 1830 in France set off shock waves in Belgium, Poland, and Italy. The Congress of Vienna had assigned Catholic Belgium to Protestant Holland; from the outset, the Belgians had protested. Stirred by the events in Paris, Belgian patriots proclaimed their independence from Holland and established a liberal government. Inspired by the uprisings in France and Belgium, Polish students, intellectuals, and army officers took up arms against their Russian overlords. The revolutionaries wanted to restore Polish independence, a dream that poets, musicians, and intellectuals had kept alive. Polish courage, however, was no match for Russian might, and Warsaw fell in 1831. The tsar took savage revenge on the revolutionaries. In 1831–1832, the Austrians suppressed another insurrection by the Carbonari in the Papal States. During these uprisings, the peasants gave the Carbonari little support; indeed, they seemed to side with the traditional rulers.

THE REVOLUTIONS OF 1848: FRANCE

In 1848, often called the Year of Revolution, uprisings for political liberty and nationhood erupted throughout Europe. The economic crisis of the previous two years had aggravated discontent with the existing regimes, but "it was the absence of liberty," concludes historian Jacques Droz, "which . . . was most deeply resented by the peoples of Europe and led them to take up arms."[1]

The February Revolution

An uprising in Paris set in motion the revolutionary tidal wave that was to engulf much of Europe in 1848. The Revolution of 1830 had broken the back of the ultras in France. There would be no going back to the Old Regime. But King Louis Philippe and his ministers, moderates by temperament and philosophy, had no intention of going forward to democracy.

The government of Louis Philippe was run by a small elite consisting of bourgeois bankers, merchants, and lawyers, as well as aristocrats who had abandoned the hope of restoring the Old Regime. This ruling elite championed the revolutionary ideas of equal treatment under the law and of careers open to talent but feared

democracy and blocked efforts to broaden the franchise. (Only about 3 percent of adult French males were qualified to vote.) The opposition—radical republicans, or democrats—wanted to abolish the monarchy and grant all men the vote. The situation reached a climax in February 1848, when the bourgeoisie, as well as students and workers, took to the streets to demand reforms; this led to a violent confrontation with soldiers. Unable to pacify the enraged Parisians, Louis Philippe abdicated, and France became a republic.

The June Days: Revolution of the Oppressed

The new bourgeois leaders were committed to political democracy, but only a few favored the social reforms demanded by the laboring poor. A meager harvest in 1846 and an international financial crisis in 1847 that drastically curtailed French factory production aggravated the misery of the working class. Workers who could find

THE BARRICADES. In February 1848, republican revolutionaries forced Louis Philippe to abdicate. This picture shows one of the barricades set up by the revolutionaries.

Carl Schurz: Revolution Spreads to the German States

The February Revolution in Paris was eagerly received by German liberals and nationalists who yearned for a Germany governed by a national parliament and a constitution that guaranteed basic liberties. In the following excerpt from his Reminiscences, *Carl Schurz (1829–1906), then a student at the University of Bonn, recalled the expectations of German liberal-nationalists. After the revolution failed, Schurz fled to Switzerland and eventually went to the United States, where he had a distinguished career as a senator, cabinet member, and journalist.*

Now had arrived in Germany the day for the establishment of "German Unity," and the founding of a great, powerful national German Empire. In the first line the convocation of a national parliament. Then the demands for civil rights and liberties, free speech, free press, the right of free assembly, equality before the law, a freely elected representation of the people with legislative power, responsibility of ministers, self-government of the communes, the right of the people to carry arms, the formation of a civic guard with elective officers, and so on—in short, that which was called a "constitutional form of government on a broad democratic basis." Republican ideas were at first only sparingly expressed. But the word democracy was soon on all tongues, and many, too, thought it a matter of course that if the princes should try to withhold from the people the rights and liberties demanded, force would take the place of mere petition. Of course the regeneration of the fatherland must, if possible, be accomplished by peaceable means. A few days after the outbreak of this commotion I reached my nineteenth birthday. I remember to have been so entirely absorbed by what was happening that I could hardly turn my thoughts to anything else. Like many of my friends, I was dominated by the feeling that at last the great opportunity had arrived for giving to the German people the liberty which was their birthright and to the German fatherland its unity and greatness, and that it was now the first duty of every German to do and to sacrifice everything for this sacred object. We were profoundly, solemnly in earnest. . . .

Great news came from Vienna. There the students of the university were the first to assail the Emperor of Austria with the cry for liberty and citizens' rights. Blood flowed in the streets, and the downfall of Prince Metternich was the result. The students organized themselves as the armed guard of liberty. In the great cities of Prussia there was a mighty commotion. Not only Cologne, Coblenz and Trier, but also Breslau, Königsberg and Frankfurt-on-the-Oder, sent deputations to Berlin to entreat the king. In the Prussian capital the masses surged upon the streets, and everybody looked for events of great import.

Question for Analysis

1. What were the goals of Schurz and many of his colleagues? How did they seek to reconcile nationalism and liberalism?

Carl Schurz, *The Reminiscences of Carl Schurz* (New York: The McClure Co., 1907), Vol. I, see pp. 112–117.

---

jobs labored twelve to fourteen hours a day under brutalizing conditions. In some districts, one out of three children died before the age of five, and everywhere in France, beggars, paupers, prostitutes, and criminals were evidence of the struggle to survive. Prevented by law from striking, unable to meet the financial requirements for voting, and afflicted with massive unemployment, the urban workers wanted relief.

The middle-class leaders of the new republic, however, had little understanding of the workers' plight and little sympathy for it. By reason of occupation and wealth, the middle class saw itself as separate from the working class. To the bourgeoisie, the workers were dangerous creatures, "the wild ones," "the vile mob." But the inhabitants of the urban slums could no longer be ignored. They felt, as Alexis de Tocqueville, the astute statesman and political theorist, stated, "that all that is above them is incapable and unworthy of governing them; that the present distribution of goods [prevalent until now] . . . is unjust; that property rests on a foundation which is not an equitable foundation."[2]

Although the new leaders gave all adult males the vote and abolished censorship, they made only insincere and halfhearted attempts to ease the distress of the urban poor. The government limited the workday to ten hours, legalized labor unions, and established national workshops, which provided food, medical benefits, and employment on public works projects. But to the workers, this was a feeble effort to deal with their monumental hardships. To the property-owning peasantry and bourgeoisie, the national workshops were a hateful concession to socialist radicalism and a waste of government funds. When the government closed the workshops, working-class hostility and despair turned to open rebellion. Again barricades went up in the streets of Paris.

The June revolution in Paris was a revolt against poverty, a cry for the redistribution of property, and a yearning to create a society that would serve the common good. What distinguished the revolution, said Alexis de Tocqueville,

> is that it did not aim at changing the form of government, but at altering the order of society. It was not, strictly speaking, a political struggle . . . but a combat of class against class. . . . We behold in it nothing more than a blind and rude, but powerful, effort on the part of the workmen to escape from the necessities of their condition, which had been depicted to them as one of unlawful oppression . . . [3]

The approximately ten to fifteen thousand insurgents, most from the working class, stood alone. To the rest of the nation, they were barbarians attacking civilized society. Aristocrats, bourgeois, and peasants feared that no one's property would be safe if the revolution succeeded. From hundreds of miles away, Frenchmen flocked to Paris to crush what they considered to be the madness within their midst. After three days of vicious street fighting and atrocities on both sides, the army extinguished the revolt. Some one thousand four hundred and sixty lives had been lost, including four generals. The government summarily executed in cold blood at least one thousand and five hundred suspected insurgents and eventually deported to Algeria many of the one thousand and two hundred it arrested. The June Days left deep scars on French society. For many years, workers would never forget that the rest of France had united against them; the rest of France would remain terrified of working-class radicalism.

In December 1848, the French people, in overwhelming numbers, elected Louis Napoleon—nephew of the great emperor—president of the Second Republic. They were attracted by the magic of Louis Napoleon's name, and they expected him to safeguard society and property from future working-class disorders. The election, in which all adult males could vote, demonstrated that most Frenchmen were socially conservative; they were unsympathetic to working-class poverty and deeply suspicious of socialist programs.

THE REVOLUTIONS OF 1848: GERMANY, AUSTRIA, AND ITALY

Like an epidemic, the fever of revolution that broke out in Paris in February raced across the Continent. Liberals, excluded from participation in political life, fought for parliaments and constitutions; many liberals were also nationalists who wanted unity or independence for their nations.

The German States: Liberalism Discredited

After the Congress of Vienna, Germany consisted of a loose confederation of thirty-nine independent states, of which Austria and Prussia were the most powerful. Jealous of their own states' independence and determined to preserve their own absolute authority, the ruling princes detested liberal and nationalist ideals, which, urged on by Metternich, they tried to repress through censorship and the regulation of student associations.

The German nationalism that had emerged during the French occupation intensified during the restoration (the post-Napoleonic period).

Inspired in part by the ideas of the romantics, intellectuals insisted that Germans, who shared a common language and culture, should also be united politically. During the restoration, the struggle for German unity and liberal reforms continued to be waged primarily by students, professors, writers, lawyers, and other educated people. The great mass of people, knowing only loyalty to their local prince, remained unmoved by appeals for national unity.

The successful revolt against Louis Philippe, hostility against absolute princes, and the general economic crisis combined to produce uprisings in the capital cities of the German states in March 1848. Throughout Germany, liberals clamored for constitutions, parliamentary government, freedom of thought, and an end to police intimidation. Some called for the creation of a unified Germany governed by a national parliament and headed by a constitutional monarch. The poor of town and countryside, their plight worsened by the great depression of the 1840s, joined the struggle.

Terrified that these disturbances would lead to anarchy, the princes made concessions to the liberals, whom they had previously censored, jailed, and exiled. During March and April 1848, the traditional rulers in Prussia and other German states replaced reactionary ministers with liberals, eased censorship, established jury systems, framed constitutions, formed parliaments, and ended peasant obligations to lords.

Liberals took advantage of their successes to form a national assembly charged with the task of creating a unified and liberal Germany. Representatives from all the German states attended the assembly, which met at Frankfurt. After many long debates, the Frankfurt Assembly approved a federation of German states. The new German union would have a parliament and would be headed by the Prussian king. Austria, with its many non-German nationalities, would be excluded from the federal union. The deputies selected Frederick William IV as emperor of the new Germany, but the Prussian king refused; he would never wear a crown given to him by common people during a period of revolutionary agitation. While the delegates debated, the ruling princes recovered from the first shock of revolution and ordered their armies to crush the revolutionaries. One by one the liberal governments fell.

The rulers of the various German states, supported by the army, the aristocracy, and the bureaucracy, retained their power. German liberalism had failed to unite Germany or to create a constitutional government dominated by the middle class. Liberalism, never securely rooted in Germany, was discredited. In the following decades, many Germans, identifying liberalism with failure, abandoned liberal values and turned to authoritarian Prussia for leadership in the struggle for unification. The fact that authoritarians hostile to the spirit of parliamentary government eventually united Germany had deep implications for future German and European history.

In 1848, German political aspirations—the creation of a constitutional government—coincided with the goals of liberals in Western European lands. However, in the late nineteenth century, while Western European states were becoming more liberal, Germany moved in an authoritarian direction. The political systems that prevailed after 1848 stifled the growth of liberal, constitutional government.

Austria: Hapsburg Dominance

The Hapsburg (Austrian) Empire, the product of dynastic marriage and inheritance, had no common nationality or language; it was held together only by the reigning Hapsburg dynasty, its army, and its bureaucracy. The ethnic composition of the empire was enormously complex. The Germans dominated; concentrated principally in Austria, they constituted about 25 percent of the empire's population. The Magyars predominated in the Hungarian lands of the empire. The great bulk of the population consisted of Slavs: Czechs, Poles, Slovaks, Slovenes, Croats, Serbs, and Ruthenians. In addition, there were Italians in northern Italy and Romanians in Transylvania. The Hapsburg dynasty, aided by the army and the German-dominated civil service, prevented the multinational empire from collapsing into anarchy.

Metternich, it is often said, suffered from a "dissolution complex": he understood that the new forces of nationalism and liberalism could break up the Austrian Empire. Liberal ideas could lead Hapsburg subjects to challenge the authority of the emperor, and nationalist feelings could

St. Petersburg

RUSSIAN EMPIRE

Black Sea

OTTOMAN EMPIRE

GREECE
(Independence, 1829)

Morea

SWEDEN AND NORWAY

Baltic Sea

DENMARK

Warsaw
POLAND

Jassy

Bucharest

Lemberg

Kolozsvar

Debrecen

Blaj

PRUSSIA Posen

Cracow

AUSTRIAN EMPIRE

Pressburg

Budapest
HUNGARY

Agram

HANOVER

Berlin

Dresden

Prague

BOHEMIA

Brno

Vienna

Salzburg

Bari

KINGDOM OF THE
TWO SICILIES

Reggio

Sicily

Palermo

North Sea

PRUSSIA

Frankfurt

BAVARIA

Munich

SWITZ.

Milan

Venice

Modena

Florence

Macerata

PAPAL
STATES

Rome

Naples

Salerno

Turin

Genoa

KINGDOM OF
PIEDMONT-
SARDINIA

KINGDOM
OF THE
NETHERLANDS

BEL.

Brussels

Paris

Lyon

FRANCE

Mediterranean Sea

Barcelona

Valencia

Glasgow

GREAT BRITAIN

Bristol

London

IRELAND Manchester

Birmingham

Saragossa

Pamplona

Oviedo

Madrid

SPAIN

La Coruña

Cadiz

PORTUGAL

Lisbon

ATLANTIC
OCEAN

Boundaries after Congress of Vienna, 1815

Boundary of German Confederation

Centers of revolution, 1820s

Centers of revolution, 1830s

Centers of popular unrest
in Britain, 1815–1848

Principal states affected
by revolution, 1848

Centers of
revolution, 1848

400 Mi.

400 Km.

200

200

0

0

© 2016 Cengage Learning.

Erich Lessing/Art Resource, N.Y.

REVOLUTION IN VIENNA, MAY 1848. A student leads armed railway workers.

But the revolutionaries' victory was only temporary, and the defeat of the old order only illusory. The Hapsburg government soon began to recover its balance. The first government victory came with the crushing of the Czechs in Bohemia. In 1848, Czech nationalists wanted the Austrian Empire reconstructed along federal lines that would give the Czechs equal standing with Germans. General Alfred zu Windischgrätz bombarded Prague, the capital of Bohemia, into submission and re-established Hapsburg control.

In October 1848, the Hapsburg authorities ordered the army to attack Vienna. Against the regular army, the courageous but disorganized and divided students and workers had little hope. In March 1849, the Hapsburg rulers replaced the liberal constitution drafted by the popularly elected Constitutional Assembly with a more conservative one drawn up by their own ministers.

The most serious threat to the Hapsburg realm came from the Magyars in Hungary. Some 12 million people lived in Hungary, five million of whom were Magyars. The other nationalities consisted of South Slavs (Croats and Serbs) and Romanians. Louis Kossuth (1802–1894), a member of the lower nobility, called for both social reform and a deepening of national consciousness in Hungary. Led by Kossuth, the Magyars demanded local autonomy. Hungary would remain within the Hapsburg Empire but have its own constitution and national army and control its own finances. The Hungarian leadership introduced liberal reforms: suffrage for all males who could speak Magyar and owned some property, freedom of religion, freedom of the press, the abolition of serfdom, and the end of the privileges of the nobles and the church. Within a few weeks, the Hungarian parliament changed Hungary from a feudal to a modern liberal state.

But the Hungarian leaders' nationalist dreams towered above their liberal ideals. The Magyars intended to incorporate lands inhabited by Croats, Slovaks, and Romanians into their state

cause the different peoples of the empire to rebel against German domination and Hapsburg rule. To keep these ideas from infecting Austrian subjects, Metternich's police imposed strict censorship, spied on professors, and expelled from the universities students caught reading forbidden books. Despite Metternich's political police, the universities still remained hotbeds of liberalism.

In 1848, revolutions spread throughout the Austrian Empire, starting in Vienna. Aroused by the abdication of Louis Philippe, Viennese liberals denounced Hapsburg absolutism and demanded a constitution, relaxation of censorship, and restrictions on the police. Intimidated by the revolutionaries, the government allowed freedom of the press, accepted Metternich's resignation, and promised a constitution. The Constitutional Assembly was convened and in August voted the abolition of serfdom. At the same time that the Viennese insurgents were tasting the heady wine of reform, revolts in other parts of the empire—Bohemia, Hungary, and northern Italy—added to the distress of the monarchy.

◀ *Map 14.1* **Europe's Age of Revolutions**
In the decades after the Vienna settlement, Europe experienced a wave of revolution based chiefly on liberalism and nationalism.

(Magyars considered these lands an integral part of historic Hungary) and to transform these peoples into Hungarians. In the spring of 1849, the Hungarians renounced their allegiance to the Hapsburgs and proclaimed Hungary an independent state, with Kossuth as president.

The Hapsburg rulers took advantage of the ethnic animosities inside and outside Hungary. They encouraged Romanians and Croats to resist the new Hungarian government. When Hapsburg forces moved against the Magyars, they were joined by an army of Croats, whose nationalist aspirations had been flouted by the Magyars. The Emperor Francis Joseph, who had recently ascended the Hapsburg throne, also appealed to Tsar Nicholas I for help. The tsar complied, fearing that a successful revolt by the Hungarians might lead the Poles to rise up against their Russian overlords. The Hungarians fought with extraordinary courage but were overcome by superior might.

Italy: Continued Fragmentation

Eager to end the humiliating Hapsburg occupation and domination and to link the disparate states into a unified and liberal nation, Italian nationalists, too, rose in rebellion in 1848. Revolution broke out in Sicily six weeks before the February revolution in Paris. Bowing to the revolutionaries' demands, King Ferdinand II of Naples granted a liberal constitution. The Grand Duke of Tuscany, King Charles Albert of Piedmont-Sardinia, and Pope Pius IX, ruler of the Papal States, also felt compelled to introduce liberal reforms.

Then the revolution spread to the Hapsburg lands in the north. After "Five Glorious Days" (March 18–22) of street fighting, the citizens of Milan forced the Austrians to withdraw. The people had liberated their city. On March 22, the citizens of Venice declared their city free from Austrian rule and set up a republic. King Charles Albert, who hoped to acquire Lombardy and Venetia, declared war on Austria. Intimidated by the insurrections, the ruling princes of the Italian states and Hapsburg Austria had lost the first round.

But soon everywhere in Italy the forces of reaction recovered and reasserted their authority. The Austrians defeated the Piedmontese and reoccupied Milan, and Ferdinand II crushed the revolutionaries in the south. Revolutionary disorders in Rome had forced Pope Pius IX to flee in November 1848; in February 1849, the revolutionaries proclaimed Rome "a pure democracy with the glorious title of the Roman Republic." Heeding the pope's call for assistance, Louis Napoleon, the newly elected French president, attacked Rome, destroyed the infant republic, and allowed Pope Pius to return. The last city to fall to the reactionaries was Venice, which the Austrians subjected to a merciless bombardment. Italy was still a fragmented nation.

THE REVOLUTIONS OF 1848: AN ASSESSMENT

The revolutions of 1848 began with much promise, but they all ended in defeat. "We stood on the threshold of paradise—but the gates slammed in our faces," wrote one dejected intellectual.[4] The revolutionaries' initial success was due less to their strength than to the governments' hesitancy to use their superior force. However, the reactionary leaders of Europe overcame their paralysis and moved decisively to smash the revolutions. The courage of the revolutionaries was no match for the sheer power of regular armies. Thousands were killed and imprisoned; many fled to America.

Class divisions weakened the revolutionaries. The union between middle-class liberals and workers, which brought success in the opening stages of the revolutions, was only temporary. Bourgeois liberals favoring political reforms—constitution, parliament, and protection of basic rights—grew fearful of the laboring poor, who demanded social reforms, that is, jobs and bread. To the bourgeois, the workers were radical Jacobins, a mob driven by dark instincts, and a threat to property. When the working class engaged in revolutionary action, a terrified middle class deserted the cause of revolution or joined the old elites in subduing the workers. These class divisions showed that the liberals' concern for political reforms—the extension of suffrage and parliamentary government—did not satisfy workers who were mired in poverty. The events of 1848 also showed that social issues—the demands of the working class for an alleviation of their misery—would become a prime consideration of European political life in the generations to come.

Intractable nationalist animosities helped to destroy all the revolutionary movements against absolutism in Central Europe. In many cases, the different nationalities hated one another more than they hated the reactionary rulers. Hungarian revolutionaries dismissed the nationalist yearnings of the Croats and Romanians living in Hungary, who in turn helped the Hapsburg dynasty extinguish the nascent Hungarian state. The Germans of Bohemia resisted Czech demands for self-government and the equality of the Czech language with German. When German liberals at the Frankfurt Assembly debated the boundary lines of a united Germany, the problem of Prussia's Polish territories emerged. In 1848, Polish patriots wanted to re-create the Polish nation, but German delegates at the convention, by an overwhelming majority, opposed returning the Polish lands seized by Prussia in the late eighteenth century.

Before 1848, democratic idealists envisioned the birth of a new Europe of free people and liberated nations. The revolutions in Central Europe showed that nationalism and liberalism were not natural allies and that nationalists were often indifferent to the rights of other peoples. Disheartened by these nationalist antagonisms, John Stuart Mill, the English liberal statesman and philosopher, lamented that "the sentiment of nationality so far outweighs the love of liberty that the people are willing to abet their rulers in crushing the liberty and independence of any people not of their race or language."[5] In the revolutions of 1848, concludes the British historian Lewis Namier, "'nationality,' the passionate creed of the intellectuals, invades the politics of central and east-central Europe, and with 1848 starts the Great European War of every nation against its neighbors."[6]

Even though the liberal and nationalist aims of the revolutionaries were not realized, liberal gains were not insignificant. All French men obtained the right to vote and slavery was abolished throughout the French Empire. Peasant obligations to lords—a survival of medieval serfdom—were either abolished or greatly reduced in the German states and Austria, and parliaments were established in Prussia and other German states.

For German liberalism, however, 1848 was a crucial defeat. Controlled by monarchs and aristocrats hostile to the democratic principles of 1848, the postrevolutionary governments, using the methods of a police state, intimidated and persecuted liberals, large numbers of whom were forced to emigrate. The failure of the revolution and the reactionary policies of the postrevolutionary governments thwarted the growth of a democratic parliamentary system in Germany. Discredited by the failure of 1848, weakened by government intimidation and the loss of many liberals to emigration, and less committed to liberal ideals—which brought no gains in 1848—the German middle class in the period immediately after 1848 became apolitical or willing to sacrifice liberal principles to achieve a united and powerful Germany. Nationalism would supersede liberalism as the principal concern of the German middle class. The failure of liberalism to take strong root in Germany would have dire consequences in the early twentieth century.

In later decades, liberal reforms, including legal guarantees of basic rights, would be introduced peacefully in several European countries—in Germany too, but there power still remained in the hands of preindustrial, semifeudal elites, not with the middle class—for the failure of the revolutions of 1848 convinced many people, including liberals, that popular uprisings were ineffective ways of changing society. The Age of Revolution, initiated by the French Revolution of 1789, had ended.

THE UNIFICATION OF ITALY

In 1848, liberals had failed to drive the Austrians out of Italy and unite the Italian nation. By 1870, however, Italian unification had been achieved, mainly through the efforts of three men: Mazzini, Cavour, and Garibaldi.

Mazzini: The Soul of the Risorgimento

Giuseppe Mazzini (1805–1872) dedicated his life to the creation of a united and republican Italy—a goal he pursued with extraordinary moral intensity and determination. Mazzini was both a romantic and a liberal. As a liberal, he fought for republican and constitutional government and held that national unity would enhance individual liberty. As a romantic, he believed that an awakened Italy would lead to the regeneration of humanity. Mazzini was convinced that just as Rome had provided law and unity in the ancient world and the Roman pope had led Latin Christendom during the Middle Ages, so a third Rome, a newly united Italy, would usher in a new age of free nations, personal liberty, and equality.

Mazzini had great charisma, determination, courage, and eloquence; he was also a prolific writer. His idealism attracted the intelligentsia and youth and kept alive the spirit of national unity. He infused the *Risorgimento*, the movement for Italian unity, with spiritual intensity. After his release from prison for participating in the insurrection of 1831, Mazzini went into exile and founded a new organization, Young Italy. Consisting of dedicated revolutionaries, many of them students, Young Italy was intended to serve as the instrument for the awakening of Italy and the transformation of Europe into a brotherhood of free peoples. Mazzini believed that a successful revolution must come from below—from the people, moved by a profound love for their nation. They must overthrow the Hapsburg princes and create a democratic republic.

Cavour and Victory over Austria

The failure of the revolutions of 1848 contained an obvious lesson: that Mazzini's approach, an armed uprising by aroused masses, did not work. The masses were not deeply committed to the nationalist cause, and the revolutionaries were no match for the Austrian army. Italian nationalists now hoped that the kingdom of Piedmont-Sardinia, ruled by an Italian dynasty, would expel the Austrians and lead the drive for unity. Count Camillo Benso di Cavour (1810–1861), the chief minister of Piedmont-Sardinia, became the architect of Italian unity.

Unlike Mazzini, Cavour was neither a dreamer nor a speechmaker but a tough-minded practitioner of *realpolitik*, "the politics of reality." Focusing on the world as it actually was, he

dismissed ideals as illusions. A cautious and practical statesman, Cavour realized that mass uprisings could not succeed against Austrian might. Moreover, mistrusting the common people, he did not favor Mazzini's goal of a democratic republic. Cavour had no precise blueprint for unifying Italy. His immediate aim was to increase the territory of Piedmont by driving the Austrians from northern Italy and incorporating Lombardy and Venetia into Piedmont-Sardinia.

To improve Piedmont's image in foreign affairs, Cavour launched a reform program to strengthen the economy. He reorganized the currency, taxes, and the national debt; in addition, he had railways and steamships built, fostered improved agricultural methods, and encouraged new businesses. Within a few years, Piedmont had become a progressive modern state.

In 1855, Piedmont joined England and France in the Crimean War against Russia. Cavour had no quarrel with Russia but sought the friendship of Britain and France and a chance to be heard in world affairs. At the peace conference, Cavour was

VICTOR EMMANUEL AND GARIBALDI AT THE BRIDGE OF TEANO (1860). The unification of Italy was the work of the romantic liberal Giuseppe Mazzini, the practical politician Count Cavour, and the seasoned revolutionary Giuseppe Garibaldi. Selflessly, Garibaldi turned over his conquests in the south to Victor Emmanuel in 1861.

granted an opportunity to denounce Austria for occupying Italian lands. He soon found a supporter in Napoleon III (the former Louis Napoleon), the French emperor, who hoped that a unified northern Italy would become an ally and client of France.

In 1858, Cavour and Napoleon III reached a secret agreement. If Austria attacked Piedmont, France would aid the Italian state. Piedmont would annex Lombardy and Venetia and parts of the Papal States. For its assistance, France would obtain Nice and Savoy from Piedmont. With this agreement in his pocket, Cavour cleverly maneuvered Austria into declaring war, for it had to appear that Austria was the aggressor. He did so by strengthening Piedmont's army and encouraging volunteers from Austrian-controlled Lombardy to join it.

Supported by French forces and taking advantage of poor Austrian planning, Piedmont conquered Lombardy and occupied Milan. But Napoleon III quickly had second thoughts. If Piedmont took any of the pope's territory, French Catholics would blame their own leader. Even more serious was the fear that Prussia, suspicious of French aims, would aid Austria. For these reasons, Napoleon III, without consulting Cavour, signed an armistice with Austria. Piedmont would acquire Lombardy, but no more. An outraged Cavour demanded that his state continue the war until all northern Italy was liberated, but King Victor Emmanuel of Piedmont accepted the Austrian peace terms. The victory of Piedmont-Sardinia, however, proved greater than Cavour had anticipated. During the conflict, patriots in Parma, Modena, Tuscany, and Romagna (one of the Papal States) had seized power. These new revolutionary governments voted to join with Piedmont.

Garibaldi and Victory in the South

Piedmont's success spurred revolutionary activity in the Kingdom of the Two Sicilies. In the spring of 1860, some one thousand red-shirted adventurers and patriots landed in Sicily. Led by Giuseppe Garibaldi (1807–1882) who, like Mazzini, was a professional revolutionary, they were determined to liberate the land from its Bourbon ruler. Garibaldi held progressive views for his day. He supported the liberation of all subject nationalities, female equality, the right of workers to organize, racial equality, and the abolition of capital punishment.

But the cause of Italian national unity was his true religion. After the liberation, Garibaldi that same year invaded the mainland. He occupied Naples without a fight and prepared to advance on Rome.

Cavour, however, feared that an assault on Rome by Garibaldi would lead to French intervention. Napoleon III had pledged to defend the pope's lands, and a French garrison had been stationed in Rome since 1849. Besides, Cavour considered Garibaldi too impulsive and rash, too attracted to republican ideals, and too popular with the masses to lead the struggle for unification.

To head off Garibaldi, Cavour persuaded Napoleon III to approve an invasion of the Papal States by Piedmont. A papal force offered only token opposition, and the Papal States of Umbria and the Marches soon voted for union with Piedmont, as did Naples and Sicily. Refusing to trade on his prestige with the masses to fulfill personal ambition, Garibaldi turned over his conquests to Piedmont's King Victor Emmanuel, who was declared king of Italy in 1861.

Italian Unification Completed

Two regions still remained outside the control of the new Italy: the city of Rome, ruled by the pope and protected by French troops; and Venetia, occupied by Austria. Cavour died in 1861, but the march toward unification continued. During the conflict between Prussia and Austria in 1866, Italy sided with the victorious Prussians and was rewarded with Venetia. During the Franco-Prussian War of 1870, France withdrew its garrisons from Rome; much to the anger of the pope, Italian troops marched in, and Rome was declared the capital of Italy.

THE UNIFICATION OF GERMANY

In 1848, German liberals and nationalists, believing in the strength of their ideals, had naïvely underestimated the power of the conservative old order. After the failed revolution, some disenchanted revolutionaries retained only a half-hearted commitment to liberalism or embraced conservatism. Others fled the country, weakening the liberal leadership. All liberals came to doubt the effectiveness of revolution as a way to transform Germany into a unified state; all gained a new respect for the realities of power. Abandoning idealism for realism, liberals now thought that German unity would be achieved through Prussian arms, not liberal ideals.

Prussia, Agent of Unification

During the late seventeenth and eighteenth centuries, Prussian kings had fashioned a rigorously trained and disciplined army. The state bureaucracy, often staffed by ex-soldiers, perpetuated the military mentality. As the chief organizations in the state, the army and the bureaucracy drilled into the Prussian people a respect for discipline and authority.

The Prussian throne was supported by the Junkers. These powerful aristocrats, who owned vast estates farmed by serfs, were exempt from most taxes and dominated local government in their territories. The Junkers' commanding position made them officers in the royal army, diplomats, and leading officials in the state bureaucracy. The Junkers knew that a weakening of the king's power would lead to the loss of their own aristocratic prerogatives.

In France in the late 1700s, a powerful and politically conscious middle class had challenged aristocratic privileges. The Prussian monarchy and the Junkers had faced no such challenge, for the Prussian middle class at that time was small and without influence. The idea of the rights of the individual did not deeply penetrate Prussian consciousness or undermine the Prussian tradition of obedience to military and state authority. Liberalism did not take firm root in Germany.

In 1834, under Prussian leadership, the German states, with the notable exception of Austria, established the *Zollverein*, a customs union that abolished tariffs between the states. The customs union stimulated economic activity and promoted a desire for greater unity. The Zollverein led many Germans to view Prussia, not Austria, as the leader of the unification movement.

Bismarck and the Road to Unity

Austria was the chief barrier to the extension of Prussian power in Germany. This was one reason why William I (1861–1888) called for a drastic reorganization of the Prussian army.

But the liberals in the lower chamber of the Prussian parliament blocked passage of the army reforms, for they feared that the reforms would greatly increase the power of the monarchy and the military establishment. Unable to secure passage, William withdrew the reform bill and asked the lower chamber for additional funds to cover government expenses. When parliament granted these funds, he used the money to institute the army reforms. Learning from its mistake, the lower chamber would not approve the new budget in 1862 without an itemized breakdown. If the liberals won this conflict between the liberal majority in the lower chamber and the crown, they would, in effect, establish parliamentary control over the king and the army.

At this critical hour, King William asked Otto von Bismarck (1815–1898) to lead the battle against parliament. Descended on his father's side from an old aristocratic family, Bismarck was a staunch supporter of the Prussian monarchy and the Junker class and a devout patriot. He yearned to increase the territory and prestige of his beloved Prussia and to protect the authority of the Prussian king, who, Bismarck believed, ruled by the grace of God. Like Cavour, Bismarck was a shrewd and calculating practitioner of realpolitik.

Liberals were outraged by Bismarck's domineering and authoritarian manner and his determination to preserve monarchical power and the aristocratic order. Set on continuing the reorganization of the army and not bowing to parliamentary pressure, Bismarck ordered the collection of taxes without parliament's approval—an action that would have been unthinkable in Britain or the United States. He dismissed the lower chamber, imposed strict censorship on the press, arrested outspoken liberals, and fired liberals from the civil service. The liberals protested against these arbitrary and unconstitutional moves. What led to a resolution of the conflict was Bismarck's extraordinary success in foreign affairs.

Wars with Denmark and Austria. To Bismarck, a war between Austria and Prussia seemed inevitable, for only by removing Austria from German affairs could Prussia extend its dominion over the other German states. Bismarck's first move, however, was not against Austria but against Denmark—in 1864, over the disputed

Three Lions/Getty Images

WILLIAM I OF PRUSSIA. The German emperor in the Hall of Mirrors at Versailles (1871).

duchies of Schleswig and Holstein. Austria joined as Prussia's ally because it hoped to prevent Prussia from annexing the territories. After Denmark's defeat, Austria and Prussia quarreled over the ultimate disposition of these lands. Bismarck used the dispute to goad Austria into war. The Austrians, on their side, were convinced that Prussia must be defeated if Austria wanted to retain its influence over German affairs.

In the Austro-Prussian war of 1866, Prussia, with astonishing speed, assembled its forces and overran Austrian territory. At the battle of Sadowa (or Königgrätz), Prussia decisively defeated the main Austrian forces, and the Seven Weeks' War ended. Prussia took no territory from Austria, but the latter agreed to Prussia's annexation of Schleswig and Holstein and a number of small German states. Prussia, moreover, organized a confederation of North German states, from which Austria was excluded. In effect, Austria was removed from German affairs, and Prussia became the dominant power in Germany.

The Triumph of Nationalism and Conservatism over Liberalism.

The Prussian victory had a profound impact on political life within Prussia. Bismarck was the man of the hour, the great hero who had extended Prussia's power. Most liberals forgave Bismarck for his authoritarian handling of parliament. The liberal press, which had previously denounced Bismarck for riding roughshod over the constitution, embraced him as a hero. Prussians were urged to concentrate on the glorious tasks ahead and to put aside the constitutional struggle, which seemed petty by contrast.

Bismarck recognized the great appeal of nationalism and used it to expand Prussia's power over other German states and strengthen Prussia's voice in European affairs. By heralding his state as the champion of unification, he gained the support of nationalists throughout Germany. In the past, the nationalist cause had belonged to the liberals, but Bismarck appropriated it to promote Prussian expansion and conservative rule.

Prussia's victory over Austria, therefore, was a triumph for conservatism and nationalism and a defeat for liberalism. The liberal struggle for constitutional government in Prussia collapsed. The Prussian monarch retained the right to override parliamentary opposition and act on his own initiative. In 1848, Prussian might had suppressed a liberal revolution; in 1866, many liberals, beguiled by Bismarck's military triumphs, gave up the struggle for responsible parliamentary government. They had traded political freedom for Prussian military glory and power.

The capitulation of Prussian liberals demonstrated the essential weakness of the German liberal tradition. German liberals displayed a diminishing commitment to the principles of parliamentary government and a growing fascination with force, military triumph, and territorial expansion. Enthralled by Bismarck's achievement, many liberals abandoned liberalism and threw their support behind the authoritarian Prussian state. Germans of all classes acquired an adoration for Prussian militarism and for the power state, with its Machiavellian guideline that all means are justified if they result in the expansion of German power. In 1848, German liberals had called for "Unity and Freedom." What Bismarck gave them was unity and authoritarianism.

War with France. Prussia emerged from the war with Austria as the leading power in the North German Confederation; the Prussian king controlled the armies and foreign affairs of the states within the confederation. To complete the unification of Germany, Bismarck would have to draw the South German states into the new German confederation. But the South German states, Catholic and hostile to Prussian authoritarianism, feared being absorbed by Prussia.

Bismarck hoped that a war between Prussia and France would ignite the nationalist feelings of the South Germans, causing them to overlook the differences that separated them from Prussia. If war with France would serve Bismarck's purpose, it was also not unthinkable to Napoleon III, the emperor of France. The creation of a powerful North German Confederation had frightened the French, and the prospect that the South German states might one day add their strength to the new Germany was terrifying. Both France and Prussia had parties that advocated war.

A cause for war arose over the succession to the vacated Spanish throne. King William of Prussia discussed the issue with the French ambassador and sent Bismarck a telegram informing him of what had ensued. With the support of high military leaders, Bismarck edited the telegram. The revised version gave the impression that the Prussian king and the French ambassador had insulted each other. Bismarck wanted to inflame French feeling against Prussia and arouse German opinion against France. He succeeded. In both Paris and Berlin, crowds of people, gripped by war fever, demanded satisfaction. When France declared a general mobilization, Prussia followed suit; Bismarck had his war.

As Bismarck had anticipated, the South German states came to the aid of Prussia. Quickly and decisively routing the French forces and capturing Napoleon III, the Prussians went on to besiege Paris. Faced with starvation, Paris surrendered in January 1871. France was compelled to pay a large indemnity and to cede to Germany the border provinces of Alsace and Lorraine—a loss that French patriots could never accept.

The Franco-Prussian War completed the unification of Germany. On January 18, 1871, at Versailles, the German princes granted the title of German kaiser (emperor) to William I. A powerful nation had arisen in Central Europe. Its people were educated, disciplined, and efficient; its industries and commerce were rapidly expanding; its army was the finest in Europe. Vigorous, confident, and intensely nationalistic, the new German Empire was eager to play a greater role in world affairs. No nation in Europe was a match for the new Germany. Metternich's fears had been realized: a Germany dominated by Prussia had upset the balance of power. The unification of Germany created fears, tensions, and rivalries that would culminate in world wars.

NATIONALITY PROBLEMS IN THE HAPSBURG EMPIRE

In Italy and Germany, nationalism had led to the creation of unified states; in Austria, nationalism eventually caused the destruction of the centuries-old Hapsburg dynasty. A mosaic of different peoples, each with its own history and traditions, the Austrian Empire could not weld together and reconcile antagonistic nationalities when nationalistic consciousness was high. The empire's collapse in the final stages of World War I marked the end of years of hostility among its various subjects.

In the first half of the nineteenth century, the Germans, who constituted less than one-quarter of the population, were the dominant national group in the empire. But Magyars, Poles, Czechs, Slovaks, Croats, Romanians, Ruthenians, and Italians were experiencing national self-awareness. Poets and writers who had been educated in Latin, French, and German began to write in their mother tongue and extol its splendor. By searching their past for glorious ancestors and glorious deeds, writers kindled pride in their native history and folklore and aroused anger against past and present injustices.

In 1848–1849, the Hapsburg monarchy had extinguished the Magyar bid for independence, the Czech revolution in Prague, and the uprisings in the Italian provinces of Lombardy and Venetia. Greatly alarmed by these revolutions, the Austrian power structure resolved to resist pressures for political rights by strengthening autocracy and tightening the central bureaucracy. German and Germanized officials took over administrative and judicial duties formerly handled on a local level. An expanded secret police stifled liberal and nationalist expressions. The various nationalities, of course, resented these efforts at centralization and repression.

The defeats by France and Piedmont in 1859 and by Prussia in 1866 cost Austria its two Italian provinces. The defeat by Prussia also forced the Hapsburg monarchy to make concessions to the Magyars, the strongest of the non-German nationalities: without a loyal Hungary, the Hapsburg monarchy could suffer other humiliations. The Settlement of 1867 split the Hapsburg territories into Austria and Hungary. The two countries retained a common ruler, Francis Joseph (reigned 1848–1916), who was emperor of Austria and king of Hungary. Hungary gained complete control over its internal affairs, the administration of justice, and education. A ministry composed of delegates from both lands conducted foreign and military affairs and dealt with common financial concerns.

With the Settlement of 1867, Magyars and Germans became the dominant nationalities in the empire. The other nationalities felt that the German–Magyar political, economic, and cultural domination blocked their own national aspirations. Nationality struggles in the half-century following the Settlement of 1867 consumed the energies of the Austrians and Hungarians. In both lands, however, the leaders failed to solve the problem of minorities—a failure that helped to precipitate World War I and that ultimately led to the dissolution of the empire during the last weeks of the war.

❖ ❖ ❖

NOTES

1. Jacques Droz, *Europe Between Revolutions, 1815–1848* (New York: Harper Torchbooks, 1967), 248.

2. *The Recollections of Alexis de Tocqueville,* trans. Alexander Teixeira de Mattos (Cleveland, Ohio: Meridian Books, 1969), 11–12.

3. Ibid., 250.

4. Quoted in Adam Zamoyski, *Holy Madness: Romantics, Patriots and Revolutionaries, 1776–1871* (London: Weidenfeld & Nicolson, 1999), 356.

5. Quoted in Hans Kohn, *Nationalism: Its Meaning and History* (Princeton, N.J.: Van Nostrand, 1965), 51–52.

6. Lewis Namier, *1848: The Revolution of the Intellectuals* (Garden City, N.Y.: Doubleday, Anchor, 1964), 38.

Chapter 15

Thought and Culture in the Mid-Nineteenth Century: Realism, Positivism, Darwinism, and Social Criticism

- Realism and Naturalism
- Positivism
- Darwinism
- Religion in a Secular Age
- Marxism
- Liberalism in Transition
- Feminism: Extending the Principle of Equality

Focus Questions

1. Why is the mid-nineteenth century described as the Age of Realism? How does realism differ from romanticism?

2. How did Darwin's theory affect conceptions of time, human origins, religious doctrines, and nationalism?

3. How did Strauss and Feuerbach undermine Christianity? How did Kierkegaard defend it?

4. What did Marx have in common with the philosophes of the Enlightenment? What relationship did he see between economics and politics? Between economics and thought?

5. How was the evolution of liberalism exemplified in the theories of Mill, Green, and Spencer?

6. How may the feminist movement be regarded as an outgrowth of certain ideals that had emerged during the course of Western history?

*T*he second half of the nineteenth century was marked by great progress in science, a surge in industrialism, and a continuing secularization of life and thought. The main intellectual currents of the century's middle decades reflected these trends. Realism, positivism, Darwinism, Marxism, and liberalism all reacted against romantic, religious, and metaphysical interpretations of nature and society, focusing instead on the empirical world. Adherents of these movements relied on careful observation and strove for scientific accuracy. This emphasis on objective reality helped to stimulate a growing criticism of social ills, for despite unprecedented material progress, reality was often sordid, somber, and dehumanizing. ❖

REALISM AND NATURALISM

Realism, the dominant movement in art and literature in the mid-nineteenth century, opposed the romantic veneration of the inner life and romantic sentimentality. The romantics exalted passion and intuition, let their imaginations transport them to a presumed idyllic medieval past, and sought inner solitude amid nature's wonders. Realists, on the other hand, concentrated on the actual world: social conditions, contemporary manners, and the familiar details of everyday life. With clinical detachment and meticulous care, they analyzed how people looked, worked, and behaved.

Like scientists, realist writers and artists carefully investigated the empirical world. For example, Gustave Courbet (1819–1877), who exemplified realism in painting, sought to practice what he called a "living art." He painted common people and commonplace scenes: laborers breaking stones, peasants tilling the soil or returning from a fair, a country burial, wrestlers, bathers, family groups. In a matter-of-fact style that sought to reproduce the environment just as it is, without any attempt at glorification or deviation, realist artists also depicted floor scrapers, rag pickers, prostitutes, and beggars.

Seeking to portray life as it is, realist writers frequently dealt with social abuses and the sordid aspects of human behavior and social life. In his

novels, Honoré de Balzac (1799–1850) described how social and economic forces affected people's behavior. Ivan Turgenev's *Sketches* (1852) portrayed rural conditions in Russia and expressed compassion for the brutally difficult life of serfs. In *War and Peace* (1863–1869), Leo Tolstoy vividly described the manners and outlook of the Russian nobility and the tragedies that attended Napoleon's invasion of Russia. The novels of Charles Dickens—*Bleak House* (1853), *Hard Times* (1854), and several others—depicted the squalor of life, the hypocrisy of society, and the drudgery of labor in British industrial cities.

Many regard Gustave Flaubert's *Madame Bovary* (1857) as the quintessential realistic novel; it tells the story of a self-centered wife who shows her hatred for her devoted, hardworking, but dull husband by committing adultery. Commenting on the realism of *Madame Bovary*, one critic noted that it "represents an obsession with description. Details are counted one by one, all are given equal value, every street, every house, every book, every blade of grass is described in full."[1]

Literary realism evolved into naturalism when writers tried to demonstrate a causal relationship between human character and the social environment: that certain conditions of life produced predictable character traits in human beings. The belief that the law of cause and effect governed human behavior reflected the immense prestige attached to science in the closing decades of the nineteenth century. The leading naturalist novelist, Émile Zola (1840–1902), probed the slums, brothels, mining villages, and cabarets of France, examining how people were conditioned by the squalor of their environment. Henrik Ibsen (1828–1906), a Norwegian and the leading naturalist playwright, examined with rigorous precision and uncompromising truth the commercial and professional classes, their personal ambitions and family relationships. His *Pillars of Society* (1877) scrutinized bourgeois social pretensions and hypocrisy. In *A Doll's House* (1879), he took up a theme that shocked the late-nineteenth-century bourgeois audience: a woman leaving her husband to seek a more fulfilling life.

In striving for a true-to-life portrayal of human behavior and the social environment, realism and naturalism reflected attitudes shaped by science,

INTERIOR, 1868–1869, BY EDGAR DEGAS. Set in a world of poor shopkeepers and clerks, *Thérèse Raquin*(1867) was Émile Zola's first great success as a naturalist novelist. This Degas painting depicts the sexual tension and violent emotions that Zola sought to uncover in his work.

industrialism, and secularism, which stressed the importance of the external world. The same outlook also gave rise to positivism in philosophy.

POSITIVISM

Positivists viewed science as the highest achievement of the mind and sought to apply a strict empirical approach to the study of society. They believed that the philosopher must proceed like a scientist, carefully assembling and classifying data and formulating general rules that demonstrate regularities in the social experience. Such knowledge, based on concrete facts, would provide the social planner with useful insights. Positivists rejected metaphysics, which, in the tradition of Plato, tried to discover ultimate principles through reason alone, rather than through observation of the empirical world. For positivists, any effort to go beyond the realm of experience to a

deeper reality would be a mistaken and fruitless endeavor.

Auguste Comte (1798–1857), the father of positivism, called for a purely scientific approach to history and society: only through a proper understanding of the laws governing human affairs could society, which was in a state of intellectual anarchy, be rationally reorganized. Comte named his system *positivism* because he believed that it rested on sure knowledge derived from observed facts and was therefore empirically verifiable. Like others of his generation, Comte believed that scientific laws operate in human affairs as they do in the physical world, and could be discovered through the methods of the empirical scientist— that is, through recording and systematizing observable data.

One of the laws that Comte believed he had discovered was the "law of the three stages." The human mind, he asserted, had progressed through three broad historical stages: the theological, the metaphysical, and the scientific. In the theological stage, the most primitive of the three, the mind found a supernatural explanation for the origins and purpose of things, and society was ruled by priests. In the metaphysical stage, which included the Enlightenment, the mind tried to explain things through abstractions—such as "nature," "equality," "natural rights," or "popular sovereignty"—that rested on hope and belief rather than on empirical investigation. The metaphysical stage was a transitional period between the infantile theological stage and the highest stage of society, the scientific, or positive, stage. In this culminating stage, the mind breaks with all illusions inherited from the past, formulates laws based on careful observation of the empirical world, and reconstructs society in accordance with these laws. People remove all mystery from nature and base their social legislation on laws of society similar to the laws of nature discovered by Newton.

DARWINISM

In a century distinguished by scientific discoveries, perhaps the most important scientific advance was the theory of evolution formulated by Charles Darwin (1809–1882), an English naturalist. Darwin did for his discipline what Newton had done for physics: he made biology an objective science based on general principles. The Scientific Revolution of the seventeenth century had given people a new conception of space; Darwin radically altered our conception of time and biological life, including human origins.

Natural Selection

During the eighteenth century, almost all people had adhered to the biblical account of creation contained in Genesis: God had instantaneously created every river and mountain and the various species of animal and plant life, giving each species a finished and permanent form distinct from that of every other species. God had designed the bird's wings so that it could fly, the fish's eyes so that it could see under water, and the human

being's legs so that people could walk. All this, it was believed, had occurred some five or six thousand years ago.

Gradually, this view was questioned. In 1794, Erasmus Darwin, the grandfather of Charles Darwin, published *Zoonomia, or the Laws of Organic Life*, which offered evidence that the earth had existed for millions of years before the appearance of people and that animals experienced modifications, which they passed on to their offspring. Nearly forty years later, Sir Charles Lyell published his three-volume *Principles of Geology* (1830–1833), which showed that the planet had evolved slowly over many ages.

In December 1831, Charles Darwin sailed as a naturalist on the H.M.S. *Beagle*, which surveyed the shores of South America and some Pacific islands. During the five-year expedition, Darwin collected and examined specimens of plant and animal life; he concluded that many animal species had perished, that new species had emerged, and that there were links between extinct and living species. In *The Origin of Species* (1859) and *The Descent of Man* (1871), Darwin used empirical evidence to show that the wide variety of animal species was due to a process of development over many millennia, and he supplied a convincing theory that explained how evolution operates.

Darwin adopted the Malthusian idea (see Chapter 12) that the population reproduces faster than the food supply, causing a struggle for existence. Not all infant organisms grow to adulthood; not all adult organisms live to old age. The principle of *natural selection* determines which members of the species have a better chance of survival in a world of myriad dangers and limited resources. The offspring of lions, giraffes, or insects are not exact duplicates of their parents. A baby lion might have the potential for being slightly faster or stronger than its parents; a baby giraffe might grow up to have a longer neck than its parents; an insect might have a slightly different color.

These small, random variations give the organism a crucial advantage in the struggle for food and against natural enemies. The organism favored by nature is more likely to reach maturity, to mate, and to pass on its superior qualities to its offspring, some of which will acquire the advantageous trait

Primary Source

Charles Darwin: *The Descent of Man*

In The Descent of Man *(1871), Charles Darwin argued that human beings have evolved from lower forms of life.*

The main conclusion here arrived at, and now held by many naturalists who are well competent to form a sound judgment, is that man is descended from some less highly organized form. The grounds upon which this conclusion rests will never be shaken, for the close similarity between man and the lower animals in embryonic development, as well as in innumerable points of structure and constitution, both of high and of the most trifling importance . . . are facts which cannot be disputed. They have long been known, but until recently they told us nothing with respect to the origin of man. Now when viewed by the light of our knowledge of the whole organic world, their meaning is unmistakable. The great principle of evolution stands up clear and firm, when these groups of facts are considered in connection with others, such as the mutual affinities of the members of the same group, their geographical distribution in past and present times, and their geological succession. It is incredible that all these facts should speak falsely. He who is not content to look, like a savage, at the phenomena of nature as disconnected, cannot any longer believe that man is the work of a separate act of creation. He will be forced to admit that the close resemblance of the embryo of man to that, for instance, of a dog—the construction of his skull, limbs and whole frame on the same plan with that of other mammals, independently of the uses to which the parts may be put—the occasional reappearance of various structures, for instance of several muscles, which man does not normally possess, but which are common to the Quadrumana*— and a crowd of analogous facts—all point in the plainest manner to the conclusion that man is the co-descendant with other mammals of a common progenitor. . . .

Man may be excused for feeling some pride at having risen, though not through his own exertions, to the very summit of the organic scale; and the fact of his having thus risen, instead of having been aboriginally placed there, may give him hope for a still higher destiny in the distant future. But we are not only here concerned with hopes or fears, only with the truth as far as our reason permits us to discover it; and I have given the evidence to the best of my ability. We must, however, acknowledge, as it seems to me, that man with all his noble qualities, with sympathy which feels for the most debased, with benevolence which extends not only to other men but to the humblest living creature, with his god-like intellect which has penetrated into the movements and constitution of the solar system—with all these exalted powers—Man still bears in his bodily frame the indelible stamp of his lowly origin.

Question for Analysis

1. What did Darwin mean when he said that we "cannot any longer believe that man is the work of a separate act of creation"?

---

*An order of mammals, Quadrumana includes all primates (monkeys, apes, and baboons) except human beings; the primates' hind feet and forefeet can be used as hands because they have opposable first digits.

Charles Darwin, *The Descent of Man* (New York: D. Appleton, 1976), 606–607.

to an even greater degree than the parent. Over many generations, the favorable characteristic becomes more pronounced and more widespread within the species. Over millennia, natural selection causes the death of old, less adaptable species and the creation of new ones, for genetic changes within a segment of a species can so differentiate its members from the rest of the species that interbreeding is no longer possible. Very few of the species that dwelt on earth 10 million years ago still survive, and many new ones, including human beings, have emerged. People themselves are products of natural selection, evolving from earlier, lower, nonhuman forms of life.

Darwinism and Christianity

Like Newton's law of universal gravitation, Darwin's theory of evolution had revolutionary consequences in areas other than science. Evolution challenged traditional Christian belief. To some, it undermined the infallibility of Scripture and the conviction that the Bible was indeed the Word of God. Natural selection, which Darwin insisted was unplanned and undesigned, could explain the development of the organic world without reference to any divine arrangement or ultimate purpose.

Darwin's theory touched off a great religious controversy between fundamentalists, who defended a literal interpretation of Genesis, and advocates of the new biology. A Methodist publication contended: "We regard this theory, which seeks to eliminate from the universe the immediate, ever-present, all pervasive action of a living and personal God, which excludes the possibility of the supernatural and the miraculous . . . as practically destructive of the authority of divine revelation, and subversive of the foundation of religion and morality."[2] In time, most religious thinkers tried to reconcile evolution with the Christian view that there was a creation and that it had a purpose. These Christian thinkers held that modifications within a species were made by an intelligent creator—that God created and then directed the evolutionary process, that he steered evolution so that it would culminate in the human being.

Darwinism ultimately helped end the practice of relying on the Bible as an authority in questions of science, completing a trend initiated earlier by Galileo. Darwinism contributed to the waning of religious belief and to a growing secular attitude that dismissed or paid scant attention to the Christian view of a universe designed by God and a soul that rises to heaven.

For many, the conclusion seemed inescapable: nature contained no divine design or purpose, and the human species itself, including its vaunted power of the mind, was a chance product of impersonal forces. The core idea of Christianity—that people were children of God participating in a drama of salvation—rested more than ever on faith rather than reason. Some even talked openly about the death of God. The notion that people are sheer accidents of nature was shocking. Copernicanism had deprived people of the comforting belief that the earth had been placed in the center of the universe just for them; Darwinism deprived people of the privilege of being God's special creation, thereby contributing to a feeling of anxiety that persists to the present.

Social Darwinism

Darwin's theories were extended by others beyond the realm in which he had worked. Social thinkers recklessly applied Darwin's conclusions to the social order and produced theories that had dangerous consequences for society. Occasionally, Darwin himself departed from his rigorous empiricism and drew murky conclusions about the mentally and physically handicapped and what he termed the "savage races." But he never intended his discoveries, which applied to the natural world, to serve as a guide for a ruthless social policy that glorified war and justified genocide. Social Darwinists—those who transferred Darwin's scientific theories to social and economic issues—used the terms "struggle for existence" and "survival of the fittest" to buttress an often brutal economic individualism and political conservatism. Successful businessmen, they said, had demonstrated their fitness to prevail in the competitive world of business. Their success accorded with nature's laws and therefore was beneficial to society; those who lost out in the socioeconomic struggle demonstrated their unfitness. Traditionally, failure had been ascribed to human wickedness or to God's plan. Now, it was being attributed to an inferior hereditary endowment.

The loose application of Darwin's biological concepts to the social world also buttressed imperialism, racism, nationalism, and militarism—doctrines that preached relentless conflict. Social Darwinists insisted that nations and races were engaged in a struggle for survival in which only the fittest survive and deserve to survive. In their view, war was nature's way of eliminating the unfit. Karl Pearson, a British professor of mathematics, wrote in *National Life from the Standpoint of Science* (1900): "History shows me only one way, and one way only in which a higher state of civilization has been produced, namely the struggle of race with race, and the survival of the physically and mentally fitter race."[3] "We are a conquering race," said U.S. Senator Albert J. Beveridge. "We must obey our blood and occupy new markets, and if necessary, new lands."[4] "War is a biological necessity of the first importance,"[5] asserted the Prussian general Friedrich von Bernhardi in *Germany and the Next War* (1911).

Darwinian biology was used to promote the belief in Anglo-Saxon (British and American) and Teutonic (German) racial superiority. Social Darwinists attributed to racial qualities the growth of the British Empire, the expansion of the United States to the Pacific, and the extension of German power. The domination of other peoples—American Indians, Africans, Asians, Poles—was regarded as the natural right of the superior race.

Social Darwinism also affected racial attitudes in the United States. Too willingly, scholars, joining antiblack polemicists, attributed an inferior biological inheritance to blacks, and some predicted their extinction, seeing them as losers in the Darwinian struggle for existence. Thus, in 1905, William B. Smith, a Tulane University professor, wrote: "The vision . . . of a race vanishing before its superior is not at all dispiriting, but inspiring. . . . The doom that awaits the Negro has been prepared in like measures for all inferior races."[6]

The theory of evolution was a great achievement of the rational mind, but in the hands of the Social Darwinists it served to undermine the Enlightenment tradition. Whereas the philosophes emphasized human equality, Social Darwinists divided humanity into racial superiors and inferiors.

Image Select/Art Resource, N.Y.

A CARICATURE OF DARWIN. Darwin's theory of evolution created much controversy and aroused considerable bitterness. In this caricature, the apelike Darwin, holding a mirror, is explaining his theory of evolution to a fellow ape.

The philosophes believed that states would increasingly submit to the rule of law to reduce violent conflicts; Social Darwinists, on the other hand, regarded racial and national conflict as a biological necessity, a law of history, and a means to progress. In propagating a tooth-and-claw version of human and international relations, Social Darwinists dispensed with the humanitarian and cosmopolitan sentiments of the philosophes and distorted the image of progress. Their views promoted territorial aggrandizement and military buildup and led many to welcome World War I.

The Social Darwinist notion of the struggle of races for survival became a core doctrine of the Nazi Party after World War I and helped to provide the "scientific" and "ethical" justification for genocide.

RELIGION IN A SECULAR AGE

In addition to Darwinism, other developments in the middle of the nineteenth century served to undermine traditional Christian belief. A growing secular attitude pushed religion to the periphery of human concerns for many people. Several intellectuals, in the tradition of the Enlightenment, attacked religion as an obstacle to progress. New trends in biblical scholarship questioned the established opinion about the authenticity of the text of the Bible. Fortified by the discoveries of anthropologists and psychologists, "higher critics" examined the Old and New Testaments and the rise of Christianity in a historical and critical way.

In his *Life of Jesus* (1835), David Friedrich Strauss (1808–1874), a German theologian, examined the Gospels in a critical spirit, attempting to discern what was historically valid. He maintained that the New Testament was replete with inherited legends and with myths—including the virgin birth and the resurrection—that were unconscious inventions by the Gospel writers, who embellished Jesus' life and words with their own messianic longings. The Gospels contain much mythical–religious content, Strauss said, but little history. Prior to the publication of Strauss's work, most students of religion had viewed the Gospels as a reliable historical source. But Strauss argued that the Jesus of faith is not the same as the Jesus of history. The belief that history, as presented in the Gospels, provided a firm basis for belief in Christian teachings was permanently undermined. Strauss' work created an uproar pitting religious authorities against secular-minded thinkers.

In *The Essence of Christianity* (1841), Ludwig Feuerbach (1804–1872), a German philosopher and theologian, argued that God is a human creation, a product of human feelings and wishes. Human beings believe in the divine because they seek assistance from it in life and fear death. Feuerbach treated religion as an expression of mythical thinking and God as an unconscious projection of human hopes, fears, and self-doubts. Christianity diminishes human beings in order to affirm God, said Feuerbach; Christians deny their own worth and goodness that they might ascribe all value to God. The human being, weak and self-hating, "sets God before him as the antithesis of himself. . . . God is holy, man sinful. . . . God is the absolutely positive; . . . . man the absolutely negative."[7] Humanity liberates itself, said Feuerbach, when it rejects God's existence and religion's claim to truth. He declared that it was his aim to change the friends of God into friends of human beings and the seekers of heaven into active, productive, and life-affirming individuals.

Confronted by this assault on orthodox belief, some Christians continued to believe that the Bible was true in all its parts; that it was the divinely inspired storehouse of knowledge about God and the world. These defenders of traditional Christianity rejected evolution and any other scientific discoveries that appeared to be in conflict with their reading of Scripture.

The Danish philosopher and Lutheran pastor Søren Kierkegaard (1813–1855) argued that true Christians commit themselves to beliefs that are seemingly unintelligible. For Kierkegaard, the highest truth is that human beings are God's creatures. However, God's existence cannot be demonstrated by reason; the crucial questions of human existence can never be resolved in a logical and systematic way. In Kierkegaard's view, the individual knows God through a leap of faith, not through systematic reasoning. In contrast to the Christian apologists who sought to demonstrate that Christian teachings did not conflict with reason, Kierkegaard denied that Christian doctrines were objectively valid. For him, Christian beliefs were absurd and irrational and could not be harmonized with reason. However, said Kierkegaard, true Christians confidently embrace beliefs that are incomprehensible, if not absurd. Because Christian truths surpass reason, Kierkegaard said that true Christians, strengthened by faith, plunge with confidence into the absurd. But it is this leap of faith that enables Christians to conquer the agonizing feeling that life, in its deepest sense, means nothing and to give meaning to their own existence. Such a faith, based on total commitment, is thus the true avenue of self-discovery.

Catholic modernism, a movement of Catholic intellectuals, sought to liberalize the church, to make it more accepting of modern liberal political ideals and modern science, and to reexamine the Gospels and Catholic teaching in the light of modern biblical scholarship. In many of these instances, modernists took positions that directly challenged core Catholic principles. Thus, Alfred Firmin Loiry (1857–1940), a scholarly priest, questioned the historicity of the virgin birth and the bodily resurrection of Jesus, rejected the infallibility of papal and council pronouncements, and contended that Jesus did not impart God's permanent truths; that both he and the Gospels have to be interpreted within the context of their historical times. Pope Pius X (1903–1914) strongly condemned Catholic modernism for undermining revelation and fostering agnosticism. The church also suppressed modernist writings, dismissed some modernist instructors, and excommunicated a number of the movement's staunchest supporters.

MARXISM

The failure of the revolutions of 1848 and a growing fear of working-class violence led liberals to abandon revolution and to press for reforms through the political process. In the last part of the nineteenth century, Marxists became the chief proponents of revolution. Both liberalism and Marxism shared common principles derived from the Enlightenment. Their adherents believed in the essential goodness and perfectibility of human nature and claimed that their doctrines rested on rational foundations. They wanted to free individuals from the accumulated superstition, ignorance, and prejudices of the past and to fashion a more harmonious and rational society. Both liberals and Marxists believed in social progress and valued the full realization of human talents.

Despite these similarities, liberalism and Marxism differed profoundly. The goal of Marxism—the seizure of power by the working class and the destruction of capitalism—was inimical to bourgeois liberals. So, too, was the Marxist belief that violence and struggle were the essence of history, the instruments of progress, and the vehicle to a higher stage of humanity. Liberals, who placed the highest value on the individual, held that through education and self-discipline people could overcome inequality and poverty. Marxists, however, insisted that without a transformation of the economic system, individual effort by the downtrodden would amount to very little.

Karl Marx (1818–1883) was born of German-Jewish parents (both descendants of prominent rabbis*). To save his job as a lawyer, Marx's father converted to Protestantism. Enrolled at a university to study law, Marx switched to philosophy. In 1842, he was editing a newspaper, which was soon suppressed by the Prussian authorities for its outspoken ideas. Leaving his native Rhineland, Marx went to Paris, where he met another German, Friedrich Engels (1820–1895), who was the son of a prosperous textile manufacturer. Marx and Engels entered into a lifelong collaboration and became members of socialist groups. In February 1848, they published the *Communist Manifesto*, which called for a working-class revolution to overthrow the capitalist system. Forced to leave France in 1849 because of his political views, Marx moved to London, where he remained to the end of his life. There he spent years writing *Capital*—a study and critique of the modern capitalistic economic system, which, he predicted, would be destroyed by a socialist revolution.

A Science of History

Like other nineteenth-century thinkers, Marx believed that human history, like the operations of nature, was governed by law. Marx was a strict materialist: rejecting all religious and metaphysical interpretations of both nature and history, he sought to fashion an empirical science of society. He viewed religion as a human creation—a product of people's imagination and feelings, a consolation for the oppressed—and the happiness it brought as an illusion. Real happiness would come, said Marx, not by transcending the natural world but by improving it. Rather than deluding oneself by seeking refuge from life's misfortunes in an imaginary world, one must confront the ills of society and reform them. This last point

---

*In his writings, Marx at times expressed contempt for Jews and Judaism, which he identified with capitalist exploitation.

was crucial: "The philosophers have only *interpreted* the world in different ways; the point is to *change* it."[8]

The world could be rationally understood and changed, said Marx. People were free to make their own history, but to do so effectively, they must grasp the inner meaning of history: the laws governing human affairs in the past and operating in the present. Marx adopted Hegel's view that history was not an assortment of unrelated and disconnected events, but a progressive development, which, like the growth of a plant, proceeded ineluctably according to its own inner laws (see the section on Hegel in Chapter 13). For both Hegel and Marx, the historical process was governed by objective and rational principles. Marx also adopted Hegel's view that history advanced dialectically—that the clash of opposing forces propelled history into higher stages.

However, Marx also broke with Hegel in crucial ways. For Hegel, it was the dialectical clash of opposing ideas that moved history into the next stage; for Marx, it was the clash of classes representing conflicting economic interests—what is called dialectical materialism—that accounted for historical change and progress. In Hegel's view, history was the unfolding of the metaphysical Spirit, and a higher stage of development was produced by the synthesis of opposing ideas. According to Marx, Hegel's system suffered from mystification. It transcended the realities of the known world. Marx saw Hegel's abstract philosophy as diverting attention from the real world and its problems, which cried out for understanding and solution; it was a negation of life.

For Marx, history was explainable solely in terms of natural processes—empirically verifiable developments. Marx valued Hegel's insight that history is a progressive and purposeful process, but he criticized Hegel for embedding his insights in metaphysical, theological fantasy. Hegel, said Marx, had made a mystical principle the real subject of history and thought. But, in truth, it is the real human being, the person living in and conditioned by the objective world—the only true reality—who is the center of history. History is not Spirit aspiring to self-actualization but people becoming fully human, fulfilling their human potential.

For Marx, the moving forces in history were economic and technological factors: the ways in which goods are produced and wealth distributed. They accounted for historical change and were the basis of all culture—politics, law, religion, morals, and philosophy. "The history of humanity," he concluded, "must therefore always be studied and treated in relation to the history of industry and exchange."[9] Marx said that material technology—the methods of cultivating land and the tools for manufacturing goods—determined society's social and political arrangements and its intellectual outlook. For example, the hand mill, the loose yoke, and the wooden plow had given rise to feudal lords, whereas power-driven machines had spawned the industrial capitalists.

Class Conflict

Throughout history, said Marx, there has been a class struggle between those who own the means of production and those whose labor has been exploited to provide wealth for this upper class. The opposing tension between classes has pushed history forward into higher stages. In the ancient world, when wealth was based on land, the struggle was between master and slave, patrician and plebeian; during the Middle Ages, when land was still the predominant mode of production, the struggle was between lord and serf. In the modern industrial world, two sharply opposed classes were confronting each other: the capitalists who owned the factories, mines, banks, and transportation systems, and the exploited wage earners (the proletariat).

According to Marx and Engels, the class with economic power also controlled the state. That class used political power to protect and increase its property and to hold down the laboring class. "Thus the ancient State was above all the slave-owners' state for holding down the slaves," said Engels, "as a feudal State was the organ of the nobles for holding down the . . . serfs, and the modern representative State is the instrument of the exploitation of wage-labor by capital."[10]

Furthermore, Marx and Engels asserted, the class that controlled material production also controlled mental production: that is, the ideas held by the ruling class became the dominant ideas of society. These ideas, presented as laws of nature or moral and religious standards, were regarded as the truth by oppressor and oppressed alike. In reality, however, these ideas merely reflected the special economic interests of the ruling class. Thus, said Marx, bourgeois ideologists would insist that natural rights and laissez-faire economics were laws of nature having universal validity. But these "laws" were born of the needs of the bourgeoisie in its struggle to wrest power from an obsolete feudal regime and to protect its property from the state. Similarly, nineteenth-century slave owners convinced themselves that slavery was morally right—that it had God's approval and was good for the slave. Slave owners and capitalist employers alike may have defended their labor systems by citing universal principles that they thought were true, but in reality their systems rested on a simple economic consideration: slave labor was good for the pocketbook of the slave owner, and laissez-faire was good in the same way for the capitalist. They were unaware of the real forces motivating their thinking.

The Destruction of Capitalism

Under capitalism, said Marx, workers knew only poverty. They worked long hours for low wages, suffered from periodic unemployment, and lived in squalid, overcrowded dwellings. Most monstrous of all, they were forced to send their young children into the factories.

Capitalism, as Marx saw it, also produced another kind of poverty: poverty of the human spirit. Under capitalism, the factory worker was reduced to a laboring beast, performing tedious and repetitive tasks in a dark, dreary, dirty cave—an altogether inhuman environment that deprived people of their human sensibilities. Unlike the artisans in their own shops, factory workers found no pleasure and took no pride in their work; they did not have the satisfaction of creating a finished product that expressed their skills. Work, said Marx, should be a source of fulfillment for people. It should enable people to affirm their personalities and develop their potential. By treating people not as human beings but as cogs in the production process, capitalism alienated people from their work, themselves, and one another.

© Mary Evans/Marx Memorial Library/The Image Works.

Karl Marx (right) and Friedrich Engels (left) with Marx's Three Daughters, 1860s. Interpreting history in economic terms, Marx predicted that socialism would replace capitalism. He called for the proletariat to overthrow capitalism and to establish a classless society.

Marx believed that capitalist control of the economy and the government would not endure forever; capitalist society produced its own gravediggers—the working class. The capitalist system would perish just as the feudal society of the Middle Ages and the slave society of the ancient world had perished. From the ruins of a dead capitalist society, a new socioeconomic system, socialism, would emerge.

Marx predicted how capitalism would be destroyed. Periodic unemployment would increase the misery of the workers and intensify their hatred of capitalists. Owners of small businesses and shopkeepers, unable to compete with the great capitalists, would sink into the ranks of the working class, greatly expanding its numbers. Society would become polarized into a small group of immensely wealthy capitalists and a vast proletariat, poor, embittered, and desperate.

Growing increasingly conscious of their misery, the workers—aroused, educated, and organized by Communist intellectuals—would revolt. "Revolution is necessary," said Marx, "not only because the *ruling class* cannot be overthrown in any other way, but also because only in a revolution *can the class which overthrows it* rid itself of the accumulated rubbish of the past and become capable of reconstructing society."[11] The working-class revolutionaries would smash the government that helped the capitalists maintain their dominance. Then they would confiscate the property of the capitalists, abolish private property, place the means of production in the workers' hands, and organize a new society. The *Communist Manifesto* ends with a ringing call for revolution: "The Communists . . . openly declare that their ends can be attained only by the forcible overthrow of all existing social conditions. Let the ruling classes tremble at a Communist revolution. The proletarians have nothing to lose but their chains. They have a world to win. Workingmen of all countries, unite!"[12]

Marx did not say a great deal about the new society that would be ushered in by the socialist revolution. With the destruction of capitalism, no longer would society be divided into capitalist and workers, haves and have-nots, and oppressor and oppressed. Since this classless society would contain no exploiters, there would be no need for a state, which was merely an instrument for maintaining and protecting the power of the exploiting class. Thus, the state would eventually wither away. The production and distribution of goods would be carried out through community planning and communal sharing, which would replace the capitalist system of competition. People would work at varied tasks, rather than being confined to one form of employment. No longer factory slaves, people would be free to fulfill their human potential, to improve their relationships on a basis of equality with others, and to work together for the common good.

Marxism had immense appeal both for the downtrodden and for intellectuals. It promised to end the injustices of industrial society; it claimed the certainty of science; and it assured adherents that the triumph of their cause was guaranteed by history. In many ways, Marxism was a secular religion: the proletariat became a chosen class, endowed with a mission to achieve worldly salvation for humanity.

Marx's influence grew during the second wave of industrialization, in the closing decades of the nineteenth century, when class bitterness between the proletariat and the bourgeoisie seemed to worsen. Many workers thought that liberals and conservatives had no sympathy for their plight and that the only way to improve their lot was through socialist parties.

Critics of Marx

Critics point out serious weaknesses in Marxism. The rigid Marxist who tries to squeeze all historical events into an economic framework is at a disadvantage. Economic forces alone will not explain the triumph of Christianity in the Roman Empire, the fall of Rome, the Crusades, the French Revolution, modern imperialism, World War I, the rise of Hitler, or the mindset of contemporary Islamic terrorists. Economic explanations fall particularly flat in trying to account for the emergence of modern nationalism, whose appeal, resting on deeply ingrained emotional needs, crosses class lines. The world wars of the twentieth century were not between classes but between nations, and today conflict is often fueled by religious and ethnic hatreds.

Many of Marx's predictions or expectations failed to materialize. Workers in Western lands did not become the oppressed and impoverished proletariat that Marx had described in the mid-nineteenth century. Because of increased productivity and the efforts of labor unions and reform-minded governments, Western workers improved their lives considerably and totally abandoned revolution. The tremendous growth of a middle class of professionals, civil service employees, and small businesspeople belies Marx's prediction that capitalist society would be polarized into a small group of very rich capitalists and a great mass of destitute workers.

Marx believed that socialist revolutions would break out in the advanced industrialized lands. But the socialist revolutions of the twentieth century occurred in underdeveloped, predominantly agricultural countries. The state in Communist lands, far from withering away, grew more centralized, powerful, and oppressive. In no country where Communist revolutionaries seized power did people achieve the liberty that Marx desired. Nor, indeed, have orthodox Communists been able to sustain a viable economic system. The phenomenal collapse of Communist regimes in the former Soviet Union and Eastern Europe in recent years testifies to Marxism's failure. All these failed predictions and expectations seem to contradict Marx's claim that his theories rested on an unassailable scientific foundation.

LIBERALISM IN TRANSITION

In the early part of the nineteenth century, European liberals were preoccupied with protecting the rights of the individual against the demands of the state. They championed laissez-faire because they feared that state interference in the economy to redress social evils would threaten property rights and the free market, which they thought were essential to personal liberty. They favored property requirements for voting and office-holding because they were certain that the unpropertied and uneducated masses lacked the wisdom and experience to exercise political responsibility.

In the last part of the century, liberals began to support—though not without reservation and qualification—both extended suffrage and government action to remedy the abuses of unregulated industrialization. This growing concern for the welfare of the laboring poor coincided with and was influenced by an unprecedented proliferation of humanitarian movements on both sides of the Atlantic. Nurtured by both the Enlightenment and Christian teachings, reform movements called for the prohibition of child labor, schooling for the masses, humane treatment for prisoners and the mentally ill, equality for women, the abolition of slavery, and an end to war. By the beginning of the twentieth century, liberalism had evolved into liberal democracy, and laissez-faire had been superseded by a reluctant acceptance of some social legislation and government regulation. But from beginning to end, the central concern of liberals remained the protection of individual rights.

John Stuart Mill

The transition from laissez-faire liberalism to a more socially conscious and democratic liberalism is seen in the thought of John Stuart Mill (1806–1873), a British philosopher and statesman. Mill's *On Liberty* (1859) is the classic statement of individual freedom and minority rights: that the government and the majority may not interfere with the liberty of another human being whose actions do no injury to others.

Mill regarded freedom of thought and expression and the toleration of opposing and unpopular viewpoints as necessary preconditions for the shaping of a rational, moral, and civilized citizen. Political or social coercion, said Mill, is also a barrier to the full development of the individual. Liberty is a supreme good that benefits both the individual and the community. When we silence an opinion, said Mill, we hurt present and future generations. If the opinion is correct, "we are deprived of the opportunity of exchanging error for truth." If the opinion is wrong—and of this we can never be entirely certain—we "lose the

CHILD LABOR. At times children were beaten by supervisors, as in this English cotton factory.

clearer perception and livelier impression of truth produced by its collision with error."[13] Therefore, government has no right to force an individual to hold a view "because it will be better for him to do so, or because it will make him happier, or because in the opinions of others, to do so would be wise, or even right. These are good reasons for remonstrating with him, or reasoning with him, or persuading him, or entreating him, but not for compelling him or visiting him with any evil in case he do otherwise."[14]

Mill would place limits on the power of government, for in an authoritarian state citizens cannot develop their moral and intellectual potential. Although he feared the state as a threat to individual liberty, Mill also recognized the necessity for state intervention to promote individual self-development: the expansion of individual moral, intellectual, and esthetic capacities. For example, he maintained that it was permissible for the state to require children to attend school against the wishes of their parents, to regulate hours of labor, to promote health, and to provide workers' compensation and old-age insurance.

Thomas Hill Green

Thomas Hill Green (1836–1882), an Oxford University professor, argued that laissez-faire protected the interests of the economically powerful class and ignored the welfare of the nation. For example, Green valued private property but could not see how this principle helped the poor. "A man who possesses nothing but his powers of labor and who has to sell these to a capitalist for bare daily maintenance, might as well . . . be denied rights of property altogether."[15]

Green argued that the do-nothing state advocated by traditional laissez-faire liberalism condemned many citizens to destitution, ignorance, and despair. The state must preserve individual liberty and at the same time secure the common good by promoting conditions favorable for the self-development of the majority of the population.

Liberalism, for Green, encompassed more than the protection of individual rights from an oppressive government. A truly liberal society, he said, gives people the opportunity to fulfill their moral potential and human capacities. And social reforms initiated by the state assisted in the realization of this broader conception of liberty. Green and other advocates of state intervention contended that the government has a moral obligation to create social conditions that permit individuals to make the best of themselves. Toward that end, the state should promote public health, ensure decent housing, and provide for education. The uneducated and destitute person cannot be morally self-sufficient or a good citizen, Green and other progressives argued.

Green and his colleagues remained advocates of capitalism but rejected strict laissez-faire, which, they said, benefitted only a particular class at the expense of the common good. Overcoming a traditional liberal mistrust of state power, they viewed the state as an ethical institution, assigned it a positive role in improving social conditions, and insisted that state actions need not threaten individual freedom.

In general, by the beginning of the twentieth century, liberals in Britain increasingly acknowledged the need for social legislation; the foundations for the British welfare state were being laid. In several other countries, liberalism was expanding into political and social democracy, a trend that would continue in the twentieth century.

FEMINISM: EXTENDING THE PRINCIPLE OF EQUALITY

Another example of the expansion of liberalism was the emergence of feminist movements in Western Europe and the United States. Feminists insisted that the principles of liberty and equality expressed by the philosophes and embodied in the French Declaration of the Rights of Man and of the Citizen and the American Declaration of Independence be applied to women. Thus, Olympe de Gouges's *Declaration of the Rights of Women* (1791), modeled after the Declaration of the Rights of Man and of the Citizen, the French Revolution's tribute to Enlightenment ideals, stated: "Woman is born free and remains equal to man in rights. . . . The aim of every political association is the preservation of the natural . . . rights of man and woman."[16] And in 1837, English novelist and economist Harriet Martineau observed: "One of the fundamental principles announced in the Declaration of Independence is that governments derive their just power from the consent of the governed. How can the political condition of women be reconciled with this?"[17]

In the United States in the 1830s, Angelina and Sarah Grimké spoke in public—something women rarely did—against slavery and for women's rights. In 1838, Sarah Grimké published *Letters on the Equality of the Sexes and the Condition of Women*, in which she stated emphatically: "Men and women were Created Equal: they are both moral and accountable beings, and whatever is *right* for man to do is *right* for

women. . . . How monstrous, how anti-Christian, is the doctrine that woman is to be dependent on man!"[18] The Woman's Suffrage Movement, holding its first convention in 1848 in Seneca Falls, New York, drew up a Declaration of Statements and Principles that broadened the Declaration of Independence: "We hold these truths to be self-evident: that all men and women are created equal." The document protested "that woman has too long rested satisfied in the circumscribed limits which corrupt customs and a perverted application of the Scriptures have marked out for her" and called for the untiring effort of both men and women to secure for women "an equal participation with men in the various trades, professions, and commerce."[19]

In their struggle for equality, feminists had to overcome deeply ingrained premises about female inferiority and deficiencies. Opponents of women's rights argued that feminist demands would threaten society by undermining marriage and the family. An article in the *Saturday Review*, an English periodical, declared that "it is not the interest of States . . . to encourage the existence of women who are other than entirely dependent on man as well for subsistence as for protection and love. . . . Married life is a woman's profession."[20] This concern for the family combined with the traditional, biased view of woman's capacity to reason.

In contrast to most of their contemporaries, some prominent men did support equal rights for women. The poet Shelley, social theorist Jeremy Bentham, and political economist William Thompson, who wrote *Appeal of One Half of the Human Race* (1825), all supported female suffrage. John Stuart Mill thought that differences between the sexes (and between the classes) were due far more to education than to inherited inequalities. Believing that all people—women as well as men—should be able to develop their talents and intellects as fully as possible, Mill was an early champion of female equality, including women's suffrage. In 1867, Mill, as a member of Parliament, proposed that the suffrage be extended to women, but the proposal was rejected by a vote of 194 to 74.

In 1851, Mill had married Harriet Taylor, a longtime friend and a recent widow. An ardent feminist, Harriet Mill influenced her husband's thought. In *The Subjection of Women* (1869),

SHE. IT IS TIME I GOT OUT OF THIS PLACE. WHERE SHALL I FIND THE KEY?

CONVICTS LUNATICS AND WOMEN! HAVE NO VOTE FOR PARLIAMENT

Library of Congress Prints and Photographs Division/LC-USZC4-6888.

POSTER PUBLISHED BY THE ARTISTS' SUFFRAGE LEAGUE, DESIGNED BY EMILY HARDING ANDERES, C. 1908. This suffragette poster illustrates the fact that British women could not vote in the early twentieth century. The cap and gown of the woman college graduate does not help her find the key that will release her from the imprisoning categorization with felons and the mentally ill, who couldn't vote for Parliament either.

Mill argued that male dominance of women constituted a flagrant abuse of power. He described female inequality as a single relic of an old outlook that had been exploded in everything else. It violated the principle of individual rights and hindered the progress of humanity:

> ... the principle which regulates the existing social relations between the two sexes—the legal subordination of one sex to the other—is wrong in itself, and now one of the chief

> hindrances to human improvement ... it ought to be replaced by a principle of perfect equality, admitting no power or privilege on the one side, nor disability on the other.[21]

Mill considered it only just that women be free to take on all the functions and enter all the occupations until then reserved for men. The struggle for female rights became a major issue in several lands at the end of the nineteenth century and the beginning of the twentieth.

❖   ❖   ❖

NOTES

1. Quoted in Leonard J. Davis, "Gustave Flaubert," in *The Romantic Century*, Vol. 7 of *European Writers*, ed. Jacques Barzun and George Stade (New York: Charles Scribner's Sons, 1985), 1382.

2. Excerpted in Richard Olson, ed., *Science as Metaphor* (Belmont, Calif.: Wadsworth, 1971), 124.

3. Karl Pearson, *National Life from the Standpoint of Science* (London: Adam & Charles Black, 1905), 21.

4. Quoted in H. W. Koch, "Social Darwinism in the 'New Imperialism,'" in *The Origins of the First World War*, ed. H. W. Koch (New York: Taplinger, 1972), 345.

5. Friedrich von Bernhardi, *Germany and the Next War*, trans. Allen H. Powles (New York: Longman, Green, 1914), 18.

6. Quoted in George M. Fredrickson, *The Black Image in the White Mind* (New York: Harper Torchbooks, 1972), 26–27.

7. Ludwig Feurbach, *The Essence of Christianity*, trans. George Eliot (New York: Harper Torchbooks. 1957), 33.

8. Karl Marx, *Theses on Feuerbach*, excerpted in *Karl Marx: Selected Writings in Sociology and Social Philosophy*, ed. T. B. Bottomore and Maximilien Rubel (London: Watts, 1956), 69.

9. Karl Marx, *The German Ideology* (New York: International Publishers, 1939), 18.

10. Friedrich Engels, *The Origin of the Family, Private Property & the State*, in *A Handbook of Marxism*, ed. Emile Burns (New York: Random House, 1935), 330.

11. Marx, *German Ideology*, 69.

12. Karl Marx, *Communist Manifesto*, trans. Samuel Moore (Chicago: Henry Regnery, 1954), 81–82.

13. John Stuart Mill, *On Liberty* (Boston: Ticknor & Fields, 1863), 36.

14. Ibid., 22.

15. Thomas Hill Green, *Lectures on the Principles of Political Obligation* (Ann Arbor: University of Michigan Press, 1967), 219.

16. Excerpted in Eleanor S. Riemer and John C. Fout, eds., *European Women: A Documentary History, 1789–1945* (New York: Schocken Books, 1980), 63–64.

17. Excerpted in Gayle Graham Yates, ed., *Harriet Martineau on Women* (New Brunswick, N.J.: Rutgers University Press, 1985), 134.

18. Excerpted in Miriam Schneir, ed., *Feminism: The Essential Historical Writings* (New York: Vintage Books, 1972), 40–41.

19. Ibid., 76, 82.

20. Quoted in J. A. Banks and Olive Banks, *Feminism and Family Planning in Victorian England* (Liverpool: Liverpool University Press, 1965), 43.

21. John Stuart Mill, *The Subjection of Women*, in *On Liberty, Etc.* (London: Oxford University Press, 1924), 427.

Chapter 16

Europe in the Late Nineteenth Century: Modernization, Nationalism, Imperialism

- ■ The Advance of Industry
- ■ Great Britain: Reform and Unrest
- ■ France: A Troubled Nation
- ■ Germany: The Power State
- ■ Italy: Unfulfilled Expectations
- ■ Russia: Tsarist Autocracy
- ■ The Rise of Racial Nationalism
- ■ The Emergence of the New Imperialism
- ■ European Domination of Asia
- ■ The Scramble for Africa
- ■ The Legacy of Imperialism

Focus Questions

1. Why is the last part of the nineteenth century called the Second Industrial Revolution?
2. What domestic problems were faced by Britain, France, Germany, Italy, and Russia in the late nineteenth century?
3. Why is racial nationalism a repudiation of the Enlightenment tradition and a regression to mythical thinking?
4. What is the relationship between medieval and modern anti-Semitism? How does anti-Semitism demonstrate the immense power of mythical thinking?

5. What factors contributed to the rise of the new imperialism in the last part of the nineteenth century?
6. Why and how were Europeans able to dominate African and Asian lands?
7. What is the legacy of imperialism for the contemporary world?

*I*n the last part of the nineteenth century, the accelerated pace of industrialization and urbanization continued the process of modernization that had begun earlier with the Industrial Revolution and had transformed European and American societies. Simultaneously, Western nations built governmental machinery for dealing with great numbers of citizens. This strengthening and centralizing process—*state building*, in modern terminology—became the major activity of Western governments. State building meant not only strengthening central authority but also absorbing previously excluded classes into the nation, primarily through the power of nationalism, which governments fostered. A state's power grew enormously as its government affected the lives of ordinary citizens through military conscription, public education, and broad taxation.

Industrialization facilitated the trends toward centralization by concentrating factory workers in cities and loosening traditional rural ties. It greatly affected international relations as well. The amount of coal and iron produced, the mileage and tonnage of railways and navies, the mechanization of industry, and the skill of the populace became important components of national power.

Nationalism, which intensified during the last part of the nineteenth century, was to turn into the dominant spiritual force of European life. It grew increasingly belligerent, intolerant, and irrational, threatening both the peace of Europe and the liberal, humanist tradition of the Enlightenment. Nationalism and industrialization were the principal forces behind imperialism, leading European nations and the United States to extend their power over Asian, African, and Latin American lands. ❖

The Advance of Industry

Historians call the second half of the nineteenth century the Second Industrial Revolution because of the great increase in the speed and scale of technological advances and social transformation. It was also characterized by the rise of the middle class to political and social power corresponding to its economic power.

At the midcentury, farming was still the main occupation of people everywhere—even in Britain, where industrialization was most advanced. Even Britain had more domestic servants than factory workers and twice as many agricultural laborers as textile and clothing workers. Large factories were few, and handicrafts still flourished. Sailing ships still outnumbered steamships, and horses carried more freight than trains. This situation, however, changed radically in two spurts: the first between 1850 and 1870, and the second from the 1890s until World War I.

During the first spurt, in Europe and America the shift from hand to machine production accelerated, leading to the concentration of factory workers in industrial cities and the growth of unions. The standard of living for most workers rose. New machines and processes, legislation, and trade union bargaining relieved the worst conditions of early industrialization. At the same time, the first regulations of urban development and sanitation began to improve living conditions. In the more advanced industrial areas, the social organization of the workplace changed: the introduction of heavy equipment resulted in men replacing women and children in the factories. However, women forced out of factories (they would return during World War I) took jobs as domestics, pieceworkers, seamstresses, or laundresses. Children became students as the state and the economy demanded that they acquire at least a minimal education.

The scale of development changed markedly during the second spurt. Giant firms run by boards of directors, including financiers, operated far-flung enterprises of enormous, mechanized factories. These industrial giants were able to control the output, price, and distribution of commodities. They dominated smaller firms, financed and controlled research and development, and expanded far beyond their national frontiers. The "captains of industry"—the owners or managers of these large firms—possessed such extraordinary economic power that they often commanded political power as well. The emergence and concentration of heavy industry in large firms, capitalized by specialist banks, characterized the post-1890 period all over Europe.

Revolutionary technological changes furthered the growth of industry. At the midcentury, all of Europe caught the railroad mania that had seized Britain in the 1840s. This epic expansion of railroads was paralleled in shipping. In 1850, steam-powered ships constituted only 5 percent of the world's tonnage; by 1893, the figure had risen to half of all tonnage. At the turn of the century, two German engineers, Gottlieb Daimler and Karl Benz, joined to perfect the internal combustion engine. Then, an American, Henry Ford, using mass-production assembly-line techniques, brought out his Model T for "the ordinary man," and the automobile age was born. The invention of the diesel engine by another German in 1897 meant that cheaper, more efficient fuel could be used. Diesel engines soon replaced steam engines on giant cargo ships, warships, and luxury liners. In communications, the advent of the telegraph, telephone, and later radio also revolutionized people's lives.

However, economic development was extremely uneven. Central, Southern, and Eastern Europe remained overwhelmingly agricultural and stayed so until World War I and after.

Accelerated Urbanization

More rapid industrialization increased the numbers of northwestern Europeans and Americans

Chronology 16.1 ❖ Expansion of Western Power

1839–1842	Opium War: the British defeat the Chinese, annexing treaty ports in China and opening them to Western trade
1851–1852	Louis Napoleon Bonaparte overthrows Second Republic, becoming Emperor Napoleon III
1853	Commodore Perry, with U.S. naval forces, opens Japan to trade
1857–1858	Sepoy Mutiny; Britain replaces the East India Company and begins ruling India through a viceroy
1867	Second Reform Bill doubles the English electorate
1869	Opening of the Suez Canal
1870	Third French Republic is established
1870–1871	Franco-Prussian War; Paris Commune; creation of German Empire, with William I as kaiser and Bismarck as chancellor
1876	Stanley sets up posts in the Congo for Leopold II of Belgium
1882	Britain occupies Egypt
1884	Berlin Conference on Africa; Reform Bill grants suffrage to most English men
1894–1906	Dreyfus affair in France
1898	Spanish–American War: United States acquires the Philippines and Puerto Rico and occupies Cuba; battle of Omdurman
1899–1902	Boer War between the British and the Afrikaners
1900	Boxers rebel against foreign presence in China
1904–1905	Russo-Japanese War: the Japanese defeat the Russians
1911	Parliament Act limits power of the House of Lords
1919	Britain grants a legislative assembly in India; Gandhi's passive resistance movement broadens with the Amritsar Massacre

who lived in cities, which became more numerous, larger, and more densely populated. Although not an industrial city, London had become a megalopolis of five million people by 1880 and was home to seven million by 1914. Paris increased from two million to three million between 1850 and World War I. Berlin, a city of only half a million in 1866, reached two million by World War I. There were only three German cities of more than a hundred thousand on the eve of unification, but by 1903 there were fifteen.

In the cities, the middle class rose to political, economic, and social prominence, often expressing its newfound importance and prosperity through civic activity. As machinery replaced handicraft, the artisan working class experienced a sharp decline. Factory workers, their ranks swelled by peasants and displaced artisans, emerged as an important social group in cities. Industrialization also created a new, "white-collar" group of clerks, who tried to differentiate themselves from factory workers.

As a gesture of protest, in 1913 one militant threw herself to death under the king's horse at the races. In 1913, Pankhurst carried her appeal to the United States where she reiterated the anguish and logic of feminism:

> *Now gentlemen, in your heart of hearts you . . . know perfectly well that if the situation were reversed, if you had no constitutional rights and we had all of them, if you had the duty of praying and obeying and trying to look . . . pleasant, and we were the proud citizens who could decide our fate and yours, because we knew what was good for you better than you knew yourselves, you know perfectly well that you wouldn't stand for it a single day, and you would be perfectly justified in rebelling against such intolerable conditions.*[1]

When feminists were arrested for violating the law, they staged hunger strikes. Ugly situations resulted, with the police force-feeding the demonstrators and subjecting them to ridicule and rough treatment.

Feminists continued to press for the right to vote. When women played a major part on the home front in World War I, many of the elite changed their minds, and in 1918, British women over the age of thirty gained the vote. In 1928, Parliament lowered the voting age for women to twenty-one, the same qualifying age as that for male voters.

The Irish Question

Feminist agitation was one explosive issue confronting prewar Britain. Another was the Irish question. While moderate Irish nationalists called for *home rule* (self-government within the British Empire), something favored by many members of Parliament, Irish Catholic militants such as the Irish Republican Brotherhood and the Gaelic League pressed for full independence. Fearing Catholic domination, the Protestant Irish (Ulstermen) in the northern counties of Ulster strongly opposed independence for Ireland. The Ulster Volunteers recruited a large private army and openly trained it for revolution in the event that home rule was enacted. Gangs smuggled guns, soldiers fired on demonstrators, violence bred violence, and civil war seemed close.

In 1916, the Easter Rebellion, an Irish insurrection, was suppressed and its leaders executed. But the English cabinet was moved to proceed with home rule at once. The Irish revolt of 1919–1920 brought matters to a head: Ireland was divided, the overwhelmingly Catholic south gaining independence, and the six predominantly Protestant counties of Ulster remaining part of the United Kingdom.

At the beginning of the twentieth century, labor, Irish, and female militancy marred Britain's image of a stable, liberal, constitutional regime. Nevertheless, British parliamentary government survived every crisis and proved itself able to carry the nation successfully through a grueling world war.

FRANCE: A TROUBLED NATION

The Enlightenment and the French Revolution gave rise in France to a liberal-democratic tradition that valued individual rights and parliamentary government. At the same time, these developments produced a counter ideology that detested this outlook and sought to reshape France in accordance with its monarchial, aristocratic, and Catholic traditions. The struggle between these two Frances endured until the end of World War II.

In 1852, Louis Napoleon Bonaparte (1808–1873), who had been elected president of the Second French Republic in 1848, took the title of emperor in the tradition of his illustrious uncle. Napoleon III ruled in an authoritarian manner, permitting no opposition, censoring the press, and allowing the legislature little power. But in the 1860s, in a drastic shift, he introduced liberal reforms, pardoning political prisoners, removing press censorship, allowing workers the right to form unions, and approving a new constitution with safeguards for individual liberty. His reforms have perplexed historians. Was Napoleon III a sincere believer in liberal ideals who waited until his power was firmly established before implementing these ideals, or did he introduce reforms only because he feared unrest?

Defeat in the Franco-Prussian War (1870–1871) brought down the empire of Napoleon III. Bitter frustration with defeat and hatred of the Prussian invaders led the people of Paris to rise against the armistice signed by the provisional government—the politicians who had replaced Napoleon III. The Paris Commune (1871) began as a patriotic refusal to accept defeat and as a rejection of Napoleon's rule, but it became a rejection of the provisional government as well. Ultimately, the Communards (as those who resisted the Prussians and the provisional government were called) also challenged property owners.

The Communards included followers of the anarchist Joseph Proudhon and groups of republican and socialist veterans of the revolution of 1848, gathered from prisons, from hiding, and from exile. For two months in the spring of 1871, these revolutionaries ruled Paris. Then, Adolphe Thiers, head of the provisional government that still governed the rest of France, ordered an attack on Paris. The fighting was bitter and desperate, with many acts of terrorism and violence. Both sides in this civil war set fires that destroyed large parts of the city they loved. The Communards were defeated and treated as traitors: twenty thousand of them were executed without trial, and those who were tried received harsh sentences—death, life imprisonment, and deportation to prison colonies. Governing classes across Europe viewed the Paris Commune as a sign that the people should be ruled with an iron fist.

At first it seemed that a monarchy would succeed the empire of Napoleon III. But disunity among the monarchists enabled France to become a republic by default. Unlike Britain with its two-party system, the Third French Republic had many political parties, which contributed to instability. No one party had sufficient weight in parliament to provide strong leadership. Prime ministers resigned in rapid succession; cabinets rose and fell frequently, giving the impression of a state without direction. Yet in the process, legislation was enacted that made elementary education free and compulsory and legalized trade unions. The Third Republic survived, though not without major crises; the principal one was the Dreyfus affair, which left France deeply divided.

In 1894, Captain Alfred Dreyfus, an Alsatian-Jewish artillery officer, was wrongly accused of having sold secrets to the Germans. In reality, the true culprit was Major Ferdinand Walsin-Esterhazy, an amoral swindler who was constantly in debt. After a court martial, Dreyfus was condemned to life imprisonment on Devil's Island and ceremoniously stripped of his military insignia. Anti-Semitic elements joined with the Republic's opponents—monarchists, army leaders, clerics, and nationalists—to denounce and block every attempt to clear Dreyfus of the charges against him. In the beginning, few people defended Dreyfus; the vast majority felt that the honor of France and the army was at stake. Then individuals, mainly radical republicans, came to his defense, including the writers Anatole France and Émile Zola and the future republican leader Georges Clemenceau, along with university students. In what has been called a battle for the soul of France, they protested and demonstrated, insisting on a retrial and a revision of the verdict. In some fifty towns and cities, rioting anti-Semites shouted "Death to the Jews," looted Jewish shops, and desecrated synagogues. After many humiliations, Dreyfus was finally cleared in 1906.

The result of the victory of the radical republicans, however, was a fierce campaign to root out those opposing The Third Republic. The radicals expelled Catholic religious orders, confiscated their property, and waged a vigorous campaign to replace the influence of the parish priest with that of the district schoolmaster. Complete separation of church and state was ordered; taxes no longer supported the parishes and religious schools. The Dreyfus Affair intensified anti-Semitism within the French Right. In a position of power during World War II, the French Right cooperated with the Nazi occupiers in deporting Jews to their deaths.

Despite progress in the middle of the nineteenth century, French economic development lagged. France had fewer and smaller industries than Britain or Germany, and more French people lived in rural areas and small communities. In the 1880s, both trade unionism and political parties with a socialist program began to make headway and to press for social reform through the democratic parliamentary institutions of the Republic. However, France was very slow to enact social measures such as pensions and regulations governing working conditions, wages, and hours.

AFTER THE FALL: LA ROQUETTE PRISONERS BEFORE THE FIRING SQUAD. The repression of the Paris Commune, which resisted the French provisional government when it tried to make peace with the Prussians, was a brutal bloodbath with atrocities on both sides. When it was over, almost eight thousand were sent into exile, five thousand imprisoned and fined, and many executed. Few could have predicted that the republic established then would survive to World War II.

These measures, which might have improved the lives of ordinary people, were regarded by the ruling elite as hateful socialism; socialists, on the other hand, viewed them as token offerings to buy off workers.

France was a troubled country, and the Third Republic was not a popular regime. The church, the army, socialism, and even memories of the monarchy and the empire inspired deeper passions than did the Republic, which survived only because the dissension among its enemies allowed it to survive. France approached World War I as a deeply divided country. Yet when World War I broke out, the French people rallied to defend the nation.

GERMANY: THE POWER STATE

Prussia's victory over France in the Franco-Prussian War of 1870–1871 completed the struggle for German unification. The new government, the German Reich (empire), was headed by the king of Prussia. Though the Reichstag (lower house) was elected by universal suffrage, the real power lay in the hands of the emperor and Bismarck, the "Iron Chancellor," who was responsible only to the emperor. The German kaiser (emperor), unlike the British monarch, had considerable control over lawmaking and foreign affairs and commanded the army and navy. The emperor alone could remove the chancellor or the cabinet members from office. The sole control over Bismarck was the Reichstag's refusal to pass the budget, an extreme measure that politicians were usually unwilling to take. German politics after unification was dominated by conservative Prussian landowners (the Junkers) and industrialists—a ruling elite that held the key positions in the army, the diplomatic service, and the state bureaucracy and used its political power to thwart democracy and socialism.

Bismarck's political practices weakened liberal and democratic elements. Nor did German liberals vigorously struggle for basic political and civil liberties; they tolerated evasions of principles and practices that British politicians would never have allowed. While Britain, France, the United States, and other Western states were becoming more democratic, Germany remained a semi-autocratic state. The failure of democratic attitudes and procedures to take root in Germany was to have dangerous consequences for the future.

Bismarck regarded parties as incapable of making policy for the country. In Bismarck's mind, the Catholics and the socialists were internationalists who did not place the interests of Germany first. He began to persecute Catholics, who made up about 40 percent of the population. The *Kulturkampf* (struggle for culture) was a series of laws passed in 1873 to subject the church to the state. The laws discriminated against the Jesuits and required state supervision of the church and training of priests in state schools. Catholics had to be married by the state. Churchmen who refused to accept these laws were imprisoned or exiled. German liberals did not defend the civil liberties of the Catholics against these laws. Persecution only strengthened the German Catholics' loyalty to their church, however, and the Catholic Center Party gained support. Prussian conservatives, though Protestant, resented Bismarck's anticlerical policy, which could hurt Lutherans as well as Catholics. With the succession of Leo XIII to the papacy in 1878, Bismarck quietly opened negotiations for peace with the church.

When two attempts were made on William I's life in 1878, Bismarck demanded that the socialists be suppressed. In reality, the socialists, few in number, were not a threat; their immediate practical program was a demand for civil liberties and democracy in Germany. Only the narrowest of conservative views would have labeled the socialists as dangerous, but many in Germany, particularly the aristocratic Junker class, held such a narrow view. The liberals once again did not oppose Bismarck's special legislation—aimed at the socialists—outlawing subversive organizations and authorizing the police to ban meetings and newspapers. The Social Democratic Party, like the Catholic Center Party before, survived the persecution. It grew stronger and better disciplined as the liberals grew weaker, discredited by their unwillingness to act.

Bismarck's policy was not merely repressive. He tried to win the workers by paternalistic social legislation. Like many conservatives, he was disturbed by the effects of industrialization, which had developed at a rapid pace in the 1850s and 1860s. Germany was the first state to enact a program of social legislation for the proletariat; it included insurance against sickness, disability, accidents, and old age. The employer, the state, and the worker each contributed small amounts to an insurance fund.

Despite Bismarck's attempts to woo the workers away from socialism, the German working class continued to support the Social Democratic Party in elections. On the eve of World War I, union membership was roughly three million, and the Social Democratic Party was the largest single party in Germany. The socialists talked revolution, but the unions—the largest and most powerful in Europe—and many party members favored policies of gradual reform. Great numbers of German workers were patriotic, even imperialistic, and thought that their government deserved their loyalty.

By 1900, Germany had caught up with, and in some areas surpassed, Britain in economic growth. Aided by the skill of its scientists and inventors, Germany became a leader in the chemical and electrical industries. It possessed the most extensive sector of large-scale, concentrated industrial and corporate capitalism of any Great Power. Within a short period, Germany had become a strong, industrialized state, ready and eager to play an important role in world affairs. Its growing industrial and military might, linked with an aggressive nationalism, alarmed other countries. This combination of German vitality, aggressiveness, and the fears of its rivals helped lead to World War I.

ITALY: UNFULFILLED EXPECTATIONS

Italian nationalists expected greatness from the unification of their country, so long conquered, plundered, divided, and ruled by absolute princes. But the newly unified Italy faced serious problems. An overwhelmingly Roman Catholic country, it was split by religious controversy. Liberals and republicans wanted a secular state, with civil marriage and public education, which was anathema to the church. Furthermore, few Italians could participate in the constitutional monarchy. Of the 27 million citizens, only about two million could vote—even after the reforms of 1881, which tripled the electorate. Liberals could point out that almost every literate male could vote, but this achievement was small consolation to those who had fought for unification but now were denied voting privileges because they did not pass a literacy test.

Among Italian workers, cynicism about the government was so deep that many turned to radical movements, which advocated the rejection of authority and the tactics of terrorism, assassination, and general strikes. Disgust with parliamentary government led the workers to believe that direct action would gain more than elections and parties. Peasants in some rural areas, particularly in the south, were strongly Catholic, loyal to their landlords, and bitterly unhappy with their economic situation; they saw few signs of the new state other than hateful taxation and military conscription.

The ruling elite brushed aside Italy's difficult social and economic problems, concentrating instead on military glory and imperial expansion. The politicians trumpeted Italy's ambitions for Great Power status to justify military expenditures beyond the means of such a poor state. They presented Italy's scramble for African and Mediterranean territories as the solution to all its social ills. The profits from exploiting others would pay for badly needed social reforms, and the raw materials gained would fuel industrialization. None of these promises came true, which deepened the cynicism of a disillusioned people. As a foreign and as a domestic policy, this pursuit of glory was too costly for the fragile nation.

Before World War I, Italy was deeply divided politically. A wave of strikes and rural discontent gave sufficient warning to political leaders so that they declared neutrality, deciding, unlike Russia, not to risk the shaky regime by entering the war. But the appeals of expansionism were too great for them to maintain this policy.

RUSSIA: TSARIST AUTOCRACY

In the middle of the nineteenth century, Russia differed fundamentally from Western Europe. The great movements that had shaped the outlook of the modern West—Renaissance, Reformation, Scientific Revolution, Enlightenment, and Industrial Revolution—had barely penetrated Russia. Autocracy, buttressed by the Orthodox church, reigned supreme; the small and insignificant middle class did not possess the dynamic, critical, and individualistic spirit that characterized the Western bourgeoisie, and the vast majority of the people were illiterate serfs.

After Napoleon's defeat in 1814, some returning Russian officers, asking why Russia could not share the civilized life they had seen in Western Europe, turned revolutionary. The unsuccessful Decembrist uprising in 1825, during the brief interlude between the death of Alexander I (1801–1825) and the accession of Nicholas I (1825–1855), was the effort of a small group of conspirators demanding a constitution. Fear of revolution determined the character of the reign of Nicholas I and of tsarist governments thereafter.

Aware of the subversive influence of foreign ideas, Nicholas decreed an ideology of Russian superiority, called *official nationality*. The Russian people were taught to believe that the Orthodox creed of the Russian church, the autocratic rule of the tsar, and Russia's Slavic culture made the Russian Empire superior to the West. To enforce this contrived invincibility, Nicholas I created the Third Section, a secret agency of police spies, and controlled access to his country from Europe. Indeed, toward the end of his reign, he drew a virtual iron curtain to keep out dangerous influences. His ideal was a monolithic country, run like an army by a vigorous administration centered on the monarch; all Russians were to obey his wise and fatherly commands. Nicholas's successor, Alexander II (1855–1881), was determined to preserve autocratic rule. However, he wanted Russia to achieve what had made Western Europe strong: the energetic support and free enterprise of its citizens. Whether stimulating popular initiative was possible without undermining autocracy was the key puzzle for him and for his successors to the end of the tsarist regime.

Alexander's boldest reforms included the emancipation of the serfs in 1861. They were liberated from bondage to the nobility and given land of their own, but not individual freedom. They remained tied to their villages and to their households, which owned the land collectively. Emancipation did not transform the illiterate peasants into enterprising and loyal citizens. For the non-peasant minority, a package of other reforms brought new opportunities: limited self-government for selected rural areas and urban settlements, an independent judiciary, trial by jury, and the introduction of a profession novel to Russians: the practice of law.

Meanwhile, Alexander reopened the borders, allowing closer ties with Europe and westernizing Russian society. The rising class of businesspeople and professional experts looked west and conformed to Western middle-class standards. There was some relaxation in the repression of non-Russian minorities. Railroads were constructed, which facilitated agricultural exports and permitted the import of Western goods and capital. For some years, the economy boomed.

More significant in the long run was the flowering of Russian thought and literature among the intelligentsia. These were educated Russians whose minds were shaped by Western schooling and travel, yet who still were prompted by the "Russian soul." They quarreled with fierce sincerity over whether Russia should pursue superiority by imitating the West or by cultivating its own Slavic genius, possibly through a Pan-Slavic movement. Pan-Slavism, which glorified the solidarity of Russians with other Slavic peoples of Eastern Europe, was a popular cause. Even more than the tsars, the intelligentsia hoped for a glorious Russia that would outshine the West.

Yet tsarist autocracy undercut their hopes. The tsar would not permit open discussion likely to provoke rebellion. Liberals advocating gradual change were thwarted by censorship and the police. The 1860s saw the rise of self-righteous fanatics who were ready to match the chicanery of the police and foment social revolution. By the late 1870s, they organized themselves into a secret terrorist organization. In 1881, they assassinated the tsar. The era of reforms ended.

The next tsar, Alexander III (1881–1894), a firm if unimaginative ruler, returned to the repressive policies of Nicholas I. In defense against the revolutionaries, he perfected the police state, even enlisting anti-Semitism in its cause. He updated autocracy and stifled dissent but also promoted economic development. Russia had relied too heavily on foreign loans and goods; it had to build up its own resources. It also needed more railroads to bind its huge empire together. So in 1891, the tsar ordered the construction of the Trans-Siberian Railroad. Soon afterward, Minister of Finance Sergei Witte used railroad expansion to boost heavy industry and industrialization generally.

Yet forced industrialization also brought perils. It propelled the country into alien and often hated ways of life and created a discontented new class of workers. In addition, it promoted literacy and contact with Western Europe and thus helped to increase political agitation. Indispensable for national self-assertion and survival, industrialization strained the country's fragile unity.

The first jolt, the revolution of 1905, followed Russia's defeat by Japan in the Russo-Japanese War. Fortunately for Nicholas II (1894–1917), his soldiers stayed loyal. The autocracy survived, although, as a concession to the revolution, it was now saddled with a parliament, called the Imperial Duma. The new regime, inwardly rejected by Nicholas II, started auspiciously. Under its freedoms, Russian art and literature flourished and the economy progressed. Agrarian reforms introduced the incentives of private property and individual enterprise in the villages. The supporters of the new constitutional experiment hoped for a liberal Russia at last, but in vain.

THE RISE OF RACIAL NATIONALISM

In the first half of the nineteenth century, European nationalism and liberalism went hand in hand. Liberals sought both the rights of the individual and national independence and unification. Liberal nationalists believed that a unified state free of foreign subjugation was in harmony with the principle of natural rights, and they insisted that love of country led to love of humanity. As nationalism grew more extreme, however, its profound difference from liberalism became more apparent. The extreme nationalism of the late nineteenth and early twentieth centuries contributed to World War I and to the rise of Fascism after the war; it was the seedbed of totalitarian nationalism. Nationalism proved more successful than liberalism in attracting allegiance; it was often expressed by a total commitment to the nation and the different classes uniting in a common cause.

Concerned exclusively with the greatness of the nation, extreme nationalists rejected the liberal emphasis on political liberty. Liberals regarded the state as a community of individuals voluntarily bonded by law and citizenship and entitled to the same rights. To extreme nationalists, however, the state was the highest development of a folkish-racial spirit inherited from their ancestors. In their eyes, profound and irreconcilable differences separated "their people" from those who did not share this ancestry. Even if others had dwelled in the land for centuries, such people were seen as unwanted and dangerous aliens. Increasingly, nationalists attacked parliamentary government as an obstacle to national power and greatness and maintained that authoritarian leadership was needed to meet national emergencies. The needs of the nation, they said, transcended the rights of the individual.

Extreme nationalists also rejected the liberal ideal of equality. Placing the nation above everything, nationalists accused national minorities of corrupting the nation's spirit, and they glorified war as a symbol of the nation's resolve and will. In the name of national power and unity, they persecuted minorities at home and stirred up hatred against other nations. Increasingly, they embraced militaristic, imperialistic, and racist doctrines. At the founding of the Nationalist Association in Italy in 1910, one leader declared: "Just as socialism teaches the proletariat the value of class struggle, so we must teach Italy the value of international struggle. But international struggle is war? Well, then, let there be war! And nationalism will arouse the will for a victorious war . . . the only way to national redemption."[2]

Similar sentiments were voiced in 1913 by a German nationalist: "Let us regard war as holy, like the purifying force of fate, for it will awaken in our people all that is great and ready for selfless sacrifice, while it cleanses our soul of the mire of petty egotistical concerns."[3]

Interpreting politics with the logic of emotions, extreme nationalists insisted that they had a sacred mission to regain lands once held in the Middle Ages, to unite with their kinfolk in other lands, or to rule over peoples considered inferior. Loyalty to the nation-state was elevated above all other allegiances. The ethnic state became an object of religious reverence; the spiritual energies that formerly had been dedicated to Christianity were now channeled into the worship of the nation-state, igniting primitive, dark, cruel feelings.

By the beginning of the twentieth century, conservatives had become the staunchest advocates of nationalism, and the nationalism preached by conservative extremists was stripped of Mazzini's humanitarian ideals of liberty, equality, and the fellowship of nations. Particularly in Germany, landholding aristocrats, generals, and clergy, often joined by big industrialists, saw nationalism as a convenient instrument for gaining a mass following in their struggle against democracy, social reform, and socialism. Championing popular nationalist myths and dreams and citing Social Darwinist doctrines, a newly radicalized right, dominated by the elite of German society, hoped to harness the instinctual energies of the masses, particularly the peasants and the lower middle class—shopkeepers, civil servants, and white-collar workers—to conservative causes. Peasants viewed liberalism and a godless Marxism as threats to traditional values, while the lower bourgeoisie feared the power of an organized proletariat. These people were receptive to the rhetoric of ultranationalists, who denounced democracy and Marxism as threats to national unity and Jews as aliens endangering the nation. Nationalism was presented as a victory of idealism over materialism and as the subordination of class and personal interests to the general good of the nation.

Volkish Thought

Extreme nationalism was a general European phenomenon, but it proved especially dangerous in Germany. Bismarck's triumphs lured Germans into a dream world. Many started to yearn for the extension of German power throughout the globe. The past, they said, belonged to France and Britain; the future, to Germany.

The most ominous expression of German nationalism (and a clear example of mythical thinking) was *Volkish* thought. (*Volk* means "folk" or "people"; in this context, "ethnic" might be the best meaning.) German Volkish thinkers sought to bind the German people together through a deep love of their language, traditions, and fatherland. These thinkers felt that Germans were animated by a higher spirit than that found in other peoples. To Volkish thinkers, the Enlightenment and parliamentary democracy were foreign ideas that corrupted the pure German spirit. With fanatical devotion, Volkish thinkers embraced all things German—the medieval past, the German landscape, the simple peasant, the village—and denounced the liberal, humanist tradition of the West as alien to the German soul.

Volkish thought attracted Germans frightened by all the complexities of the modern age—industrialization, urbanization, materialism, class conflicts, and alienation. Seeing their beloved Germany transformed by these forces of modernity, Volkish thinkers yearned to restore the sense of community, the spiritual unity, that they attributed to the preindustrial age. Only by identifying with their sacred soil and sacred traditions could modern Germans escape from the evils of industrial society. Only then could the different classes band together in an organic unity.

The Volkish movement had little support from the working class, which was concerned chiefly with improving its standard of living. The movement appealed mainly to farmers and villagers, who regarded the industrial city as a threat to native values and a vehicle for spreading foreign ideas; to artisans and small shopkeepers, threatened by big business; and to scholars, writers, teachers, and students, who saw in Volkish nationalism a cause worthy of their idealism. The schools were leading agents for the dissemination of Volkish ideas.

Volkish thinkers glorified the ancient Germanic tribes that had overrun the Roman Empire; they contrasted their courageous and vigorous German ancestors with the effete and degenerate Romans.

A few tried to harmonize ancient Germanic religious traditions with Christianity. Such attitudes led Germans to see themselves as a heroic people fundamentally different from and better than the English and the French. It also led them to regard German culture as unique—innately superior and opposed to the humanist outlook of the Enlightenment. Like their romantic predecessors, Volkish thinkers held that the German people and culture had a special destiny and a unique mission. They pitted the German soul against the Western intellect—feeling, intuition, spirit, and

Cover of an edition of "The Jewish Danger: The Protocols of the Learned Elders of Zion," c. 1940 (colour litho), French School, (20th century)/ Private Collection/Archives Charmet/The Bridgeman Art Library.

THE PROTOCOLS OF THE ELDERS OF ZION. This infamous forgery, commissioned by the Russian secret police, became an international bestseller and contributed to outrages against Jews. Anti-Semitic organizations continue to publish and circulate it today. The picture is the actual cover of a French edition of the *Protocols*, c. 1934.

idealism against a drab rationalism. To be sure, the Western humanist tradition had many supporters in Germany, but the counterideology of Volkish thought was becoming increasingly widespread. This murky, irrational, radically nationalist, and anti-liberal outlook shaped by these Volkish thinkers in the late nineteenth century would later undermine support for the democratic Weimar Republic established in Germany after World War I and provide Hitler with receptive listeners. Many of Hitler's supporters hoped that he would transform these Volkish longings into political realities.

Racist doctrines had an especially strong appeal for Volkish thinkers. According to these doctrines, race was the key to history; not only physical features, but also moral, esthetic, and intellectual qualities distinguished one race from another. For racist thinkers, a race demonstrated its vigor and achieved greatness when it preserved its purity; intermarriage between races was contamination that would result in genetic, cultural, and military decline. Unlike liberals, who held that anyone who accepted German law was a member of the German nation, racists argued that a person's nationality was a function of his or her "racial soul" or "blood." Like their Nazi successors, Volkish thinkers claimed that the German race was purer than, and therefore superior to, all other races. Its superiority was revealed in such physical characteristics as blond hair, blue eyes, and fair skin—all signs of inner qualities lacking in other races.

German racial nationalists insisted that Germany had a unique mission; as a superior race, Germans had a national right to dominate other peoples, particularly the "racially inferior" Slavs of the East. The Pan-German Association, whose membership included professors, schoolteachers, journalists, lawyers, and aristocrats, spread racial and nationalist theories and glorified war as an expression of national vitality. A statement from the association's journal sums up its philosophy: "The racial biological ideology tells us that there are races that lead and races that follow. Political history is nothing but the history of struggles among the leading races. Conquests, above all, are always the work of the leading races. Such men can conquer, may conquer, and shall conquer."[4]

Anti-Semitism: The Power and Danger of Mythical Thinking

German racial nationalists singled out Jews as a wicked race and a deadly enemy of the German people. Anti-Semitism, which was widespread in late-nineteenth-century Europe, provides a striking example of the perennial appeal, power, and danger of mythical thinking—of elevating to the level of objective truth ideas that have no basis in fact but provide all-encompassing, emotionally satisfying explanations of life and history. By manufacturing the myth of the wicked Jew, the radical Right confirmed the insight reached by the political theorist Georges Sorel (see the section on Sorel under "Irrationalism" in Chapter 17): that people are moved and united by myths that offer simple, clear, and emotionally gratifying resolutions to the complexities of the modern world.

Anti-Semitic organizations and political parties sought to deprive Jews of their civil rights, and anti-Semitic publications proliferated. Edouard Drumont, a French journalist, argued that the Jews, racially inferior and believers in a primitive religion, had gained control of France. Like medieval Christian anti-Semites, Drumont accused Jews of deicide and of using Christian blood for ritual purposes. Drumont's newspaper (established with Jesuit funds) blamed all the ills of France on the Jews, called for their expulsion from the country, and predicted that they would be massacred. French politicians played the anti-Semitic card in order to gain popularity and votes. Fully one-third of the Chamber of Deputies wanted to deprive Jews of the civil rights that they had gained during the French Revolution.

Romania barred most Jews from holding office and from voting, imposed various economic restrictions on them, and limited their admission into secondary schools and universities. The Romanian government even financed an international congress of anti-Semites, which met in Bucharest in 1886. In German-speaking Austria, Karl Lueger, a leader of the Christian Social Party, founded by conservative German nationalists, exploited anti-Semitism to win elections in overwhelmingly Catholic Vienna. Georg von Schönerer, founder of the German National Party in Austria, wanted to eliminate Jews from all areas of public life.

Primary Source

The Pan-German League: Extreme Racial Nationalism

Organized in 1894, the ultranationalist and imperialist Pan-German League called for German expansion both in Europe and overseas. It often expressed blatantly Social Darwinist and racist views, as illustrated in the following article, which appeared in 1913 in the league's principal publication.

The historical view as to the biological evolution of races tells us that there are dominant races and subordinate races. Political history is nothing more than the history of the struggles between the dominant races. Conquest in particular is always a function of the dominant races. . . . Where now in all the world does it stand written that conquering races are under obligations to grant after an interval political rights to the conquered? Is not the practice of political rights an advantage which biologically belongs to the dominant races? . . . What are [these] rights? . . . In my opinion, the rights of men are, first, personal freedom; secondly, the right of free expression of opinion—as well as freedom of the press; . . . and, finally, the right to work, in case one is without means. . . .

. . . The man with political rights sets up schools, and the speech used in the instruction is his speech. . . . The purpose must be to crush the [individuality of the] conquered people and its political and lingual existence. . . .

The conquerors are acting only according to biological principles if they suppress alien languages and undertake to destroy strange popular customs. . . . Only the conquering race must be populous, so that it can overrun territory it has won. Nations that are populous are, moreover, the only nations which have a moral claim to conquest, for it is wrong that in one country there should be overpopulation while close at hand—and at the same time on better soil—a less numerous population stretches its limbs at ease.

[As to the inferior races:] From political life they are to be excluded. They are eligible only to positions of a non-political character, to commercial commissions, chambers of commerce, etc. . . . The principal thing for the conqueror is the outspoken will to rule and the will to destroy the political and national life of the conquered. . . .

Question for Analysis

1. Why is an ideology based on biological racism particularly dangerous?

Conquest and Kultur, compiled by Wallace Notestein and Elmer E. Stoll (Washington, D.C.: Government Printing Office, 1917), 90–91.

Russia placed a quota on the number of Jewish students admitted to secondary schools and higher educational institutions, confined Jews to certain regions of the country, and, "to purify the sacred historic capital," expelled about twenty thousand Jews from Moscow. Some government officials encouraged or did nothing to stop *pogroms* (mob violence) against Jews. Between 1903 and 1906, pogroms broke out in 690 towns and villages, most of them in the Ukraine, traditionally a hotbed of anti-Semitism. (Ukrainian folksongs and legends glorified centuries-old massacres of Jews.) The attackers looted, burned, raped, and murdered, generally with impunity. In Russia and several other lands, Jews were put on trial for slaughtering Christian children as part of a Passover ritual—a deranged accusation that survived from the Middle Ages.

Defeat in the Opium War also forced changes on the Manchu emperor. He drew on China's mandarins (high officials) to revitalize the Manchu bureaucracy by cleaning out much of the official corruption, which weighed heavily on the poorest taxpayers, and by strengthening China against the Westerners, sometimes by hiring Westerners to train Chinese armies. Nevertheless, widespread economic discontent, hatred of the Manchu (who were regarded by many Chinese as foreign conquerors, even though the conquest had taken place some two hundred years earlier), and religious mysticism led to the Taiping Rebellion of 1850–1864. This uprising seriously threatened the dynasty, which called on Western assistance to suppress the rebels. For this aid, Britain and France extorted additional concessions from the emperor.

For a time, the Europeans seemed content with trading rights in coastal towns and preferential treatment for their subjects. But the Sino-Japanese War of 1894–1895, which Japan won easily because of China's weakness, encouraged the Europeans to mutilate China. Britain, France, Russia, and Germany all scrambled for concessions, protectorates, and spheres of influence. The United States, which insisted that it be given any trading concession that any other state received, proclaimed an "Open Door" policy: that trade should be open to all and that the Great Powers should respect China's territorial integrity. The U.S. action may have restrained the Western powers from partitioning China, but it was also a way to safeguard American interests there.

Chinese traditionalists organized secret societies to expel foreigners and to punish those Chinese who accepted Christianity or any other form of westernization. In 1900, encouraged by Empress Tzuhsi, the Society of Righteous and Harmonious Fists (called the Boxers by Europeans) attacked foreigners throughout the north of China. An international army of Europeans, Japanese, and Americans suppressed the rebellion, seized Chinese treasures, and forced China to pay an indemnity. They also made China agree to the stationing of foreign troops on its soil.

Chinese discontent with the Manchu dynasty deepened, as did unrest and nationalistic opposition to the foreigners. When the Japanese defeated the Russians in 1905, many Chinese argued that the only way to protect their country was to imitate the West, as the Japanese had done. Many signs of growing nationalism appeared. In 1911, nationalist revolutionaries, strongly present among soldiers, workers, and students, overthrew the Manchu and declared a republic. Sun Zhongshan (Sun Yatsen, 1866–1925), who was in the United States when the revolution broke out, returned to China to become the first president of the republic and the head of the Nationalist Party.

Espousing the Western ideas of democracy, nationalism, and social welfare (the three principles of the people, as Sun called them), the republic struggled to establish its authority over a China torn by civil war and ravaged by foreigners. Russia was claiming Mongolia, and Britain was claiming Tibet. The northern warlords, who were regional leaders with private armies, resisted any attempt to strengthen the republic's army because it might diminish their power. In the south, however, the republic more or less maintained control. After Sun's death, the Guomindong (Kuomintang), under the authoritarian leadership of Jiang Jieshi (Chiang Kai-shek, 1887–1975), tried to westernize by using the military power of the state and introducing segments of a modern economic system. But attacked both from within by the Communists led by Mao Zedong (Mao Tsetung, 1893–1976), and by the Japanese after 1931, the Guomindong made slow progress. A divided China continued to be at the mercy of outside interests until after World War II.

Japan

Japan, like China, was opened to the West against its will. The Japanese had expelled Europeans in the seventeenth century, remaining isolated for the next two hundred years. By the 1850s, however, as in India and China, social dissension within Japan and foreign pressure combined to force the country to admit outside trade. Americans

◄ *Map 16.1* ASIA IN 1914 In addition to the lands depicted in the map under European and American domination, Western states also exercised control over technically sovereign states, particularly China and Siam (Thailand).

in particular refused to accept Japanese prohibitions on commercial and religious contacts. Like China, Japan succumbed to superior technological power. In 1853, Commodore Matthew C. Perry sailed into Tokyo Bay, making a show of American strength and forcing the Japanese to sign a number of treaties that granted Westerners extraterritoriality and control over tariffs.

A flood of violence surged over Japan. Determined to preserve Japan's independence, a group of *samurai*, the warrior nobility, seized the government. This takeover—the Meiji Restoration of 1867—returned power to the emperor, or Meiji, from the feudal aristocracy, which had ruled in his name for almost seven hundred years. The new government enacted a series of reforms, turning Japan into a powerful, modern, unitary state. Large landowners were persuaded to give their estates to the emperor in exchange for compensation and high-level positions in the government. All classes were made equal before the law. As in France and Germany, universal military service was required, which diminished social privilege and helped to imbue Japanese of all classes with nationalism. The Japanese modeled their constitution on Bismarck's: there was a parliament, but the emperor held the most authority, which he delegated to his ministers to govern in his name without much control from the parliament.

The Meiji regime introduced modern industry and economic competition. Japanese visited factories all over the West and hired Westerners to teach industrial skills. The government built defense industries, backed heavy industry and mining, and developed a modern communications system of railways, roads, and telegraphs. Industry in Japan adopted traditional Japanese values and emphasized cooperation more than competition; relations between employer and employee were paternalistic rather than indifferent and deferential rather than hostile. Within little more than a generation of the Meiji Restoration, Japan moved from economic backwardness to a place among the top ten industrial nations. To underdeveloped countries, Japan became a model of a nation that borrowed from the West yet preserved its traditional values and social structure.

By 1900, Japan had ended the humiliating treaties with the West and become an imperialist power in its own right. It had won Taiwan and Korea in its war with China in 1894–1895, although the Great Powers intervened, forcing the Japanese to return some of the spoils of victory while they themselves grabbed greater spheres of influence from the helpless Chinese. Their self-serving maneuvering infuriated the Japanese. Finally, in 1904, conflict over influence in Manchuria brought Japan and Russia to war, which Japan won. The victory of an Asian power over a Western power had a tremendous impact on Asian nationalists. If Japan could unite its people with nationalism and strong leadership, others should be able to do likewise. Japan's victory inspired anti-Western and nationalist movements throughout China, Indochina, India, and the Middle East.

In the 1930s, extreme militarist and nationalistic groups, which were set on imperial expansion in China, gained the upper hand in Japan. To Asians in the 1930s, Japan seemed to champion Asian racial equality and to oppose Western imperialism. Many leaders of nationalist movements in Burma, India, Indochina, and Indonesia were attracted for a time by Japan's pose. World War II, however, brought Japanese occupation and exploitation, not freedom and equality for Asians.

THE SCRAMBLE FOR AFRICA

The most rapid European expansion took place in Africa. Until the 1870s, Great Power interest in Africa seemed marginal and likely to decline even further. As late as 1880, European nations ruled just a tenth of the continent. Only three decades later, by 1914, Europeans had claimed all of Africa except Liberia (a small territory of freed slaves from the United States) and Ethiopia, which had successfully held off Italian invaders at Adowa in 1896.

The activities of Leopold II, the king of Belgium, spurred expansion. In 1876, as a private entrepreneur, he formed the International Association for the Exploration and Civilization of Central Africa. Leopold sent Henry Stanley (1841–1904) to the Congo River Basin to establish trading posts, sign treaties with the chiefs, and claim the territory for the association. Stanley, an adventurer and a newspaper reporter who had fought on both sides of the American Civil War, had earlier led an expedition to Central Africa in search of David Livingstone, the popular missionary explorer, who was believed to be in danger. For men like Stanley, Leopold's private development efforts promised profit and adventure. For the Africans, they promised brutal exploitation. The French responded to Leopold's actions by immediately establishing a protectorate on the north bank of the Congo. The scramble was on.

The Berlin Conference

Bismarck and Jules Ferry, the premier of France, called an international conference of the Great Powers in Berlin in 1884 to lay some ground rules for the development of Africa south of the Sahara. The Berlin Conference established the rule that a European country had to occupy territory in order to claim it. This led to a mad race to the interior of Africa; it was a field day for explorers and soldiers. As Europeans rushed to claim territory, they ignored both natural and cultural frontiers. Even today, the map of Africa reveals many straight (and thus artificial) boundary lines, rather than the irregular lines of natural boundaries, such as rivers and mountains.

The conference declared that Leopold (as an individual, not as the king of Belgium) was the personal ruler of the Congo Free State. Before long, Leopold's Congo Association was trying to turn a profit with practices as vicious as those of the African slave traders. At the turn of the century, Edward D. Morel, an English humanitarian, produced evidence that slavery, mutilation, brutality, and murder were commonly practiced to force blacks to work for the rubber plantations in the Congo. In response to the outcry of public opinion, in 1908 the Belgian parliament declared the territory a Belgian colony, thus putting an end to Leopold's private enterprise.

The British in Africa

For much of the nineteenth century, British interest in Africa was minimal. The opening in 1869 of the Suez Canal, which Britain viewed as a vital highway to India, greatly increased the strategic value of Egypt. Officially a part of the Ottoman Empire, Egypt had in effect been independent of the Ottoman sultan since the 1830s. When a nearly bankrupt Egypt could not pay its foreign debts and was threatened with internal rebellion, Britain intervened as "protector" in 1882. Prime Minister Gladstone, a "little Englander" (one who opposed empire), promised to withdraw British troops once the situation stabilized.

Not only did the British fail to withdraw from Egypt, they also moved further south into the Sudan to quell a Muslim holy war against Egyptian authority and British influence. In 1885, the Sudanese, led by the Mahdi, who viewed himself as the successor to Muhammad, captured Khartoum and killed the popular General Charles Gordon, the recently appointed governor-general of the Sudan. In 1898, the British, armed with machine guns, mowed down charging Muslims at Omdurman by the thousands, suffering only slight casualties themselves.

Immediately after the battle, British forces confronted the French at Fashoda in the Sudan. In the diplomatic crisis that followed, Britain and France were brought to the brink of war, and public passions were inflamed. However, since France was too divided by the Dreyfus affair at home to risk a showdown with Britain, the French cabinet ordered retreat.

The British also sought territory in South Africa. Cecil Rhodes (1853–1902), who had gone to South Africa for his health in 1870 and made a fortune in diamonds and gold, dreamed of expanding the British Empire. "The British," he declared, "are the finest race in the world and the more of the world we inhabit the better it is for the human race."[8] Rhodes was responsible for acquiring Rhodesia (Zimbabwe), a sizable and wealthy territory, for Britain. He also plotted to involve Britain in a war with the Boers, Dutch farmers and cattlemen who had settled in South Africa in the seventeenth century.

During the Napoleonic wars, the British had gained Cape Town at the southern tip of Africa, a useful provisioning place for trading ships bound for India. Despising British rule and refusing to accept the British abolition of slavery in 1833, the

TANGIER
Casablanca
MOROCCO
Madeira Is.
(Portugal)
Algiers
TUNISIA
Mediterranean Sea
Canary Is.
(Spain)
Ifni (Sp.)
Tripoli
Cyrene
ALGERIA
LIBYA
Cairo
RIO DE ORO
EGYPT
Red Sea
Nile R.
ARABIA
FRENCH WEST AFRICA
SENEGAL
GAMBIA
Niger R.
L. Chad
Khartoum
ERITREA
PORT.
GUINEA
ANGLO-EGYPTIAN
SUDAN
Adowa
FRENCH
SOMALILAND
SIERRA LEONE
NIGERIA
Fashoda
BRITISH
SOMALILAND
IVORY
COAST
TOGO
LIBERIA
CAMEROONS
ETHIOPIA
GOLD
COAST
RIO MUNI
FRENCH EQUATORIAL AFRICA
Ubangi R.
ITALIAN
SOMALILAND
Congo R.
UGANDA
BRITISH
EAST AFRICA
ATLANTIC OCEAN
CABINDA
(Port.)
BELGIAN
CONGO
L. Victoria Nyanza
L. Tanganyika
Mombasa
GERMAN
EAST AFRICA
Zanzibar (Gr. Br.)
INDIAN
OCEAN
0   500   1000 Km.
0   500   1000 Mi.
ANGOLA
NYASALAND
RHODESIA
MOZAMBIQUE
MADAGASCAR
GERMAN
SOUTHWEST
AFRICA
BECHUANALAND
TRANSVAAL
ORANGE
FREE STATE
SWAZILAND
UNION OF
SOUTH AFRICA
NATAL
BASUTOLAND
Cape Town

ARAB AND BERBER PEOPLES
SAHARA
(Gr. Br.)
Sudanese Empires
(Port.)
(Gr. Br.)
(Sp.)
Swahili language
Bantu Kingdoms
AFRICA IN 1878

British	Portuguese
French	Belgian
German	Spanish
Italian	Independent African states

© 2016 Cengage Learning.

Boers moved northward in a migration called the Great Trek (1835–1837), warring with African tribes along the way. They established two republics, the Transvaal and the Orange Free State, whose independence the British recognized in the 1850s. The republics' democratic practices did not extend to black Africans, who were denied political rights. In 1877, the British annexed the Transvaal, but Boer resistance forced them in 1881 to recognize the Transvaal's independence again.

The discovery of rich deposits of gold and diamonds in the Boer lands reinforced Rhodes's dream of building a great British empire in Africa. In 1895, his close friend Leander Jameson led some six hundred armed men into the Transvaal, hoping to create a pretext for a British invasion. Although the raid failed and both Jameson and Rhodes were disgraced, tensions between Britain and the Boer republics worsened, and in 1899, the Anglo-Boer War broke out.

The Boers were formidable opponents—farmers by day and commandos by night, armed with the latest French and German rifles. To deal with their stubborn foe, the British herded, or "concentrated," thousands of Boers, including women and children, into compounds surrounded by barbed wire, where some twenty-five thousand perished. The nasty war ended in 1902. Hoping to live together in peace with the Boers, the British drew up a conciliatory treaty. In 1910, the former Boer republics were joined with the British territories into the Union of South Africa. Self-government within the British Empire for the British settlers and the Boers did not help the majority black population; it still had to cope with the Boers' deeply entrenched racist attitudes.

Other European Countries in Africa

The cost of imperialism in Africa seemed high not only to the British, but to other imperialists as well. The Italians' defeat at Adowa (1896) by Ethiopians belied Italian dreams of empire and

◀ *Map 16.2* Africa in 1914 Africa's rapid dismemberment is pictured in these two maps. In 1878, there were few enclaves of Europeans along the coasts. By 1914, Africa had been carved up, and all but Ethiopia and Liberia had been claimed.

national glory. (Bismarck scoffed that the Italians had enormous appetites but very poor teeth.) Germans could take little heart from their African acquisitions—Southwest Africa (Namibia), East Africa (Tanzania, but not Zanzibar, which was British), the Cameroons, and Togo (part of Ghana today).

The German colonies were the most efficiently governed—critics said the most ruthlessly controlled. Racist theory determined the attitudes and behavior of colonial administrators in German Southwest Africa. Blacks were barred from riding horses, walking on footpaths, or entering libraries. One missionary observed: "The average German looks down upon the natives as being about on the same level as the higher primates (baboon being their favorite term for natives) and treats them like animals."[9] In 1904, General Adolf Lebrecht von Troth ordered the extermination of the Herero people in Southwest Africa. Driven into the desert, some eighty thousand Hereros, almost the entire nation, perished from dehydration and starvation. German colonies yielded few benefits other than pride of ownership, because they were costly to govern. And the Belgians had obviously gained no prestige from the horrors perpetrated in the Congo. Serious thinkers, contemplating the depths to which Europeans would sink in search of fortune and fame, began to suggest that barbarity characterized the Europeans more than the Africans. The Europeans seemed to be the moral barbarians, as novelist Joseph Conrad and others pointed out. For the most part, honor was fleeting and profits illusory in these new African empires.

THE LEGACY OF IMPERIALISM

World War I was a turning point in the history of imperialism. The principle of self-determination, championed for European nationalities at the peace conference, was seized on by Asian and African intellectuals, who intensified their anti-imperialist efforts. After World War II, the exhausted colonial powers were reluctant to fight rebellious colonies. Moreover, after waging war to destroy Nazi imperialism and racism, European colonial powers had little moral justification to deny other peoples self-determination.

© Bettman/CORBIS.

SLAVES DRYING COFFEE ON A PLANTATION IN TERREIROS, RIO DE JANEIRO (C. 1882). Brazilian slaves toiled to produce one of Brazil's main exports to the world market. The world economy, which developed during the commercial revolution, emerged full force with the age of imperialism as more and more resources of the non-European world were produced, bought, and sold for overseas consumption.

Decades after the decolonization of most of the world, the consequences of imperialism persist. To former colonial peoples, imperialism has been a source of great bitterness, not only because of its economic exploitation but also because of its encouragement of racism and callous disregard of other cultures. Thus, non-Western nationalism has often included anti-Western elements.

Imperialism accelerated the growth of a global market economy, completing the trend that started with the Commercial Revolution of the sixteenth and seventeenth centuries. At the beginning of the twentieth century, in many parts of Europe even the working classes and the peasantry were able

to buy goods from faraway places—goods that had previously been available only to the very wealthy. The underdeveloped areas of the world, in turn, found markets for their crops and were able to buy European goods—at least, the wealthy could.

Imperialism has also fostered the spread of Western civilization around the globe. The influence of Western ideas, institutions, techniques, language, and culture is apparent everywhere. English and, to some extent, French are international languages. African and Asian lands have adopted, often with limited success, democracy and parliamentary government from the West. Socialism, a Western ideology, has been transplanted in some Third World countries. Industrialism and modern science, both achievements of the West, have become globalized. So, too, have Western agricultural techniques, business practices, medicine, legal procedures, school curricula, architecture, music, and dress. That Turkish women are no longer required to wear the veil, that Chinese women no longer have their feet bound, that Indians have outlawed untouchability, that (with exceptions) Arabs, Africans, and Indians no longer practice slavery—all these changes have occurred under the influence of Western ideas. (To be sure, cultural forms have not moved in only one direction: African and Asian ways have also influenced Western lands.) The impact of Western ways on Asian and African lands is one of the most crucial developments of our time.

NOTES

1. Excerpted in Jane Marcus, ed., *Suffrage and the Pankhursts* (London: Routledge & Kegan Paul, 1967), 160–161.

2. Cited in Edward R. Tannenbaum, *1900: The Generation Before the Great War* (Garden City, N.Y.: Doubleday, 1976), 337.

3. Quoted in Roger Chicklering, *Imperial Germany and the Great War, 1914–1918* (Cambridge: Cambridge University Press, 1998), 9.

4. Cited in Horst von Maltitz, *The Evolution of Hitler's Germany* (New York: McGraw-Hill, 1973), 33.

5. Quoted in Raul Hilberg, *The Destruction of the European Jews* (Chicago: Quadrangle, 1967), 10–11.

6. Quoted in Helmut Krausnick, Hans Buchheim, Martin Broszat, and Hans-Adolf Jacobsen, *Anatomy of the SS State*, trans. Richard Barry et al. (London: William Collins Sons, 1968), 9.

7. Quoted in Peter G. J. Pulzer, *The Rise of Political Anti-Semitism in Germany and Austria* (New York: Wiley, 1964), 299.

8. Joseph E. Flint, *Cecil Rhodes* (Boston: Little, Brown, 1974), 248.

9. Quoted in Niall Ferguson, *Civilization: The West and the Rest* (New York: Penguin, 2011), 177.

Chapter 17

Modern Consciousness: New Views of Nature, Human Nature, and the Arts

- ■ **Irrationalism**
- ■ **Freud: A New View of Human Nature**
- ■ **Social Thought: Confronting the Irrational and the Complexities of Modern Society**
- ■ **The Modernist Movement**
- ■ **Modern Physics**
- ■ **The Enlightenment Tradition in Disarray**

Focus Questions

1. In what ways did late modern thought and the arts break with the Enlightenment tradition?
2. Why did Nietzsche disdain both Christianity and democracy?
3. How did the thought of Nietzsche, Bergson, and Sorel exemplify the growing power and appeal of irrationalism?
4. What did Freud contribute to an understanding of irrationalism? What is his relationship to the Enlightenment tradition?
5. How did the modernist movement in the arts break with the standards of esthetics that had governed European culture since the Renaissance?
6. How did modern physics alter the Newtonian conception of the universe?
7. In what ways was the Enlightenment tradition in disarray by the early twentieth century?

The modern mentality may be said to have passed through two broad phases: early modernity and late modernity. Formulated during the era of the Scientific Revolution and the Enlightenment, early modernity stressed confidence in reason, science, human goodness, and humanity's capacity to improve society. Then, in the late nineteenth and early twentieth centuries, a new outlook took shape. Late modern thinkers and scientists achieved revolutionary insights into human nature, the social world, and the physical universe; writers and artists opened up hitherto unimagined possibilities for artistic expression.

These developments produced a shift in European consciousness. The mechanical model of the universe, which had dominated the Western outlook since Newton, was fundamentally altered. The Enlightenment view of human rationality and goodness was questioned, and the belief in natural rights and objective standards governing morality came under attack. Rules of esthetics that had governed the arts since the Renaissance were discarded. Shattering old beliefs, late modernity left Europeans without landmarks—without generally accepted cultural standards or agreed-upon conceptions about human nature and the meaning of life.

The late modern period was marked by extraordinary creativity in thought and the arts. Yet imaginative and fruitful as these changes were for Western intellectual and cultural life, they also helped to create the disoriented, fragmented, and troubled era that characterized the twentieth century. ❖

IRRATIONALISM

While many intellectuals continued to adhere to the outlook identified with the Enlightenment, some thinkers in the late nineteenth century challenged the basic premises of the philosophes and their nineteenth-century heirs. In particular, they repudiated the Enlightenment conception of human rationality, stressing instead the irrational side of human nature. Regarding reason as sovereign, the philosophes had defined human beings by their capacity to think critically; now

thinkers saw blind strivings and animal instincts as the primary fact of human existence. It seemed that reason exercised a very limited influence over human conduct, and that impulses, drives, and instincts—all forces below the surface—determined behavior much more than did logical consciousness. Carrying this view further, intellectuals argued that the universal principles advanced by rational thought often expressed self-interest, not truth.

The problem of irrationalism is manifold. Some thinkers, while recognizing the weakness of reason, continued to value it and sought to preserve it as an essential ingredient of civilized life. Some studied manifestations of the irrational in myth, religion, the arts, and politics in a logical and systematic way in order to gain a more complete understanding of human nature and human behavior. Others, concentrating on the creative potential of the irrational, urged nourishing the feelings, which they considered vital to artistic creativity and a richer existence. Still others celebrated violence as a healthy expression of the irrational.

The new insights into the irrational side of human nature and the growing assault on reason had immense implications for political life. In succeeding decades, these currents of irrationalism would become ideologized and politicized by unscrupulous demagogues, who sought to mobilize and manipulate the masses. The popularity of Fascist movements, which openly denigrated reason and exalted race, blood, action, and will, demonstrated the naïveté of nineteenth-century liberals, who believed that reason had triumphed in human affairs.

Nietzsche

The principal figure in the "dethronement of reason" and the glorification of the irrational was the German philosopher Friedrich Nietzsche (1844–1900). Nietzsche's writings are not systematic treatises but collections of aphorisms, often containing internal contradictions. Consequently, his philosophy lends itself to misinterpretation and misapplication. For example, Nazi theorists distorted Nietzsche to justify their notions of the German master race.

FRIEDRICH NIETZSCHE (1844–1900). Possessing the intuitive genius of a great poet, Nietzsche grasped the crucial problem afflicting the modern European soul: What path should the individual take in a world where God is dead? Nietzsche's answer to this question—the overman who creates his own values—lent itself to considerable misinterpretation and distortion and had little constructive social value.

© Bettmann/Corbis.

Nietzsche attacked the accepted views and convictions of his day as a hindrance to a fuller and richer existence. He denounced social reform, parliamentary government, and universal suffrage; ridiculed the vision of progress through science; condemned Christian morality; and mocked the liberal belief in human beings' essential goodness and rationality. We must understand, he said, that life, which is replete with cruelty, injustice,

uncertainty, and absurdity, is not governed by rational principles. There exist no absolute standards of good and evil whose truth can be demonstrated by reflective reason. Nothing is true; there is no higher purpose or sense to the universe or human existence. There is only the naked individual living in a godless and absurd world.

Modern bourgeois society, said Nietzsche, was decadent and enfeebled—a victim of the excessive development of the rational faculties at the expense of will and instinct. Against the liberal-rationalist stress on the intellect, Nietzsche urged recognition of the dark, mysterious world of instinctual desires—the true forces of life. Smother the will with excessive intellectualizing, and you snuff out the spontaneity that sparks cultural creativity and ignites a zest for living. The critical and theoretical outlook destroys the creative instincts. To realize his multifaceted potential, man must stop relying on the intellect and nurture again the instinctual roots of human existence.

Christianity, with all its prohibitions, restrictions, and demands to conform, also stifles the human impulse for life, said Nietzsche, the son of a Lutheran pastor. Christian morality must be obliterated, for it is fit only for the weak, the slave. According to Nietzsche, the triumph of Christianity in the ancient world was an attempt of the resentful slave and the slave-like plebeian to prevent their aristocratic superiors from expressing their heroic natures and to strike back at those noble spirits, whom they envied. Their way of striking back was to condemn as evil the very traits that they themselves lacked—strength, power, assertiveness, and a zest for life—and to make their own base, wretched, and life-negating values (meekness, self-denial, humility, and compassion) the standard of all things. Then they saddled people with guilt if they deviated from these contemptible values. This transvaluation of values engineered by Christianity, said Nietzsche, led to a deterioration of life and culture.

Although the philosophes had rejected Christian doctrines, they had largely retained Christian ethics. Unlike the philosophes, however, Nietzsche did not attack Christianity because it was contrary to reason. He attacked it because, he said, it gave man a sick soul. It was life-denying. Blocking the free and spontaneous exercise of human instincts, it made humility, weakness, and self-abnegation virtues and pride a vice. In short, Christianity extinguished the spark of life in man. This spark of life, this inner yearning that fosters self-creation, must again burn.

"God is dead," proclaimed Nietzsche. God is man's own creation. Dead also are all the inherited truths based on nature and reason. There are no higher worlds, no transcendent or metaphysical truths, no morality derived from God or nature, and no natural rights, scientific socialism, or inevitable progress. We wander through an eternal nothing in which all the old values and truths have lost their intelligibility. This *nihilism*—the belief that moral and social values have no validity—had caused a crisis in European life. But the death of God and of all transcendental truths could mean the liberation of man, insisted Nietzsche. Man can surmount nihilism by adopting a new orientation that gives primacy to the superior man—the *overman* or *superman* who asserts his will, gives order to chaotic passions, makes great demands on himself, and lives life with a fierce joy. The overman aspires to self-perfection; without fear or guilt he rejects traditional religion and morality and creates his own values and defines his own self, his own life. Such a man could overcome the deadening uniformity and mediocrity of modern civilization. He could undo democracy and socialism, which have made masters out of cattle-like masses, and surmount the shopkeeper's spirit, which had made man soft and degenerate.

European society, as Nietzsche saw it, lacked heroic figures; everyone belonged to a vast herd, but there were no shepherds. Europe could be saved only by the emergence of such a higher type of man—one who would not be held back by the egalitarian rubbish preached by Christians, democrats, and socialists. "A declaration of war on the masses by *higher* man is needed," said Nietzsche, to end "the dominion of *inferior* men." Europe required "the annihilation of *suffrage universal,* i.e., the system through which the lowest natures prescribe themselves as laws for the higher."[1] Europe needed a new breed of rulers, a true aristocracy of masterful men.

Nietzsche conceived of the overman as a new kind of man who breaks with accepted morality and sets his own standards. He does not repress his instincts but asserts them. He destroys old values and asserts his prerogative as master. Free of Christian guilt, he proudly affirms his own being; dispensing with Christian "thou shalt not," he instinctively says, "I will." He dares to be himself. Because he is not like other people, traditional definitions of good and evil have no meaning for him. He does not allow his individuality to be stifled. He makes his own values, those that flow from his very being. He knows that life is meaningless but lives it laughingly, instinctively, fully.

The overman understands and exemplifies the ultimate fact of life: that "the most fearful and fundamental desire in man [is] his drive for power,"[2] that human beings crave and strive for power ceaselessly and uncompromisingly. It is perfectly natural for human beings to want to dominate nature and other human beings; inherent in human nature is the desire "to overpower . . . to overthrow . . . to become master, [to] thirst for enemies and antagonisms and triumphs."[3] This will to power is not a product of rational reflection but flows from the very essence of human existence. As the motivating force in human behavior, it governs everyday life and is the determining factor in political life. The enhancement of power brings supreme enjoyment: "The love of power is the demon of men. Let them have everything—health, food, a place to live, entertainment—they are and remain unhappy and low-spirited; for the demon waits and waits and will be satisfied. Take everything from them and satisfy this and they are almost happy—as happy as men and demons can be."[4] The masses, cowardly and envious, will condemn the higher man as evil; this has always been their way. Thus, Nietzsche castigates democracy because it "represents the disbelief in great human beings and an elite society,"[5] and Christianity because it imposes an unnatural morality, one that affirms meekness, humility, and compassion.

The influence of Nietzsche's philosophy is still a matter of controversy and conjecture. Perhaps better than anyone else, Nietzsche grasped the crucial problem of modern society and culture: that with the "death of God," traditional moral values had lost their authority and binding power. In a world where nothing is true, all is permitted. Nietzsche foresaw that the future, an age without values, would be violent and sordid, and he urged individuals to face themselves and life free of illusions, pretense, and hypocrisy. Nietzsche is also part of the general nineteenth-century trend that sought to affirm the human being and earthly aspirations rather than God or salvation. Furthermore, Nietzsche's rejection of God and metaphysics, as well as of all-embracing theories of history (Hegelianism and Marxism, for example) that attempt to impose rational patterns on the past and the present, is crucial to the development of existentialism (see "Existentialism" in Chapter 19) and the movement in contemporary thought called postmodernism.

However, no helpful social policy could be derived from Nietzsche's heroic individualism, which taught that "there are higher and lower men and that a single individual can ... justify the existence of whole millennia."[6] Nietzsche thought only of great individuals, humanity's noblest specimens, who overcome mediocrity and the artificiality of all inherited values; the social community and social injustice did not concern him. "The weak and ill-constituted shall perish: first principle of our philanthropy. And one shall help them to do so."[7] Surely, these words offer no constructive guidelines for dealing with the problems of modern industrial civilization.

Likewise, Nietzsche had no constructive proposals for dealing with the disintegration of rational and Christian certainties. Instead, his vitriolic attack on European institutions and values helped erode the rational foundations of Western civilization. This assault appealed immensely to intellectuals in Central Europe, who saw Nietzsche's philosophy as liberating an inner energy. Thus, many young people, attracted to Nietzsche, welcomed World War I; they viewed it as a way of realizing Nietzsche's command to live dangerously; they saw it as a creative and aesthetic experience that would overcome bourgeois decadence and clear a path to a new heroic age. They took Nietzsche's words literally: "A society that definitely and *instinctively* gives up war and conquest is in decline."[8]

Nazi theorists tried to make Nietzsche a forerunner of their movement. They sought from him a philosophical sanction for their own thirst for power, contempt for the weak, ruthlessness, and glorification of action. They also wanted this sanction for their cult of the heroic and their Social Darwinist revulsion for human equality. Recasting Nietzsche in their own image,

the Nazis viewed themselves as Nietzsche's supermen: members of a master race who, by force of will, would conquer all obstacles and reshape the world according to their self-created values. Some German intellectuals were drawn to Nazism because it seemed a healthy affirmation of life, the life with a new purpose for which Nietzsche called.

Detesting German nationalism and militarism, Nietzsche himself scoffed at the notion of German racial superiority, disdained (despite some unfortunate remarks) anti-Semitism, and denounced state worship. He would have abhorred Hitler and would have been dismayed at the twisting of his idea of the will to power into a prototype Fascist principle. The men that he admired were passionate but self-possessed individuals who, by mastering their own chaotic passions, would face life and death courageously, affirmatively, and creatively. Such men make great demands on themselves. Nevertheless, as Janko Lavrin points out, "Practically all the Fascist and Nazi theories can find some support in Nietzsche's texts, provided one gives them the required twist."[9]

Nietzsche's extreme and violent denunciation of Western democratic principles, including equality, his praise of power, his call for the liberation of the instincts, his elitism, which denigrates and devalues all human life that is not strong and noble, and his spurning of humane values provided a breeding ground for violent, anti-rational, anti-liberal, and inhumane movements. His philosophy, which included loose talk about the virtues of pitiless warriors, the breeding of a master race, and the annihilation of the weak and the ill constituted, is conducive to a politics of extremes that knows no moral limits.

Bergson

Another thinker who reflected the growing irrationalism of the age was Henri Bergson (1859–1941), a French philosopher of Jewish background. Originally attracted to positivism, Bergson turned away from the positivistic claim that science could explain everything and fulfill all human needs. Such an emphasis on the intellect, said Bergson, sacrifices spiritual impulses,

Primary Source

Friedrich Nietzsche: *The Will to Power*

First published in 1901, one year after Nietzsche's death, The Will to Power *consists of the author's notes written in the years 1883–1888. The following passages from this work show Nietzsche's contempt for democracy and socialism and proclaim the will to power.*

728 (March–June 1888)

. . . A society that definitely and *instinctively* gives up war and conquest is in decline: it is ripe for democracy and the rule of shopkeepers. . . .

752 (1884)

. . . Democracy represents the disbelief in great human beings and an elite society: "Everyone is equal to everyone else." "At bottom we are one and all self-seeking cattle and mob."

753 (1885)

I am opposed to 1. socialism, because it dreams quite naively of "the good, true, and beautiful" and of "equal rights"—(anarchism also desires the same ideal, but in a more brutal fashion); 2. parliamentary government and the press, because these are the means by which the herd animal becomes master.

765 (Jan–Fall 1888)

. . . Another Christian concept, no less crazy, has passed even more deeply into the tissue of modernity: the concept of the "equality of souls before God." This concept furnishes the prototype of all theories of equal rights: mankind was first taught to stammer the proposition of equality in a religious context, and only later was it made into morality: no wonder that man ended by taking it seriously, taking it practically!—that is to say, politically, democratically, socialistically. . . .

854 (1884)

In the age of *suffrage universel*, i.e., when everyone may sit in judgment on everyone and everything, I feel impelled to reestablish *order of rank*.

861 (1884)

A declaration of war on the masses by *higher men* is needed! Everywhere the mediocre are combining in order to make themselves master! Everything that makes soft and effeminate, that serves the ends of the "people" or the "feminine," works in *favor of suffrage universel*, i.e., the dominion of *inferior* men. But we should take reprisal and bring this whole affair (which in Europe commenced with Christianity) to light and to the bar of judgment.

862 (1884)

A doctrine is needed powerful enough to work as a breeding agent: strengthening the strong, paralyzing and destructive for the world-weary.

The annihilation of the decaying races. Decay of Europe.—The annihilation of slavish evaluations.—Dominion over the earth as a means of producing a higher type.—The annihilation of the tartuffery [hypocrisy] called "morality." . . . The annihilation of *suffrage universel*; i.e., the system through which the lowest natures prescribe themselves as laws for the higher.—The annihilation of mediocrity and its acceptance. . . .

870 (1884)

The root of all evil: that the slavish morality of meekness, chastity, selflessness, absolute obedience, has triumphed. . . .

874 (1884)

The degeneration of the rulers and the ruling classes has been the cause of the greatest mischief in history! Without the Roman Caesars and Roman society, the insanity of Christianity would never have come to power.

997 (1884)

I teach: that there are higher and lower men, and that a single individual can under certain circumstances justify the existence of whole millennia—that is, a full, rich, great, whole human being in relation to countless incomplete fragmentary men.

Question for Analysis

1. Why did Friedrich Nietzsche attack democracy, socialism, and Christianity? How do you respond to his attack?

From *The Will to Power* by Friedrich Nietzsche, edited by R. J. Hollingdale, translated by Walter Kaufmann, copyright © 1967 by Walter Kaufmann. Used by permission of Random House, Inc.

---

imagination, and intuition and reduces the soul to a mere mechanism.

The methods of science cannot reveal ultimate reality, Bergson insisted. European civilization must recognize the limitations of scientific rationalism. Our capacity for intuition, whereby the mind achieves an immanent relationship with the object—participates in it—tells us more about reality than the method of analysis employed by science. The intuitive experience—something like the artist's instant comprehension of a natural scene—is a direct avenue to truth that is closed to the calculations and measurements of science. Bergson's philosophy pointed away from science toward religious mysticism.

To his admirers, Bergson's philosophy liberated the person from the constraints of positivism, mechanism, and materialism. It extolled the creative potential of intuition, the mystical experience, and the poetic imagination—those forces of life that resist categorization by the scientific mind. A protest against modern technology and bureaucracy and against all the features of mass society that seemed to stifle individual uniqueness and spontaneity, it sought to reaffirm the primacy of the individual in an increasingly mechanized and bureaucratic world. The popularity of Bergson's intuitionism and vitalism, with their depreciation of reason, symptomized the unsuspected strength and appeal of the nonrational—another sign that people were

searching for new alternatives to the Enlightenment worldview.

Sorel

Nietzsche proclaimed that irrational forces constitute the essence of human nature, and Bergson held that a nonrational intuition brought insights unattainable by scientific thinking. Georges Sorel (1847–1922), a French social theorist, recognized the political potential of the nonrational. Like Nietzsche, Sorel was disillusioned with contemporary bourgeois society, which he considered decadent, soft, and unheroic. Whereas Nietzsche called for the higher man to rescue society from decadence and mediocrity, Sorel placed his hopes in the proletariat, whose position made them courageous, virile, and determined. Sorel wanted the proletariat to destroy the existing order. This overthrow, said Sorel, would be accomplished through a general strike: a universal work stoppage that would bring down governments and give power to the workers.

Sorel saw the general strike as having the appeal of a great mobilizing myth. What was important was not that the general strike actually take place, but that its image stir all the anticapitalist resentments of the workers and inspire them to carry out their revolutionary responsibilities. Sorel understood the extraordinary potency of myth for eliciting total commitment and inciting heroic action. Because it appeals to the imagination and feelings, myth is an effective way of moving the masses to revolt. By believing in the myth of the general strike, workers would soar above the moral decadence of bourgeois society and bear the immense sacrifices that their struggle called for. Sorel thought that the only recourse for workers was direct action and violence, which he regarded as ennobling, heroic, and sublime—a means of restoring grandeur to a flabby world.

Sorel's pseudoreligious exaltation of violence and mass action, his condemnation of liberal democracy and rationalism, and his recognition of the power and political utility of fabricated myths would find concrete expression in the Fascist movements after World War I. Sorel heralded the age of mass political movements committed to revolutionary violence and of myths manufactured by propaganda experts determined to destroy democracy.

FREUD: A NEW VIEW OF HUMAN NATURE

In many ways, Sigmund Freud (1856–1939), an Austrian-Jewish physician who spent most of his adult life in Vienna, was a child of the Enlightenment. Like the philosophes, Freud identified civilization with reason and regarded science as the avenue to knowledge. But in contrast to the philosophes, Freud focused on the massive power and influence of nonrational drives. Whereas Nietzsche glorified the irrational and approached it with a poet's temperament, Freud recognized its potential danger. He sought to comprehend it scientifically and wanted to regulate it in the interests of civilization. Unlike Nietzsche, Freud did not belittle the rational but always strove to salvage respect for reason. Better than anyone, Freud recognized reason's limitations and the power of the nonrational, but he never wavered in his support of reason.

Freud's explorations of the world of the unconscious had a profoundly upsetting impact on our conception of the self. Freud himself viewed his theories as a great blow to human pride, to "man's craving for grandiosity."

> *Humanity has, in the course of time, had to endure from the hands of science two great outrages upon its naive self-love. The first was when it realized that our earth was not the center of the universe, but only a tiny speck in a world-system of a magnitude hardly conceivable; this is associated in our minds with the name of Copernicus. . . . The second was when biological research robbed man of his peculiar privilege of having been specially created, and relegated him to a descent from the animal world, implying an ineradicable animal nature in him: this transvaluation has been accomplished in our own time upon the investigations of Charles Darwin. . . . But man's craving for grandiosity is now suffering the third and most bitter blow from present-day psychological research which is endeavoring to show the "ego" of each of us that he is not even master in his own house, but that he must remain content with the veriest scrap of information about what is going on unconsciously in his own mind.*[10]

Freud held that people are not fundamentally rational; human behavior is governed primarily by powerful inner forces, which are hidden from consciousness. These instinctual strivings, rather than rational faculties, constitute the greater part of the mind. Freud's great achievement was his exploring of the world of the unconscious with the tools and temperament of a scientist. He showed that the irrational contained a structure that could be empirically explained and rationally explored.

After graduating from medical school, Freud specialized in the treatment of nervous disorders. His investigations led him to conclude that childhood fears and experiences, often sexual in nature, accounted for neuroses: disorders in thinking, feeling, and behavior that interfere with everyday acts of personal and social life.

Neuroses can take several forms, including hysteria, anxiety, depression, and obsessions. So painful and threatening were these childhood emotions and experiences that his patients banished them from conscious memory to the realm of the unconscious.

To understand and treat neurotic behavior, Freud said, it was necessary to look behind overt symptoms and bring to the surface emotionally charged experiences and fears—childhood traumas—that lie buried in the unconscious, along with primitive impulses. The key to the

FREUD AND HIS DAUGHTER ANNA (1912). Sigmund Freud, the father of psychoanalysis, penetrated the world of the unconscious in a scientific way. He concluded that powerful drives govern human behavior more than reason does. His explorations of the unconscious produced an image of the human being that broke with the Enlightenment's view of the individual's essential goodness and rationality.

unconscious, in Freud's view, was the interpretation of dreams. An individual's dreams, said Freud, reveal his or her secret wishes—often socially unacceptable desires and frightening memories. Too painful to bear, they get locked up in the deepest dungeons of our unconscious. But even in their cages, the demons remain active, continuing to haunt us and to generate conflicts. Our distress is real and even excruciating, but we do not know its source.

The *id*, the subconscious seat of the instincts, said Freud, is a "cauldron full of seething excitations," which constantly demand gratification. The id is primitive and irrational. It knows no values and has no awareness of good and evil. Unable to endure tension, it demands sexual release, the termination of pain, the cessation of hunger. When the id is denied an outlet for its instinctual energy, we become frustrated, angry, and unhappy. Gratifying the id is our highest pleasure. But the full gratification of instinctual demands is detrimental to civilized life. That is why the *ego*, which stands for reason, seeks to hold the id in check, to bring it in line with reality.

Freud postulated a harrowing conflict between the relentless strivings of our instinctual nature and the requirements of civilization. Civilization, for Freud, required the renunciation of instinctual gratification and the mastery of animal instincts, a thesis he developed in *Civilization and Its Discontents* (1930). Although Freud's thoughts in this work were no doubt influenced by the great tragedy of World War I and the rise of Fascist movements in several European lands, the main theme could be traced back to his earlier writings. Human beings derive their highest pleasure from sexual fulfillment, said Freud, but unrestrained sexuality drains off psychic energy needed for creative artistic and intellectual life; it also directs energies away from work needed to preserve communal life. Hence society, through the family, the priest, the teacher, and the police, imposes rules and restrictions on our animal nature. In effect, it implants a conscience in human beings that serves to check antisocial drives.

But this is immensely painful. The human being is caught in a tragic bind. Society's demand for repression of instincts in the interest of civilization causes terrible frustration. Equally

The Scream, 1893, by Edvard Munch (1863–1944). The dark forces of emotional torment and sexual aberration fill the canvases of the Norwegian postimpressionist Edvard Munch.

distressing, the violation of society's rules under the pressure of instinctual needs evokes terrible feelings of guilt. Either way, people suffer; civilized life simply entails too much pain for people. It seems that the price we pay for civilization is neurosis. Most people cannot endure the amount of instinctual renunciation that civilization requires. There are times when our elemental human nature rebels against all the restrictions and "thou shalt nots" demanded by society, against all the misery and torment imposed by civilization.

"Civilization imposes great sacrifices not only on man's sexuality but also on his aggressivity,"[11] said Freud. People are not good by nature, as the philosophes had taught, but are predisposed to behave cruelly and brutally. They are "creatures among whose instinctual endowments is to be reckoned a powerful share of aggressiveness." Their first inclination is not to love their neighbor, but to "satisfy their aggressiveness on him, to exploit his capacity for work without compensation, to use him sexually without his consent, to seize his possessions, to humiliate him, to cause him pain, to torture and to kill him."[12]

Man is wolf to man, Freud concluded. "Who has the courage to dispute it in the face of all the evidence in his own life and in history?"[13] Civilization "has to use its utmost efforts in order to set limits to man's aggressive instincts," but "in spite of every effort these endeavors of civilization have not so far achieved very much."[14] People find it difficult to do without "the satisfaction of this inclination to aggression."[15] When circumstances are favorable, this primitive aggressiveness breaks loose and "reveals man as a savage beast to whom consideration towards his own kind is something alien."[16] For Freud, "the inclination to aggression is an original self-subsisting disposition in man" and it "constitutes the greatest impediment to civilization."[17] Aggressive impulses drive people apart, threatening society with disintegration. Freud believed that an unalterable core of human nature is ineluctably in opposition to civilized life. To this extent, everyone is potentially an enemy of civilization.

Freud's awareness of the irrational and his general pessimism regarding people's ability to regulate it in the interests of civilization did not lead him to break faith with the Enlightenment tradition, for Freud did not celebrate the irrational. He was too cognizant of its self-destructive nature for that. Civilization is indeed a burden, but people must bear it because the alternative is far worse. In the tradition of the philosophes, Freud sought truth based on a scientific analysis of human nature and believed that reason was the best road to social improvement. Like the philosophes, he was critical of religion, regarding it as a pious illusion—a fairy tale in conflict with reason. Freud wanted people to throw away what

In actuality, a small group of party leaders controls the political system. Pareto also rejected as naïve Marx's vision of the end of the class struggle.

In the tradition of Machiavelli, Pareto held that a successful ruling elite must—with cunning and if necessary with violence—exploit the feelings and impulses of the masses to its own advantage. Democratic states, he said, delude themselves in thinking that the masses are really influenced by rational argument. Pareto predicted the emergence of new political leaders who would master the people through propaganda and force, always appealing to sentiment rather than to reason. To this extent, Pareto was an intellectual forerunner of Fascism, which preached an authoritarian elitism. Mussolini praised Pareto and proudly claimed him as a source of inspiration.

Weber

Probably the most prominent social thinker of the age, the German academic Max Weber (1864–1920) was a leading shaper of modern sociology. Weber believed that Western civilization, unlike the other civilizations of the globe, had virtually eliminated myth, mystery, and magic from its conception of nature and society. This process of rationalization—the "disenchantment of the world," as Weber called it—was most conspicuous in Western science, but it was also evident in politics and economics. Weber considered Western science an attempt to understand and master nature through reason, and Western capitalism an attempt to organize work and production in a rational manner. The Western state has a rational, written constitution, rationally formulated law, and a bureaucracy of trained government officials that administers the affairs of state according to rational rules and regulations.

Weber understood the terrible paradox of reason. Reason accounts for brilliant achievements in science and economic life, but it also despiritualizes life by ruthlessly eliminating centuries-old traditions, denouncing deeply felt religious beliefs as superstition, and regarding human feelings and passions as impediments to clear thinking. The process of disenchantment shattered the basis for belief in transcendental values; in a thoroughly disenchanted world, life is without ultimate purpose or intrinsic meaning and the individual is soulless. This is the dilemma of modern individuals, said Weber. Secular rationality is shaping a world in which standards cannot claim ultimate sanction. A disenchanted world contains no inherited truths, no God-given answers to the human being's desperate need for meaning. We are now confronted with an immense and unprecedented burden: how to create for ourselves values that give meaning to life in a world deprived of certainty.

Secular rationality has produced still another awesome problem, said Weber. It has fostered self-liberation, for it enables human beings to overcome illusions and take control of the environment and of themselves, but it is also a means of self-enslavement, for it produces institutions, giant public and corporate bureaucracies, that depersonalize life. Modern officials, said Weber, are emotionally detached. Concerned only with the efficient execution of tasks, they employ reason in a cold and calculating way; such human feelings as compassion and affection are ruled out as hindrances to effectiveness. In the name of efficiency, people are placed in "steel cages"— that is, treated impersonally as mere objects—and thus are deprived of their autonomy. The prospect existed that people would refuse to endure this violation of their spiritual needs and would reverse the process of disenchantment by seeking redemption in the irrational. Weber himself, however, was committed to the ideals of the Enlightenment and to perpetuating the rational scientific tradition.

Like Freud, Weber was aware of the power of the irrational in social life. One expression of the irrational that he analyzed in considerable depth was the charismatic leader who attracts people by force of personality. Charismatic leaders may be religious prophets, war heroes, demagogues, or others who possess this extraordinary personality that attracts and dominates others. People yearn for charismatic leadership, particularly during times of crisis, when they feel disoriented and helpless. The leader claims a mission—a sacred duty—to lead the people during the crisis; the leader's authority rests on the people's belief in the mission and their faith in the leader's extraordinary abilities, which set him apart from ordinary people. A common allegiance to the charismatic leader unites the community. In an age that has seen its share of dictators and demagogues, the question of why people are drawn to the charismatic savior—why they succumb to his authority, and why they alter their lives in order to implement his vision—is of crucial concern to historians and social theorists.

THE MODERNIST MOVEMENT

At the same time that Freud and the social theorists were breaking with the Enlightenment view of human nature and society, artists and writers sought to liberate the imagination from traditional forms of artistic and literary expression that had governed European cultural life since the Renaissance. They adhered to Nietzsche's dictum: "What is needed above all is an absolute scepticism toward all inherited concepts."[19] Rejecting both classical and realist models, they subordinated form and objective reality to the inner life—to feelings, imagination, and the creative process. These avant-garde writers and artists found new and creative ways to express the explosive primitive forces within the human psyche that increasingly had become the subject of contemporary thinkers. Their experimentations produced a great cultural revolution called *modernism* that still profoundly influences the arts. In some ways, modernism was a continuation of the Romantic Movement, which had dominated European culture in the early nineteenth century. Both movements subjected to searching criticism cultural styles that had been formulated during the Renaissance and that had roots in ancient Greece.

Breaking with Conventional Modes of Esthetics

Even more than romanticism, modernism aspired to an intense introspection—a heightened awareness of self—and saw the intellect as a barrier to the free expression of elemental human emotions. Modernist artists and writers abandoned conventional literary and artistic models and experimented with new modes of expression. They liberated the imagination from the restrictions of conventional forms and enabled their audience, readers, and viewers alike, to share in the process of creation, often unconscious, and to discover fresh insights into objects, sounds, people, and social conditions. They believed that there were further discoveries to be made in the arts, further possibilities of expression, that past masters had not realized. The consequence of their bold venture, wrote the literary critic and historian Irving Howe, was nothing less than the "breakup of the traditional unity and continuity of Western culture."[20]

Like Freud, modernist artists and writers probed beyond surface appearances for a more profound reality hidden in the human psyche. Writers such as Thomas Mann, Marcel Proust, James Joyce, August Strindberg, D. H. Lawrence, Joseph Conrad, and Franz Kafka explored the inner life of the individual and the psychopathology of human relations in order to lay bare the self. They dealt with the predicament of alienated and estranged men and women who rejected the values and customs of their day, and they depicted the anguish of people burdened by guilt, torn by internal conflicts, driven by an inner self-destructiveness and disfigured by moral collapse. Like Freud, several modernist writers explored the dark side of human nature. Besides showing the overwhelming might of the irrational and the seductive power of the primitive and the instinctual, they also broke the silence about sex that had prevailed in Victorian literature.

From the Renaissance through the Enlightenment and into the nineteenth century, Western esthetic standards had been shaped by the conviction that the universe embodied an inherent mathematical order. A corollary of this conception of the outer world as orderly and intelligible was the view that art should imitate reality, that it should mirror nature. Since the Renaissance, artists had deliberately made use of laws of perspective and proportion; musicians had used harmonic chords, which brought rhythm and melody into a unified whole; writers had produced works according to a definite pattern, which included a beginning, middle, and end.

Modernist culture, however, acknowledged no objective reality of space, motion, and time that has the same meaning to all observers. Rather, reality can be grasped in many ways; a multiplicity of frames of reference applies to nature and human experience. Consequently, reality is what the viewer perceives it to be through the prism of the imagination. "There is no outer reality," said the modernist German poet Gottfried Benn, "there is only human consciousness, constantly building, modifying, rebuilding new worlds out of its own creativity."[21] Modernism is concerned less with the object itself than with how the artist experiences it—with the sensations that an object evokes in the artist's very being and with the meaning the artist's imagination imposes on reality. Sociologist Daniel Bell makes this point in reference to painting:

> *Modernism ... denies the primacy of an outside reality, as given. It seeks either to rearrange that reality, or to retreat to the self's interior, to private experience as the source of its concerns and aesthetic preoccupations. ... There is an emphasis on the self as the touchstone of understanding and on the activity of the knower rather than the character of the object as the source of knowledge. ... Thus one discerns the intentions of modern painting ... to break up ordered space.*[22]

Dispensing with conventional forms of esthetics, which stressed structure and coherence, modernism propelled the arts onto uncharted seas. Modernists abandoned the efforts of realists and naturalists to produce a clinical and objective description of the external world; instead, they probed subjective views and visions and the inner world of the unconscious, searching within its primitive layer for an authentic inner self. Recoiling from a middle-class, industrial civilization, which prized rationalism, organization, clarity, stability, and definite norms and values, modernist writers and artists were fascinated by the bizarre, the mysterious, the unpredictable, the primitive, the irrational, and the formless. Writers, for example, experimented with new techniques to convey the intense

struggle between the conscious and the unconscious and to explore the aberrations and complexities of human personality and the irrationality, absurdity, and cruelty of human behavior. In particular, they devised a new way, the stream of consciousness, to exhibit the mind's every level—both conscious reflection and unconscious strivings—and to capture how thought is punctuated by spontaneous outbursts, disconnected assertions, random memories, hidden desires, and persistent fantasies. The stream of consciousness is not narrated memory but a flow of feelings and thoughts in which the boundary between consciousness and unconsciousness is blurred. It attempts to reveal the mystery and complexity of the inner person, the hidden drives, desires, torments, and obsessions that intrigued Freud.

Modern artists deliberately plunged into the world of the unconscious in search of the instinctual, the fantastic, the primitive, and the mysterious, which they believed yielded a truth higher than that given by analytical thought. They embarked on a voyage into the mind's interior in the hopes of finding fantastic stimulants that would spark the creative imagination. Composers engaged in open revolt against the conventional rules and standards of musical composition. For example, the Austrian composer Arnold Schöenberg (1874–1951) purposefully abandoned traditional scales and harmonic chords to produce atonal music that "seeks to express all that swells in us subconsciously like a dream."[23] The Russian composer Igor Stravinsky (1882–1971) experimented with both atonality and primitive rhythms. When Stravinsky's ballet *The Rite of Spring* was performed in Paris in 1913, the theater audience rioted to protest the composition's break with tonality, its use of primitive, jazz-like rhythms, and its theme of ritual sacrifice.

Modern Art

The modernist movement, which began near the end of the nineteenth century, was in full bloom before World War I and would continue to flower in the postwar world. Probably the

Digital Image © The Museum of Modern Art/Licensed by SCALA/Art Resource, N.Y.

THE STARRY NIGHT (1889), BY VINCENT VAN GOGH. Van Gogh experienced wide mood swings—from extreme agitation to melancholy. His tumultuous temperament found expression in his paintings. *The Starry Night* conveys van Gogh's impression of a night sky.

clearest expression of the modernist viewpoint is found in art. In the late nineteenth century, artists began to turn away from the standards that had characterized art since the Renaissance. No longer committed to depicting how an object appears to the eye or to organizing space mathematically, they searched for new forms of representation. Increasingly, artists sought to penetrate the deepest recesses of the unconscious, which they saw as the wellspring of creativity and the dwelling place of a higher truth. Inspired by dreams, nightmares, and powerful emotions, they often represented the world in a startling manner that deviated from the Renaissance's search for form and the ideal. Paul Klee (1879–1940), a prominent Swiss painter, described modern art in these words: "Each [artist] should follow where the pulse of his own heart leads. . . . Our pounding heart drives us down, deep down to the source of all. What springs from this source, whether it may be called dream, idea or phantasy—must be taken seriously."[24]

Between 1909 and 1914, a new style, *cubism*, was developed by Pablo Picasso (1881–1973) and Georges Braque (1882–1963). Exploring the interplay between the flat world of the canvas and the three-dimensional world of visual perception, they sought to paint a reality deeper than what the eye sees at first glance. One art historian describes cubism as follows: "The cubist is not interested in usual representational standards. It is as if he were walking around the object he is analyzing, as one is free to walk around a piece of sculpture for successive views. But he must represent all these views at once."[25] The cubists' effort to depict something from multiple perspectives rather than from a single point in space and their need to deliberately deform objects in order to achieve this effect mark a radical break with artistic conventions.

Throughout the period from 1890 to 1914, artists were deemphasizing subject matter and stressing the expressive power of such formal qualities as line, color, and space. It is not surprising that some artists, such as Piet Mondrian (1872–1944), a Dutch painter, and Wassily Kandinsky (1866–1944), a Russian residing in Germany, finally created abstract art, a nonobjective art totally devoid of reference to the visible world. In breaking with the Renaissance view of the world as inherently orderly and rational and stressing the power of the imagination, modern artists opened up new possibilities for artistic expression. They also exemplified the growing appeal and force of the nonrational in European life.

MODERN PHYSICS

Until the closing years of the nineteenth century, the view of the universe held by the Western mind was based on the classical physics of Newton. It included the following principles: (1) time, space, and matter were objective realities that existed independently of the observer; (2) the universe was a giant machine, whose parts obeyed strict laws of cause and effect; (3) the atom, indivisible and solid, was the basic unit of matter; (4) heated bodies emitted radiation in continuous waves; and (5) through further investigation it would be possible to gain complete knowledge of the physical universe.

Between the 1890s and the 1920s, this view of the universe was shattered by a second Scientific Revolution. The discovery of X-rays by William Conrad Roentgen in 1895, of radioactivity by Henri Becquerel in 1896, and of the electron by J. J. Thomson in 1897 led scientists to abandon the conception of the atom as a solid and indivisible particle. Rather than resembling a billiard ball, the atom consisted of a nucleus of tightly packed protons separated from orbiting electrons by empty space.

In 1900, Max Planck (1858–1947), a German physicist, proposed the quantum theory, which holds that a heated body radiates energy not in a continuous, unbroken stream, as had been believed, but in intermittent spurts, or jumps, called quanta. Planck's theory of discontinuity in energy radiation challenged a cardinal principle of classical physics: that action in nature was strictly continuous. In 1913, Niels Bohr, a Danish scientist, applied Planck's theory of energy quanta to the interior of the atom and discovered that the Newtonian laws of motion could not fully explain what happened to electrons orbiting an atomic nucleus. As physicists explored the behavior of the atom further, it became apparent

Ascet **(1903), by Pablo Picasso.** This depiction of a gaunt old man conveys a sorrowful if not tragic mood.

that its nature was fundamentally elusive and unpredictable.

Newtonian physics says that, given certain conditions, we can predict what will follow. For example, if an airplane is flying north at four hundred miles per hour, we can predict its exact position two hours from now, assuming that the plane does not alter its course or speed. Quantum mechanics teaches that in the subatomic realm we cannot predict with certainty what will take place; we can only say that, given certain conditions, it is *probable* that a certain event will follow. This principle of uncertainty was developed in 1927 by the German scientist Werner Heisenberg, who showed that it is impossible to determine at one and the same time both an electron's precise speed and its position. In the small-scale world of the electron, we enter a universe of uncertainty, probability, and statistical relationships. No improvement in measurement techniques will dispel this element of chance and provide us with complete knowledge of the universe.

The theory of relativity, developed by Albert Einstein (1879–1955), a German-Swiss physicist of Jewish lineage, was instrumental in shaping modern physics; it altered classical conceptions of space and time. Newtonian physics had viewed space as a distinct physical reality, a stationary medium through which light traveled and matter moved. Time was deemed a fixed and rigid framework that was the same for all observers and existed independently of human experience. For Einstein, however, neither space nor time had an independent existence; neither could be divorced from human experience. Once asked to explain briefly the essentials of relativity, Einstein replied: "It was formerly believed that if all material things disappeared out of the universe, time and space would be left. According to the relativity theory, however, time and space disappear together with the things."[26]

Contrary to all previous thinking, the relativity theory holds that time differs for two observers traveling at different speeds. Imagine twin brothers involved in space exploration, one as an astronaut and the other as a rocket designer who never leaves earth. The astronaut takes off in the most advanced spaceship yet constructed, one that achieves a speed close to the maximum attainable in our universe—the speed of light. After traveling several trillion miles, the spaceship turns around and returns to earth. According to the experience of the ship's occupant, the whole trip took about two years. But when the astronaut lands on earth, he finds totally changed conditions. His brother has long since died, for according to earth's calendars some two hundred years have elapsed since the rocket ship set out on its journey. Such an occurrence seemed to defy all common-sense experience, yet experiments supported Einstein's claims.

Einstein's work encompassed motion, matter, and energy as well. Motion, too, is relative: the only way we can describe the motion of one body is to compare it with another moving body. This means that there is no motionless, absolute, fixed frame of reference anywhere in the universe. In his famous equation, $E = mc^2$, Einstein showed that matter and energy are not separate

AP Images.

ALBERT EINSTEIN (1879–1955), A PRINCIPAL ARCHITECT OF MODERN PHYSICS. Forced to flee Nazi Germany, Einstein became a U.S. citizen. He was appointed to the Institute for Advanced Study at Princeton, New Jersey.

categories, but rather two different expressions of the same physical entity. The source of energy is matter, and the source of matter is energy. Tiny quantities of matter could be converted into staggering amounts of energy. The atomic age was dawning.

The discoveries of modern physics transformed the world of classical physics. Whereas nature had been regarded as something outside the individual—an objective reality existing independently of ourselves—modern physics teaches that our position in space and time determines what we mean by reality and that our very presence affects reality itself. When we observe a particle with our measuring instruments, we are interfering with it, knocking it off its course; we are participating in reality. Nor is nature fully knowable, as the classical physics of Newton had presumed; uncertainty, probability, and even mystery are inherent in the universe.

We have not yet felt the full impact of modern physics, but there is no doubt that it has been part of a revolution in human perceptions. Jacob Bronowski, a student of science and culture, concludes:

> One aim of the physical sciences has been to give an exact picture of the material world. One achievement of physics in the twentieth century has been to prove that that aim is unattainable. . . . There is no absolute knowledge. . . . All information is imperfect. We have to treat it with humility. That is the human condition; and that is what quantum physics says. . . . The Principle of Uncertainty . . . fixed once and for all the realization that all knowledge is limited.[27]

Like Darwin's theory of human origins, Freud's theory of human nature, and the transformation of classical space by modern artists, the modifications of the Newtonian picture by modern physicists have enlarged our understanding. At the same time, they have contributed to the sense of uncertainty and disorientation that characterized the twentieth century.

THE ENLIGHTENMENT TRADITION IN DISARRAY

Most nineteenth-century thinkers carried forward the spirit of the Enlightenment, particularly in its emphasis on science and its concern for individual liberty and social reform. In the tradition of the philosophes, nineteenth-century thinkers regarded science as humanity's greatest achievement and believed that through reason society could be reformed. The spread of parliamentary government and the extension of education, along with the many advances in science and technology, seemed to confirm the hopes of the philosophes for humanity's future progress.

But at the same time, the Enlightenment tradition was being undermined. In the early nineteenth century, the romantics revolted against the Enlightenment's rational-scientific spirit in favor of human will and feeling. Romantic nationalists valued the collective soul of the nation—ancient traditions rooted in a hoary and dateless past—over reason and individual freedom. Conservatives emphasized the limitations of reason and attacked the political agenda of the Enlightenment and the French Revolution. In the closing decades of the nineteenth century, the Enlightenment tradition was challenged by Social Darwinists, who glorified violence and saw conflict between individuals and between nations as a law of nature. They considered domination by domestic elites and powerful states to be a right of nature, beyond good and evil, and they castigated humanitarianism as weakness. Echoing Sorel, several thinkers trumpeted the use of force in social and political controversies.

Furthermore, a number of thinkers, rejecting the Enlightenment view of people as fundamentally rational, held that subconscious drives and impulses govern human behavior more than reason does. If this is so, then individuals are not essentially autonomous, masters of their own selves. Several of these thinkers urged celebrating and extolling the irrational, which they regarded as the true essence of human beings and of life. They glorified an irrational vitality, or Nietzsche's will to power, which transcended considerations of right and wrong. "I have always considered myself a voice of what I believe to be a greater renaissance—the revolt of the soul against the intellect—now beginning in the world," wrote the Irish poet William Butler Yeats.[28] German advocates of "life philosophy" explicitly called the mind "the enemy of the soul."

Even the theorists who studied the individual and society in a scientific way pointed out that below a surface of rationality lies a substratum of irrationality, which constitutes a deeper reality. The conviction was growing that reason was a puny instrument when compared with the volcanic strength of nonrational impulses, that these impulses pushed people toward destructive behavior and made political life precarious, and that the nonrational did not bend very much to education. The Enlightenment's image of the autonomous individual who makes rational decisions after weighing the choices (a fundamental premise of liberalism and democracy) no longer seemed tenable. Often the individual is not the master of his or her own person, human volition is limited by human nature.

Liberalism, which owed much to the Enlightenment, was also undermined by theorists who rejected the idea of natural rights. The view that all individuals are born with inalienable rights had provided the philosophical basis of classical liberalism. It was now argued, however, that natural rights were not a law of nature or a higher truth; rather, they were simply a human creation, a product of a specific set of circumstances at a particular stage in history, notably the emergence of the bourgeoisie. Could commitment to parliamentary government, the rule of law, and other liberal-democratic institutions and practices survive this assault on the core principle of liberalism?

Other theorists argued that the ideas of right, truth, and justice do not have an independent value; rather, they are merely tools used by elites in their struggle to gain and maintain power. Opponents of liberalism and democracy utilized the theory of elites advanced by Pareto, as well as the new stress on human irrationality, as proof that the masses were incapable of self-government and

that they had to be led by their betters. Many intellectuals of the Right employed the new social theories to devalue the individualist and rational bases of liberal democracy bequeathed by the Enlightenment.

At the beginning of the twentieth century, the dominant mood remained that of confidence in Europe's future progress and in the values of European civilization. However, certain disquieting trends were already evident; they would grow to crisis proportions in succeeding decades. Although few people may have realized it, the Enlightenment tradition was in disarray.

The thinkers of the Enlightenment believed in an orderly, machinelike universe; natural law and natural rights operating in the social world; objective rules that gave form and structure to artistic productions; the essential rationality and goodness of the individual; and science and technology as instruments of progress. This coherent worldview, which had produced an attitude of certainty, security, and optimism, was in the process of dissolution by the early twentieth century. The commonsense Newtonian picture of the physical universe, with its inexorable laws of cause and effect, was fundamentally altered; the belief in natural rights and objective standards governing morality was undermined; rules and modes of expression that were at the very heart of Western esthetics were abandoned; and confidence in human rationality and goodness weakened. Furthermore, science and technology were accused of forging a mechanical, bureaucratic, and materialistic world that stifled intuition and feelings, thereby diminishing the self. To redeem the self, some thinkers urged a heroic struggle, which easily was channeled into primitive nationalism and martial crusades.

This radical attack on the moral and intellectual values of the Enlightenment, as well as on liberalism and democracy, included the denunciation of reason, exaltation of force, quest for the heroic, and yearning for a new authority; it constitutes the intellectual background of the Fascist movements that emerged after World War I. Holding the Enlightenment tradition in contempt and fascinated by power and violence, many people, including intellectuals, would exalt Fascist ideas and lionize Fascist leaders.

When the new century began, most Europeans were optimistic about the future, some even holding that European civilization was on the threshold of a golden age. Few suspected that European civilization would soon be gripped by a crisis that threatened its very survival. The powerful forces of irrationalism that had been hailed by Nietzsche, analyzed by Freud, and creatively expressed in modernist culture would erupt with devastating fury in twentieth-century political life, particularly in the form of extreme nationalism and racism that extolled violence. Confused and disillusioned people searching for new certainties and values would turn to political ideologies that openly rejected reason, lauded war, and scorned the inviolability of the human person. Dictators, utilizing the insights into the unconscious and the nonrational advanced by Freud and the social theorists, succeeded in manipulating the minds of the masses to an unprecedented degree.

These currents began to form at the end of the nineteenth century, but World War I brought them together in a tidal wave. World War I accentuated the questioning of established norms and the dissolution of Enlightenment certainties. It caused many people to see Western civilization as dying and beyond redemption. Exacerbating the spiritual crisis of the preceding generation, the war shattered Europe's political and social order. It also gave birth to totalitarian ideologies that nearly obliterated the legacy of the Enlightenment. The world wars of the twentieth century, with their millions of dead and mutilated, and the totalitarian experiments, which trampled on human dignity, bore out Nietzsche's warning that in a nihilistic world all is permitted.

❖ ❖ ❖

NOTES

1. Friedrich Nietzsche, *The Will to Power*, trans. Walter Kaufmann and R. J. Hollingdale, ed. Walter Kaufmann (New York: Vintage Books, 1968), 458–459.

2. Ibid., 383–384.

3. Friedrich Nietzsche, *The Genealogy of Morals*, Essay 1, sec. 13 (New York: The Modern Library, 1954), 656.

4. Quoted in R. J. Hollingdale, *Nietzsche* (London: Routledge & Kegan Paul, 1973), 82.

5. Nietzsche, *Will to Power*, 397.

6. Ibid., 518.

7. Friedrich Nietzsche, *Twilight of the Idols and The Anti-Christ*, trans. R. J. Hollingdale (New York: Penguin, 1972), 116.

8. Nietzsche, *Will to Power*, 386.

9. Janko Lavrin, *Nietzsche* (New York: Charles Scribner's Sons, 1971), 113.

10. Sigmund Freud, *A General Introduction to Psychoanalysis*, trans. Joan Riviere (Garden City, N.Y.: Garden City Publishing Co., 1943), 252.

11. Sigmund Freud, *Civilization and Its Discontents* (New York: Norton, 1961), 62.

12. Ibid., 58.

13. Ibid.

14. Ibid., 59.

15. Ibid., 61.

16. Ibid., 59.

17. Ibid., 69.

18. Émile Durkheim, *Suicide: A Study in Sociology*, trans. John Spaulding and George Simpson (New York: The Free Press, 1951), 391.

19. Quoted in Christopher Butler, *Early Modernism: Literature, Music, and Painting in Europe, 1900–1916* (New York: Oxford University Press), 2.

20. Irving Howe, ed., *The Idea of the Modern in Literature and the Arts* (New York: Horizon Press, 1967), 16.

21. Ibid., 15.

22. From *The Cultural Contradictions of Capitalism* by Daniel Bell, 110, 112. Copyright © 1976 by Basic Books. Reprinted by permission

of Basic Books, a member of Perseus Books Group.

23. Excerpted in Piero Weiss and Richard Taruskin, eds., *Music in the Western World: A History in Documents* (New York: Schirmen Books, 1984), 428.

24. Paul Klee, *On Modern Art*, trans. Paul Findlay (London: Faber & Faber, 1948), 51.

25. John Canaday, *Mainstreams of Modern Art* (New York: Holt, 1961), 458.

26. Quoted in A. E. E. McKenzie, *The Major Achievements of Science* (New York: Cambridge University Press, 1960), vol. 1, 310.

27. Jacob Bronowski, *The Ascent of Man* (Boston: Little, Brown, 1973), 353.

28. Quoted in Roland N. Stromberg, *Redemption by War*, 65. University Press of Kansas, 1982. Copyright © 1982 by University Press of Kansas. All rights reserved. Reprinted with permission.

Chapter 18

World War I: The West in Despair

- Aggravated Nationalist Tensions in Austria-Hungary
- The German System of Alliances
- The Triple Entente
- The Drift Toward War
- War as Celebration
- Stalemate in the West
- Other Fronts
- The Collapse of the Central Powers
- The Peace Conference
- The Russian Revolution of 1917
- The War and European Consciousness

Focus Questions

1. How did the nationality problem in Austria-Hungary contribute to the outbreak of World War I?
2. In assessing responsibility for the war, what arguments have been advanced by historians for each of the major countries involved?
3. Why did many Europeans celebrate the coming of war?
4. Why was trench warfare so deadly?
5. Why did the United States enter the war?
6. What was President Wilson's peace program? What obstacles did he face?
7. What was Germany's reaction to the Treaty of Versailles?
8. Why did the Provisional Government and liberal democracy fail in Russia in 1917?
9. How did World War I transform the consciousness of Europeans?

*P*rior to 1914, the dominant mood in Europe was one of pride in the accomplishments of Western civilization and confidence in its future progress. Advances in science and technology, the rising standard of living, the spread of democratic institutions, and Europe's position of power in the world all contributed to a sense of optimism, as did the expansion of social reform and the increase in literacy for the masses. Furthermore, since the defeat of Napoleon, Europe had avoided a general war, and since the Franco-Prussian War (1870–1871), the Great Powers had not fought each other. Few people recognized that the West's outward achievements masked an inner turbulence that was propelling Western civilization toward a cataclysm. The European state system was failing.

By 1914, national states, answering to no higher power, were fueled by an explosive nationalism and were grouped into alliances that faced each other with ever-mounting hostility. Nationalist passions, overheated by the popular press and expansionist societies, poisoned international relations. Nationalist thinkers propagated pseudoscientific racial and Social Darwinist doctrines that glorified conflict and justified the subjugation of other peoples. Committed to enhancing national power, statesmen lost sight of Europe as a community of nations sharing a common civilization. Caution and restraint gave way to belligerency in foreign relations.

The failure of the European state system was paralleled by a cultural crisis. Some European intellectuals attacked the rational tradition of the Enlightenment and celebrated the primitive, the instinctual, and the irrational. Increasingly, young people were drawn to philosophies of action that ridiculed liberal, bourgeois values and viewed war as a purifying and ennobling experience. Colonial wars, colorfully portrayed in the popular press, ignited the imagination of bored factory workers and daydreaming students and reinforced a sense of duty and an urge for gallantry among soldiers and aristocrats. These "splendid" little colonial wars helped fashion an attitude that made war acceptable, if not laudable. Yearning to break loose from their ordinary lives and to embrace heroic values, many Europeans regarded violent conflict as the highest expression of individual and national life. "If only there were a war, even an unjust one," wrote George Heym, a young German writer, in 1912. "This peace is so rotten."[1] The popular historian Heinrich von Treitschke (1834–1896), whose lectures influenced many students who were to rise to positions of importance in the German army and administration, expressed the prevailing mood: "Those who preach the nonsense about everlasting peace do not understand the life of the [German] race. . . . To banish war from history would be to banish all progress."[2] Although technology was making warfare more brutal and dangerous, Europe retained a romantic illusion about combat.

While Europe was seemingly progressing in the art of civilization, the mythic power of nationalism and the primitive appeal of conflict were driving European civilization to the abyss. Few people recognized the potential crisis—certainly not the statesmen whose reckless blundering and horrific miscalculations allowed the Continent to stumble into war. ❖

AGGRAVATED NATIONALIST TENSIONS IN AUSTRIA-HUNGARY

On June 28, 1914, a young terrorist, with the support of a secret Serbian nationalist society called Union or Death (more popularly known as the Black Hand), murdered Archduke Francis Ferdinand, heir to the throne of Austria-Hungary. Six weeks later, the armies of Europe were on the march; an incident in the Balkans had sparked a world war. An analysis of why Austria-Hungary felt compelled to attack Serbia and why the other powers became enmeshed in the conflict shows how explosive Europe was in 1914. And nowhere were conditions more volatile than in Austria-Hungary, the scene of the assassination.

With its several nationalities, each with its own history and traditions and often conflicting aspirations, Austria-Hungary stood in opposition to nationalism, the most powerful spiritual force of the age. Perhaps the supranational Austro-Hungarian Empire was obsolete in a world of states based on the principle of nationality.

Primary Source

Friedrich von Bernhardi: *Germany and the Next War*

A militaristic attitude that glorified war was widespread in Germany prior to World War I. The following excerpt comes from Friedrich von Bernhardi's work Germany and the Next War *(1911), which was immensely popular in his country.*

. . . War is a biological necessity of the first importance, a regulative element in the life of mankind which cannot be dispensed with, since without it an unhealthy development will follow, which excludes every advancement of the race, and therefore all real civilization. "War is the father of all things." The sages of antiquity long before Darwin recognized this.

The struggle for existence is, in the life of Nature, the basis of all healthy development. . . . The law of the stronger holds good everywhere. Those forms survive which are able to procure themselves the most favourable conditions of life, and to assert themselves in the universal economy of Nature. The weaker succumb. . . .

Struggle is, therefore, a universal law of Nature, and the instinct of self-preservation which leads to struggle is acknowledged to be a natural condition of existence.

Strong, healthy, and flourishing nations increase in numbers. From a given moment they require a continual expansion of their frontiers, they require new territory for the accommodation of their surplus population. Since almost every part of the globe is inhabited, new territory must, as a rule, be obtained at the cost of its possessors—that is to say, by conquest, which thus becomes a law of necessity.

The right of conquest is universally acknowledged. . . .

. . . Vast territories inhabited by uncivilized masses are occupied by more highly civilized States, and made subject to their rule. Higher civilization and the correspondingly greater power are the foundations of the right to annexation. . . .

Lastly, in all times the right of conquest by war has been admitted. It may be that a growing people cannot win colonies from civilized races, and yet the State wishes to retain the surplus population which the mother-country can no longer feed. Then the only course left is to acquire the necessary territory by war. Thus the instinct of self-preservation leads inevitably to war, and the conquest of foreign soil. It is not the possessor, but the victor, who then has the right. . . .

In such cases might gives the right to occupy or to conquer. Might is at once the supreme right, and the dispute as to what is left is decided by the arbitrament of war. War gives a biologically just decision, since its decisions rest on the very nature of things. . . .

The knowledge, therefore, that war depends on biological laws leads to the conclusion that every attempt to exclude it from international relations must be demonstrably untenable.

Question for Analysis

1. What conclusions did Friedrich von Bernhardi draw from his premise that war was a biological necessity?

Friedrich von Bernhardi, *Germany and the Next War*, trans. Allan H. Fowles (New York: Longmans, Greens, 1914), 18, 21–24.

Chronology 18.1 ❖ World War I

1882	Formation of the Triple Alliance of Germany, Austria-Hungary, and Italy
1894	Alliance between Russia and France
1904	Anglo-French Entente
1907	Anglo-Russian Entente
1908	Bosnian crisis
June 28, 1914	Archduke Francis Ferdinand of Austria is assassinated at Sarajevo
August 4, 1914	Germans invade Belgium
September 1914	First Battle of the Marne saves Paris
May 1915	Italy enters the war on the Allies' side
Spring 1915	Germany launches offensive that forces Russia to abandon Galicia and most of Poland
February 1916	General Pétain leads French forces at Verdun; Germans fail to capture the fortress town
July–November 1916	Battle of the Somme: the Allies suffer 600,000 casualties
January 1917	Germany launches unrestricted submarine warfare
April 6, 1917	United States declares war on Germany
November 1917	Bolsheviks take power in Russia
March 1918	Russia signs the Treaty of Brest-Litovsk, losing territory to Germany and withdrawing from the war
March 21, 1918	Germans launch a great offensive to end the war
June 3, 1918	Germans advance to within fifty-six miles of Paris
August 8, 1918	British victory at Amiens
October 1918	Turkey is forced to withdraw from the war after several British successes
November 3, 1918	Austria-Hungary signs armistice with the Allies
November 11, 1918	Germany signs armistice with the Allies, ending World War I
January 1919	Paris Peace Conference
June 28, 1919	Germany signs the Treaty of Versailles

Dominated by Germans and Hungarians, the empire remained unable either to satisfy the grievances or to contain the nationalist aims of its minorities, particularly the Czechs and South Slavs (Croats, Slovenes, and Serbs).

Heightened agitation among the several nationalities, which worsened in the decade before 1914, created terrible anxieties among Austrian leaders. The fear that the empire would be torn apart by rebellion caused Austria

407

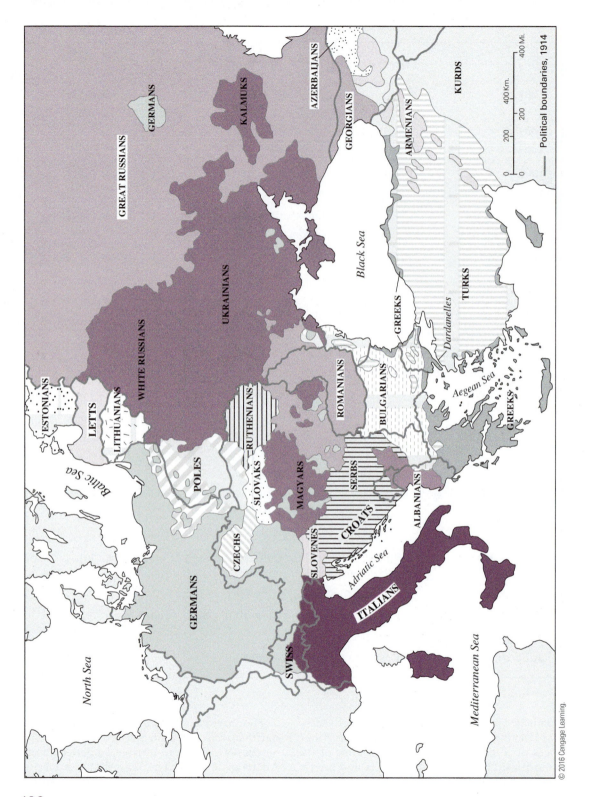

GREAT RUSSIANS

GERMANS

KALMUKS

AZERBAIJANS

GEORGIANS

ARMENIANS

KURDS

Political boundaries, 1914

400 Mi.

400 Km.

200

200

Black Sea

TURKS

Dardanelles

GREEKS

Aegean Sea

GREEKS

UKRAINIANS

WHITE RUSSIANS

ROMANIANS

BULGARIANS

ESTONIANS

LETTS

LITHUANIANS

Baltic Sea

RUTHENIANS

POLES

SLOVAKS

MAGYARS

SERBS

CROATS

SLOVENES

ALBANIANS

ITALIANS

CZECHS

GERMANS

SWISS

Adriatic Sea

North Sea

Mediterranean Sea

© 2016 Cengage Learning.

to pursue a forceful policy against any nation that fanned the nationalist feelings of its Slavic minorities. In particular, this policy meant worsening tensions between Austria and small Serbia, which had been independent of the Ottoman Empire since 1878.

Captivated by Western ideas of nationalism, the Serbs sought to create a Greater Serbia by uniting with their racial kin, the South Slavs who dwelled in Austria-Hungary. Since some seven million South Slavs lived in the Hapsburg Empire, the dream of a Greater Serbia, shrilly expressed by Serbian nationalists, caused nightmares in Austria. Fearing that continued Serbian agitation would encourage the South Slavs to press for secession, some Austrian leaders urged the destruction of the Serbian menace.

The tensions arising from the multinational character of the Austro-Hungarian Empire in an age of heightened nationalist feeling set off the explosion in 1914. Unable to solve its minority problems and fearful of Pan-Serbism, Austria-Hungary felt itself in a life-or-death situation. This sense of desperation led it to lash out at Serbia after the assassination of Archduke Francis Ferdinand.

THE GERMAN SYSTEM OF ALLIANCES

The war might have been avoided, or might have remained limited to Austria and Serbia, had Europe in 1914 not been divided into two hostile alliance systems. Such a situation contains inherent dangers. For example, knowing that it has the support of allies, a country might pursue a more provocative and reckless course and be less conciliatory during a crisis. Furthermore, a conflict between two states might spark a chain reaction, drawing in the other powers and transforming a limited war into a general war. That is what happened after the assassination. This dangerous alliance system originated with Bismarck and the Franco-Prussian War.

◄ *Map 18.1* Various Ethnic Groups in Europe Before World War I.

The New German Empire

The unification of Germany in 1870 and 1871 turned the new state into an international power of the first rank, upsetting the balance of power in Europe. For the first time since the wars of the French Revolution, a nation was in a position to dominate the European continent. To German nationalists, the unification of Germany was both the fulfillment of a national dream and the starting point for an even more ambitious goal: extending German power in Europe and the world.

As the nineteenth century drew to a close, German nationalism became more extreme. Believing that Germany must either grow or die, nationalists pressed the government to build a powerful navy, acquire colonies, gain a much greater share of the world's markets, and expand German interests and influence in Europe. Sometimes these goals were expressed in the language of Social Darwinism: that nations are engaged in an eternal struggle for survival and domination. Decisive victories against Austria (1866) and France (1871), the formation of the German Reich, rapid industrialization, and the impressive achievements of German science and scholarship had molded a powerful and dynamic nation. Imbued with great expectations for the future, Germans became increasingly impatient to see the fatherland gain its "rightful" place in world affairs—an attitude that alarmed non-Germans.

Bismarck's Goals

Under Bismarck, who did not seek additional territory but wanted only to preserve the recently achieved unification, Germany pursued a moderate and cautious foreign policy. One of Bismarck's principal goals was to keep France isolated and friendless. Deeply humiliated by its defeat in the Franco-Prussian War and the loss of Alsace and Lorraine, France found its nationalists yearning for a war of revenge against Germany. Even though the French government, aware of Germany's strength, was unlikely to initiate such a conflict, the issue of Alsace-Lorraine increased tensions between the two countries.

Bismarck also hoped to prevent a war between Russia and Austria-Hungary, for such a conflict

© Bettmann/Corbis.

THE ASSASSINATION OF ARCHDUKE FRANCIS FERDINAND. Immediately after the assassination, Austrian authorities arrest one of the assassins.

Constantinople. Because it was on the victorious side, landlocked Serbia gained the Albanian coast and thus a long-desired outlet to the sea. Austria was determined to keep its enemy from reaping this reward, and Germany, as in the Bosnian crisis, supported its ally. Unable to secure Russian support, Serbia was forced to surrender the territory, which became the state of Albania.

Incensed Serbian nationalists accelerated their campaign of propaganda and terrorism against Austria. Believing that another humiliation would irreparably damage its prestige, Russia vowed to back Serbia in its next confrontation with Austria. And Austria had exhausted its patience with Serbia. Emboldened by German encouragement, Austria wanted to end the Serbian threat once and for all. Thus, the ingredients for war between

Austria and Serbia, a war that might easily draw in Russia and Germany, were present. Another incident might well start a war. It came in 1914.

Assassination of Francis Ferdinand

On June 28, 1914, Francis Ferdinand was assassinated while making a state visit to Sarajevo, the capital of Bosnia. Young Gavrilo Princip, who was part of a team of Bosnian terrorists linked to the Black Hand, fired two shots at close range into the archduke's car. Francis Ferdinand and his wife died within fifteen minutes. By killing the archduke, the terrorists hoped to bring tensions in the Hapsburg Empire to a boiling point and to prepare the way for revolution.

For many years, leaders of Austria had yearned for war with Serbia in order to end the agitation for the union of the South Slavs. Now, they reasoned, the hour had struck. But war with Serbia would require the approval of Germany. Believing that Austria was Germany's only reliable ally and that a diminution of Austrian power and prestige threatened German security, German statesmen encouraged their ally to take up arms against Serbia. Both Germany and Austria wanted a quick strike, a localized conflict, to overwhelm Serbia before other countries were drawn into the conflict.

Germany Encourages Austria

Confident of German backing, on July 23 Austria presented Serbia with an ultimatum and demanded a response within forty-eight hours. The terms of the ultimatum were so harsh that it was next to impossible for Serbia to accept them. This reaction was the one that Austria intended, as it sought a military solution to the crisis rather than a diplomatic one. But Russia would not remain indifferent to an Austro-German effort to liquidate Serbia. Russia feared that an Austrian conquest of Serbia was just the first step in an Austro-German plan to dominate the Balkans. Such an extension of German and Austrian power in a region bordering Russia was unthinkable to the tsar's government. Moreover, after suffering repeated reverses in foreign affairs, Russia would not tolerate another humiliation. As Germany had decided to back its Austrian ally, Russia resolved not to abandon Serbia.

Serbia responded to Austria's ultimatum in a conciliatory manner, agreeing to virtually all Austrian demands. But it refused to let Austrian officials enter Serbia to investigate the assassination. Having already discarded the idea of a peaceful settlement, Austria insisted that Serbia's failure to accept one provision meant that the entire ultimatum had been rejected. It ordered the mobilization of the Austrian army.

This was a crucial moment for Germany. Would it continue to support Austria, knowing that an Austrian attack on Serbia would probably bring Russia into the conflict? Determined not to desert Austria and believing that a showdown with Russia was inevitable anyway, the German war party, with the military cajoling and persuading the civilian authorities, continued to urge Austrian action against Serbia. They argued that it was better to fight Russia in 1914 than a few years later, when the tsar's empire, which already had a huge reserve of manpower and was rapidly building strategic railroads and expanding its Baltic fleet, would be stronger. Confident of the superiority of the German army, the war party claimed that Germany could defeat both Russia and France and that Britain's army was too weak to make a difference.

On July 28, 1914, Austria declared war on Serbia. Russia, with the assurance of French support, proclaimed partial mobilization aimed at Austria alone. But the military warned that partial mobilization would throw the slow-moving Russian war machine into total confusion if the order had to be changed suddenly to full mobilization. Moreover, the only plans the Russian general staff had drawn up called for full mobilization, that is, for war against both Austria and Germany. Pressured by his generals, the tsar gave the order for full mobilization on July 30. Russian forces would be arrayed against Germany as well as Austria.

Because the country that struck first gained the advantage of fighting according to its own plans rather than having to improvise in response to the enemy's attack, generals tended to regard mobilization by the enemy as an act of war. Therefore, when Russia refused a German warning to halt mobilization, Germany, on August 1, ordered a general mobilization and declared war on Russia. Two days later, Germany also declared war on France, believing that France would support its Russian ally. Besides, German battle plans were based on a war with both Russia and France. Thus, a war between Germany and Russia automatically meant a German attack on France.

When Belgium refused to allow German troops to march through Belgian territory into France, Germany invaded the small nation, which brought Britain, pledged to guarantee Belgian neutrality, into the war. Britain could never tolerate German troops directly across the English Channel in any case, nor could it brook German mastery of Western Europe.

The Question of Responsibility

The question of whether any one power was mainly responsible for the war has intrigued historians. In assessing blame, historians have focused on Germany's role. German historian Fritz Fischer argues that Germany's ambition to dominate Europe was the underlying cause of the war. Germany encouraged Austria to strike at Serbia, knowing that an attack on Serbia could mean war with Russia and its French ally. Believing that it had the military advantage, Germany was willing to risk such a war. Hence, "her leaders must bear a substantial share of the historical responsibility for the outbreak of general war in 1914."[3]

Attracted by Social Darwinist ideas that foresaw an inevitable racial struggle between Germans and Slavs, by militarist doctrines that glorified war, and by a nationalist drive for *Lebensraum* (more living space), continues Fischer, Germany sought to become the foremost economic and political power in Europe and to play a far greater role in world politics; to achieve this goal, it was willing to go to war. Fischer supports his position by pointing to Germany's war aims, drawn up immediately after the outbreak of war, which called for the annexation of neighboring territories and the creation of satellite states, that is, imposing German hegemony over Europe. Fischer's thesis had distressed Germans for it implies that there is continuity between Germany's territorial ambitions at the time of World War I and Hitler's territorial goals—that Nazi imperialism was not an aberration in

FOR MANY PEOPLE, THE DECLARATION OF WAR WAS A CAUSE FOR CELEBRATION.
Few Europeans realized what a horror the war would turn out to be.

Archives Larousse, Paris, France/Giraudon/The Bridgeman Art Library International.

German history but coincided with the wishes of Germany's traditional ruling elite. Fischer's critics stress, however, that Social Darwinism and militarism enthralled other nations besides Germany and that this was not peculiarly German, but rather part of a general European sickness. They argue further that Germany would have preferred a limited war between Austria and Serbia and before the war had no plans to annex and dominate neighboring lands.

Historians also attribute blame to the other powers. Austria bears responsibility for its determination to crush Serbia and for its insistent avoidance of a negotiated settlement. Serbia's responsibility stems from its pursuing an aggressive Pan-Serbian policy and tolerating terrorist networks within the country, which set it on a collision course with Austria-Hungary. In 1913, Sir Fairfax Cartwright, the British ambassador to Vienna, warned: "Serbia will some day set Europe by the ears, and bring about a universal war on the Continent. I cannot tell you how exasperated people are getting here at the continual worry which that little country causes to Austria."[4] Russia bears responsibility for being the first country to institute general mobilization, a momentous decision that turned a limited war between Austria-Hungary and Serbia into a European war; France, for failing to restrain Russia and indeed for encouraging its ally to mobilize; and England, for failing to make clear that it would support its allies. Had Germany seen plainly that Britain would intervene, it might have been more cautious. Finally blame falls on diplomats and statesmen for their ineptness and their lack of imagination in dealing with a crisis that could have been resolved without war.

Some historians, dismissing the question of responsibility, regard the war as an obvious sign that European civilization was in deep trouble. Viewed in the broad perspective of European history, the war marked a culmination of dangerous forces in European life: the belief expressed by some theorists that violent conflict was a natural, inevitable, and worthy feature of human relations and a belligerent nationalism that pitted nation against nation in a struggle for survival. It also pointed to the flaws and perils of the alliance system, which set off a chain reaction, and the failure of the European state system that glorified national power at the expense of a common European civilization. Nor do European leaders and statesmen escape blame. Had Austro-Hungarian and Russian policymakers been more willing to compromise and less willing to risk war and had German and French officialdom tried to restrain their allies, the tragedy could have been averted.

WAR AS CELEBRATION

When war was certain, an extraordinary phenomenon occurred. Crowds gathered in capital cities and expressed their loyalty to the fatherland and their readiness to fight. Particularly in Germany, clergy, theologians, scientists, scholars, journalists, and literary figures justified the nation's participation in the war. The sentiments of a German theologian voiced in the opening stage of the war were not uncommon: "Our battles are God's battles. Our cause is sacred. . . . We are God's chosen among the nations. That our prayers for victory will be heard is entirely to be expected, according to the religious and moral order of the world."[5]

It seemed as if people wanted violence for its own sake. War seemed to offer an escape from the dull routine of classroom, job, and home and from the emptiness, drabness, mediocrity, and pettiness of bourgeois society—from "a world grown old and cold and weary," as Rupert Brooke, a young British poet, put it.[6] To some, war was a "beautiful . . . sacred moment" that satisfied an "ethical yearning."[7] To many people, especially youth and intellectuals, war seemed a healthy and heroic antidote to what was regarded as an unbearably decadent and soul-destroying machine age and to the bourgeois preoccupation with work, profits, and possessions. But more significantly, the outpouring of patriotic sentiments demonstrated the immense power that nationalism exercised over the European mind. With extraordinary success, nationalism welded millions of people into a collectivity ready to devote body and soul to the nation, especially during its hour of need. All believed that their country was a victim of aggression.

In Paris, men marched down the boulevards singing the stirring words of the French national anthem, the "Marseillaise," while women showered young soldiers with flowers. A participant in these days recalls: "Young and old, civilians and military men burned with the same excitement. . . . [T]housands of men eager to fight would jostle one another outside recruiting offices, waiting to join up. . . . The word 'duty' had a meaning for them, and the word 'country' had regained its splendor."[8] The term *union sacrée* (sacred union) was coined to express the sense of oneness, inclusiveness, and devotion to the nation that gripped French men and women at the time.

Similarly, in Germany, "flowers were thrown at us from every window; everyone wanted to shake hands with the departing soldiers. . . . Musicians played. . . . People cried and sang at the same time. . . . Nobody could resist the ebullient feeling."[9] "It is a joy to be alive," editorialized one newspaper. "We wished so much for this hour. . . . The sword which has been forced into our hand will not be sheathed until our aims are won and our territory extended as far as necessity demands."[10] Writing about those momentous days, the British mathematician-philosopher Bertrand Russell recalled his horror and "amazement that average men and women were delighted at the prospect of war. . . . [T]he anticipation of carnage was delightful to something like ninety percent of the population. I had to revise my views on human nature."[11]

Soldiers bound for battle and wives and sweethearts seeing them off at train stations were in a holiday mood. "My dear ones, be proud that you live in such a time and in such a nation and that you . . . have the privilege of sending those you love into so glorious a battle," wrote a young German law student to his family.[12] The young warriors yearned to do something noble and altruistic, to win glory, and to experience life at its most intense.

The martial mood also captivated many of Europe's most distinguished intellectuals. They shared Rupert Brooke's sentiments: "Now God be thanked Who has matched us with His hour / And caught our youth, and wakened us from sleeping."[13] To the prominent German historian Friedrich Meinecke, August 1914 was "one of the great moments of my life which suddenly filled my soul with the deepest confidence in our people and the profoundest joy."[14] In November 1914, Thomas Mann (see "Intellectuals and Artists

in Troubled Times" in Chapter 19), the distinguished German writer, saw the war as "purification, liberation . . . an enormous hope; [it] set the hearts of poets aflame. . . . How could the artist, the soldier in the artist," he asked, "not praise God for the collapse of a peaceful world with which he was fed up, so exceedingly fed up?"[15] Besides being gripped by a thirst for excitement and a quest for the heroic, some intellectuals welcomed the war because it unified the nation in a spirit of fraternity and altruism. It was a return, some felt, to the organic roots of human existence, a way of overcoming a sense of individual isolation. War, in the view of some intellectuals, would spiritually regenerate the nation. It would resurrect glory, honor, and heroism; it would awaken a spirit of self-sacrifice and dedication and give life an overriding purpose in a world suffocating from bourgeois materialism and drabness.

Thus, a generation of European youth marched off to war joyously, urged on by their teachers and cheered by their delirious nations. It must be emphasized, however, that the soldiers who went off to war singing and the statesmen and generals who welcomed war or did not try hard enough to prevent it expected a short, decisive, gallant conflict. Few envisioned what World War I turned out to be: four years of barbaric, senseless slaughter. The cheers of deluded chauvinists, naïve idealists, and fools drowned out the words of those—principally socialists, labor leaders, pacifists, and left-leaning liberals—who realized that Europe was stumbling into darkness. "The lamps are going out all over Europe," said British Foreign Secretary Edward Grey. "We shall not see them lit again in our lifetime."

STALEMATE IN THE WEST

On August 4, 1914, the German army invaded Belgium. German war plans, drawn up years earlier, chiefly by General Alfred von Schlieffen, called for the army to swing through Belgium

Map 18.2 World War I, 1914–1918 ▶
This map shows Europe divided into competing alliances and German advances into France and Eastern Europe once war broke out.

Art as History: The Renaissance to the Present

Michelangelo Buonarotti: *David*, 1504. A towering marble sculpture, Michelangelo's David is one of the crowning masterpieces of the High Renaissance. During the Middle Ages, artists depicted the nude figure for specific, often moral, reasons: tormented sinners at the Last Judgment, for example. Michelangelo's use of nudity breaks with this tradition. What does his heroic, idealized portrayal of the biblical David reveal about the secular spirit of the Renaissance? (© Asier Villafranca/Shutterstock.com)

T he visual arts are a particularly rich source of information for historians of the modern West. Revolutionary changes in art styles reflect the stages and complexities of the modern age. What insights into modern history can be derived from examining these works of art?

Pieter Brueghel the Elder: *Hunters in the Snow*, **1565.** Brueghel's treatment of landscape art resulted from the technique he acquired when he studied in Italy during the Renaissance. His depiction of objects in three-dimensional space achieves a depth of perspective that is entirely new, virtually ushering in a new age in art, and superseding the "flat" two-dimensional space of medieval art. Compare Brueghel's painting with the manuscript illustration "April" from Les Très Riches Heures of Jean, Duke of Berry (see the art essay in Chapter 7). How does it differ? What makes it "modern"? (Erich Lessing/Art Resource, N.Y.)

Rembrandt van Rijn (1606–1669): *Self-Portrait at Old Age*, **1669.** Rembrandt was influenced in his early years by Italian painters' use of light. He also was highly introspective and produced a series of sixty-two self-portraits during his lifetime. The portraits revealed a variety of attitudes and poses, ranging from youthful and flamboyant to aging and distraught. In this painting, the fifty-fifth of the self-portraits, Rembrandt stares back at us with the calm assurance of a man who has mastered his art and life. What words would you use to describe the emotions conveyed in this self-portrait? How does Rembrandt use light and darkness in this painting? (Fine Art/Corbis.)

Jacques Louis David: *The Death of Marat*, **1793.** This painting was done during the French Revolution by David, a foremost exponent of the neoclassical style and an ardent revolutionary. It shows Marat, a revolutionary leader, after he had been stabbed to death by a crazed woman who had handed him a personal petition to read. What does this stark depiction of the death scene reveal about David's perception of the episode and his indebtedness to the classical style of antiquity? How does his treatment of the moment of death differ from a work such as the Laocoön group's treatment of the same theme? (Sergio Anelli/Electa/Mondadori Portfolio/Getty Images.)

J. M. W. Turner (1775–1851): *Burning of the Houses of Parliament*, **c. 1835.** Turner was preoccupied with shimmering light. Although he often used literary themes for his paintings, in accordance with romantic taste the people, buildings, and ships were often obscured. What does this painting reveal about his temperament and perception of the world? (Philadelphia Museum of Art: The John Howard McFadden Collection, 1928)

Georges Seurat (1859–1891): *The Seine at La Grande Jatte*, **1888.** Seurat belonged to a late-nineteenth-century artistic movement called impressionism, which wanted to depict objects in the instant they impress themselves on the passive human eye. Painting in oil, Seurat used a measured technique—what has been called the "science behind color"—to create light and vibrant colors. This position was opposed to the early-nineteenth-century movement of romanticism, which wanted to reveal how the act of seeing an object expresses a mood or feeling. Describe what Seurat's painting contains. How does it compare to a romantic work, such as Turner's *Burning of the Houses of Parliament?*

Pablo Picasso (1881–1973): *Les Demoiselles d'Avignon,* 1907. The cubists distorted perspective to give viewers the feeling of seeing objects and people "in the round" and over time. In this picture, Picasso painted the female nude in the strong cubist style to express the forces of nature: he goes beyond the conscious level. Can a correlation be made between some twentieth-century art and the scientific examination of the unconscious? (© 2014 Estate of Pablo Picasso/Artists Rights Society (ARS), New York, Digital Image © The Museum of Modern Art/Licensed by SCALA/Art Resource, N.Y.)

Edward Hopper (1882–1967): *Hotel Lobby*, 1943. American painter Edward Hopper is one of the most notable American realist artists of the twentieth century. In his *Hotel Lobby*, the harsh light creates an uncomfortable feeling which exemplifies a sense of loneliness and alienation. What other details besides lighting does Hopper use to convey this sense of loneliness? What historical events in 1942 might Hopper have been responding to in this painting?

Jackson Pollock (1912–1956): *Convergence*, 1952. American artist Jackson Pollock poured and splattered his colors on the canvas instead of applying them with a brush or palette knife. This style of painting, known as action painting, allowed Pollock to walk around the canvas and work on it from all sides and angles. His *Convergence* may at first seem to be a canvas used as a drop cloth, but each application of color was made in a controlled and studied manner. Pollock was part of the abstract-expressionist movement, in which artists strived to express their emotions through color and abstract, nonrepresentational forms. What emotions does this painting convey to you? Why might it have been important for an abstract-expressionist like Pollock to move around the canvas instead of painting in a more traditional manner?

Frank O. Gehry (1929–): Guggenheim Museum at Bilbao, Spain, 1997.
American architect Frank Gehry is famous for his innovative use of materials—
twisting, bending, and turning metal into shapes that affect the emotions. Gehry
views architecture as an art form, like painting and sculpture, that is expressive
of human feeling and emotion. His Guggenheim Museum in Bilbao, Spain
consists of organically interrelated, contrasting shapes composed of a multiplicity
of materials, ranging from limestone and glass to titanium. It provides the city
of Bilbao with a dramatic architectural centerpiece that attracts thousands of
visitors each year. In what ways does this museum prove Gehry's assertion that
architecture is an art form capable of stirring human emotion? (© Steve Vidler/Superstock.)

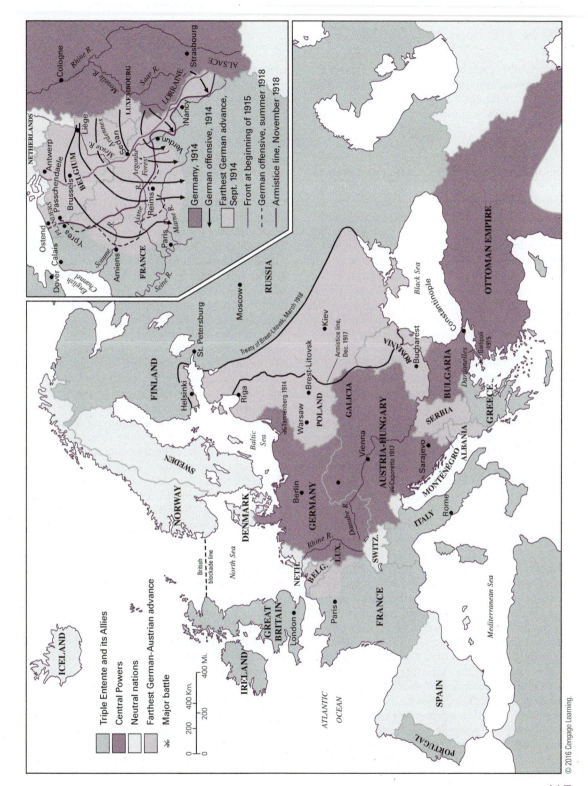

Germany, 1914
German offensive, 1914
Farthest German advance,
Sept. 1914
Front at beginning of 1915
German offensive, summer 1918
Armistice line, November 1918

Cologne
Rhine R.
Moselle R.
Strasbourg
ALSACE
LUXEMBOURG
LORRAINE
Saar R.
NETHERLANDS
Antwerp
Liège
Nancy
Ardennes
Meuse R.
BELGIUM
Sedan
Verdun
Argonne
Forest
Aisne R.
Reims
Passchendaele
Brussels
FLANDERS
Ypres
Ostend
Dover
Calais
Marne R.
English Channel
Somme
Amiens
Paris
FRANCE
Seine R.

Triple Entente and its Allies
Central Powers
Neutral nations
Farthest German–Austrian advance
Major battle

0   200   400 Mi.
0   200   400 Km.

ICELAND

NORWAY

SWEDEN

FINLAND
Helsinki

St. Petersburg

Moscow

RUSSIA

Treaty of Brest-Litovsk, March 1918

Kiev
Armistice line,
Dec. 1917

Riga
×Tannenberg 1914
Warsaw
Brest-Litovsk
POLAND
GALICIA

Black Sea

Constantinople

Bucharest
ROMANIA

OTTOMAN EMPIRE

Dardanelles
Gallipoli
1915

BULGARIA
SERBIA
GREECE

Vienna
AUSTRIA-HUNGARY
Sarajevo
×Caporetto 1917
MONTENEGRO
ALBANIA

Berlin
GERMANY
Danube R.
Rhine R.

Baltic
Sea

DENMARK

North Sea

British
blockade line

GREAT
BRITAIN
London

IRELAND

NETH.
BELG.
LUX.
SWITZ.

FRANCE
Paris

ITALY
Rome

Mediterranean Sea

SPAIN

PORTUGAL

ATLANTIC
OCEAN

© 2016 Cengage Learning.

417

to outflank French border defenses, envelop the French forces, and destroy the enemy by attacking its rear. With the French army smashed and Paris isolated, German railroads—an extensive system of tracks, carefully planned by the general staff, had been constructed in the previous decade—would rush the victorious troops to the Eastern front to bolster the small force that had been assigned to hold off the Russians. Everything depended on speed. France must be taken before the Russians could mobilize sufficient numbers to invade Germany. The Germans were confident that they would defeat France in two months or less.

But things did not turn out the way the German military had anticipated. Moving faster than the Germans expected, the Russians invaded East Prussia, which led General Helmuth von Moltke to transfer troops from the French front, hampering the German advance. By early September, the Germans had reached the Marne River, forty miles from Paris. With their capital at their backs, the regrouped French forces, aided by the British, fought with astounding courage and resolve. Moreover, in their rush toward Paris, the Germans had unknowingly exposed their flank, which the French attacked. The British then penetrated a gap that opened up between the German armies, forcing the Germans to retreat. The First Battle of the Marne had saved Paris. German military planners had been denied the quick victory they had anticipated. With no side achieving a decisive victory, the war entered a new and unexpected phase: the deadlock of trench warfare.

For over four hundred miles across northern France, from the Alps to the North Sea, the opposing sides both constructed a vast network of trenches. These trenches had underground dugouts, and barbed wire stretched for yards before the front trenches as a barrier to attack. Behind the front trenches were other lines to which soldiers could retreat and from which support could be sent. Between the opposing armies lay "no man's land," a wasteland of mud, shattered trees, torn earth, and broken bodies. In the trenches, soldiers were reduced to a primitive existence. Sometimes they stood knee-deep in freezing water or slimy mud; the stench from human waste, rotting corpses, and unwashed bodies overwhelmed the senses; rats, made more fecund and larger by easy access to food, including decaying flesh, swarmed

over the dead and scampered across the wounded and the sleeping; and ubiquitous lice caused intense discomfort and disease, which frequently required hospitalization for several weeks. After days of uninterrupted, fearsome, earsplitting bombardment by artillery, even the most stouthearted were reduced to shivering, whimpering creatures. Unless the dugouts were fortified with concrete, soldiers rarely survived a direct hit; sometimes they were simply burned alive or torn apart and made unrecognizable by exploding shells. Artillery accounted for about 70 percent of casualties. The agonizing cries and pleas of the wounded, left to die on the battlefield because it was too dangerous to attempt a rescue, shattered the nerves of the men in the trenches. Trench warfare was a futile battle of nerves, endurance, and courage, waged to the constant thunder of heavy artillery, which pulverized both ramparts and men. And in April 1915, the Germans introduced poison gas, which added to the war's horror. It was also butchery. As attacking troops climbed over their trenches and advanced bravely across no man's land, they were decimated by heavy artillery and chewed up by rapid machine-gun fire from weapons that could fire 500 or more rounds a minute. If they did penetrate the frontline trenches of the enemy, they would soon be thrown back by a counterattack.

Despite a frightful loss of life, little land changed hands. The Allied generals in particular, unfeeling and totally lacking in imagination, persisted in ordering greater but still ineffective frontal attacks by masses of infantry, hoping to wear down German manpower, which was inferior to their own. Once German reserves could not replenish losses, they reasoned, a breakthrough would be possible. But this strategy achieved nothing. The generals ordered still greater attacks to end the stalemate; this only increased the death toll, for the advantage was always with the defense, which possessed machine guns, magazine rifles, and barbed wire. Tanks could redress the balance, but the generals, committed to old concepts, did not make effective use of them. And whereas the technology of the machine gun had been perfected, the motorized tanks, a newly developed weapon, often broke down. Gains and losses of land were measured in yards, but the lives of Europe's youth were squandered by the

TROOPS LEAVING BERLIN, 1914. "The sword has been forced into our hand," said Germans at the outbreak of war. German troops mobilized eagerly and efficiently; here a trainload is leaving for the Western front.

hundreds of thousands. Against artillery, barbed wire, and machine guns, human courage had no chance, but the generals—uncomprehending, unfeeling, and incompetent—persisted in their mass attacks. This futile effort at a breakthrough wasted untold lives to absolutely no purpose.

In 1915, neither side could break the deadlock. Hoping to bleed the French army dry and force its surrender, the Germans, in February 1916, attacked the town of Verdun. Knowing that the French could never permit a retreat from this ancient fortress, they hoped that France would suffer such a loss of men that it would be unable to continue the war. France and Germany suffered more than a million casualties at Verdun—including some 300,000 dead—which one military historian calls "the greatest battle in world history."

When the British opened a major offensive on July 1, however, the Germans had to channel their reserves to the new front, relieving the pressure on Verdun.

At the end of June 1916, the British, assisted by the French, attempted a breakthrough at the Somme River. On July 1, after seven days of intense, unprecedented bombardment intended to destroy German defenses, the British climbed out of their trenches and ventured into no man's land. But German positions had not been destroyed. Emerging from their deep dugouts, German machine gunners fired repeatedly at the British, who had been ordered to advance in rows. Marching into concentrated machine-gun fire and desperately searching for a way through the still-intact German wire, few British troops ever made it across no man's land. Out of the 110,000 who attacked, some 57,000 fell dead or wounded—most in the first hour of the assault—"the heaviest loss ever suffered in a single day by a British army or by any army in the First World War."[16] When the battle of the Somme ended in mid-November, Britain and France had suffer more than 600,000 casualties and the military situation remained essentially unchanged. The only victor was the war itself, which was devouring Europe's youth at an incredible rate.

In December 1916, General Robert Nivelle was appointed commander in chief of the French forces. Having learned little from past French failures to achieve a breakthrough, Nivelle ordered another mass attack for April 1917. The Germans discovered the battle plans on the body of a French officer and withdrew to a shorter line on high ground, constructing the strongest defense network of the war. Knowing that the French had lost the element of surprise and pushing aside the warnings of leading statesmen and military men, Nivelle went ahead with the attack. "The offensive alone gives victory; the defensive gives only defeat and shame," he told the president and the minister of war.[17]

The Nivelle offensive, which began on April 16, was another bloodbath. Sometimes the fire was so intense that the French could not make it out of their own trenches. Although French soldiers fought with courage, the situation was hopeless. Still, Nivelle persisted with the attack; after ten days, French casualties numbered 187,000, including thousands of soldiers recruited from French African colonies. The disgraced Nivelle was soon relieved of his command.

OTHER FRONTS

While the Western front hardened into a stalemate, events moved more decisively on the Eastern Front. In August 1914, the Russians, with insufficient preparation, invaded East Prussia. After some initial successes, which sent a scare into the German general staff, the Russians were soundly defeated at the battle of Tannenberg (August 26–30, 1914) and forced to withdraw from German territory, which remained inviolate for the rest of the war.

Meanwhile, Germany's ally Austria was having no success against Serbia and Russia. An invasion of Serbia was thrown back, and an ill-conceived offensive against Russia cost Austria its Galician provinces. Germany had to come to Austria's rescue. In the spring of 1915, the Germans made a breakthrough that forced the Russians to abandon Galicia and most of Poland. In June 1916, the Russians launched an offensive that opened a wide breach in the Austrian lines, but they could not maintain it. A German counteroffensive forced a retreat and cost the Russians more than a million casualties.

In March 1917, food shortages and disgust with the great loss of life exploded into a spontaneous revolution in Russia, and the tsar was forced to abdicate. The new government, dominated by liberals, opted to continue the war despite the weariness of the Russian masses. In November 1917, a second revolution brought to power the Bolsheviks, or Communists, who promised "Peace, Land, Bread." In March 1918, the Bolsheviks, to end the war, signed the punitive Treaty of Brest-Litovsk, in which Russia surrendered Poland, the Ukraine, Finland, and the Baltic provinces to Germany.

Several countries that were not belligerents in August 1914—among them the Ottoman Empire and Italy—joined the war later. That autumn, the Ottoman Turks entered the conflict as allies of Germany. Before the war, Germany had cultivated the Ottoman Empire's friendship by training the Turkish army; for their part, the Turks wanted German help in case Russia attempted to seize the Dardanelles. Hoping to supply Russia and, in turn, obtain badly needed Russian grain, the Allies did decide to capture the Dardanelles. In April 1915, a combined force of British, French, Australian, and New Zealander troops stormed the Gallipoli Peninsula on the European side of the Dardanelles. Ignorance of amphibious warfare, poor intelligence, and the fierce resistance of the Turks prevented the Allies from getting off the beaches and taking the heights. The Gallipoli campaign cost the Allies 252,000 casualties, and they had gained nothing.

Although a member of the Triple Alliance, Italy remained neutral when war broke out. In May 1915, on the promise of receiving Austrian territory, Italy entered the war on the side of the

Allies. The Austrians repulsed a number of Italian offensives along the frontier and in 1916 took the offensive against Italy. A combined German and Austrian force finally broke through the Italian lines in the fall of 1917 at Caporetto, and the Italians retreated in disorder, leaving behind huge quantities of weapons. Germany and Austria took some 275,000 prisoners.

THE COLLAPSE OF THE CENTRAL POWERS

The year 1917 seemed disastrous for the Allies. The Nivelle offensive had failed, the French army had mutinied, a British attack at Passchendaele did not bring the expected breakthrough and added some three hundred thousand casualties to the list of butchery, and the Russians, torn by revolution and gripped by war weariness, were close to making a separate peace. But there was one encouraging development for the Allies. In April 1917, the United States declared war on Germany.

American Entry

From the outset, America's sympathies lay with the Allies. To most Americans, Britain and France were democracies, threatened by an autocratic and militaristic Germany. These sentiments were reinforced by British propaganda, which depicted the Germans as cruel "Huns." Since most war news came to the United States from Britain, anti-German feeling gained momentum. What precipitated American entry was the German decision of January 1917 to launch a campaign of unrestricted submarine warfare. The Germans were determined to deprive Britain of war supplies and to starve it into submission. Their resolve meant that German U-boats would torpedo both enemy and neutral ships in the war zone around the British Isles. Since the United States was Britain's principal supplier, American ships became a target of German submarines.

Angered by American loss of life and materiel, as well as by the violation of the doctrine of freedom of the seas, and fearing a diminution of prestige if the United States took no action,

President Woodrow Wilson (1856–1924) pressed for American entry. Also at stake was American security, which would be jeopardized by German domination of Western Europe. Leading American statesmen and diplomats worried that such a radical change in the balance of power would threaten American national interests. As German submarines continued to attack neutral shipping, President Wilson, on April 2, 1917, urged Congress to declare war on Germany. It did so on April 6.

Germany's Last Offensive

With Russia out of the war, General Erich Ludendorff prepared for a decisive offensive before the Americans could land sufficient troops in France to help the Allies. A war of attrition now favored the Allies, who could count on American supplies and manpower. Without an immediate and decisive victory, Germany could not win the war. On March 21, 1918, the Germans launched an offensive that was intended to bring victory in the west.

Suddenly, the deadlock was broken; it was now a war of movement. Within two weeks, the Germans had taken some 1,250 square miles. But British resistance was astonishing, and the Germans, exhausted and short of ammunition and food, called off the drive. A second offensive against the British, in April, also had to be called off, as the British contested every foot of ground. Both campaigns depleted German manpower, while the Americans were arriving in great numbers to strengthen Allied lines and uplift morale. At the end of May, Ludendorff resumed his offensive against the French. Attacking unexpectedly, the Germans broke through and advanced to within fifty-six miles of Paris by June 3. However, reserves braced the French lines, and in the battle of Belleau Wood (June 6–25, 1918), the Americans checked the Germans.

In mid-July, the Germans tried again, crossing the Marne River in small boats. Although in one area they advanced nine miles, the offensive failed against determined American and French opposition. By August 3, the Second Battle of the Marne had ended. The Germans had thrown everything they had into their spring and summer offensives, but it was not enough. The Allies had bent, but,

WILSON AND CLEMENCEAU ARRIVE AT VERSAILLES, JUNE 18, 1919. The idealism of President Wilson (center) clashed with Premier Clemenceau's (left) determination to enhance France's security.

reinforced and encouraged by American arms, they did not break. Now they began to counterattack, with great success.

Meanwhile, German allies, deprived of support from a hard-pressed Germany, were unable to cope. An Allied army of Frenchmen, Britons, Serbs, and Italians compelled Bulgaria to sign an armistice on September 29. Shortly afterward, British successes in the Middle East forced the Turks to withdraw from the war. In the streets of Vienna, people were shouting "Long live peace! Down with the monarchy!" The Austro-Hungarian Empire was rapidly disintegrating into separate states based on nationality.

By early October, the last defensive position of the Germans had crumbled. The army's spirit collapsed as well; war-weary soldiers, sensing that the war was lost, surrendered in large numbers and refused orders to return to the front. Fearing that the Allies would invade the fatherland and shatter the reputation of the German army, Ludendorff wanted an immediate armistice. However, he needed to find a way to obtain favorable armistice terms from President Wilson and to shift the blame for the lost war from the military and the kaiser to civilian leadership. Cynically, he urged the creation of a popular parliamentary government in Germany.

But events in Germany went further than the general had anticipated. Whereas Ludendorff sought a limited monarchy, the shock of defeat and widespread hunger sparked a revolution that forced the kaiser to abdicate. On November 11, the new German Republic signed an armistice ending the hostilities.

THE PEACE CONFERENCE

In January 1919, representatives of the Allied Powers assembled in Paris to draw up peace terms; President Wilson was also there. The war-weary masses turned to Wilson as the prophet who would have the nations beat their swords into plowshares.

Wilson's Hope for a New World

For Wilson, the war had been fought against autocracy. He hoped that a peace settlement based on liberal-democratic ideals would sweep away the foundations of war, and he expressed these hopes in several speeches, including the famous Fourteen Points of January 1918. None of Wilson's principles seemed more just than the idea of self-determination: the right of a people to have its own state, free of foreign domination. In particular, this goal meant (or was interpreted to mean) the return of Alsace and Lorraine to France, the creation of an independent Poland, a readjustment of the frontiers of Italy to incorporate Austrian lands inhabited by Italians, and an opportunity for Slavs of the Austro-Hungarian Empire to form their own states.

Aware that a harshly treated Germany might well seek revenge, engulfing the world in another cataclysm, Wilson insisted that there should be a "peace without victory." A just settlement would encourage a defeated Germany to work with the victorious Allies in building a new Europe. To preserve peace and help remake the world, Wilson urged the formation of the League of Nations, an international parliament to settle disputes and discourage aggression. Wilson wanted a peace of justice to preserve Western civilization in its democratic and Christian form.

Problems of Peacemaking

Wilson's negotiating position was undermined by the Republican Party's victory in the congressional elections of November 1918. Before the election, Wilson had appealed to the American people to cast their ballots for Democrats as a vote of confidence in his diplomacy. But instead, Americans sent twenty-five Republicans and only fifteen Democrats to the Senate. Whatever the motives of the American people in voting Republican—apparently their decision rested on local and national, not international, issues—the outcome diminished Wilson's prestige at the conference table. To his fellow negotiators, Wilson was trying to preach to Europe when he could not command the support of his own country. Since the Senate must ratify any American treaty, European diplomats worried that what Wilson agreed to the Senate might reject, which is precisely what happened.

Another obstacle to Wilson's peace program was France's demand for security and revenge. Nearly the entire war on the Western front had been fought on French territory. Many French industries and farms had been ruined; the country mourned the loss of half its young men. Representing France at the conference table was Georges Clemenceau (1841–1929), nicknamed "the Tiger." Nobody loved France or hated Germany more. Cynical, suspicious of idealism, and not sharing Wilson's hope for a new world or his confidence in the future League of Nations, Clemenceau demanded that Germany be severely punished and its capacity to wage war destroyed.

Seeing Germany's greater population and superior industrial strength as a long-term threat and doubting that its military tradition would let it resign itself to defeat, Clemenceau wanted guarantees that the wars of 1870–1871 and 1914–1918 would not be repeated. The latter war had shown that without the help of Britain and the United States, France would have again been at the mercy of Germany. Since there was no certainty that these states would again aid France, Clemenceau wanted to use his country's present advantage to cripple Germany.

The intermingling of European nationalities was another barrier to Wilson's program. Because in so many regions of Central Europe there was a mixture of nationalities, no one could create a Europe completely free of minority problems; some nationalities would always feel that they had been treated shabbily. And the various nationalities were not willing to moderate their demands or lower their aspirations. For example, Wilson's Fourteen Points called for the creation of an independent Poland with secure access to the sea. But between Poland and the sea lay territory populated by Germans. Giving this land to Poland would violate German self-determination; denying it to Poland would mean that the new country had little chance of developing a sound economy. No matter what the decision, one people would regard it as unjust. Similarly, to provide the new Czechoslovakia with defensible borders, it would be necessary to give it territory inhabited mostly by Germans. This, too, could be viewed as a denial of German self-determination, but not granting the territory to Czechoslovakia would mean that the new state would not be able to defend itself against Germany.

Secret treaties drawn up by the Allies during the war also interfered with Wilson's program. These agreements dividing up German, Austrian, and Ottoman territory did not square with the principle of self-determination. For example, to entice Italy into entering the war, the Allies had promised it Austrian lands that were inhabited predominantly by Germans and Slavs. Italy was not about to repudiate its prize because of Wilson's principles.

Finally, the war had generated great bitterness, which persisted after the guns had been silenced. Both the masses and their leaders demanded retribution and held exaggerated hopes for territory and reparations. In such an atmosphere of postwar enmity, the spirit of compromise and moderation could not overcome the desire for spoils and punishment.

The Settlement

After months of negotiations, often punctuated by acrimony, the peacemakers hammered out a settlement. Five treaties made up the Peace of Paris: one each with Germany, Austria, Hungary, Bulgaria, and Turkey. Of the five, the Treaty of Versailles, which Germany signed on June 28, 1919, was the most significant.

France regained Alsace and Lorraine, lost to Germany in the Franco-Prussian War of 1870–1871. The treaty also barred Germany from placing fortifications in the Rhineland. The French military had wanted to take the Rhineland from Germany and break it up into one or more republics under French suzerainty. Under this arrangement, French control would extend to the Rhine River, which was a natural defensive border; one had only to destroy the bridges to prevent a German invasion of France. With Germany deprived of this springboard for invasion, French security would be immensely improved. Recognizing that the German people would never permanently submit to the amputation of the Rhineland, which was inhabited by more than five million Germans and contained key industries, Wilson and British Prime Minister David Lloyd George (1863–1945) resisted these French demands.

Faced with the opposition of Wilson and Lloyd George, Clemenceau backed down and agreed instead to Allied occupation of the Rhineland for fifteen years, the demilitarization of the region, and an Anglo-American promise of assistance if Germany attacked France in the future. This last point, considered vital by France, proved useless. The alliance went into effect only if both the United States and Britain ratified it. Since the Security Treaty did not get past the U.S. Senate, Britain also refused to sign it. The French people felt that they had been duped and wronged.

A related issue concerned French demands for annexation of the coal-rich Saar Basin, which adjoined Lorraine. By obtaining this region, France would weaken Germany's military potential and strengthen its own. France argued that this would be just compensation for the deliberate destruction of the French coal mines by the retreating German army at the end of the war. But here, too, France was disappointed. The final compromise called for a League of Nations commission to govern the Saar Basin for fifteen years, after which the inhabitants would decide whether their territory would be ceded to France or returned to Germany.

In eastern Germany, in certain districts of Silesia that had a large Polish population, a plebiscite determined the future of the region. Part of Upper Silesia was ceded to Poland. The settlement also gave Poland a corridor cut through West Prussia and terminating in the Baltic port of Danzig; Danzig itself was declared an international city, to be administered by a League of Nations commission. The Germans would never resign themselves to this loss of territory that separated East Prussia from the rest of Germany.

The victorious nations were awarded control of German colonies and Ottoman lands. However, these nations held colonies not outright but as mandates under the supervision of the League, which would protect the interests of the native peoples. The mandate system implied the ultimate end of colonialism, for it clearly opposed the exploitation of colonial peoples and asserted independence as the rightful goal for subject nations.

Other issues revolved around the German military forces and reparations. To prevent a resurgence of militarism, the German army was limited to one hundred thousand volunteers and deprived of heavy artillery, tanks, and warplanes. The German navy was limited to a token force, which did not include submarines. The issue of war reparations caused great bitterness between Wilson and his French and British adversaries. The American delegation wanted the treaty to fix a reasonable sum that Germany would have to pay and specify the period of years allotted for payment. But no such items were included; they were left for future consideration. The Treaty of Versailles presented Germany with an open-ended bill that would probably take generations to pay. Moreover, Article 231, which preceded the reparation clauses, placed sole responsibility for the war on Germany and its allies. The Germans responded to this accusation with contempt.

In separate treaties, the conference dealt with the dissolution of the Hapsburg Empire. During the final weeks of the war, the Austro-Hungarian Empire had crumbled as the various nationalities proclaimed their independence from Hapsburg rule. In most cases, the peacemakers ratified with treaties what the nationalities had already accomplished in fact. Serbia joined with Austrian lands inhabited by Croats and Slovenes to become Yugoslavia. Czechoslovakia arose from the predominantly Czech and Slovak regions of Austria. Hungary, which broke away from Austria to become a separate country, had to cede considerable land to Romania and Yugoslavia. Austria turned over to Italy the South Tyrol, inhabited by two hundred thousand Austrian Germans. This clear violation of the principle of self-determination greatly offended liberal opinion. Deprived of its vast territories and prohibited from union with Germany, the new Austria was a third-rate power.

Assessment and Problems

The Germans unanimously denounced the Treaty of Versailles, for in their minds the war had ended not in German defeat but in a stalemate. They regarded the armistice as the prelude to a negotiated settlement among equals, based on Wilson's call for a peace of justice. Instead, the Germans were barred from participating in the negotiations. And they viewed the terms of the treaty as humiliating and vindictive—designed to keep Germany militarily and economically weak.

When the United States had entered the war, the Germans protested, Wilson had stated that the enemy was not the German people but their government. Surely, the Germans now argued, the new German democracy should not be punished for the sins of the monarchy and the military. To the Germans, the Treaty of Versailles was not the dawning of the new world that Wilson had promised, but an abomination—a vile crime.

Critics in other lands also condemned the treaty as a punitive settlement in flagrant violation of Wilsonian idealism. The peacemakers, they argued, should have set aside past hatreds and, in cooperation with the new democratic German republic, forged a just settlement to serve as the foundation of a new world. Instead, they burdened the fledgling German democracy with reparations that were impossible to pay, insulted it with the accusation of war guilt, and deprived it of territory in violation of the principle of self-determination. All these provisions, said the critics, would only exacerbate old hatreds and fan the flames of German nationalism. This was a poor beginning for democracy in Germany and for Wilson's new world.

The treaty's defenders, however, insisted that if Germany had won the war, it would have imposed a far harsher settlement on the Allies. They pointed to German war aims, which called for the annexation of parts of France and Poland, the reduction of Belgium and Romania to satellites, and German expansion in central Africa. They pointed also to the treaty of Brest-Litovsk, which Germany had compelled Russia to sign in 1918, as an example of Germany's ruthless appetite. An insatiable Germany gained 34 percent of Russia's population, 32 percent of its farmland, 54 percent of its industrial enterprises, and 89 percent of its coal mines. Moreover, they maintained that the peace settlement did not repudiate Wilson's principles. The new map of Europe was the closest approximation of the ethnic distribution of its peoples that Europe had ever known.

What is most significant about the Treaty of Versailles is that it did not solve the German problem. Germany was left weakened but unbroken—its industrial and military power only temporarily contained, and its nationalist fervor not only undiminished but stoked higher by a peace treaty that all political parties viewed as unjust, dictated, and offensive to national pride. The real danger in Europe was German unwillingness to accept defeat or surrender the dream of expansion.

Would France, Britain, and the United States enforce the treaty against a resurgent Germany? The war had demonstrated that an Allied victory depended on American intervention. But in 1920, the U.S. Senate, angry that Wilson had not taken Republicans with him to Paris and fearing that membership in the League of Nations would involve America in future wars, refused to ratify the Treaty of Versailles. Britain, feeling guilty over the treatment of Germany, lacked the will for enforcement and even came to favor revising the treaty. Therefore, the responsibility for preserving the settlement rested primarily with France, which was not encouraging. Germany had greater industrial potential than France and, with Russia now Communist, France could not count on Russian manpower to balance Germany's much larger population. The Paris peace settlement left Germany resentful but potentially powerful, and to the east lay small and weak states—some of them with sizable German minorities—that could not check a rearmed Germany.

THE RUSSIAN REVOLUTION OF 1917

One consequence of the war that influenced the course of European and world history in momentous ways was the Russian Revolution of 1917 and the resultant triumph of the Bolsheviks. The people of Russia had initially responded to the war with a show of patriotic fervor. But the realities of war quickly dimmed this ardor. The ill-equipped and poorly led Russian armies suffered huge losses. In July 1915, the minister of war wrote this dismal report:

> *The soldiers are without doubt exhausted by the continued defeats and retreats. Their confidence in final victory and in their leaders is undermined. Ever more threatening signs of impending demoralization are evident. Cases of desertion and voluntary surrender to the enemy are becoming more frequent. It is difficult to expect enthusiasm and selflessness from men sent into battle unarmed and ordered to pick up the rifles of their dead comrades.*[18]

By 1916, the home front began to fall apart. Shops were empty, money had no value, and hunger and cold stalked the working quarters of cities and towns. Factory workers, many of them women replacing husbands, brothers, and sons who were at the front, toiled long hours for wages that could not keep up with the accelerating inflation. When they protested, the government resorted to heavy-handed repression. By January 1917, nearly all Russians, soldiers and civilians alike, had lost trust in their autocratic government. But Tsar Nicholas II, determined to preserve autocracy, resisted any suggestion that he liberalize the regime for the sake of the war effort.

Autocracy was ready to collapse at the slightest blow. In early March (February 23 by the calendar then in use*), a strike, riots in the food lines,

and street demonstrations in Petrograd (formerly Saint Petersburg) flared into sudden, unpremeditated revolution. The soldiers, who in 1905 had massacred peaceful protesters, now rushed to support the striking workers. The Romanov dynasty, after three hundred years of rule (1613–1917), came to an end. The Provisional Government was set up—provisional until a representative Constituent Assembly, to be elected as soon as possible, could establish a permanent regime.

The Problems of the Provisional Government

The collapse of autocracy was followed by what supporters in Russia and the West hoped would be a liberal-democratic regime pledged to give Russia a constitution. In reality, however, the course of events from March to November 1917 resembled a free-for-all—a no-holds-barred fight for the succession to autocracy, with only the fittest surviving. Events demonstrated the desperate state of the Russian Empire. Its vast size promoted internal disunity; increasing hardships raised the fury of the accumulated resentments to raw brutality among the masses. National minorities took advantage of the anarchy to dismember the country.

Among the potential successors to the tsars, the liberals of various shades seemed at first to enjoy the best chances. They represented the educated and forward-looking elements in Russian society that had arisen after the reforms of the 1860s: lawyers, doctors, professional people of all kinds, intellectuals, businesspeople and industrialists, many landowners, and even some bureaucrats. Liberals had opposed autocracy and earned a reputation for leadership.

The liberals had joined the March revolution only reluctantly, for they were afraid of the masses and the violence of the streets. They dreaded social revolution that could result in the seizure of factories, dispossession of landowners, and tampering with property rights. Although most leaders of the Provisional Government had only modest means, they were capitalists, believing in private enterprise as the means of promoting economic progress. Their ideal was a constitutional monarchy, its leadership entrusted to the educated

---

*Until March 1918, events in Russia were dated by the Julian calendar, thirteen days behind the Gregorian calendar used in the West. By the Julian calendar, the first revolution occurred in February and the second in October.

WOMEN DEMONSTRATE IN PETROGRAD, 1917. The collapse of the tsarist regime was followed by a period of political fermentation, meetings, and concern about food shortages. Women demonstrated for increased bread supplies. The poster reads, "Comrades, workers, and soldiers, support our demands!"

and propertied elite familiar with the essentials of statecraft.

Unfortunately, the liberals misunderstood the mood of the people. Looking to the Western democracies—including, after April 1917, the United States—for political and financial support, the liberals decided to continue the war on the side of the Allies. The decision antagonized the war-weary masses, along with the Russian soldiers, almost two million of whom had deserted. The liberals also antagonized the Russian peasants by not confiscating and redistributing the landlords' lands free of charge, and industrial workers, whose economic conditions continued to deteriorate. As Russian nationalists who wanted their country to remain undivided, the liberals opposed national minorities—Finns, Ukrainians, Georgians, and others—who sought self-determination; hence, they lost the minorities' support.

Frustrated by the Provisional Government's inaction on the land question, peasants began taking matters into their own hands. They seized the nobles' land and torched their estates, sometimes putting them to death. The peasants began to divide the landlords' land among themselves, which encouraged more soldiers to desert in order to claim a share of the land. The breakdown of the railways stopped factory production; enraged workers ousted factory managers and owners. Consumer goods grew scarce and prices soared, and the peasants could see no reason to sell their crops if they could buy nothing in return. Thus, the specter of famine in the cities arose. Hardships and anger mounted. Adding to the disorder were the demands of the non-Russian nationalities for self-determination and even secession.

Freedom in Russia was leading to dissolution and chaos. The largely illiterate peasant masses had no experience with or understanding of the institutions, habits, and attitudes of a free society. Without their cooperation, Russian liberalism collapsed. This outcome demonstrated the difficulty of establishing Western liberal-democratic forms of government in countries lacking a sense of unity, a strong middle class, and a tradition of responsible participation in public affairs.

By July 1917, when Aleksandr Kerensky (1881–1970), a radical lawyer of great eloquence, took over the leadership of the Provisional Government, it had become clear that law and order could be upheld only by brute force. In late August and early September, a conspiracy led by a right-wing general, Lavr Kornilov, sought to establish a military dictatorship. Kornilov had the support not only of the officer corps and the tsarist officials, but also of many liberals who were fed up with anarchy. What stopped the general was not Kerensky's government (which had no troops), but the workers of Petrograd. Their agitators demoralized Kornilov's soldiers, proving that a dictatorship of the right had no mass support. The workers also repudiated Kerensky and the Provisional Government, as well as their own moderate leaders; henceforth, they supported the Bolsheviks.

Lenin and the Rise of Bolshevism

Revolutionary movements had a long history in Russia, going back to the early nineteenth century, when educated Russians began to compare their country unfavorably with Western Europe. They, too, wanted constitutional liberty and free speech in order to make their country modern. Prohibited from speaking out in public, they went underground, giving up their liberalism as ineffective. They saw revolutionary socialism, with its idealistic vision and compassion for the multitude, as a better ideology in the harsh struggle with the tsar's police. By the 1870s, many socialists had evolved into austere and self-denying professional revolutionaries who, in the service of the cause, had no moral scruples, just as the police had no scruples in the defense of the tsars. Bank robbery, murder, assassination, treachery, and terror were not seen as immoral if they served the revolutionary cause.

In the 1880s and 1890s, revolutionaries had learned industrial economics and sociology from Marx; from Marxism they had also acquired a vision of a universal and inevitable progression toward socialism and Communism that satisfied their semireligious craving for salvation in this world, not the next. Marxism also allied them with socialist movements in other lands, giving them an internationalist outlook. History, they believed, was on their side, as it was for all the proletarians and oppressed peoples in the world.

By 1900, a number of able young Russians had rallied to revolutionary Marxism; almost all of them were educated or came from privileged families. The most promising was Vladimir Ilyich Ulyanov, known as Lenin (1870–1924), the son of a teacher and school administrator who had attained the rank of a nobleman. Lenin had studied law but practiced revolution instead. His first contribution lay in adapting Marxism to Russian conditions; to do so, he took considerable liberties with Marx's teaching. His second contribution followed from the first: outlining the organization of an underground party capable of surviving against the tsarist police. It was to be a tightly knit conspiratorial elite of professional revolutionaries. Its headquarters would be safely located abroad, and it would have close ties to the masses, that is, to the workers and other potentially revolutionary elements.

Two other prominent Marxists close to Lenin were Leon Trotsky (1879–1940) and Joseph Stalin (1879–1953). Trotsky, whose original name was Lev Bronstein, was the son of a prosperous Jewish farmer from southern Russia and was soon known for his brilliant pen. Less prominent until after the Revolution, Stalin (the man of steel) was originally named Iosif Dzhugashvili; he was from Georgia, beyond the Caucasus Mountains. Bright enough to be sent to the best school in the area, he dropped out for a revolutionary career. While they were still young, Lenin, Trotsky, and Stalin were all hardened by arrest, imprisonments, and exile to Siberia. Lenin and Trotsky later lived abroad, while Stalin, following a harsher course, stayed in Russia; for four years before 1917, he was banished to bleakest northern Siberia and conditioned to ruthlessness for life.

In 1903, the Russian Marxists split into two factions, the moderate Mensheviks, so named after finding themselves in a minority (*menshinstvo*) at a rather unrepresentative vote at the Second Party Congress, and the extremist Bolsheviks, who at that moment were in the majority (*bolshinstvo*). They might more accurately have been called the "softs" and the "hards." The "softs" (Mensheviks) preserved basic moral scruples; they would not stoop to crime or undemocratic methods for

V. I. LENIN. Red Army soldiers leaving for battle in the civil war are addressed by Lenin in Moscow in May 1920.

the sake of political success. For that the "hards" (Bolsheviks) ridiculed them, noting that a dead, imprisoned, or unsuccessful revolutionary was of little use.

Meanwhile, Lenin perfected Bolshevik revolutionary theory. He violated Marxist tradition by paying close attention to the revolutionary potential of peasants (thereby anticipating Mao Zedong). Lenin also looked closely at the numerous peoples in Asia who had recently fallen under Western imperialist domination. These people, he sensed, constituted a potential revolutionary force. In alliance with the Western—and Russian—proletariat, they might overthrow the worldwide capitalist order. The Bolsheviks, the most militant of all revolutionary socialists, were ready to assist in that gigantic struggle.

Lenin was a Russian nationalist as well as a socialist internationalist; he had a vision of a modern and powerful Russian state destined to be a model in world affairs. Russian Communism was thus nationalist Communism. The Bolsheviks saw the abolition of income-producing property by the dictatorship of the proletariat as the most effective way of mobilizing the country's resources. Yet the Bolshevik mission was also internationalist. The Russian Revolution was intended to set off a world revolution, liberating all oppressed classes and peoples around the world and achieving a higher stage of civilization.

Lenin's Opportunity

On April 16, 1917, Lenin, with German help, arrived in Petrograd from exile in Switzerland. (The Germans provided Lenin with a secret train to take him to Petrograd; they hoped that the Bolshevik leader, who wanted Russia to withdraw from the "capitalist" war, would initiate a revolution and gain power.) The Provisional Government, he said, could not possibly preserve Russia from disintegration. Most of the soldiers, workers, and peasants would repudiate the Provisional Government's cautious liberalism in favor of a regime expressing their demand for peace and land. Nothing would stop them from avenging themselves for centuries of oppression. Lenin also felt that only complete state control of the economy could rescue the country from disaster. The sole way out, he insisted, was the dictatorship of the proletariat backed by *soviets* (councils) of soldiers, workers, and peasants, particularly the poorer peasants.

Lenin prepared his party for the second stage of the Revolution of 1917: the seizure of power by the Bolsheviks. His slogan, "Peace, Land, and Bread," held a magnetic attraction for the desperate Russian masses. The Bolsheviks' determined effort to win over the disheartened soldiers proved particularly effective. Many of the people who supported the Bolsheviks interpreted Lenin's other powerful slogan—"All Power to the Soviets"—to mean that the Bolsheviks aimed to create a democratic socialist state that would institute needed social reforms. They did not anticipate the creation of Bolshevik dictatorship.

Conditions favored the Bolsheviks, as Lenin had predicted. The Bolsheviks obtained majorities in the soviets. The peasants were in active revolt, seizing the land themselves. The Provisional Government lost all control over the course of events. On November 6 (October 24 by the old calendar), Lenin urged immediate action: "The government is tottering. It must be *given the death blow* at all costs. To delay action is fatal."[19] On the following day, the Bolsheviks, meeting little resistance, seized power. Lenin permitted the elections for the Constituent Assembly that had been scheduled by the Provisional Government. In a free election, the Bolsheviks received only 24 percent of the vote. After meeting once in January 1918, however, the Constituent Assembly was disbanded by the Bolsheviks.

The Bolsheviks Survive

Lenin contended that he was guiding the Russian proletariat and all humanity toward a higher social order, symbolizing—in Russia and much of the world—the rebellion of the disadvantaged against Western (or "capitalist") dominance. That is why in 1918 he changed the name of his party from Bolshevik to Communist, which implied a concern for the human community. For Lenin, as for Marx, a world without exploitation was humanity's noblest ideal.

But staggering adversity confronted Lenin after his seizure of power. In the prevailing anarchy, Russia lay open to the German armies. Under the Treaty of Brest-Litovsk, signed in March 1918—the lowest point in Russian history for over two hundred years—Russia lost Finland, Poland, and the Baltic provinces, all regions inhabited largely by non-Russians. It also lost the rebellious Ukraine, its chief industrial base and breadbasket. Yet Lenin had no choice but to accept the humiliating terms.

THE WAR AND EUROPEAN CONSCIOUSNESS

"There will be wars as never before on earth," Nietzsche had predicted. World War I bore him out. Modern technology enabled the combatants to kill with unprecedented efficiency; modern nationalism infused both civilians and soldiers with the determination to fight until the enemy was totally beaten. Exercising wide control over its citizens, the modern state mobilized its human, material, and spiritual resources to wage total war. As the war hardened into a savage and grueling fight, the statesmen did not press for a compromise peace; instead, they demanded ever more mobilization, ever more escalation, and ever more sacrifices.

The Great War profoundly altered the course of Western civilization, deepening the spiritual crisis that had helped to produce it. How could one speak of the inviolability of the individual when Europe had become a slaughterhouse, or of the primacy of reason when nations permitted slaughter to go unabated for four years? How could the mind cope with this spectacle of a civilization turning against itself, destroying itself in an orgy of organized violence? A young French soldier, shortly before he was killed at Verdun, expressed the disillusionment that gripped the soldiers in the trenches: "Humanity is mad! It must be mad to do what it is doing. What a massacre! What scenes of horror and carnage, I cannot find words to translate my impressions. Hell cannot be so terrible. Men are mad!"[20] The war, said British poet Robert Graves, provoked an "inward scream" that still reverberates. The agony caused by the astronomical casualty figures—some 9.4 million dead and 21 million wounded, many of them pathetically mutilated and disfigured or mentally deranged—touched millions of homes. About 300,000 of French fatalities were unidentifiable, their bodies blown apart by artillery shelling. For a generation, millions of grieving widows and orphaned children were a tragic reminder of Europe's descent into savagery. Now only the naïve could believe in continuous progress. Western civilization had entered an age of violence, anxiety, and doubt.

The war left many with the gnawing feeling that Western civilization had lost its vitality and was caught in a rhythm of breakdown and disintegration. It seemed that Western civilization was fragile and perishable, that Western people, despite their extraordinary accomplishments, were never more than a step or two away from barbarism. Surely, any civilization that could allow such senseless slaughter to last had entered its decline and could look forward to only the darkest of futures.

European intellectuals were demoralized and disillusioned. The orderly, peaceful, rational world of their youth had been wrecked, and they knew in their hearts that it would never be restored. Their foreboding was not misplaced, for without World War I it is highly doubtful that the Communists would have gained power in Russia or that a Nazi Party would have even emerged in Germany. The Enlightenment worldview, weakened in the nineteenth century by the assault of romantics, Social Darwinists, extreme nationalists, race mystics, and glorifiers of the irrational, was now disintegrating. The enormity of the war had destroyed faith in the capacity of reason to deal with crucial social and political questions. Civilization seemed to be fighting an unending and hopeless battle against the irrational elements in human nature. It appeared that war would be a recurring phenomenon in the twentieth century.

Scientific research had produced more efficient weapons to kill and maim Europe's youth. The achievements of Western science and technology, which had been viewed as a boon for humanity and the clearest testament to the superiority of European civilization, were called into question. Confidence in the future gave way to doubt. The old beliefs in the perfectibility of humanity, the blessings of science, and ongoing progress now seemed an expression of naïve optimism and post-Christian myths; the war had exposed them as fraudulent. As A. J. P. Taylor concludes,

> *The First World War was difficult to fit into the picture of a rational civilization advancing by ordered stages. The civilized men of the twentieth century had outdone in savagery the barbarians of all preceding ages, and their civilized virtues—organization, mechanical skill, self-sacrifice—had made war's savagery all the more terrible. Modern man had developed powers which he was not fit to use. European civilization had been weighed in the balance and found wanting.*[21]

This disillusionment heralded a loss of faith in liberal-democratic values—a loss of faith that contributed to the widespread popularity of Fascist ideologies in the postwar world. Having lost confidence in the power of reason to solve the problems of the human community, in liberal doctrines of individual freedom, and in the institutions of parliamentary democracy, many people turned to Fascism as a simple saving faith. Far from making the world safe for democracy, as Wilson and other liberals had hoped, World War I gave rise to totalitarian movements that would nearly destroy democracy.

The war produced a generation of young people who had reached their maturity in combat. Violence had become a way of life for millions of soldiers hardened by battle and for millions of civilians aroused by four years of propaganda. The relentless massacre of Europe's young men had a brutalizing effect. Violence, cruelty, suffering, and even wholesale death seemed to be natural and acceptable components of human existence. The sanctity of the individual seemed to be liberal and Christian claptrap.

To be sure, many people, including veterans repelled by the slaughter, abandoned the popular romantic view that war was glorious and heroic. But the fascination with violence and contempt for life persisted in the postwar world. Many returned veterans yearned for the excitement of battle and the fellowship of the trenches—what one French soldier called "the most tender human experience." After the war, a young English officer reminisced: "There was an exaltation, in those days of comradeship and dedication, that would have come in few other ways."[22] A fraternal bond united the men of the trenches. But many veterans also shared a primitive attraction to war's fury. A Belgian veteran expressed it this way:

> *The plain truth is that if I were to obey my native animal instincts—and there was little hope for anything else while I was in the trenches—I should enlist again in any future war, or take part in any sort of fighting, merely to experience again that voluptuous thrill of the human brute who realizes his power to take away life from other human beings who try to do the same to him. What was first accepted as a moral duty became a habit . . . had become a need.*[23]

The British novelist D. H. Lawrence (1885–1930) understood that the brutality and hate unleashed by the war ruined old Europe and would give rise to even greater evils. On the day the armistice was signed, he warned prophetically:

> *I suppose you think the war is over and that we shall go back to the kind of world you lived in before it. But the war isn't over. The hate and evil is greater now than ever. Very soon war will break out again and overwhelm you. . . . The crowd outside thinks that Germany is crushed forever. But the Germans will soon rise again. Europe is done for. . . . The war isn't over. Even if the fighting should stop, the evil will be worse because the hate will be damned up in men's hearts and will show itself in all sorts of ways.*[24]

Particularly in Germany, the veterans who aspired to recapture the exhilaration experienced in combat, and men who had been too young to fight but were inspired by the heroic deeds of their elders, made ideal recruits for extremist political movements that glorified action and brutality and promised to rescue society from a decadent liberalism. Both Hitler and Mussolini, themselves ex-soldiers imbued with the ferocity of the front, knew how to appeal to veterans. The lovers of violence and the harbingers of hate who became the leaders of Fascist parties would come within a hairsbreadth of destroying Western civilization. The intensified nationalist hatreds following World War I also helped fuel the fires of World War II. The Germans swore to regain lands lost to the Poles. Many Germans, like the embittered Hitler, were consumed by anguish over a defeat that they believed never should have happened and over the humiliating Treaty of Versailles; a desire for revenge festered in their souls. Italy, too, felt aggrieved because it had not received more territory from the dismembered Austro-Hungarian Empire.

Yet, while some veterans clung to an aggressive militarism, others aspired to build a more humane world. Such veterans embraced democratic and socialist ideals and resolved that the horror should never be repeated. Tortured by the memory of the Great War, European intellectuals wrote pacifist plays and novels and signed pacifist declarations. In the 1930s, an attitude of "peace at any price" discouraged resistance to Nazi Germany in its bid to dominate Europe.

The war impacted on women. In order to release men for military service, women in England, France, Germany, and later the United States, responded to their countries' wartime needs. They took jobs in munitions factories, worked on farms, and drove ambulances, mail trucks, and buses. They worked as nurses, laboratory assistants, plumbers' helper, and bank clerks. By performing effectively in jobs formerly carried out by men, women demonstrated that they had an essential role to play in their countries' economic life. The employment of women in many areas of the workplace did encounter strong resistance, and after the war many female workers were dismissed from their new positions. Nevertheless, by the end of the war, little opposition remained to granting women political rights.

During World War I, new weapons were introduced, particularly the tank and the fighter plane, which revolutionized the future of warfare. Prior to World War II, imaginative military planners recognized that planes and tanks, properly deployed, could penetrate and smash the enemy's defenses, circumventing the stalemate of trench warfare. Planes also meant terror from the skies, for bombs could pulverize a city, killing and maiming tens of thousands of civilians.

World War I was total war; it encompassed the entire nation and was without limits. States

Hulton Archive/Stringer/Getty Images.

BRITISH MUNITIONS WORKERS. With millions of men in the military, women took jobs formerly held only by men. Women drove trucks and buses, operated cranes, and worked in armament factories. Their patriotism and productive labor caused opposition to women's suffrage to dissipate.

demanded total victory and total commitment from their citizens. They regulated industrial production, developed sophisticated propaganda techniques to strengthen morale, and exercised ever-greater control over the lives of their people, organizing and disciplining them like soldiers. This total mobilization of nations' human and material resources provided a model for future dictators. With ever-greater effectiveness and ruthlessness, dictators would centralize power and manipulate thinking. The ruthless dictatorships that emerged in Russia, Germany, and Italy were products of the war. The war gave Communists the opportunity to seize power in Russia, and the mentality of the front helped to mold the Fascist movements that emerged in Italy and Germany. And both Hitler and Stalin drew a moral lesson from the immense loss of life in the trenches: a desired political end justifies vast human sacrifice. The barbarism of the trenches would be eclipsed by the horrors inflicted on people by totalitarian regimes and a second world war begot by World War I. The noble sentiment, widely publicized during the war that this was to be "the war to end all wars," proved to be still another naïve fantasy.

❖   ❖   ❖

NOTES

1. Quoted in Roland N. Stromberg, *Redemption by War*, 24. University Press of Kansas, 1982. Copyright © 1982 by University Press of Kansas. All rights reserved. Reprinted with permission.

2. Heinrich von Treitschke, *Politics*, excerpted in *Germany's War Mania* (New York: Dodd, Mead, 1915), 222–223.

3. Fritz Fischer, *Germany's Aims in the First World War* (New York: Norton, 1967), 88.

4. Quoted in Joachim Remak, *The Origins of World War I* (New York: Holt, 1967), 135.

5. Quoted in Michael Burleigh, *Earthly Power: The Clash of Religion and Politics in Europe from the French Revolution to the Great War* (New York: HarperCollins, 2007), 445.

6. Rupert Brooke, "Peace," in *Collected Poems of Rupert Brooke* (New York: Dodd, Mead, 1941), 111.

7. Quoted in Joachim C. Fest, *Hitler* (New York: Harcourt Brace Jovanovich, 1973), 66.

8. Roland Dorgelès, "After Fifty Years," excerpted in *Promise of Greatness*, ed. George A. Panichas (New York: John Day, 1968), 14–15.

9. Quoted in Joseph E. Persico, *Eleventh Month, Eleventh Day, Eleventh Hour: Armistice Day, 1918* (New York: Random House, 2004), 27.

10. Quoted in Barbara Tuchman, *The Guns of August* (New York: Macmillan, 1962), 145.

11. Bertrand Russell, *The Autobiography of Bertrand Russell, 1914–1944* (Boston: Little, Brown, 1951, 1956), Vol. 2, 4–6.

12. Quoted in Robert G. L. Waite, *Vanguard of Nazism* (New York: Norton, 1969), 22.

13. Brooke, "Peace," 111.

14. Quoted in James Joll, "The Unspoken Assumptions," in *The Origins of the First World War*, ed. H. W. Koch (New York: Taplinger, 1972), 318.

15. Quoted in Peter Gay, *Freud: A Life for Our Time* (New York: Norton), 348.

16. A. J. P. Taylor, *A History of the First World War* (New York: Berkeley, 1966), 84.

17. Quoted in Richard M. Watt, *Dare Call It Treason* (New York: Simon & Schuster, 1963), 169.

18. Excerpted in Ronald Kowalski, ed., *The Russian Revolution, 1917–1921* (New York: Routledge, 1997), 20.

19. From *Collected Works of V. I. Lenin*, Vol. 26, 4th edition (Moscow, 1960–1967), 235.

20. Quoted in Alistair Horne, *The Price of Glory* (New York: Harper, 1967), 240.

21. A. J. P. Taylor, *From Sarajevo to Potsdam* (New York: Harcourt, Brace & World), 1966, 55–56.

22. Quoted in Modris Eksteins, *Rites of Spring: The Great War and the Birth of the Modern Age* (New York: Doubleday Anchor Books, 1989), 232.

23. Quoted in Eric J. Leed, *No Man's Land: Combat and Identity in World War I* (New York: Cambridge University Press, 1979), 201.

24. Quoted in Samuel Hynes, *A War Imagined* (New York: Atheneum, 1991), 266.

Chapter 19

An Era of Totalitarianism

- The Nature of Totalitarianism
- Communist Russia
- The Stalin Revolution
- The Nature and Appeal of Fascism
- The Rise of Fascism in Italy
- The New German Republic
- The Rise of Hitler
- Nazi Germany
- Liberalism and Authoritarianism in Other Lands
- Intellectuals and Artists in Troubled Times
- Existentialism
- The Modern Predicament

Focus Questions

1. What are the distinctive features of a totalitarian state?
2. What motivated Stalin to make terror a government policy? What motivated Communist bureaucrats to participate in Stalin's inhumanities?
3. What were the essential features of the Fascist movements that arose in Europe after World War I?
4. What were Hitler's attitudes toward liberalism, war, race, the Jews, and propaganda?
5. In what ways did Nazism conflict with the core values of both the Enlightenment and Christianity? Why did the Nazi regime attract so many supporters?
6. What lessons might democratic societies draw from the Nazi experience?
7. Why and how did European intellectual and cultural life convey a mood of pessimism and disillusionment after World War I?
8. How did art and literature express a social conscience during the 1920s and 1930s?

9. What were the different ways that intellectuals struggled with the crisis of European society in an era of world wars and totalitarianism?
10. What were some of the conditions that gave rise to existentialism? What are the basic principles of existentialism?

*I*n the 1930s, the term *totalitarianism* was used to describe the Fascist regime in Italy, the National Socialist regime in Germany, and the Communist regime in the Soviet Union. To a degree that far exceeds the ancient tyrannies and early modern autocratic states, these dictatorships aspired to and, with varying degrees of success, attained control over the individual's consciousness and behavior and all phases of political, social, and cultural life. To many people, it seemed that a crisis-riddled democracy was dying and that the future belonged to these dynamic totalitarian movements.

Totalitarianism was a twentieth-century phenomenon, for such all-embracing control over the individual and society could be achieved only in an age of modern ideology, technology, and bureaucracy. The totalitarian state was more completely established in Germany and the Soviet Union than in Italy, where cultural and historic conditions impeded the realization of the totalitarian goal of monolithic unity and total control.

The ideological aims and social and economic policies of Hitler and Stalin differed fundamentally. However, both Soviet Russia and Nazi Germany shared the totalitarian goal of total domination of both the individual and institutions, and both employed similar methods to achieve it. Mussolini's Italy is more accurately called authoritarian, for the party-state either did not intend to control all phases of life or lacked the means to do so. Moreover, Mussolini hesitated to use the ruthless methods that Hitler and Stalin employed so readily. ❖

THE NATURE OF TOTALITARIANISM

Striving for total unity, control, and obedience, the totalitarian dictatorship is the antithesis of liberal democracy. Seeking to obliterate the democratic state that preceded it (the short-lived Provisional Government in Russia and the Weimar Republic in Germany), both Communist Russia and Nazi Germany abolished all competing political parties, suppressed individual liberty, eliminated or regulated private institutions, and utilized the modern state's bureaucracy and technology to impose its ideology and enforce its commands. The party-state determined what people should believe—what values they should hold. There was no room for individual thinking, private moral judgment, or individual conscience, all considered evils that threatened the totalitarian ideology and party. The individual possessed no natural rights that the state must respect. The state regarded individuals merely as building blocks, the human material to be hammered and hewed into a new social order. It sought to create an efficiently organized and stable society—one whose members did not raise troublesome questions or hold unorthodox opinions.

Nevertheless, the totalitarian dictatorship was also an unintended consequence of liberal democracy. It emerged in an age in which, because of the French and Industrial Revolutions, the masses had become a force in political life. The totalitarian leader sought to gain and preserve power by harnessing mass support. Hitler, in particular, built a party within the existing constitutional system and exploited the electoral process in order to overthrow the democratic government.

Unlike previous dictatorial regimes, the dictatorships of both the Left and the Right sought to legitimatize their rule by gaining the masses' approval. They claimed that their governments were higher and truer expressions of the people's will. The Soviet and Nazi dictatorships established their rule in the name of the people—the German Volk or the Soviet proletariat.

A distinctive feature of totalitarianism is the overriding importance of the leader, who is seen as infallible and invincible. The masses' slavish adulation of the leader and their uncritical acceptance of the dogma that the leader or the party is always right promote loyalty, dedication, and obedience and distort rational thinking.

Totalitarian leaders want more than power for its own sake; they engage in vast projects of social engineering intending to transform the world according to an all-embracing ideology, a set of convictions and beliefs, which, says Hannah Arendt, "pretend[s] to know the mysteries of the whole historical process—the secrets of the past, the intricacies of the present, the uncertainties of the future."[1] The ideology constitutes a higher truth based on a law of history and contains a dazzling vision of the future—a secular New Jerusalem—that strengthens the will of the faithful and attracts converts. Like a religion, the totalitarian ideology provides its adherents with beliefs that make society and history intelligible, that explain all of existence in an emotionally gratifying way.

The ideology satisfies a human yearning for complete certitude. Like a religion, it creates true believers, who feel that they are participating in a great cause—a heroic fight against evil—that gives meaning to their lives. During World War II, a German soldier fighting on the Eastern front wrote to his brother that the battle "is for a new ideology, a new belief, a new life! I am glad that I can participate . . . in this war of light and darkness."[2] Also like a religion, the totalitarian party gives isolated and alienated individuals a sense of belonging, a feeling of camaraderie; it enables a person to lose himself or herself in the comforting and exhilarating embrace of a mass movement.

Not only did the totalitarian religion-ideology supply followers with a cause that claimed absolute goodness, it also provided a Devil. For the Soviets, the source of evil and the cause of all the people's hardships were the degenerate capitalists, reactionary peasants who resisted collectivization, the traitorous Trotskyites, or the saboteurs and foreign agents who impeded the realization of the socialist society. For the Nazis, the Devil was the conspirator Jew. These "evil" ones must be eliminated in order to realize the totalitarian movement's vision of the future.

Thus, totalitarian regimes liquidate large segments of the population designated as "enemies of the people." Historical necessity or a higher purpose demands and justifies their liquidation. The appeal to historical necessity has all the power of a great myth. Presented as a world-historical struggle between the forces of good and the forces of evil, the myth incites fanaticism and numbs the conscience. Traditional rules of morality have no meaning; seemingly decent people engage in terrible acts of brutality with no remorse, convinced that they are waging a righteous war.

Totalitarians are utopians inspired by idealism; they seek the salvation of their nation, their race, or humanity. They believe that the victory of their cause will usher in the millennium, a state of harmony and bliss. Such a vision is attractive to people burdened by economic insecurity or spiritual disorientation. The history of the twentieth century demonstrates how easily utopian beliefs can be twisted into paranoid fantasies, idealistic sentiments transformed into murderous fanaticism, and destructive components of human nature mobilized and directed by demagogues who see themselves as possessors of an overarching historical truth.

Unlike earlier autocratic regimes, the totalitarian dictatorship is not satisfied with its subjects' outward obedience; it demands the masses' unconditional loyalty and enthusiastic support. It strives to control the inner person—to shape thoughts, feelings, and attitudes in accordance with the party ideology, which becomes an official creed. It does not rule by brute force alone but seeks to create a "new man," one who dedicates himself body and soul to the party and its ideology. Such unquestioning, faithful subjects can be manipulated by the party. The disinterested search for truth, justice, and goodness—the exploration of those fundamental moral, political, and religious questions that have characterized the Western intellectual tradition for centuries—is abandoned. Truth, justice, and goodness are what the party deems them to be, and ideological deviation is forbidden.

The totalitarian dictatorship deliberately politicizes all areas of human activity. Ideology pervades works of literature, history, philosophy, art, and even science. It dominates the school curriculum and influences everyday speech and social relations. The state is concerned with everything its citizens do; there is no distinction between public and private life, and every institution comes under the party-state's authority. If voluntary support for the regime cannot be generated by indoctrination, then the state unhesitatingly resorts to terror and violence to compel obedience. People live under a constant strain. Fear of the secret police is ever present; it produces a permanent state of insecurity, which induces people to do everything that the regime asks of them and to watch what they say and do.

COMMUNIST RUSSIA

In 1918, the infant Soviet government was threatened with civil war. Tsarist officers had gathered troops in the south; other anti-Communist centers rose in Siberia, and still others in the extreme north and along the Baltic coast. The political orientation of these anti-Communist groups, generally called Whites in contrast to the Communist Reds, combined all shades of opinion, from moderate socialist to reactionary, the latter usually predominating. Generally the Whites were monarchists who identified with the old tsarist regime. The Whites received support from foreign governments, which freely intervened. Until their own revolution in November 1918, the Germans occupied much of southern Russia. England, France, and the United States sent troops to points in northern and southern European Russia; England, Japan, and the United States also sent troops to Siberia. At first, they wanted to offset German expansion, but later they hoped to overthrow the Communist regime. In May and June 1918, Czech prisoners of war, about to be evacuated, precipitated anti-Communist uprisings along the Trans-Siberian Railroad, bringing the civil war to fever pitch. In July 1918, the Communists murdered Nicholas II and his entire family.

The Communists speeded the buildup of their own Red Army. Recruited from the remnants of the tsarist army and its officer corps, the Red Army was reinforced by compulsory military service and strict discipline, including the execution of deserters. Trotsky reintroduced the death penalty, which had been outlawed by the Provisional Government. Threatened with death if they refused, many tsarist officers served in the Red Army. They were closely watched by Trotsky's ruthless political commissars, who were also responsible for the political reliability and morale of the troops. Trotsky ordered the formation of "blocking units" to machine-gun retreating soldiers. The civil war was brutal; both sides butchered civilians and their own comrades.

Hard-pressed as Lenin's party was, by the autumn of 1920 it had prevailed over its enemies. The Whites were divided among themselves and discredited by their association with the tsarist regime; the Communists had greater popular support, the advantage of interior communications, and superior political skills. The war-weary foreign interventionists called off their efforts to overthrow the Bolshevik regime by force.

The Communist victory in the civil war exacted a staggering price. Reds and Whites alike carried the tsarist tradition of political violence to a new pitch of horror. Some 1.2 million combatants on both sides perished. In addition, the Communists killed some 250,000 peasants who resisted grain requisitions and executed tens of thousands of political opponents. Adding to the death toll were some 100,000 Jews, victims of pogroms perpetrated largely by Whites and Ukrainian nationalists. Compounding the nation's anguish was the famine of 1921–1922, which claimed some five million victims.

War Communism and the New Economic Policy

Besides the extreme misery brought on by the world war and civil war, the Russian people had to endure the rigors of the policy known as War Communism. It was introduced in 1918 to deal with plummeting agricultural and economic production, rampant inflation, and desperate hunger in the cities. Under War Communism, the state took over the means of production and greatly limited the sphere of private ownership; it conscripted labor and, in effect, confiscated grain from the peasants in order to feed workers in the cities. War Communism devastated the economy even further and alienated workers and peasants. The state-run factories were mismanaged, workers stayed away from their jobs or performed poorly, and peasants resisted the food requisition detachments that the government sent to seize their grain.

There was even open rebellion. In March 1921, sailors at the Kronstadt naval base and workers in nearby Petrograd—people who in 1917 had been ready to give their lives for the Revolution—rose against the repression that had been introduced during the civil war; they called for the establishment of socialist democracy. Trotsky ruthlessly suppressed that uprising, but the lesson was clear: the Communist regime had to implement a strategic retreat from War Communism and to restore a measure of stability to the country.

In 1921, the Communist Party adopted the New Economic Policy, called NEP, which lasted until 1928. Under a system that Lenin characterized as "state socialism," the government retained control of finance, industry, and transportation—"the commanding heights" of the economy—but allowed the rest of the economy to return to private enterprise. The peasants, after giving part of their crops to the government, were free to sell the rest in the open market; traders could buy and sell as they pleased. With the resumption of small-scale capitalism, an air of normal life returned.

One-Party Dictatorship

While the Communists were waging a fierce struggle against the Whites, they instituted a militant dictatorship run by their party. Numbering about five hundred thousand members in 1921, the Communist Party was controlled by a small, tight core of professional political leaders, the best of them unusually disciplined in personal dedication to the Revolution.

Sovfoto.

IDEALIZED PORTRAIT OF STALIN. Like Lenin, Stalin's public image was idealized, but the real man was ruthless. He was determined to reshape the Soviet people's consciousness through a totalitarian revolution. His policy of forced collectivization and his purges killed millions, many of them after being deported to the gulag. The father of the little girl shown on the banner here was assassinated by Stalin that very same year. Her mother was arrested and died under "mysterious" circumstances a few years later.

Under its constitution, the Russian Communist Party, as its formal title read, was a democratic body. Its members elected delegates to periodic party congresses; these in turn elected the membership of the central committee, which originally held the reins of leadership. However, power soon shifted to a smaller and more intimate group, the *politburo* (political bureau), which assumed a dictatorial role. The

key leaders—Lenin, Trotsky, Stalin, and a few others—determined policy, assigned tasks, and appointed important officials. The party dominated all public agencies; its leaders held the chief positions in government. No other political parties were tolerated, and trade unions became agents of the regime. Never before had the people of Russia been forced into such abject dependence on their government.

Impatient with the endless disputes among righteous and strong-willed old revolutionaries, Lenin, in agreement with other top leaders, demanded unconditional submission to his decisions. He even ordered that dissidents be disciplined and political enemies be terrorized. No price was too high to achieve monolithic party unity and total commitment to the party's policies. Believing that they were creating a new and better society that would serve as a model for the rest of humanity, the Communists felt no moral objection to the use of force or even terror, including executions and forced-labor camps. The dreaded Cheka, a ruthless secret police organization, executed some two hundred thousand people from 1919 to 1925. The means Lenin employed for ruling his backward country denied the human values that Marx had taken from the Enlightenment and put into his vision of a socialist society. Lenin was perfectly willing to use state terror to promote the class struggle.

The Communists abolished the power of the Orthodox church, which was the traditional ally of tsarism and the enemy of innovation. They were militant atheists, believing with Marx that religion was the "opium of the people"; God had no place in their vision of a better society.

The Communists also simplified the alphabet, changed the calendar to the Gregorian system prevailing in the capitalist West, and brought theater and all arts, until then reserved for the elite, to the masses. Above all, they wiped out—by expropriation, discrimination, expulsion, and execution—the educated upper class of bureaucrats, landowners, professional people, and industrialists.

In the spring of 1918, Lenin argued that the Russian workers had not yet matched capitalist performance: "The Russian worker is a bad worker compared with the workers of the advanced, i.e., western countries." To overcome this fatal handicap, Lenin relentlessly hammered home the need for "iron discipline at work" and "unquestioning obedience" to a single will, that of the Communist Party. There was no alternative: "Large-scale machinery calls for absolute and strict unity of will, which directs the joint labors of hundreds and thousands and tens of thousands of people. A thousand wills are subordinated to one will."[3] In these words lay the essence of subsequent Soviet industrialization. The entire economy was to be monolithic, rationally planned in its complex interdependence, and pursuing a single goal: overcoming the weaknesses of Russia, so disastrously demonstrated in the war.

In attempting to transform their Soviet Russia into a modern, industrialized, socialist state that would serve as a model for the world, the Communists imposed a new autocracy even more authoritarian than tsarism. The minds of the people came under unprecedented government control. In education, from kindergarten through university, in press and radio, and in literature and the arts, the Communist Party tried to fashion people's thoughts to create the proper "consciousness." The party made Marxism-Leninism the sole source of truth, eliminating as best it could all rival creeds, whether religious, political, or philosophical. Minds were to be as reliably uniform as machine processes and totally committed to the party, and they were to be protected against all subversive capitalist influences.

Lenin molded the Soviet Union into an international revolutionary force, the champion of anticapitalism and of the liberation of colonial peoples. The Russian Revolution inspired nationalistic ambitions for political self-determination and cultural self-assertion among a growing number of peoples around the world, especially in Asia. It appealed particularly to intellectuals educated in the West (or in westernized schools) yet identifying themselves with their downtrodden compatriots.

To have a political tool for world revolution, Lenin created the Communist—or Third—International (Comintern). The most radical successor to earlier socialist international associations, it helped organize small Communist parties in Western Europe, which in time became dependable, although rather powerless, agents of Soviet Russia. In Asia, where no proletariat existed, Lenin tried to work closely with incipient nationalist movements. Lenin and the Bolshevik Revolution gained the admiration and instinctive loyalty of colonial and semicolonial peoples in what would come to be called the Third World. Soviet Russia now stood out as the Communist alternative to the capitalist West.

THE STALIN REVOLUTION

Lenin died in 1924, and the task of achieving the goal that he had set was taken up by Stalin. The "man of steel" was crude and vulgar, toughened by the revolutionary underground and tsarist prisons and by the roughest aspects of Russian life. Relentlessly energetic but relatively inconspicuous among key Communists, Stalin had been given, in 1922, the unwanted and seemingly routine task of general secretary of the party. Shrewd and methodical, he used this position to his own advantage, building up a reliable party cadre—apparatus men, or *apparatchiki*, as they came to be called—and dominating the party as not even Lenin had done. When he was challenged, particularly by Trotsky and his associates, in the protracted struggles for the succession to Lenin, it was too late to unseat him. None of Stalin's rivals could rally the necessary majorities at the party congresses; none could match Stalin's skill in party infighting or in making rough and anarchic people into docile members of the Communist Party apparatus.

Modernizing Russia: Industrialization and Collectivization

To Stalin, Russia's most pressing need was not world revolution, but the fastest possible buildup of Soviet power through industrialization. The country could not afford to risk near-annihilation again, as it had done in the world war and then in the civil war. Communist pride dictated that the country be made as strong as possible. Stalin set forth the stark reckoning of Russian history in a speech delivered in 1931, three years after launching a program of massive industrialization.

> *Those who fall behind get beaten. But we do not want to be beaten. No, we refuse to be beaten. One feature of the history of old Russia was the continual beatings she suffered for falling behind, for her backwardness. All beat her—for her backwardness, for military backwardness, cultural backwardness, political backwardness, for industrial backwardness, for agricultural backwardness. She was beaten because to do so was profitable and could be done with impunity. . . . You are backward, you are weak—therefore you are wrong, hence you can be beaten and enslaved. You are mighty, therefore you are right, hence we must be wary of you. Such is the law of the exploiters. . . . That is why we must no longer lag behind.*[4]

Stalin decided on all-out industrialization at the expense of the toiling masses. Peasants and workers, already poor, would be required to make tremendous sacrifices of body and spirit to overcome the nation's weaknesses. Abandoning the NEP, Stalin decreed a series of Five-Year Plans, the first and most experimental one commencing in 1928. The industrialization drive was heralded as a vast economic and social revolution, undertaken by the state according to a rational plan. The emphasis lay on heavy industry: the construction of railroads, power plants, steel mills, and military hardware such as tanks and warplanes. Production of consumer goods was cut to the minimum, and all small-scale private trading, revived under the NEP, came to an end—with disastrous results for the standard of living. Having just come within sight of their pre-1914 standard of living, Russians now found their expectations dashed for decades.

Thus, a new, grim age began, with drastic material hardships and profound anguish. Harsh punishments, including denial of food cards and imprisonment, were meted out for lateness, slowness, or incompetence. But many people, particularly the young, were fired to heroic exertions. They were proud to sacrifice themselves for the building of a superior society. And many common factory workers had the opportunity to attend school and become engineers and administrators, which tied them to the regime. When the Great Depression in the capitalist countries put millions out of work, no Soviet citizen suffered from unemployment; gloom pervaded the West, but confidence and hope, artificially fostered by the party, buoyed up many people in Soviet Russia. The first two Five-Year Plans dramatically and rapidly increased Russia's industrial infrastructure as factories, mines, dams, and railroads were feverishly constructed. At no time, though, did the planning produce Western-style efficiency, and workers, who labored in a herculean way, actually suffered a decline in real wages. The regime concentrated on heavy industry, not consumer goods or improving the standard of living.

Meanwhile, a second and far more brutal revolution overtook Soviet agriculture, for the peasants had to be forcibly integrated into the planned economy through collectivization. Agriculture—the peasants, their animals, and their fields—had to submit to the same rational control as industry. Collectivization meant the pooling of farmlands, animals, and equipment for the sake of more efficient, large-scale production. The Bolshevik solution for the backwardness of Russian agriculture was for the peasants to be organized like factory workers. But knowing the peasants' distaste for the factory, their attachment to their own land, and their stubbornness, the party had hesitated to carry out its ambitious scheme. In 1929, however, Stalin believed that, for the sake of industrialization, he had no choice. If the Five-Year Plan was to succeed, the government had to receive planned crops of planned amounts and quality at planned times. This could only be accomplished, Stalin thought, by destroying the independent peasantry and creating huge agricultural factories. With collectivization, the ascendancy of the party over the people of Russia became almost complete.

The peasants paid a ghastly price. Stalin declared war on the Russian countryside. He ordered that the *kulaks*, the most enterprising and well-to-do peasants, be "liquidated as a class." Designated as "enemies of the people" and dehumanized as "swine," "scum," and "vermin," between 1929 and 1932 some 10 million kulaks were forcibly removed from their homes and land. Large numbers were killed outright and millions were deported to forced labor camps in the far north where many ultimately perished from hunger, cold, or abuse. Their poorer and less efficient neighbors were herded onto collective farms at the point of a bayonet.

The peasants struck back, sometimes in pitched battles. The horror of forced collectivization broke the spirit even of hardened officials. "I am an old Bolshevik," sobbed a secret police colonel to a fellow passenger on a train; "I worked in the underground against the Tsar and then I fought in the civil war. Did I do all that in order that I should now surround villages with machine guns and order my men to fire indiscriminately into crowds of peasants? Oh, no, no!"[5] Typically, however, the local officials and activists who stripped the peasants of their possessions and searched for hidden grain viewed themselves as idealists building a new society that was in the best interests of a suffering humanity, an outlook that justified ruthlessness. Their dedication to the triumph of Communism overcame all doubts caused by the sight of starving people and the sounds of wailing women and children.

Defeated but unwilling to surrender their livestock, the peasants slaughtered their animals, gorging themselves in drunken orgies against the days of inevitable famine. The country's cattle herds declined by one-half, inflicting irreparable secondary losses as well. The number of horses, crucial for rural transport and farm work, fell by one-third. Crops were not planted or not harvested, the Five-Year Plan was disrupted, and from 1931 to 1933 millions starved to death.

The suffering was most cruel in the Ukraine, where famine killed some three million people, many after extreme abuse and persecution. In order to buy industrial equipment abroad so that industrialization could proceed on target, the Soviet Union had to export food, as much of it as possible and for prices disastrously lowered by the Great Depression. Let the peasants in the Ukrainian breadbasket starve so that the country could grow strong! Moreover, Stalin relished the opportunity to punish the Ukrainians for their disloyalty during the civil war and their resistance to collectivization.

By 1935, practically all farming in Russia was collectivized. The kulaks had been wiped out as a class, and the peasants grumbled about the rise of a new serfdom.

Stalin had hoped to create technically efficient "factory farms" that would provide inexpensive

Scala/Art Resource, N.Y.

A COLLECTIVE FARM FESTIVAL (1936–1937), BY SERGEI GERASIMOV. This propaganda painting of a festival on a collective farm glorifies the new agricultural system that Stalin imposed on the Russian peasantry by force.

food for the massive industrial labor force. But in reality, collectivization stifled agricultural production. Enraged peasants had slaughtered livestock rather than turn it over to the state; mismanagement and unenthusiastic collective farmers resulted in a precipitous decline in agricultural production. For decades collective farming failed to achieve the levels of production previously reached in the 1920s.

Total Control

To quash resistance and mold a new type of suitably motivated and disciplined citizen, Stalin unleashed a third revolution, the revolution of totalitarianism. Only Communist regimentation and monolithic control by the party over state and society, he believed, could liberate Russia from its historic inferiority. The Five-Year Plans obliterated private enterprise; virtually every worker and peasant was now an employee of the state. Moreover, the totalitarian state accorded with his desire to exercise total control over the party and the nation. Stalin's totalitarianism aimed at a complete reconstruction of state and society, down to the innermost recesses of human consciousness. It called for a "new man" suited to the needs of Soviet industrialism. In many ways Stalin's totalitarianism fulfilled Lenin's policies.

The revolution of totalitarianism encompassed all cultural activity. Religion, which offered an alternative worldview, came under attack. Priests were jailed, organized worship discouraged, and churches converted into barns. All media of communication—literature, the arts, music, the stage—were forced into subservience to the Five-Year Plan and Soviet ideology. In literature, as in all other art, an official style was promulgated. Called *socialist realism*, it was expected to describe the world as the party saw it or hoped to shape it. Novels in the social realist manner told how the romances of tractor drivers and milkmaids or of lathe operators and office secretaries led to new victories of production under the Five-Year Plan. Composers found their music examined for remnants of bourgeois spirit; they were to write simple tunes suitable for heroic times. Everywhere huge, high-color posters showed men

and women hard at work with radiant faces, calling others to join them; often Stalin, the wise father and leader, was shown among them. In this way, artistic creativity was locked into a dull, utilitarian straitjacket of official cheerfulness; creativity was allowed only to boost industrial productivity. Behind the scenes, all artists were disciplined to conform to the will of the party or be crushed.

Education, from nursery school to university, was likewise harnessed to train dutiful and loyal citizens, and Soviet propaganda made a cult of Stalin that bordered on deification. Thus, a writer declared in 1935:

> *Centuries will pass and the generations still to come will regard us as the happiest of mortals, as the most fortunate of men, because we . . . were privileged to see Stalin, our inspired leader. Yes, and we regard ourselves as the happiest of mortals because we are the contemporaries of a man who never had an equal in world history. The men of all ages will call on thy name, which is strong, beautiful, wise, and marvelous. Thy name is engraven on every factory, every machine, every place on the earth, and in the hearts of all men.[6]*

To break stubborn wills and compel conformity, Stalin, calculating, cunning, cold, cruel, and cynical, unleashed raw terror. Terror had been used as a tool of government ever since the Bolshevik Revolution (and the tsars had also used it, intermittently). After the start of the first Five-Year Plan, show trials were staged that denounced as saboteurs the engineers who disagreed with Stalin's production timetable. The terror used to herd the peasants onto collective farms was even greater. Stalin also used terror to crush opposition and to instill an abject fear both in the ranks of the party and in Russian society at large.

Purges had long been used to rid the party of weaklings. After 1934, however, they became an instrument of Stalin's drive for unchallenged personal power. Stalin's paranoia, which defied all logic and morality, led him to see enemies and threats to his rule everywhere. In 1936, his vindictive terror broke into the open. The first batch of victims, including many founders of the Communist Party, were accused of conspiring with the exiled Trotsky to set up a "terrorist center" and of scheming to terrorize the party. After being sentenced to death, they were immediately executed. Included among the millions that Stalin consigned to death were close friends and comrades in the Bolshevik Revolution. In 1937, the next group, including prominent Communists of Lenin's day, was charged with cooperating with foreign intelligence agencies and wrecking "socialist reconstruction," the term for Stalin's revolution; they too were executed. Shortly afterward, a secret purge decimated the military high command—for which the country paid a heavy price when Germany attacked in 1941. Almost half the country's seventy thousand officers were either shot or sent to the camps—after the Nazi invasion many of these prisoners were rehabilitated and restored to active duty.

In 1938, the last and biggest show trial advanced the most bizarre accusation of all: sabotage, espionage, and attempting to dismember the Soviet Union and kill all its leaders (including Lenin in 1918). In the public hearings, some defendants refuted the public prosecutor, but in the end all confessed, usually after torture and threats to their family, before being executed. Western observers were aghast at the cynical charges and at the physical and mental tortures used to obtain the confessions. Under Stalin, the revolution was devouring its own children at a rate that far surpassed earlier revolutions.

The great trials, however, involved only a small minority of Stalin's victims; many more perished in silence without the benefit of legal proceedings. The terror first hit members of the party, especially the Old Bolsheviks, who had joined before the Revolution; they were the most independent-minded members and therefore the most dangerous to Stalin. But Stalin also diminished the cultural elite that had survived the Lenin revolution. Thousands of engineers, scientists, industrial managers, scholars, and artists disappeared; accused of counterrevolutionary crimes, they were shot or sent to forced-labor camps, where many perished. No one was safe. To frighten the common people in all walks of life, men, women, and even children were dragged into the net of Stalin's

secret police, leaving the survivors with a soul-killing reminder: submit or else. "In the years of the terror," recalled one victim, "there was not a house in the country where people did not sit trembling at night."[7]

The 476 forced-labor camps to which Stalin's victims were deported played an important role in the Soviet economy. Slave labor constructed the White Sea–Baltic Canal, which the regime held up as a monument of Communist achievement. Mining, logging, and construction enterprises in remote parts of the country also depended on forced labor. It is estimated that from 1929 to the death of Stalin in 1953, some 18 million people were confined to the Gulag, as Stalin's system of concentration camps came to be known. Many perished from abuse, starvation, and bone-crushing labor in freezing weather. Organized executions of vanloads of victims were common. As in Nazi concentration camps, administrators and guards deliberately dehumanized and brutalized the prisoners, whom the regime designated as "filth" and "enemies of the people."

Stalin may have orchestrated the terror, but large numbers of party members believed that terror, which was decimating their own ranks, was necessary. The memory of the vicious civil war, when domestic and foreign enemies sought to overthrow the new Bolshevik regime, and the resistance of the kulaks to collectivization created a siege mentality among the Communist leadership. Everywhere they saw anti-Soviets plotting against the party; they defined these enemies as Trotskyites, former kulaks, Whites who had fought in the civil war, members of outlawed anti-Soviet political parties, foreign agents, criminals, cattle and horse thieves, contraband smugglers, bandits, and so on. Party officials saw terror as a legitimate way both of protecting the party—to which they were ideologically committed and from which they derived prestige, power, and material benefits—and of protecting the Soviet experiment, which they viewed as humanity's best hope.

The toll of the purges is reckoned in many millions; it included Trotsky, who in 1940 was murdered in Mexico. The bloodletting was ghastly, as Stalin's purge officials themselves followed each other into death and ignominy. Although it might take decades for some to realize it, Stalin's criminal rule blackened the ideal of a humane socialist society.

Stalin was untroubled by the waste of life. He believed that without the total obedience of the Russian people, the Soviet economy could not be effectively and quickly mobilized, and that terror was necessary to compel compliance. In Stalin's mind, totalitarianism was necessary to save Russia from foreign enemies that would devour it. No doubt, the terror was also an expression of his craving for personal power and his vengeful and suspicious, some say clinically paranoid, nature. He saw enemies everywhere, took pleasure in selecting victims, and reveled in his omnipotence. By showing party officials and the Russian masses how vulnerable they were, how dependent they were on his will, Stalin frightened them into servility. For good reason, Stalin has been called a twentieth-century Ivan the Terrible. Like the sixteenth-century tsar, for whom he expressed admiration, Stalin stopped at no brutality to establish personal autocracy.

But more than a craving for personal power motivated Stalin. He regarded himself as Lenin's heir, responsible for securing and expanding the Revolution and defending it against foreign and domestic enemies. The only way to do this was to create a powerful Soviet Union through rapid modernization.

THE NATURE AND APPEAL OF FASCISM

Liberals viewed the Great War as a conflict between freedom and autocracy and expected an Allied victory to accelerate the spread of democracy throughout Europe. Right after the war, it seemed that liberalism would continue to advance as it had in the nineteenth century. The collapse of the autocratic German and Austrian Empires had led to the formation of parliamentary governments throughout Eastern and Central Europe. Yet within two decades, in an extraordinary turn of events, democracy seemed in its death throes. In Spain, Portugal, Italy, and Germany, and in all the newly created states of Central and Eastern Europe except Czechoslovakia, democracy collapsed, and various forms of authoritarian government emerged. The defeat of democracy and the surge of authoritarianism was best exemplified by the triumph of Fascist movements in Italy and Germany.

The emergence of Fascist movements in more than twenty European lands after World War I was a sign that liberal society was in a state of disorientation and dissolution. The cultural pessimism, disdain for reason, elitism, romantic glorification of action and heroism, and contempt for liberal values voiced by many intellectuals and nationalists before the war found expression after the war in the antidemocratic and irrational Fascist ideologies, which altered European political life. Fascism marked the culmination of the dangerous trends inherent in the extreme nationalism and radical conservatism of the late nineteenth century and in the repudiation of modern Western civilization by disenchanted intellectuals.

As a Europe-wide phenomenon, Fascism was a response to a postwar society afflicted with spiritual disintegration, economic dislocation, political instability, and thwarted nationalist hopes. A general breakdown of meaning and values led people to search for new beliefs and new political arrangements. Fascism was an expression of fear that the Bolshevik Revolution would spread westward. It was also an expression of hostility to democratic values and a reaction to the failure of liberal institutions to solve the problems of modern industrial society; with brutal frankness, Fascist leaders proclaimed that individual freedom, a relic of a dying liberal age and a barrier to national greatness, would be dispensed with. Anything seemed better than the ineffectual parliaments that appeared helpless in the face of mounting misery. Moreover, in many European lands, democracy had shallow roots. Having little familiarity with or appreciation of the procedures and values of constitutional government, people were susceptible to antidemocratic ideologies and demagogues.

Fascist movements were marked by a determination to eradicate liberalism and Marxism—to undo the legacy of the French Revolution of 1789 and the Bolshevik Revolution of 1917. Fascists believed that theirs was a spiritual revolution, that they were initiating a new era in history and building a new civilization on the ruins of liberal democracy. "We stand for a new principle in the world," said Mussolini. "We stand for the sheer, categorical, definitive antithesis to the world of democracy . . . to the world which still abides by the fundamental principles laid down in 1789."[8] The chief principle of Nazism, said Hitler, "is to abolish the liberal concept of the individual and the Marxist concept of humanity, and to substitute for them the Volk community, rooted in the soil and united by the bond of its common blood."[9] The Fascists' uniforms, songs, flags, parades, mass rallies, and cult of physical strength and violence all symbolized this call for a reawakened and reunited people.

Fascists accused liberal society of despiritualizing human beings and transforming them into materialistic creatures whose highest ideal was moneymaking. Regarding liberalism as bankrupt and parliamentary government as futile, many people yearned for an authoritarian government led by military men and nationalists. To Fascists and their sympathizers, democracy seemed an ineffective and enfeebled old order ready to be overthrown. Idealistic youth and intellectuals rejoiced in Fascist activism. They saw Fascism as a revolt against the mediocrity of the liberal state and modern mass society and a reaffirmation of the noblest human qualities: heroism and dedication to one's people. Fascists saw themselves as participants in a dynamic mass movement that would rectify the weaknesses and irresolution of parliamentary government and rid the nation of corrosive foreign influences. For them, the triumph of Fascism would mark a new beginning for their nation and a new era in world history.

The Fascist vision of a regenerated nation—a new order led by a determined and heroic elite—arising from the ruins of a decadent old order had the appeal of great myth; it evoked belief, commitment, and loyalty. The myth of rebirth—a nation cured of evil and building a new and vigorous society—had a profound impact on people dissatisfied with liberal society and searching for new beliefs. The myth of the nation reborn answered a metaphysical yearning to give meaning to life and history. It provided an emotionally gratifying worldview at a time when many people had lost their confidence in liberal-democratic ideals and institutions.

Fascists regarded Marxism as another enemy, for class conflict divided and weakened the state.

To Fascists, the Marxist call for workers of the world to unite meant the death of the national community. Fascism, in contrast, would reintegrate the proletariat into the nation and end class hostilities by making people at all levels feel that they were a needed part of the nation. Fascism thus offered a solution to the problem of insecurity and isolation in modern industrial society.

Attacking the rational tradition of the Enlightenment, Fascism exalted will, blood, feeling, and instinct. Intellectual discussion and critical analysis, said Fascists, cause national divisiveness; reason promotes doubt, enfeebles the will, and hinders instinctive, aggressive action. Fascism made a continual appeal to the emotions as a means of integrating the national community. This flow of emotion fueled irrational and dangerous desires, beliefs, and expectations that blocked critical judgment and responsible action. Glorifying action for its own sake, Fascists aroused and manipulated brutal and primitive impulses and carried into politics the combative spirit of the trenches. They formed private armies, which attracted veterans—many of them rootless, brutal, and maladjusted men who sought to preserve the loyalty, camaraderie, and violence of the front.

Fascists exalted the leader—who, according to the Fascist view, intuitively grasped what was best for the nation—and called for rule by an elite of dedicated party members. The leader and the party would relieve the individual of the need to make decisions. Convinced that the liberal stress on individual freedom promoted national divisiveness, Fascists pressed for monolithic unity: one leader, one party, one ideology, and one national will.

Fascism drew its mass support from the lower middle class: small merchants, artisans, white-collar workers, civil servants, and peasants of moderate means, all of whom were frightened both by big capitalism and by Marxism. They hoped that Fascism would protect them from the competition of big business and prevent the hated working class from establishing a Marxist state, which would threaten their property. The lower middle class saw in Fascism a non-Communist way of overcoming economic crises and restoring traditional respect for family, native soil, and nation. Furthermore, many of these people saw

Fascism as a way of attacking the existing social order, which denied them opportunities for economic advancement and social prestige.

Although a radicalized middle class gave Fascist movements their mass support, the Fascists could not have captured the state without the aid of existing ruling elites: landed aristocrats, industrialists, and army leaders. In Russia, the Bolsheviks had to fight their way to power; in Italy and Germany, the old ruling order virtually handed power to the Fascists. In both countries, Fascist leaders succeeded in reassuring the conservative elite that they would not institute widespread social reforms or interfere with private property and would protect the nation from Communism. Even though the old elite abhorred Fascist violence and demagoguery, it entered into an alliance with the Fascists to protect its interests.

In their struggle to bring down the liberal state, Fascist leaders aroused primitive impulses and tribal loyalties; they made use of myths and rituals to mobilize and manipulate the masses. Organizing their propaganda campaigns with the rigor of a military operation, Fascists stirred and dominated the masses and confused and undermined their democratic opposition, breaking its will to resist. Fascists were most successful in countries with weak democratic traditions. When parliamentary government faltered, it had few staunch defenders, and many people were drawn to charismatic demagogues who promised direct action.

The proliferation of Fascist movements demonstrated that the habits of democracy are not quickly learned, easily retained, or even desired. Particularly during times of crisis, people lose patience with parliamentary discussion and constitutional procedures, sink into nonrational modes of thought and behavior, and are easily manipulated by unscrupulous politicians. For the sake of economic or emotional security and national grandeur, they will often willingly sacrifice political freedom. Fascism starkly manifested the immense power of the irrational; it humbled liberals, making them permanently aware of the limitations of reason and the fragility of freedom.

The Fascist goal of maximum centralization of power was furthered by developments during World War I: the expansion of bureaucracy, the concentration of industry into giant monopolies, and the close cooperation between industry and the state. The instruments of modern technology—radio, motion pictures, public address systems, telephone, and teletype—made it possible for the state to indoctrinate, manipulate, and dominate its subjects.

THE RISE OF FASCISM IN ITALY

Postwar Unrest

Although Italy had been on the winning side in World War I, the country resembled a defeated nation. Food shortages, rising prices, massive unemployment, violent strikes, workers occupying factories, and peasants squatting on the uncultivated periphery of large estates created a climate of crisis. Italy required effective leadership and a reform program, but party disputes paralyzed the liberal government. With several competing parties, the liberals could not organize a solid majority that could cope with the domestic crisis.

The middle class was severely stressed. To meet its accelerating expenses, the government had increased taxes, but the burden fell unevenly on small landowners, owners of small businesses, civil service workers, and professionals. Large landowners and industrialists feared that their nation was on the verge of a Bolshevik-style revolution. In truth, Italian socialists had no master plan to seize power. Peasant squatters and urban strikers were responding to the distress in their own regions and did not significantly coordinate their efforts with those in other localities. Besides, when workers realized that they could not keep the factories operating, their revolutionary zeal waned and they started to abandon the plants. The workers' and peasants' poorly led and futile struggles did not portend a Red revolution. Nevertheless, the industrialists and landlords, with the Bolshevik Revolution still vivid in their minds, were taking no chances.

Adding to the unrest was national outrage at the terms of the World War I peace settlement. Italians felt that despite their sacrifices—five hundred thousand dead and one million wounded—they had been robbed of the fruits of victory. Italy had been denied the Dalmatian coast, the Adriatic port of Fiume, and territory in Africa and the

Middle East. Nationalists blamed the liberal government for what they called a "mutilated victory." In 1919, a force of war veterans, led by the poet and adventurer Gabriele D'Annunzio (1863–1938), seized Fiume, to the delirious joy of Italian nationalists and the embarrassment of the government. D'Annunzio's occupation of the port lasted more than a year, adding fuel to the flames of Italian nationalism and demonstrating the weakness of the liberal regime in imposing its authority on rightist opponents.

Mussolini's Seizure of Power

Benito Mussolini (1883–1945), a former socialist and World War I veteran, exploited the unrest in postwar Italy in order to capture control of the state. In 1919, he organized the Fascist Party, which attracted converts from among the discontented, the disillusioned, and the uprooted. Many Italians viewed Mussolini as the leader who would gain Fiume, Dalmatia, and colonies and win for Italy its rightful place of honor in international affairs. Hardened battle veterans joined the Fascist movement to escape the boredom and idleness of civilian life. They welcomed the opportunity to wear the uniforms of the Fascist militia (called the Black Shirts), parade in the streets, and fight socialist and labor union opponents. Squads of the Black Shirts (*squadristi*) raided socialist and trade union offices, destroying property and beating the occupants. As socialist Red Shirts responded in kind, Italy soon appeared to be drifting toward civil war.

Hoping that Mussolini would rescue Italy from Bolshevism, industrialists and landowners contributed large sums to the Fascist Party. The lower middle class, fearful that the growing power of labor unions and the Socialist Party threatened their property and social prestige, viewed Mussolini as a protector. Middle-class university students, searching for adventure and an ideal, and army officers, dreaming of an Italian empire and hostile to parliamentary government, were also attracted to Mussolini's party. Mussolini's philosophy of action intrigued intellectuals disenchanted with liberal politics and parliamentary democracy. His nationalism, activism, and anti-Communism gradually seduced elements of the

AP Images.

MUSSOLINI WITH HIS TROOPS. The Italian dictator deliberately tried to sustain an image of a virile warrior. Although Mussolini established a one-party state, he was less successful than Hitler or Stalin in creating a totalitarian regime.

power structure: capitalists, aristocrats, army officers, the royal family, and the church. Regarding liberalism as bankrupt and parliamentary government as futile, many of these people yearned for a military dictatorship.

In 1922, Mussolini made his bid for power. Speaking at a giant rally of his followers in late October, he declared: "Either they will give us the government or we shall take it by descending on Rome. It is now a matter of days, perhaps hours." A few days later, the Fascists began their march on Rome. It would have been a relatively simple matter to crush the twenty thousand Fascist marchers, who were armed with little more than pistols and rifles, but King Victor Emmanuel III (1869–1947) refused to act. The king's advisers, some of them sympathetic to Mussolini, exaggerated the strength of the Fascists. Believing that he was rescuing Italy from terrible violence, the king appointed Mussolini prime minister.

Mussolini had bluffed his way to power. Fascism had triumphed not because of its own strength—the Fascist Party had only 35 of 535 seats in parliament—but because the liberal government, indecisive and fearful of violence, did not counter force with force. In the past, the liberal state had not challenged Fascist acts of terror; now it feebly surrendered to Fascist blustering and threats. No doubt liberals hoped that, once in power, the Fascists would forsake terror, pursue moderate aims, and act within the constitution. But the liberals were wrong; they had completely misjudged Fascism's antidemocratic character.

The Fascist State in Italy

Gradually, Mussolini moved toward establishing a dictatorship. In 1925 and 1926, he eliminated non-Fascists from his cabinet, dissolved opposition parties, smashed the independent trade unions, suppressed opposition newspapers, replaced local mayors with Fascist officials, and organized a secret police to round up troublemakers. Many anti-Fascists fled the country or were deported.

Mussolini was less successful than Hitler and Stalin in fashioning a totalitarian state. The industrialists, the large landowners, the church, and to some extent even the army never fell under the complete domination of the party. Nor did the regime possess the mind of its subjects with the same thoroughness as the Nazis did in Germany. Life in Italy was less regimented and the individual less fearful than in Nazi Germany or Communist Russia.

Like Communist Russia and Nazi Germany, however, Fascist Italy used mass organizations and mass media to control minds and regulate behavior. As in the Soviet Union and the Third Reich, the regime created a cult of the leader. "Mussolini goes forward with confidence, in a halo of myth, almost chosen by God, indefatigable and infallible, the instrument employed by Providence for the creation of a new civilization," wrote the philosopher Giovanni Gentile.[10] To convey the image of a virile leader, Mussolini had

himself photographed bare-chested or in a uniform and a steel helmet. Elementary school textbooks depicted him as the savior of the nation, a modern-day Julius Caesar.

Fascist propaganda urged that the grandeur of the Roman Empire be restored through conquest. It also inculcated habits of discipline and obedience: "Mussolini is always right." "Believe! Obey! Fight!" Propaganda also glorified war: "A minute on the battlefield is worth a lifetime of peace." The press, radio, and cinema idealized life under Fascism, implying that Fascism had eradicated crime, poverty, and social tensions. Schoolteachers and university professors were compelled to swear allegiance to the Fascist government and to propagate Fascist ideals, while students were urged to criticize instructors who harbored liberal attitudes. Millions of youths belonged to Fascist organizations, in which they participated in patriotic ceremonies and social functions, sang Fascist hymns, and wore Fascist uniforms. They submerged their own identities in the group.

Denouncing economic liberalism for promoting individual self-interest, Fascists also attacked socialism for instigating conflicts between workers and capitalists, which divided and weakened the nation. The Fascist way of resolving tensions between workers and employers was to abolish independent labor unions, prohibit strikes, and establish associations or corporations that included both workers and employers within a given industry. In theory, representatives of labor and capital would cooperatively solve their particular industry's labor problems; in practice, however, the representatives of labor turned out to be Fascists who protected the interests of the industrialists. Although the Fascists lauded the cooperative system as a creative approach to modern economic problems, in reality it played a minor role in Italian economic life. Big business continued to make its own decisions, paying scant attention to the corporations.

Nor did the Fascist government solve Italy's longstanding economic problems. To curtail the export of capital and to reduce the nation's dependence on imports in case of war, Mussolini sought to make Italy self-sufficient. To win the "battle of grain," the Fascist regime brought marginal lands under cultivation and urged farmers to concentrate on wheat rather than other crops. While wheat production increased substantially, total agricultural output fell because wheat had been planted on land more suited to animal husbandry and fruit cultivation. To make Italy industrially self-sufficient, the regime limited imports of foreign goods, with the result that Italian consumers paid higher prices for goods manufactured in Italy. Mussolini posed as the protector of the little people, but under his regime the power and profits of big business grew and the standard of living of small farmers and urban workers slipped.

Although anticlerical since his youth, Mussolini was also expedient. He recognized that coming to terms with the church would improve his image with Catholic public opinion. The Vatican regarded Mussolini's regime as a barrier against atheistic Communism and as less hostile to church interests and more amenable to church direction than a liberal government. Pope Pius XI (1922–1939) was an ultraconservative whose hatred of liberalism and secularism led him to believe that the Fascists would increase the influence of the church in the nation.

In 1929, the Lateran Accords recognized the independence of Vatican City, repealed many of the anticlerical laws passed under the liberal government, and made religious instruction compulsory in all secondary schools. Relations between the Vatican and the Fascist government remained fairly good throughout the decade of the 1930s. When Mussolini invaded Ethiopia and intervened in the Spanish Civil War, the church supported him. Although the papacy criticized Mussolini for drawing closer to Hitler and introducing anti-Jewish legislation, it never broke with the Fascist regime.

THE NEW GERMAN REPUBLIC

In the last days of World War I, a revolution brought down the German government, a semi-authoritarian monarchy, and led to the creation of a democratic republic. The new government, headed by Chancellor Friedrich Ebert (1871–1925), a Social Democrat, signed the armistice agreement ending the war. Many Germans blamed the creators of the new democratic leadership for the defeat—a baseless accusation, for the German generals, knowing that the war was lost, had sought an armistice. In February 1919, the recently elected National Assembly met at Weimar and proceeded to draw up a constitution for the new state. The Weimar Republic—born in revolution, which most Germans detested, and military defeat, which many attributed to the new government—faced an uncertain future. The legend that traitors, principally Jews and Social Democrats, cheated Germany of victory was created and propagated by the conservative Right—generals, high-ranking bureaucrats, university professors, and nationalists, who wanted to preserve the army's reputation and bring down the new and hated democratic Weimar Republic.

THE SPELLBINDER. Hitler was a superb orator who knew how to reach the hearts of his listeners. The masses, he said, are aroused by the spoken, not the written, word.

Threats from Left and Right

Dominated by moderate socialists, the infant republic faced internal threats from both the radical Left and the radical Right. In January 1919, the newly established German Communist party, or Spartacists, disregarding the advice of their leaders Rosa Luxemburg and Karl Liebknecht, took to the streets of Berlin and declared Ebert's government deposed. To crush the revolution, Ebert turned to the Free Corps: volunteer brigades of ex-soldiers and adventurers led by officers loyal to the emperor, who had been fighting to protect the eastern borders from encroachments by the new states of Poland, Estonia, and Latvia. The men of the Free Corps relished action and despised Bolshevism, and many of them would later become prominent in Hitler's party. They suppressed the revolution and murdered Luxemburg and Liebknecht on January 15.

The Spartacist revolt and the short-lived "soviet" republic in Munich (and others in Baden and Brunswick) had a profound effect on the German psyche. The Communists had been easily subdued, but fear of a Communist insurrection remained deeply embedded in the middle and upper classes—a fear that drove many of their members into the ranks of the Weimar Republic's right-wing opponents.

Refusing to disband as the government ordered, in March 1920, the right-wing Free Corps marched into Berlin and declared a new government, headed by Wolfgang Kapp, a staunch German nationalist. Insisting that it could not fire on fellow soldiers, the German army, the *Reichswehr*, made no move to defend the republic. A general strike called by the labor unions prevented Kapp from governing, and the coup collapsed. However, the Kapp Putsch demonstrated that the loyalty of the army to the republic was doubtful and that important segments of German society supported the overthrow, by violence if necessary, of the Weimar Republic and its replacement by an authoritarian government driven by a nationalist credo.

Economic Crisis

In addition to uprisings by the Left and Right, the republic was burdened by economic crisis. Unable to meet the deficit in the national budget, the government simply printed more money, causing the value of the German mark to decline precipitously. In 1919, the mark stood at 8.9 to the dollar; in November 1923, a dollar could be exchanged for 4 billion marks. Bank savings, war bonds, and pensions, representing years of toil and thrift, became worthless. Blaming the government for this disaster, the ruined middle class became more receptive to ultra-rightist movements that aimed to bring down the republic.

A critical factor in the collapse of the German economy was the French occupation of the Ruhr in January 1923. With the economy in shambles, the republic had defaulted on reparation payments. The French premier, Raymond Poincaré (1860–1934), ordered French troops into the Ruhr—the nerve center of German industry. Responding to the republic's call for passive resistance, factory workers, miners, and railway workers in the Ruhr refused to work for the French. Paying salaries to striking workers and officials contributed to the mark's free fall.

Gustav Stresemann, who became chancellor in August 1923, skillfully placed the republic on the path to recovery. He declared Germany's willingness to make reparation payments and issued a new currency, backed by a mortgage on German real estate. To protect the value of the new currency, the government did not print another issue. Inflation receded, and confidence was restored.

A new arrangement regarding reparations also contributed to the economic recovery. In 1924, the parties accepted the Dawes Plan, which reduced reparations and based them on Germany's economic capacity. During the negotiations, France agreed to withdraw its troops from the Ruhr—another step toward easing tensions for the republic.

From 1924 to 1929, economic conditions improved. Foreign capitalists, particularly Americans, were attracted by high interest rates and the low cost of labor. Their investments in German businesses stimulated the economy. By 1929, iron, steel, coal, and chemical production exceeded prewar levels. The value of German exports also surpassed that of 1913. Real wages were higher than before the war, and improved unemployment benefits also made life better for the workers. It appeared that Germany had achieved political stability, as threats from the extremist parties of the Left and the Right subsided. And Weimar Germany was distinguished by a flourishing intellectual and cultural life unmatched in Europe. Given time and continued economic stability, democracy might have taken firmer root in Germany. But then came the Great Depression. The global economic crisis that began in October 1929 starkly revealed how weak the Weimar Republic was.

Fundamental Weaknesses of the Weimar Republic

German political experience provided poor soil for transplanting an English democratic parliamentary system. Before World War I, Germany had been a semiautocratic state, ruled by an emperor who commanded the armed forces, controlled foreign policy, appointed the chancellor, and called and dismissed parliament. This authoritarian system blocked the German people from acquiring democratic habits and attitudes; still accustomed to rule from above, still adoring the power-state, many Germans sought to destroy the democratic Weimar Republic.

Traditional conservatives—the upper echelons of the civil service, judges, industrialists, large landowners, and army leaders—scorned democracy and hated the republic. They regarded the revolution against the monarchy in the last weeks of the war as a treacherous act and the establishment of a democratic republic as a violation of Germany's revered tradition of hierarchical leadership. Nor did the middle class feel a commitment to the liberal-democratic principles on which the republic rested. The traditionally nationalistic middle class identified the republic with the defeat in war and the humiliation of the Versailles treaty. Rabidly antisocialist, this class saw the leaders of the republic as Marxists who would impose on Germany a working-class state. Right-wing intellectuals often attacked democracy as a barrier to the true unity of the German nation. In the tradition of nineteenth-century Volkish thinkers, they disdained reason and political freedom, glorifying instead race, instincts, and action. By doing so, they turned many Germans against the republic,

eroding the popular support on which democracy depends.

The Weimar Republic also showed the weaknesses of the multiparty system. With the vote spread over a number of parties, no one party held a majority of seats in the parliament (Reichstag), so the republic was governed by a coalition of several parties. But because of ideological differences, the coalition was always unstable and in danger of failing to function. This is precisely what happened during the Great Depression. When effective leadership was imperative, the government could not act. Political deadlock caused Germans to lose what little confidence they had in the democratic system. Support for the parties that wanted to preserve democracy dwindled, and extremist parties that aimed to topple the republic gained strength. Seeking to bring down the republic were the Communists on the left and two rightist parties—the Nationalists and the National Socialist German Workers' Party, led by Adolf Hitler.

THE RISE OF HITLER

Adolf Hitler (1889–1945) was born in Austria on April 20, 1889, the fourth child of a minor civil servant. A poor student in secondary school, although by no means unintelligent, Hitler left high school and lived idly for more than two years. In 1907 and again in 1908, the Vienna Academy of Fine Arts rejected his application for admission. Hitler did not try to learn a trade or to work steadily but earned some money by painting picture postcards. He read a lot, especially in art, history, and military affairs. He also read the racist, nationalist, anti-Semitic, and Pan-German literature that abounded in multinational Vienna. The racist treatises preached the danger posed by mixing races, called for the liquidation of racial inferiors, and marked the Jew as the embodiment of evil and the source of all misfortune.

In Vienna, Hitler came into contact with Georg von Schönerer's Pan-German movement. For Schönerer, the Jews were evil not because of their religion or because they rejected Christ but because they possessed evil racial qualities. Schönerer's followers wore watch chains with pictures of hanged Jews attached. Hitler wave of enthusiasm. Their despair over the condition of their nation turns to hope, and they derive a sense of belonging and mission. They feel that they are participants in a mighty movement that is destined to regenerate the German nation and initiate a new historical age. "The man who enters such a meeting doubting and wavering leaves it inwardly reinforced; he has become a link to the community."[17]

Hitler Gains Power

After serving only nine months of his sentence, Hitler left prison in December 1924. He continued to build his party and waited for a crisis that would rock the republic and make his movement a force in national politics. The Great Depression, which began in the United States at the end of 1929, provided that crisis. Desperate and demoralized people lined up in front of government unemployment offices. Street peddlers, beggars, and youth gangs proliferated; suicides increased, particularly among middle-class people shamed by their descent into poverty, idleness, and uselessness. As Germany's economic plight worsened, the German people became more amenable to Hitler's radicalism. His propaganda techniques worked. The Nazi Party went from 810,000 votes in 1928 to 6,400,000 in 1930, and its representation in the Reichstag soared from 12 to 107.

To the lower middle class, the Nazis promised effective leadership and a solution to the economic crisis. But Nazism was more than a class movement. It appealed to the discontented and disillusioned from all segments of the population: embittered veterans, romantic nationalists, idealistic intellectuals, industrialists and large landowners frightened by Communism and social democracy, rootless and resentful people who felt they had no place in the existing society, the unemployed, lovers of violence, and newly enfranchised youth yearning for a cause. And always there was the immense attraction of Hitler, who tirelessly worked his oratorical magic on increasingly enthusiastic crowds, confidently promising leadership and national rebirth. Many Germans were won over by his fanatical sincerity, his iron will, and his conviction that he was chosen by fate to rescue Germany.

In the election of July 31, 1932, the Nazis received 37.3 percent of the vote and won 230 seats—far more than any other party, but still not a majority. Franz von Papen, who had resigned from the chancellorship, persuaded the aging president, Paul von Hindenburg (1847–1934), to appoint Hitler as chancellor. In this decision, Papen had the support of German industrialists and aristocratic landowners, who regarded Hitler as a useful instrument to fight Communism, block social reform, break the backs of organized labor, and rebuild the armament industry.

Never intending to rule within the spirit of the constitution, Hitler, who took office on January 30, 1933, quickly moved to assume dictatorial powers. In February 1933, a Dutch drifter with Communist leanings set a fire in the Reichstag. Hitler persuaded Hindenburg to sign an emergency decree suspending civil rights on the pretext that the state was threatened by internal subversion. The chancellor then used these emergency powers to arrest, without due process, Communist and Social Democratic deputies.

In the elections of March 1933, the German people elected 288 Nazi deputies in a Reichstag of 647 seats. With the support of 52 deputies of the Nationalist Party and in the absence of Communist deputies, who were under arrest, the Nazis now had a secure majority. Later that month, Hitler bullied the Reichstag into passing the Enabling Act, which permitted the chancellor to enact legislation independently of the Reichstag. With astonishing passivity, the political parties had allowed the Nazis to dismantle the government and make Hitler a dictator with unlimited power. Hitler had used the instruments of democracy to destroy the republic and create a totalitarian state.

NAZI GERMANY

The Nazis moved to subjugate all political and economic institutions and all culture to the will of the party. The party became the state and its teachings the soul of the German nation. There could be no separation between private life and politics and no rights of the individual that the state must respect. Ideology must pervade every phase of daily life, and all organizations must come under party control. For both Communists and Nazis, ideology was "a grand transcendent fiction [or] metamyth" that provided adherents with answers to the crucial questions of life and history.[18] Joseph Goebbels (see the upcoming section "Shaping the 'New Man'") summed up this totalitarian goal as follows: "It is not enough to reconcile people more or less to our regime, to move them towards a position of neutrality towards us, we want rather to work on people until they are addicted to us."[19] An anonymous Nazi poet expressed the totalitarian credo in these words:

> *We have captured all the positions*
> *And on the heights we have planted*
> *The banners of our revolution.*
> *You had imagined that that was all that we*
>   *wanted*
> *We want more*
> *We want all*
> *Your hearts are our goal*
> *It is your souls we want.*[20]

The Leader-State

The Third Reich was organized as a leader-state, in which Hitler, the *führer* (leader), embodied and expressed the real will of the German people, commanded the supreme loyalty of the nation, and held omnipotent power. His authority was neither limited by constitutional checks or individual rights.

In June 1933, the Social Democratic Party was outlawed, and within a few weeks the other political parties simply disbanded on their own. In May 1933, the Nazis had seized the property of the trade unions, arrested the leaders, and ended collective bargaining and strikes. The newly established German Labor Front, an instrument of the party, became the official organization of the working class.

Unlike the Bolsheviks, the Nazis did not destroy the upper classes of the old regime. Hitler made no war against the industrialists. He wanted from them loyalty, obedience, and a war machine. German businessmen prospered but exercised no influence on political decisions. The profits of industry rose, and workers lauded the regime for

ending the unemployment crisis through an extensive program of public works, the restoration of conscription, and rearmament.

Nazism conflicted with the core values of Christianity. "The heaviest blow that ever struck humanity was the coming of Christianity," said Hitler to intimates during World War II.[21] Because Nazism could tolerate no other faith alongside itself, the Nazis, recognizing that Christianity was a rival claimant for the German soul, moved to repress the Protestant and Catholic churches. In the public schools, religious instruction was cut back and the syllabus was changed to omit the Jewish origins of Christianity. Christ was depicted not as a Jew, heir to the prophetic tradition of Hebrew monotheism, but as an Aryan hero. The Gestapo (secret state police) censored church newspapers, scrutinized sermons and church activities, forbade some clergymen to preach, dismissed the opponents of Nazism from theological schools, and arrested some clerical critics of the regime.

The clergy were well represented among the Germans who resisted Nazism; some were sent to concentration camps or were executed. But these courageous clergy were not representative of the German churches, which, as organized institutions, capitulated to and cooperated with the Nazi regime. Both the German Evangelical (Lutheran) and German Catholic churches demanded that their faithful render loyalty to Hitler; both turned a blind eye to Nazi persecution of Jews. Even before World War II and the implementation of genocide, many Evangelical churches banned baptized Jews from entering their temples and dismissed pastors with Jewish ancestry. Some clergy, reared in a traditional anti-Semitic theological environment, regarded Nazi measures as just punishment for a people who had rejected Christ. During the war, both Catholic and Evangelical churches condemned resistance and found much in the Third Reich to admire, and both supported Hitler's war. The prominent Lutheran theologian who "welcomed that change that came to Germany in 1933 as a divine gift and miracle" voiced the sentiments of many members of the clergy.[22]

The Nazis instituted many anti-Jewish measures designed to make outcasts of the Jews. Thousands of Jewish doctors, lawyers, musicians, artists, and professors were barred from practicing their professions, and Jewish members of the civil

Primary Source

Ernst Huber: "The Authority of the Führer Is . . . All-Inclusive and Unlimited"

In Verfassüngsrecht des grossdeutschen Reiches *(Constitutional Law of the Greater German Reich), legal scholar Ernst Rudolf Huber (1903–1990) offered a classic explication of the basic principles of National Socialism. The following excerpts from that work describe the nature of Hitler's political authority.*

The Führer-Reich of the [German] people is founded on the recognition that the true will of the people cannot be disclosed through parliamentary votes and plebiscites but that the will of the people in its pure and uncorrupted form can only be expressed through the Führer. Thus a distinction must be drawn between the supposed will of the people in a parliamentary democracy, which merely reflects the conflict of the various social interests, and the true will of the people in the Führer-state, in which the collective will of the real political unit is manifested. . . .

It would be impossible for a law to be introduced and acted upon in the Reichstag which had not originated with the Führer or, at least, received his approval. The procedure is similar to that of the plebiscite: The lawgiving power does not rest in the Reichstag; it merely proclaims through its decision its agreement with the will of the Führer, who is the lawgiver of the German people.

The Führer unites in himself all the sovereign authority of the Reich; all public authority in the state as well as in the movement is derived from the authority of the Führer. We must speak not of the state's authority but of the Führer's authority if we wish to designate the character of the political authority within the Reich correctly. The state does not hold political authority as an impersonal unit but receives it from the Führer as the executor of the national will. The authority of the Führer is complete and all-embracing; it unites in itself all the means of political direction; it extends into all fields of national life; it embraces the entire people, which is bound to the Führer in loyalty and obedience. The authority of the Führer is not limited by checks and controls, by special autonomous bodies or individual rights, but it is free and independent, all-inclusive and unlimited.

Question for Analysis

1. Point out several ways that Ernst Huber's views represent a rejection of Western liberalism.

Raymond E. Murphy et al., *National Socialism: Basic Principles* (Washington, D. C.: Government Printing Office, 1943), 34, 36–38.

service were dismissed. A series of laws tightened the screws of humiliation and persecution. Marriage or sexual encounters between Germans and Jews were forbidden. Universities, schools, restaurants, pharmacies, hospitals, theaters, museums, and athletic fields were gradually closed to Jews. The propaganda machine, including the schools and media, conditioned Germans to see the Jew as an evil, alien, and dangerous parasite. The Nazis also expropriated Jewish property, an act of thievery that benefited numerous individual Germans and business firms.

In November 1938, using as a pretext the assassination of a German official in Paris by a seventeen-year-old Jewish youth whose family the Nazis had mistreated, the Nazis organized an extensive pogrom. Nazi gangs murdered scores of Jews, destroyed 267 synagogues, and burned and vandalized 7,500 Jewish-owned businesses all over Germany—an event that became known as Night of the Broken Glass *(Kristallnacht)*. In many communities local citizens joined the Nazis in the pogrom, often brutalizing neighbors. Many Germans were also shamed by this relapse into barbarism. Some thirty thousand Jews were thrown into concentration camps where they were systematically humiliated and brutalized. The Reich then imposed on the Jewish community a fine of one billion marks. These measures were a mere prelude, however. During World War II, the genocidal murder of European Jewry became a cardinal Nazi objective. As a rule, German academic and clerical elites did not protest; indeed, many agreed with the National Socialists' edicts. The Jews were simply abandoned.

Shaping the "New Man"

The Ministry of Popular Enlightenment, headed by Joseph Goebbels (1897–1945), controlled the press, book publishing, the radio, the theater, and the cinema. Nazi propaganda sought to condition the mind to revere the führer and to obey the new regime. Its intent was to deprive individuals of their capacity for independent thought. By concentrating on the myth of race and the cult of the infallible führer—the German messiah sent by destiny to redeem the fatherland—Nazi propaganda tried to disorient the rational mind and to give the individual new standards to believe in and obey. Propaganda aimed to mold the entire

ADOLF HITLER BEFORE HIS LABOR ARMY AT NUREMBERG, GERMANY, SEPTEMBER 1938. In the monster rallies staged at Nuremberg, thousands of Nazi supporters worshipped at their leader's feet.

nation to think and respond as the leader-state directed.

The regime made a special effort to reach young people. All youths between the ages of ten and eighteen were urged and then required to join the Hitler Youth, and all other youth organizations were dissolved. At camps and rallies, young people paraded, sang, saluted, and chanted: "We were slaves; we were outsiders in our own country. So were we before Hitler united us. Now we would fight against Hell itself for our leader."[23] The schools, long breeding grounds of nationalism, militarism, antiliberalism, and anti-Semitism, now indoctrinated the young in Nazi ideology. The Nazis instructed teachers how certain subjects were to be taught, and to ensure obedience members of the Hitler Youth were asked to report teachers who did not conform.

In May 1933, professors and students proudly burned books, many of them written by Jews, considered a threat to Nazi ideology, in a display of cultural barbarism that gave prophetic meaning to the famous words of Heinrich Heine, the great nineteenth-century German-Jewish poet: "Wherever they burn books they will also, in the end, burn people." As books removed from public and private libraries were hurled into the flames, students danced.

Many academics praised Hitler and the new regime. Some 10 percent of the university faculty, principally Jews, Social Democrats, and liberals, were dismissed, and their colleagues often approved. "From now on it will not be your job to determine whether something is true but whether it is in the spirit of the National Socialist revolution," the new minister of culture told university professors.[24] Numerous courses on "racial science" and Nazi ideology were introduced into the curriculum. Many German academics, some of them noted scholars, willingly, if not enthusiastically, loaned their talents and learning to the new regime.

Symbolic of the Nazi regime were the monster rallies staged at Nuremberg. Scores of thousands roared, marched, and worshiped at their leader's feet. These true believers, the end product of Nazi indoctrination, celebrated Hitler's achievements and demonstrated their loyalty to their savior. Everything was brilliantly orchestrated to impress Germans and the world with the irresistible power, determination, and unity of the Nazi movement and the greatness of the führer. Armies of youths waving flags, storm troopers bearing weapons, and workers shouldering long-handled spades paraded past Hitler, who stood at attention, his arm extended in the Nazi salute. The endless columns of marchers, the stirring martial music played by huge bands, the forest of flags, the chanting and cheering of spectators, and the burning torches and beaming spotlights united the participants into a racial community. "Wherever Hitler leads we follow," thundered thousands of Germans in a giant chorus.

Terror was another means of ensuring compliance and obedience. The instruments of terror were the Gestapo and the *Schutzstaffel* (SS), which was organized in 1925 to protect Hitler and other party leaders and to stand guard at party meetings. Under the leadership of Heinrich Himmler

NAZI CULTURE. The Nazis considered jazz to be racially degenerate Jewish and black music.

(1900–1945), a fanatical believer in Hitler's racial theories, the SS was molded into an elite force of disciplined, dedicated, and utterly ruthless men. Many Germans, seduced by Nazi propaganda, accepted terror as a legitimate weapon against subversives and racial defilers who threatened the new Germany. Informers often denounced to the security forces fellow Germans suspected of Communist leanings, having business or sexual relations with Jews, or criticizing Hitler. Recent research shows the Gestapo, relatively few in number, could not function effectively without the assistance of civilians willing to inform on their neighbors and even family members.

Mass Support

The Nazi regime became a police state characterized by arrests of innocents, the persecution of Jews, and concentration camps that institutionalized terror. But since the secret police arrested mainly Communists and Jews, average Germans had nothing to fear. In many ways life seemed normal for them. The Nazis skillfully established the totalitarian state without upsetting the daily life of the great majority of the population. Moreover, Hitler, like Mussolini, was careful to maintain the appearance of legality. By not abolishing parliament or repealing the constitution, he could claim that his was a legitimate government.

To people concerned with little except family, job, and friends—and this includes most people in any country—life in the first few years of the Third Reich seemed quite satisfying. Most Germans believed that the new government was trying to solve Germany's problems in a vigorous and sensible manner, in contrast to the ineffective Weimar leadership. By 1936, the invigoration of the economy, stimulated in part by rearmament, had virtually eliminated unemployment, which had stood at six million jobless when Hitler took power. An equally astounding achievement in

© Topham/The Image Works.

Young Nazis Burning Books in Salzburg, Austria, 1938. Heinrich Heine, the great nineteenth-century German-Jewish poet, once said that people who burn books end up burning people.

the eyes of the German people was Hitler's bold termination of the humiliating Versailles treaty, the rebuilding of the German war machine, and the restoration of German power in international affairs. It seemed to most Germans that Hitler had awakened a sense of self-sacrifice and national dedication among a people dispirited by defeat and economic depression.

To many Germans, Hitler was exactly as Nazi mythology depicted him, a man of destiny and a savior of the nation who "stands like a statue grown beyond the measure of earthly man."[25] When Hitler rode into Nuremberg in preparation for a giant rally, observed American journalist William L. Shirer, "wildly cheering Nazis packed the narrow streets. . . . [T]en thousand hysterics . . . jammed the moat in front of Hitler's hotel. . . . [W]hen Hitler finally appeared on the balcony for a moment . . . They looked at him as if he were a Messiah, their faces transformed into something positively inhuman."[26]

The frenzied adoration shown by the German people for Hitler both in peacetime and in war and their faith in his mission to regenerate the German nation is an extraordinary phenomenon that continues to intrigue historians and social psychologists and to astonish new generations of Europeans, including Germans. It was considerably different for other dictators of Hitler's generation. Whatever devotion the Italians felt for Mussolini quickly faded once he brought the country into war. And the Soviet people's bonds to Stalin, particularly for non-Russian ethnic groups, were often based more on fear than genuine adulation. The German people's hero worship of Hitler and their positive view of his dictatorship were not driven by terror and for many endured for the duration of the war. Nor did ordinary Germans have to be coerced to support and serve the Nazi state, even as collaborators in persecution and genocide during World War II. Rarely in history has a nation been so spellbound by a leader.

There was some opposition to the Hitler regime. Social Democrats and Communists in particular organized small cells. Some conservatives, who considered Hitler a threat to traditional German values, and some clergy, who saw Nazism as a pagan religion in conflict with Christian morality, also formed small opposition groups. But only the army could have toppled Hitler. Some generals, even before World War II, urged resistance, but the overwhelming majority of German officers either preferred the new regime—which had smashed Marxism within Germany, destroyed an ineffective democracy, and restored Germany's military might and pride—or considered it dishonorable to break their oath of loyalty to Hitler. Most of these officers would remain loyal until the bitter end. Very few Germans realized that their country was passing through a long night of barbarism, and still fewer considered resistance. The great majority of Germans would remain loyal to their führer and would serve the Nazi regime until its collapse.

LIBERALISM AND AUTHORITARIANISM IN OTHER LANDS

After World War I, in country after country, parliamentary democracy collapsed and authoritarian leaders came to power. In most of these countries, liberal ideals had not penetrated deeply. Proponents of liberalism met resistance from conservative elites.

The Spread of Authoritarianism

Spain and Portugal. In both Spain and Portugal, parliamentary regimes faced strong opposition from the church, the army, and large landowners. In 1926, army officers overthrew the Portuguese republic that had been created in 1910, and gradually Antonio de Oliveira Salazar (1889–1970), a professor of economics, emerged as dictator. In Spain, after antimonarchist forces won the election of 1931, King Alfonso XIII (1902–1931) left the country, and Spain was proclaimed a republic. But the new government, led by socialists and liberals, faced the determined opposition of the traditional ruling elite. The reforms introduced by the republic—expropriation of large estates, reduction of the number of army officers, dissolution of the Jesuit order, and the closing of church schools—only intensified the old order's hatred.

The difficulties of the Spanish republic mounted: workers, near starvation, rioted and engaged in violent strikes; the military attempted a coup; and Catalonia, with its long tradition of separatism, tried to establish its autonomy. Imitating France (see the upcoming section on France), the parties of the Left, including the Communists, united in the Popular Front, which came to power in February 1936. In July 1936, General Francisco Franco (1892–1975), stationed in Spanish Morocco, led a revolt against the republic. He was supported by army leaders, the church, monarchists, landlords, industrialists, and the Falange, a newly formed Fascist party. Spain was torn by a bloody civil war. Aided by Fascist Italy and Nazi Germany, Franco won in 1939 and established a ruthless dictatorship.

Eastern and Central Europe.

Parliamentary government in Eastern Europe rested on weak foundations. Predominantly rural, these countries lacked the sizable professional and commercial classes that had promoted liberalism in Western Europe. Only Czechoslovakia had a substantial native middle class with a strong liberal tradition. The rural masses of Eastern Europe, traditionally subjected to monarchical and aristocratic authority, were not used to political thinking or civic responsibility. Students and intellectuals, often gripped by a romantic nationalism, were drawn to antidemocratic movements. Right-wing leaders also played on the fear of Communism. When parliamentary government failed to solve internal problems, the opponents of the liberal state seized the helm. Fascist movements, however, had little success in Eastern Europe. Rather, authoritarian regimes headed by traditional ruling elites—army leaders or kings—extinguished democracy there.

The Western Democracies

While liberal governments were everywhere failing, the great Western democracies—the United States, Britain, and France—continued to preserve democratic institutions. In Britain and the United States, Fascist movements were merely a nuisance. In France, however, Fascism was more of a threat because it exploited a deeply ingrained hostility in some quarters to the liberal ideals of the French Revolution.

The United States.

The central problem faced by the Western democracies was the Great Depression, which started in the United States. In the 1920s, hundreds of thousands of Americans had bought stock on credit; this buying spree sent stock prices soaring well beyond what the stocks were actually worth. In late October 1929, the stock market was hit by a wave of panic selling, causing prices to plummet. Within a few weeks, the value of stocks listed on the New York Stock Exchange fell by some $26 billion. A ruinous chain reaction followed over the next few years. Businesses cut production and unemployment soared; farmers who were unable to meet mortgage payments lost their land; banks that had made poor investments closed down. American investors withdrew the capital they had invested in Europe, causing European banks and businesses to fail. Throughout the world, trade declined and unemployment rose.

When President Franklin Delano Roosevelt (1882–1945) took office in 1933, more than 13 million Americans—one-quarter of the labor force—were out of work. Hunger and despair showed on the faces of the American people. Moving away from laissez-faire, Roosevelt instituted a comprehensive program of national planning, economic experimentation, and reform known as the New Deal. Although the American political and economic system faced a severe test, few Americans turned to Fascism or Communism; the government engaged in national planning but did not break with democratic values and procedures.

Britain.

Even before the Great Depression, Britain faced severe economic problems. Loss of markets to foreign competitors hurt British manufacturing, mining, and shipbuilding; rapid development of water and oil power reduced the demand for British coal, and outdated mining equipment put Britain in a poor competitive position. To decrease costs, mine owners in 1926 called for salary cuts; the coal miners countered with a strike and were joined by workers in other industries. To many Britons, the workers were leftist radicals trying to overthrow the government. Many wanted the state to break the strike. After nine days, industrial workers called it off, but the miners held out for another six months; they returned to work with longer hours and lower pay.

The general strike had failed. However, because the workers had not called for revolution and had refrained from violence, the fear that British workers would follow the Bolshevik path abated.

The Great Depression cast a pall over Britain. The Conservative Party leadership tried to stimulate exports by devaluing the pound and to encourage industry by providing loans at lower interest rates, but in the main it left the task of recovery to industry itself. Not until Britain began to rearm did unemployment decline significantly. Despite the economic slump of the 1920s and the Great Depression, Britain remained politically stable, a testament to the strength of its parliamentary tradition. Neither the Communists nor the newly formed British Union of Fascists gained mass support.

France. In the early 1920s, France was concerned with restoring villages, railroads, mines, and forests that had been ruined by the war. From 1926 to 1929, France was relatively prosperous; industrial and agricultural production expanded, tourism increased, and the currency was stable. Although France did not feel the Great Depression as painfully as the United States and Germany, the nation was hurt by the decline in trade and production and the rise in unemployment. The political instability that had beset the Third Republic virtually since its inception continued, and hostility to the republic mounted. The rift between liberals and conservatives, which had divided the country since the Revolution and had grown worse with the Dreyfus affair (see "France: A Troubled Nation" in Chapter 16), continued to plague France during the Depression. As the leading parties failed to solve the nation's problems, a number of Fascist groups gained strength.

Fear of growing Fascist strength at home and in Italy and Germany led the parties of the left to form the Popular Front. In 1936, Léon Blum (1872–1950), a socialist and a Jew, became premier. Blum's Popular Front government instituted more reforms than any other ministry in the history of the Third Republic. To end a wave of strikes that tied up production, Blum gave workers a forty-hour week and holidays with pay and guaranteed them the right to collective bargaining. He took steps to nationalize the armaments and aircraft industries. To reduce the influence of the wealthiest families,

he put the Bank of France under government control. By raising prices and buying wheat, he aided farmers. Conservatives and Fascists denounced Blum as a Jewish socialist who was converting the fatherland into a Communist state. "Better Hitler than Blum," grumbled French rightists.

Despite significant reforms, the Popular Front could not revitalize the economy. His political support eroding, Blum resigned in 1937, and the Popular Front, always a tenuous alliance, soon fell apart. Through democratic means, the Blum government had tried to give France its own New Deal, but the social reforms passed by the Popular Front only intensified hatred between the working classes and the rest of the nation. France had preserved democracy against the onslaught of domestic Fascists, but it was a demoralized and divided nation that confronted a united and dynamic Nazi Germany.

INTELLECTUALS AND ARTISTS IN TROUBLED TIMES

The presuppositions of the Enlightenment, already eroding in the decades before World War I, seemed near collapse after 1918—another casualty of trench warfare. Economic distress, particularly during the Great Depression, also profoundly disoriented the European mind. Westerners no longer possessed a frame of reference, a common outlook for understanding themselves, their times, or the past. The core values of Western civilization—the self-sufficiency of reason, the inviolability of the individual, and the existence of objective norms—no longer seemed inspiring or binding.

The crisis of consciousness evoked a variety of responses. Some intellectuals, having lost faith in the essential meaning of Western civilization, turned their backs on it or found escape in their art. Others sought a new hope in the Soviet experiment or in Fascism. Still others reaffirmed the rational humanist tradition of the Enlightenment. Repelled by the secularism, materialism, and rootlessness of the modern age, Christian thinkers urged Westerners to find renewed meaning and purpose in their ancestral religion. A philosophical movement called existentialism, which rose to prominence after World War II, aspired to make life authentic in a world stripped of universal values.

Postwar Pessimism

After World War I, Europeans looked at themselves and their civilization differently. It seemed that in science and technology they had unleashed powers that they could not control, and belief in the stability and security of European civilization appeared to be an illusion. Also illusory was the expectation that reason would banish surviving signs of darkness, ignorance, and injustice and usher in an age of continual progress. European intellectuals felt that they were living in a "broken world." In an age of heightened brutality and mobilized irrationality, the values of old Europe seemed beyond recovery. "All the great words," wrote D. H. Lawrence "were cancelled out for that generation."[27] The fissures discernible in European civilization before 1914 had grown wider and deeper. To be sure, Europe also had its optimists—those who found reason for hope in the League of Nations and in the easing of international tensions and improved economic conditions in the mid-1920s. However, the Great Depression and the triumph of totalitarianism intensified feelings of doubt and disillusionment.

Expressions of pessimism abounded after World War I. In 1919, Paul Valéry stated: "We modern civilizations have learned to recognize that we are mortal like the others. We feel that a civilization is as fragile as life."[28] "We are living today under the sign of the collapse of civilization,"[29] declared humanitarian Albert Schweitzer in 1923. German philosopher Karl Jaspers noted in 1932 that "there is a growing awareness of imminent ruin tantamount to a dread of the approaching end of all that makes life worthwhile."[30]

T. S. Eliot's *The Waste Land* (1922) also conveys a sense of foreboding. In his image of a collapsing European civilization, Eliot creates a macabre scenario. Hooded hordes, modern-day barbarians, swarm over plains and lay waste to cities. Jerusalem, Athens, Alexandria, Vienna, and London—each once a great spiritual or cultural center—are now "falling towers." Amid this destruction, one hears "high in the air/Murmur of

maternal lamentation."[31] In 1936, Dutch historian Johan Huizinga wrote in a chapter entitled "Apprehension of Doom":

> *We are living in a demented world. And we know it. . . . Everywhere there are doubts as to the solidity of our social structure, vague fears of the imminent future, a feeling that our civilization is on the way to ruin. . . . almost all things which once seemed sacred and immutable have now become unsettled, truth and humanity, justice and reason. . . . The sense of living in the midst of a violent crisis of civilization, threatening complete collapse, has spread far and wide.*[32]

The most influential expression of pessimism was Oswald Spengler's *The Decline of the West*. The first volume was published in July 1918, as the Great War was drawing to a close, and the second volume in 1922. The work achieved instant notoriety, particularly in Spengler's native Germany, shattered by defeat. Spengler viewed history as an assemblage of many different cultures, which, like living organisms, experience birth, youth, maturity, and death. What contemporaries pondered most was Spengler's insistence that Western civilization had entered its final stage and that its death could not be averted.

To an already troubled Western world, Spengler offered no solace. The West, like other cultures and like any living organism, was destined to die; its decline was irreversible and its death inevitable, and the symptoms of degeneration were already evident. Spengler's gloomy prognostication buttressed the Fascists, who claimed that they were creating a new civilization on the ruins of the dying European civilization.

Literature and Art: Innovation, Disillusionment, and Social Commentary

Postwar pessimism did not prevent writers and artists from continuing the cultural innovations begun before the war. In the works of D. H. Lawrence, Marcel Proust, André Gide, James Joyce, Franz Kafka, T. S. Eliot, and Thomas Mann, the modernist movement achieved a brilliant flowering. Often these writers gave expression to the troubles and uncertainties of the postwar period.

Franz Kafka (1883–1924), a Czech Jew, grasped the dilemma of the modern age perhaps better than any other novelist of his generation. In Kafka's world, human beings are caught in a bureaucratic web that they cannot control. They live in a nightmare society dominated by oppressive, cruel, and corrupt officials and amoral torturers: a world where cruelty and injustice are accepted facts of existence, power is exercised without limits, and victims cooperate in their own destruction. Traditional values and ordinary logic do not operate in such a world. In *The Trial* (1925), for example, the hero is arrested without knowing why, and he is eventually executed, a victim of institutional evil that breaks and destroys him "like a dog." In these observations, Kafka proved to be a prophet of the emerging totalitarian state. (Kafka's three sisters perished in the Holocaust.)

Kafka expressed the feelings of alienation and isolation that characterize the modern individual; he explored life's dreads and absurdities, offering no solutions or consolation. In Kafka's works, people are defeated and unable to comprehend the irrational forces that contribute to their destruction. The mind yearns for coherence, but, Kafka tells us, uncertainty, if not chaos, governs human relationships. We can be sure neither of our own identities nor of the world we encounter, for human beings are the playthings of unfathomable forces, too irrational to master.

Before World War I, German writer Thomas Mann (1875–1955) had earned a reputation for his short stories and novels, particularly *Buddenbrooks* (1901), which portrays the decline of a prosperous bourgeois family. In *The Magic Mountain* (1924), Mann reflected on the decomposition of bourgeois European civilization. The setting for the story is a Swiss sanitarium whose patients, drawn from several European lands, suffer from tuberculosis. The sanitarium symbolizes Europe, and it is the European psyche that is diseased. *The Magic Mountain* raised, but did not resolve, crucial questions. Was the epoch of rational humanist culture drawing to a close? Did Europeans welcome their spiritual illness in the same way that some of the patients in the sanitarium had a will to illness? How could Europe rescue itself from decadence?

In 1931, two years before Hitler took power, Mann, in an article entitled "An Appeal to Reason," described National Socialism and the extreme nationalism it espoused as a rejection of the Western rational tradition and a regression to primitive and barbaric modes of behavior. Nazism, he wrote, "is distinguished by . . . its absolute unrestraint, its orgiastic, radically anti-humane, frenziedly dynamic character. . . . Everything is possible, everything is permitted as a weapon against human decency. . . . Fanaticism turns into a means of salvation . . . politics becomes an opiate for the masses . . . and reason veils her face."[33]

Shattered by World War I, disgusted by Fascism's growing strength, and moved by the suffering caused by the Depression, many writers became committed to social and political causes. Erich Maria Remarque's *All Quiet on the Western Front* (1929) was one of many antiwar novels. George Orwell's *The Road to Wigan Pier* (1937) recorded the bleak lives of English workers. In *The Grapes of Wrath* (1939), John Steinbeck captured the anguish of American farmers driven from their land by the Dust Bowl and foreclosure during the Depression. Few issues stirred the conscience of intellectuals as did the Spanish Civil War, and many of them volunteered to fight with the Spanish republicans against the Fascists. Ernest Hemingway's *For Whom the Bell Tolls* (1940) expressed the sentiments of these idealists.

The new directions taken in art before World War I—abstractionism and expressionism—continued in the postwar decades. Picasso, Mondrian, Kandinsky, Matisse, Rouault, Braque, Modigliani, and other masters continued to refine their styles. In addition, new art trends emerged, mirroring the trauma of a generation that had experienced the war and lost its faith in Europe's moral and intellectual values.

In 1915 in Zurich, artists and writers founded a movement, called Dada, to express their revulsion against the war and the civilization that spawned it. From neutral Switzerland, the movement spread to Germany and Paris. Dada shared in the postwar mood of disorientation and despair. Dadaists viewed life as essentially absurd (*Dada* is a nonsense term) and cultivated indifference. "The acts of life have no beginning or end. Everything happens in a completely idiotic way,"[34] declared the poet Tristan Tzara, one of Dada's founders and its chief spokesman. Dadaists expressed contempt for artistic and literary standards and rejected both God and reason. "Through reason man becomes a tragic and ugly figure," said one Dadaist; "beauty is dead," said another. Tzara declared:

> *What good did the theories of the philosophers do us? Did they help us to take a single step forward or backward? . . . We have had enough of the intelligent movements that have stretched beyond measure our credulity in the benefits of science. What we want now is spontaneity. . . . because everything that issues freely from ourselves, without the intervention of speculative ideas, represents us.*[35]

For Dadaists, the world was nonsensical and reality disordered; hence, they offered no solutions to anything. "Like everything in life, Dada is useless,"[36] said Tzara. Despite their nihilistic aims and "calculated irrationality," however, Dadaist artists, such as Marcel Duchamp, were innovative and creative.

Dada ended as a formal movement in 1924 and was succeeded by surrealism. Surrealists inherited from Dada a contempt for reason; they stressed fantasy and made use of Freudian insights and symbols in their art to reproduce the raw state of the unconscious and to arrive at truths beyond reason's grasp. In their attempt to break through the constraints of rationality to reach a higher reality—that is, a "surreality"—leading surrealists such as Max Ernst (1891–1976), Salvador Dali (1904–1989), and Joan Miro

Erich Lessing/Art Resource, N.Y. © 2011 Artists Rights Society [ARS], New York/VGBild-Kunst, Bonn.

THE NIGHT **(1918–1919)**, BY MAX BECKMANN **(1884–1950)**. Max Beckmann's paintings gave expression to the disillusionment and spiritual unease that afflicted postwar Germany. When the Nazis included his works in the Degenerate Art Exhibition (1937), he left the country. In *The Night*, Beckmann, himself a veteran of the front, depicts brutal men engaging in terrible violence.

(1893–1983) used unconventional techniques to depict an external world devoid of logic and normal appearances.

Like writers, artists expressed a social conscience. George Grosz combined a Dadaist sense of life's meaninglessness with a new realism to depict the moral degeneration of middle-class German society. In *After the Questioning* (1935), Grosz, then living in the United States, dramatized Nazi brutality; in *The End of the World* (1936), he expressed his fear of another impending world war. Käthe Kollwitz, also a German artist, showed a deep compassion for the sufferer: the unemployed, the hungry, the ill, and the politically oppressed. William Gropper's *Migration* (1932) dramatized the suffering of the same dispossessed farmers described in Steinbeck's novel *The Grapes of Wrath*. Philip Evergood, in *Don't Cry Mother* (1938–1944), portrayed the apathy of starving children and their mother's terrible helplessness.

In his etchings of maimed, dying, and dead soldiers, German artist Otto Dix produced a powerful visual indictment of the Great War's cruelty and suffering. Max Beckmann's service in the German army during World War I made him acutely aware of violence and brutality, which he expressed in *The Night* (1918–1919) and other paintings. Designated a "degenerate artist" by the Nazis, Beckmann went into exile. In *Guernica* (1937), Picasso memorialized the Spanish village decimated by saturation bombing during the Spanish Civil War. In the *White Crucifixion* (1938), Marc Chagall, a Russian-born Jew who had settled in Paris, depicted the terror and flight of Jews in Nazi Germany.

Communism: "The God That Failed"

The economic misery of the Depression and the rise of Fascist barbarism led many intellectuals to find a new hope, even a secular faith, in Communism. They considered the Soviet experiment a new beginning that promised a better future for all humanity. These intellectuals praised the Soviet Union—a "workers' paradise"—for supplanting capitalist greed

with socialist cooperation, for replacing a haphazard economic system marred by repeated depressions with one based on planned production, and for providing employment for everyone when joblessness was endemic in capitalist lands. American literary critic Edmund Wilson said that in the Soviet Union one felt at the "moral top of the world where the light never really goes out."[37] To these intellectuals, it seemed that in the Soviet Union a vigorous and healthy civilization was emerging and that only Communism could stem the tide of Fascism. For many, however, the attraction was short lived. Sickened by Stalin's purges and terror, the denial of individual freedom, and the suppression of truth, they came to view the Soviet Union as another totalitarian state and Communism as another "god that failed."

One such intellectual was Arthur Koestler (1905–1983). Born in Budapest of Jewish ancestry and educated in Vienna, Koestler worked as a correspondent for a leading Berlin newspaper chain. He joined the Communist Party at the very end of 1931 because he "lived in a disintegrating society thirsting for faith," was moved by the misery caused by the Depression, and saw Communism as the "only force capable of resisting the onrush of the primitive [Nazi] horde."[38] Koestler visited the Soviet Union in 1933, experiencing firsthand both the starvation brought on by forced collectivization and the propaganda that grotesquely misrepresented life in Western lands. While his faith was shaken, he did not break with the party until 1938, in response to Stalin's liquidations.

In *Darkness at Noon* (1941), Koestler explored the attitudes of the Old Bolsheviks who were imprisoned, tortured, and executed by Stalin. These dedicated Communists had served the party faithfully, but Stalin, fearing opposition, hating intellectuals, and driven by megalomania, denounced them as enemies of the people. In *Darkness at Noon*, the leading character, the imprisoned Rubashov, is a composite of the Old Bolsheviks. Although innocent, Rubashov, without being physically tortured, publicly confesses to political crimes that he never committed.

Rubashov is aware of the suffering that the party has brought to the Russian people:

> [I]n the interests of a just distribution of land we deliberately let die of starvation about five million farmers and their families in one year. . . . [To liberate] human beings from the shackles of industrial exploitation . . . we sent about ten million people to do forced labour in the Arctic regions . . . under conditions similar to those of antique galley slaves.[39]

Pained by his own complicity in the party's crimes, including the betrayal of friends, Rubashov questions the party's philosophy that the individual should be subordinated and, if necessary, sacrificed to the regime. Nevertheless, Rubashov remains the party's faithful servant; true believers do not easily break with their faith. By confessing, Rubashov performs his last service for the revolution. For the true believer, everything—truth, justice, and the sanctity of the individual—is properly sacrificed to the party.

Reaffirming the Christian Worldview

By calling into question core liberal beliefs—the essential goodness of human nature, the primacy of reason, the efficacy of science, and the inevitability of progress—World War I led thinkers to find in Christianity an alternative view of the human experience and the crisis of the twentieth century. Christian thinkers, including Karl Barth, Paul Tillich, Reinhold Niebuhr, Christopher Dawson, Jacques Maritain, and T. S. Eliot, affirmed the reality of evil in human nature. They assailed liberals and Marxists for holding too optimistic a view of human nature and human reason and for postulating a purely rational and secular philosophy of history. For these thinkers, the Christian conception of history as a clash between human will and God's commands provided an intelligible explanation of the tragedies of the twentieth century. They agreed with the leading French Catholic thinker Jacques Maritain (1882–1973), who argued that "anthropomorphic humanism," which held that human beings

by themselves alone can define life's purpose and create their own values, had utterly failed. Without guidance from a transcendental source, Maritain insisted, reason is powerless to control irrational drives, which threaten to degrade human existence. Without commitment to God's values, we find substitute faiths in fanatic and belligerent ideologies and unscrupulous leaders. For democracy to survive, he said, it must be infused with Christian love and compassion.

Reaffirming the Ideals of Reason and Freedom

Several thinkers tried to reaffirm the ideals of rationality and freedom that had been trampled by totalitarian movements. In *The Treason of the Intellectuals* (1927), Julien Benda (1867–1956), a French cultural critic of Jewish background, castigated intellectuals for intensifying hatred between nations, classes, and political factions. "Our age is indeed the age of the *intellectual organization of political hatreds*," he wrote. These intellectuals, said Benda, do not pursue justice or truth but proclaim that "even if our country is wrong, we must think of it in the right." They scorn outsiders, extol harshness and action, and proclaim the superiority of instinct and will to intelligence; or they "assert that the intelligence to be venerated is that which limits its activities within the bounds of national interest." The logical end of this xenophobia, said Benda, "is the organized slaughter of nations and classes."[40]

José Ortega y Gasset (1883–1955), descendant of a noble Spanish family and a professor of philosophy, gained international recognition with the publication of *The Revolt of the Masses* (1930). According to Ortega, European civilization, the product of a creative elite, was degenerating into barbarism because of the growing power of the masses, for the masses lacked the mental discipline and commitment to reason needed to preserve Europe's intellectual and cultural traditions. Ortega did not equate the masses with the working class and the elite with the nobility; it was an attitude of mind, not a class affiliation, that distinguished the "mass-man" from the elite.

The mass-man, said Ortega, has a commonplace mind and does not set high standards for himself. Faced with a problem, he "is satisfied with thinking the first thing he finds in his head," and "crushes . . . everything that is different, everything that is excellent, individual, qualified, and select. Anybody who is not like everybody, who does not think like everybody, runs the risk of being eliminated."[41] Such intellectually vulgar people, declared Ortega, cannot understand or preserve the processes of civilization. The Fascists, for him, exemplified this revolt of the masses:

> Under Fascism there appears for the first time in Europe a type of man who does not want to give reasons or to be right, but simply shows himself resolved to impose his opinions. This is the new thing: the right not to be reasonable, the "reason of unreason." Hence I see the most palpable manifestation of the new mentality of the masses, due to their having decided to rule society without the capacity for doing so.[42]

Since the mass-man does not respect the tradition of reason, he does not enter into rational dialogue with others or defend his opinions logically, said Ortega. Rejecting reason, the mass-man glorifies violence—the ultimate expression of barbarism. As Ortega saw it, if European civilization was to be rescued from Fascism and Communism, the elite must sustain civilized values and provide leadership for the masses.

A staunch defender of the Enlightenment tradition, Ernst Cassirer (1874–1945), a German philosopher of Jewish lineage, emigrated after Hitler came to power, eventually settling in the United States. Just prior to Hitler's triumph, in 1932, Cassirer wrote about the need to uphold and reenergize that tradition: "More than ever before, it seems to me, the time is again ripe for applying . . . self-criticism to the present age, for holding up to it that bright clear mirror fashioned by the Enlightenment. . . . The age which venerated reason and science as man's highest faculty cannot and must not be lost even for us."[43]

In his last work, The Myth of the State (1946), Cassirer described Nazism as the triumph of mythical thinking over reason. The Nazis, he wrote, cleverly manufactured myths—of the race, the leader, the party, the state—that disoriented the intellect. The Germans who embraced these myths surrendered their capacity for independent judgment, leaving themselves vulnerable to manipulation by the Nazi leadership. To contain the destructive powers of political myths, Cassirer urged strengthening the rational humanist tradition and called for the critical study of political myths.

George Orwell (1903–1950), a British novelist and political journalist, wrote two powerful indictments of totalitarianism: Animal Farm (1945) and 1984 (1949). In Animal Farm, based in part on his experiences with Communists during the Spanish Civil War, Orwell satirized the totalitarian regime built by Lenin and Stalin in Russia. In 1984, Orwell, who was deeply committed to human dignity and freedom, warned that these great principles were now permanently menaced by the concentration and abuse of political power. "If you want a picture of the future, imagine a boot stamping on a human face forever," says a member of the ruling elite as he tortures a victim in the dungeons of the Thought Police.[44]

The society of 1984 is ruled by the Inner Party, which constitutes some 2 percent of the population. Heading the Party is Big Brother—most likely a mythical figure created by the ruling elite to satisfy people's yearning for a leader. The Party indoctrinates people to love Big Brother, whose picture is everywhere. The Ministry of Truth resorts to thought control to dominate and manipulate the masses and to keep Party members loyal and subservient. Independent thinking is destroyed. Objective truth no longer exists. Truth is whatever the Party decrees at the moment. If the Party were to proclaim that two plus two equals five, it would have to be believed. In this totalitarian society of the future, all human rights are abolished, people are arrested merely for their thoughts, and children spy on their parents.

EXISTENTIALISM

The philosophical movement that best exemplified the anxiety and uncertainty of Europe in an era of world wars was existentialism. Like writers and artists, existentialist philosophers were responding to a European civilization that seemed to be in the throes of dissolution. Although existentialism was most popular after World War II,

JEAN PAUL SARTRE AND SIMONE DE BEAUVOIR. Existentialism was a major philosophical movement of the twentieth century. Sartre and de Beauvoir were two of its principle exponents.

expressing the anxiety and despair of many intellectuals who had lost confidence in reason and progress, several of its key works were written prior to or during the war.

What route should people take in a world where old values and certainties had dissolved, where universal truth was rejected and God's existence denied? How could people cope in a society where they were menaced by technology, manipulated by impersonal bureaucracies, and overwhelmed by feelings of anxiety? If the universe lacks any overarching meaning, what meaning could one give to one's own life? These questions were at the crux of existentialist philosophy.

Existentialism does not lend itself to a single definition, for its principal theorists did not adhere to a common body of doctrines. For example, some existentialists were atheists, like Jean Paul Sartre, or omitted God from their thought, like Martin Heidegger; others, like Karl Jaspers, believed in God but not in Christian doctrines; still others, like Gabriel Marcel and Nikolai Berdyaev, were Christians; and Martin Buber was a believing Jew.

That there are no timeless truths that exist independently of and prior to the individual human being and that serve as ultimate standards of virtue is a core principle of existentialism. Existence—our presence in the here-and-now—precedes and takes precedence over any presumed absolute values. The moral and spiritual values that society tries to impose cannot define the individual person's existence. Our traditional morality rests on no foundation whose certainty can be either demonstrated by reason or guaranteed by God. There are simply no transcendent absolutes; to think otherwise is to surrender to illusion. It is the first principle of existentialism, said Jean Paul Sartre (1905–1980), the prominent French existentialist, that we must choose our own ethics, define ourselves, and give our own meaning to our life.

For existentialists, human nature is not fixed or constant; each person is like no other. Self-realization comes when one affirms one's own uniqueness. One becomes less than human when one permits one's life to be determined by a mental outlook—a set of rules and values—imposed by others.

Existentialists maintained that we are alone in a universe that is indifferent to our expectations and needs, and death is ever stalking us. Awareness of this elementary fact of existence evokes a sense of overwhelming anxiety and depression. Existence is essentially absurd. There is no purpose to our presence in the universe. We simply find ourselves here; we do not know and will never find out why. Compared with the eternity of time that preceded our birth and will follow our death, the short duration of our existence seems trivial and inexplicable. And death, which irrevocably terminates our existence, testifies to the ultimate absurdity of life. We are free. We must face squarely the fact that existence is purposeless and absurd. In doing so, we can give our life meaning. It is in the act of choosing freely from among different possibilities that the individual shapes an authentic existence. There is a dynamic quality to human existence; the individual has the potential to become more than he or she is.

THE MODERN PREDICAMENT

The process of fragmentation in European thought and arts, which had begun at the end of the nineteenth century, accelerated after World War I. Increasingly, philosophers, writers, and artists expressed disillusionment with the rational humanist tradition of the Enlightenment. They no longer shared the Enlightenment's confidence in either reason's capabilities or human goodness, and they viewed perpetual progress as an illusion.

For some thinkers, the crucial problem was the great change in the European understanding of truth. Since the rise of philosophy in ancient Greece, Western thinkers had believed in the existence of objective, universal truths: truths that were inherent in nature and applied to all peoples at all times. (Christianity, of course, also taught the reality of truth as revealed by God.) It was held that such truths—the natural rights of the individual, for example—could be apprehended by the intellect and could serve as a standard for individual aspirations and social life. The recognition of these universal principles, it was believed, compelled people to measure the world of the here-and-now in the light of rational and universal norms and to institute appropriate reforms. It was the task of philosophy to reconcile human existence with the objective order.

During the nineteenth century, the existence of universal truth came into doubt. A growing historical consciousness led some thinkers to maintain that what people considered truth was merely a reflection of their culture at a given stage in history—their perception of things at a specific point in the evolution of human consciousness. These thinkers held that universal truths were not woven into the fabric of nature. There were no natural rights of life, liberty, and property that constituted the individual's birthright; there were no standards of justice or equality inherent in nature and ascertainable by reason. Rather, people themselves elevated the beliefs and values of an age to the status of objective truth. The normative principles—the self-evident truths proclaimed by Jefferson—which for the philosophes constituted a standard for political and social reform and a guarantee of human rights, were no longer linked to the natural order, to an objective reality that could be confirmed by reason. As Hannah Arendt noted, "We certainly no longer believe, as the men of the French Revolution did, in a universal cosmos of which man was a part and whose natural laws he had to imitate and conform to."[45]

This radical break with the traditional attitude toward truth contributed substantially to the crisis of European consciousness that marked the first half of the twentieth century. Traditional values and beliefs, whether those inherited from the Enlightenment or those taught by Christianity, no longer gave Europeans a sense of certainty and security. People were left without a normative order to serve as a guide to living—and without such a guide might be open to nihilism. For if nothing is fundamentally true—if there are no principles of morality and justice that emanate from God or can be derived from reason—then it can be concluded, as Nietzsche understood, that everything is permitted. Some scholars interpreted Nazism as the culminating expression of a nihilistic attitude grown ever more brutal.

By the early twentieth century, the attitude of Westerners toward reason had undergone a radical transformation. Some thinkers, who had placed their hopes in the rational tradition of the Enlightenment, were distressed by reason's inability to resolve the tensions and conflicts of modern industrial society. Moreover, the growing recognition of the nonrational—of human actions determined by hidden impulses—led people to doubt that reason played the dominant role in human behavior. Other thinkers viewed the problem of reason differently. They assailed the attitude of mind that found no room for Christianity because its teachings did not pass the test of reason and science. Or they attacked reason for fashioning a technological and bureaucratic society that devalued and crushed human passions and stifled individuality. These thinkers insisted that human beings cannot fulfill their potential, cannot live wholly, if their feelings are denied. They agreed with D. H. Lawrence's critique of rationalism: "The attribution of rationality to human nature, instead of enriching it, now seems to me to have impoverished it. It ignored certain powerful and valuable springs of feeling. Some of the spontaneous, irrational outbursts of human nature can have a sort of value from which our schematism was cut off."[46]

While many thinkers focused on reason's limitations, others, particularly existentialists, pointed out that reason was a double-edged sword: it could demean, as well as ennoble and liberate, the individual. These thinkers attacked all theories that subordinated the individual to a rigid ideological or political system.

Responding to the critics of reason, its defenders insisted that it was necessary to reaffirm the rational tradition first proclaimed by the Greeks and given its modern expression by the Enlightenment. Reason, they maintained, was indispensable to civilization. What these thinkers advocated was broadening the scope of reason to accommodate the insights into human nature advanced by the romantics, Nietzsche, Freud, modernist writers and artists, and others who explored the world of feelings, will, and the subconscious. They also stressed the need to humanize reason so that it could never threaten to reduce a human being to a thing—a mere instrument used to realize some socioeconomic blueprint.

In the decades shaped by world wars and totalitarianism, intellectuals raised questions that went to the heart of the dilemma of modern life. How can civilized life be safeguarded against human irrationality, particularly when it is channeled into political ideologies that idolize the state, the leader, the party, or the race? How can individual human personality be rescued from a relentless rationalism that organizes the individual as it would any material object? Do the values associated with the Enlightenment provide a sound basis on which to integrate society? Can the individual find meaning in what many now regarded as a meaningless universe? World War II and the Holocaust gave these questions a special poignancy.

❖   ❖   ❖

NOTES

1. Hannah Arendt, *The Origins of Totalitarianism* (New York: World, Meridian Books, 1958), 469.

2. Quoted in Omer Bartov, *Hitler's Army: Soldiers, Nazis, and War in the Third Reich* (New York: Oxford University Press, 1992), 166.

3. V. I. Lenin, "The Immediate Tasks of the Soviet Government," in *The Lenin Anthology*, ed. Robert C. Tucker (New York: Norton, 1975), 448 ff.

4. J. V. Stalin, "Speech to Business Executives" (1931), in *A Documentary History of Communism from Lenin to Mao*, ed. Robert V. Daniels (New York: Random House, 1960), Vol. 2, 22.

5. Quoted in Isaac Deutscher, *Stalin: A Political Biography* (New York: Oxford University Press, 1966), 325.

6. Excerpted in T. H. Rigby, ed., *Stalin* (Englewood Cliffs, N.J.: Prentice-Hall, 1966), 111.

7. Quoted in Jonathan Glover, *Humanity: A Moral History of the Twentieth Century* (New Haven, Conn.: Yale University Press, 1999), 241.

8. Quoted in Zeev Sternhill, "Fascist Ideology," in *Fascism: A Reader's Guide*, ed. Walter Laqueur (Berkeley: University of California Press, 1976), 338.

9. Quoted in John Weiss, *The Fascist Tradition* (New York: Harper & Row, 1967), 9.

10. Quoted in Max Gallo, *Mussolini's Italy* (New York: Macmillan, 1973), 218.

11. Adolf Hitler, *Mein Kampf*, trans. Ralph Manheim (Boston: Houghton Mifflin, 1962), 161.

12. Quoted in Joachim C. Fest, *Hitler*, trans. Richard and Clara Winston (New York: Harcourt Brace Jovanovich, 1974), 162.

13. *Hitler's Secret Conversations, 1941–1944*, with an introductory essay by H. R. Trevor Roper (New York: Farrar, Straus & Young, 1953), 28.

14. Quoted in Lucy S. Dawidowicz, *The War Against the Jews, 1933–1945* (New York: Holt, Rinehart & Winston, 1975), 21.

15. Quoted in Uri Tal, "Consecration of Politics in the Nazi Era," in *Judaism and Christianity Under the Impact of National Socialism*, ed. Otto Dov Kulka and Paul R. Mendes Flohr (Jerusalem: Historical Society of Israel, 1987), 70.

16. Adolf Hitler, *Mein Kampf*, 107.

17. Ibid., 479.

18. Quoted in Zbigniew Brzezinski, *Out of Control* (New York: Charles Scribner's Sons, 1993), 19.

19. Quoted in David Welch, ed., *Nazi Propaganda* (Totowa, N.J.: Barnes & Noble, 1983), 5.

20. Quoted in J. S. Conway, *The Nazi Persecution of the Churches* (New York: Basic Books, 1968), 202.

21. Hitler's *Secret Conversations*, 6.

22. Quoted in Hermann Graml et al., *The German Resistance to Hitler* (Berkeley: University of California Press, 1970), 206.

23. Quoted in T. L. Jarman, *The Rise and Fall of Nazi Germany* (New York: New York University Press, 1956), 182.

24. Quoted in Karl Dietrich Bracher, *The German Dictatorship*, trans. Jean Steinberg (New York: Praeger, 1970), 268.

25. Quoted in Fest, *Hitler*, 532.

26. William L. Shirer, *Berlin Diary: The Journal of a Foreign Correspondent, 1934–1941* (New York: Galahad Books, 1945), 16–17.

27. Quoted in Barbara Tuchman, *The Guns of August* (New York: Macmillan, 1962), 489.

28. Quoted in Hans Kohn, "The Crisis in European Thought and Culture," in *World War I: A Turning Point in Modern History*, ed. Jack J. Roth (New York: Alfred A. Knopf, 1967), 28.

29. Quoted in Franklin L. Baumer, "Twentieth-Century Version of the Apocalypse," *Cahiers d'Histoire Mondiale (Journal of World History)*, 1 (January 1954), 624.

30. Ibid.

31. T. S. Eliot, "The Waste Land," in *Collected Poems*, 1909–1962 (New York: Harcourt, Brace, 1970), 67.

32. Johan Huizinga, *In the Shadow of Tomorrow* (London: Heinemann, 1936), 1–3.

33. Thomas Mann, "An Appeal to Reason," excerpted in *Sources of the Western Tradition*, 8th ed. Marvin Perry ed., (Boston: Wadsworth, Cengage Learning, 2012), Vol. 2, 349–350.

34. Tristan Tzara, "Lecture on Dada (1922)," trans. Ralph Mannheim, in *The Dada Painters and Poets*, ed. Robert Motherwell (New York: Witterborn, Schultz, 1951), 250.

35. Ibid., 248.

36. Ibid., 251.

37. Quoted in David Caute, *The Fellow Travellers* (New York: Macmillan, 1973), 64.

38. Richard Crossman, ed., *The God That Failed* (New York: Bantam Books, 1951), 15, 21.

39. Arthur Koestler, *Darkness at Noon* (New York: Macmillan, 1941), 158–159.

40. Julien Benda, *The Betrayal of the Intellectuals*, trans. Richard Aldington (Boston: Beacon, 1955), 21, 38, 122, 162. The book is commonly known by its first translation, *The Treason of the Intellectuals*.

41. José Ortega y Gasset, *The Revolt of the Masses* (New York: Norton, 1957), 63, 18.

42. Ibid., 73.

43. Ernst Cassirer, *The Philosophy of the Enlightenment*, trans. Fritz C. A. Koelln and James P. Pettegrove (Boston: Beacon, 1955), xi–xii.

44. George Orwell, *1984* (New York: Harcourt, Brace, 1949; paperback, The New American Library, 1961), 220.

45. Cited in Harry S. Kariel, *In Search of Authority* (Glencoe, Ill.: The Free Press, 1964), 246.

46. Quoted in Anthony Arblaster, *The Rise and Decline of Western Liberalism* (Oxford: Basil Blackwell, 1984), 81.

Chapter 20

World War II: Western Civilization in the Balance

- **The Road to War**
- **The Nazi Blitzkrieg**
- **The New Order**
- **The Turn of the Tide**
- **The Legacy of World War II**

Focus Questions

1. What were Hitler's foreign policy aims?
2. Why did Britain and France pursue a policy of appeasement, and with what effect?
3. What factors contributed to the German victory over Poland? Over France?
4. Why was Britain able to win the air battle in the summer of 1940?
5. Why was Germany unable to conquer Russia?
6. What was the nature of the new order Germany established in conquered Europe? Why were Jews marked for extermination?
7. What factors led to Germany's defeat?
8. In your opinion, what is the meaning of the Holocaust for Western civilization? For Jews? For Christians? For Germans?
9. What is the legacy of World War II?

*F*rom the early days of his political career, Hitler dreamed of forging a vast German empire in Central and Eastern Europe. He believed that only by waging a war of conquest against Russia could the German nation gain the living space and security it required and, as a superior race, deserved. War was an essential component of National Socialism's racist ideology, which postulated an eternal struggle between races and the shaping of a new order in Europe based on race; war also accorded with Hitler's temperament. For the former corporal from the trenches, the Great War had never ended. Hitler aspired to political power because he wanted to mobilize the material and human resources of the German nation for war and conquest.

Although historians may debate the question of responsibility for World War I, few would deny that World War II was Hitler's war. Most would concur with the assessment of French historian Pierre Renouvin: "It appears to be an almost incontrovertible fact that the Second World War was brought on by the actions of the Hitler government, that these actions were the expression of a policy laid down well in advance in *Mein Kampf,* and that this war could have been averted up until the last moment if the German government had so wished."[1] Western statesmen had sufficient warning that Hitler was a threat to peace and to the essential values of Western civilization. In the 1920s, Hitler had openly proclaimed his commitment to a war of revenge and expansion, and in the 1930s, he scrapped the Versailles Treaty and openly prepared for such a conflict. But Western statesmen, not fully grasping Hitler's ruthlessness and ideological obsession with creating a German racial empire and underestimating his Machiavellian cunning in foreign policy, failed to rally their people and take a stand until Germany had greatly increased its capacity to wage aggressive war. ❖

THE ROAD TO WAR

After consolidating his power and mobilizing the nation, Hitler moved to implement his foreign policy objectives: the destruction of the Versailles treaty, the conquest and colonization of Eastern Europe, and the domination and exploitation of racial inferiors. In foreign affairs, Hitler demonstrated the same blend of opportunism and singleness of purpose that had brought him to power. Here, too, he displayed an uncanny understanding of his opponents' weaknesses; and here, too, his opponents underestimated his skills and intent. As in his climb to power, he made use of propaganda

to undermine his opponents' will to resist. The Nazi propaganda machine, which had effectively won the minds of the German people, became an instrument of foreign policy. To promote social and political disorientation in other lands, the Nazis propagated anti-Semitism worldwide. Nazi propagandists also tried to draw international support for Hitler as Europe's best defense against the Soviet Union and Bolshevism.

British and French Foreign Policies

As Hitler had anticipated, the British and the French backed down when faced with his violations of the Versailles treaty and threats of war. Haunted by the memory of World War I, Britain and France went to great lengths to avoid another catastrophe—a policy that had the overwhelming support of public opinion. Because Britain believed that Germany had been treated too severely by the Versailles treaty and knew that its own military forces were woefully unprepared for war, from 1933 to 1938 the British were amenable to making concessions to Hitler. Although France had the strongest army on the Continent, it was prepared to fight only a defensive war—the reverse of its World War I strategy. France built immense fortifications, called the Maginot Line, to protect its borders from a German invasion, but it lacked a mobile striking force that could punish an aggressive Germany. The United States, concerned with the problems of the Great Depression and standing aloof from Europe's troubles, did nothing to strengthen the resolve of France and Britain. Since both France and Britain feared and mistrusted the Soviet Union, the grand alliance of World War I was not renewed. There was an added factor: suffering from a failure of leadership and political and economic unrest that eroded national unity, France was experiencing a decline in morale and a loss of nerve. It consistently turned to Britain for direction.

British statesmen championed a policy of appeasement: giving in to Germany in the hope that a satisfied Hitler would not drag Europe through another world war. British policy rested on the disastrous illusion that Hitler, like his Weimar predecessors, sought peaceful revision of the Versailles treaty and that he could be contained through concessions. Accepting the view that Nazi

HITLER AND HIS AIDES IN FRONT OF THE EIFFEL TOWER. In 1940, after military successes in Belgium and Holland, the German forces overcame France. Hitler (center, right) saw the fall of France as a proof of the invincibility of the Reich and a predestined reversal of the humiliation felt by Germans at their defeat in World War I.

propaganda cleverly propagated and exploited, some British appeasers also regarded Hitler as a defender of European civilization and the capitalist economic order against Soviet Communism. Appeasement, which in the end was capitulation to blackmail, failed. Germany grew stronger and the German people more devoted to the führer. Hitler did not moderate his ambitions, and the appeasers did not avert war.

Breakdown of Peace

To realize his foreign policy aims, Hitler required a formidable military machine. Germany must rearm. The Treaty of Versailles had limited the size of the German army to a hundred thousand volunteers; restricted the navy's size; forbidden the production of military aircraft, heavy artillery, and tanks; and disbanded the general staff. In March 1935, Hitler declared that Germany was no longer bound by the Versailles treaty. Germany would restore conscription, build an air force (which it had been doing secretly), and strengthen its navy. France and Britain offered no resistance.

A decisive event in the breakdown of peace was Italy's invasion of Ethiopia in October 1935. The League of Nations called for economic sanctions against Italy, and most League members restricted trade with the aggressor. But Italy continued to receive oil, particularly from American suppliers, and neither Britain nor France sought to restrain Italy. Mussolini's subjugation of Ethiopia discredited the League of Nations, which had already been weakened by its failure to deal effectively with Japan's invasion of the mineral-rich Chinese province of Manchuria in 1931. The fall of Ethiopia, like that of Manchuria, evidenced the League's reluctance to check aggression with force.

Remilitarization of the Rhineland. On March 7, 1936, Hitler marched troops into the Rhineland, violating the Versailles treaty, which called for the demilitarization of these German border lands. German generals had cautioned Hitler that such a move would provoke a French invasion of Germany, which the German army could not repulse. But Hitler gambled that France and Britain, lacking the will to fight, would take no action.

Hitler had assessed the Anglo-French mood correctly. The remilitarization of the Rhineland did not greatly alarm Britain. After all, Hitler was not expanding Germany's borders but only sending soldiers to its frontier. Such a move, reasoned British officials, did not warrant risking a war, and France would not act alone. Moreover, the French general staff overestimated German military strength and thought only of defending French soil from a German attack, not of initiating a strike against Germany.

Spanish Civil War. The Spanish Civil War of 1936–1939 was another victory for Fascism. Nazi Germany and Fascist Italy aided Franco (see "Liberalism and Authoritarianism in Other Lands" in Chapter 19); the Soviet Union supplied the Spanish Republic. By October 1937, some sixty thousand Italian "volunteers" were fighting in Spain. Hitler sent between five thousand and six thousand men and hundreds of planes, which proved decisive in winning the war. By comparison, the Soviet Union's aid was meager. Viewing the conflict as a struggle between democracy and Fascism, thousands of Europeans and Americans volunteered to fight for the republic.

Without considerable help from France, the Spanish Republic was doomed, but Prime Minister Léon Blum feared that French intervention might lead to war with Germany. Moreover, supplying the republic would have dangerous consequences at home because French rightists were sympathetic to Franco's conservative-clerical authoritarianism. In 1939, the republic fell, and Franco established a dictatorship, imprisoning or banishing to labor camps more than one million Spaniards and executing another two hundred thousand. The Spanish Civil War provided Germany with an opportunity to test weapons and pilots and demonstrated again that France and Britain lacked the determination to fight Fascism.

Anschluss with Austria. One of Hitler's aims was incorporation of Austria into the Third Reich, but the Treaty of Versailles had expressly prohibited the union (Anschluss) of the two German-speaking countries. In March 1938, under the pretext of preventing violence, Hitler ordered his troops into Austria, which was made a province of the German Reich.

Many Austrians welcomed the Anschluss. The idea of a Greater Germany appealed to their Pan-German sentiments, and they hoped that Hitler's magic would produce economic recovery. Moreover, depriving Jews of their rights, property, and occupations had widespread appeal among traditionally anti-Semitic Austrians. The Viennese celebrated by ringing church bells, waving swastika banners, and spontaneously beating, robbing, and humiliating Jews, including tearing Torah scrolls, shearing the beards of rabbis, and forcing whole families to scrub sidewalks. The Austrians' euphoria over the Anschluss and their treatment of Jews astonished many observers, including the German occupiers.

Sudetenland, Munich, Prague. Hitler obtained Austria merely by threatening to use force. Another threat would give him the Sudetenland of Czechoslovakia. Of the 3.5 million people living in the Sudetenland, some 2.8 million were ethnic Germans. Encouraged and instructed by Germany, the Sudeten Germans, led by Konrad Henlein, shrilly denounced the Czech government for "persecuting" its German minority and depriving it of its right to self-determination. The Sudeten Germans agitated for local autonomy and the right to profess the National Socialist ideology. Behind this demand was the goal of German annexation of the Sudetenland and the destruction of Czechoslovakia.

While negotiations between the Sudeten Germans and the Czech government proceeded, Hitler's propaganda machine accused the Czechs of hideous crimes against the German minority and warned of retribution. Hitler also ordered his generals to prepare for an invasion of Czechoslovakia. Fighting between Czechs and Sudeten Germans heightened the tensions. Seeking to preserve peace, Prime Minister Neville Chamberlain (1869–1940) of Britain offered to confer with Hitler, who then extended an invitation.

Britain's position regarding Czechoslovakia—the only democracy in Eastern Europe—was somewhat different from that of France. In 1924, France and Czechoslovakia had concluded an agreement of mutual assistance in the event that either was attacked by Germany. Czechoslovakia had a similar agreement with Russia, but with the provision that Russian assistance depended on France first fulfilling the terms of its agreement. Britain had no commitment to Czechoslovakia. Swallowing Hitler's propaganda, some British officials believed that the Sudeten Germans were indeed a suppressed minority entitled to self-determination and that the Sudetenland, like Austria, was not worth a war that could destroy Western civilization. Hitler, they said, only wanted to incorporate Germans living outside Germany; he was only carrying the noble principle of self-determination to its logical conclusion. Once these Germans lived under the German flag, argued these British officials, Hitler would be satisfied. In any case, Britain's failure to rearm between 1933 and 1938 weakened its position. The British chiefs of staff believed that the nation was not prepared to fight and that it was necessary to sacrifice Czechoslovakia to buy time.

Czechoslovakia's fate was decided at the Munich Conference (September 1938), attended by Chamberlain, Hitler, Mussolini, and Prime Minister Édouard Daladier (1884–1970) of France. The Munich Pact gave the Sudetenland to Germany. Both Chamberlain and Daladier were showered with praise by the people of Britain and France for keeping the peace. Hitler regarded these Western leaders as "little worms."

Chamberlain's critics have insisted that the Munich agreement was an enormous blunder and tragedy. Chamberlain, they say, was a fool to believe that Hitler, who sought domination over Europe, could be bought off with the Sudetenland. Hitler regarded concessions by Britain and France as signs of weakness; they only increased his appetite for more territory. Furthermore, argue the critics, it would have been better to fight Hitler in 1938 than a year later, when war actually did break out. To be sure, in the year following the Munich agreement, Britain increased its military arsenal, but so did Germany, which built submarines, planes, and heavy tanks; strengthened western border defenses; and trained more pilots. The Czechs had a sizable number of good tanks, and the Czech people were willing to fight to preserve their nation's territorial integrity. While the main elements of the German army were battling the Czechs, the French, who could mobilize a hundred divisions, could have broken through the German West Wall, which was defended by only five regular and four reserve divisions; then they could have invaded the Rhineland and devastated German industrial centers in the Ruhr. (Such a scenario, of course, depended on the French overcoming their psychological reluctance to take the offensive, which was doubtful given the attitude of the French general staff.)

After the annexation of the Sudetenland, Hitler plotted to crush Czechoslovakia out of existence. He encouraged the Slovak minority in Czechoslovakia, led by a Fascist priest, Josef Tiso, to demand complete separation. On the pretext of protecting the Slovak people's right of self-determination, Hitler ordered his troops to enter Prague. In March 1939, Czech independence ended.

The destruction of Czechoslovakia was a different matter from the remilitarization of the Rhineland, the Anschluss with Austria, and the annexation of the Sudetenland. In all these previous cases, Hitler could claim the right of self-determination, Woodrow Wilson's grand principle. However, the occupation of Prague and the end of Czech independence showed that Hitler really sought European hegemony. Outraged statesmen now demanded that the führer be deterred from further aggression.

Poland. After Czechoslovakia, Hitler turned to Poland and demanded, among other things, that Danzig be returned to Germany. Poland refused to restore the port, which was vital to its economy. On May 22, 1939, Hitler and Mussolini entered into the Pact of Steel, promising mutual aid in the event of war. The following day, Hitler told his officers that Germany's real goal was the destruction of Poland. "Danzig is not the objective. It is a matter of expanding our living space in the East, of making our food supplies secure. . . . There is therefore no question of sparing Poland, and the decision remains to attack Poland at the first suitable opportunity."[2]

Britain, France, and the Soviet Union had been engaged in negotiations since April. The Soviet Union wanted a mutual assistance pact, including joint military planning, and demanded bases in Poland and Romania in preparation for a German attack. Britain was reluctant to endorse these demands, fearing that a mutual assistance pact with Russia might cause Hitler to embark on a mad adventure that would drag Britain into war. Moreover, Poland would not allow Russian troops on its soil, fearing Russian expansion.

At the same time, Russia was conducting secret talks with Nazi Germany. Unlike the Allies, Germany could tempt Stalin with territory that would serve as a buffer between Germany and Russia. Besides, a treaty with Germany would give Russia time to strengthen its armed forces. On August 23, 1939, the two totalitarian states signed a nonaggression pact, stunning the world. A secret section of the pact called for the partition of Poland between Russia and Germany and Russian control over Lithuania, Latvia, and Estonia. By signing such an agreement with his enemy, Hitler had pulled off an extraordinary diplomatic coup: he blocked the Soviet Union, Britain, and France from duplicating their World War I alliance against Germany. The Nazi–Soviet Pact was the green light for an invasion of Poland, and at dawn on September 1, 1939, German troops crossed the frontier. When Germany did not respond to their demand for a halt to the invasion, Britain and France declared war.

THE NAZI BLITZKRIEG

The Conquest of Poland

Germany struck at Poland with speed and power. The German air force, the *Luftwaffe,* destroyed obsolete Polish planes, struck railways, hampering Polish mobilization; attacked tanks; pounded defense networks; and bombed Warsaw, terrorizing the population. Tanks opened up breaches in the Polish defenses, and mechanized columns overran the foot-marching Polish army, trapping large numbers of soldiers. The Polish high command could not cope with the incredible speed and co-ordination of German air and ground attacks. By September 8, the Germans had advanced to the outskirts of Warsaw. On September 17, Soviet troops invaded Poland from the east. On September 27, Poland surrendered. In less than a month, the Nazi *blitzkrieg* (lightning war) had vanquished Poland.

The Fall of France

For Hitler, the conquest of Poland was only the prelude to a German empire stretching from the

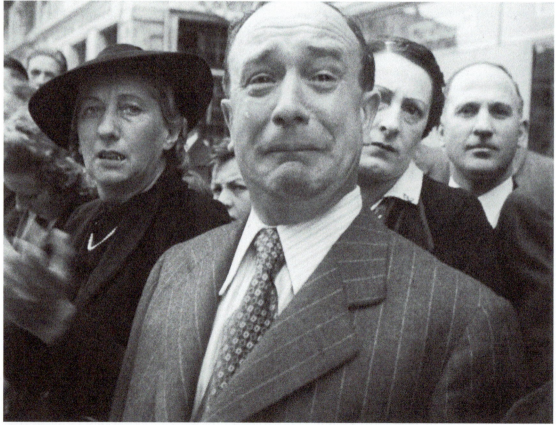

THE FALL OF FRANCE. French civilians of Marseilles show the shock of defeat in 1940. Hitler's army accomplished what the German generals of World War I had planned but not brought about: the defeat of France. The might of motorized warfare had prevailed over the French army and its outmoded World War I methods.

Atlantic to the Urals. When weather conditions were right, he would unleash a great offensive in the west. In early April 1940, the Germans struck at Denmark and Norway. Denmark surrendered within hours. A British and French force tried to assist the Norwegians, but the landings, badly coordinated and lacking in air support, failed.

On May 10, 1940, Hitler launched his offensive in the west with an invasion of neutral Belgium, Holland, and Luxembourg. On May 14, after the Luftwaffe had bombed Rotterdam, destroying the center of the city and killing many people, the Dutch surrendered. Meeting almost no resistance, German panzer (tank) divisions had moved through the narrow mountain passes of Luxembourg and the dense forest of Ardennes in southern Belgium. Thinking that the forest of Ardennes could not be penetrated by a major German force, the French had only lightly fortified the western extension of the Maginot Line. But on May 12, German units were on French soil near Sedan. Then the Germans raced across northern France to the sea, which they reached on May 20, cutting the Anglo-French forces in two.

The Germans now sought to surround and annihilate the Allied forces converging on the French seaport of Dunkirk, the last port of escape. But probably fearing that German tanks would lose mobility in the rivers and canals around Dunkirk, Hitler called them off just as they prepared to take the port. Instead, he ordered the Luftwaffe to wipe out the Allied troops, but fog and rain prevented German planes from operating at full strength, and British pilots inflicted heavy losses on the attackers. While the Luftwaffe bombed the beaches, some 338,000 British and French troops were ferried across the English Channel by destroyers, merchant ships, motorboats, fishing boats, tugboats, and private yachts. Hitler's personal decision to hold back his tanks made "the miracle of Dunkirk" possible.

Meanwhile, the battle for France was turning into a rout. With authority breaking down, demoralization spreading, and resistance dying, the French cabinet appealed for an armistice. It was signed on June 22 in the same railway car in which Germany had agreed to the armistice ending World War I.

How can the collapse of France be explained? France had somewhat fewer pilots and planes, particularly bombers, than Germany, but many French planes never left the airfields. France had planes, but the High Command either did not use them—which is still a cause of astonishment—or did not deploy them properly. In contrast, the German air force was an integral part of an offensive operation, providing support for advancing tanks and infantry and bombing behind enemy lines. As for tanks, the French had as many as the Germans, and some were superior, but they were spread among the infantry divisions, unlike the Germans, who organized their tanks in large formations in order to drive through enemy lines. Nor was German manpower overwhelming. France met disaster largely because its military leaders, unlike the German command, had not mastered the psychology and technology of motorized warfare. Put succinctly, the French were badly outgeneraled. One senses also that there was a loss of will among the French people—the result of internal political disputes, poor leadership, the years of appeasement and lost opportunities, and German propaganda, which depicted Nazism as irresistible and the führer as a man of destiny. It was France's darkest hour.

According to the terms of the armistice, Germany occupied northern France and the coast. The French military was demobilized, and the French government, now located at Vichy in the south, would collaborate with the German authorities in occupied France, even to the point of passing racial laws and assisting the Germans in deporting seventy-five thousand Jews, including eight thousand children under the age of thirteen, to the Nazi murder factory at Auschwitz. The leaders of Vichy and their supporters, many of them prominent intellectuals and anti-Dreyfusards in their youth, shared in the antidemocratic, anti-Marxist, and anti-Semitic tradition of the radical Right that had arrayed itself against the Third French Republic since the late nineteenth century. Refusing to recognize defeat, General Charles de Gaulle (1890–1970) escaped to London and organized the Free French forces. The Germans gloried in their revenge; the French wept in their humiliation; and the British gathered their courage, for they now stood alone.

GERMAN ATROCITIES. The invading Germans treated the Russian people, whom they regarded as racial inferiors, in a savage manner. They deliberately starved to death Russian prisoners of war and engaged in atrocities against civilians. Here Russians are looking for relatives and friends among seven thousand Crimean villagers slaughtered by the Germans.

The Battle of Britain

Hitler expected that, after his stunning victories in the West, Britain would make peace. The British, however, continued to reject Hitler's peace overtures, for they envisioned only a bleak future if Hitler dominated the Continent. After the German victory in Norway, Chamberlain's support in the House of Commons had eroded, and he had been replaced by Winston Churchill, who had opposed appeasement. Dynamic, courageous, and eloquent, Churchill had the capacity to stir and lead his people in the struggle against Nazism. "The Battle of Britain is about to begin," Churchill told them. "Upon this battle depends the survival of Christian civilization. . . . [I]f we

fail, then . . . all we have known and cared for will sink into the abyss of a new Dark Age."[3]

Finding Britain unwilling to come to terms, Hitler proceeded in earnest with invasion plans. But a successful crossing of the English Channel and the establishment of beachheads on the English coast depended on control of the skies. Marshal Hermann Goering assured Hitler that his Luftwaffe could destroy the British Royal Air Force (RAF), and in early August 1940, the Luftwaffe began massive attacks on British air and naval installations. Virtually every day during the battle of Britain, weather permitting, hundreds of planes fought in the sky above Britain. Convinced that Goering could not fulfill his promise to destroy British air defenses and unwilling to absorb more losses in planes and trained pilots, Hitler called off the invasion. The development of radar by British scientists, the skill and courage of British fighter pilots, and the unwillingness of Germany to absorb more losses in planes and pilots saved Britain in its struggle for survival. With the invasion of Britain called off, the Luftwaffe concentrated on bombing English cities, industrial centers, and ports in the hopes of eroding Britain's military potential and undermining civilian morale. Every night for months, the inhabitants of London sought shelter in subways and cellars to escape German bombs, while British planes rose time after time to make the Luftwaffe pay the price. British morale never broke during the "Blitz."

Britain, by itself, had no hope of defeating the Third Reich. What ultimately changed the course of the war were Germany's invasion of the Soviet Union in June 1941 and Japan's attack on the United States on December 7, 1941. With the entry of these two powers, a coalition was created that had the human and material resources to reverse the tide of battle.

The Invasion of Russia

The obliteration of Bolshevism and the conquest, exploitation, and colonization of Russia by the German master race were cardinal elements of Hitler's ideology. To prevent any interference with the forthcoming invasion of Russia, the Balkan flank had to be secured. On April 6, 1941, the Germans struck at both Greece, where an Italian attack had failed, and Yugoslavia. Yugoslavia was quickly overrun, and Greece, although aided by fifty thousand British, New Zealander, and Australian troops, fell at the end of April.

For the war against Russia, Hitler had assembled a massive force: some four million men, thirty-three hundred tanks, and two thousand planes. Evidence of the German buildup abounded, but a stubborn Stalin ignored these warnings. Desperate to avoid war with Nazi Germany, Stalin would take no action that he feared might provoke Hitler. Consequently, the Red Army was vulnerable to the German blitzkrieg. In the early hours of June 22, 1941, the Germans launched their offensive over a wide front. Raiding Russian airfields, the Luftwaffe destroyed 1,200 aircraft on the first day. The Germans drove deeply into Russia, cutting up and surrounding the disorganized and unprepared Russian forces. The Russians suffered horrendous losses. In a little more than three months, 2.5 million Russian soldiers had been killed, wounded, or captured and 14,000 tanks destroyed. Describing the war as a crusade to save Europe from "Jewish Bolshevik subhumans," German propaganda claimed that victory was assured.

But there were also disquieting signs for the Nazi invaders. The Russians, who had a proven capacity to endure hardships, fought doggedly and courageously for the motherland, and the government would not consider capitulation. Russian reserve strength was far greater than the Germans had estimated. Far from its supply lines, the Wehrmacht (German army) was running short of fuel, and trucks and cars had to contend with primitive roads that turned into seas of mud when the autumn rains came. Compounding the supply problem were attacks behind German lines by Russian partisans determined to inflict pain on the hated invaders. Early and bitter cold weather hampered the German attempt to capture Moscow. The Germans advanced to within twenty miles of Moscow, but on December 6, a Red Army counterattack forced them to postpone the assault on the Russian capital.

By the end of 1941, Germany had conquered vast regions of Russia but had failed to bring the country to its knees. There would be no repetition of the collapse of France. Moreover, by moving machinery and workers east far beyond the German reach, the Soviets were able to replenish their military hardware, which was almost totally destroyed during the first six months of the war. Driven by patriotic fervor—and by fear of the omnipresent NKVD agents searching for malingerers—Russian factory workers, many of them the wives and daughters of soldiers at the front, toiled relentlessly, heroically. Employing modern production methods, acquired in large measure from American technical assistance provided before the war, the Soviets were soon producing more planes and tanks than Germany. The Russian campaign demonstrated that the Russian people would make incredible sacrifices for their land and that the Nazis were not invincible.

SOVIET UNION

Caspian Sea

Russian Front, Dec. 1941

Stalingrad

Volga R.

Russian Front, Nov. 1942

Don R.

SYRIA

TRANS-JORDAN (Br. Mandate)

TURKEY

•Moscow

•Tula

Ankara•

LEBANON

•Smolensk

Kiev•

Bucharest•

PALESTINE (Br. Mandate)

Suez Canal

Black Sea

•Yalta

Athens•

Alexandria•

•Cairo

Nile R.

El Alamein (Summer 1942)

EGYPT

Russian Front, Spring 1944

Pinsk•

UKRAINE

ROMANIA

Sofia•

BULGARIA

Crete

Mediterranean Sea

L. Ladoga

Leningrad

FINLAND

Helsinki•

Riga•

Russian Front, Feb. 1945

Warsaw•

Posen•

POLAND

Krakow•

SLOVAKIA

HUNGARY

Budapest•

Vienna•

GREECE

Malta (Gr. Br.)

Stockholm•

Baltic Sea

SWEDEN

Copenhagen•

Berlin•

Elbe R.

GERMANY

CZECHOSLOVAKIA

AUSTRIA

YUGOSLAVIA

ALBANIA

Italian Front, Feb. 1945

Monte Cassino (May 1944)

Salerno (Sept. 1943)

LIBYA

NORWAY

Oslo•

DENMARK

North Sea

Rotterdam•

Antwerp•

NETHERLANDS

BELGIUM

Battle of the Bulge (Dec. 1944)

Rhine R.

ITALY

Rome•

Anzio•

Bologna•

Rommel defeated in Tunisia (May 1943)

Tunis•

TUNISIA

GREAT BRITAIN

Battle of Britain (Fall 1940)

London•

Dunkirk•

Bastogne•

Sedan•

Western Front, Feb. 1945

SWITZERLAND

Sicily (July 1943)

NORTHERN IRELAND

IRELAND

English Channel

Invasion of Normandy (June 6, 1944)

NORMANDY

Paris•

FRANCE

Vichy•

VICHY FRANCE (Occupied Nov. 1942)

Algiers•

ALGERIA (Vichy France)

ATLANTIC OCEAN

Madrid•

SPAIN

Gibraltar (Gr. Br.)

SP. MOROCCO

FRENCH MOROCCO

PORTUGAL

Lisbon•

Casablanca (Nov. 1942)

Hitler's Greater Germany

Allied with Germany

Occupied by Germany and its allies

Advances by Allied forces

Major battle

400 Mi.

400 Km.

200

200

0

0

© 2016 Cengage Learning.

THE NEW ORDER

By 1942, Germany ruled virtually all of Europe, from the Atlantic to deep into Russia. Some conquered territory was annexed outright; other lands were administered by German officials; in still other countries, the Germans ruled through local officials sympathetic to Nazism or willing to collaborate with the Germans. On this vast empire, Hitler and his henchmen imposed a new order designed to serve the interests of the master race.

Exploitation and Terror

The Germans systematically looted the countries they conquered, taking gold, art treasures, machinery, and food supplies back to Germany and exploiting the industrial and agricultural potential of non-German lands to aid the German war economy. The Nazis also made slave laborers of conquered peoples. Some seven million people from all over Europe were wrested from their homes and transported to Germany. These forced laborers, particularly the Russians, Poles, and Jews, whom Nazi ideology classified as a lower form of humanity, lived in wretched, unheated barracks and were poorly fed and overworked; many died of disease, hunger, and exhaustion. Many of Germany's most prominent firms collaborated in the enslavement and brutalization of foreign workers. The ransacking of occupied lands, the seizure of Jewish property throughout Europe, and the exploitation of foreign forced labor kept Germans largely prosperous and content until the last year of the war.

The Nazis ruled by force and terror. The prison cell, the torture chamber, the firing squad, and the concentration camp symbolized the new order. In the Polish province annexed to Germany, the Nazis jailed and executed intellectuals and priests, closed all schools and most

◀ *Map 20.1* World War II: The European Theater By 1942, Germany ruled virtually all of Europe from the Atlantic to deep into Russia. Germany's defeat at Stalingrad in Russia and El Alamein in North Africa were decisive turning points.

churches, and forbade Poles to hold professional positions. In the region of Poland administered by German officials, most schools above the fourth grade were shut down. The Germans were especially ruthless toward the Russians. Soviet political officials were immediately executed; many prisoners of war were herded into camps and deliberately starved to death. In all, the Germans took some 5.5 million Russian prisoners, of whom about 3.5 million perished, primarily from starvation.

German soldiers routinely abused innocents: they stripped Russian peasants of their winter clothing and boots before driving them into the freezing outdoors to die of cold and starvation, slaughtered large numbers of hostages, burned whole villages to the ground in reprisal for partisan attacks, and deported massive numbers of people for slave labor. To the German invaders drenched in Nazi ideology, the Russians were "Asiatic bestial hordes" led by sinister "subhuman" Jews who aimed to destroy Germany. Recent studies, largely by German historians, demonstrate how committed the Wehrmacht command—and not just the SS who committed genocide and other atrocities—was to Nazi ideological aims, how willingly senior and junior officers propagated Nazi ideology among the troops. Letters and diaries reveal how ideologically devoted average soldiers were to Nazism. Both the high command and common soldiers, who represented a cross section of German society, were implicated in war crimes, including the extermination of the Jews.

The Holocaust

Against the Jews of Europe, the Germans waged a war of extermination. The task of imposing the "Final Solution of the Jewish Problem" was given to Himmler's SS. Himmler fulfilled his grisly duties with fanaticism and bureaucratic efficiency. He and the SS believed that they had a holy mission to rid the world of worthless life—a satanic foe that was plotting to destroy Germany. Regarding themselves as righteous and courageous idealists who were writing a glorious chapter in the history of Germany, the SS tortured and murdered with immense dedication.

Special squads of the SS—the *Einsatzgruppen,* trained for mass murder—followed on the heels of the German army into Russia. Entering captured villages and cities, they rounded up Jewish men, women, and children, herded them to execution grounds, and slaughtered them with machine-gun and rifle fire at the edge of open trenches, which sometimes were piled high with thousands of victims, including severely wounded people who would suffocate to death when the pit was filled with earth. Aided by Ukrainian, Lithuanian, and Latvian auxiliaries, the Einsatzgruppen massacred some 1.3 million Russian Jews—the commanders kept meticulous records of each *Aktion.* Not just the SS, but units of the regular German army, the Wehrmacht, actively participated in the rounding up of Jews and sometimes in the shootings. Despite the denials of staff officers after the war, evidence from their own files reveals that they knew full well that the extermination of the Jews was state policy that their soldiers were helping to implement. To speed up the Final Solution, extermination camps were built in Poland. Jews from all over Europe were rounded up, jammed into sealed cattle cars, and shipped to Treblinka, Auschwitz, and other death camps, where they entered another world:

> *Corpses were strewn all over the road; bodies were hanging from the barbed wire fence; the sound of shots rang in the air continuously. Blazing flames shot into the sky; a giant smoke cloud ascended about them. Starving, emaciated human skeletons stumbled forward toward us, uttering incoherent sounds. They fell down right in front of our eyes gasping out their last breath.*
>
> *Here and there a hand tried to reach up, but when this happened an SS man came right away and stepped on it. Those who were merely exhausted were simply thrown on the dead pile. . . . Every night a truck came by, and all of them, dead or not, were thrown on it and taken to the crematory.*[4]

SS doctors quickly inspected the new arrivals— "the freight," as they referred to them. Those unfit for work, including children, were immediately exterminated in gas chambers. Those not gassed faced a living death in the camp, which also included non-Jewish inmates. The SS relished their absolute power over the inmates and took sadistic pleasure in humiliating and brutalizing their Jewish victims. When exhausted, starved, diseased, and beaten prisoners became unfit for work, generally within a few months, they were sent to the gas chambers.

Many of the SS were true believers, committed to racist and Social Darwinist fantasies. To realize their mythic vision of ultimate good, they had to destroy the Jews, whom Nazi ideology designated as less-than-human but also immensely evil, powerful, and dangerous enemies of Germany and Aryan civilization. For these racist ideologues, Jews were unworthy of life. A Jewish physician-inmate at Auschwitz asked one of the Nazi doctors who selected Jews for the gas chamber how he could reconcile extermination with the Hippocratic oath he took to preserve life. The Nazi replied:

> *Of course I am a doctor and I want to preserve life. And out of respect for human life I would remove a gangrenous appendix from a diseased body. The Jew is the gangrenous appendix in the body of mankind.*[5]

Assisting the SS was an army of bureaucrats, transportation employees, town officials, local police, and other involved in rounding up and deporting Jews to the death camps. Many Germans and their collaborators in occupied lands were ordinary people doing their duty as they had been trained to do, following orders the best way they knew how. They were morally indifferent bureaucrats, concerned with techniques and effectiveness, and careerists and functionaries seeking to impress superiors with their ability to get the job done. Sharing in the Nazi vision, many of these "ordinary people" were willing if not dedicated participants in genocide. Thus, as Konnilyn G. Feig notes, thousands of German railway workers "treated the Jewish cattle-car transports as a special business problem that they took pride in solving so well."[6] German physicians who selected Jews for the gas chambers were concerned only with technical problems and efficiency, and those doctors who performed unspeakable medical experiments on Jews viewed their subjects as laboratory animals. German industrialists who worked Jewish slave laborers to death considered only cost—effectiveness in their operations. So, too, did the firms that built the gas chambers and the furnaces, whose durability and performance they guaranteed.

An eyewitness reports that engineers from Topf and Sons experimented with different combinations of corpses, deciding that "the most economical and fuel-saving procedure would be to burn the bodies of a well-nourished man and an emaciated woman or vice versa together with that of a child, because, as the experiments had established, in this combination, once they had caught fire, the dead would continue to burn without any further coke being required."[7] Rudolf Hoess, the commandant of Auschwitz, who exemplified the bureaucratic mentality, noted that his gas chambers were more efficient than those used at Treblinka because they could accommodate far more people. The Germans were so concerned with efficiency and cost that—to conserve ammunition or gas and not slow down the pace from the time victims were ordered to undress until they were hurried into the gas chambers—toddlers were taken from their mothers and thrown live into burning pits or mass graves.

When the war ended, the SS murderers and those who had assisted them returned to families and jobs, resuming a normal life, free of remorse and untroubled by guilt. "The human ability to normalize the abnormal is frightening indeed," observes sociologist Rainer C. Baum.[8] Mass murderers need not be psychopaths. It is a "disturbing psychological truth," states Robert Jay Lifton, that "ordinary people can commit demonic acts."[9]

There have been many massacres during the course of world history. And the Nazis murdered many non-Jews in concentration camps and in reprisal for acts of resistance. What is unique about the Holocaust—the systematic extermination of European Jewry—was the Nazis' determination to murder, without exception, every single Jew who came within their grasp, and the fanaticism, ingenuity, cruelty, and systematic way (industrialized murder) with which they pursued this goal. Despite the protests of the army, the SS murdered Jews whose labor was needed for the war effort, and when Germany's military position was desperate, the SS still diverted military personnel and railway cars to deport Jews to the death camps.

The Holocaust was the grisly fulfillment of Nazi racial theories. Believing that they were cleansing Europe of a lower and dangerous race that threatened the German people, Nazi executioners performed their evil work with dedication and resourcefulness, with precision and moral indifference—a gruesome testament to human irrationality and wickedness. Using the technology and bureaucracy of a modern state, the Germans killed approximately six million Jews—*two-thirds* of the Jewish population of Europe. Some 1.5 million of the murdered were children; almost 90 percent of Jewish children in German-occupied lands perished. Tens of thousands of entire families were wiped out without a trace. Centuries-old Jewish community life vanished, never to be restored. Burned into the soul of the Jewish people was a wound that could never entirely heal. For generations to come Germans would be compelled to reflect on this most shameful period in their history. Written into the history of Western civilization was an episode that would forever cast doubt on the Enlightenment conception of human goodness, rationality, and the progress of civilization.

Resistance

Each occupied country had its collaborators, including government officials, business elites, and right-wing intellectuals, who welcomed the demise of democracy, saw Hitler as Europe's best defense against Communism, and profited from the sale of war materiel. Each country also produced a resistance movement that grew stronger as Nazi barbarism became more visible and the prospects of a German defeat more likely. The Nazis retaliated by torturing and executing captured resistance fighters and killing hostages—generally fifty for every German killed.

In Western Europe, the resistance rescued downed Allied airmen, radioed military intelligence to Britain, and sabotaged German installations. Norwegians blew up the German stock of heavy water needed for atomic research. The Danish underground sabotaged railways and smuggled into neutral Sweden almost all of Denmark's eight thousand Jews just before they were to be deported to the death camps. After the

© Topham Picturepoint/The Image Works.

CONCENTRATION CAMP SURVIVORS. Thousands of emaciated and diseased inmates of German concentration camps died in the weeks after liberation by the Allies. These camps will forever remain a monument to the capacity of human beings for inhumanity.

Allies landed on the coast of France in June 1944, the French resistance delayed the movement of German reinforcements and liberated sections of the country.

In Eastern Europe, resistance took the form of guerrilla warfare and sabotage. In August 1944, with Soviet forces approaching Warsaw, the Poles staged a full-scale revolt against the German occupiers. The Poles appealed to the Soviets, camped ten miles away, for help. Thinking about a future Russian-dominated Poland, the Soviets did not move. After sixty-three days of street fighting and the massacre of Polish hostages, remnants of the Polish underground surrendered, and the Germans methodically destroyed what was left of Warsaw. In the Soviet Union, Russian partisans

numbered several hundred thousand men and women. Operating behind the German lines, they sabotaged railways, destroyed trucks, and killed thousands of German soldiers in hit-and-run attacks. In Yugoslavia, the mountains and forests provided excellent terrain for guerrilla warfare. The leading Yugoslav resistance army was headed by Josip Broz (1892–1980), better known as Tito. Moscow-trained, intelligent, and courageous, Tito organized his partisans into a disciplined fighting force that tied down a huge German army and ultimately liberated the country from German rule. Jews participated in the resistance in all countries and were particularly prominent in the French resistance. Specifically Jewish resistance organizations emerged in Eastern Europe, and revolts took place in the ghettos and concentration camps. In the spring of 1943, the surviving Jews of the Warsaw ghetto, armed with only a few guns and homemade bombs, fought the Germans for several weeks.

Italy and Germany also had resistance movements. After the Allies landed in Italy in 1943, bands of Italian partisans helped to liberate Italy from Fascism and the German occupation. In Germany, army officers plotted to assassinate the führer. On July 20, 1944, Colonel Claus von Stauffenberg planted a bomb at a staff conference attended by Hitler, but the führer escaped serious injury. In retaliation, some five thousand suspected anti-Nazis were imprisoned, two hundred of whom were immediately tortured and executed in barbarous fashion. More would be executed in succeeding months.

THE TURN OF THE TIDE

While Germany was subduing Europe, its ally, Japan, was extending its dominion over much of Asia. Seeking raw materials and secure markets for Japanese goods and driven by a xenophobic nationalism, Japan in 1931 had attacked Manchuria in northern China. Quickly overrunning the province, the Japanese established the puppet state of Manchukuo in 1932. After a period of truce, the war against China was renewed in July 1937. Japan captured leading cities, including China's principal seaports, and inflicted heavy casualties on the poorly organized Chinese forces, obliging the government of Jiang Jieshi (Chiang Kai-shek) to withdraw to Chungking in the interior.

The Japanese Offensive

In 1940, after the defeat of France and with Britain standing alone against Nazi Germany, Japan eyed Southeast Asia—French Indochina, British Burma and Malaya, and the Dutch East Indies. From these lands, Japan planned to obtain the oil, rubber, and tin vitally needed by Japanese industry and enough rice to feed the nation. Japan hoped that a quick strike against the American fleet in the Pacific would give it

time to enlarge and consolidate its empire. On December 7, 1941, the Japanese struck with carrier-based planes at Pearl Harbor in Hawaii. Taken by surprise—despite warning signs—the Americans suffered a total defeat: the attackers sank 17 ships, including 7 of the 8 battleships; destroyed 188 airplanes and damaged 159 others; and killed 2,403 men. The Japanese lost only 29 planes. After the attack on Pearl Harbor, Germany declared war on the United States. Now the immense American industrial capacity could be put to work against the Axis powers—Germany, Italy, and Japan. American factories produced planes, tanks, and ships at a pace and scale that astonished both friend and foe. The American arsenal supplied Britain and the Soviet Union with badly needed equipment.

Defeat of the Axis Powers

By the spring of 1942, the Axis powers held the upper hand. The Japanese empire included the coast of China, Indochina (Vietnam), Thailand, Burma, Malaya, the Dutch East Indies (Indonesia), the Philippines, and other islands in the Pacific. Germany controlled Europe almost to Moscow. When the year ended, however, the Allies seemed assured of victory. Three decisive battles—Midway, Stalingrad, and El Alamein—reversed the tide of war.

In June 1942, the main body of the Japanese fleet headed for Midway, eleven hundred miles northwest of Pearl Harbor; another section sailed toward the Aleutian Islands, in an attempt to divide the American fleet. But the Americans had broken the Japanese naval code and were aware of the Japanese plan. On June 4, 1942, the two navies fought a strange naval battle; it was waged entirely by carrier-based planes, for the fleets were too far from each other to use their big guns. American pilots destroyed four Japanese aircraft carriers stacked with planes. The battle of Midway cost Japan the initiative. With American industrial production accelerating, the opportunity for a Japanese victory had passed.

After being stymied at the outskirts of Moscow in December 1941, the Germans renewed their offensive in the spring and summer of 1942.

Japanese Empire, 1931
Japanese Empire, 1942
Extent of Japanese expansion
Allied advances

SOVIET UNION

ASIA

MONGOLIA

MANCHURIA

Peiping
(Beijng)

KOREA

CHINA

Hiroshima

Shanghai

Nagasaki

JAPAN

Tokyo

Attu

Kiska
1943

Aleutian Is.

PACIFIC OCEAN

Midway 1942

Taiwan

BURMA

Hong Kong

THAILAND

FRENCH
INDOCHINA

MALAYA

Singapore

Sumatra

Borneo

Dutch East Indies

Java

INDIAN OCEAN

Iwo Jima
1945

Okinawa
1945

Mariana Is.

Saipan

Guam
1944

Manila

Philippine Is.

Leyte 1944

Wake

Marshall
Is.

Caroline Is.

Hawaiian Is.
Pearl Harbor

Tawara
1943

Gilbert Is.

New
Guinea

Solomon Is.

Guadalcanal
1942

AUSTRALIA

Brisbane

0   500   1000 Km.

0   500   1000 Mi.

Hitler's goal was Stalingrad, the great industrial center located on the Volga River; control of Stalingrad would give Germany command of vital rail transportation and access to the oil fields of the Caucasus. The battle of Stalingrad was an epic struggle in which Russian soldiers and civilians fought for every building and street of their city. In this urban battlefield, scarred by mile after mile of destroyed buildings and mountains of rubble, the combatants were separated by mere yards; snipers, some of them Russian women, lurked in the maze of ruins; and tough Russian soldiers stealthily and ceaselessly attacked at night with bayonets and daggers; here the blitzkrieg, which had brought the Germans immense success in their earlier offensives, did not apply. So brutal was the fighting that at night half-crazed dogs sought to escape the city by swimming across the river. One German soldier wrote in his diary at the end of December: "The horses have already been eaten . . . the soldiers look like corpses or lunatics looking for something to put in their mouths. They no longer take cover from Russian shells; they haven't the strength to walk, run away and hide."[10]

A Russian counterattack in November, planned by General (later Marshal) Georgi Zhukov, caught the Germans in a trap. With his soldiers exhausted and desperately short of food, medical supplies, weapons, and ammunition, Friedrich Paulus, commander of the Sixth Army, urged Hitler to order a withdrawal before the Russians closed the ring. The führer refused. After suffering tens of thousands of additional casualties, their position hopeless, the remnants of the Sixth Army surrendered on February 2, 1943. Some 260,000 German soldiers had perished in the battle of Stalingrad, and another 110,000 were taken prisoner.

The Soviet High Command, which had performed terribly in the early days of the German offensive, distinguished itself at Stalingrad. At the battle of Kursk in July 1943, Russian military leaders again demonstrated an increasing ability to master the technique of modern warfare. Analyzing correctly that the Germans would attack the Kursk salient, Marshal Georgi Zhukov turned the area into a fortress. Although Soviet casualties were greater than the Germans, the Red Army had beaten back the best combat units of the Wehrmacht, inflicting heavy losses of men and materiel in the process. The operation, which included an epic tank battle, had depleted the German military of almost all its reserves on the Eastern Front. The momentum had turned. The Wehrmacht and its panzer armies were now on the defensive. The initiative had passed to the Red Army.

In January 1941, the British were routing the Italians in northern Africa. Hitler assigned General Erwin Rommel (1891–1944) to halt the British advance. Rommel drove the British out of Libya and, with strong reinforcements, might have taken Egypt and the Suez Canal. But Hitler's concern was with seizing Yugoslavia and Greece and preparing for the invasion of Russia. Early, in 1942, Rommel resumed his advance, intending to conquer Egypt. The British Eighth Army, commanded by General Bernard L. Montgomery, stopped him at the battle of El Alamein in October 1942. The victory of El Alamein was followed by an Anglo-American invasion of northwest Africa in November 1942. By May 1943, the Germans and Italians were defeated in northern Africa.

After securing northern Africa, the Allies, seeking complete control of the Mediterranean, invaded Sicily in July 1943 and quickly conquered the island. Mussolini's fellow Fascist leaders turned against him, and the king dismissed him as prime minister. In September, the new government surrendered to the Allies, and in the following month, Italy declared war on Germany. Italian partisans—their number would grow to three hundred thousand—resisted the occupying German troops, who were determined to hold on to central and northern Italy. At the same time, the Allies fought their way up the peninsula. Captured by partisans, Mussolini was executed on April 28, 1945, and his dead body, hanging upside down, was publicly displayed.

◀ *Map 20.2* World War II: The Pacific Theater The battle of Midway was a major turning point in the Pacific theater. The map also shows the island-hopping of the Americans that brought them closer to Japan. The battles of Iwo Jima and Okinawa were particularly brutal.

Primary Source

Historical Division, War Department:
Omaha Beachhead

Ultimately the success of the Allied invasion of France, D-day, depended on what happened during the first few hours. If the Allies had failed to secure beachheads, the operation would have ended in disaster. As the following reading illustrates, some of the hardest fighting took place on Omaha Beach, which was attacked by the Americans. This extract, published in 1945, comes from a study prepared in the field by the Second Information and Historical Service attached to the First Army and by the Historical Section, European Theater of Operations.

The outstanding fact about these first two hours of action is that despite heavy casualties, loss of equipment, disorganization, and all the other discouraging features of the landings, the assault troops did not stay pinned down behind the sea wall and embankment. At half-a-dozen or more points on the long stretch, they found the necessary drive to leave their cover and move out over the open beach flat toward the bluffs. Prevented by circumstance of mislandings from using carefully rehearsed tactics, they improvised assault methods to deal with what defenses they found before them. In nearly every case where advance was attempted, it carried through the enemy beach defenses. . . .

Various factors, some of them difficult to evaluate, played a part in the success of these advances. . . . But the decisive factor was leadership. Wherever an advance was made, it depended on the presence of some few individuals, officers and noncommissioned officers, who inspired, encouraged, or bullied their men forward, often by making the first forward moves. On Easy Red a lieutenant and a wounded sergeant of divisional engineers stood up under fire and walked over to inspect the wire obstacles just beyond the embankment. The lieutenant came back and, hands on hips, looked down disgustedly at the men lying behind the shingle bank. "Are you going to lay there and get killed, or get up and do something about it?" Nobody stirred, so the sergeant and the officer got the materials and blew the wire. On the same sector, where a group advancing across the flat was held up by a marshy area suspected of being mined, it was a lieutenant of engineers who crawled ahead through the mud on his belly, probing for mines with a hunting knife in the absence of other equipment. When remnants of an isolated boat section of Company B, 116th Infantry, were stopped by fire from a well-concealed emplacement, the lieutenant in charge went after it single-handed. In trying to grenade the rifle pit he was hit by three rifle bullets and eight grenade fragments, including some from his own grenade. He turned his map and compass over to a sergeant and ordered his group to press on inland. . . .

. . . Col. George A. Taylor arrived in the second section at 0815 and found plenty to do on the beach. Men were still hugging the embankment, disorganized, and suffering casualties from mortar and artillery fire. Colonel Taylor summed up the situation in terse phrase: "Two kinds of people are staying on this beach, the dead and those who are going to die—now let's get the hell out of here." Small groups of men were collected without regard to units, put under charge of the nearest noncommissioned officer, and sent on through the wire and across the flat, while engineers worked hard to widen gaps in the wire and to mark lanes through the minefields.

Question for Analysis

1. What drove the almost paralyzed American soldiers to move across the open beaches and attack German positions?

Omaha Beachhead, prepared by the Historical Division, War Department (Washington D.C.: U.S. Government Printing Office, 1945), 58–59, 71.

On June 6, 1944, D-day, the Allies landed on the beaches of Normandy in France. They had assembled a massive force for the liberation of Europe: two million men and over seven thousand vessels. The success of D-day depended on securing the beaches, which the Allies did despite stubborn German resistance. On some beaches the soldiers struggled ashore in the face of intense enemy fire. At Omaha Beach, the Americans almost did not make it. Landing craft packed with soldiers were destroyed by German mines. Weighed down by heavy equipment, men drowned as they were tossed by high waves; others were killed or wounded by machine-gun fire before reaching the beach. Much of the heavy armor was lost. Those who stumbled ashore hugged the embankment and sheltered themselves behind whatever barrier they could find to escape the German guns firing from the cliffs. Traumatized by ferocious German fire and the wounded and dead surrounding them, and often leaderless, the soldiers, many of them facing combat for the first time, seemed paralyzed. But amid the chaos, men began to advance and overwhelm the German positions.

By the end of July, the Allies had built up their strength in France to a million men, and after much hard fighting, by the end of August drove the Germans out of most of France.

After their heady victories in France, Allied commanders thought that Germany was virtually finished, that the war would be over before the end of the year. But Germany mobilized its remaining manpower and regrouped divisions that had been shattered in France. And through a herculean effort, the German armaments industry continued to function at a high level, despite massive Allied bombardments. In the autumn, the Allied advance was halted as the revamped German forces inflicted heavy casualties on the Allies in southern Holland, the German border city of Aachen, and the Huertgen Forest on the border of Belgium and Germany. Nevertheless, as winter approached the situation looked hopeless for Germany. Brussels and the vital port of Antwerp fell to the Allies; Allied planes mass bombed German cites in terror raids that took a horrendous toll of life, creating a morale problem. Although German civilians continued to perform their duties in the workplace, many had lost hope in a German victory and only wanted the war to end. By destroying fuel depots and the transportation network, the air bombardments helped erode Germany's industrial potential.

Desperate, Hitler made one last gamble. In mid-December 1944, he launched an offensive to split the Allied forces and regain the vital port of Antwerp. The Allies were taken by surprise in the Battle of the Bulge, but a heroic defense by the Americans at Bastogne—an important road junction—helped stop the German offensive. German losses in Hitler's failed gamble proved insurmountable. With its reserve strength now depleted beyond restitution and its industrial capacity eroded by Allied bombings, Germany lacked the manpower, tanks, planes, and fuel to forestall an Allied assault into its heartland from the west or to turn back the Red Army.

In June 1944, the Russians launched a major offensive advancing into the Baltic states, Poland, and Hungary. By February 1945, they stood within one hundred miles of Berlin. Yet German soldiers continued to fight with remarkable skill, inflicting proportionately greater casualties than they suffered. They were driven by a fanatic devotion to Hitler and Nazi racial ideology, loyalty to their comrades and the endangered fatherland, and fear of both vengeful Russians and the SS and other special units charged with executing "defeatists."

By April 1945, British, American, and Russian troops were penetrating deeper into Germany from east and west. From his underground bunker near the chancellery in Berlin, Hitler, physically exhausted and emotionally unhinged, engaged in wild fantasies about new German victories. On April 30, 1945, with the Russians only blocks away, the führer took his own life. On May 7, 1945, a demoralized and devastated Germany surrendered unconditionally.

In the Pacific war, after the victory at Midway in June 1942, American forces attacked strategic islands held by Japan. American troops had to battle their way up beaches and through jungles tenaciously defended by Japanese soldiers, who believed that death was preferable to the disgrace of surrender. In March 1945, twenty-one thousand Japanese perished on Iwo Jima; another hundred thousand died on Okinawa in April 1945 as they contested for every inch of the island.

On August 6, 1945, the United States dropped an atomic bomb on Hiroshima, killing more than seventy-eight thousand people and demolishing 60 percent of the city. President Harry S Truman said that he ordered the atomic attack to avoid

© Bettmann/Corbis.

HIROSHIMA AFTER THE ATOMIC BOMB. The mass destruction of Hiroshima ushered in a new age. Nuclear weapons gave humanity the capacity to destroy civilization.

an American invasion of the Japanese homeland, which would have cost hundreds of thousands of lives. Truman's decision has aroused considerable debate. Some analysts maintain that dropping the bomb was unnecessary. They say that Japan, deprived of oil, rice, and other essentials by an American naval blockade and defenseless against unrelenting aerial bombardments, was close to surrender and had indicated as much. It has been suggested that because the Soviet Union was about to enter the conflict against Japan, Truman wanted to end the war immediately, thus depriving the U.S.S.R. of an opportunity to extend its influence in East Asia. On August 8, Russia did enter the war against Japan, invading Manchuria. After a second atomic bomb was dropped on Nagasaki on August 9, the Japanese asked for peace.

THE LEGACY OF WORLD WAR II

World War II was the most destructive war in history. The total war waged by the combatants also enveloped civilians, who were victims of reprisals, genocide, slave labor, and aerial bombardment of cities. Estimates of the number of dead range as high as 50 million, including some 25 million Russians (one in three Russians lost a father) who sacrificed more than the other participants in both population and material resources. (In comparison, the United States suffered 400,000 service deaths.)

Material costs were staggering. Everywhere cities were in rubble; bridges, railway systems, waterways, and harbors destroyed; farmlands laid waste; livestock killed; coal mines wrecked. Homeless and hungry people wandered the streets and roads. Europe faced the gigantic task of rebuilding. Yet Europe did recover from this material blight, and with astonishing speed.

The war produced a vast migration of peoples unparalleled in modern European history. The Soviet Union annexed the Baltic lands of Latvia, Lithuania, and Estonia, forcibly deporting many of the native inhabitants into central Russia. The bulk of East Prussia was taken over by Poland, and Russia annexed the northeastern portion. Millions of Germans fled the invading Russians, who, bent on revenge for the misery the

Nazis had inflicted on their kin and country, committed numerous atrocities, including indiscriminate killing and mass rape, before Soviet authorities ended the mayhem. Millions more Germans were driven out of Poland, Czechoslovakia, Yugoslavia, Romania, and Hungary—places where their ancestors had lived for centuries—by vengeful Eastern Europeans. Moreover, leaders in these countries, driven by nationalist aspirations, welcomed an opportunity to rid their nations of an ethnic minority, particularly since so many of these Germans had aided the Nazi occupiers. In 1945 and 1946, some 12 million to 13 million Germans were driven westward. Expelled from their homes, often with only a few minutes' warning, they had to leave almost everything behind. Those herded into internment camps were brutalized by Polish and Czech guards who relished the opportunity to torment Germans. Hundreds of thousands died from malnutrition, disease, exposure, and mistreatment and suicide. Ironically, the German expellees who managed to start a new life in West Germany escaped the Communist dictatorships imposed on the Czechs and Poles who had expelled them, often with great cruelty.

After the war many German war criminals went into hiding, changed their identity, lied about their wartime record, or fled to other countries, particularly South America. A substantial number of escapees, including major war criminals involved in mass murder, were aided by Austrian, German, and Croatian clerics, some of them important figures at the Vatican. They provided fleeing Nazis with safe houses, money, and forged documents. With the Cold War looming, Nazi war criminals escaped justice by working with American, British, and Soviet intelligence services that protected them. Thousands of East European collaborators, including those who had participated in mass murder, hid their past and found asylum in the United States, Canada, Australia, and Britain. Nevertheless, over the years in Germany and other countries, a significant number of war criminals were indicted, imprisoned, and some executed. In 1945–1946, twenty-two leading Nazis stood trial at Nuremberg before the international Military Tribunal, comprised of representatives of the United States, Great Britain, the Soviet Union, and France. The court sentenced twelve to death by hanging and one in absentia; seven were given jail sentences from ten years to life; and three were acquitted.

Women in the belligerent countries served in the armed forces, and in the Soviet Union they were actively involved in combat. Some 2,000 Soviet women fought as snipers, some with great effectiveness. Soviet women also flew fighter planes and drove tanks and some 200,000 fought with partisans. Women were active in the resistance movements in occupied Europe, and some were captured, tortured, and killed by the Nazis. Britain also planted female spies in occupied France, some of whom fell victim to the Nazis.

In the United States and Britain, women volunteers performed such noncombat duties as flight testing, ferrying planes to different bases, driving ambulances, serving as telegraphers and mechanics, and caring for the wounded in hospitals. Thousands of nurses served in the different branches of service. The role of British women in tracking incoming German planes proved invaluable in the Battle of Britain.

In both the United States and Britain, with men going off to war, large numbers of women, many of them housewives, worked in factories producing armaments needed for the war effort. While some 70 to 75 percent of American women chose to remain at home, that same percentage of British women were employed. When the war ended, many American women were forced to give up their jobs to provide work for the returning soldiers and resumed being housewives, a role that they and their husbands often preferred. Nevertheless, the new possibilities created by the war gave women more confidence in their abilities and in time helped spark a woman's movement that pressed for equal opportunity in employment and education.

The war produced a shift in power arrangements. The United States and the Soviet Union emerged as the two most powerful states in the world. The traditional Great Powers—Britain, France, and Germany—were now dwarfed by these *superpowers*. The United States had the atomic bomb and immense industrial might; the Soviet Union had the largest army in the world and was extending its dominion over Eastern Europe. With Germany defeated, the principal incentive for Soviet–American cooperation had evaporated.

After World War I, nationalist passions had intensified. After World War II, Western Europeans progressed toward unity. The Hitler years had convinced many Europeans of the dangers inherent in extreme nationalism, and fear of the Soviet Union prodded them toward greater cooperation.

World War II accelerated the disintegration of Europe's overseas empires. The European states could hardly justify ruling over Africans and Asians after they had fought to liberate European lands from German imperialism. Nor could they ask their people, exhausted by the Hitler years and concentrating all their energies on reconstruction, to fight new wars against Africans and Asians pressing for independence. In the years just after the war, Great Britain surrendered India, France lost Lebanon and Syria, and the Dutch departed from Indonesia. In the 1950s and 1960s, virtually every colonial territory gained independence. Where a colonial power resisted granting the colony independence, the price was bloodshed.

The consciousness of Europe, already profoundly damaged by World War I, was again grievously wounded. Nazi racial theories showed that even in an age of advanced science, the mind remains attracted to irrational beliefs and mythical imagery; Nazi atrocities proved that people will torture and kill with religious zeal and machinelike indifference. This regression to mythical thinking and savagery bears out Walter Lippmann's contention that "men have been barbarians much longer than they have been civilized. They are only precariously civilized, and within us there is the propensity, persistent as the force of gravity, to revert under stress and strain, or under temptation, to our first natures."[11] And the behavior of German intellectuals also contained a painful lesson, says German historian Karl Dietrich Bracher: "The intellectuals who supported the Nazis in one way or another all document that the mind can be temporarily seduced, that people can be bribed with careers and fame, that thinking people, especially, are tempted by an irrational cult of action and are peculiarly susceptible to 'one-dimensional' answers and promises of salvation."[12]

The Nazi assault on reason and freedom demonstrated anew the fragility of Western civilization. This assault would forever cast doubt on the Enlightenment conception of human goodness, secular rationality, and the progress of civilization through advances in science and technology.

The Holocaust was heightened irrationality and organized evil on an unprecedented scale.

Auschwitz, Treblinka, Sobibor, and the other death factories represent the triumph of human irrationality over reason—the surrender of the mind to a bizarre racial mythology that provided a metaphysical and pseudoscientific justification for mass murder. They also represent the ultimate perversion of reason. A calculating reason manufactured and organized lies and demented beliefs into a structured system with its own inner logic and employed sophisticated technology and administrative techniques to destroy human beings spiritually and physically. Science and technology, venerated as the great achievement of the Western mind, had made mass extermination possible. The philosophes had not foreseen the destructive power inherent in reason. Historian Omer Bartov poses this disturbing question about the failure of reason and the Western humanist tradition:

> *What was it that induced Nobel Prize-winning scientists, internationally respected legal scholars, physicians known throughout the world for their research into the human body and their desire to ameliorate the lot of humanity, to become not merely opportunist accomplices, but in many ways the initiators and promoters of this attempt to subject the human race to a vast surgical operation by means of mass extermination of whole categories of human beings? What was there (or is there) in our culture that made the concept of transforming humanity by means of eugenic and racial cleansing seem so practical and rational?*[13]

Both the Christian and the Enlightenment traditions had failed the Germans and many other Europeans. Conversely, Hitler's supporters had betrayed civilization, as Joachim Wieder, a German officer and veteran of Stalingrad, concluded after the war:

> *By means of a destructive battle against universal educational and cultural powers of classic antiquity, humanism, and Christianity, an anti-intellectual political religion of power had successfully extracted the German people from the best of the commonly-held European body of human thought and thereby also out of the commitment to the objective concepts of truth, compassion, and justice.*[14]

And "what is both historically unique and persistently disturbing about the Holocaust," notes Bernhard Schlink, a prominent German novelist, "is that Germany, with its cultural heritage and place among civilised nations, was capable of those kinds of atrocities. It elicits troubling questions: if the ice of culturally-advanced civilisation upon which one fancied oneself safely standing, was in fact so thin at that time, then how safe is the ice we live upon today?"[15]

Auschwitz marked a rupture in the progressive development of European civilization. It demonstrated that against the forces of mythical thinking, fanaticism, and human beings' propensity for evil, our rational faculties, so admired by the philosophes of the Enlightenment and their liberal heirs, have limited power. Some intellectuals, shocked by the irrationality and horrors of the Hitler era, drifted into despair. To these thinkers, life was absurd, without meaning; human beings could neither comprehend nor control it. In 1945, only the naïve could have faith in continuous progress or believe in the essential goodness of the individual. The future envisioned by the philosophes seemed more distant than ever. Nevertheless, this profound disillusionment was tempered by hope. Democracy had, in fact, prevailed over Nazi totalitarianism and terror. A year before he perished at Normandy, a young British soldier wrote to a friend in words that would aptly describe the sentiments of many people immediately after the war: "To . . . admit any hope of a better world is definitely foolish, as foolish as it is to stop working for it."[16]

Finally, World War II saw major advances in weaponry, none more significant than the atomic bomb, which made war more lethal. That states now possess nuclear weapons capable of destroying one another, and even civilization and the planet, is another ever-present, ever-terrifying legacy of World War II.

❖   ❖   ❖

NOTES

1. Pierre Renouvin, *World War II and Its Origins* (New York: Harper & Row, 1969), 167.

2. *Documents on German Foreign Policy, 1918–1945* (London: Her Majesty's Stationery Office, 1956), Vol. 6, series D, no. 433.

3. Winston S. Churchill, *The Second World War: Their Finest Hour* (Boston: Houghton Mifflin, 1949), Vol. 2, 225–226.

4. Judith Sternberg Newman, *In the Hell of Auschwitz* (New York: Exposition, 1964), 18.

5. Quoted in Robert Jay Lifton, *The Nazi Doctors* (New York: Basic Books, 1986), 16.

6. Konnilyn G. Feig, *Hitler's Death Camps* (New York: Holmes & Meier, 1979), 37.

7. Quoted in Steven T. Katz, "Technology and Genocide: Technology as a 'Form of Life,'" in *Echoes from the Holocaust*, ed. Alan Rosenberg and Gerald E. Meyers (Philadelphia: Temple University Press, 1988), 281.

8. Rainer C. Baum, "Holocaust: Moral Indifference as the Form of Modern Evil," in *Echoes from the Holocaust*, ed. Rosenberg and Meyers, 83.

9. Lifton, *The Nazi Doctors*, 5.

10. Richard Overy, *Why the Allies Won* (New York: W. W. Norton, 1955), 82.

11. Walter Lippmann, *The Public Philosophy* (Boston: Little, Brown, 1955), 86.

12. Karl Dietrich Bracher, *Turning Points in Modern Times*, trans. Thomas Dunlap (Cambridge, Mass.: Harvard University Press, 1995), 198.

13. Omer Bartov, *Germany's War and the Holocaust: Disputed Histories* (Ithaca, N.Y.: Cornell University Press, 2003), 136.

14. Joachim Wieder, *Stalingrad: Memories and Assessments*, trans. Helmut Bogler (London: Arms and Armor, 1993), 87.

15. Bernhard Schlink, *Guilt About the Past* (Toronto: House of Anansi, 2009), 29.

16. Paul Fussell, ed., *The Norton Book of Modern War* (New York: W. W. Norton, 1991), 381.

Part Six

The Contemporary World

The Destruction of the World Trade Center's Twin Towers.

Politics and Society	Thought and Culture
1940 Yalta agreement (1945)	Koestler, *Darkness at Noon* (1940)
United Nations established (1945)	Hemingway, *For Whom the Bell Tolls* (1940)
Marshall Plan for recovery of Europe (1947)	Camus, *The Stranger* (1942)
Cold War starts (1947)	von Hayek, *The Road to Serfdom* (1944)
State of Israel established (1948)	Wiener, *Cybernetics* (1948)
North Atlantic Treaty Organization (NATO) established (1949)	Orwell, *1984* (1949)
Division of Germany (1949)	de Beauvoir, *The Second Sex* (1949)
Triumph of Communism in China (1949)	
1950 Korean War (1950–1953)	Camus, *The Rebel* (1951)
European Economic Community (EEC) established (1957)	Discovery of DNA by Crick and Watson (1951–1953)
Sputnik launched: space age begins (1957)	Djilas, *The New Class* (1957)
	Chomsky, *Syntactic Structures* (1957)
	Grass, *The Tin Drum* (1959)
	Snow, *The Two Cultures and the Scientific Revolution* (1959)
1960 Berlin Wall built (1961)	Carson, *Silent Spring* (1962)
Cuban missile crisis (1962)	Pope John XXIII, *Pacem in Terris* (Peace on Earth) (1963)
Vietnam War (1963–1973)	McLuhan, *Understanding Media* (1964)
	Levi-Strauss, *The Savage Mind* (1966)
1970 Détente in East-West relations (1970s)	Solzhenitsyn, *The Gulag Archipelago* (1974–1978)
	Wilson, *Sociobiology* (1975)
	Lyotard, *The Postmodern Condition* (1979)
1980 Gorbachev becomes leader of Soviet Union (1985)	Creation of the Internet (1983)
Explosion at Chernobyl nuclear power plant (1986)	Dawkins, *The Blind Watchmaker* (1986)
Peaceful overthrow of Communist governments in Eastern Europe (1989)	Gorbachev, *Perestroika* (1987)
Berlin Wall demolished (1989)	Grossman, *Life and Fate* (1988)
1990 Reunification of Germany (1990)	Fukuyama, *The End of History and the Last Man* (1992)
Charter of Paris for a New Europe (1990)	Huntington, *The Clash of Civilizations and the Remaking of the World Order* (1998)
Official end of Cold War (1990)	Hawkins, *A Brief History of Time* (1998)
Persian Gulf War (1991)	
Yugoslav federation breaks up and civil war begins (1991)	
Collapse of the Soviet Union (1991)	
European Union ratifies the Maastricht Treaty (1993)	
Dayton Agreement ends civil war in former Yugoslavia (1995)	
2000 Terrorist attack on World Trade Center (2001)	
U.S.-led war in Iraq; fall of Saddam Hussein (2003)	

Chapter 21

Europe After World War II: Recovery and Realignment, 1945–1989

- ■ **The Cold War**
- ■ **Decolonization**
- ■ **Building a New Europe: Unity and Recovery**
- ■ **The Soviet Bloc**

Focus Questions

1. What were the origins of and key developments in the Cold War?
2. What conditions made possible the "revolution" of 1989 in Eastern Europe?
3. What are the main problems confronting the European Union?
4. What factors led to the collapse of Communism and the end of the Cold War?
5. What is the historical significance of Communism's collapse?

*A*t the end of World War II, Winston Churchill described Europe as "a rubble heap, a charnel house, a breeding ground for pestilence and hate."[1] Millions had perished. Industry, transportation, and communication had come to a virtual standstill; bridges, canals, dikes, and farmlands were ruined. Ragged, worn people picked among the rubble and bartered their valuables for food.

Europe was politically cut in half, for in pursuing Hitler's armies, Soviet troops had overrun Eastern Europe and penetrated into the heart of Germany. Europe's future now depended on two countries, the United States and the Soviet Union, which soon became embroiled in a bitter Cold War. The Soviet Union, exhausted by World War II and anxious about security, imposed its grim tradition of Communist dictatorship on Eastern Europe, while the United States, virtually unharmed by the war, brought the boon of its wealth and power to help rebuild Western Europe. Henceforth, the United States stood out as the heir to and guardian of the Western tradition, a political giant come into its own. ❖

THE COLD WAR

Origins

The Cold War (the American financier Bernard Baruch coined the phrase in 1947) stemmed from the divergent historical experiences and the incompatible ideologies and political ambitions of the United States and the Soviet Union. The wartime coalition of the United States, Britain, and the Soviet Union was based solely on temporary political expediency—the need to defeat the common enemy. Both the United States and Britain had long disdained the repressive Communist system and feared its spread to Western Europe, and the Soviet Union had a profound distrust for Western capitalist states, particularly Germany, which in both world wars had invaded Russia, leaving behind death and destruction. Fearing a revival of German power, Stalin was determined to protect Soviet security by annexing border regions and establishing subservient Communist governments throughout Eastern Europe.

Protecting the Soviet Union from its capitalist enemies was one major concern for Stalin. The other was to retain his absolute personal rule. The epic struggle against the Nazi invaders had further hardened Stalin. Sixty-six years old in 1945, Stalin displayed in his last years an unrelenting ruthlessness and paranoid suspiciousness. And as leader in the victorious war against Nazi Germany, his authority was unquestioned and his stature had grown immensely. The cult of the great leader

was shaped and propagated by a vast propaganda machine that included the state-controlled media and educational institutions.

As the Red Army fought its way west in 1944 and 1945, Eastern European Communists, trained in the Soviet Union, followed. The Baltic states (Lithuania, Latvia, and Estonia), seized after the Nazi–Soviet Pact of 1939 and then lost to Hitler, were reincorporated into the Soviet Union. The Soviet Union also annexed part of East Prussia; Ruthenia in eastern Czechoslovakia, whose population was predominantly Ukrainian; parts of Romania; and eastern Poland, for which the Poles were compensated with German territory, including much of East Prussia. Elsewhere, Stalin respected, at least outwardly, the national sovereignty of the occupied countries by ruling through returning native Communists and whatever sympathizers he could find. In the Soviet-occupied zone of Germany, Stalin arranged for the establishment of Communist rule. Stalin knew that in free elections Communists had little chance of winning and that left to their own devices these countries would return to their traditional anti-Russian orientation. In these new Soviet client states, Stalin retained a morbid fear of nationalist and anti-Communist insurgencies backed by the capitalist West. Poles, for example, had bitter historical memories of being under Russian rule until after World War I. Strongly Catholic, they also hated the atheistic Communist ideology and resented the Soviet Union for invading eastern Poland in 1939 and deporting hundreds of thousands of Poles to desolate regions of the Soviet Union, for massacring thousands of Polish officers during the war, and for not helping the Polish insurrection against the Nazis in 1944. And it would be extremely difficult to win the hearts of Czechs and Hungarians, who are exceedingly patriotic and identified with Western Europe, and of the Baltic nations, who hated Russian domination. Feeling a desperate need for allies as a security buffer, Soviet leadership would use military force to keep the satellite countries of Eastern Europe in line.

Under the leadership of the pugnacious Marshal Tito, who had led the Yugoslav resistance movement against Nazi occupation, Yugoslavia alone successfully defied Stalin. A hardened Communist, Tito was also a Yugoslav patriot

Primary Source

Milovan Djilas: *The New Class*

In 1956, Milovan Djilas (1911–1995), a Yugoslav Communist and political commentator who traveled to Moscow during and after the war, wrote The New Class, *an early and devastating critique of the Communist system. Under Communism, he said, government bureaucrats, all members of the Communist Party, constitute a privileged "exploiting and governing class."*

Earlier revolutions, particularly the so-called bourgeois ones, attached considerable significance to the establishment of individual freedoms immediately following cessation of the revolutionary terror . . . The final results of earlier revolutions were often greater legal security and greater civil rights. This cannot be said of the Communist revolution. . . .

In contrast to earlier revolutions, the Communist revolution, conducted in the name of doing away with classes, has resulted in the most complete authority of any single new class. Everything else is sham and an illusion. . . .

The new class may be said to be made up of those who have special privileges and economic preference because of the administrative monopoly they hold. . . .

The mechanism of Communist power. . . . leads to the most refined tyranny and the most brutal exploitation. The simplicity of this mechanism originates from the fact that one party alone, the Communist Party, is the backbone of the entire political, economic, and ideological activity. The entire public life is at a standstill or moves ahead, falls behind or turns around according to what happens in the party forums. . . .

. . . Communist control of the social machine . . . restricts certain government posts to party members. These jobs, which are essential in any government but especially in a Communist one, include assignments with police, especially the secret police; and the diplomatic and officers corps, especially positions in the information and political services. In the judiciary only top positions have until now been in the hands of Communists. . . .

Only in a Communist state are a number of both specified and unspecified positions reserved for members of the party. The Communist government, although a class structure, is a party government; the Communist army is a party army; and the state is a party state. More precisely, Communists tend to treat the army and the state as their exclusive weapons.

The exclusive, if unwritten, law that only party members can become policemen, officers, diplomats, and hold similar positions, or that only they can exercise actual authority, creates a special privileged group of bureaucrats. . . .

A citizen in the Communist system lives oppressed by the constant pangs of his conscience, and the fear that he has transgressed. He is always fearful that he will have to demonstrate that he is not an enemy of socialism, just as in the Middle Ages a man constantly had to show his devotion to the Church. . . .

. . . Tyranny over the mind is the most complete and most brutal type of tyranny; every other tyranny begins and ends with it. . . .

History will pardon Communists for much, establishing that they were forced into many brutal acts because of circumstances and the need to defend their existence. But the stifling of every divergent thought, the exclusive monopoly over thinking for the purpose of defending their personal interests, will nail the Communists to a cross of shame in history. . . .

Question for Analysis

1. How did Milovan Djilas characterize the "new class"? What were its qualities? How did it wield its power?

Milovan Djilas, *The New Class* (New York: Frederick A. Praeger, 1957), 27, 36, 39, 70, 72, 73, 132.

who resisted Soviet occupation of his country. Backed by his people, Tito pursued an independent course, but he too resorted to oppression to maintain Communist rule.

The Communist regimes in the satellite countries could only be maintained by force and terror. And as President Ronald Reagan declared in 1982, "the regimes planted by totalitarianism have had more than 30 years to establish their legitimacy. But none—not one regime—has yet been able to risk free elections. Regimes planted by bayonets do not take root."[2]

Local populations, and their supporters in Western European lands, viewed the Soviet domination of Eastern Europe as a calamity. But unwilling to risk another war, Western countries were powerless to intervene. By the end of 1948, the lands of Eastern Europe had become Soviet satellites. Wartime cooperation between the former allies, admittedly tenuous and forced, was replaced by suspicion and hostility, initiating the era of the Cold War. For the next forty-five years, the two parts of the Continent would be two camps of opposing ideologies. In Churchill's famous words, "From Stettin in the Baltic to Trieste in the Adriatic, an iron curtain has descended across the Continent."[3]

American leaders were profoundly concerned: they had the responsibility of rallying Western Europe, and possibly the world, against universal Communism, another form of totalitarianism that threatened both freedom and the free market. And, in what was a significant consequence of the war, the three Axis powers—(West) Germany, Italy, and Japan—embraced democratic principles and sided with the United States and its allies in their hostility to Communism and Soviet expansion. The rapid growth of Communist parties throughout Western Europe and the specter of these countries ruled by Communist parties with allegiance to the Soviet Union remained a gnawing worry.

Cold War Mobilization

In March 1947, fearing Soviet penetration in the eastern Mediterranean, President Truman proclaimed the Truman Doctrine: "It must be the policy of the United States to support free peoples who are resisting attempted subjugation by armed minorities or by outside pressures."[4] The Truman Doctrine was the centerpiece of the new policy of *containment,* of holding Soviet power within its then-current boundaries. U.S. military and economic support soon went to Greece and Turkey. Thus, a sharp reversal took place in American foreign policy; prewar American isolation gave way to worldwide vigilance against any Soviet effort at expansion.

In June 1947, Secretary of State George C. Marshall announced an impressive program of economic aid, formally called the European Recovery Program but widely known as the Marshall Plan. By 1952, when the plan terminated, it had supplied Europe with a total of $13.15 billion in aid—a modest pump priming for the subsequent record upswing in the United States, Western European, and even global prosperity. Western Europe recovered, and the United States gained economically strong allies and trading partners.

In 1948, Stalin, seeking greater control in East Germany, cut off access to West Berlin. In response, the United States and Britain organized a massive airlift of supplies to the city, preserving the western outpost in East Germany.

The United States strove to contain Soviet power by establishing in 1949 the North Atlantic Treaty Organization (NATO), which linked the armed forces of the United States, Canada, Portugal, Norway, Iceland, Denmark, Italy, Britain, France, and the Benelux countries (an acronym for Belgium, the Netherlands, and Luxembourg). Greece and Turkey soon joined; West Germany was included in 1956, and Spain in 1982. In response to NATO, the Soviet Union formed the Warsaw Pact, consisting of the armed forces of the Soviet Union and its European satellites.

Military alliances and forces were backed up by ever more powerful and sophisticated armaments. Sooner than expected, in 1949, the Soviet Union exploded its own atomic device. Thereafter, the arms race escalated to hydrogen bombs and intercontinental ballistic missiles (ICBMs), which ended America's geographical invulnerability.

The U.S.–Soviet rivalry extended into outer space. In 1957, the Soviet government sent the first *sputnik* (satellite) into orbit around the earth, shocking complacent Americans into a keen

Chronology 21.1 ❖ Europe After 1945

1945	United Nations founded; Eastern Europe occupied by Red Army
1947	Cold War starts; Marshall Plan inaugurated
1948	Stalinization of Eastern Europe; Tito's Yugoslavia breaks with the Soviet Union
1949	NATO formed
1953	Stalin dies
1956	Khrushchev's secret speech on Stalin's crimes; the Polish October; the Hungarian uprising crushed
1957	*Sputnik* launched: space age begins; EEC established
1961	Berlin Wall built, dividing the city of Berlin
1962	Cuban missile crisis
1963–1973	Vietnam War
1964	Khrushchev ousted; Brezhnev and Kosygin installed as leaders in U.S.S.R.
1968	Czechoslovakia's "Prague Spring": Dubček's "socialism with a human face"
1971	Détente in East–West relations
1979	Soviet Union invades Afghanistan
1980	Solidarity trade union formed in Poland
1982	Brezhnev dies, succeeded by Andropov (d. 1984) and Chernenko (d. 1985)
1985	Gorbachev becomes U.S.S.R. leader
1988	Soviet Union withdraws from Afghanistan
1989	Year of liberation in Eastern Europe
1990	Reunification of Germany; Charter of Paris for a New Europe: official end of the Cold War
1991	Persian Gulf War; Yeltsin elected Russian president; collapse of Soviet Union; Yugoslav federation breaks up and civil war begins
1993	Czechoslovakia splits into Czech Republic and Slovakia; elections for new Russian constitution and parliament; European Union ratifies Maastricht Treaty
1994	South Africa elects multiracial government; war breaks out between Russia and Chechnya
1995	Dayton Agreement ends civil war in Bosnia
1996	Yeltsin reelected president of Russia; truce ends hostilities in Chechnya
1999	NATO invades Kosovo; Russia again attacks Chechnya
2001	Terrorist attack on World Trade Center; War on Terrorism in Afghanistan
2003	United States and Britain crush regime of Saddam Hussein

awareness of their vulnerability. For some years, the Soviet Union remained ahead in the prestigious field of space exploration, sending the first astronaut, Yuri Gagarin, into orbit in 1961. The United States caught up in 1969 by landing a man on the moon.

An Early Confrontation: The Korean War

In June 1950, war broke out in Korea, a country divided in 1945 between a pro-Soviet Communist regime in the north and a pro-American regime in the south. Eager to restore Korean national unity and mistakenly assuming U.S. nonintervention, the North Korean army invaded South Korea, with somewhat reluctant support of the Soviet Union and Communist China; the leaders of both countries thought the United States would not intervene. Immediately, however, the United States gained U.N. backing (the U.S.S.R. was temporarily boycotting the body) for a war against North Korea. Under the command of General Douglas MacArthur, South Korean and U.S. troops, assisted by a token force from other U.N. members, fought their way north toward the Chinese border. Fearing for his own security, Mao Zedong, head of Communist China, dispatched "volunteers"— as they were called—to drive back the approaching enemy in a surprise attack. Forced to retreat, General MacArthur's troops eventually withdrew from North Korea. Peace was restored in 1953, with the division of Korea reaffirmed. The Korean War was immensely costly: 36,568 Americans died in action; some 600,000 Chinese troops and more than 2 million Korean soldiers and civilians also perished. While South Korea evolved into a thriving democracy with a sophisticated economy and high standard of living, North Korea retained a ruthless dictatorship and continues to have one of the lowest standards of living in the world.

DECOLONIZATION

World War II, in which many colonial soldiers loyally fought for their masters, stirred up demands among non-Western peoples for an end to Western colonial rule and for political independence. After all, freedom and self-determination were prominent Allied war slogans. Exhausted by the war, European colonial powers had little strength left for colonial rule. In this setting, a mighty groundswell of decolonization, supported by the ideals of the United Nations, eventually propelled African and Asian lands into independent statehood.

Decolonization often sparked brutal struggles of building modern states among peoples who were ill unprepared for this effort. For example, in 1960, the Belgians pulled out of the Congo, leaving behind some thirty Congolese university graduates to fill four thousand administrative posts. Moreover, divided by historic, ethnic, and tribal animosities, newly independent states were often torn by civil war. In many African lands, army officers seized power; these ruthless rulers treated the countries as their private fiefs. Thus, Mobutu Sese Seko, who ruled mineral-rich Zaire for thirty-two years, amassed one of the world's largest fortunes and purchased luxurious mansions abroad while poverty raged among his people. For decades most African countries suffered economic stagnation and political corruption and oppression. It was extremely rare for a party or president to be voted out of office in a peaceful election.

Former Asian colonies also suffered hardships. In 1947, Britain partitioned India into two countries, Hindu India and Muslim Pakistan. The ensuing sectarian frenzy produced several hundred thousand civilian deaths, many of them victims of massacres, and over 10 million displaced persons. The animosity still persists. In 1971, Bangladesh, supported by India, fought a bloody war of liberation from Pakistan, which was compelled to grant it independence.

The Vietnam War. The United States was drawn into a particularly brutal postimperial conflict in Vietnam where the Communist regime in the north threatened to take over South Vietnam. From the north, the authoritarian regime of Ho Chi Minh (1890–1969), backed by indigenous nationalism and Soviet aid, cast its shadow over an inept and oppressive south. Providing South Vietnam with the stability and strength needed to resist Communist infiltration required increasing U.S. aid—including troops to

AP Images/Henri Huet.

BOGGED DOWN IN VIETNAM. Americans defended South Vietnam against a threatened takeover by Communist North Vietnam. Between 1964 and 1973, U.S. involvement in the unsuccessful Vietnam War polarized U.S. public opinion over the morality of the war.

fight off the Communist guerrillas, the Vietcong. If the Communists prevailed, the argument ran, all the other countries in East and Southeast Asia emerging from colonial rule would fall like dominoes. Under President Lyndon B. Johnson, who assumed office in 1963, U.S. intervention in South Vietnam became the undeclared Vietnam War.

The United States shipped to Vietnam nearly half a million soldiers, equipped with the latest weaponry and electronic equipment. Yet victory eluded the Americans. The North Vietnamese government and its people withstood the cruelest punishment of bombs and chemical weapons ever inflicted. Nor was South Vietnam spared; virtually every South Vietnamese family saw relatives killed or maimed and their livelihoods ruined.

As domestic opposition to the war increased and Vietcong resistance held firm, President Richard M. Nixon, elected in 1968, initiated negotiations with North Vietnam, while U.S. forces put pressure on the enemy by attacking Communist bases and supply routes in neighboring Cambodia and Laos. Civilians were bombed more fiercely than in World War II. In 1973, by agreement with North Vietnam, the United States withdrew its forces. In 1975, the North Vietnamese swept aside the weak South Vietnamese army and unified the country under a Communist dictatorship. Ho Chi Minh had triumphed against the mightiest nation in the world. Tragically, the Communist regime sent perhaps two million citizens to "reeducation camps" where well over one hundred thousand died, and more than two million "boat people" fled the country.

In the wake of the American withdrawal, Cambodian Communists—the Khmer Rouge— seized power under their leader, Pol Pot. He drove more than two million people from the capital city

© 2016 Cengage Learning.

Map 21.1 **Southeast Asia and the Vietnam War** The Vietcong used the Ho Chi Minh Trail to infiltrate South Vietnam.

of Phnom Penh and the countryside and tried to establish a new order based on ideologically regimented rural communes. The result was genocide in which well over one million people perished.

BUILDING A NEW EUROPE: UNITY AND RECOVERY

Although Europeans share a common cultural heritage, the diversity of their history and national temperaments cursed them in the past with warfare. After two ruinous world wars, many people at last began to feel that the price of violent conflict had become excessive; war no longer served any national interest. And the extension of Soviet power made some form of Western European unity attractive, if not imperative.

In 1951, the chief Continental consumers and producers of coal and steel, the two items most essential for the rebuilding of Western Europe, created the European Coal and Steel Community (ECSC). Its six members, France, West Germany, the Netherlands, Belgium, Luxembourg, and Italy, intended to put the Ruhr industrial complex, the heart of German industrial power, under international control, thereby promoting cooperation and reconciliation, as well as economic strength.

Emboldened by the success of the ECSC, in 1957 the six countries established the European Economic Community (EEC), also known as the Common Market, a free trade zone aimed at improving living conditions among member states. In 1973, Great Britain, Ireland, and Denmark joined the original members in what was now called the European Community (EC); in 1981 Greece and in 1986 Spain and Portugal became members. The EC constituted the world's largest single trading bloc, conducting more than one-fifth of the world's commerce. In this framework of growing cooperation, the major countries of Western Europe experienced a political and economic revival, which contributed to Western superiority in the Cold War.

A most striking fact of recent history in the West has been the unprecedented economic advance. Between the early 1950s and the late 1970s, production in Western Europe and the United States surpassed all previous records. The rapid postwar economic boom suffered a setback in the 1970s, due in part to the drastic increase in oil prices imposed by the Organization of Petroleum Exporting Countries (OPEC). Economic growth revived throughout the 1980s. However, unemployment in Western Europe remained high, even in West Germany, the strongest country economically.

Stimulated by the expansion of U.S. multinational corporations into Western Europe and by the opportunities offered by the European Community, many European companies have turned multinational and grown larger than any nationalized industry. The Western European economy came to be dominated by gigantic private and public enterprises tied to other parts of the world.

Boosted by rising standards of living and by U.S. power, the overall trend of political life in the West since World War II has been toward constitutional democracy. Although Spain and Portugal retained their prewar dictatorships until the mid-1970s and Greece for a time wavered between democracy and dictatorship, by the late 1970s even these countries had conformed to the common pattern.

Great Britain and France

Impoverished by the war and forced to dismantle its colonial empire, Great Britain lost its leading role in world politics after World War II. It peacefully dismantled its colonial empire, and British seapower was replaced by the American navy and air force. The postwar Labour government, allied with powerful trade unions, provided Britons with a measure of economic security through social programs and extensive government control over important branches of the economy. However, these policies undermined economic efficiency and output.

In 1979, at a low point in the economy, the voters elected a Conservative government led by Margaret Thatcher, the "Iron Lady" and Britain's first female prime minister. She dominated English politics for the next decade, fighting inflation and rigorously encouraging individual initiative and free enterprise. During the Thatcher

Map 21.2 **Western Europe After 1945** To counter the Communist threat from the Soviet Union, Western European countries, formerly enemies, cooperated for their mutual protection. The majority of countries joined NATO for security against Communist attack, and six countries within Europe formed the Common Market (the forerunner of the European Union) to facilitate trade and economic integration.

BERLIN WALL. The Berlin Wall, swiftly erected by the East German Communist regime in 1961, divided the city of Berlin for twenty-eight years.

years, the British economy improved, and London regained its former luster as a financial center.

Across the English Channel, France, liberated from German occupation, was reorganized democratically under the Fourth Republic and soon achieved respectable economic growth, despite frequent changes of a government's cabinet (twenty-six in twelve years). France faced serious problems with overseas possessions. In Indochina (now Vietnam), the colonial liberation movement inflicted a resounding defeat on the French army in 1954. In Algeria, French settlers and soldiers were determined to thwart independence. The long and bloody Algerian conflict had serious repercussions.

In 1958, the agitation to keep Algeria under French control, supported by certain army circles, reached a dangerous point. To prevent a right-wing coup aided by the army, General Charles de Gaulle stepped forward. He had been the leader of the Free French forces in World War II and president for a brief period after the war ended. De Gaulle established the Fifth Republic, with a strong executive authority, and sought to raise the country again to prominence by building its nuclear strength, making France independent of NATO, and renewing French influence in Africa. In 1962, he arranged a cease-fire in Algeria, allowing it to achieve independence. In 1968, demonstrations by students and workers demanding educational reform and social justice, which were supported by the Communist Party, greatly alarmed de Gaulle. He quickly called a general election, in which a frightened electorate gave him a landslide victory. However, unable to revise the constitution in his favor, he resigned in 1969.

The Fifth Republic continued under a government firmly based on a stable centrist majority, flanked by two radical parties. On the Left, the Communist Party gradually lost credibility because of its loyalty to Moscow. On the extreme Right, the ultranationalist *Front National* gained electoral strength in the early 1980s, stirring up hatred against the increasing number of Muslim immigrants from North Africa. Under the pressure of the newcomers, the French, even more than the English, feared for their national identity.

Amid the economic and political uncertainties of the times, François Mitterand, a moderate socialist who became president in 1981, maintained the Gaullist tradition. His country was the third largest nuclear power and the fourth largest economy in the world, deriving 70 percent of its energy from nuclear power plants. All along, France was a leading architect of European unity without surrendering its French character.

Italy and Germany

Italy became a democratic republic in 1946. Its government, however, was weak and unstable, with frequent changes of cabinet. A lengthy peninsula stretching out into the Mediterranean, the country offered a sharp contrast between north and south. The north was efficient and prosperous, whereas the south was backward and infiltrated by the Mafia. Centered in Sicily, the Mafia was a source of political corruption and even occasional terror against the government.

Division also characterized the political parties, from Communists to Christian Democrats. The Italian Communists, relatively free from corruption, well organized, and oriented toward Europe rather than Moscow, usually gained a quarter of the vote. On the other hand, the Christian Democrats—allied with the Vatican and constituting the majority party—were poorly disciplined, like the other non-Communist parties, and riven by corruption.

Yet the Italian economy proved to be a surprising success, despite the fact that the government was perennially in debt and unemployment ran high, especially in the south. Even more than France, Italy has been overrun by legal and illegal immigrants from Asia and Africa, straining the country's resources. It has been the most unruly of the major European countries, but no troublemaker for its neighbors.

In 1945, its cities in ruins, Germany had been defeated, occupied, and branded as a moral outcast. Divided among the four occupying powers—the United States, Britain, France, and the Soviet Union—the German nation was politically shattered. Extensive eastern lands were lost to Poland and the Soviet Union; some territory was returned to France. By 1949, two new and chastened Germanys had emerged. West Germany (the Federal Republic of Germany), formed from the three western zones of occupation, faced the hostile, Soviet-dominated East Germany (the German Democratic Republic). The former capital city of Berlin, inside East Germany, was similarly divided into western and eastern zones of occupation. The partition of Germany signified the destruction of Germany's traditional identity and ambition. The national trauma reached a climax in August 1961, when the East German government suddenly threw up a wall between East and West Berlin and tightly sealed off East from West Germany. West Germany thus became the crucial frontier of the Cold War, radiating Western superiority into the Soviet Bloc.

The Cold War proved a boon to the West Germans; it contributed to their integration into the emerging new Europe and to the reduction of old hatreds. Located next door to the Red Army, the West Germans, along with the Western armed forces stationed on their soil, were in a strategic position for defending Western Europe. Moreover, German industrial expertise was indispensable for rebuilding the Western European economy. On this basis, West Germany (far larger than its Communist counterpart to the east and the most populous of all Western European countries) began to construct a new political identity.

The architect of the new West Germany was Konrad Adenauer, its chancellor from 1949 to 1963 and a Christian Democrat. He sought to restore respect for Germany in cooperation with the leading states of Western Europe and the United States. As a patriot, he reestablished a cautious continuity with the German past. He also had Germany shoulder responsibility for the crimes of the Nazi regime and assume the payment of indemnifications and pensions to the Jewish victims and survivors of the Nazi era, as well as the payment of reparations to the state of Israel, which had been established in May 1948 and where many survivors were building a new life. Under Adenauer's guidance, the West Germans also rebuilt their economy, leading in the 1950s to the German "economic miracle." As a result, democracy put down roots among the West German people, strengthening their solidarity with their former European enemies. In 1966, Willy Brandt (1913–1992) was elected chancellor of the Federal Republic of Germany. Calling the cold war "a sterile and dangerous confrontation," he took the initiative for peaceful accommodation with the Soviet Union, neighboring Poland, and East Germany, a bold policy that earned him the Nobel Peace Prize in 1971. At the Warsaw Ghetto memorial in 1973, Brandt spontaneously fell to his knees in memory of the victims of the Holocaust. West Germany was admitted to NATO in 1957 and, together with East Germany, to the United Nations in 1972. It joined France in promoting the European Community.

During these years, West German prosperity and a generous admission policy attracted ambitious immigrants, many from Turkey, for the booming economy needed additional workers. Political extremists did not endanger political stability, except for one party, the Greens, which called attention to the destruction of the environment, industrial pollution, and the dangers of nuclear power. Loosely organized, the Greens expressed a romantic alienation from contemporary society and politics but achieved no lasting success. In 1982, the voters turned conservative, electing the leader of the Christian Democratic Union, Helmut Kohl, chancellor. He served for sixteen years and played a prominent role in strengthening the Cold War alliance against Soviet Communism.

THE SOVIET BLOC

Stalin's Last Years

For the Soviet Union, World War II was another cruel landmark in the long succession of wars, revolutions, and crises that had afflicted the country since 1914. Nothing basically changed after the war. The U.S.S.R. remained a closed society and a police state. The liberation from terror and dictatorship that many soldiers had hoped for as a reward for their heroism never occurred.

Corrupted by unlimited power and unrestrained adulation, his authority reinforced by success in defeating Nazi Germany, Stalin displayed in his last years an unrelenting ruthlessness and a suspiciousness that turned into paranoia. He found no reason to relax control. He kept the satellite nations in check with local propaganda machines and brute force. And he sent over a million returning Soviet soldiers and prisoners of war to concentration camps for fear of their disloyalty. Neglecting consumer goods, he poured vast resources into military development. Stalin's indomitable ambition, undiminished by age (he was sixty-six years old in 1945), was to build up Soviet power in his lifetime, whatever the human cost. More Five-Year Plans and more terror were needed.

On this familiar note, the Soviet Union slid from war into peace, staggering through the hardships and hunger of the war's aftermath, mourning its dead, and desperately short of men. Planning, much selfless hard work, manpower released from the army, and resources requisitioned from all occupied territories brought industrial production back to prewar levels within three years—no mean achievement.

In his last years, Stalin withdrew into virtual isolation, surrounded by a few fawning and fearful subordinates, and his paranoia worsened. Before he died, he "recognized" a plot among the doctors, most of them Jews, who treated him and other senior officials; he personally issued orders for their torture (which killed one of them), and the press circulated vicious anti-Semitic propaganda. Had Stalin not died it is likely that he would have launched a murderous campaign against Soviet Jews. When on March 5, 1953, the failing dictator died of a stroke, his advisers sighed with relief, but many people wept. To them, Stalin was the godlike leader and savior of the nation.

Khrushchev

After Stalin's death, leadership was assumed by a team headed by Nikita Khrushchev (1954–1964), who breathed fresh air into Soviet life. Khrushchev was the driving force behind the "thaw" that emptied the forced-labor camps and allowed most of the nationalities forcibly resettled during the war to return to their native regions. In a speech at the Twentieth Party Congress in February 1956, Khrushchev even dared to attack Stalin himself. His audience gasped with horror as he recited the facts: "Of the 139 members and candidates of the Party Central Committee who were elected at the 17th Congress (1934), 98 persons, i.e., 70 percent were arrested and shot."[5] In this vein, Khrushchev cited example after example of Stalin's terror. He aimed to shift the country away from terror and to increase his own stature, but without discrediting the Communist Party. Khrushchev's revelations created a profound stir around the world and prompted defection from Communist ranks everywhere.

In foreign policy, Khrushchev professed to promote peace, but also made some provocative moves. The U.S.S.R. threatened Western access to West Berlin in 1958, detonated a massive 50-megaton bomb in 1961, and authorized the building in August 1961 of the infamous "Berlin Wall" aimed to stop the massive flight of East Germans to West Germany. His most adventurous policy culminated in the Cuban missile crisis. In 1959, the dictatorship of Fulgencio Batista had been toppled by Fidel Castro (b. 1927), a left-wing revolutionary who turned Cuba into a Communist-style dictatorship. After an American attempt to overthrow him in 1961—the bungled Bay of Pigs operation—Castro was ready to turn his country into an outpost of Soviet power. Khrushchev planned to exploit this foothold in the Western Hemisphere by installing Soviet nuclear missiles in Cuba. Although the United States had stationed nuclear weapons in Turkey, within easy reach of Soviet targets, the reverse situation—a major Soviet threat close to home—alarmed the country. President John F. Kennedy demanded that Khrushchev withdraw the Soviet missiles from Cuba. The Cold War confrontation threatened to turn into a hot nuclear war. However, Khrushchev backed down—a move that contributed to his fall from power two years later.

Eager to prod his country toward full Communist development, Khrushchev presented a new party program and impatiently pressed for reforms in industry, agriculture, and party organization. His ceaseless reorganizations, impatient manner, and extravagant promises antagonized wide sections of state and party administration. In October 1964, while he was on vacation, his comrades in the Politburo unceremoniously ousted him for "ill health" or, as they later added, his "hare-brained schemes." He was retired and allowed to live out his years in peace.

Khrushchev was succeeded by a leadership team. Among these men, Leonid Brezhnev (1906–1982) gradually rose to the fore. Under his leadership, the government of the U.S.S.R. turned from a personal dictatorship into an oligarchy: the collective rule of a privileged minority. Brezhnev's style stressed reasoned agreement rather than command. Soviet officials breathed more easily, and Soviet society in turn grew less authoritarian. Citizens could engage in underground economic and countercultural activities—Western style music and dress, for example—so long as they avoided politics. More issues of state policy were opened to public debate, and more latitude was granted to artistic expression. Interest in religion revived. There were, however, limits to official leniency. Any public questioning of the Communist system or its leaders, even in literary allusion, could land one in prison or (later) in a mental institution, beginning with the trial of the "dissident" writers Andrei Sinyavsky and Yuli Daniel in 1965–1966. Yet the dissident movement gained strength.

Changes in Eastern Europe

Realizing that continued repression of the satellite countries would provoke trouble, Stalin's successors began to relax their controls. The Soviet satellites began to move toward greater national self-determination, searching for their own forms of industrialization, collectivization of agriculture, and Communist dictatorship. The history of the region after 1953 was thus a series of experiments to determine what deviations from Soviet practice in domestic politics and what measure of self-assertion in foreign policy the Kremlin would tolerate.

No event proved more crucial than Khrushchev's attack on Stalin in 1956. It set off a political earthquake throughout the bloc, discrediting Stalinists and encouraging moderates in the parties, reviving cautious discussions among

SOVIET TANKS IN BUDAPEST, HUNGARY, NOVEMBER 1956. On October 30, 1956, Soviet tanks left Budapest but returned a week later and crushed the Hungarian uprising, leaving as many as 1,500 civilians dead.

intellectuals, and even arousing visions of national self-determination.

The first rumbles of protest were heard in June 1956 in Poland—the largest and most troublesome of the satellite countries. The crisis came to a head in October: would Poland revolt, inviting invasion by the Red Army, or would Khrushchev ease Soviet control? The Soviet boss yielded in return for a Polish pledge of continued loyalty to the Soviet Union. Thereafter, Poland breathed more freely, affirming its Catholicism as a cornerstone of its national identity.

Although the "Polish October" ended peacefully, events moved to a brutal showdown in Hungary. On October 20, 1956, anti-Soviet feeling boiled over in an uprising in Budapest, forcing Soviet troops to withdraw from the country.

A moderate Communist government took over the reins. Eager to capture popular sentiment, it called for Western-style political democracy and Hungary's withdrawal from the Warsaw Pact. Thoroughly alarmed and supported by Mao and even Tito, the Soviet leaders struck back. On November 4, 1956, Soviet troops reentered Hungary and crushed all opposition, leaving some 1,500 civilians dead.

But the bold uprising left its mark. The new Communist leader of Hungary, János Kádar, was a moderate. With Khrushchev's approval, he built a pragmatic regime of consumer-oriented "goulash Communism" that granted considerable opportunity to private enterprise. Kádar's regime also allowed non-Communists to participate extensively in public affairs. Relaxation and decentralization of planning made possible in the 1970s remarkable increases in individual freedom and economic prosperity; though by contrast with Western Europe, the standard of living remained abysmally low. The Hungarian experiment became the envy of all other Soviet Bloc countries.

After 1956, Soviet leaders permitted modest social and economic change in the Eastern Bloc countries. In Czechoslovakia in 1968, a new group of Czech Communists, led by Alexander Dubček, sought to liberalize their regime to include non-Communists, permit greater freedom of speech, and rid the economy of the rigidities that for so long had prevented prosperity. Their goal was a "humanist democratic socialism," or "socialism with a human face": a Communist Party supported by public goodwill rather than by the secret police.

This program panicked Soviet Bloc leaders. On August 21, East German, Polish, Hungarian, and Soviet troops, under the Warsaw Pact, carried out a swift and well-prepared occupation of Czechoslovakia but failed to break the rebellious will of its reformers. While Soviet tanks rumbled through Prague, Czechoslovak Communist leaders met secretly and in choked fury defied the Soviets. Nonetheless, the revolt ended in failure. The party was purged, all reforms were canceled, and the country was reduced to abject hopelessness. But the Soviet Union paid a high price. A cry of moral outrage resounded around the world; protests were heard even in Moscow.

Extraordinary events occurred in Poland. Industrial workers, theoretically the real masters in Communist regimes, embarrassed their government by taking the lead in pressing for freedom and a better standard of living. When a Polish cardinal became Pope John Paul II in 1978, patriotism surged. In 1980, workers under the leadership of an electrician named Lech Walesa succeeded, with the blessing of the church, in forming an independent labor union. Called Solidarity, the union engaged in numerous strikes. In 1981, matters came to a head: some of Solidarity's more radical members spoke of bringing free elections to Poland. In December, a military dictatorship, formed suddenly under General Wojciech Jaruzelski, imposed martial law.

Walesa and other leaders of Solidarity were arrested, and protesting workers were dispersed by force.

The Gorbachev Years

Brezhnev died in 1982; his immediate successors, chosen by agreement among top party officials, were old men who survived in office only for a short time. Former KGB chief Yuri Andropov (aged sixty-eight), in poor health from the start, died in early 1984. He was replaced by Konstantin Chernenko, a man of Brezhnev's generation, likewise in poor health, who lasted until early 1985. In that year, Mikhail Gorbachev (b. 1931) took over, representing a younger and more sophisticated age group, whose members had started their careers in the calmer times after Stalin's death.

Self-confident, energetic, and articulate, Gorbachev was keenly aware of his country's problems and eager to confront them. Alcoholism was rife. Air and water pollution were at catastrophic levels. Economic growth had stagnated. The Soviet Union produced scarcely any consumer goods that could be sold on the international market. Rigid centralized planning stifled innovation. The country lagged in the design and production of computers, which handicapped military technology. Gorbachev knew that the Soviet Union had to update its industrial and agricultural productivity to compete with Japan, South Korea, Taiwan, the countries of Western Europe, and the United States in particular.

Gorbachev demanded no less than a fundamental reorganization—*perestroika*—of the Soviet system, with the Communist Party responding more readily to the plans and hopes of Soviet citizens, but without surrendering its monopoly of power. Even more than his

Map 21.3 **Eastern Europe After 1945** ▶
During and after World War II, the Soviet Union extended its rule halfway across Europe. Repressive Communist governments in Eastern Europe were controlled by Moscow. Yugoslavia, under President Tito, defied Moscow and became a Communist state with links to Western Europe and the United States.

515

predecessors, he advocated "the democratization of society," hoping to stimulate participation by ordinary citizens, especially at their places of work and in local administration. He called for multiple candidates for elected posts, a novel experience for Soviet voters. To loosen up administrative rigidity, he also granted greater freedom to local entrepreneurs in agriculture, industry, and consumer services.

Gorbachev promoted a new policy, *glasnost* (openness), in the discussion of public affairs. Let all the problems of Soviet society, hitherto kept under cover, be openly discussed: corruption, abuse of power, disregard for legality, and stifling of criticism. This policy was dramatically put to the test in late April 1986 when, because of staff misjudgment, a reactor at the nuclear power plant at Chernobyl exploded, spewing dangerous radiation high into the atmosphere; poisonous fallout covered much of Europe. It was by far the worst nuclear accident ever experienced. At first, the Soviet government, following its usual pattern, downplayed its significance. But, promoting *glasnost* in earnest, Gorbachev insisted on an unbiased investigation and discussion of the tragedy.

Domestic news began to depict Soviet reality more accurately. There was also a new candor about the Soviet past. During the seventieth anniversary of the Bolshevik Revolution, Gorbachev asserted that "the guilt of Stalin . . . for the wholesale repressive measures and acts of lawlessness is enormous and unforgivable."[6] Gorbachev then assured Soviet citizens that they should not hesitate to speak out freely. Academics, writers, and artists responded enthusiastically. As contacts with the outside world increased, Western ideals, culture, and respect for human rights entered Soviet minds as never before.

Yet the rigid Communist system was not easy to reform. Economic output and per capita consumption continued to fall. To drum up more support for change, Gorbachev advocated "the democratization of society." This involved shifting power away from the Communist Party and toward an elective Congress of People's Deputies. For the first time since 1917, citizens had the right to choose among more than one candidate. The electoral system was still stacked against non-Communists, only 12 percent of whom were elected during the election of 1989. Even

so, and contrary to his own wishes, Gorbachev had mobilized popular opposition not only to the entrenched Communist bureaucrats but to himself as well.

The End of the Cold War

Gorbachev also sought to ease international tensions. Pressure from foreign leaders, especially Ronald Reagan, Margaret Thatcher, and Pope John II, who tirelessly challenged Soviet Communism in both word and deed, lent urgency to Gorbachev's dilemma. Reagan launched an arms race the Soviets could ill afford, furnished logistical support to anti-Communist groups inside the Soviet Bloc like the Polish trade union Solidarity, supplied military aid to the Mujahideen in Afghanistan rebelling against the Soviet-backed Communist government, and insisted on building the Strategic Defense Initiative ("Star Wars"), an ultrasophisticated missile defense system the Soviets could not hope to match.

Gorbachev thought that the Soviet Union was more imperiled by internal rot than by foreign aggression. Plagued by incompetent managers, lethargic and alcoholic workers, corruption, and a loss of confidence in Communist leadership, the Soviet Union lagged far behind the capitalist West, particularly the United States. And the high cost of the Cold War impeded the reforms that his socialist country so urgently needed. In the spirit of glasnost, Gorbachev frankly admitted that the adverse prospects of his country's economy forced him to advocate not only "normal international relations," but also an end to the arms race. He cautiously lifted the restrictions barring access to the outside world. Jewish emigration was eased; foreign firms were invited to help stimulate the Soviet economy; and high-level discussions between Russians and Americans became commonplace.

By early 1989, Gorbachev withdrew the Soviet army from Afghanistan, admitting that the 1979 invasion had been a mistake. He allowed Eastern Europe to throw off Soviet domination, permitting the dissolution of the Warsaw Pact, the Soviet military alliance in the area, and gave approval to German reunification. He surrendered the Leninist claim to the superiority of Soviet Communism and stopped support for Marxist regimes in the Third World. Unilaterally demobilizing sizable units of the Red Army in 1988, he also stopped nuclear testing. At summit meetings—with President Reagan and later with President George H. W. Bush—Gorbachev successfully pressed for strategic arms reduction. In late 1991, both the United States and the Soviet Union agreed to scrap a significant part of their nuclear arsenals.

The Collapse of Communism

1989: The Year of Liberation. Resentful of Communist domination and growing economic hardships, in 1989 and 1990 Eastern Europeans demanded democratic reforms. Faced with a rising tide of popular discontent, Communist leaders resigned or agreed to reforms. People around the world cheered the opening of a new era in Eastern Europe.

In Poland, public pressure had forced General Jaruzelski to end his dictatorship and appoint a civilian government. Struggling with a deteriorating economy, Jaruzelski legalized the highly popular Solidarity union in 1989. Permitted to run against Communist Party candidates in a free election, Solidarity won an overwhelming victory. The once jailed Solidarity members now sat in the Polish parliament next to their former jailers. In December 1990, Lech Walesa, the leader of Solidarity, was elected president.

Encouraged by events in Poland, Hungary abolished its Communist bureaucracy in May 1989. By the end of the year, a multiparty system was in place, with two non-Communist parties, the Democratic Forum and the Alliance of Free Democrats, competing for leadership. Hungary had shaken off Soviet domination and embraced the ideals of democracy and free enterprise.

An even more momentous upheaval occurred in 1989 in East Germany. More than 340,000 people voted for freedom and prosperity with their feet, escaping to West Germany across the recently opened borders of Hungary and Czechoslovakia. Far larger numbers took to the streets in protest against the regime. Hoping to restore calm, Party Secretary Erich Honecker's colleagues deposed their sickly, old, hard-line boss, but antigovernment

demonstrations continued. On November 6, when almost a million demonstrators crammed the streets of East Berlin, the Communist government resigned. On November 9, in an explosion of patriotic fervor, the Berlin Wall was breached; tens of thousands of East Germans flocked into West Berlin, where they were welcomed with flowers and champagne. Liberated East Germany was soon reunited with West Germany, with Gorbachev's ultimate approval.

In Bulgaria, the dramatic events in Berlin led to the resignation of Tedor Zhivkov, the longest-serving Communist dictator in the Soviet Bloc and an opponent of reform. Bulgaria had joined the quest for democratic government and private enterprise.

While democratic reforms triumphed elsewhere, Romania's Nicholae Ceausescu, long bent on pursuing his own dictatorial course and hostile to Gorbachev's reforms, ruthlessly enforced his own rule, ordering his soldiers to shoot into a crowd of antigovernment demonstrators. But popular resentment was too powerful to contain, and even the army turned against the dictator. On December 25, 1989, Ceausescu and his wife were tried and executed. The most hardened symbol of Communist rule, defying to the last the common trend toward democratic freedom, had ignominiously fallen.

Faced with massive demonstrations in Prague and urged by Gorbachev himself to institute democratic reform, Czechoslovakia's Communist leaders resigned on November 24, 1989. Václav Havel, a leading dissident writer and outspoken advocate of democracy who had been jailed for his views, was chosen president on December 25.

Shocked by the news of Ceausescu's execution and Havel's election, the Yugoslav Communist Party caved in. Its central committee suggested the formation of a multiparty system, which was fully adopted in January 1990.

Except for Albania, where the Communist Party held on until free elections in February 1991, in 1789 all of Eastern Europe had liberated itself from Soviet domination—a breathtaking change, accomplished unexpectedly within a single year. Viewed as a whole, events in Eastern Europe had taken a surprisingly peaceful course, prompted by a number of favorable factors. First, a weakening of censorship had enabled citizens to perceive

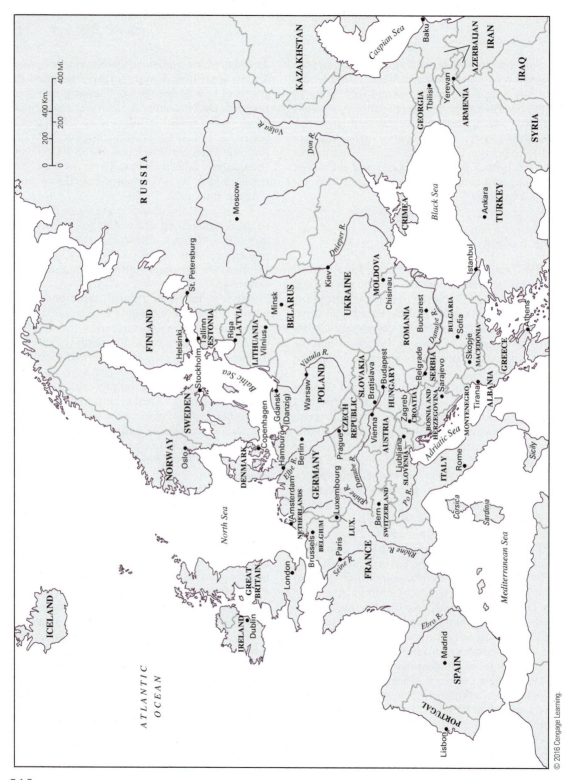

518

◀ *Map 21.4* **Post-Cold War Europe and the Former Soviet Union** Instead of the stark postwar division of Europe into three blocs—Western Europe, Eastern Europe, and the Soviet Union—the continent is now a patchwork of independent countries, some with new names. Despite the independence of former Soviet territory, Russia remains the largest country within Europe, East and West Germany are united, while Yugoslavia has split up.

the vastly higher standard of living in the free and democratic West. Second, led by intellectuals and clergy, the people united against repression, foreign domination, and economic misery, which so vividly contrasted with the prosperity of Western Europe. The revolutionary changes of 1989 constituted an overwhelming victory for Western forms of government and ways of life.

© Regis Bossu/Sygma/Corbis.

THE WALL CAME TUMBLING DOWN. The Berlin Wall, symbol of the division of Germany, was breached in November 1989. Young people excitedly clambered onto the partially demolished wall while East and West Berliners thronged the streets.

It is likely that most of the East European Communist leaders would have fought to keep power, if only their Soviet chief had given them military support. Why did Gorbachev abandon them? He wanted what most Soviet citizens longed for: "a normal life in a normal country." He cared about international criticism of his government's use of violence in the political sphere. He believed in the ideals of the self-determination of peoples and the popular will. Above all, he still believed in Soviet-style socialism and its capacity for both peaceful reform and continued popular support.

The Disintegration of the Soviet Union. The transformation and spiritual rebirth that Gorbachev hoped for the Soviet Union did not occur. In October 1990, Gorbachev conceded that "unfortunately, our society is not ready for the procedures of a law-based state. We don't have that level of political culture, those traditions. All that will come in the future."[7] Meanwhile, the Soviet Union was experiencing a breakdown of effective government, economic collapse, corruption, spiraling crime, and political agitation by national minorities in regions inhabited by non-Russian minorities with a strong national consciousness: these included Ukrainians, Lithuanians, Estonians, Latvians, Armenians, Georgians, and others. In response to the mounting crisis, the liberals, most strongly represented in Moscow and Leningrad among the young generation open to Western ways, pressed, under Boris Yeltsin's guidance, for speedy westernization, including a multiparty system and a market economy. On the opposite side, the Communist hard-liners prepared to revive the old system, relying on the army and the security forces to restore order and hold the country together. In August 1991, they staged a coup, imprisoning Gorbachev and deposing him as president of the Soviet Union. Their aim was to establish a new Communist dictatorship.

However, the conspirators, all of them high officials appointed by Gorbachev, grossly misjudged the people's revulsion against the Communist Party. The KGB's (State Security Service) vanguard forces defected to Yeltsin, who had been elected president of the Russian Federation in June 1991. At a risk to his own life, Yeltsin led a fervent popular protest against the coup. The emotional outburst in favor of democracy quickly spread from Moscow to other cities, and the coup collapsed within three days. The chief victim of the coup, apart from its leaders, was the Communist Party, now repudiated by Gorbachev himself and swept aside by public fury. Racked by the deteriorating economy and the growing nationalist sentiments among the various ethnic groups, the Soviet Union fell to pieces. The Baltic nations—Lithuania, Latvia, and Estonia—established their independence shortly after the coup, and a new Commonwealth of Independent States, consisting of eleven former republics of the collapsed Soviet Union, was proclaimed in December 1991. At the end of the month, Gorbachev, the last leader of the Soviet Union, resigned as president of a now-defunct country. Boris Yeltsin became the informal leader of the commonwealth. Its ideology discredited, its economy shattered, and its government transformed into a confederation of sovereign states; the Soviet Union had collapsed as a major force in world affairs. Only one superpower remained.

The Death of an Ideal?

The sudden and unexpected collapse of Communism in Eastern Europe in 1989 seemed to discredit Marxism irrevocably. Reformers in Eastern European lands liberated from Communist oppression expressed revulsion for the socialist past and a desire to regenerate their countries with an infusion of Western liberal ideals and institutions. Havel, the newly elected president of a free Czechoslovakia, expressed this disillusionment with the past and hope for a new democratic future:

> *The worst of it is that we live in a spoiled moral environment. We have become morally ill because we are used to saying one thing and thinking another. We have learned not to believe in anything, not to care about each other, to worry only about ourselves. . . . The previous regime, armed with a proud and intolerant ideology, reduced people into the means of production. . . . Many of our citizens died in prison in the 1950's. Many were executed. Thousands of human lives were destroyed.*

Perhaps you are asking what kind of republic I am dreaming about. I will answer you: a republic that is independent, free, democratic, a republic with economic prosperity and also social justice.[8]

Marxism had become a failed ideology propped up only by force in the few surviving Communist regimes: for many intellectuals, including once ardent Communists, "scientific socialism," which claimed to have deciphered the essential meaning and direction of history, no longer seems scientific or relevant to current needs. It is merely another idea that was given too much credence and is now ready to be swept into the dustbin of history. Political theorist Francis Fukuyama suggests that the decline of Communism and the end of the Cold War reveal a larger process at work, "the ultimate triumph of Western liberal democracy":

The twentieth century saw the developed world descend into a paroxysm of ideological violence, as liberalism contended first with the remnants of absolutism, then bolshevism and Fascism, and finally an updated Marxism that threatened to lead to the ultimate apocalypse of nuclear war. But the century that began full of self-confidence in the ultimate triumph of Western liberal democracy seems at its close to be returning full circle to where it started . . . to an unabashed victory of economic and political liberalism. The triumph of the West, of the Western idea, is evident first of all in the total exhaustion of viable systematic alternatives to Western liberalism. . . . What we may be witnessing . . . is the end point of mankind's ideological evolution and the universalization of Western liberal democracy as the final form of government.[9]

❖   ❖   ❖

NOTES

1. Quoted in Walter Laqueur, *Europe Since Hitler* (Baltimore: Penguin Books, 1970), 118.

2. Quoted in Melvyn P. Lefler, *For the Soul of Mankind: The United States, the Soviet Union, and the Cold War* (New York: Hill and Wang, 2007), 340.

3. Winston S. Churchill, "Sinews of Peace: Address, March 5, 1946," *Vital Speeches of the Day,* March 15, 1946, 3.

4. "The Truman Doctrine," in *Major Problems in American Foreign Policy: Documents and Essays,* ed. Thomas G. Paterson (Lexington, Mass.: Heath, 1978), Vol. 2, 290.

5. Nikita S. Khrushchev in *The Crimes of the Stalin Era: Special Report to the 20th Congress of the Communist Party of the Soviet Union,* annotated by Boris I. Nicolaevsky (New York: The New Leader, 1956), 20.

6. Gorbachev's speech at the seventieth anniversary of the Bolshevik Revolution, quoted in *The New York Times,* November 3, 1987, A3.

7. Quoted in Anthony Lewis, "Et Tu Eduard," *The New York Times,* December 21, 1990, A39.

8. *The New York Times,* January 2, 1990, A13.

9. Francis Fukuyama, "The End of History," *The National Interest* (Summer 1989), 3–4.

Chapter 22

The Troubled Present

- **The Post–Cold War World**
- **New and Old Problems: Muslim Immigration and the Resurgence of Anti-Semitism**
- **Culture Clash, Terrorism, and War**
- **Our Global Age: Promise and Problems**
- **Reaffirming the Core Ideals of the Western Tradition**

Focus Questions

1. How did the collapse of Communism impact politics in Russia and Eastern Europe?
2. What problems are faced by the European Union?
3. What tensions surround Muslim immigration in Europe?
4. What are the reasons for the surge of anti-Semitism in contemporary Europe?
5. What are the motivations and goals of radical Muslims? How should Europe and the United States respond to radical Islam?
6. How would you characterize Taliban leaders and their followers?
7. Why have some analysts questioned the wars in Afghanistan and Iraq?
8. The euphoria with which Westerners first greeted the Arab Spring has waned. Why?
9. In your opinion, what are the reasons to be optimistic about the contemporary world? To be pessimistic?
10. What are the essential ideals of the Western tradition? In your opinion, how can these ideals best be preserved?

Since 1989, momentous events have utterly changed the world. The superpower polarization of world politics ended, and a new, multicentered, unstable world order has emerged.

Western civilization and its ideals have fostered transcultural worldwide modernity. At the same time, however, traditional cultural diversity still simmers. On the one hand, global interdependence promotes peaceful cooperation; on the other, it causes a clash of cultural traditions, giving rise to contagious violence and extremism. ❖

THE POST-COLD WAR WORLD

Post-Communist Russia and the Former Soviet Republics

Throughout the 1990s and into the twenty-first century, the Russian Federal Republic has been struggling to bring its political and economic systems into conformity with the Western model while coping with its loss of territory and superpower status. The collapse of the Soviet Union revealed Russia to be a weak, poorly developed society beset by profound problems.

Yeltsin's "Shock Therapy."　Marred by mismanagement, waste, and lack of incentives, the Soviet economic system had failed miserably in comparison with Western capitalism. In order to reform the economy and improve the standard of living of the Russian people, which lagged far behind living standards in Western lands, President Yeltsin, emerging in 1990 as the leader of the new Russia, made a sudden switch in 1992 from a state-run economy to private ownership and a capitalist market system. This precipitous transfer of state firms to private ownership—"shock therapy"—in many ways proved a disaster. The chief beneficiaries of privatization were often the same inefficient managers who had controlled the economy during the Soviet era and amassed wealth by unscrupulous means. Industrial decline, the withdrawal of government subsidies, and ruinous inflation reduced millions of people dependent on pensions to hand-to-mouth subsistence. Many working Russians also sank into poverty as real wages plummeted some 40 percent from 1992 to 1998. Workers often had to wait two to six months for their paychecks, and unemployment soared.

With popular unrest mounting and facing opposition from Communist hard-liners, Yeltsin was forced to slow his liberalization of the economy; the social costs—public confusion over bewildering changes, a sharp decline in the standard of living, and the loss of productivity leading to shortages—were too high. "No more experiments," advised slogans spray-painted on walls.

Yeltsin consolidated his power by making alliances with a small group of businessmen, the "oligarchs," who had grown wealthy by acquiring former state-owned enterprises at extremely low prices. They plundered the firms for assets, concentrating Russia's wealth in their own hands, and they gained control of banks. As law enforcement deteriorated, organized crime became a major force in Russian life.

In 1996, the oligarchs financed Yeltsin's bid for reelection as president, which he won despite suffering a heart attack during the election campaign. In 1997, he frankly acknowledged the difficulties that he and his country faced: "After creating a new political system, we failed to outfit it with new tools of government, and we ourselves did not learn to govern in a new way."[1]

Nevertheless, by winning reelection with the support of the oligarchs, Yeltsin vanquished the Communists in the Duma, the new legislature. In addition, by permitting the oligarchs to buy up the major state enterprises, he smashed Soviet central planning. It would be impossible in these circumstances to reinstate Communism in Russia. But many key enterprises, including banks and the media, were now controlled by unscrupulous oligarchs. In return for their support of Yeltsin, they became an inner political circle in the Kremlin, controlling the country's policies. No wonder Russians began to feel that the government itself had been "privatized."

In August 1998, everything changed. The dysfunctional banking system precipitated a second currency collapse, wiping out Russians' savings and livelihoods. Among the casualties were many of the oligarchs. Some were ruined by the collapse of their banks, others went abroad, and the remainder backed out of public life. Suddenly their political influence, which had been paramount since 1995, diminished dramatically, and a new generation of businessmen began to emerge.

Yeltsin resigned the presidency on New Year's Eve 1999, becoming the first Russian leader to give up power voluntarily. He made appalling mistakes, but he was determined to go down in history as the man who made the restoration of Communism in Russia impossible. It was no mean achievement.

Putin: Clamping Down. Yeltsin's chosen successor, Vladimir Putin, was determined to make his mark as a strongman during his short term as Yeltsin's prime minister by reopening the war in Chechnya, a small Islamic enclave in the Caucasus that had opposed Russian rule since its conquest in 1864. After two years of ruthless fighting, at great political damage to Yeltsin, the defeated Russian armies withdrew in 1996, leaving the burden of the final settlement of Chechnya's independence to the future. The war resumed in 1999 when Chechen rebels invaded neighboring Dagestan (a predominantly Muslim region that is part of Russia) in an effort to establish a united, independent, Islamic state in the Caucasus. At the same time, a terrorist attack on apartment buildings in Russian cities killed more than three hundred people and maimed many more. Putin put the blame for the attack on Chechens and stormed into the Caucasus to force the invaders out of Dagestan. The Chechen capital, Grozny, was devastated; ironically, the main victims were elderly Russian residents, the rebels having already escaped to the mountains. Russian troops took control of the war-devastated Caucasus region, but the Chechen leaders remained at large and continued guerrilla attacks on Russian soldiers.

Vladimir Putin became president of Russia at a time when modest economic stability was beginning to emerge, thanks largely to a spike in the price of oil and natural gas, Russia's chief exports. His main objective was to establish a strong centralized state. To this end, he reigned in the troublesome oligarchs, dismembering an oil group and absorbing their property into the state-controlled oil and gas company. This spectacular government takeover sent a chill through the energy sector of the economy and alarmed foreign investors, who worried that property rights might exist only at the whim of the Russian government. But Putin's popularity increased among people resentful of the oligarchs' wealth and pleased by strong economic growth. New elites grew fabulously wealthy.

More alarmingly, President Putin steadily increased government control of television and eroded freedom of the press—in the 2000s numerous journalists were murdered, presumably on orders from the government. These actions drew immediate criticism from Western countries, which had hoped that Russia would follow a democratic path in allowing a free media and encouraging discussion and criticism of political issues.

The Chechen conflict sprang dramatically onto the front pages in October 2002 when pro-Chechen terrorists seized a theater in Moscow in the middle of a performance. In the resulting counterattack, all the hostage takers and 129 hostages were killed by an inept gas attack on the theater by Russian authorities. The worst terrorist attack in Russia took place on the first day of the new school year in 2004. Chechen fighters seized a school in Beslan in the Caucasus and held hundreds of children, parents, and teachers hostage. More than three hundred hostages died, many of them children. The massacre led to worldwide revulsion, and Putin denounced it as part of global Islamic terrorism.

Despite the clear influence of Islamic radicalism, the principal motive of the Chechen fighters was independence from Russia. This was unacceptable to Putin, who feared that granting independence to any region or nationality in multiethnic Russia would weaken the fabric of the fragile country.

Exhausted by years of turmoil, many Russians supported Putin; they appreciated his strong leadership that imposed order. Others saw it as authoritarianism triumphing over Russia's nascent democracy; that Putin was taking his country back to one-party rule. His immediate associates in the Kremlin were drawn from the *siloviki*, former security officials who shared his hard-line law-and-order orientation and had no patience for the uncertainties of democracy.

The Russian constitution limits the president to two consecutive terms in office. In the fall of 2007, Putin moved dramatically to continue his power by appointing obscure minister Dmitry Medvedev as his prime minister and grooming him as his successor to the presidency. Putin further announced that he would lead his party, United Russia, in the December 2007 election; its victory gave him a seat in the lower house of Parliament, from which he then became prime minister. His power had not diminished.

For Putin, a strong Russian nationalist, the demise of the Soviet Union was a catastrophe; he has sought to restore Russia's power and influence lost in the decades after the breakup of the Soviet Union. He has deliberately stirred nationalist sentiments among the Russian people, crushed the revolt in Chechnya, and invaded neighboring Georgia. Putin ordered the invasion in August 2008 when Georgia tried to retake South Ossetia, one of two regions that had broken away from Georgian control in the 1990s and achieved de facto independence. Both of these break-away regions are close to Russia, and Mikhail Saakashvili, the pro-Western president of Georgia, is close to the United States and wants his country to join NATO. In preventing Georgia from reasserting its authority over the two break-away regions, Moscow was also displaying its power to Washington. Most recently, in 2013, Putin strongly pressured Ukraine to reject membership in the European Union. Mass protests broke out in November then turned bloody in February 2014, forcing the pro-Kremlin president, Viktor F. Yanukovich, to flee the capital. Shortly after that Putin ordered the invasion of the Crimea, a region of the Ukraine inhabited by a majority of Russians, many of whom feel a greater attachment to Russia than to the Ukraine. The seizure of Ukrainian territory aroused great tension between Putin's Russia and the United States and European countries. Pro-Russian activists continued to clash with authorities in several cities and Western leaders scrambled to diffuse tensions.

The gap between Russia and the West remains enormous. Russia has vast natural resources and a well-educated population. Yet it is still a huge, poor country burdened with a crumbling infrastructure, desperate rural poverty, and crime and corruption. Russia, in tsarist times "the breadbasket of Europe," is now a net importer of agricultural and food products, though output has increased in the past decade. In recent years, huge exports of energy products and raw materials have fueled substantial economic growth and an expansion of the middle class. Russia continues to face severe health problems that have hampered family life and work, and caused a decline in life expectancy: drug addiction, alcoholism, drug-resistant tuberculosis, AIDS, and increasing heart attacks and strokes caused by excessive smoking.

Unrealistic optimism at the time of the Soviet collapse that Russia would emerge as a free, democratic, and market-oriented state has changed to pessimism. Building a democratic civic society took centuries in the West; Russia cannot achieve that in one generation. Moreover, the Communist legacy, with its bureaucratic inefficiency, stifling of individual initiative, and repression still weighs heavily on the country.

Central and Eastern Europe After 1989

After a century of war, occupation, and dictatorship, hopes ran high in the former Soviet satellite countries of Central and Eastern Europe. The countries that were closest to Western Europe geographically—Poland, Hungary, and the Czech Republic—were closest to Western political and economic systems and eager to move toward full democracy and market economies. The economic prospects began to improve with the help of increasing Western aid and trade. Thanks to economic integration with Western Europe, twelve former Soviet bloc countries joined NATO beginning in 1999, and from 2004 to 2013 eleven entered the European Union (discussed later in the chapter).

In the 1990s, the former Yugoslavia became the most troubled region of Europe. Cobbled together after World War I as an artificial state composed of sharply different ethnic groups dominated by Serbians, Yugoslavia was torn apart by the nationalist ambitions set off by the collapse of the Soviet Union. In July 1991, Slovenia seceded; Croatia and Bosnia attempted to follow in 1992, ending Serbian domination. Because there were large Serbian populations in both Croatia and Bosnia, Yugoslav president Slobodan Milosevic, a Serb nationalist, refused to give up control and unleashed the Serb army, augmented by Bosnian Serbs, on the two countries. Ethnic hatred exploded, centered on Bosnia, a splintered mountainous region. Its major ethnoreligious groups—43 percent Muslim, 17 percent Catholic

Croat, and 31 percent Orthodox Serb—were scattered in multiethnic communities; there were few ethnically consolidated areas.

Muslims, Croats, and Serbs ruthlessly fought each other. The Bosnian Serbs, hoping to join with Serbia in a Greater Serbia, conquered 70 percent of Bosnia, conducting a brutal "ethnic cleansing" of Muslims while submitting Sarajevo, Bosnia's capital, to bloody bombardment. All sides, but most of all the Serbs, committed heinous atrocities, provoking moral outrage. A U.N. force of sixty thousand peacekeepers vainly tried to halt ethnic cleansing by Serbs.

In August 1995, Croatia went on the offensive to drive Serbs out of its territory, and NATO used its air force for the first time in its fifty-year history, against the Bosnian Serbs. In November 1995, the United States stepped forward, in negotiations held in Dayton, Ohio, to promote peace. The Dayton Agreement proposed a Bosnian government equally shared by Muslims, Croats, and Serbs. While analysts praised NATO's operation to end the outrageous inhumanities of the Bosnian civil war, they were critical of both NATO and the United States for their delay in taking action.

In 1998, violence erupted between Serbs and ethnic Albanians in the Yugoslav province of Kosovo. This is a sacred place for Serbs, the site of Orthodox shrines and of the battle of Kosovo in 1389, in which the Ottoman Turks defeated the Serbs, ruling Kosovo until 1912. The Serbs regard the battle as the birth of the Serb nation. Ethnic antagonism has persisted between Serbs and the predominantly Muslim Albanians who form 90 percent of the population of two million. In 1998, President Milosevic, seeking to shore up his power by manipulating Serbian nationalist feelings, sent Serbian forces to crush Albanian separatists fighting for an independent Kosovo.

Repelled by the forced expulsions and massacres of innocent villagers, NATO felt compelled to intervene. Despite a threat of NATO air strikes, Milosevic, a dictator whose hands already were stained with the blood of thousands of victims in Bosnia, refused to allow a NATO peacekeeping force into Kosovo. NATO launched air strikes on Serbia in March 1999. At the same time special Serbian forces, determined to drive Albanians out of Kosovo, stormed into the region. Carrying the practice of ethnic cleansing in the region to a new level of brutality, they terrorized and murdered Albanians, systematically burned villages, confiscated valuables, and compelled their victims to flee the province. Hundreds of thousands of Albanian refugees streamed out of the country into neighboring lands, creating a massive humanitarian crisis.

The unrelenting NATO bombardment of Serbia, expected to be brief and decisive, continued for eleven weeks—so too did the ethnic cleansing of Kosovo—until Milosevic capitulated. Eventually the Kosovo Albanians were allowed to return to their ravaged country. A force of forty thousand NATO and U.N. troops remained in Kosovo through 2013 to assist with relief efforts, prevent revenge attacks on the remaining Serb population, and ensure Kosovo's autonomy.

The U.N. International Criminal Tribunal for the former Yugoslavia indicted President Milosevic and Bosnian Serb and Croatian leaders and military commanders on charges of genocide and crimes against humanity. Milosevic went on trial in 2002 but died in 2006 before sentencing.

After the war, the former Yugoslavia, mired in poverty and dependent on foreign aid, consisted only of a dysfunctional federation of Serbia, Montenegro, and Kosovo. Tiny Montenegro declared its independence in June 2006, while Kosovo remained part of Serbia and an international protectorate of the United Nations. Its Albanian leadership, eager for a future apart from Serbia, declared independence in February 2008. America and most European countries recognized Kosovo's independence, but Serbia, bitterly opposed to the loss of sacred historical territory in Kosovo and backed by its ally, Russia, denounced Kosovo's independence as illegal.

The European Union

After the end of World War II, six Western European nations began a slow process of economic, political, and cultural integration. The collapse of Soviet power supplied a sudden jolt for accelerating this trend. In 1991, in the Dutch city of Maastricht, the members of the European Community (EC), now twelve in number,

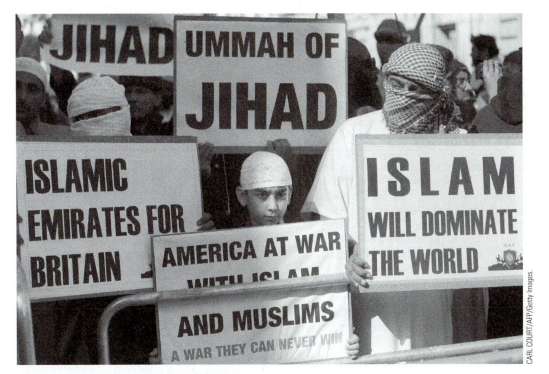

Muslim Militants in Britain Display Their Hatred of the West. Demonstrations against the West, Israel, and Jews have been frequent occurrences in Muslim lands and Europe. On September 11, 2011, the tenth anniversary of 9/11, Muslim militants demonstrated outside the U.S. embassy in London. They brandished placards that expressed hatred of the United States and their desire to extend Islamic power throughout the globe. (Ummah means the Muslim nation; an emirate is a Muslim state which the demonstrators hope to establish in Britain.)

negotiated the Maastricht Treaty, designed to shape Europe into a unified economic and political force. By 1993, the member states had ratified the treaty and, in recognition of its aims, the European Community became the European Union. In 1999, eleven members adopted a common monetary unit, the euro; by 2009, the Eurozone (countries that use the euro) had expanded to seventeen countries with several more scheduled to join, starting with Latvia in 2014. In the new Europe, goods, labor, capital, and services move freely between countries, and English has become the common language for Europeans who travel and work throughout the union.

On May 1, 2004, the European Union accepted ten new members, eight of which had been former Communist countries—the Czech Republic, Estonia, Hungary, Latvia, Lithuania, Poland, Slovakia, and Slovenia—together with Cyprus and Malta. They were followed in 2007 by Romania and Bulgaria and by Croatia in 2013, for a total of twenty-eight members. Several candidates now await entry, including Muslim Turkey. This ambitious enlargement of the EU marked the historic reintegration of a continent that had been divided for forty-five years by the iron curtain. With 500 million inhabitants, it is the world's biggest economic and trading bloc.

All the new members had made progress toward a market economy and had demonstrated acceptable standards of democracy and human rights. However, the new countries are much poorer than previous entrants to the EU and naturally hope to increase their prosperity with the help of EU economic assistance.

Many Europeans worried about the future of their countries. Were they surrendering their identity, along with their sovereignty, to the EU? Were Europeanization and globalization (the latter frequently defined as "American imperialism") going to change irrevocably their national status? Many Europeans do not identify with the EU, personified by remote Eurocrats headquartered in Brussels, Belgium. On the positive side, since a large part of EU governance involved generous subsidies to member countries, especially to their agricultural sectors, most citizens were fairly content with this arrangement.

The global financial meltdown of 2008 made it difficult for the EU member countries to maintain their heavy government spending, often for social welfare. Unemployment soared in several countries. Investor confidence fell markedly. Increased borrowing costs further drove up budget deficits. During the next few years, Greece, Portugal, Ireland, and Cyprus received huge bailouts from the Euro Monetary Union (EMU), with Germany paying the lion's share. Many richer Europeans resented having to rescue their poorer neighbors, whom they considered wasteful spenders. Drastic budget cuts were implemented throughout Europe, sparking protests and even violence.

Nevertheless, as late as summer 2013, most economies of the EU remained in the doldrums, with overall Eurozone unemployment hovering at 12 percent and joblessness among the young hitting 24 percent and more than twice that in Greece and Spain. All Europeans expect generous cradle to grave social welfare programs, yet their aging (and even declining) populations and slower growing productivity will make paying for them more and more difficult. Resolving this dilemma consumed much political attention throughout Europe in the early twenty-first century.

The three largest countries in the European Union are France, Germany, and the United Kingdom. France and Germany are the largest countries in terms of area, with populations of 62 million and 83 million, respectively; they have traditionally set the agenda for the EU. France and the United Kingdom are nuclear powers. The United Kingdom, with a population of 60 million crammed into its small islands, maintains a special relationship with the United States.

In the United Kingdom, Prime Minister Margaret Thatcher resigned in 1990 in the face of conservative criticism. Her successor, John Major, maintained an uncertain majority in Parliament, increasingly troubled by political scandals and the rising popularity of the Labour party. In the election of 1997, that party, revitalized by Tony Blair, its young and lively leader in close touch with the people, scored an impressive victory. Under his leadership, the Labour party moved to the political center, endorsing a pro-business, pro-enterprise policy that limited benefits for the poor, and jettisoned Labour's old working-class/state-ownership image. This policy gave the country an unusually strong economy, and London became a vibrant worldwide financial center.

Blaire achieved a remarkable success in Northern Ireland, where Protestant and Catholics had long been at war with each other. In 1998, he helped to end the conflict and create an elected assembly. Although at times threatening to breakdown, the experiment in power sharing continues to function. In bringing the two sides together, Blair had succeeded where every previous prime minister had failed.

Prime Minister Blair, despite strong opposition in Britain, supported the United States–led invasion of Iraq in 2003 and committed forces to the coalition. He saw his country as an important bridge between the EU and America—a stance that became increasingly unpopular both in his own country and within the EU. All the promise of Blair's early years and his extraordinary popularity were eroded by his unwavering support of the detested war in Iraq. He resigned in mid-2007 and was succeeded by Gordon Brown, who had been Blair's impressive chancellor of the Exchequer. Brown was also less supportive of the Iraq War and removed all but a small contingent of troops in 2009. Following disappointing election results in May 2010, Brown resigned and was replaced by David Cameron, a Conservative who entered into a coalition with left-leaning Liberal Democrats. A major theme of his administration has been to roll back what he considered profligate social spending by previous Labour governments. Political scandals, austerity policies, and Britain's poor economic performance (until 2013), however, weakened public support for Cameron. His support for a gay marriage bill, which became law in July 2013, set many in his party against him. Yet his demand to renegotiate Britain's membership in the EU and promise to submit that membership to a popular vote in 2017, should the Tories win reelection in 2015, enjoyed broad support.

France, including the Mediterranean island of Corsica, has the largest territorial state in the European Union. Proud of their historical tradition, the French cherish their past and are uneasy about the intrusion of alien ways, especially from the United States.

Succeeding Socialist François Mitterand in 1995, Jacques Chirac, a moderate-conservative, continued the tradition of a strong, centralized state with generous welfare benefits. Chirac had no viable opposition, apart from a perennial gadfly, Jean Marie Le Pen, an anti-immigration, anti-EU, anti-globalization, anti-Semitic, racist candidate of the far Right, who qualified (with 18 percent of the vote) for a presidential runoff election against Chirac in 2002. He lost resoundingly, but the affair revealed a troubling undercurrent in French society.

In 2004, President Chirac was at the center of a storm that divided the six million Muslims living in France. A law banned the wearing of symbols of religion in France's traditionally secular schools; it was aimed primarily at the headscarves worn by Muslim girls. This reaffirmation of the secular nature of the French state and its insistence on cultural uniformity was at odds with the policies of other EU countries, which have accepted multiculturalism and tolerate headscarves in schools.

President Chirac's stand against participation in the Iraq War in 2003 brought him renewed popularity in France. At the same time, however, France worked closely with NATO to preserve peace in the Balkans. Chirac's chief concern was cooperation with Germany in creating an effective European Union that balances French and German aspirations. Chirac was identified with a vision of a powerful, politically integrated Europe, serving as a French-led counterweight to the United States.

In 2007, Nicolas Sarkozy succeeded the aging Chirac. He came to office claiming a mandate for change that included domestic reforms, a new relationship with the United States, and an active role in the European Union, as well as fighting global poverty and global warming.

A vocal advocate of economic conservatism, Sarkozy cut taxes, increased spending on research and development, raised the minimum retirement age from 60 to 62, declined to fulfill many vacant civil service jobs, slashed government spending, and engineered a significant decline in greenhouse gas emissions; he also diminished central control over the country's universities. Sarkozy's plans to reform rules on labor, tighten welfare rules, and review public health insurance schemes started with abolishing the "special regimes" that allowed utilities and transport workers to retire at fifty on a full pension. It led to a one-day strike, but the public backed Sarkozy, not the strikers. It was a crucial change and hinted at success for future reforms.

In 2009, Sarkozy reintegrated France into the command structures of NATO, of which France was already a core member, and in 2011 spearheaded NATO's intervention in Libya (see page 544), which proved highly successful. Yet his main mission in office—to grow the economy—failed, in large part because of the euro crisis. High unemployment, slow economic growth, and a series of political scandals drove down his popularity. His 2012 budget proposed big tax increases and more spending cuts. By then, most citizens strongly disliked Sarkozy.

Germany has the largest population in the European Union and is proud of the peaceful reunification of the West and East in 1990, their leading role in the European Union, and their status as the fourth largest world economy. At the same time, the undying memory of Germany's role in World War II and the Holocaust continues to haunt the nation.

Helmut Kohl, as chancellor of West Germany, was the architect of the reunited Germany; he poured huge amounts of West German money into what had been the Communist German Democratic Republic, hoping for quick integration. However, attitudes and habits developed under Communism have persisted; having no experience with democracy, the 17 million former East Germans were somewhat disillusioned with unification. Unemployment was as high as 25 percent because Communist-era factories closed and no new industries were established. The rise in right-wing violence since reunification is particularly severe in the old East Germany, where neo-Nazis and skinheads, usually underemployed and alienated youth, have been responsible for outbreaks of lawlessness and brutality against "outsiders"—predominantly Turkish immigrants and Jews—whom they regard as parasites draining away the country's resources and diluting its national character.

Kohl's conservative chancellorship ended after sixteen eventful years. In 1998, Germans elected Gerhard Schröder, leader of the Social Democrats, as his successor. Schröder's party formed a coalition with the Greens, who scaled down their environmental and pacifist radicalism. Schröder sent combat forces to Kosovo in 1999—the first German military deployment since World War II—and Afghanistan in 2001 (over four thousand troops remained in mid-2013). Like Chirac, however, he vociferously denounced the impending Iraq War, which helped him win reelection in 2002.

In 2003, when German unemployment stood at 11.6 percent, Schröder announced Agenda 2010. It promised employers more flexibility in hiring and firing workers, curtailed unemployment benefits, and created incentives for the unemployed to accept available jobs. This was a radical shift for his party, which two decades before had stood for unions and social justice. Joblessness slid from over 15 percent in 2005 to under 10 percent in 2012.

These positive results were too late to prevent voters in 2005 electing Angela Merkel, Germany's first female chancellor and a former scientist who grew up in East Germany. Fixing the crisis of the Eurozone has been her chief end. A workaholic stateswoman of enormous talent, she became the most powerful political figure in Europe, perhaps second in the world only to Barack Obama. Under her leadership, Germany began to regain its confidence. She rejected a EU proposal to impose a quota for women company directors, supported an initiative to increase subsidies to mothers who stay home with their children, and promoted numerous women to mid-level positions in her government. By spring 2013, unemployment had fallen to 5.4 percent, compared to 12.1 percent in the Eurozone. Among the major European countries, only Germany had kept its perfect AAA credit rating.

Despite its troubles, analysts are generally optimistic about Europe's future. Its leaders peacefully and productively have integrated over two dozen countries and virtually banished warfare—a unique historical achievement. It boasts the world's highest-energy particle collider, the best and most extensive high-speed rail network, the most important financial center (London), and four of the five most energy-efficient countries (along with Japan). Europe is the second biggest producer of cars (after China) and is home to the second biggest airplane manufacturer (Airbus) and second biggest exporter (Germany). Europe vies with the United States in aerospace technology.

NEW AND OLD PROBLEMS: MUSLIM IMMIGRATION AND THE RESURGENCE OF ANTI-SEMITISM

Among the problems that have burdened Europe in the first decade of the twenty-first century are the threat of terrorism by radical Islamists, the failure of millions of Muslim immigrants to integrate into European society, and a resurgence of anti-Semitism. The issue of terrorism is discussed in the next section.

Muslim Immigration

In the 1950s and 1960s, Western Europe's booming economy created a demand for cheap labor that was met by an influx of millions of Muslims from Turkey, Pakistan, and North Africa. In succeeding decades, additional millions of Muslim immigrants from the Middle East and sub-Saharan Africa, many of them illegal, settled in various European lands. Like other immigrants, they sought to join relatives, find economic opportunities, or escape from oppressive regimes. Several of these countries, including France, Germany, Britain, Belgium, Holland, Spain, and Denmark, now have substantial Muslim populations. While some Muslims have achieved success in business and academia, Muslims remain profoundly alienated from European society and at odds with its values. European liberal democracy, which espouses religious freedom, equal rights for women, separation of church and state, and freedom of expression, noticeably conflicts with many facets of Islamic society.

In describing the failure of Muslim integration, analysts refer to the demands of some Muslim groups that they be governed by their own religious law, sharia, rather than the law of the land. They also cite the perpetuation in Europe by some Muslims of cultural mores that sanction polygamy, forced marriages between young girls and much older men, wife-beating, and so-called honor killings of "wayward" females, and require women to keep their bodies and faces hidden from view; the high crime rate among Muslims—in Britain Muslims are 2 percent of the population, but more than 8 percent of the prison population; the high rate of dependency on social welfare; and the emergence of extremist Islamist cells in European lands that have participated in several terrorist acts—much of the planning for the 9/11 attacks took place in Hamburg, Germany. British commentators have raised a difficult question. In the past, they say, immigrant Jews and recently Sikhs and Hindus have thrived in Britain, even when confronted with prejudice. Why, they ask, is the integration of Muslim immigrants in Western society so fraught with problems?

In the fall of 2005, the suburbs of Paris and scores of other French cities were convulsed by two weeks of rioting—nearly nine thousand cars were set afire and schools, shops, and churches burned to the ground—by young Muslim males from the bleak housing projects inhabited principally by North African immigrants. That the great majority of rioters were not recent immigrants but had been born in France was particularly distressing to officials, for the French government prided itself on creating a uniform French identity that superseded ethnic and religious origins. Whatever the aspirations of the government, many French citizens remain resentful of North African immigrants, whom they view as an alien minority that, unlike other immigrants, has failed to integrate into French society. They point to the immigrants' preference for native cultural traditions, the high cost of welfare payments they receive, and the high crime rate among them—Muslims, about 10 percent of the nation, constitute more than 50 percent of France's prison population. Numerous commentators, however, interpreted the riots as a rebellion by a resentful underclass protesting discrimination, segregation, poverty, and a staggering unemployment rate—as much as 40 percent—for young Muslim males.

Faced with what is perceived as a rapidly growing, unassimilable Muslim minority that is hostile to Western values, lives in isolated communities, often does not speak the host nation's language, and recruits and finances terrorists, Europe is experiencing a backlash against Muslim immigrants and multiculturalism. An increasing number of Europeans now say that the premise of multiculturalism—assigning equal value to and tolerating Islamic traditions—was a mistake, for several of these traditions undermine democracy and fragment the nation. There is the fear that extremist right-wing political parties—ultranationalistic, racist, and intolerant—will capitalize on this wave of anti-immigrant sentiment that is sweeping across Europe.

Increasingly, governments are introducing tighter immigration laws and are deporting Muslim radicals. They are also trying to work with moderate Muslims who support integration into European society and value Europe's liberal-democratic tradition. However, successful integration, say some commentators, is a two-way street. It is necessary that European society also address the socioeconomic problems burdening Muslims, overcome racist attitudes toward immigrants, and recognize the fact that numerous Muslims do work and pay taxes, respect the laws of their adopted country, and reject extremism; most importantly, Muslims must be made to feel that their religion is not being attacked and insulted. For many years to come, Europeans will be confronted with—or tormented by—the question of Islam's place in their country.

Resurgence of Anti-Semitism

In the decades following the Holocaust, overt anti-Semitism appeared to have receded in Western Europe. The outbursts of the traditionally anti-Semitic far Right did not greatly affect the surviving Jews and their descendants, who represented a model of successful integration. In recent years, however, there has been a significant upsurge of anti-Semitic incidents in European lands, including physical assaults, even murder; the firebombing of Jewish synagogues, schools, and homes; and the desecration of Jewish cemeteries with Nazi symbols—much of it, but not all, initiated by the growing number of Muslims residing in Western Europe. Denis MacShane, a Labor member of Parliament who in 2007 chaired a committee of British parliamentarians that studied anti-Semitism in Britain, concluded that "hatred of Jews has reached new heights in Europe."[2] Similar conclusions were reached by the U.S. State Department and the Parliamentary Assembly of the Council of Europe.

"It is Islamism [Muslim extremism] that has unleashed new twenty-first century anti-Semitism," observes MacShane, "and it is impossible to discuss the problem without dealing with Islamism."[3] The creation of Israel on what is perceived as inviolable Muslim land and the Jewish state's ongoing conflict with the Palestinians have stirred the cauldron of Jew-hatred in the Arab and Muslim world. Now reaching epidemic proportions, anti-Semitism has become a principal theme in the Middle Eastern media and a motivation for attacks on Jews by Muslims living in Europe. As Cardinal Tucci, the director of Vatican Radio, stated in November 2003: "Now in the whole Muslim world, in the media, the radio, television, in schools, a whole system inciting to anti-Semitism exists. It is the worst anti-Semitism that can be imagined after Nazi anti-Semitism, if not its equal."[4]

Contemporary Muslim anti-Semitism borrows considerably from traditional European anti-Semitism—Christian, nationalist, and Nazi. Like the Nazis, much of the Muslim world perceives Jews as a criminal people that threatens all humanity, blames the Jews for their misfortunes, and holds out the image of a utopian future once Israel is eradicated and the Jews eliminated. As in Nazi Germany, the media in the Arab and Muslim world are often filled with repulsive caricatures of Jews—dark, stooped, sinister, hook-nosed, devil-like creatures—many of them taken from Nazi works. In Arab sermons and classrooms and on the Internet, Jews are often referred to as "accursed," "descendants of apes and pigs," "the scum of the human race," "the rats of the world," "bacteria," "vampires," "usurers," and "whoremongers."

Reminiscent of Nazi propaganda, no accusation against Jews is too absurd not to be included in the litany of Jewish evil propagated in the Muslim media, and not just by extremists. Hamas, the radical Palestinian organization that rules Gaza, maintains that Jews were responsible for the French Revolution, the Russian Revolution, both world wars, and the atomic bombing of Hiroshima and Nagasaki. Osama bin Laden maintained that Jews "in accordance with their religion, believe that human beings are their slaves and that those who refuse [to recognize this] should be put to death."[5] The Arab media have even revived the outrageous medieval blood libel that Jews are required to murder non-Jewish children in order to obtain their blood for making unleavened bread for Passover. Holocaust denial is widespread in the Middle East; so too is celebrating Hitler's mass murder of Jews. A columnist for *Al-Akhbar*, considered a moderate newspaper sponsored by the Egyptian government, gives "thanks to Hitler of blessed memory," for taking revenge against Jews—although Muslims "do have a complaint against him for his revenge on them was not enough."[6] And Dr. Ahmed Abu Halabiyah, rector of advanced studies at the Islamic University of Gaza, is more representative than unique; similar sentiments are frequently voiced in the Arab media: "The Jews . . . must be butchered and must be killed. . . . It is forbidden to have mercy in your hearts for the Jews in any place and in any land, make war on them anywhere that you find yourself. Any place that you meet them, kill them."[7]

Propagated over the Internet and by radical imams in mosques throughout Europe, this demonization of the Jew has incited Muslim youth in Europe to acts of intimidation, physical assault, and vandalism against Jews; it has also led to organized campaigns of vilification of Jews on college campuses. On a positive note, in some European lands, Muslim and Jewish organizations are engaged in interfaith dialogue, and some Muslim intellectuals and religious leaders have condemned anti-Semitic outbursts.

In addition to the anti-Semitic incidents initiated by Muslims residing in various European lands, analysts have pointed to the ongoing Jew-hatred of the far Right, and a rather new phenomenon, a growing and insidious anti-Semitism afflicting the Left.

As in the past, European anti-Semitism remains a bulwark of the far Right, traditionally hostile to the Enlightenment's legacy of reason, political freedom, and tolerance. Principally extreme nationalists, racists, Fascists, and neo-Nazis, they propagate Holocaust denial and Jewish conspiracy theories—Jews invented a "Holocaust hoax" in order to extract compensation from Germany; Jews control the world's media and finances and are conspiring to dominate the planet; Jews are the real power behind the U.S. government; Jews are a threat to the nation.

During the Nazi era and for decades before, the Left—liberals, socialists, trade unionists, and intellectuals, including many academics—had been the strongest defenders of Jews against their detractors and oppressors. But now the distinguishing feature of the "new anti-Semitism" is its adoption by a New Left that employs anti-Semitic language and imagery—linking the Star of David with the swastika, a recognized symbol of evil—to express its support of the Palestinians and to delegitimize Israel; for them, Israelis are today's Nazis and Israel is a criminal state that should disappear.

Many Europeans are concerned about the revival of anti-Semitism. They recognize that Jew-hatred and the irrational myths associated with it, which undermine rational thinking and incite barbaric violence, transcend a purely Jewish concern. They threaten the core values of Western civilization, as Nazism so painfully demonstrated.

CULTURE CLASH, TERRORISM, AND WAR

On September 11, 2001, nineteen Muslim Arabs, most of them from Saudi Arabia, hijacked four planes: two of them they crashed into the World Trade Center in New York, bringing down both towers; a third plane rammed into the Pentagon in Washington, D.C., causing severe damage; the fourth plane, apparently headed for the White House, crashed in a field in Pennsylvania when passengers heroically attacked the hijackers. In all, almost three thousand people perished in the worst terrorist attack in history. The meticulously planned operation was the work of Al Qaeda, an international terrorist network of militant Muslims, or Islamists, as they call themselves. In 1998, it was responsible for the deadly bombings of the American embassies in Kenya and Tanzania, which killed hundreds, and in 2000, it detonated a bomb next to the U.S. destroyer *Cole* in the harbor of Aden, costing the lives of seventeen American sailors.

The leader of Al Qaeda, Osama bin Laden, scion of an immensely wealthy Saudi family, operated from Afghanistan with the protection of the radical fundamentalist Taliban, who ruled the country, transforming it into a repressive regime based on a rigid interpretation of Islamic law. In particular, the Taliban imposed oppressive rules for women, permitting beatings by male relatives, prohibiting females from working, barring them from schools, and demanding that they wear a garment—the burka—that covered them from head to foot. Violators could be severely beaten, imprisoned, or executed.

When Taliban leaders refused to turn bin Laden over to the United States, President George W. Bush, supported by an international coalition, launched a military campaign whose ultimate goal was the destruction of international terrorism. Local Afghan forces opposed to the Taliban, assisted by American airpower—which proved decisive—defeated the Taliban in a few weeks. But the new democratically elected government, backed by American and NATO troops, continues to face immense problems: local warlords who defy central authority, a resurgence of Taliban fighters—many of them coming from the lawless tribal regions of neighboring Pakistan—and a country impoverished by years of warfare and misrule. Afghan officials, many of them corrupt and inefficient, generally owe their prime loyalties to family and tribe and not to the nation.

American and coalition forces have succeeded in killing and capturing numerous mid-level Taliban leaders and forcing Taliban fighters out of key population areas. Nevertheless, lack of security continues to plague the Afghan people. To promote instability, the Taliban deliberately

Primary Source

United Nations Secretary-General: *Ending Violence Against Women*, "the Systematic Domination of Women by Men"

In October 2006, the United Nations released the Secretary-General's in-depth study of violence against women, which concluded that "the pervasiveness of violence against women across the boundaries of nation, culture, race, class and religion points to its roots in patriarchy—the systematic domination of women by men." Excerpts from the study follow.

A number of key means through which male dominance and women's subordination are maintained are common to many settings. These include: . . . control over women's sexuality and reproductive capacity; cultural norms and practices that entrench women's unequal status; State structures and processes that legitimize and institutionalize gender inequalities; and violence against women. Violence against women is both a means by which women's subordination is perpetuated and a consequence of their subordination.

Violence against women serves as a mechanism for maintaining male authority. When a woman is subjected to violence for transgressing social norms governing female sexuality and family roles, for example, the violence is not only individual but, through its punitive and controlling functions, also reinforces prevailing gender norms. . . .

When the State fails to hold the perpetrators accountable, . . . [it] sends a message to society that male violence against women is both acceptable and inevitable. As a result, patterns of violent behaviour are normalized. . . .

Cultural justifications for restricting women's human rights have been asserted by some States and by social groups within many countries claiming to defend cultural tradition. . . . [R]eligious "fundamentalisms" in diverse geographic and religious contexts has become a serious challenge to efforts to secure women's human rights. . . .

Femicide [the murder of women] takes place in many contexts . . . [including] the protection of family "honour". For example, crimes committed in the name of "honour", usually by a brother, father, husband or other male family member, are a means of controlling women's choices, not only in the area of sexuality but also in other aspects of behaviour, such as freedom of movement. . . .

Crimes against women committed in the name of "honour" may occur within the family or within the community. . . . UNFPA estimated that 5,000 women are murdered by family members each year in "honour killings" around the world. . . .

Trafficking is a form of violence against women that takes place in multiple settings and usually involves many different actors including families, local brokers, international criminal networks and immigration authorities. Trafficking in human beings takes place both between and within countries. The majority of the victims of human trafficking are women and children, and many are trafficked for purposes of sexual exploitation.

Question for Analysis

1. According to the U.N. study, what means are used to maintain male dominance and female subordination?

Ending Violence Against Women: From Words to Action, Study of the Secretary-General, October 9, 2006.

target for assassination of local Afghan officials, police, and virtually anyone cooperating with the Americans. Suicide bombings and homemade explosives placed at roadsides and in cars have caused the death of American soldiers and Afghan civilians. The Taliban also threaten working women and has forced the closing of girls' schools.

After more than twelve years of conflict—the longest war in American history—Americans have grown increasingly disenchanted with the war, and President Barack Obama, who took office in 2009, started pulling out troops in 2011 and declared that almost all American troops will be out of Afghanistan by the end of 2014.

Julien Warnand/AFP/Getty Images.

A Culture Clash The Niqab worn by this Muslim woman on a street in Brussels covers the body from head to toe, leaving only a slit for the eyes. Maintaining that such dress demeans women, Europeans are increasingly urging banning it outside the home.

Bin Laden and other Arabs from Morocco to Yemen, devoted to a militant Islam, had fought in Afghanistan to drive out the Soviets. During that conflict, bin Laden and his cohorts drew up plans for the creation of an Islamic world-state governed by Islamic law, a revival of the medieval caliphate. In 1998, bin Laden told his followers that the stationing of American troops, an army of "Crusaders," in Saudi Arabia, "the land of the two holy mosques," demonstrated that America was waging war against God, Muhammad, and Muslims. Bin Laden wanted to drive Westerners—the "infidel" they call them—and Western values out of Islamic lands and impose a narrow, intolerant version of Islam on the Muslim world. His followers are zealots who are convinced that they are doing God's will. Recruits for suicide missions are equally convinced that they are waging holy war against the enemies of God and their centers of evil, for which they will be richly rewarded in Paradise. In 1998, bin Laden called "on every Muslim who believes in Allah and wishes to be rewarded to comply with Allah's order to kill the Americans and plunder their money wherever and whenever they find it. . . . to launch the raid on Satan's U.S troops and the devil's supporters allying with them."[8]

To be sure, the actions of bin Laden and his followers violated core Islamic teachings against killing civilians. At the same time, however, terrorists find religious justification for their actions in Islamic tradition. The early followers of Muhammad, says Bernard Lewis, divided the world

> *into two houses: the House of Islam, in which a Muslim government ruled and Muslim law prevailed, and the House of War, the rest of the world . . . ruled by infidels. Between the two, there was to be a perpetual state of war until the entire world either embraced Islam or submitted to the rule of the Muslim state. . . . For Osama bin Laden, 2001 marks the resumption of the war for the religious dominance of the world that began in the seventh century. For him and his followers, this is the moment of opportunity. Today America exemplifies the civilization that embodies the leadership of the House of War, and it . . . has become degenerate and demoralized, ready to be overthrown.[9]*

After September 11, several terrorist operations in Europe and the United States were thwarted, including attempts to explode an airplane headed for Detroit and planting an explosive device in Times Square. But terrorists, either loosely or directly affiliated with Al Qaeda, succeeded in other operations in several countries, most of them suicide bombings that killed and wounded many innocents. In July 2005, Muslim suicide bombers killed more than fifty people and injured seven hundred in a terrorist attack on London's transit system. A year later, British security forces foiled a terrorist plot to blow up several transatlantic flights departing from Heathrow airport that would have killed more people than had perished on September 11. That the planners and perpetrators of these attacks were British citizens terrorizing their fellow citizens distressed analysts; they feared that the millions of Muslims dwelling in Europe were potential recruits for extremist Islamic groups, including Al Qaeda, engaged in holy war against the West and that European cities would become targets of fanatical suicide bombers. Likewise, U.S. officials are disconcerted by a number of terrorist attempts on American soil by Islamic radicals who are American citizens. (To be sure, the overwhelming number of American Muslims are loyal citizens and do not support terrorism.)

A tenacious United States, and other countries with varying degrees of determination and effectiveness, have combated militant Islam. The tracking down, capture, and killing of Al Qaeda leaders, at times using sophisticated unmanned drones, and rigorous international efforts to destabilize Al Qaeda's vast financial network had weakened the terrorist organization. Then on May 1, 2011, President Barak Obama announced that a superbly orchestrated operation by the CIA and Navy Seals killed bin Laden—not in a cave in Pakistan's remote tribal lands, where it was generally thought he was hiding, but in a large, specially built compound with tall security fences in an upscale section of a town only 70 miles from the capital.

But the death of bin Laden does not mean the end of Al Qaeda or Islamist terrorism. With Al Qaeda located in numerous countries across the Middle East and Africa, international terrorism remains a threat to world stability. Moreover, throughout the globe there are many affiliated,

but independent, Islamist groups and freelancers that are inspired by bin Laden's ideology. Like bin Laden, these offshoots regard Muslims as victims of Western exploitation and believe that their faith demands that they fight and conquer nonbelievers.

A horrific example of terrorism by freelancers that shocked the American people occurred during the running of the famed Boston Marathon in April 2013. Two Muslim brothers, refugees from the region where Russia is battling Chechen separatists (see page 530), had lived for several years in the United States, which had granted their family asylum (and education and welfare); one brother had become a naturalized citizen. After embracing Islamic extremism, they planted explosives near the finish line of the race, crowded with spectators. The attack left three people dead and some 260 injured, sixteen of whom, including children, lost legs or feet. One brother died in a fierce gun battle with police and the other is awaiting trial after recovering from serious wounds.

Despite the seizure of Al Qaeda's assets, local cells continue to receive substantial funds from wealthy Arab donors, particularly Saudi Arabians, from money contributed by the faithful purportedly for charitable causes, and from the tens of millions paid by European governments for the release of their kidnapped citizens. Nor do terrorist undertakings require great sums of money. The bombings of a night club in Bali that killed two hundred and two people, including eighty-two Australians, cost less than $35,000, the London subway bombings less than $500, and the September 11 attacks under $500,000. And Al Qaeda, with local support, has set up training camps in the remote tribal areas of Pakistan and the mountains and deserts of Yemen. Worsening the threat are jihadist sites on the Internet that inflame young Muslims and instruct them in preparing and planting explosives.

The events of September 11 may have signaled a new type of warfare for a new century. Free and open societies like the United States are vulnerable to attack, less from states that are deterred by America's might—as in the Cold War—than by stateless conspiratorial groups employing modern computers, communications, and difficult-to-trace financial operations to organize and finance terrorism. Such groups are not deterred by America's

DOWNFALL OF A TYRANT After Baghdad, the capital of Iraq, had been taken by American forces in April 2003, the twenty-foot stature of Saddam Hussein was pulled down by Iraqis with the assistance of a U.S. vehicle.

arsenal. And there is the fearful prospect that a rogue state will supply these groups with biological, chemical, and eventually nuclear weapons to wage war by proxy.

It was just such a fear that led President Bush in March 2003 to order an invasion of Iraq. The war was supported by Great Britain, which provided military assistance, but France, Germany, and Russia strongly opposed the decision. In about three weeks, U.S. and British forces, in an awesome display of operational planning and precision weaponry suffering minimal casualties, destroyed Iraq's military hardware and decimated its armies. The victorious coalition forces uncovered torture chambers, where "enemies" of Hussein's regime

were brutalized, and mass graves, where thousands were slaughtered at the tyrant's command. In December 2003, Saddam Hussein was captured. Put on trial by Iraqi authorities and found guilty of crimes against humanity, Saddam was executed by hanging at the end of December 2006.

But vexing problems remained. Could the United States install a democratic regime in a country torn by ethnic, religious, and tribal hatreds; where some Iraqis regarded the Americans as hated occupiers; and where democratic traditions and attitudes were largely lacking?

The United States declared that it had invaded Iraq to overthrow a ruthless dictator who had used poison gas against Iranian forces and Kurdish rebels in the 1980s and was now feverishly amassing an arsenal of biological and chemical weapons and was also seeking a nuclear capability. Now, warned the United States, there was a danger that Hussein would supply these weapons of mass destruction (WMD) to be used against Americans. However, American intelligence—and the intelligence of other countries—was faulty. When no such weapons were found in the months after Iraq's defeat, critics in several lands accused the United States of pursuing a reckless foreign policy.

After crushing the Iraqi army, coalition forces still faced attacks principally from militant Muslims or Jihadists, most of them were Sunni Muslims who had received favored treatment under Saddam. The insurgents also targeted Shi'ite Muslims who constitute the majority of the population and had been cruelly oppressed by Saddam. After reaching a peak in 2006 and 2007, the barbaric sectarian violence eased due in part to the intervention of coalition forces.

By the end of 2011, President Obama had withdrawn American forces from Iraq. More than 4,450 American soldiers died in the seven-and-a-half-year conflict; there were more than 160,000 Iraqi civilian fatalities, and some 1.5 million had fled the country. When it pulled its troops out, the United States declared that Iraq was on track to becoming a stable democracy, but once American troops withdrew, the Iraqi government had great difficulty controlling the insurgency and renewed religious violence, which increased the death toll and made daily life insecure. Sunni insurgents, who regard Shi'ites as heretics, felt maltreated by the Shi'ite led government—Shi'ites constitute the majority of the population—which purged them from positions in the government and the military. Determined to strike at Shi'ite power, Sunni militants carried out murderous car bombings and suicide attacks directed against Shi'ites congregating in markets, cafes, at funerals, and other crowded areas that have killed thousands of civilians.

Many Sunni militants are members of the radical Islamic State of Iraq and Syria (ISIS), a jihadist terrorist organization that vowed to create an Islamic religious state that would span Sunni-dominated regions of Syria and Iraq. ISIS intends to rule with Taliban-like rigor in areas under its control. In late spring 2014, ISIS seized vast areas of Iraq. The Iraqi army, which greatly outnumbered the insurgents, collapsed; soldiers simply fled, leaving behind stores of American-supplied arms, including heavy equipment. Even Sunnis, who do not want their lives to be regulated by Islamist extremists, have sided with ISIS, so hateful are they of the Shi'ite-led government's policies. ISIS jihadists are considered more brutal and fanatic than Al Qaeda; they have crucified and beheaded opponents and slaughtered hundreds of captured Shi'ite prisoners in a mass execution (they posted gruesome photos and videotapes of these atrocities online).

In June, 2014, ISIS declared that the territory it controlled constituted a revived caliphate—the Islamic empire that had ruled over Muslim lands for centuries. ISIS called on all jihadists worldwide to swear loyalty to the new caliph, the head of ISIS. President Obama first declared that the United States would not get embroiled again in combat in Iraq; it would only provide several hundred military advisers to help train Iraqi security forces. But as ISIS' brutality against minorities, including Christians, grew more barbaric, and fearful that ISIS' growing power posed a threat to the Western world—ISIS is an offshoot of Al Qaeda—President Obama ordered air strikes against the terrorists. The United States wanted to protect the Kurds who share Western values and have established a semi-autonomous state in fragmented Iraq.

Many analysts conclude that the Iraqi and Afghan conflicts demonstrate once more the immense difficulty of transplanting Western democratic values and institutions to regions whose history and cultural traditions do not easily mesh with democracy and whose prime allegiance to sect and ethnic group impede a sense of citizenship in a pluralistic state. And they point to a larger concern: these costly and unpopular wars—some six thousand American fatalities and expenditures of more than one trillion dollars—illustrate the limitations of American power. The American military had demonstrated the ability to wage successful counterterrorism campaigns, but, say some analysts, it should not be entrapped into nation-building, an amorphous objective fraught with uncertainty that is beyond the capacity of the military, or, indeed, of the U.S. government.

In early 2011, a wave of popular protest against autocratic rulers—what has been called the "Arab Spring"—swept across the Arab world, a region where democracy has been dismissed as an impossible dream. Many of the participants were alienated and educated youth clamoring for jobs and political freedom.

Because it held the promise of constructive change and the advancement of human rights, Western policy makers were euphoric over the democratic thrust in the Arab world. But the euphoria soon faded. The forty year tyranny of Maummar el-Qaddafi, who was killed by rebels, came to an end, but tribal conflicts, private militias, and weak central authority rather than democracy characterized the post-Qaddafi Libya. In Syria, the revolt against the tyrannical rule of President Bash-al Assad has led to a vicious civil war in which an estimated 160,000 people have perished and some two million have fled to neighboring countries. In August 2013, the Assad regime used poison gas to regain control over a Sunni Suburb of Damascus, killing, in a single night, an estimated one thousand civilians, including several hundred children, who died painfully. Enraged by this inhuman act that violated international law against the use of chemical weapons, President Obama threatened a limited punitive strike and American warships with missile weapons moved closer to Syria. Assad and the United States accepted a Russian proposal—the Russians are a principal supplier of armaments to Assad's regime—to turn Syria's stockpile of chemical weapons over to international authorities for destruction. Acting quickly, both foreign powers reached an agreement that called for the removal or destruction of Syria's chemical weapons by the middle of 2014.

There is a growing fear that the secular and democratic movement is being usurped by radical Islamists and jihadists seeking to establish an authoritarian theocratic regime that seeks to foist a rigid interpretation of Islamic law and hatred of the West. For a short period the Muslim Brotherhood, an anti-Western party that seeks to impose strict religious rule, gained power in Egypt. After massive public demonstrations against Mohamed Morsi, the Muslim Brotherhood's democratically elected president who was tightening his party's control over the country, the Egyptian military ousted him; in mass shootings, security forces killed more than a thousand of Morsi supporters protesting the coup and then jailed the leaders of the Brotherhood, including Morsi, and seized its assets. In succeeding months, the military-backed government designated the movement a terrorist organization and outlawed it.

And in Syria, Sunni extremists, several thousand of whom are volunteers from numerous lands who see themselves as holy warriors, have joined the civil war; many are members of ISIS that has succeeded Al Qaeda as the most formidable terrorist group in the Arab world. It is believed that three thousand Westerners, including more than seventy Americans, are among the jihadist volunteers; analyst worry that they will return to Europe and America as battle-hardened terrorists. The failure of the Arab Spring demonstrates how little the ethic of tolerance, the acceptance of different viewpoints, pervades Arab society.

OUR GLOBAL AGE: PROMISE AND PROBLEMS

In the twenty-first century, globalization continues relentlessly; the world is being knit ever closer together by the spread of Western ideals, popular culture (particularly American), free-market capitalism, and technology. Government officials and business and professional people all over the world dress in Western clothes. Women follow Western fashions in dress and makeup. People line up to eat at McDonald's, see a Hollywood movie, or attend a rock concert. Everywhere people are eager to adopt the latest technology that originated in the West but is now also manufactured in other, particularly Asian, lands. Advanced technology intensifies the means of communication, not only through television and radio but also with faxes, e-mail, cellular phones, and the Internet. The breakthrough in information technology has enabled companies to place production and research facilities in different lands and yet maintain direction and control with instant communication. And it allows individuals all over the world to communicate with each other instantly and inexpensively. These developments promote shared interests among individuals and businesses, some of them multinational corporations, throughout the globe, reducing the importance of national frontiers. All these factors combined are reshaping Western and non-Western societies in a relentless adjustment that holds great promise.

Generally globalization has enhanced economic growth and improved the standard of living for hundreds of millions throughout the globe. But more than two billion people are still mired in poverty, struggling to survive on less than two dollars a day. Each year eight million people—some twenty thousand a day—perish because they lack safe drinking water, proper nutrition, bed nets to protect them from malaria-carrying mosquitos, adequate hospitals, and life-saving drugs. Despite these unpleasant images of human suffering, poverty rates continue to decline. From 1990 to 2010, almost one billion people were lifted out of extreme poverty. It is hoped that continued economic growth and better income distribution will by 2030 rescue another billion people from extreme poverty.

The spread of Western science, medicine, and humanitarianism and economic progress have produced an unprecedented population explosion worldwide. For countless millennia the world's population remained almost stationary, slowly beginning to grow in the eighteenth century. In 1900, the world's population reached 1.6 billion. In 2011, the world's population passed seven billion. A spiraling population places immense pressure on the earth's resources and exacerbates both national and international problems.

The hopes analysts held that the dissemination of democratic institutions around the globe would reduce conflicts and advance human rights have somewhat diminished. The ideals of individual liberty, political democracy, religious and cultural freedom, and increasingly female equality—all historical accomplishments of Western civilization—do exert a powerful influence worldwide. But, unlike technology, these ideals and practices, which evolved from the history and traditions of the West, are often difficult to transmit to non-Western nations. This is particularly true in countries that are driven by ethnic and religious divisions that preclude a willingness to tolerate and cooperate with citizens holding different beliefs and practicing different traditions—a fundamental requirement of a pluralistic democratic society.

While some countries, particularly in Asia, have established working democracies, across the globe we see fraudulent democracies, countries that maintain the outer form of democracy—parliaments and elections—but in reality are contemporary forms of dictatorship, often led by a power-hungry despot. Even more depressing, we see people willingly supporting parties and leaders hostile to democratic principles and human rights—religious toleration and equal rights for women, for example—that conflict with deeply ingrained cultural traditions. John Agresto explains the cultural barriers impeding the implementation of democracy in the Arab world.

> *Yet it is the character of a culture that shapes the aspirations of its citizens and the nature of its democracy. A culture in which there is little religious or intellectual freedom, where adherence to the commands of imams or religious scholars is sacrosanct, a culture that believes its duty before God is to punish dissent, kill apostates, and exterminate God's supposed enemies, a culture in which there is no deep acceptance of difference—such cultures will produce illiberal souls who are hardly strong candidates to form a truly liberal and free democracy.*[10]

For decades, human rights movements throughout the globe have pressed for eliminating abuses that violate human dignity. Due to their efforts, many developing countries have instituted legal reforms protecting the rights of their citizens. But despite gains, human rights violations, particularly against the poor and women (see Primary Source, page 540) persist, particularly in developing lands. In many developing lands, it is difficult to overcome cultural traditions that confine women to a subordinate position. The publicizing of gang rapes in India and the Congo, where these cruel acts are not uncommon, and the attempted assassination by the Taliban in Pakistan of Malala Yousafzal, a young female student, for advocating education for girls created an international furor. Regarding girls' schools as symbols of Western decadence, since 2009 Taliban militants in northwestern Pakistan have bombed more than eight hundred schools.

Analysts of human rights are growing increasingly concerned with escalating religious persecution in recent years. We discussed the resurgence of anti-Semitism earlier in the chapter. In Myanmar, mobs responding to the spreading of hatred by Buddhist monks against the Muslim minority have terrorized Muslim areas, destroying and killing. Tens of thousands of Muslims, fearful of returning to their villages, are confined in camps that foreign aid workers call large outdoor jails. A similar situation has developed in India where thousands of Muslims, fleeing Hindu oppressors, are compelled to live in makeshift tent shelters. The persecution of Christians in Muslim lands, where Christians have been historically regarded as infidels, has increased dramatically. Churches, religious symbols, and the distribution of the Bible are prohibited in Saudi Arabia and Christians congregating in homes to pray risk being flogged and jailed. Iranian police, at times, raid the homes of Christian converts and imprison them. In 2013, numerous churches were torched and bombed in the Muslim world, including one in Peshawar Pakistan that killed eighty-five Christians and injured one hundred and twenty. In the turmoil accompanying the Arab Spring in Egypt, radical Muslims turned on Coptic Christians whose roots go back to the early days of Christianity in Egypt; more than eighty Coptic churches were torched and looted and scores of Coptic were maimed and killed. Bombings on Christmas day in the Christian district of Baghdad, Iraq's capital, killed thirty-seven people, some during a church service—it is not uncommon for Muslim militants to target Christian churches during Christmas and Easter. In Kenya,

Nigeria, Mali, Iraq, and Syria, Christians have been kidnapped, raped, murdered, and forcibly converted to Islam. Faced with the vandalizing of their churches and violent attacks that kill and wound, hundreds of thousands of Christians have fled Egypt, Syria, Iraq, and other Muslim lands. Christian spokespersons have lamented the failure of Muslim clergy in both Muslim and Western lands—with some exceptions—to condemn the antichristian behavior of their coreligionists.

The world remains burdened with conflicts. In recent years, civil wars have caused horrific suffering in several lands. Strife in the Congo left some 3.8 million people dead between 1998 and 2003. More than two decades of warfare in southern Sudan cost two million lives before a peace treaty was signed between the government and the rebels in 2005. The actions of Arab militias against blacks in Sudan's Darfur region have been called genocidal; despite the peace treaty, state supported militias still prey in Darfur, killing helpless civilians and driving hundreds of thousands into refugee camps. Yet, in actual fact, the early twenty-first century, says sociologist Joshua S. Goldstein, "has seen fewer war deaths than any decade in the past 100 years." There are fewer civil wars today than in 1990, and since the Korean War, which ended some sixty years ago, great powers have not taken up arms against each other.

Most frightening for the future is the development of weapons of mass destruction by states that do not share Western democratic values. North Korea, a ruthless Communist dictatorship, possesses nuclear weapons; so too does Pakistan, which is afflicted with political instability and Taliban insurgents. Iran, headed by Islamic fundamentalists who have financed and provided military assistance to terrorist organizations, is moving ahead with plans to develop nuclear energy that, despite denials, will no doubt include nuclear weapons. It is feared that a nuclear Iran might supply its militant and terrorist clients with nuclear weapons and seek to dominate its Arab neighbors, totally transforming the Middle East. (There is fierce hostility between Iranians, who are Persian and Shiites, and Arabs, who are predominantly Sunni.) Most concerned is Israel, whose destruction Iran's leaders have repeatedly called for.

Its economy devastated by the crippling sanctions imposed by the United States and its supporters, in late 2013, Iran reached an interim agreement with the United States, Britain, France, Germany, Russia, and China. While the agreement curbed Iran's nuclear enrichment program for six months, its nuclear infrastructure remained essentially intact. In return, some sanctions were lifted—but most remained in place. Critics of the agreement argued that since the accord did not dismantle Iran's nuclear infrastructure, Iran would still be able to build a nuclear weapon in a relatively short time if its leadership decided to do so. The Obama administration regarded the freeze as an interim accord, a first stage designed to halt Iran's race to build a nuclear weapon; a soon to come broader agreement, the United States believed, would put an end to Iran's nuclear weapons capacity.

There are hopeful signs for the future. Democracy has replaced repressive regimes in Central and Eastern Europe. There is hope, admittedly fading in the summer of 2014, that recent events in the Ukraine will not revive the passions of the Cold War, which seem to have ended. Compared to the generation born in the early twentieth century, people are healthier, live longer and better, and the death rate for children under five has plummeted. Impressive economic growth in many lands, including South and East Asia and now Africa has significantly broadened the middle class and reduced poverty, a testament to the effectiveness of the free market, although worldwide repercussions are still felt from the financial crisis of 2008 caused largely by wild speculation in the American mortgage market. The past decade has seen an astonishing turnaround in Africa. Famine, civil war, dictatorships, and deaths from AIDS and malaria are receding, and the economy is booming. Real income per person in the last ten years has soared by an extraordinary 30 percent, whereas it had contracted by 10 percent in the previous twenty years.

Advances in science and technology hold great promise for the future. In medicine, surgical transplants and new antibiotics are saving lives and creative research is providing new insights for the prevention and curing of disease. Abounding in every area—communications, transportation, agriculture, manufacturing, sanitation, energy, astronomy—scientific and technological breakthroughs are transforming the way we live and work often for the better. Look at what the worldwide Internet has accomplished!

How can peaceful global interdependence be advanced, given the persistent cultural and political differences that divide the world, promoting hatred and inciting violence? Can the present generation of Western peoples, above all Americans, help shape the development of the global community in accordance with the highest ideals of Western civilization?

REAFFIRMING THE CORE IDEALS OF THE WESTERN TRADITION

In recent years, modern Western civilization, whose core values were articulated during the Enlightenment, has come under severe attack from several quarters, including religious thinkers, intellectuals loosely called postmodernists, advocates of the poor and oppressed, and militant Muslims. Some religious thinkers deplore the modern age for its espousal of secular rationality, the central legacy of the Enlightenment. These thinkers argue that reason without God degenerates into an overriding concern for technical efficiency—an attitude of mind that produces Auschwitz, Stalin's labor camps, weapons of mass destruction, and the plundering and polluting of the environment. The self without God degenerates into selfish competition, domination, exploitation, and unrestrained hedonism. Human dignity conceived purely in secular terms does not permit us to recognize the *thou* of another human being, to see our neighbor as someone who has been dignified by God; and removing God from life ends in spiritual emptiness and gnawing emotional distress. These critics of the Enlightenment tradition urge the reorientation of thinking around God and transcendent moral absolutes. Without such a reorientation, they argue, liberal democracy cannot resist the totalitarian temptation or overcome human wickedness.

Postmodernists argue that modernity founded on the Enlightenment legacy, which once was viewed as a progressive force emancipating the individual from unreasonable dogmas, traditions, and authority, has itself become a source of repression through its own creations: technology, bureaucracy, consumerism, materialism, the nation-state, ideologies, and a host of other institutions, procedures, and norms. Aversion to a technoscientific culture and to its methodology leads postmodernists to devalue the principle of objectivity in the social sciences and to give greater weight to the subjective, to feelings, intuition, and fantasy, to the poetry of life. Postmodernists contend that the evaluation of data and reasoned arguments, no matter how logical they seem, reveal only personal preferences and biases. In their view, science has no greater claim to truth than does religion, myth, or witchcraft. In a world marked by cultural diversity and individual idiosyncrasies, there are no correct answers, no rules that apply everywhere and to everyone. Moreover, like those who point out the dangers of reason not directed by spiritual values, postmodernists argue that reason fosters oppressive governments, military complexes, and stifling bureaucracies. Nor has it solved our problems.

Expressing disdain for Western humanism, which ascribes an inherent dignity to human beings, urges the full development of the individual's potential, and regards the rational, self-determining human being as the center of existence, postmodernists claim that humanism has failed. The humanist vision of socialist society ended in Stalinism, and liberal humanism proved no more effective a barrier to Nazism than did Christianity. In our own day, they ask, has the rational humanist tradition been able to solve the problems of overpopulation, worldwide pollution, world hunger, poverty, and war that ravage our planet? Closer to home, has reason coped successfully with urban blight, homelessness, violence, racial tensions, or drug addiction? Moreover, postmodernists contend that the Western tradition, which has been valued as a great and creative human achievement, is fraught with gender, class, and racial bias. In their view, it is merely a male, white, Eurocentric interpretation of things, and the West's vaunted ideals are really a cloak of hypocrisy intended to conceal, rationalize, and legitimate the power, privileges, and preferences of white, European, male elites.

People who identify with victims of exploitation, discrimination, and persecution throughout the globe also attack the Western tradition. They point to the modern West's historic abuses: slavery, imperialism, racism, ethnocentrism, sexism, class exploitation, and the ravaging of the environment. They accuse Westerners of marginalizing the poor, women, and people of color by viewing them as the "other." Furthermore, they condemn the West for arrogantly exalting Western values and achievements and belittling, or even destroying, indigenous peoples and cultures. Finding Western civilization intrinsically flawed, some critics seek a higher wisdom in non-Western traditions—African, Asian, or Native American.

Radical Muslims, who were responsible for or applaud September 11, view Western civilization as a threat to traditional Islam and plot its destruction. Their vision of an Islamic society based on a strict interpretation of the Koran clashes head-on with core principles of Western democracy—separation of church and state, religious toleration, protection of basic rights, and female equality.

Defenders of the Enlightenment heritage argue that this heritage, despite its flaws, still has a powerful message for us. They caution against devaluing and undermining the modern West's unique achievements: the tradition of *rationality*, which makes possible a scientific understanding of the physical universe and human nature, the utilization of nature for human betterment, and the identification and reformation of irrational and abusive institutions and beliefs; the tradition of *political freedom*, which is the foundation of democratic institutions; the tradition of *inner freedom*, which asserts the individual's capacity for ethical autonomy, the ability and duty to make moral choices; the tradition of *humanism*, which regards individuals as active subjects, with both the right and the capacity to realize their full human potential; the tradition of *equality*, which demands equal treatment under the law; and the tradition of *human dignity*, which affirms the inviolable integrity and worth of the human personality and is the driving force behind what is now a global quest for social justice and human rights.

The modern struggle for human rights—initiated during the Enlightenment, advanced by the French Revolution, and embodied in liberalism—continues in the contemporary age. Two crucial developments in this struggle are the civil rights movement in the United States and the feminist movement. Spokespersons for these movements have used ideas formulated by Western thinkers in earlier struggles for liberty and equality. Thus, one reason for the success of Martin Luther King's policy of direct action was that he both inspired and shamed white America to live up to its Judeo-Christian and democratic principles. Though written more than thirty years ago, the insights of the French social theorist Jacques Ellul still apply.

> *The essential, central, undeniable fact is that the West was the first civilization in history to focus attention on the individual and on freedom . . . The West, and the West alone, is responsible for the movement that has led to the desire for freedom. . . . Today men point the finger of outrage at slavery and torture. Where did that kind of indignation originate? What civilization or culture cried out that slavery was unacceptable and torture scandalous? Not Islam, or Buddhism, or Confucius, or Zen, or the religions and moral codes of Africa and India! The West alone has defended the inalienable rights of the human person, the dignity of the individual. . . . The West attempted to apply in a conscious, methodical way the implications of freedom. . . . The West discovered what no one else had discovered: freedom and the individual. . . . I see no other satisfactory model that can replace what the West has produced.*[11]

The roots of these ideals are ultimately found in the West's Greek and Judeo-Christian heritage, but it was the philosophers of the Enlightenment who clearly articulated them for the modern age. To be sure, these ideals are a goal, not a finished achievement, and nothing should make Westerners more appreciative of the preciousness of these ideals and more alert to their precariousness than examining the ways they have been violated and distorted over the course of centuries. It is equally true that every age has to rethink and revitalize this tradition in order to adapt it to the needs of its own time.

Therefore, it is crucial in this age of globalism, with its heightened sense of ethnic and cultural diversity, that Westerners become sensitized to the histories and traditions of all cultures. But it is equally crucial in an era of global interdependence and tension that Westerners continuously affirm and reaffirm the core values of their heritage and not permit this priceless legacy to be dismissed or negated. As the history of the twentieth century demonstrates, when we lose confidence in this heritage, we risk losing our humanity, and civilized life is threatened by organized barbarism.

NOTES

1. Boris Yeltsin, "Yeltsin Addresses Parliament on the State of the Nation," *Current Digest of the Post-Soviet Press*, April 9, 1997, 1.

2. Denis MacShane, "The New Anti-Semitism," *The Washington Post*, September 4, 2007, A17.

3. Denis MacShane, *Globalising Hatred: The New Antisemitism* (London: Weidenfeld & Nicolson, 2008), xi.

4. Quoted in Bat Ye'or, *Eurabia: The Euro-Arab Axis* (Madison, N.J.: Fairleigh Dickinson University Press, 2005, 2006), 240–241.

5. Quoted in Raymond Ibrahim, ed. and trans., *The Al Qaeda Reader* (New York: Broadway Books, 2007), 277.

6. Quoted in Gabriel Schoenfeld, *The Return of Anti-Semitism* (San Francisco: Encounter Books, 2004), 13.

7. Quoted in Itamar Marcus and Barbara Crook, "Kill a Jew—Go to Heaven: The Perception of the Jew in Palestinian Society," *Jewish Political Studies Review*, vol. 17, nos. 3–4 (Fall 2005), 127. Copyright © 2005 Jerusalem Center for Public Affairs. Reprinted with permission.

8. From www.fas.org/irp/world/para/docs/980223-Fatwa.htm

9. Bernard Lewis, "Revolt of Islam," *The New Yorker*, November 19, 2001, 52, 62.

10. John Agresto, "Was Promoting Democracy a Mistake?" *Commentary*, December 2012, Vol. 134: No 5.

11. Jacques Ellul, *The Betrayal of the West*, trans. J. O'Connell (New York: Seabury, 1978), 17–19, 29.

Index

Note: Page numbers followed by *ph* refer to photographs. Page numbers followed by *m* refer to maps